W9-ATB-049

ALSO BY BRYAN MAGEE

The New Radicalism

The Democratic Revolution

Aspects of Wagner

Modern British Philosophy

The Gays Among Us
(originally published as *One in Twenty*)

Men of Ideas

The Philosophy of Schopenhauer

Philosophy and the Real World
(originally published as *Karl Popper*)

The Great Philosophers

On Blindness

Confessions of a Philosopher

Confessions of a

Philosopher

A JOURNEY THROUGH
WESTERN PHILOSOPHY

BRYAN MAGEE

RANDOM HOUSE

NEW YORK

Copyright © 1997 by Bryan Magee

All rights reserved under International and Pan-American
Copyright Conventions. Published in the United States
by Random House, Inc., New York.

This work was originally published in Great Britain
by Weidenfeld & Nicolson, a division of the Orion
Publishing Group Ltd., London, in 1997.

Grateful acknowledgment is made to Farrar, Straus & Giroux, Inc., for permission to
reprint seven lines from "Aubade" from *Collected Poems* by Philip Larkin.
Copyright © 1988, 1989 by the Estate of Philip Larkin. Reprinted by
permission of Farrar, Straus & Giroux, Inc.

Library of Congress Cataloging-in-Publication Data
Magee, Bryan.
Confessions of a philosopher/Bryan Magee.
p.   cm.
Includes index.
ISBN 0-375-50028-6 (alk. paper)
1. Magee, Bryan.   2. Philosophy—Introductions.   3. Philosophers—
Great Britain—Biography.   I. Title.
B1647.M186A3   1998
192—dc21   [B]   97-26479

Random House website address: http://www.randomhouse.com/

Printed in the United States of America on acid-free paper

24689753

First U.S. Edition

For Jenny, Josefin and Niklas

Contents

This book introduces the reader to philosophy and its history through the story of one person's encounter with them. So it is about ideas: the autobiographical element is medium, not message.

Confessions of a Philosopher

1

Scenes from Childhood

Until I was five I shared a bed with my sister, three and a half years older than me. After our parents had switched out the light we would chatter away in the darkness until we fell asleep. But I could never afterwards remember falling asleep. It was always the same: one moment I was talking to my sister in the dark, and the next I was waking up in a sunlit room having been asleep all night. Yet every night there must have come a time when I stopped talking and settled down to sleep. It was incomprehensible to me that I did not experience that, and never remembered it.

When I confided my bafflement to my sister she was dismissive. "Nobody remembers it," she said in confident tones of finality, as if that were all there was to it. I remained dissatisfied. *How does she know?* I thought. *All that means is* she *doesn't remember it. I bet she's never talked about it to anybody else.* So I set myself to keep a keen watch on my self, so that I would know when I was falling asleep, in the same sort of way as people try to catch the light in a refrigerator going out when they close the door. But it was no use. Everything continued just as before. One moment I'd be chattering away to my sister in the darkness on, say, a Monday evening, and the next thing I knew I'd be waking up in broad daylight and it would be several hours into Tuesday. That going to sleep was something I did every night yet never experienced was for years a source of active mystification to me.

I retain a vivid memory of myself, two or three years after that, when I was seven or eight, standing in a shaft of sunlight in the corner of the kitchen by our back door, between a barred window and a green wooden wall, focusing my eyes keenly on the index finger of my right hand, which I held pointed upwards in front of my face. *I'm going to count to three,* I was saying to myself, *and when I say "three" my finger's going to bend.* Then I counted: *One, two, thr——* And sure enough on *three* my finger bent. How did I do it? I did it again. Then I thought: *This time I'll count to four.* And on *four* my finger bent. Next time I counted to five. My finger bent on *five.* I tried dragging out the counting so as to catch my finger out: *one, two . . . three . . . four . . .* [wait for it] *. . . five!* But on *five* my finger, not caught napping at all, bent. I could bend my finger whenever I liked. Or not, just as I decided. Yet no matter how hard I concentrated I couldn't grasp anything at all about how I did it. How could something that was so completely within my command, solely and entirely a matter of my own conscious decision, be a nothing for me, just simply no experience whatever, and yet happen? From that day to this the problem has fascinated me.

When I was a teenager, and had acquired the concept of willed activity, and knew that the decision to crook my finger was something taking place in my head, I tried all ways I could think of to catch, in experience, whatever it was that was happening between my brain and my finger. The result was always total failure. I would take the decision inside my head to crook my finger and *simultaneously* my finger would crook; and between my head and my finger there was an emptiness. The simultaneity presented me with an additional problem: Why wasn't there a time lag? How could a decision be the cause of something that happened at the same time as itself?

For a period of two or three years between the ages of about nine and twelve I was in thrall to puzzlement about time. I would lie awake in bed at night in the dark thinking something along the following lines. I know there was a day before yesterday, and a day before that, and a day before that, and so on, as far back as I can remember. But there must also have been a day before the first day I can remember. I know I was born on 12 April 1930, and there must have been a day before that. And a day before that. And so on—and so on—and so on. Before every day there must have been a day before. So it must be possible to go back like that for ever and ever and ever . . . Yet is it? The idea of going back for ever and *ever* was something I could not get a hold of: it seemed impossible. So perhaps, after all, there must have been a beginning somewhere. But if there was a beginning, what had been going on before that? Well, obviously, nothing—nothing at all—otherwise it could not be the beginning. But if there was nothing, how could anything have got started? Where could it have come from? Time couldn't just suddenly pop into existence—bingo!—out of *nothing,* and start going, all by itself. Nothing is nothing, not anything. So the idea of a beginning was unimaginable, which somehow made it seem impossible too. The upshot was that it seemed impossible for time to have had a beginning and impossible for it not to have had a beginning.

I must be missing something here, I came to think. There are only these two alternatives, so one of them must be right. They can't both be impossible. So I would switch my concentration from one to the other and then, when it had exhausted itself, back again, trying to work out where I had gone wrong; but I never discovered. I became enslaved by the problem, and started to get lost in it not only in bed at night but increasingly during the day. There were adults who I thought at first might be able to help me, so I put it to them, but their responses left me more bewildered than before. Either they admitted they could not solve it, and then went on to talk about other things, as if this particular question were not interesting enough even to discuss, or else they actively pooh-poohed it with superior little laughs and remarks like "Oh, you don't want to go wasting your time worrying about things like that." I couldn't make this out. If they were as unable as I was to answer the question, how could they feel superior to it? Why weren't they disconcerted, and why didn't they find it even interesting? After several perplexing rebuffs I stopped talking to people about it and just got on with thinking about it by myself.

I had realized almost immediately that the same problem operated forward as backward. After tomorrow there would be another day, and then another day after that, and then another; and it was inconceivable that time should ever end—for what was there for it to end in, if not time (perhaps another time, or a different sort of time), and so one would always be able to ask what happened after that. On the other hand, it was inconceivable that time could go on for ever and ever and ever and ever—for that would be eternity in this world, in fact it would be the eternity of this world. As I thought about it more and more, what came to me were not possible answers but more problems. One of these was that if it were necessary for infinite time to have elapsed before the present moment were reached it would be impossible for us ever to have reached it. Another was that for something to *exist,* it must have some sort of identity, and that meant there must be something it wasn't, and that meant it must have limits, so it couldn't both *be* and *be endless,* or *be* and *be beginningless.* I became convinced that a beginningless or endless time was impossible—yet on the other hand I was no nearer grasping the possibility of a beginning or an end.

Again, almost immediately, I realized that a similar problem existed with regard to space. I remember myself as a London evacuee in Market Harborough—I must have been ten or eleven—lying on my back in the grass in a park and trying to penetrate a cloudless blue sky with my eyes and thinking something like this: "If I went straight up into the sky, and kept on going in a straight line, why shouldn't I just be able to keep on going for ever and ever? But that's impossible. Why isn't it possible? Surely, eventually, I'd have to come to some sort of an end? But why? If I bumped up against something eventually, wouldn't that have to be a something in space? And if it was in space, wouldn't there have to be something on the other side of it, if only more space? On the other hand, if there was no limit, endless space couldn't just *be,* any more than endless time could be."

After a lot of puzzling about this I began to think that perhaps my key mistake was to suppose that what I couldn't conceive of couldn't be. Perhaps there was a difference between what I could think and what could be the case. For after all, there *was* a sense in which I could think about something going on and on for ever and ever because I could always keep on asking: *What next? What next? What next? What next?* But still it seemed to me self-evident that this was only something I could think and not anything that could actually be. I could think infinity, but infinity couldn't exist. For instance, there couldn't actually *be* an infinite number of stars . . . Or was I now falling back into the mistake I was trying to climb out of? In any case, whatever the truth about this—even if something I could think couldn't exist, and something I couldn't think could exist—it wouldn't help me solve my real problem, because it didn't tell me what the truth was about whether time did or didn't have a beginning. Which of those two alternatives was the truth?

The more I thought about time and space, the more the problems proliferated. One thing that came to puzzle me very much indeed was that the future was specific yet unknown. The thought first came to me in connection with a football match. It was a Friday evening, and the following day my two favourite teams were going to play against each other. My over-excited impatience to know the result bordered on the uncontainable. At first it was merely to calm myself that I said to myself: "This time tomorrow I'll know the result. Only three things can have happened: either Arsenal will have won, or Spurs will have won, or it'll be a draw. And whatever it is, I'll know it for the rest of my life." But then I found myself thinking: "Whatever the truth is, it's true *now.* If Spurs win, then it's true *now* that Spurs are going to win. And if the score is 3–2, then it's true *now* that the score is going to be 3–2. These things'll have been true since the beginning of time. If an ancient Roman or an Old Testament prophet had said them thousands of years ago they would have been just as true even then. So why can't I know them the day before? They'll have been true from the beginning of time, and they'll be true till the end of time, and yet I shall only be able to know what they are at some particular moment tomorrow afternoon."

And then, inevitably, the fact struck me that the same applied to every event throughout the whole of time: whatever was true of it was true now, and always had been true, and always would be true. Some of these truths we knew and some we didn't, but all of them were equally true. The fact that we knew some and not others seemed to be, so to speak, a fact about us and not a fact about the truths, which were all equally eternal. Those we knew we called the past, those we didn't know we called the future; but that seemed scarcely anything more than *our* way of dividing them up. In fact the dividing point actually *was* us: *we* were the shifting division between past and future. For anyone who had lived in the past, the period between his time and mine was future for him, past for me—unknowable by him, knowable by me. But my own future, unknowable by me, would be the knowable past for people in the future. Yet the truths themselves were all in the same boat. How come we were in this strange position of knowing some and not others—and of different people knowing, and not knowing, different ones? It seemed essentially a matter of our situation as individuals.

The more I thought about this the more frustrated I became. It was during these reflections that the terrifying thought occurred to me that if everything was true now, nothing we did could ever change it. It was true *now* that everything that was going to happen to me during the course of my life was going to happen to me. It was also true *now* that nothing else apart from those things was ever going to happen to me. It was true *now* that I was going to do everything I would ever do. And it was true *now* that I would never, ever, do anything else, apart from those things. It seemed, then, that everything was fixed and unalterable *now.* But if that was the case there was no such thing as free will. I was a helpless object at the mercy of fate. I found this thought so frightening that it had a seriously disturbing effect on my equilibrium. I felt real terror every time it entered my mind, and I started trying to prevent myself from thinking about it.

That was the first problem of this kind ever to crop up in my reflections that upset me emotionally. Most such problems I found frustratingly absorbing, infuriating yet fascinating; and therefore, in spite of their unsettling nature, pleasurable to think about in some inexplicable but deep-lying way.

One day when I was throwing a ball around, it occurred to me that at any given moment the ball must be some actual where. At every single instant it must, whole and entire, be in some actual position. At no instant could it be in two places, nor could its position in even one place be ambiguous or blurred. It could only be, wholly and precisely, where it was. But in that case I didn't see how it could move. Obviously, though, it did move. Again, something that, it seemed to me, must happen wasn't happening; and whatever it was that was happening was something I couldn't find a way of getting my mind round.

It was during these same years, about the ages nine to twelve, that what had long been the pleasure of listening to music on the gramophone became an addiction. Once, when I was playing records, I found myself imagining a rod sticking out from the turntable with a sideways-on cup at the end. And I imagined a ball perched on a golf tee at the right distance from the edge of the turntable for the cup to catch it as it spun round. And I imagined ball, cup and rod as being made of an absolutely hard material—or, as I might put it now, I imagined them as being perfectly inelastic. What happened when the turntable was spinning at top speed and the cup scooped the ball up? Did the ball change instantaneously from being at rest to moving at the same speed as the cup, without passing through any of the speeds in between? That seemed impossible, and impossible in the same way as those earlier things: impossible to imagine, *unthinkable*. On the other hand, if the cup and the ball and the rod were all 100 per cent hard there was no alternative: it *had* to happen, it was the only thing that could possibly happen. So here yet again, there was something I found impossible to conceive of as happening, and yet impossible to conceive of as not happening.

And so it went on as the years went by. The more things I thought about, the more problems I acquired. But I never seemed to acquire any solutions. And yet, it seemed to me, solutions there had to be. Something or other must be the case with regard to each one of these questions, if only I could find out what it was. Furthermore, if something just self-evidently did happen, like a ball moving, then there had to be something wrong with any way of looking at it that said it didn't. And there had to be a flaw in any argument that said it couldn't. This being so, it seemed highly peculiar to me that I could never discover what any of these mistakes were, no matter how hard I thought. I came to see the ordinary world I was living in as a place crammed with self-contradiction and mystery. Whatever you thought about you were almost immediately led into paradox and inconceivabilities. And this gave me a thirst to understand. This drive became almost as strong as my strongest other instincts, like physical thirst or hunger, and as compelling. An ever-present curiosity became for most of the time my strongest felt emotion, sometimes the mode I lived in.

Perhaps I should make it explicit, in case there are readers whose own beliefs or whose own experience of childhood causes them to assume otherwise, that none of this had anything in my mind to do with religion. No such connection entered my head. All the problems that plagued me were questions about the situation in which I immediately found myself. Some of them were questions about me, some were questions about the world around me, but all of them were practical questions, which is to say questions about how things are, to which something or other had to constitute a true answer, or so it seemed to me. To none of these questions would the existence of a God have constituted an answer, and I never felt any inclination, no matter as how young a child, to believe in one. There is a story that G. E. Moore, when asked why he had never addressed himself to questions about God, replied that he had never seen any reason for taking such questions seriously, and the same applied in those days to me. The postulation of a God seemed to me a cop-out, a refusal to take serious problems seriously; a facile, groundless and above all evasive response to deeply disturbing difficulties: it welcomed the self-comforting delusion that we know what we do not know, and have answers that we do not have, thereby denying the true mysteriousness, indeed miraculousness, of what is. By sheer chance I had the good fortune to grow up in a family in which religion was never mentioned. I have just said that there was never an age at which I believed in God: still less have I ever been a Christian. But perhaps even more important than either of those things, I have never felt any need to react against such beliefs. That is something for which I am deeply grateful. There was a good deal of carry-on about them at school, but my attitude to anything to do with school—or rather to anything organized by the authorities, such as classes and religious services—was one of boredom and indifference. None of it seemed to me to have anything to do with real life, and I never thought any of it mattered, so I never gave any of it a moment's consideration outside the classroom. And it was outside the classroom that everything real and exciting was waiting with open arms to sweep me up into itself as soon as the bell rang. Nor did it ever occur to me to think of any of the problems I have been discussing as abstract or theoretical, still less as other-worldly. They were real, gripping problems, and they were problems *about reality,* about the actual world I was living in, and the life I was living, and me. I *had* them, whether I liked it or not. There was no choice about it. I'd got these problems.

Although none of these experiences had anything in my mind to do with religion or religious thoughts, it so happened that it was in the school chapel, in the middle of a hymn, that the realization came to me that if I closed my eyes then the visual scene of hundreds of boys facing me in that huge, high-ceilinged building, with all those vast paintings and windows, simply disappeared. *They* did not disappear, of course, but the visual image of them did, the scene. And when I opened my eyes, the scene came back again. *They* had been there all the time, and would have been there just the same if I had not been in the chapel at all, but the only apprehension I had of them consisted in the seeing of them plus the hearing of them, and those were in my head. If I stopped my ears and eyes they ceased to have any existence for me. Up to that moment I had always taken it for granted that I was in immediate contact with the people and things outside me, and that their presence was something I experienced in an unmediated way; but now, suddenly, I realized that their existence was one thing and my awareness of it something radically other. Their existence was out there, independent of me: but all the awareness and experience and knowledge I could ever have of it was inside my head, and that could pop into or out of existence irrespective of them, provided of course that they were there. I could make it come and make it go whenever I liked, simply by opening and closing my eyes. With a horrible churning over of my stomach I realized that the natural way of putting this into words was to say: "When I close my eyes they disappear."

Even now, after all these years, what I cannot put into words is how indescribably appalling I found that moment of insight, how nightmarish. I was inundated by crashing great tidal waves of nausea, claustrophobia, and isolation, as if I were for ever cut off from everything that existed—apart from myself—and as if I were trapped for life inside my own head. I thought I was going to throw up or faint. I was overwhelmed by panic and a need to escape from the situation—just get out. Groping and blundering, I lurched along the row of boys in my pew, and under the eyes of the whole school that rose up above my head in serried ranks on both sides—they faced each other four hundred to four hundred across a centre aisle—I veered distraught down the channel between them and out of the building. What everyone commented on afterwards was the colour of my face, which was apparently green—so no one doubted that I had felt ill, and therefore no one questioned me about why I had walked out.

From that day on I wrestled with demons for at least a part of every day of my life, especially when I was alone and otherwise unoccupied, which meant most of all in bed at night in the dark. The prospect of going to chapel induced panic, and often I used to hide in the lavatories when the bell for it rang. When I did go to the services I was twanging with tension, sometimes literally shaking. Often the prospect of going was so dreadful that I willingly accepted punishment instead. And there was no way I could explain any of this to anyone. I considered trying to explain it to the school doctor, and asking him to get permission for me to be excused chapel; but he was a hearty extrovert of the old-fashioned public-school type, and I knew he would never understand. In fact I was afraid he would think I was mad. So I kept my terrors to myself.

There was one occasion when I thought myself I was going mad because of this. I was coming out of a cinema one afternoon during the school holidays and suddenly, in the foyer, I was engulfed by the realization that, for me and for the whole of my life, absolutely everything in so far as I could ever possibly be aware of it—not only my own life and thoughts and memories but other people too, and the whole of the present-day world, whatever I read about in the newspapers, all history, all art, the cosmos itself, *everything*—existed only in my head; that this always had been so, and always must be so; and that I should never, ever be able to have any consciousness of anything at all other than of what was in my own mind. The thought was not solipsism—not that everything existed only in my mind—but the opposite: that everything (except, of course, for my experience) existed *outside* my mind, and I was cut off from it for ever and always, unrescuably alone, trapped for life inside the tiny box of my skull, never, never, *never* able to get out and be part of the rest of everything there was. The feeling, again, was one of total, permanent and unsalvageable isolation from everything and everybody, combined with intolerable claustrophobia, a waking nightmare of being locked up inside myself. I tried to flee these terrors by forcibly distracting my thoughts, but then the second barrel of the shotgun went off: *nothing you can ever do can make you experience anything other than the deliverances of your own consciousness.* The only alternative to them is oblivion. I felt about to explode as the only way of breaking out of myself and escaping my own confines, in the way a hand grenade shatters its own casing when it goes off. In that moment I really did believe I was going out of my mind.

And all this was the result of seeing reality in a certain way. Everything, I thought, exists independently of me in a framework of space and time, which exist also independently. The only way I, as one of the objects in that space and time, can get to know about any of the other objects in it is if it impinges on one of my senses, and that conveys a stimulus to my brain which is translated into a sensory image. So the only conscious awareness I can ever have of any part of reality other than myself is of images—which are always, and can only ever be, in my head—and I have to infer back from these images to the existence of the objects of which they are representations. And the representation is the only conception I can form of the *nature* of the object. With objects themselves I had no means of direct, unmediated contact. They existed permanently on the other side of an uncrossable frontier constituted by the limits of the possibility of awareness.

The next insight I had following on from this way of seeing things was that there was no way in which objects could be "like" my perceptions of them. This came to me for the first time in the living room of my parents' flat, when I was about thirteen. In this room there were two armchairs facing each other with a sofa between them on one side and a fireplace on the other, and beside one of the armchairs stood a tall standard lamp. I was sitting in the armchair opposite the lamp, looking at it. There it was, with a dark brown, square wooden base out of which grew a stem of the same colour and material, culminating in a conical lampshade made of a soft textile of lighter brown. That was it, the standard lamp: and I couldn't conceptualize it in any other terms. And that's how it would be for an observer anywhere else in the room, except—it suddenly struck me—in one unique position, namely the position occupied by the standard lamp itself. In that room it was only if you *were* the standard lamp that you would not be able to *see* the standard lamp. And in the absence of mirrors, you would have no conception of what you looked like. In other words, whatever your conception of yourself was it couldn't possibly take the form that for me and anyone else was the only form it could take. I sat there trying to imagine what it was to *be* the standard lamp—putting myself in its place, so to speak. And the same thoughts reasserted themselves. It could see everything in the room except itself. And no matter where it was it would never be able to see itself. This made me realize that I knew what my own face looked like only because I had seen its reflection in mirrors and windows, and photographs of it—in other words, because I had seen images that were other than myself and extraneous to myself. From inside my face I had no way of knowing how my face was. So if you *were* something you weren't it in the terms in which everyone else perceived it and, as a result of that, conceived it. And what's more you couldn't be. Looking at the same situation from the other end, everyone perceiving or conceiving anything *had no alternative* but to do so in terms in which it wasn't possible for that thing to *be*. So things as they were in themselves must be unimaginably different from any idea we could form of them.

For a couple of years I was constantly trying to imagine what it was to be an inanimate object, and always with this contradictory thought that it must be unconceptualizably different from anything I could imagine . . . What was it to *be* that building, what was it to *be* that rugger boot? There they were, they existed, they had being. What was that being? Not what was it *like* but what *was* it—for the one thing I was certain of was that it couldn't be like any image or conception I was able to form of it. Although I knew that my attempt to put myself in the place of that book, that tree, that piece of furniture, was in this very way self-contradictory, I could not stop myself from doing it. *Being,* it seemed to me, was the ultimate mystery, *the ultimately unconceptualizable.* And yet there wasn't anything that wasn't. Everything was. So how could it be a mystery? Here, it seemed to me, was the last word in paradoxes: everything that actually exists is unknowable, and the whole of whatever it is we experience is image only, with no existence independent of our experience.

In my middle teens I came across a book in the school library called *The Bible of the World* containing the main writings of the world's great religions. Out of curiosity I read it all. The only part of the book that stirred my imagination really deeply was the Upanishads. Here, to my astonishment, I found it said that the entire world of human knowledge and experience consisted of images only, which were fleeting and had no abiding reality, whereas *real* reality, that which existed permanently, was something we could have no direct knowledge of, and therefore could form no clear and determinate conception of. I was astounded to see my own thought there before me on the page, and in writings thousands of years old. The Upanishads then went on to offer an explanation that had not occurred to me. They said that what presented this indefinite number of variegated images to our minds was not an equal number of un-get-at-able somethings corresponding to the separate images, but just one big something. We became differentiated from it when we came into existence as individuals, and we dissolved back into it when we died; and that, actually, was ultimately all there was. It was only images that were disparate, individual, separate. And because images *were* images, and were subjective and ephemeral, and above all because we had a natural tendency to mistake them for independently existing things, they could not unreasonably be classed as illusions. Separate things, then—separate *any* things, including people— were illusions. In reality everything was one.

This intrigued me as an idea without involving my emotions. It neither commended itself nor failed to commend itself to my intuitions, and I felt agnostic about it. I did not see how we could know it to be true even if it were. But it did drive home to me one essential fact: that without realizing that I was doing so I had continued to assume that reality was "like" our conception of it in one fundamental respect, namely that it was variegated—and that I had no grounds for this assumption. In fact, on consideration, it seemed to me that I had no basis whatsoever for any beliefs about what ultimate reality might be.

However, no matter what it was that existed, it seemed to me extraordinary beyond all wonderment that it should. It was astounding that anything existed at all. Why wasn't there nothing? By all the normal rules of expectation—the least unlikely state of affairs, the most economical solution to all possible problems, the simplest explanation—*nothing* is what you would have expected there to be. But such was not the case, self-evidently. And yet although it was impossible to know what there was, and therefore impossible to *say* what it was, and perhaps therefore even impossible to assert that there *was* any *thing, something was unquestionably going on.* Yet how could anything be going on? In what medium? Nothingness? Impossible to conceive: and yet undeniably something was happening.

Although more and more given to talk and discussion and argument as I grew older, for several years I never encountered anyone who felt the same fascination as I did with these questions. By the time I had grown into adulthood I had become familiar with a number of general attitudes to experience that seemed to embrace among themselves most people, at least most of those I met, but none of them was at all like mine. There seemed to be three main groupings. First, there were people who took the world for granted as they found it: that's how things are, and it's obvious that that's how they are, and talking about it isn't going to change it, so there's no purpose that perpetually questioning it is going to serve; discussing it is really a waste of time, even *thinking* about it much is a waste of time; what we have to do is get on with the practical business of living, not indulge in a lot of useless speculation and ineffectual talk. That seemed to be roughly the outlook of most people. Then there were others who regarded that attitude as superficial, on religious grounds. According to them, this life was no more than an overture, a prelude to the real thing. There was a God who had made this world, including us, and had given us immortal souls, so that when our bodies died after a brief sojourn on earth the souls in them would go on for ever in some "higher" realm. Such people tended to think that in the eye of eternity this present world of ours was not all that important, and whenever one raised questions about the self-contradictory nature of our experience they would shrug their shoulders and attribute this to the inscrutable workings of a God. It was not that they used this as the answer to all questions, because what such people said seldom answered any actual questions: they felt under no pressure to do so. God knew all the answers to all the questions, and his nature was inscrutable to us, therefore the only thing for us to do was to put our trust in him and stop bothering ourselves with questions to which we could not possibly know the answers until after we died. It seemed to me that this attitude was at bottom as incurious as the first; it just offered a different reason for not asking questions; and equally obviously it did not really *feel* the problems. There was no awareness in it of the real extraordinariness of the world: on the contrary, people who subscribed to it were often marked by a certain complacency, not to say smugness. They seemed to be happily lulling themselves to sleep with a story which might or might not be true but which they had no serious grounds for believing.

Finally, there were people who condemned both of these other sets of attitudes as uncomprehending and mistaken, on what one might call rationalistic grounds. They critically questioned both the way things are and traditional religious beliefs, and challenged the adherents of either for proof, or at least good evidence; for some justification, or at least good argument. These tended in spirit to be either children of the enlightenment or children of the age of science, and in either case to have a kind of outlook that did not begin to exist until the seventeenth century. They seemed to believe that everything was explicable in the light of reason, that rational enquiry would eventually make all desirable discoveries, and that in principle if not altogether in practice all problems could be solved by the application of rationality. Most of my friends and fellow spirits seemed to fall into this third category, and indeed I tended to agree with their criticisms of the other two. My problem was that their own positive beliefs seemed to me manifestly untenable, and their attitudes—well, perhaps not quite as comfortable and complacent as those they criticized, but comfortable and complacent none the less. They seemed to think that the world was an intelligible place, and I did not see how in the light of a moment's thought this belief could be entertained. Their faith in the power of reason seemed to me almost unbelievably unreflecting and misplaced in view of the fact that it was the application of reason that perpetually gave rise to insoluble problems, problems that were brought into existence by thinking but could not be removed by it. With many such people, belief in the power of reason was an ideology. They believed in it uncritically and on principle, and were totally dismissive of any dissenting voice. They never reflected seriously on the narrowness of the range within which reason is applicable, or its propensity for self-contradiction, or its manifest inability to solve most of the fundamental questions about experience. Any attempt on my part (or anyone else's) to draw their attention to these things smacked to them of religion, which they equated with superstition, and of which they tended to be contemptuous. It was self-evident to them that this world of experience is all there is, and anything we do not as yet understand about it we can reasonably hope to discover in the course of time. All meaning and all purpose inhabit this world: value and morality are created by human beings, which in practice means that value and morality are created socially and historically. Any suggestion that reality is hidden was to them unintelligible, and therefore any suggestion that the significance of our experience might lie outside the range of our understanding a kind of gobbledygook—and again, crypto-religious. What cut me off most deeply of all from this attitude, and what I also found hardest to understand about it, was its lack of any sense of the amazingness of our existence, indeed of the existence of anything at all—the sheer miraculousness of everything. After all, you do not have to reflect deeply, you do not need even to go beyond what a child is capable of thinking, to realize that our experience is unintelligible to ourselves in its most general and basic features—and yet the sort of people I am talking about seemed not to have made that discovery. To them it seemed self-evident that some sort of commonsense view of things must be, by and large, right, whereas I saw it as self-evident that common sense could not possibly be right, since reasoning logically from it as a starting point led one almost immediately into a morass of incomprehensibility and self-contradiction. In fact, to put it baldly yet truthfully, they found the denial of the commonsense view of the world ridiculous whereas I found the acceptance of the commonsense view of the world ridiculous. Their whole outlook was one that could survive for only so long as they did not reflect on its foundations. Not only was it superficial in the extreme, it was also detached, floating in mid-air, unsupported and unsustainable. Any fundamental questioning of it by anyone was dismissed as uninteresting and pointless. If one drew their attention to the fact that there seemed to be no way in which our reasoning powers could make sense of this or that basic feature of the world or of our experience, this was seen by them as a reason for not raising the question. What they wanted to do was confine their lives to the domain within which they *could* make sense of things. So at an only slightly deeper and more critical level they really turned out to share most of the attitudes of the first of the three groups.

Growing to adulthood as I did, absorbed by a sense of wonder about the world, and engrossed in some of the seemingly insoluble problems it presented—especially problems connected with time, space, our perception of physical objects and their intrinsic nature—this to a small extent had the effect of cutting me off from other people. Not only did I never find anyone I could discuss these questions with, I learnt that I was likely to be looked on as peculiar if I raised them. I was not a solitary, for there were other aspects of life in which I was very much a social creature—I always had friends, and after the age of seventeen love affairs; I hugely enjoyed partying, besides being a voracious music-lover and theatre-goer—but my baffled absorption in the whole metaphysical dimension of experience was something I learnt to keep to myself, even though I lived with it daily. What more than anything else made it a source of isolation was its overwhelming importance. These questions were fundamental to our nature, and the nature of the world we lived in, and I could never understand why not everybody was fascinated by them. It seemed to me bizarre that I should be associating all the time with intelligent people yet as if under some sort of informal ban on discussing the most crucial and interesting questions of all.

Until I went to university it never entered my head to associate any of these questions with the word "philosophy." I shall never forget the sheer incredulity with which I discovered that this is what they were, and that they had been addressed by some of the greatest geniuses among mankind over a period of three thousand years. Every one of the problems I have described in this chapter turned out to be a familiar one in the history of philosophy. Some of them even had established names: my bafflement that a ball could move was known as "Zeno's arrow." Wittgenstein, it turned out, had dealt with the same point regarding death as had puzzled me so much about falling asleep: we expect it to be an experience but it cannot be, he said, because, by definition, we are not conscious through it, and therefore not conscious of it. Above all, though it was a longer time before this happened, the discovery was lying in wait for me that I had grown up a natural Kantian, beginning with the antinomies of time and space and going on to the unconceptualizability of things as they are in themselves independently of our modes of experience. My undying sense of astonishment that anything exists at all was first put into words by, so far as I know, Leibniz, and given its most dramatic and compelling expression by one of Kant's most immediate followers, Schelling. It pervades the work of Kant's most illuminating successor, Schopenhauer, in which I also discovered what in most essentials are the same doctrines as I had stumbled across in the Upanishads—though arrived at in Schopenhauer's case, as for that matter in mine, by considerations not of a religious but of an essentially Kantian nature, and therefore (in his case) by a mode of thinking in the very centre of the mainstream of Western philosophy. Before and apart from all that, there was the problem of free will, and the question whether an act of will was the cause of a willed action or the same event apprehended in a different way, and these were questions which Schopenhauer also dealt with profoundly.

From what Hume had to say about the nervous breakdown he experienced when he was young, and its connection with his philosophical reflections, I suspected that his terrifying psychological experiences had had some similarity with my own. Especially given the nature of his philosophy, that seems to me likely. (It is striking, incidentally, how many famous philosophers had breakdowns in youth.) Like the character in Molière who discovered to his astonishment that he had been speaking prose all his life, I discovered to my astonishment that I had been immersed in philosophical problems all my life. And I had been drawn into the same problems as great philosophers by the same felt need to make sense of the world and my experience of it, followed hard-on-heel by the same realization that these were inexplicable in terms of common sense—which, on the contrary, spawned self-contradictions where it did not remain unhelpfully silent. The chief difference between me and them, of course, was that whereas they had something to offer by way of solutions to the problems, I had failed even to formulate very rich or sophisticated versions of the problems, let alone work my way through to defensible solutions for them. In consequence I fell on their work like a starving man on food, and it has done a great deal to nourish and sustain me ever since.

Professional philosophy as I discovered it for the first time in the Oxford of the early 1950s was scarcely concerned with any of this—certainly not with much of it, except perhaps for our perception of material objects—having pretty well abandoned philosophy's traditional task of trying to understand the world, and therefore very largely turned its back on the subject's past. But that failed to deter me from anything, except perhaps from becoming a professional philosopher in the contemporary mode. Unlike such people at that time, I actually had philosophical problems, real ones, which were about the nature of reality and of my relationship to the rest of it, and indeed about the nature of my self. And these were not just confusions into which I had fallen as a result of misuse of language.

2

My Introduction to Academic Philosophy

The fact that my metaphysical problems were in the mainstream tradition of Western philosophy, whereas Oxford philosophy had repudiated that tradition, had for me the unlucky consequence that it was some time after I arrived in Oxford that I realized that my problems were philosophical, so I did not opt to study philosophy for my first degree. If only I had known I would have plunged into it from the beginning, indeed before I got there. But as things were, it took me three or four years to discover where my true academic interests lay.

At my school, far and away the most gifted master had been the teacher of the history specialists, a man called David Roberts. He possessed what could almost be called a genius for teaching, such as I have seen surpassed by only one person since. It was for that reason, and not because of the subject, that I became a history specialist, to be taught by him; in fact I was no more interested in history than in several other subjects. So although I left school with a scholarship in history to Oxford, the two years of specialization this had already entailed were enough for me, and I had no desire to embark on three more years of specialization in history at Oxford.

In those days there was compulsory military service between school and university, so when I was in England on army leave from Austria I visited Oxford to see the head of my college. I asked him if I could study music, this being then, as it always has been, my ruling passion. He tried to talk me out of it, I persisted, he prevaricated, and in the end he postponed a decision until such time as I should arrive at the college as a student. When that time came, however, the college refused to allow me to make the change, on the ground that I had been elected to an open scholarship that had been endowed under somebody's will for the study of history, so that if I were to change subjects the scholarship would have to be taken away from me. As a result I spent my first three years at Oxford studying history against my declared wishes. I do not think this could happen nowadays. The whole idea of forcing a student to study as his main subject something he does not want to do is now, quite rightly, seen as absurd. In those days it was not all that uncommon.

So it was while studying history at Oxford that I made my first acquaintance with academic philosophy, chiefly through my friendships with undergraduates who were studying it. It came as a revelation to me that one of the problems they were concerned with was that of our perception of material objects. With even greater astonishment I discovered that there had been philosophers not merely hundreds but thousands of years ago who wrote what are still regarded as works of genius on the subject, works which my friends were now studying, discussing with their tutors, arguing about with one another, and writing essays on. It made me deeply envious. There were, I was told, classic works in the English language by people called Locke, Berkeley and Hume. At school I had known David Hume for his *History of Great Britain.* Public readings of his description of the death of King Edward II were perennially popular, and in the massive fireplace of a room reserved for the use of history specialists there had been a poker of prodigious size that was ritually brandished during such recitals. But I had had no idea that Hume had also written about our perception of material objects.

Certain works of political philosophy were part of the history course: Aristotle's *Politics,* Hobbes's *Leviathan,* Locke's *Second Treatise of Civil Government* and his *Letter Concerning Toleration.* In addition to these I started dipping into mainstream philosophy for myself, in a somewhat scattered, random way: Plato's *Republic* and *Symposium,* Aristotle's *Ethics* and *Poetics,* Marx's *Das Kapital,* Nietzsche's *Also Sprach Zarathustra,* A. J. Ayer's *Language, Truth and Logic*—and, in the hope of getting an overview, Bertrand Russell's *History of Western Philosophy.* For my special subject in my history degree I chose the Italian Renaissance, and the history of the arts and of ideas soon took over the direction of my historical interests. Unfortunately for me, though, it figured very little in the syllabus. I asked my history tutors if they would pay special attention to the intellectual and cultural aspects of the history they were teaching me, but they were disconcerted by this and declined to be budged from their accustomed ways. "History" in the Oxford of those days meant the history of politics and administration, and of very little else. Furthermore, the views of the world and the past that were embodied in it were

Eurocentric to a degree that now seems unbelievable: for most purposes "foreign history" and even "world history" meant the history of Continental Europe as against Britain. I had quite a row with the man who taught me seventeenth-century English history: I complained that he had never so much as mentioned Newton, whose work had transformed not only the entire outlook of Western man but, through science and technology, the world we ourselves lived in, yet we had discussed the Stuart queens at length and I had been required to write an essay on Archbishop Laud. He replied dismissively that of course if *that* was the sort of thing I was interested in there was nothing at all to stop me reading about it in my spare time.

I despaired of my tutors, and sought out philosophy students to discuss their subject with them. Soon they began to seek me out too, for that was the heyday of what was known as "ordinary-language philosophy," and they were constantly wanting to know how a non-philosopher would respond to such-and-such a question, or what he would spontaneously understand by such-and-such an expression. The upshot of this was that I became more involved in philosophy than in history. My degree in history came with second-, not first-, class honours, but was good enough to entitle me to move on to a higher degree. However, what I wanted to do more than anything else was study philosophy, be taught it in a disciplined way; so instead of taking a higher degree I read for another undergraduate degree, this time in philosophy.

Wisely, Oxford (unlike Cambridge) does not allow undergraduates to read philosophy in isolation, but insists on their studying it together with some other subject or subjects. So I combined it with politics and economics in the famous PPE course. Having already taken one undergraduate degree I was allowed only one academic year in which to do what was in fact a three-year course. But my vivid interest in philosophy stimulated me academically, with the result that (despite being President of the Oxford Union during that year) I did better in my PPE examinations than I had in History.

That, then, is the story of how philosophy came to be, in academic terms, my "subject." As things turned out it was not at Oxford that I received my most valuable training in it. That was to come at Yale, to which I was awarded a post-graduate fellowship in philosophy two years after taking my second Oxford degree.

When I went up to Oxford I had a very low opinion of academic pursuits and academic life in general. My supreme love was music, and from an early age I had boozed and swilled it—first at home, on records and radio; then, from before my teens, as a concert-goer and opera-goer in London. After music in my affections came theatre—I went to more live theatre than music simply because there was a great deal more of it available. Then came poetry, mostly by people who were then living and writing, above all T. S. Eliot, W. H. Auden and Dylan Thomas. Then came novels. Alongside all this I was an impassioned schoolboy socialist, revelling in political talk and argument. So it happened quite naturally that when I began to read newspapers seriously these were the things I wanted to read about. The journalistic feast of the week was the *Sunday Times:* Ernest Newman on music, James Agate on theatre, Desmond MacCarthy and others on books—not to mention Dilys Powell on films. From reading such people it was only a short step to reading some of the books they reviewed or referred to, and then another short step to reading other books on the same subjects. One way and another I got a great deal more education from these activities than ever I got from school.

Because music, theatre and politics seemed so much the most exciting, interesting and important things in life, and because I had had the good luck to be born into a family that took an active interest in them, and lived in central London, I grew up somewhat limitedly metropolitan in my outlook and assumptions. A life of personal interest in public affairs, and almost daily music and theatre in professional performances, seemed to me the only sort of life that was seriously worth having; and therefore the only sort of place worth living in seemed to me a place where such a life was possible. This meant only a small handful of the world's great cities. When at the age of seventeen I was sent as an exchange boarder to the Lycée Hôche in Versailles I went into Paris at every opportunity to go to the Opéra and the Opéra-Comique, the Comédie-Française, the picture galleries. When at eighteen I was sent to Austria for a year on military service I made straight for Vienna each time I got local leave, and went to the opera every night regardless of what was being performed. I co-ordinated my single allowance of home leave with the first post-war production of *The Ring* at Covent Garden. And in all these cities what I loved above all else were the human surroundings in which my activities were embedded: the busy streets with people all around, the eating places, the street-corner vendors, the urbanized rivers, the squares and parks, the churches and cathedrals, the public buildings—as well as the bookshops and theatres, the concert halls, the opera houses and the art galleries. Feeling myself as much a Londoner as an Englishman, and having grown up in one of the famous old pre-war street-markets, I had without even thinking about it something like a Dickensian feeling for the life of big-city streets. (One of the shrewdest things ever said about Dickens as a novelist is that he sees most of his characters as one sees people in the street.)

All of this seemed to me unconnected with academic life, which I perceived as provincial, shallow, and thin, a colourless, lightweight world unrelated to real life. I took university to be more or less a continuation of school, and professors to be the next level up of schoolmaster, people who lived their lives in closed institutions devoting all their working energies to the same sort of sub-jects as were pursued in school classrooms: Latin, Greek, history, geogra-phy . . . I found these subjects easy to "do," but had never seen much point in doing them. What seemed to me to penetrate life to the core—and therefore to be, ultimately, what living was for, in addition to relationships with other peo-ple—was the creation and absorption of works of art. Artistic experience, it seemed to me, was in a totally different category from any other sort of experi-ence, except sexual experience, when it came to glory and significance. It was the distilled essence of living. If you could choose your talent the obvious thing to be was a creative artist. If you hadn't got what it took to be that, then the next best thing was to be an interpretive artist—a conductor, or some other sort of musical performer, or an actor. If you couldn't be an artist at all, then at the head of the other professions, in a class by itself, stood politics. And whichever of these things you pursued, alongside it would go a massive interest in, and consumption of, the others—and together they would come close to filling your life. As for myself, I saw my future as being probably that of a writer; but if I should find that I lacked the creative ability to be a good enough writer I would fall back into politics. Perhaps I might do both—a lot of people had.

This, then, was my general standpoint when I was a teenager; and looking at life from this position I was unable to understand people who were inter-ested in academic pursuits. It seemed to me there must be something drasti-cally limited about them, for only people to whom all these things meant little or nothing could imagine that what went on in classrooms and lecture halls was the stuff of life. I remember believing for most of my teens that if some-one wrote only non-fiction books it must mean that he wasn't up to writing novels, hadn't the talent for the real thing. Almost every great artist I read about—and I did a lot of reading about them—seemed to be openly contemp-tuous and dismissive of academics, not only in their relation to his own work but in their relation to art.

My present view of those long-past attitudes is that they were severely im-poverished. In a narrow way, and only up to a point, I was right about what the most important things in life are, but there was something blinkered in the way I was bound up in them. Other things are important too, and can enrich life, and can yield deep satisfactions. Also, it is neither possible nor desirable that all of us should be interested in the same things. However, the greatest of the many defects of these attitudes is that they completely fail to appreciate the value and importance of the life of the mind. I had no notion then of the mo-mentous role of science in the spiritual adventure of mankind, and no notion of the indispensability of scholarship to any continuing culture or civilization, nor any notion of the profound joys for the individual that can accrue from pursuing those activities. The truth is that I had not learnt to distinguish the intellectual from the artistic—indeed, I thought the artistic *was* the intellectual. I took the term "an intellectual" to mean someone who was interested—or, still more so, actively involved—in the arts, archetypally a poet. It was, I think, the commonest use of the term at that time; people used to talk about "long-haired intellectuals," and by this they meant mainly poets and musical people, though also left-wing politicos (and I was all of those things—I was even long-haired). This use of the term had the bizarre consequence that Einstein did not count as an intellectual. But so it was.

When I went up to Oxford my overwhelming first reaction to it was that the things I cared about most in life were absent. I felt cut off from them, and was conscious all the time of being in a little town, a county and market town, where not much happened. For proper concerts and theatre I had to go to London; and I remained London-oriented for a long time. It was all a great disappointment. What shocked me most was the apparent indifference of most academics to the arts, and also to ideas generally. Their outlook seemed poky. It was only slowly that I began to learn the value of what Oxford did have to offer. And perhaps in the end the most important single thing it did for me intellectually was teach me that intellectual values exist independently of artistic values—and what they are; and to make me care about them. In my first year the discovery that there were intelligent and sympathetic individuals who were devoted more to them than to anything else came as a culture shock to me, and for a long time I was flummoxed by it: I saw clearly *that* they were but did not see how they could be. Only slowly, through daily intercourse with them, did I begin to understand it; and not until my third year did I start to ingest some of these values myself. I never did so to the point of putting them on a par with artistic values, and in that I remain convinced I was right, but they became an essential part of me, and permanently enriched my life and outlook.

Incidentally, I think that going through this experience helped me towards a deeper understanding of intelligent people who, for whatever reason, have not had a university education, and so have not themselves gone through it. I believe I know what it is like to see things as they do; and I empathize with them, because I might quite easily have been one of them myself. The greatest gift a formal education can bestow is to develop in us a conception of the world that is not merely an enlargement of our own views and attitudes and interests and assumptions; and in the nature of the case we are not able to do this without help from others who are free of our limitations. But from this, alas, it follows that the self-educated can never be more than half-educated, a regrettable but inescapable fact.

Of the specific omissions in my outlook when I went up to Oxford the most important, in view of my subsequent development, was philosophy. I had no conception of philosophy as an intellectual discipline, and not the remotest idea of what it was capable of in the work of a thinker like Kant. At that level it does, I now believe, stand close to great art among the most valuable and important of human concerns, and for a similar reason: both are truth-seeking activities pursued at the deepest level that human beings are capable of penetrating to. Both are trying to see into the ultimate nature of things, the ultimate mystery of existence; and if they fail it is only at the limits of human understanding that they fail. As Schopenhauer put it, the philosopher is doing *in abstracto* what the artist is doing *in concreto.* The philosopher has no recourse but to articulate his findings in concepts, and it may be that from the ineluctable generality of concepts it follows that philosophy cannot bite as deep as art can, but at the same time there are things that it can do that art cannot. When Iris Murdoch said, "For better and worse art goes deeper than philosophy,"* she was right to imply that there are some respects in which philosophy surpasses art, and also right to imply that it comes short of it overall.

The history of philosophy is part of a more general history of ideas, and this in turn can be subsumed under the notion of "cultural history," which of course must include the history of the arts. It is somewhere in this territory that my academic field lies. I am fully aware that art is not an intellectual, still less an academic, activity, but there are interesting and worthwhile things to be said *about* art that can be said only from a background of cultural history. It is because of this, and because of the passion I have developed for a conception of philosophy that includes its history, that an academic side to my nature was able belatedly to come into existence and grow, and then slowly to integrate with what is preponderantly a non-academic self. Although I developed academic interests late in the day, when they did come they caused me to feel a spontaneous empathy with people who were driven by them in other fields. Ever since the period I spent at Yale in my mid-twenties I have regarded myself as having at least part of one foot in the academic world, whatever other things I may have been doing at the same time.

Of the five years I devoted to specializing in history (two at school and three at university) one general legacy remains, and several specific ones. The general legacy is that I carry in my head a rough and ready outline knowledge of the history of the West from the ancient Greeks until now which is more or less continuous, sketchy though parts of it are. The fact that such a thing takes years of reading to acquire means, unavoidably, that most people, even most well-educated people, do not have it. It deeply influences the way I apprehend things, for it means that there is always a historical dimension to my view, whether of music, theatre, politics, philosophy, or anything else. I tend to see

* Bryan Magee, *Men of Ideas,* p. 277.

everything at least partially in terms of how it came to be what it is, and how it is likely to continue to change. I tend also to locate past figures in a wider context—to be aware of what sort of society it was they were living in; what was going on around them, and elsewhere, at the time they were active; what had not yet happened, and what they could not possibly have known. In particular I am conscious of the reality of perpetual change, and know that there is nothing privileged about the present. I do not, as so many people seem to, assume that the whole of the past has been leading up to now, and that what is happening now is of privileged significance. On the contrary, I am aware that the present is as temporary as every previous now, and will soon be no more than another moment in the general past. All human beings—past, present and future—find their lives embedded at some arbitrary point in the middle of a rich, complex and unceasing historical flow that is ever-changing and goes on after their death. No one point in it is privileged as against any other, and none either more or less real than any other. This realization, that cuts to the centre of me, pervades my attitude both to the arts and to intellectual life.

In society as a whole, artistic and intellectual life are both for the most part lived in thrall to fashion. People in each generation tend to believe that what matters most is what is being done by themselves and their contemporaries. And I always see this as a delusion. Nearly all of what is done in any generation is quickly forgotten. Only a tiny amount, if any, survives to become part of the accumulating treasure of an ever-extending remembered past. Nearly everything of lasting value and significance that is available to each generation is already in its past. The fashionable concerns of the day are not worth bothering about unless they happen to coincide with what is lastingly important—and then they are worth bothering about anyway, not because they are fashionable but because they are lastingly important. What is lastingly important can easily be unfashionable in its day, like the music of Bach; or old-fashioned, like the music of Brahms. What matters about an artist is not how his work relates to his time but how good it is regardless of that consideration. Indeed, whether it survives or not will depend entirely on what value it has for times other than his own. Innovation, novelty, up-to-dateness, contemporaneity, relevance to current concerns, are all characteristics of short duration. They are not values, they are irrelevant features when it comes to quality. A work can have all of them and be trifling, or none of them and be great. Equally, of course, it can have all of them and be great, and none of them and be trifling. If one says this to most people who are professionally concerned in artistic or intellectual life it seems to them obviously false, when it ought to seem to them obviously true. This is because they are irretrievably lost in the concerns of their own time. And I have found this to be as true of philosophy as it is of the arts.

Philosophy, like the arts, does not progress. Just as no poet or dramatist since Shakespeare has been better than Shakespeare, so Plato—who happens to be the first philosopher whose works have come down to us—continues to be regarded by many as the greatest philosopher of all time. Whitehead, who famously said that the whole of Western philosophy is footnotes to Plato, once remarked that it is possible to be provincial in time as well as in place; and the unfortunate truth is that all but a handful of people are narrowly provincial in time.

The more specific legacies that I have inherited from my years of immersion in the study of history are two or three periods of special historical knowledge, and the impact of a number of books. Two books in particular made an impression on me during my three years of history at Oxford, and it is characteristic of my situation there that neither of them was read at the behest of a tutor. They were *Religion and the Rise of Capitalism* by R. H. Tawney, and Karl Marx's *Das Kapital.* The latter had a tremendous effect on me. During the Easter vacation of my second year I found digs in East Oxford where for at least a fortnight I did nothing morning, afternoon and evening but live my way through *Das Kapital*—taking it at its own pace, putting the book down whenever I wanted to ruminate on what it was saying, feeling free to continue these reflections for as long as I liked before picking it up again, going out for walks to mull over crucial passages, thinking about it in bed at night. It was the first book I ever absorbed in this way, and in the course of my life I do not think there have been more than a dozen others—the dialogues of Plato, the New Testament, Hume's *A Treatise of Human Nature,* Kant's *Critique of Pure Reason,* Schopenhauer's *The World as Will and Representation,* the Upanishads, Popper's *The Open Society and Its Enemies,* Einstein's General Theory of Relativity. These are the writings that have changed me. That is to say, I have absorbed them to such a degree that they have entered into the way I see things, so that I would not now feel myself to be the person I am if I had not read them. I take it there are few books of which any of us can say that. There is at least one playwright, Shakespeare, of whom the corresponding thing is true for me, and perhaps seven or eight composers. Obviously there is a sense in which all of one's reading, theatre-going and listening to music has a drip-drip-drip effect on one's outlook and personality, changing them by imperceptible degrees; but the number of individual creators to whom one can attribute felt and identifiable change in one's *self* remains small. Of the bodies of written work I have instanced, half are by writers from the German-speaking world, and this fact—to which might be added the fact that most of the composers come from that world too, and during the same historical period—says something about the nature of my inner life.

Most of *Das Kapital* is a history of the Industrial Revolution in England; but it is an argued history, expounded to make a case. I did not emerge from my reading of it a Marxist: I saw straight away that the Labour Theory of Value, which Marx himself makes foundational to his system, was a metaphysical concept without any real content; and I also rejected from the beginning his belief in the scientific predictability of historical change. Nevertheless my thinking was greatly influenced by Marx; and although that influence diminished the more I thought about his work, it has never disappeared—and nor would I wish it to, for in my opinion he offers insights which are of permanent value. He is also a magnificent writer, full of character—if overly judgmental, Jehovah-like in his wrath and judgment. I cannot think how the idea ever got about that *Das Kapital* is a boring and indigestible tome, unless as an excuse given to themselves for not reading it by people who were put off by its size. It is a great book. And it must surely go without saying that it has been one of the most influential books in the history of the world.

After reading it I read the most significant of Marx's other writings. There are many readily available one-volume collections of these, and the most important of the works appear in them all. These writings embody a whole view of the world, and of the history of the world, within which economic and class factors are allotted decisive roles; and although Marx may be wrong about the nature of those roles, as well as exaggerating their relative importance in the overall scheme of things, he nevertheless casts floods of new light upon them. It is difficult now to realize that before him they were accorded scarcely any significance at all as agents of historical change. No serious thinker today could be guilty of such blindness—he would not be regarded as a serious thinker if he were—but that this is so is owing to Marx. Also, until Marx came along, economic and class factors were taken to be altogether extraneous to aesthetic ones in the creation and interpretation of works of art; but no one nowadays would seriously maintain that. These are examples of how Marx has influenced all of us, not only those who are or have been Marxists. The world is a different place because of him, not only objectively but also in the way we look at it.

There were three books that I had read at school and now re-read at Oxford that became lifelong possessions: Machiavelli's *The Prince,* Jacob Burkhardt's *The Civilization of the Renaissance in Italy,* and John Stuart Mill's *On Liberty.* The first of these, again, is a much misrepresented work. What it does is tell home truths about what people do to get power and keep it, wherever *Realpolitik* rules. Its insights are wonderfully penetrating, and in most cases valid. Much of it consists of situational logic, and has universal application. For instance, Machiavelli warns you that if someone plays a key role in hoisting you up into a position of power higher than the one he himself occupies he will almost inevitably become disaffected and a source of danger to you. He will be perpetually conscious of the fact that it is only through him that you have reached your position, and this will make him feel that he is as good as you are but is not regarded as such by others. So he will feel that you ought to lift *him* up more, show him more gratitude, reward him more, take more notice of him and of his special interests and his advice to you. As his resentment grows he will be tempted by the thought that his having placed you in your position means that he could place someone else in it if he set his mind to it. So he is likely eventually to start plotting against you, or at least sympathizing with your enemies. For all these reasons, if you have been raised to power by another person and want to be secure, you should seek to eliminate that person as soon as you can safely do without him. I have seen this insight borne out over and over again in different walks of life, not only in politics but in office politics, and in academic politics, even in the politics of voluntary organizations. Short though it is, *The Prince* teems with perceptions of this calibre. As an education in the ways of the world, especially in the more brutal of life's realities, there is no book to surpass it. Regardless of whether you yourself are ever going to behave in the ways it describes, the book is an eye-opener to what you must expect to happen around you in many areas of your life. I take it the need for such alertness on the part of people who are themselves of the purest integrity is what Jesus meant when he said, "Be ye therefore wise as serpents, and harmless as doves" (Matthew 10:16). If I am right in that interpretation then Jesus would have approved of people reading Machiavelli.

John Stuart Mill's *On Liberty* is a flawed book, but its central thesis—that individuals should be free to live as they wish, to the maximum extent that is compatible with their not significantly injuring others—has been my basic political belief all my life. The changes of political opinion I have gone through have been changes in belief about how we can come closest to that aim. When most people in Britain were poor, badly housed and ill-educated, I believed that only large-scale government provision could sufficiently increase the number and magnitude of the life-chances open to them. Two things about that have changed during my adult lifetime: most people in Britain have ceased to be poor and badly housed; and I have become disillusioned with the efficacy of many sorts of state intervention. So I have changed from being a liberal socialist to being a liberal non-socialist. But I have always had the same end in view, namely personal freedom. Mill's advocacy of this remains, I think, the best short introduction to the basic ideas involved, and to some of the ways in which the most obvious objections can be answered.

Two books that I read at Oxford for the first time were Aristotle's *Politics* and Tocqueville's *L'Ancien Régime et la Révolution,* both of which were set texts for the preliminary examination in history that I faced at the end of my second term. The Aristotle was my introduction to ancient philosophy. And what a revelation it was! I still remember my naive astonishment that someone living hundreds of years B.C. could speak to me directly with such a largeness of outlook and knowledge, such a range of penetrating analysis and intelligent argument, all of which seemed to have application to my own world. I was astounded that there was nothing primitive about any of it: on the contrary, it moved at a higher intellectual level, and a higher level of worldly sophistication, than I was used to encountering in the people around me. It was through this gateway that I entered the incredible world of the ancient Greeks; and to this day my imagination is perplexed by how much the members of so small a society achieved in so short a time, especially when so little had been done to prepare the ground for them at anything like the level on which they moved. I came gradually to feel that my own deepest roots are in a culture which they more than anyone inaugurated, a culture which was not to return to the levels they set until more than two thousand years after them, with the equally incredible civilization of the German-speaking world in the short period between the late eighteenth and early twentieth centuries—the period whose representative figures include Mozart, Kant, Haydn, Beethoven, Schubert, Goethe, Schiller, Schopenhauer, Hegel, Marx, Brahms, Wagner, Nietzsche, Mahler, Freud and Einstein.

Tocqueville was someone I had simply never heard of, and he was in every way a discovery for me. One insight that everyone who has read *L'Ancien Régime* seems to carry away from it and retain for life is that if a revolution is going to occur it will probably come not when social conditions are at their worst but when they have started to improve after a long period of deprivation and repression—in other words, revolutions happen when things are getting better, not when things are getting worse. Indeed, the regimes that are overthrown by them are usually carrying out programmes of rapid and radical reform. It is the profusion in his work of wonderfully counter-intuitive insights such as this that makes Tocqueville the only sociologist of true genius that there has ever been, unless one counts Marx as a sociologist. His book *Democracy in America* leaves today's reader lost in admiration at the detailed accuracy of his prophecies about how the United States was going to turn out, an accuracy which proves how deep and right his understanding of that infant society in the early nineteenth century was. In the United States (because he was the greatest of all analysts of American society) and in France (because he was French) he is valued at something like his true worth, but in Britain he is far too little known—I suspect not only because he wrote about those two foreign societies and not about Britain, but also because for several generations his liberalism rendered him inimical to both of the bodies of political thought that had mass representation in Britain, namely conservatism and socialism. If only he rather than Marx had become the chief theoretical inspiration of left-of-centre Britons the history of the democratic left in that country would be a great deal happier and more successful than it has been. The undeniable fact is that although Marxist thought has had more influence, on issue after issue it is Tocqueville who has turned out to be right as against Marx—as in the case I just instanced about when revolutions occur. Tocqueville's *Democracy in America* is still the first book I would recommend to anyone wanting to acquire a more than superficial understanding of the United States. The very length of time that has elapsed between when it was written and now helps it to reveal the deep structure that lies beneath, and sustains, the modern surface.

I will not be so tedious as to enumerate all the books I read as a history student that relate to the history of ideas—and hence to philosophy, if only via political philosophy, or the philosophy of sociology. As for the strengths and weaknesses of my knowledge of history itself, these are in many ways arbitrary. Everyone who read history at Oxford when I did was required to study English history from the beginning; and at my school, history specialists had to specialize in medieval history; so I have been formally taught my way through English medieval history twice. On the other hand, when the old School Certificate offered a choice between English and German nineteenth-century history my school chose the German option for us all (probably because the main modern language at the school was German) without passing the choice on to us; and at Oxford my history tutors simply ran out of time at 1832, and I went no further with them; and when I went on to read PPE in one year there was no time to receive tuition in more than six of the eight papers, so I was deemed already to have covered English nineteenth-century political history; so I have never been taught nineteenth-century English history. Most English people I know who have never been history specialists have spent a year or two being taught about Gladstone and Disraeli, Peel and Palmerston, but I have not. Of course I have acquired some knowledge of the period in the course of my life, but it does not have the support structure that is acquired by disciplined and lengthy study.

History students at Oxford had to choose a period of "general history" to specialize in, so I chose the most recent one, which included the First World War, the Russian Revolution, the rise of Mussolini and Hitler, the Spanish Civil War, and ended with the outbreak of the Second World War, which had finished only four years before I went up to the university. Young though I was, I was studying events that had taken place during my own lifetime, and I remain permanently pleased to have done that. It vastly enriches one's understanding of the social and historical context in which one's own life is being lived; and in my case at least it cleared my mind of a good deal of bigotry and illusion.

From my historical studies in general I learnt a great many lessons that were absorbed into my political outlook. One was that violent internal revolutions never achieve their aims. This is partly because so much more of the old society always continues into the new one than the revolutionaries want or realize, and partly for another reason. There is a situational logic to such revolutions. Disparate groups unite to overthrow an existing regime, but once they have succeeded in doing so the cause that brought them together has gone, and they then fight one another to fill the power vacuum that they themselves have created. These internecine struggles, usually savage, among erstwhile allies perpetuate the revolutionary breakdown of society far beyond the overthrow of the old regime, and delay the establishment of a new order. The population at large begins to feel itself threatened by unending social chaos, and in these circumstances a strong man who can bring the warring factions to heel and impose order comes forward and meets with widespread support, or at least acquiescence. Thus an internal revolution carried out in the name of civil liberties, or equality, or to bring a tyranny to an end, will itself end by putting into power a Cromwell, a Napoleon or a Stalin. All internal revolutions are uncontrollable, and all such revolutions are betrayed. It is in their nature that these things should be so. This fact makes belief in violent revolution as a method of changing society not only irrational and delusory but profoundly immoral.

A related thing that I learnt was the indispensability of the rule of law to civilized life. I perceived how law developed in England over the centuries not only from the top downwards but partly as the only effective shield for the individual against arbitrary authority. In societies where government is not bound by laws the individual has no such protection, and all the evils of totalitarian societies are made possible by the fact that the political parties who rule them govern above the law. I saw that Marxists' attacks on legality for allegedly representing only the interests of the ruling class were not merely misconceived and invalid but positively disastrous, for when successful they have the effect of removing from everybody, not least the poor and the powerless, their chief defence. Without law, everything becomes a matter of arbitrary power—as indeed it was in the societies of that day that were defended by British Marxists, societies in which the governments routinely suppressed, imprisoned, exiled, or killed their opponents. Ironically, it was in Communist societies more than any others that the law was used cynically by the ruling class in its own self-interest as an instrument of tyrannical government. From Plato I learnt that for those who come to power not to suppress their opponents but to deal with them in accordance with laws to which the rulers themselves are subject was the most important single step between barbarism and civilization. Plato is repeatedly insistent on this. He is right, and the societies approved of by Communists were indeed in a state of barbarism.

Something else I learnt, less easy to express in words, is respect for reality as against all the many alternatives to it—conventional assumptions, fashionable ways of looking at things, ideologies, social or personal aspirations, fears, intentions, wishful thinking, religious claims, and the rest. Whatever people may write, say, want or believe, the only reality is what actually happens. In T. S. Eliot's famous lines: "What might have been is an abstraction remaining a perpetual possibility only in a world of speculation." This insight was first brought home to me in real terms, perhaps not surprisingly, in relation to one of my own fundamental beliefs. Ever since becoming a socialist in childhood I had believed, as most socialists in those days did, in the inevitability of socialism. Indeed, there were quite a lot of non-socialists who believed in the inevitability of socialism. But one day, at the age of twenty-one or -two, I was sitting reading about Lenin in the Radcliffe Camera (the history library at Oxford which was architecturally the central point of the university) when suddenly the thought invaded my mind with almost traumatic clarity: "It's never going to happen. There just isn't ever actually going to *be* socialism." And once I realized this, it became obvious that no matter how attractive the idea might be, and no matter how good it would have been in practice if it could have come into existence, to advocate socialism was worse than useless because it meant being divorced from reality. For anyone, being serious about politics means thinking in terms of what can actually be done, and this therefore involves, among other things, not being a socialist. As a result of this realization I felt for the first time inclined to support the Labour Party, which I had always hitherto regarded as pragmatic and compromising, and therefore not really as socialist. When I told my friends that the reason I had begun to support the Labour Party was that I had ceased to be a socialist they thought this a witty remark, but it was simple truth.

I came to realize, then, that what matters above all else in politics is what happens, not what people say about it. And for the most part what happens is independent of my wishes. In politics especially, people tend to allow their wishes to influence their assessment of reality, and to mix up the two even at conscious levels of thinking. For instance, all my life I have bet on elections, and all my life I have found that many people assume that what I am betting on is what I wish to occur. If I say to a group of people, "I've just put some money on the Conservatives to win the election," I can count on at least one of them to say, "I didn't know you were a Conservative." Some people carry the mistake even further and assert that for someone who is not a Conservative to bet on a Conservative victory is wrong, in the sense of not morally right. Some even go so far as to assert that if you support a political party you *ought to think that that party is going to win:* in other words you positively ought to let your practical judgment be distorted by your wishes. Alas, the human tendency to think in this way extends into metaphysics. I have innumerable times heard people say that it would be intolerable if the existence of the universe were a meaningless accident, and life were without any larger purpose or significance; and therefore that there *must* be some meaning to it all. At least as often I have heard people advocate belief in God on the ground that such belief is comforting. Again, if I say to them, "But it might just *be* the case that there is no significance to it all; after all, we know that lots of things certainly are the case that we don't like, sometimes things that we find horrifying, like torture and death," someone is almost bound to say, usually angrily, "Do you want life to be pointless, then?"

The study of history did much to develop in me a respect for unpalatable truth. It brought vividly alive for me the realization that what the truth is has nothing to do with my preferences, or with what I consider ought to happen. To say that such-and-such a group of people cannot possibly have terrorized and slaughtered millions of other people because it would be too terrible to contemplate is just plain wrong if in fact they did; and to say that it was a wicked thing to do leaves the fact that they did unaltered. If a reality is something appalling and horrible, it is not any the less a reality for that, and what is more there is nothing that can make it not a reality. Wishful thinking is incompatible with serious thinking, and anyone who goes in for it is refusing to take part in the pursuit of truth.

From all these things it will be evident that my five years as a history specialist left a permanent mark on me. The most important point to make in this book is that they influenced my approach to ideas, including philosophical ideas. Even so, because of the narrowness of "history" as conceived at the Oxford of my undergraduate days it is as a passionate student of philosophy during the time since then that I have acquired most of my knowledge of the history of ideas; and it is as a passionate lover of the arts that I have acquired most of my knowledge of cultural history. The most instructive of all my disciplines in these fields has been the need to write. Lord Acton said that one should learn as much from writing as from reading. It is a profound saying. Writing about a subject forces one to study it in an organized way and with a focused aim; to read all the important literature about it; to cover the whole ground, not leaving material gaps; and it gives one a powerful motive to get even the most trivial details right, not to let errors creep in. Most important of all, it forces one to *think* about the subject—and to organize one's thoughts, as well as one's material, into coherent structures. I have written several of my books (and made broadcast series on television and radio that were then turned into books) because I wanted to master a subject: producing a book about it was the best, if not the only, way I could force myself to work really hard and systematically at it over a long period of time. I can sit and think for a while, but not for months on end—unless I write.

3

Logical Positivism
and Its Refutation

The golden age of what came to be known internationally as "Oxford philosophy" was roughly the decade and a half between the end of the Second World
War in 1945 and the death of J. L. Austin in 1960. I was pitched into it at its
height, my student years in Oxford being 1949–53, and then again, as a post-
graduate, 1954–5.

I have to say at the outset that I was trained in Oxford philosophy without
ever subscribing to it. I seem to have learnt to do it as well as some of its practitioners, but I never believed in its validity *as a conception of philosophy*—
though I always perceived that as a form of intellectual training it had
considerable merits. It taught students to be hyper-careful about what they
said, and to make sure they understood it as well as meant it; to treat subtle
differences of meaning as if they mattered; and to try to achieve these things
with clarity and humour. The fact, too, that so much of it involved face-to-face
argument made it a training in mental agility and public debate, though this
carried with it the disadvantage of being unaccommodating to people who
were deep-thinking but slow-moving: in live argument the cleverest people
quite often lost out while the superficially clever shone. Whenever someone
says anything philosophically interesting to me my natural reaction is to want
to go away and think about it, not to give it some impromptu, off-the-top-of-
my-head response and then continue the discussion from *there,* of all places.
Philosophical discussion that moves forward in that way simply passes from
one instant response to the next instant response. Of course these instant re-

sponses are informed by previous reflections, but they cannot take account of the new. And this is the way most philosophical discussion in professional circles proceeds. My most deeply felt criticism of it is that it trains its practitioners in quickness and cleverness while precluding depth. However, be that as it may, for all the usefulness of Oxford philosophy as a tool for sharpening the wits, I could never understand how anyone could take seriously the view that the subject matter of philosophy was linguistic, and this was something that all the various forms of Oxford philosophy had in common.

I say "all the various forms of Oxford philosophy" because in fact the expression "Oxford philosophy" was an umbrella term that covered more than one approach. From the turn of the century until the Second World War the chief centre of philosophical activity in Britain had been Cambridge, with Whitehead, Russell, Moore and Wittgenstein as the most notable figures, surrounded by an impressive number of individuals of substantial if lesser ability. But after the Second World War the centre shifted to Oxford. In the first phase of the Oxford hegemony the dominant influence was that of logical positivism, and the most influential book *Language, Truth and Logic* by A. J. Ayer—which had been published in 1936 but whose full impact had been delayed by the war.*

Logical positivism had originated not in Oxford but in Vienna, during the period between the two world wars. Ayer, then a very junior research fellow, only twenty-three when he wrote his most famous book, did nothing to originate it but only introduced it to the English-speaking world. It became all the rage in Oxford first of all; and—at least as far as Britain was concerned—that university was to remain the centre of it. Its influence, by no means confined to philosophy, reached its greatest height in the years immediately after the Second World War, and it was this intellectual fashion that brought Oxford to the forefront in philosophy.

The central concern of the logical positivists was to find a criterion of demarcation between sense and non-sense. The original members of the so-called Vienna Circle were all native German speakers who quite naturally oriented themselves towards the intellectual and cultural traditions of the German-speaking world, and they were convinced that most of the metaphysicians best known in that world—people like Fichte, Schelling and Hegel, and their more recent epigones—were talking high-flown nonsense. The British logical positivists harboured the same conviction towards the work of British neo-Hegelian philosophers of the late nineteenth and early twentieth centuries such as Bradley and McTaggart. In ordinary life one knows that it is possible even with the best of intentions to utter words and yet say nothing—we are ac-

* See *Men of Ideas*, p. 130.

customed to hearing decent men do it from pulpits; and empty utterance is the order of the day throughout the mass media, including the so-called quality press. Given that speaking without saying anything is compatible with both high intelligence and good intentions, how are we to distinguish between statements that really do say something (whether true or false is a separate question) and statements that say nothing at all—and therefore can be neither true nor false, because they do not mean anything?

The answer at which the logical positivists arrived ran as follows. For present purposes meaningful statements fall into one of two categories. One kind is either true or false by virtue of the terms that are used. If I say to you: "The man who lives next door to me is a bachelor with a wife and two children," you know that this cannot be true (unless his surname is Bachelor and I am making a pun). "Bachelor" means "unmarried man," and therefore my neighbour cannot be both a bachelor and married. So you do not need to investigate to find out whether what I say is true or false; the very terms of my statement tell you that it is false. So you can confidently pronounce its falsity without stirring out of your armchair. Statements whose truth or falsity can be established in this way, by analysing the statement itself, are known as "analytic statements." The logical positivists held that all definitions, and all statements in logic and mathematics, are of this kind, together with all statements whose validity is based on conventions, such as the rules of games, or statements in a field like heraldry. The alternative category of statement consists of those whose truth or falsity cannot be established by analysis but only by checking the facts. If I say to you, "There are fourteen red-headed people living in my village," this may be true or it may be false. It could be either, and the terms of the statement itself do not tell you which. The only way to find out is to look at all the inhabitants of my village and count the redheads. Because the truth or falsity of statements of this kind can be established only by setting them against a reality outside themselves they are known as "synthetic statements." Now whereas the negation of a true analytic statement is a self-contradiction, the negation of a true synthetic statement is not self-contradictory: it is a statement that could well have been true but happens not to be. There might have been six redheads in my village, or fifteen, or none. Each of these alternatives is perfectly possible, and there is nothing intrinsically self-contradictory about my asserting any of them. Not more than one such statement can be true, though, and all of those I make may well be false, so the only way to find out is to check.

The members of the Vienna Circle had all, or nearly all, been trained as scientists or mathematicians, not as philosophers, so they may well not have known that the distinction between analytic and synthetic statements went back a long way in the history of philosophy. It had first been made persuasively and at length (although not using the terms "analytic" and "synthetic") by Leibniz, and then again, after Leibniz but independently, by Hume. Hume had applied it with the same radicalism and ruthlessness as the logical positivists now went on to do. If you utter any indicative statement at all, they said, it has to be either analytic or synthetic. If it is analytic we shall establish by analysis whether it is true or false. If it is synthetic there must, at least in principle, be something we can observe, something we can check, that will tell us whether it is true or false. If it possesses any real content at all its truth or falsity has to make some difference to something. And if what you are talking about is the world of possible experience then there must be some possible experience that would register that difference. If no conceivable experience would serve to verify or falsify your statement, then the statement is unconnected with how things are, at least in the world of possible experience—which is the only world we can know. So your statement tells us nothing at all. It can be neither true nor false, and is therefore meaningless. The sentence may be grammatically well formed and look deceptively like other sentences that tell us something, but actually it is empty.

Thus the famous Verification Principle was arrived at. Only assertions that were in principle verifiable by observation or experience could convey factual information. Assertions that there could be no imaginable way of verifying must either be analytic or meaningless.

The worldview that lay behind this doctrine was that of the science of its day. In fact the Vienna Circle, who as I have said were themselves scientists and mathematicians, were explicit about this: to the manifesto they published they gave the title "The Scientific View of the World." They tended to believe that all discoverable truths about the world were discoverable by the methods of science. The matter of which the world consists was being explained with ever-increasing success by physics and chemistry and, as far as living organisms were concerned, by the life sciences. Human beings were being further explained by psychology, linguistics, the behavioural sciences, social science, political science, and the rest. Scientific methods were being introduced with ever more impressive results into economics, history, anthropology and so on. Astronomy was telling us more and more about the universe as a whole. There was no corner of the world of possible experience—precisely because it *is* the realm of experience—that was not amenable to investigation by scientific methods of one sort or another, and in response to such investigation our knowledge of it was galloping ahead at a rate unprecedented in history. This was the only really reliable way of acquiring knowledge—which, to be really *knowledge,* had to satisfy the conditions either of the sciences, if the subject matter were synthetic, or of mathematics or logic, if it were analytic. Synthetic statements that did not satisfy the criteria of science were just empty claims to knowledge—expressions of conventional or religious belief, or personal viewpoint, ungrounded assumption, speculation, superstition, wishful thinking, prejudice, perhaps feeling or emotion of some kind, but certainly not knowledge in any objective or intellectually serious sense. The logical positivists' all-embracing, dismissive, and contemptuous term for beliefs of this kind was "metaphysics"—chiefly, I think, because of their determination to sweep into limbo all religious ways of thinking as well as all metaphysical philosophy in the Hegelian tradition, and to stop people talking about the world in either of these ways. They were always insistent that the only world of which we could claim *knowledge* was the world of actual and possible experience.

The effect of all this was to assimilate every meaningful utterance about the world to utterances about direct experience (common sense) or utterances in the contemporary language of science (which they took to be common sense rendered self-critical and made systematic). Either something is scientific, or capable of becoming a science, or it is merely an expression of opinion or feeling, in which case it is subjective, not factual. This, of course, was a world-view not peculiar to the Vienna Circle but widely held among educated Westerners through most of the nineteenth and twentieth centuries. What the logical positivists did was provide it with what they took to be its philosophical underpinning.

This, however, raises the question of the place of philosophy in a world such as that presented to us by the logical positivists, a world no part of which is unamenable to scientific investigation. The task of philosophy as traditionally conceived is to understand the world. But if every element of that task is taken over by science then clearly none of it is left for philosophy to carry out. But does this leave philosophy with any *raison d'être?* Yes, said the logical positivists, it does, but philosophy's task is now a second-order one. We should no longer look to philosophy to further our direct understanding of the world. For that we should look to the apposite science. However, the sciences are in a process of unceasing development, as are mathematics and logic, so there is perpetual need for re-evaluation and reformulation of their tasks and methods. There is also perpetual need for clarification of the new concepts that come into existence as scientific knowledge expands. And there is perpetual need for a critical self-awareness about our utterances in every field— precisely what we mean by them, and what our justification for making them is, and what the logical consequences of them are. All these tasks are tasks for the philosopher, and they point up the areas that constitute his legitimate field of activity: method, logic, the clarification of concepts, the elucidation of meaning. Logical positivism is itself the exemplar of philosophy in this sense, and shows what it can do. It has swept away whole libraries of misguided and fruitless speculation, and clarified definitively the terms on which legitimate intellectual activity of every kind takes place.

Thus it came about that people who regarded their view of the world and of knowledge as solidly science-based nevertheless put a high valuation on philosophy, but at the same time regarded it as a second-order activity. It was at that point in its history that philosophy in the empiricist tradition stopped regarding its task as the understanding of the world and saw itself as clarifying formulations in language—formulations of concepts, of logical implications of arguments, of presuppositions, of methods, of research programmes, and of their outcomes. Historically, it was a turning point.

Perhaps in putting the matter in these terms I am making everything seem a little too clear-cut historically, too independent of its own immediate pre-history. Between Leibniz and Hume on the one hand and the logical positivists on the other I have left a historical gap unaccounted for. There were in fact developments of great importance for logical positivism in between. Not only had the rise of modern science taken place. The intellectual developments I have been describing had vital connections with the (to them recent) logical and philosophical work of Bertrand Russell and—in Britain at any rate— G. E. Moore. This pre-history is the subject of a book by A. J. Ayer whose title itself makes the point: *Russell and Moore: The Analytical Heritage.* Russell had done more than any other individual to propagate the revolutionary developments that took place in logic in the period straddling the nineteenth and twentieth centuries, and to apply new techniques of logical analysis not only to traditional problems of philosophy but to utterances in ordinary language. For these reasons he was revered as a sort of intellectual godfather by logical positivists everywhere, including Vienna. But he never regarded the application of these new developments in logic as constituting more than a redoubtable intellectual technology that would help philosophy in its traditional task of understanding the world. They might, he believed, render some hitherto unsolved philosophical problems soluble, and be for that reason of the very greatest importance to philosophy, but they were certainly not *in themselves* philosophy, still less were they what philosophy was "about." So although he sympathized with much of what the logical positivists were doing he never thought of himself as one of them, and he always viewed their overall conception of philosophy as rather crude and limited, for all its perceived merits. In so far as they exercised a reciprocal influence on him he came later to feel that this influence had not been entirely to the good.

Whereas Russell's standing and influence were international, Moore's never extended much beyond the English-speaking world. But within that world his influence was immense. First and foremost must be reckoned the influence on Russell. As young men at Cambridge Moore and Russell, who were lifelong friends, were neo-Hegelians of a kind that was characteristic of their time and place. The first of them to break with German idealism was Moore, and Russell followed close behind. Together they embraced, with the enthusiasm of converts, the British empiricist tradition represented by Locke, Berkeley, Hume and Mill. Moore continued for the rest of his life to exercise direct influence on most of the leading philosophers practising in Britain—an influence that seems to me (and came to seem eventually to most of them) out of all proportion to his merits as a philosopher. Indeed, such an influence on his part was not confined to the world of philosophy. He was the greatest intellectual influence on the whole ethos of the Bloomsbury Group, which produced outstanding figures in other fields, several of whom were of much greater ability than Moore.

Like the logical positivists, Moore thought that we human beings were already in secure possession of a reliable source of knowledge and understanding of the world, though in his case this source was not so much science as common sense. To him it seemed self-evident that the commonsense view of the world was, with appropriate qualifications, right, and what is more that we all in our heart of hearts knew it to be right: for instance, that each one of us knows that he has a body, and lives in a world whose existence in the dimensions of time and space is independent of whether he himself exists or not; and that this world contains a large number of other material bodies, some of which are people like himself and have experiences similar to his. So when philosophers come along and say that time and space are forms of human sensibility, and that we ourselves unconsciously carry out the process of synthesizing material objects in the act of perceiving them; or that we cannot really know for certain that there are minds other than our own; this is just a sort of high-faluting humbug. People who say this sort of thing do not themselves actually, in their lived lives, believe it. The philosopher who says that time is an illusion knows nothing with greater certainty than that he ate his breakfast this morning after he got up but before he left home, and that to deny this would be to utter a falsehood. The philosopher who says we cannot be certain of the existence of an external world does not actually regard the existence of his house or his car as being in doubt. The philosopher who says we cannot be sure of the existence of other minds has no doubt whatsoever about the independent existence of his wife. In short, philosophers say all sorts of things that they themselves know to be untrue. And Moore saw his task as exposing this kind of nonsense for what it was.

So, strictly speaking, it was with Moore that the task of philosophy first came to be seen as talk about talk, at least in the anglophone world. And his influence on Oxford philosophers of both the main schools, not only logical positivists but also the linguistic analysts who came after them, was enormous. To cite evidence for this concerning only the leaders of the two movements, A. J. Ayer once said: "I was very much influenced by Moore, and also influenced by the problems in which Moore was interested—not the Moore of *Principia Ethica* but the later Moore, who was very much concerned with the problem of perception, for example. And one of the unresolved problems in the Vienna Circle was the status of observation statements themselves. They held that everything had to be reduced to observation statements, that in the end what science was about was what was observable, but they weren't at all agreed on what was observable. They were divided between one wing, headed by Schlick, who wanted to reduce everything to so-called sensation statements, that is statements recording people's actual and possible sensations, and another wing led by Carnap and Neurath who wanted to stop at statements describing physical objects."*

As for J. L. Austin, the doyen of the school of linguistic analysis which succeeded logical positivism, the following exchange once took place between me and one of his closest colleagues, Geoffrey Warnock, who after Austin's death became one of his literary executors:

> WARNOCK: He is on record as actually saying at one point "Moore's my man"—certainly meaning by that that this is what he liked, the way he liked to see the subject done.
> MAGEE: And also meaning, presumably, that he didn't like seeing it done in Russell's way.
> WARNOCK: I think, on that occasion, yes—the relevant contrast was with Russell . . .†

In the same conversation Warnock put forward an admirably lucid summary of Moore's influence in general. "First, I'm sure that his way of doing philosophy—the extreme plainness and care and clarity, the taste for small steps and small points—was very influential. Predominantly, people came to adopt this cool, cautious manner of philosophical argument. Then, secondly, his example led many philosophers to think that philosophy is *entirely* analysis—that the philosopher does not, so to speak, assert propositions on his own account, but *only* analyses propositions asserted by others. Moore himself didn't say this, but others did; and Moore's *practice* seemed to support their view. But I think, in fact, his actual defence of common sense was very important too—I mean his insistence that there are vastly many things which as

---

* Bryan Magee, *Modern British Philosophy,* p. 50.
† *Modern British Philosophy,* p. 93.

a matter of fact we all know for certain to be true, and that there must be something seriously wrong if philosophers seem to be denying or questioning these. . . . This, I think, has since Moore become a very generally held view, at any rate among English-speaking philosophers. . . . And this has been very important, I think, in changing the way philosophers look at what they're doing. . . . This is an important change of angle among philosophers, which is largely attributable to Moore's influence."*

Anyone who has read Chapter One of this book will understand without further explanation that, and why, I regard this enthronement of common sense as an intellectual catastrophe. Quite apart from everything that has been said there, and all other considerations that might be described as philosophical, modern science has shown that behind our moment-to-moment experience of the everyday world teem truths and realities that common sense is totally unaware of, that are frequently astounding and often counter-intuitive, and sometimes deeply difficult to grasp even when we know them to be true. For instance, that every physical object in our environment is a whirl of molecules and atoms made up of subatomic particles in random motion at speeds approaching that of light. That all this is transmutable into energy—that every physical object is a space filled with force—is not at all the commonsense way of looking at things. Nor is the fact that the air around us is full of invisible waves of information-bearing kinds, to wit television and radio waves, and has a great many other analysable properties too. Even something so basic as that we are living on the surface of a giant ball that is rotating on its axis at surface speeds of up to a thousand miles an hour while at the same time hurtling through space is (I am tempted to say, violently) counter-intuitive, impossible to see or feel even when we know it to be true, and so contrary to common sense that the first people to put it forward, only a few hundred years ago, were denounced as either ludicrous fantasists or dangerous liars whose wild falsehoods would, if believed, undermine all true religion and (therefore) true morality. So we know for a fact—it is not a matter of opinion—that common sense does not come anywhere near to giving us even a truthful let alone adequate picture of our situation. And everything revealed to us by special and general relativity, everything revealed to us by quantum physics, shows that our immediate physical surroundings are bizarre beyond anything imaginable by human beings until recently, so far from common sense that every student of such matters, no matter how intelligent, finds serious difficulty in understanding them. In these circumstances attempts to defend the commonsense view of the world are doomed before they begin. They constitute

* *Modern British Philosophy,* pp. 91–2.

anachronism and obscurantism at their most unimaginative. They are dinosaur-ism of the deepest dye.

To understate the matter as politely as I can, the commonsense view of the world can be the metaphysics only of the insufficiently seriously reflective. Russell, ruder than I, described it as the metaphysics of savages. The words of his that I have quoted elsewhere more often than any others constitute the last sentence in the following passage from his book *The Problems of Philosophy* (p. 38—his italics): ". . . common sense leaves us completely in the dark as to the true intrinsic nature of physical objects, and if there were good reason to regard them as mental, we could not legitimately reject this opinion merely because it strikes us as strange. The truth about physical objects *must* be strange."

The greatest tragedy of academic philosophy in the twentieth century in the English-speaking world is that it was developed as a profession largely by people to whom these things were not obvious, people who did not themselves have philosophical problems and who—perhaps for that reason—operated with a commonsense view of the world, and equated philosophical activity with conceptual analysis. A related tragedy lay in the fact that the most conspicuous alternative models of philosophy that were on offer during this period either contained religious' elements or were in the oracular traditions stemming from Hegel and Nietzsche, which meant that many generations of serious students saw themselves as confronted with the subject in only these alternative forms. A consequence of this was that many of the ablest of them turned away from it altogether, while some of those who remained saw the conceptual analysis view of it as justified by the alternatives.

To pin the blame for all this on G. E. Moore would be unfair. Some such development would have taken place if he had never existed. I doubt whether many members of the Vienna Circle were familiar with his work, if indeed any of them were. The fact that he exerted the influence he did in the anglophone world is largely, I believe, a matter of historical accident: he happened to be the leading figure of that particular sort in the right place at the right time. Indirectly, at least, this appears to be supported by the terms in which Geoffrey Warnock has compared Moore's influence with Austin's. "Moore will be judged historically to have made more difference, but that's at least partly because of the historical context in which he began to work; philosophy was much dottier and more extraordinary when Moore hit the scene than when Austin did—there was more difference to be made, so to speak, and partly for that reason I suppose Moore did actually make more difference."* Another point that lends support to the view that Moore's influence was a matter of his-

* *Modern British Philosophy*, p. 99.

torical accident is that active interest in his work is now much diminished. And whereas the work of some disregarded philosophers is such that one can imagine interest in it reviving, this does not seem to me to be the case with Moore's.

I have read, I think, all of Moore's work, and know of no more telling demonstration in the whole of philosophical literature of how narrow, petty and point-missing a high intelligence can be. The lack of imagination is near total. This particular combination is familiar enough in academic life, but most people manage to put the best of themselves (rather than the whole of themselves) into their work. Moore, however, was blessed with abnormal simplicity of heart, naivety and lack of self-consciousness—everyone who knew him seems to be agreed on that—and the result is a kind of naked self-revelation in the work. His is like the voice of a clever infant who as yet knows nothing of the world and has no real understanding that there can be points of view other than his own, and quizzes what the grown-ups say with disconcerting intelligence yet without self-awareness, never thinking to turn the same sort of questioning against his own assumptions. I once said something to this effect to Russell, who had of course known Moore intimately, and his response was: "Moore's whole approach to philosophy was based on the unshakable belief that everything that had been said to him before the age of six must be true."

Now to return to logical positivism. Rather like Marxism, it had seductive appeal and therefore an enormous vogue because it was clear-cut, easy to grasp, and provided all the answers. Like Marxism too, it constituted a ready-to-hand instrument of intellectual terrorism. At the university in which I arrived as a freshman in 1949 there were many who prided themselves on their mastery of it for this purpose. Almost regardless of what anyone said to them on any subject they would run him through with a "How would you go about verifying that statement?" or a "What kind of an answer do you want to that question?" Clever young people were exhilarated by the sense of mastery this gave them. A lot of excited discussion took place on the basis of it—and to give it its due it did have the effect of clearing away a great deal of woolly thinking, and of giving people an altogether new alertness to the logical status of what it was they were saying. However, the more it itself was subjected to critical examination, the more trouble it ran into. The Verification Principle was neither analytic nor empirically verifiable, and therefore, according to its own criterion, it was meaningless. Furthermore, philosophical statements generally tended to be of this kind, neither tautological nor empirically verifiable, so the Verification Principle had the effect of outlawing more or less the whole of philosophy apart from logic. Once people ceased to be cowed they stopped agreeing that value judgments such as "Toscanini was a better orchestral conductor than Edward Heath" were empty of cognitive significance, or that statements about events in the past turned out on analysis to be statements about the presently available evidence for their having occurred. People began to realize that this glittering new scalpel was, in one operation after another, killing the patient. In every case it destroyed too much. There was a period in which several of the cleverest philosophers became reluctant to say anything at all, because almost nothing that might be deemed to be worth saying was, unless it was factually provable, permissible.

The logical positivists conceded the existence of other forms of discourse besides those of science, but they tended, or tried, to evaluate them by the standards of science. And in Oxford, at least, the most influential rebellion against the hegemony of logical positivism, when finally it came, took the form of rejecting the view that all meaningful utterance about the world ought to approximate to scientific utterance. The counter-assertion was that there were many different and useful ways of talking about the world and our experience of it, each of which had a *raison d'être* of its own. From this it seemed to follow that the right way of distinguishing the meaningful from the meaningless was not by blanket application of a single criterion but by the carrying out of separate and careful analyses of the way different, or even sometimes the same, concepts functioned in different areas of human thought and activity, to see what the legitimate uses were to which they could be put in each separate case. If you found that the way a concept was being used in a certain context would have been legitimate only in a different one then you had before you an example of conceptual confusion which was soluble, or dissoluble, by conceptual analysis. This became the basic approach (indeed the whole conception of philosophy) of linguistic analysis, which usurped the throne of logical positivism as the reigning orthodoxy in Oxford while I was there, so I lived through the changeover.

Gilbert Ryle's book *The Concept of Mind,* the most influential work of linguistic analysis ever published by an Oxford philosopher, appeared in the same month as I arrived at the university, October 1949. Most people there who were involved in philosophy seemed, sooner or later, to start arguing under its sway, and to be changing their own thinking in its direction; and within two or three years what it represented had pretty well driven logical positivism out of the field. Individuals who had previously developed a hardened logical positivist mind-set remained under the influence of that in much the same sort of way as even the most anti-Communist of ex-Communists go on being perceptibly influenced by Communism in their way of thinking. Even so, at the end of my undergraduate period at Oxford one of the questions in an examination paper was: "Does anything survive of the influence of logical positivism?" No doubt the setting of this question was a bit of fall-out from aggression between colleagues, but still, it made its point, and forcefully.

What was almost comically typical of Britain's, and especially Oxford's, parochialism is that a completely effective demolition of logical positivism had already been published before A. J. Ayer introduced it into the English-speaking world in the first place. In 1934, in Vienna, a book had appeared called *Logik der Forschung,* by Karl Popper. It was not to come out in English translation until a quarter of a century later, when it was published in 1959 under the title *The Logic of Scientific Discovery.* In it there were many criticisms of logical positivism, including some I have mentioned already, but its central and most devastating one was that logical positivism claimed to be first and foremost a (indeed the) scientific view of the world, and yet its central tenet, the Verification Principle, wiped out the whole of science. This criticism, if clinched—and few people today would deny that Popper's book pretty well clinched it—spelled total shipwreck for logical positivism.

Popper's argument can be summarized as follows. From Newton until the time of the logical positivists the central task of science had been seen as the search for natural laws, these being unrestrictedly general statements about the world that were known to be invariantly true. Examples are: "Every physical object in the universe attracts every other physical object in the universe with a force which is directly proportional to their masses and inversely proportional to the square of the distance between them" (Newton's Inverse Square Law) or "At a constant temperature the volume of a given quantity of any gas is inversely proportional to the pressure of the gas" (Boyle's Law) or "$E = mc^2$" (one of the consequences of Einstein's General Theory of Relativity). I have chosen familiar examples, but of course the physical sciences virtually consist of such laws and constants and equations, of which there are untold thousands. When the question was raised how we knew them to be true, the answer was that they had been arrived at in the first place by practical observation which had then been corroborated by crucial experiments, and that whenever they had subsequently been used they had invariably yielded accurate results. To spell this out a little more, it was believed that scientists amassed large amounts of data in the course of their work from which general patterns or features would begin to emerge that might suggest the possibility of some unrestrictedly general statement or equivalence of a law-like character. Some enterprising scientist would perceive this possibility and formulate a hypothesis. He would then try to work out a crucial experiment that would test the hypothesis. If the experiment was well constructed, and had no loopholes, it would establish for certain whether the hypothesis was true or false. In these circumstances, inevitably, it was the fate of most hypotheses to be proved false; but if the experiment confirmed the hypothesis a new scientific law, or a new constant equation, had been discovered.

Statements such as these laws are never analytic, and indeed, if they were they would give us no information about the world. Their truth does not follow by deductive logic from the definitions of their terms, nor would denial of them be self-contradictory. On the contrary, their discovery nearly always comes as a revelation. What they give us is empirical information which is of interest, and often of great practical value, about the way things contingently are in the world, information which observation is able only to suggest and rigorous experiment to corroborate. However, to the astonishment of most of those who understood it, what Popper demonstrated in *Logik der Forschung* is that scientific laws are not empirically verifiable. Nowadays people are inclined to attribute the origination of this revelation to Popper himself, but in fact, as he always acknowledged, it had been made by Hume two and a half centuries before; but although Hume's exposition was clear and unequivocal it was so bombshell-like in its implications that only the very greatest of subsequent thinkers, such as Kant, Schopenhauer and Einstein, really took it fully on board. Nevertheless it was Hume who first pointed out, and with all his customary lucidity, that from no finite number of observations, however large, could any unrestrictedly general conclusion be drawn that would be defensible in logic. It might well be that if every time I let go of something it falls, I conclude eventually that all unsupported objects fall, but if so the conclusion has been reached from the premises not by a logical process but by a psychological one. If you see an A, and it has the characteristic *x*, it does not follow logically from this that the next A you see will also have the characteristic *x*. Either it may or it may not—there may be some A's with this characteristic and some without—unless of course you make the conjunction true by definition, which is to say you stipulate that something is to count as an A *only* if it has the characteristic *x*. But in that case the statement "All A's are *x*" is a tautology, and conveys no empirical information.

Not only does the non-tautologous conclusion "All A's are *x*" not follow from a single observation of an A, it does not follow from two such observations, nor from two thousand, nor from two billion. The best-known example that has been used in illustration of this point has to do with swans. For thousands of years before the discovery of Australia all the swans that any Westerner had ever seen had been white, and everyone seems to have taken it for granted that all swans were white—expressions like "swan-white" or "as white as a swan" were common, and the very statement "All swans are white" had been made familiar by being used as a recurrent example in a standard textbook of logic that was in common use at the time of the Reformation and after. But when Europeans discovered Australia they encountered, for the first time, black swans. Now they could have reacted to this by saying that because these birds were black they were not swans, but a different sort of bird, and then given them another name. That would have been to empty the statement "All swans are white" of informational content by making it true by definition. Instead they accepted that these birds were indeed swans, and that the statement "All swans are white" was false. But what this means is that however many swans had been observed on however many occasions by however many millions of people over however many thousands of years, and without one single exception in all that time being seen to be white, it had never followed that all swans were white. As Hume put it: "However easy this step may seem, reason would never, to all eternity, be able to make it." But this in turn means that unrestrictedly general statements of the form "All A's have the characteristic x" are, of their very nature, not empirically verifiable. And the disconcerting fact is that scientific laws are characteristically statements of this kind. So their unrestricted generality makes it permanently impossible to verify them empirically, by no matter how many observations—trillions, zillions, any number anyone cares to name. So, said Popper, from the Verification Principle it follows that scientific laws are meaningless statements, and are empty of informational content. The Verification Principle rules out all scientific laws, and therefore the whole of science.

Fully to understand Popper it is essential to realize that he was not a thinker who was following the same line of enquiry as the logical positivists and arriving at a different conclusion from them. He was on a different path altogether. They, it will be remembered, were in search of a criterion of meaningfulness, a criterion of demarcation between sense and non-sense. Popper always held that this, the search for a criterion of meaning, was a mistake. He pointed out that much the most useful knowledge we have, and the biggest body of it, is contained in the natural sciences, yet scientists are not given to debating the meanings of their fundamental terms, terms as widely different in kind as *physics, observation, measurement, light, mass, energy*— not to mention all the terms involved in the mathematics they use (what is a number?—what is mathematics?). Scientists leave this, for the most part, undiscussed, and get on with doing more science. And, said Popper, they are right. The clinging notion that if we are to have a worthwhile discussion we need first to define our terms is demonstrably self-contradictory. Every time we define a term we have to introduce at least one new term into the definition, otherwise the definition is circular. But then we are under an obligation to define our new term. And so we are launched into an infinite regress. Attempts to clarify all our terms must, and can only, result in discussions of words and meanings to which it is logically impossible that there should ever be a conclusion. So discussion, if it is to take place at all, has no alternative but to make use of undefined terms. And this is at bottom the logical justification for what scientists do in this regard. And as their example makes clear, it is no bar whatsoever to rapid, successful and continuous growth in our knowledge and understanding of the world. The only thing that discussion of the meanings of words extends our understanding of is the meanings of words: it does nothing, or next to nothing, to extend our understanding of non-linguistic reality.

For these as well as other reasons, Popper asserted from the beginning that, both in fact and in logic, for a philosopher to be centrally concerned with the meanings of words was a disastrous error. It precluded him from ever getting down to the discussion of matters of real substance. The very endlessness of the processes in which it involved its participants meant that it could not but be unproductive as regards the primary level of discussion, and in consequence of that, boring to anyone for whom it was not an end in itself. In practice it was bound to lead to interminable word-spinning, logic-chopping, and in the end scholasticism. So not only was he not in search of a criterion of meaningfulness, he perceived that those who were had waded into a quicksand from which they would never emerge unless and until they renounced the search.

Popper's own starting point had little to do with language. His first job was as a schoolteacher in mathematics and physics. And as a young man in the Vienna of his day he had seen most of the intellectuals around him in thrall to one or both of two worldviews that claimed to be scientific: Marxism and psychoanalysis. In the course of time he came to realize that both of these were pseudo-sciences. This is not to say that they were without valuable insights. On the contrary, both of them were unusually rich in suggestive and original ideas. But they claimed something other than that for themselves: they claimed, explicitly, to be *science,* and that is not the same thing. After all, the mythology of ancient Greece is exceptionally rich in ideas of the profoundest insight, yet it is not scientific. And the plain fact is, as Popper realized, that Marxism and psychoanalysis are not scientific either. Yet why not? How is real science to be distinguished from everything that is not science, even though some of it may be teeming with good ideas and claim to be science? That was the question the young Popper set himself. He was in quest of a criterion not between sense and non-sense but between science and non-science.

His contemporaries, including the members of the Vienna Circle, believed—as had virtually everyone since Newton—that a science was an edifice of certain and secure knowledge that was built up by logically deductive argument on the basis of scientific laws that had been conclusively verified. The Hume-Popper demonstration that this cannot possibly be so is seismic in its consequences, for it means that the entire conception of science that had prevailed for getting on for three hundred years cannot be right. The rug is pulled out from under what had been the very basis of Western thought for centuries. So many things go when this goes that I cannot begin even to enumerate them; but an obvious and major question is raised which Popper took up and which we have already introduced, namely: if science is not what it has hitherto been taken to be, what is it? In other words, what is the criterion of demarcation between science and non-science?

A turning point in Popper's thought that was to lead him to the transformed conception of science that he introduced—and not only of science but eventually of human knowledge as such, and hence of human life as such, so that this one insight was to beget consequences across the whole range of philosophy—was the perception of a radical asymmetry between verification and falsification. He saw that although unrestrictedly general empirical statements are not verifiable they are falsifiable. Although no number of observations can prove that a statement of the form "All A's have the characteristic x" (e.g., "All swans are white") is true, one single observation of an A that does not have the characteristic x (e.g., a black swan) conclusively proves it to be false. This means that scientific laws, although not verifiable, are falsifiable, *and that means they can be tested.* This last step is the crucial one. If a theory can explain anything that happens, no matter what, this must mean that all possible observations are consistent with its truth. But in that case no actual observations can ever be cited as evidence in its favour. So not only can it not be falsified, it cannot be corroborated either. No such theory, said Popper, can count as scientific. To count as scientific, a theory must be empirically testable, and since the only form of testing that is logically possible is falsification this means that only statements that are empirically falsifiable can have scientific status. Empirical falsifiability, he concluded, was the criterion of demarcation between science and non-science.

It was the fact that Marxism and psychoanalysis could provide explanations for everything that could possibly happen that did more than anything else to convince their adherents that they must be true, but Popper perceived that it was precisely this that constituted their decisive flaw. It meant that their truth could never be put to the test, and this made them literally a matter of faith: they were more in the nature of ideologies than sciences. They were in clear contrast to theories in the real sciences, any one of which could be eliminated by well-attested observations that contradicted it. One of the most spectacular examples of this in the history of science occurred during the very years when Popper was growing up. Einstein published first his Special Theory of Relativity and then his General Theory of Relativity. In some aspects these were incompatible with Newtonian physics, which had been accepted throughout the West for over two hundred years as definitive and incorrigible fact—Newton's laws were commonly referred to, and taught in schools, as "laws of nature." But when Einstein came along it was realized that he and Newton could not both be right. Crucial experiments were devised to determine which was nearer the truth, experiments in which Einstein's theories exposed themselves nakedly to refutation by predicting results that were incompatible with Newton's. And in every case the empirical evidence favoured Einstein. This meant not that Einstein's theories were thereby proved to be "true," any more than Newton's theories had previously been proved by observation and experiment to be true—this, as we now understand, is impossible—but it did mean that they had been shown to be nearer to whatever the truth is than Newton's.

Popper was thrilled by these events, and drew from them several lessons that became fundamental to his developing philosophy. First of all, we had not "known" Newtonian science all along, in the then conventionally accepted sense of the word "known," which meant being certain and holding unshakable grounds for our certainty. Here was the most spectacular illustration imaginable of Hume's dictum that unrestrictedly general empirical statements can never be conclusively verified. No body of such statements could have received more, and more apparently conclusive, corroboration than those of Newtonian science. Every machine incorporated its principles, and thus the whole of modern technology up to that time had been based on it—and hence the Industrial Revolution—and hence, in a sense, the modern world, throughout which its laws and equations were being put to practical use millions of times a day. It had revealed the natural world to us with the same astonishing degree of accuracy: it had explained to us the workings of the entire solar system, and enabled us to predict with mathematical precision a whole mass of natural phenomena ranging from the movements of the tides to the existence and orbit of a planet hitherto not known to exist. In Pope's words, quoted so often:

> Nature and Nature's laws lay hid in night:
> God said, Let Newton be! and all was light.

Yet even after this unimaginable quantity of apparent verification over two hundred years—after, indeed, a whole historical epoch, the Industrial Age, had been successfully built on it—Newtonian science turned out not to have been conclusively verified, and to be in some respects wrong. This led Popper to realize that scientifically we could never "know," in the traditional sense, anything at all. The search for certainty that had been the central preoccupation of Western philosophy since Descartes was an error: it was a search for something that it was logically impossible we should ever find. Human knowledge as it actually is and can only ever be is not a revelation of something objectively and timelessly true, an assured grasp of something existing "out there" independently of ourselves. It is what we have the best grounds at any given time for believing. Because this is what it is, it does indeed provide the best possible basis for our suppositions and actions. But it always remains *our* belief, *our* conjecture, *our* hypothesis, *our* theory; and, as such, fallible— and also, as such, a creation of the human mind. Newton's laws had not been laws of Nature, they had been laws of Newton. They were the product of his incredible genius, the greatest single achievement in the intellectual (in which term I do not include the artistic or the moral) history of mankind. They had not been embodied in the world, sitting out there waiting to be read off by someone with acute enough perception and then decoded by the first person clever enough to do so: they had been thought up by Newton. And they were so much closer than anything that had gone before to whatever the truth is as to constitute the biggest intellectual breakthrough there has ever been. But still they remained corrigible, which is to say replaceable by a better theory—and now they had been replaced by a better theory. And this theory itself was now, of course, in the same case. Einstein himself understood this very clearly, and spent the second half of his life looking for a theory that would subsume and supersede his own theories of relativity, in exactly the same sort of way as he had superseded Newton.

Popper saw in this whole situation the paradigm of knowledge as such; and also of the way, and why, it grows. The world exists independently of us, but our knowledge of the world does not and cannot exist independently of us, for it is we who form it. Human knowledge is human. It is made by us. It is intrinsically conjectural, and can always be refuted or corrected by reality in the form of new experiences, new observations, new discoveries—and then replaced by a more accurate or informative theory. For although we never have adequate grounds for regarding the truth of a theory as definitively established, we can have—and do frequently have, and perpetually act upon—good grounds for discarding one theory in favour of a better one. And of course, even if such a theory were then to be completely and unqualifiedly true, we could still not know that, and in logic it would always remain potentially falsifiable.

These arguments constituted a wholesale demolition not just of the logical positivists' doctrines but of their entire programme and agenda. But for a long time the positivists themselves did not understand this. What they did—as people nearly always do with any approach that is radically at variance with their own—was to see it in terms of their own already existing categories and commitments, and therefore to interpret it in terms of what they themselves were currently doing; and thus to misunderstand it. Since the question they were addressing themselves to was "What is it that renders some statements

about the world meaningful, even if false, and others not?" they took it that
what this man who kept arguing with them was doing was disputing their answer to that question. And because they were becoming increasingly aware of
some of the difficulties involved in defending empirical verifiability as a criterion of meaning they saw Popper as cunningly attempting to meet these difficulties by proposing falsifiability instead. In other words, they saw him as
involved in the same game as themselves but imparting an ingenious twist to
the ball. For many years their references to him (including the one in A. J.
Ayer's *Language, Truth and Logic*) embodied this misunderstanding. It also
lay behind Neurath's nicknaming him "the Official Opposition." In taking this
attitude towards him they gave themselves full marks for giving him full
marks for cleverness on a single point. The knee-jerk reaction to the name
"Popper" became "falsifiability."

But in the annals of this misunderstanding we now come to what is the real
twist. When Popper tried to get the logical positivists to understand that he
was not putting forward a criterion for meaningfulness at all, and what is more
that he considered it a serious mistake for anyone to do so—that he was
proposing falsifiability as the criterion of demarcation between science and
non-science—they responded by asserting that it came to the same thing. This
was because, given their assumption that the only forms of meaningful utterance about the world were those of science (and its progenitor, common
sense), for anyone to propose a criterion of demarcation between scientific utterances about the world and non-scientific utterances about the world *was* to
propose a criterion of demarcation between sense and non-sense. But here
again they were mistaken, both in and by themselves and about Popper's
views. Their assumption about the scientific character of all meaningful utterance was wrong, and Popper had never shared that assumption. On the contrary, he had pointed out that as a matter of historical fact all science had
emerged by gradual steps out of non-science, out of what logical positivists
characterized and dismissed as "metaphysics"; and he maintained that it was
credible neither logically nor historically that scientific theories should have
evolved from predecessor-theories that were meaningless. Popper had never
looked on astrology, alchemy, magic, myth, religion, or metaphysical beliefs
as such as meaningless or as nonsense. On the contrary, he saw them as being,
like science itself, attempts on the part of human beings to understand, and
possibly to gain a degree of control over, their world and their experience of
it. They were primitive sets of ideas, in most cases, and sweepingly wrong, but
they often contained important insights, and it was sometimes these that had
turned into—through a centuries-long and continuous feedback process of
change based on criticism, elimination, adaptation, revision, imaginative addition, and so on—our sciences, or parts of our sciences. Furthermore, Popper

held that all of us must inevitably hold metaphysical beliefs about the world, whether we like it or not, and he mischievously gave as a genuine example in his own case his belief in the existence of regularities in nature.

All this fell on deaf ears. The logical positivists continued to regard him as an off-shoot of themselves in spite of the fact that in his already published work he had torn up and burnt their roots. And because they and their work remained in the forefront of philosophical debate for several years more, their assumptions about him were widely propagated. This fact was to be seized on and exploited for polemical purposes in the 1960s by participants in the terminal revival of Marxism that occurred in that decade. By then Popper had produced the most comprehensive and effective of all demolitions of Marxism in his book *The Open Society and Its Enemies,* which had been published in 1945. In their anxiety to discredit and dismiss him the neo-Marxists referred to him always as a positivist—logical positivism being by that time regarded generally as a burnt-out case, and the implication therefore being that Popper's views no longer compelled anyone's serious attention. A general consequence of these and other developments is that even now, as I write these words in the late 1990s, it is not uncommon to hear Popper referred to by philosophers of widely differing and incompatible schools as if he were some sort of positivist whose work belongs to a past that will never return. The Marxists have themselves by and large disappeared into that past, but adherents of the view that philosophy is conceptual analysis remain as readily given to misunderstanding Popper as the Marxists were—and for a not dissimilar reason: Popper is formidably opposed to their whole way of doing philosophy, and if only they can be confident in identifying him as belonging to a school of thinkers whose time has gone they can safely regard him as someone they have no need to take notice of, and can ignore his criticisms. When anyone refers to Popper as any sort of positivist it is a sure sign that the person in question has little serious acquaintance with his work.

4

Linguistic Analysis

We have seen that "Oxford philosophy" was an umbrella term covering more than one approach, and that the earlier and later parts of its period had ruling orthodoxies of different kinds. During the earlier period logical positivism reigned, but it was eventually brought down by what Marxists would have called its own internal contradictions. So it was gradually superseded by what came to be known under two names equally, linguistic analysis and linguistic philosophy, the two terms being interchangeable. Many individual philosophers, at Oxford and elsewhere, passed from the first to the second by a seemingly natural progression: first they adopted logical positivism, but as they became increasingly aware of the insoluble problems to which it gave rise they shifted to a more linguistic-analytic approach. However, although at the time they were acutely conscious of the differences between the two, what are more striking now are the similarities.

First and foremost, both of them renounced philosophy's traditional task of understanding the world. Both took it for granted that philosophy's main job was analysing verbalized concepts and other linguistic formulations. However, whereas logical positivism had a rationale for this, linguistic analysis had none. Logical positivists believed that the reason why philosophy could make no direct contribution to our understanding of the world—the reason why, so to speak, there could be no such thing as first-order philosophy—was that the whole of this task had now been taken over, and properly so, by the sciences, which meant that at a first-order level there was nothing left for philosophy to do. Linguistic analysts rejected the view that our knowledge of the world was exclusively the province of science, yet they retained the conception of philosophy for which that view had been the justification. In other words they rejected the reason for regarding philosophy as talk about talk but continued to practise it as if it were. Their chief assumption about the whole nature of the subject lacked any adequate foundation. In so far as they had to call on something else to fill the vast gaps left by science in the provenance of our first-order conception of the world the appeal was to common sense and its concomitant use of language. The resultant view of philosophy is one to which lapidary expression was given by Peter Strawson. "It seems to me that ordinary people employing ordinary language—and the emphasis on language isn't always essential here—ordinary people employing the ordinary conceptual resources of mankind have at their disposal not a crude, rough-and-ready instrument, but an enormously sophisticated instrument, for thinking; and that it's an immensely and inexhaustibly interesting task to trace the various connections between the concepts which people handle in their ordinary life with no particular difficulty. There are enormously difficult and interesting problems about the *structure* of this whole conceptual scheme which ordinary people manage so easily in the ordinary course of events. The difficulty consists in saying what the structure *is,* in saying how the notions of perception, action, personal identity, ethics—all the ordinary notions which we handle quite easily—are related to each other. Their complexities, and the interest of this structure, seem to me quite inexhaustible, and have seemed inexhaustible, I should say, to many philosophers throughout the history of the subject."*

This view of philosophy seems to me to be immediately open to three devastating objections. First of all, it assumes that our normal use of concepts stands in need of a theory. But does it? If someone were to say, "Violin playing contributes to some of the profoundest experiences of which human beings are capable; therefore it is a matter of the greatest importance to us to acquire as full a theoretical understanding as we possibly can of violin playing," everyone would see the confusion at once. Violin playing is, of its nature, something that could not possibly be the instantiation of a theory. No theory, no matter how flexible, finely particularized and subtle, could do it justice: it inhabits a realm theories cannot reach. Yet even if such a thing were possible, a theory of violin playing would be more of an encumbrance than a help to violinists, and would do nothing to increase listeners' appreciation of the music. It would be both superfluous and harmful. The same goes for theories of most of the most important human activities: we do not seek, and we are right not

---

* *Modern British Philosophy,* pp. 136–7.

to seek, a systematic theoretical understanding of marriage, or of parenthood, of love or of friendship, of eating or drinking or sleeping. It is simply not true to say that if an activity is important then it is desirable for us to have a theoretical understanding of it. Whoever seeks a theoretical understanding of sexual love? In most cases there is no purpose that such a theory could serve, and, worse, it would get in the way, it would detract. There is something wrong with the whole conception of life that anyone has who thinks we need theories of such things. Indeed, there is something lacking in anyone who does not see that it would be impossible to formulate a theory of such an activity anyway. Life, real life, is not like that—it is not the instantiation of theories. In fact one of the most tragic and familiar examples of inauthenticity is of individuals who try to live in accordance with theories.

So the first two points to be made about Strawson's programme are that it calls, one, for something that is impossible, and, two, for something which would be worse than useless if we had it. A third criticism is that it is unconnected with the growth of first-order knowledge or understanding without supplying any good reason for this limitation. It takes for granted the conceptual scheme of ordinary common sense and sees the main task of philosophy as being to investigate its structure. But common sense is a wholly inadequate instrument for understanding the world. It stands baffled before the most rudimentary questions concerning experience. Are we therefore not to ask those questions? Philosophers of a Strawsonian persuasion say: "No. We do not know how to answer them, and should therefore not ask them. Let's get on with questions we know how to handle." What this means in practice is: let us stay within the limits of the outlook we already have and try to improve our understanding of its structure and implications. This would be a sustainable view if the structure in question were determined by our biology and could not be changed, but it cannot seriously be argued that this is the case. Of the very examples that Strawson gives—the notions of perception, action, personal identity, ethics—at least the last three are to some extent culture-dependent (the last one obviously so) and I would argue that all of them, even the notion of perception, can be shown to be different in radically different cultures. Even within our own culture some people conceive of perception as Berkeley did, as God's mode of communication with the observer. Strawson, it must be said, has pursued his investigations with outstanding brilliance, but still not in a way that meets these objections.

In pursuing this subject we need to take both a more detailed and a wider view of linguistic philosophy than we have done so far.

I have already mentioned that the most influential work of linguistic analysis to be published by an Oxford philosopher was Gilbert Ryle's *The Concept* *of Mind.* That book was written undisguisedly under the influence of the later philosophy of Wittgenstein, with whom Ryle had formerly been on terms of friendship—they had even been on a number of walking holidays together. Wittgenstein was still alive when *The Concept of Mind* was published—he was to die eighteen months later, in April 1951, in Cambridge—and was on record as saying that Ryle was one of only two people who really understood his philosophy.*

During his lifetime Wittgenstein published only one book, and one article. The book, *Tractatus Logico-Philosophicus,* was published in 1921, and made an international reputation both for itself and for Wittgenstein. But during the years of its greatest influence he came to the conclusion that it was fundamentally mistaken. So at the very time when philosophers in many countries were discovering it, and in some cases ardently becoming disciples of it, he himself was rejecting it and developing a new approach that was at odds with it. Perhaps not surprisingly, the starting point of the new approach was the point at which he thought his earlier philosophy had gone wrong, which thus became the point about which, more than any other, the differences between the two philosophies turned. However, he did not during his lifetime publish any of his later philosophy. Rumours about his change of direction circulated underground, but the only people with any way of knowing what it consisted in were those who had direct access either to him or to his immediate circle, or to certain privately distributed manuscripts. Thus it came about that the first book-length piece of philosophizing in the manner of the later Wittgenstein that was published and commanded attention was not by Wittgenstein himself but by Ryle—a fact that is said to have caused Wittgenstein a great deal of chagrin. What is nowadays standardly referred to as "the later philosophy of Wittgenstein" did not present itself to the public until the posthumous publication of his book *Philosophical Investigations* in 1953.

In Oxbridge it was to an important degree under the influence of these two books that the hegemony of logical positivism succumbed during the 1950s to that of linguistic analysis—though, at the grass-roots level, in Oxford itself it was J. L. Austin who was the dominating figure, with Ryle resentfully playing second fiddle, while in Cambridge, Wittgenstein ruled from beyond the grave. The fact that Austin in his lifetime, like Wittgenstein, exerted intellectual influence more through teaching and discussion than publication helped to keep that influence fairly tightly centered on Oxford. But of course he had pupils who moved on to teach elsewhere, as did Ryle; and in the Britain of those days there were only twenty-something universities. It was always confidently asserted that Ryle was the most influential king-maker throughout the whole

* Ray Monk, *Ludwig Wittgenstein: The Duty of Genius,* p. 436.

country when it came to academic appointments in philosophy. So most universities, inevitably, were affected.

One of the fundamental beliefs of the linguistic analysts was that there can justifiably be no such thing as a philosophical system. So if one tries to describe their approach one finds that there is not a coherent body of doctrine to expound. Austin was always insistent that in any philosophical enquiry we must start not from theoretical considerations but from reality, from what actually happens, which includes what people do in fact say. It is pointless, he held, for us to rack our brains about what such-and-such an assertion could possibly mean when there are no imaginable circumstances in which anyone would utter it. If it has no possible use then it has no meaning. The same line of thought, looked at from the opposite end, provided him with one of his standard methods of approach. When confronted with any expression or proposition, or other piece of linguistic usage, he would ask himself, "In what circumstances would anyone actually *say* this?"—and then in pinning down its possible use he would, he thought, be pinning down its meaning. He believed that this brought out something that philosophers had characteristically behaved badly about down the ages: they had tended to take up an assertion or argument and examine it in isolation as a self-contained formulation in language, without any consideration of the flesh-and-blood circumstances in which it would be used. He was, perhaps more than any philosopher has ever been, acutely conscious that talking and thinking are things that we *do*. They are forms of human behaviour—in some ways the most important forms of human behaviour, the ones that differentiate us most of all from the rest of the animal kingdom. Every time we say something we are doing something, and our everyday vocabulary contains an enormous number of words that name these different actions (including naming, itself)—telling, asking, repeating, implying, explaining, insisting, describing, narrating, warning, scolding, ordering, recommending, protesting, denying, and so on and so forth. Austin claimed that there were over a thousand verbally distinguishable such acts that we perform when we speak. And to say this is to make no reference to the range of further nuance made available within each act by its location in context, and our choice of words, tone of voice, body language, and so on. This notion of speech as behaviour, and the term "speech-act," were given common currency in philosophy by Austin.

One category of speech that he differentiated, and that seemed to catch people's imaginations especially, was what he called "performative utterances." These were utterances the very making of which performed the act they designated. Common examples are "I thank you," "I promise," "I apologize," "Congratulations!" or, spoken in the context of a marriage ceremony, just simply "I will." When someone utters a statement of this kind he is not describing or reporting something that he is doing, he is doing it. And one of Austin's points was that most such utterances are unquestionably complete, meaningful and useful statements in the indicative, yet they do not seem to come under the analytic-synthetic distinction, nor would it appear meaningful to ask of them whether they are true or false. From a great many considerations such as these Austin developed the first of his broad criticisms of the logical positivists, namely that there is not, as everything about their interests and practices seemed to presuppose, one premier use of non-analytic utterances, namely the making of statements about the world that must be either true or false: there are literally hundreds of different sorts of legitimate uses of indicative statements.

It goes without saying that wherever there is a possible use there is a possible misuse. Philosophical puzzles and confusions characteristically arise, Austin thought, because we tend to use the refined and subtle instrument that is our natural language in crude problem-creating ways. The logical positivists themselves yielded numerous examples. Since scientific discourse was their touchstone of meaningful utterance they tended to regard statements in, say, ethics or aesthetics as if they were scientific statements for which we have inadequate evidence, when in fact they are not that sort of statement at all but quite different sorts of statements, to be understood differently. The logical positivists perpetrated this sort of mistake wholesale, thereby landing themselves with philosophical problems that were really pseudo-problems, the creation of their own misuse of categories. Austin came to see the main task of philosophy as being to unpick such conceptual tangles by the methods of painstakingly careful linguistic analysis, and as a result of doing so to not so much solve the philosophical problem in question as dissolve it, in other words to show that it did not properly arise. An incidental bonus of this approach was to make perspicuous the legitimate uses of our concepts. Since these did not fit into a unifying abstract system, or fall conveniently under any simplifying formula, the only way to go about the job was piecemeal, concept by concept. The word "piecemeal" was often used by Austin and his followers as a term of recommendation to describe their own approach.

It was in the context of ideas such as these that Ryle's *The Concept of Mind* made such a great reputation. Brilliantly written, the whole book was devoted to our alleged misuse of a single concept. It became, and long remained, the most famous example of any such single analysis. What Ryle was attacking was Cartesian dualism. Firmly established in the mainstream tradition of Western thinking ever since Descartes has been a view of human beings as consisting of two different sorts of entity mysteriously conjoined, a body and a mind. We have tended to think of the mind as something that can have its own experiences independently of the body—we can say of an individual, for example, that he has a healthy body but a sick mind—and we have even tended to think of the mind as an immaterial entity that inhabited the body and operated it from inside, like someone driving a car. Ryle's famous expression for this was "the ghost in the machine." On the basis of this distinction we thought of everyone, including ourselves, as having an inner life that was different from his outer one. We often thought of the mind as sitting there invisibly, inside the body, enjoying secret access to a flow of private, non-bodily experiences all of its own. The mind, we supposed, was an entity that existed and did things and had experiences and a history, but was not the same as the body, which was also an entity that existed and did things and had experiences and a history.

This common view of what we are was Ryle's target. My sketch of it may surprise some readers by fathering dualism so specifically on Descartes when in fact it, or something obviously like it, has constituted humanity's standard conception of itself since primitive times. Man has nearly always regarded himself as consisting of a body plus some nonbodily component which inhabited his body, and which he has called at different times his spirit or his soul or his mind; and he has nearly always seen this as having, or as having the potential for, some degree of separate existence. I once challenged Ryle with this fact, and his reply was: "No one could think Descartes invented this mistake. The point was he put nice firm edges and labels on to it so that there it was, a doctrine or a dogma from his time. Descartes said, in effect, what Shakespeare and the Bible didn't, that my mind is one substance and my body is another substance. They sometimes talked *as if* this were the case. Descartes said that it *was* the case."*

I do not think this is true, as a matter of fact, but be that as it may, Ryle's central thesis is that dualism is an error because there is no such entity as a mind. On the basis of extensive analyses, which constitute the book, he argues that what we humans do is to categorize certain aspects of our own behaviour and experience as mental and then attribute them to a different subject from the rest—and then reify that subject as a mind. He holds that careful investigation of our use of mental concepts shows that we do not have justification for doing this, indeed that the human being is a single entity, one subject of behaviour and experience, with a single identity and a single history. We are not two entities mysteriously laced together. We have made what he calls a category mistake (a term to which he gave wide currency in philosophy): we treat the concept of mind as if it designated one sort of thing when in fact it designates a quite different sort of thing. We think of mind as a separately existing entity that does things and has experiences, when all the time it is merely an

* *Modern British Philosophy,* p. 110.

umbrella term for certain among our various modes of behaviour—performance, disposition, experience and so on—all of which should correctly be attributed to a single subject. This category mistake breeds a whole population of other mistakes in our assumptions about ourselves, and in our various ways of thinking and talking about ourselves. It is a prime example of a philosophical error, and it infects huge areas of our thinking. Ryle's book is a paradigm example of how a linguistic analyst goes about clearing up such a problem.

Throughout the period in which successive schools of Oxford philosophy had their day there were, as is only to be expected, dissident groups and maverick individuals who had significant differences from, as well as affinities with, what was going on around them, and even some who dissociated themselves from it entirely. But common to all the different and even conflicting approaches that got themselves bracketed as "Oxford philosophy" was, as I have said, a central concern with language. Philosophers of all those different sorts seemed to take it for granted that we think in words. So it seemed to them self-evident that the most solidly based way of addressing a philosophical problem was first of all to get it clearly formulated in language and then to set about analysing the formulation. The result was that what they were addressing was never direct experience but always a linguistic formulation. For example, what for me had been existential problems thrust into my face by my perception of physical objects, problems that were sometimes so terrifying that I felt as if they were imperilling my sanity, were translated by Oxford philosophers into puzzles about the nature of observation statements, and then dealt with in that form. The earlier ones would ask questions like: *What exactly are we saying when we say we perceive something? What count as adequate grounds for making such statements? Is the logic of them such that they are deduced from, i.e., presuppose, more basic statements about sensory data—or not? Is the logical object of their reference really something internal to us, or something external? If the former, how can we be justified in deducing from them statements about the latter? How would the validity of such inferences be verified? Does their logic possess special features?* And so on and so forth. Later ones would be more inclined to ask: *What are the sorts of circumstances in which observation statements are normally used? How do ordinary people in fact formulate them in the natural course of their daily lives? Let us examine this use, working through particular examples, and ask ourselves in what sort of conditions such-and-such an observation statement would spontaneously be uttered. Do we have difficulty in understanding any of them? Do we confuse their logic, and make or understand them as if they were statements of a different sort? If none of these things, what exactly is the problem? Are we sure there is a problem at all?* And so on.

Philosophers of a specifically Austinian bent went in for asking questions like: *How do we distinguish between seeing, perceiving, watching, observing and noting?*—just as they asked: *What are the differences between performing the same action unwillingly, involuntarily, inadvertently, by chance, by accident, by mistake, and negligently?* If challenged about the value of raising such an enquiry they would reply that it had a bearing on the ascription of moral responsibility, and might even have practical consequences in a court of law.

Whatever the kind of "Oxford philosopher," the problems, no matter how they had arisen in the first place, would be dealt with by being translated into questions about language which would then be "elucidated." So if one studied philosophy at Oxford during that period, nearly all discussions and investigations were about some piece of linguistic utterance. In practice they tended to be about an exiguously narrow range of the characteristics attributable to linguistic utterance: meaning above all, but also sense, reference, truth and ordinary usage. "*What exactly do you mean by . . .*" became the commonest opening to a challenging question, and "*Suppose we wanted to say . . .*" the commonest introduction to a conjecture; and in both cases this would be followed by a discussion of the word, or form of words, thus introduced. "*I don't understand what you mean*" became accepted shorthand for "*What you've just said can't be made to stand up*" (i.e., can't be formulated without self-contradiction, and therefore can't properly be made sense of).

The classic assertion of the validity of an exclusively linguistic approach to philosophy had been published as early as 1931 by the young Gilbert Ryle in his paper "Systematically Misleading Expressions":

> . . . there is, after all, a sense in which we can properly inquire and even say "what it really means to say so and so." For we can ask what is the real form of the fact recorded when this is concealed or disguised and not duly exhibited by the expression in question. And we can often succeed in stating this fact in a new form of words which does exhibit what the other failed to exhibit. And I am for the present inclined to believe that this is what philosophical analysis is, and that this is the sole and whole function of philosophy.

I believe it was Ryle, too, who coined the famous definition of philosophy as "talk about talk."

Inevitably, after a generation of this, philosophy came to be widely seen as being *about* language, its central activity being the elucidation of concepts as expressed in words. In consequence of that, all legitimate problems of philosophy came to be viewed as being problems about language and its use or misuse, problems such as were to be solved or dissolved by logical or linguistic analysis. The philosophers engaged in this activity believed sincerely that they were doing definitive work: truth is a property of statements, and once you get a question or a position formulated clearly in language you can bring to bear on it the whole armoury of logic—and logic had itself made spectacular advances in the twentieth century. Often analysis would reveal that what had traditionally been thought of as one problem was several problems that had been gathered together under a single description, and needed to be tackled separately. Sometimes when a problem had been formulated sufficiently clearly it would be fairly obvious what the answer was—in other words, there was not too much of a problem at all. Sometimes it would emerge that what had been thought to be a problem could not be formulated clearly—in other words it had been incoherently conceived, so that again, though for a different sort of reason, there was no real problem. A great deal of the rhetorical or high-faluting stuff being produced by contemporary philosophers on the Continent dissolved under this treatment, and stood exposed as empty. Most Oxford philosophers believed the same to be true for some of the most famous figures of the past. When they wrote about dead philosophers of whom they approved it was to recast them in a contemporary mould, translating both their problems and their solutions into the linguistic mode, revealing them to their great credit as having been Oxford philosophers before their time. Most remarkable of all, it was widely and genuinely believed by Oxford philosophers that they were finally disposing of their own subject by settling its outstanding problems for ever. In his maturity Peter Strawson observed of his younger self and colleagues, with admirable detachment: "When one turned to problems in the theory of knowledge, the nature of perception, memory, imagination, free-will and determinism and so on, one had the feeling that the use of this new technique would really dissolve the problems, they'd just vanish away. . . ."* Similarly Bernard Williams, speaking later still of the beliefs of the same group of people during the same period, said that "[when you] had analytically taken the problems apart, you'd find that many of the traditional questions of philosophy had not been solved but had disappeared. You no longer needed to ask them. And the promise this offered was very great—and extremely exciting. There really were people who were saying that the whole of philosophy would be over in fifty years. It would all be finished."†

For reasons which the first chapter of this book will have made self-evident, when I arrived on this scene and encountered people holding such attitudes they seemed to me like non-music-lovers who had sneaked into a concert without paying. They failed on two separate counts to meet the entrance requirement to be where they were. They were studying philosophy in the belief

---

* *Modern British Philosophy,* p. 117.

† *Men of Ideas,* p. 139.

that it was something quite other than what it was, and they had no under-standing at all of the true nature of philosophical problems. Both things were fundamentally due to the fact that they did not themselves have philosophical problems, and never had had them, or any idea what it was like to have them. Nevertheless, since what they regarded themselves as doing was nothing less than disposing of the accumulated problems of two and a half thousand years of Western philosophy, their activity became a magnet for the intellectually ambitious. It was the most fashionable field for bright undergraduates to move into. And because most of it took the form of discussion and argument it gave the brilliant unparalleled opportunities to shine. As a result the subject was pursued by people of unusual gifts, the best of them of very considerable an-alytic ability and dialectical skill. And the fact that they were solving all the traditional problems of philosophy by techniques that were new meant that many of them felt they had little or no need for the so-called great philoso-phers of the past. Some made a public show of their ignorance of past philos-ophy (as had, egregiously, Wittgenstein—whose example in this, as in so many other things, was not so much followed as imitated).

Given all this, especially the philosophers' conception of what they were doing, and the intrinsically public nature of discussion and argument, a noto-rious arrogance developed. Oxford philosophers tended to assume that if somebody did not share their view of their own activity this meant merely that he did not understand it. This was openly declared and re-endorsed by one of its leading representatives as late as 1973, in an article which Geoffrey Warnock published about Austin's famous "Saturday mornings." The piece is so revealing, for all its ironic tone, that it is worth quoting at length from the lead-up to the point in question.

We compared and contrasted such substantives as "tool," "instrument," "im-plement," "utensil," "appliance," "equipment," "apparatus," "gear," "kit"—even "device" and "gimmick." Here I remember Austin inviting us to classify *scissors;* kitchen scissors, I think we thought, were utensils, and gar-den shears were probably tools (or implements?), but the sort of scissors used in, for instance, dressmaking were something of a problem. (Sewing "materials" would probably *include* scissors, but that is not quite an answer to the question.) And I remember that he asked why, awaiting an operation, one would be disconcerted if the surgeon said, "Right, I'll just go and get my tools." Then once—I am really not sure why, or in the hope of what—the Lo-gician's use of "class" led us on to a string of such words as "group," "set," "collection" (what sort of thing does one have to do, to be a *collector?*), "as-semblage," "range," even "crowd," and "heap."

I must confess (no doubt it is a sign of changed times that I use the defen-sive word "confess") that I always found this sort of thing enormously enjoyable, exactly to my taste. I did not believe that it was likely to contribute to the solution of the problems of the post-war world; I did not believe that it would contribute, certainly or necessarily, to the solution of any problems of philosophy. But it was enormously enjoyable; it was not easy; it exercised the wits; and those who think they know that it cannot ever be valuably instructive have simply never tried, or perhaps are no good at it.*

The attitude nakedly revealed in this last sentence was characteristic of Oxford philosophers altogether. The undisguised complacency with which they gave anyone who questioned the value of what they were doing to understand "simply" that he was either ignorant or incapable of doing it himself rankled with their colleagues in other fields, many of whom felt themselves to be no less intelligent than the philosophers, and to be engaged in work of more solid merit. The fracture of goodwill was compounded by the fact that quite a few of the philosophers were not just passively smug but actively aggressive. They used their dialectical skills for purposes of intellectual terrorism which included the triumphant carving up in public of opponents, or even merely of the uninitiated. If one witnessed one of these scenes (I witnessed many) it was impossible to regard the pursuit of truth as having much of a part in what was going on. The way these philosophers conducted themselves sowed a lasting hostility towards philosophy among gifted people in other disciplines, many of whom either saw or suspected—accurately, to my mind—that the philosophers were self-deluded and that most of their work was superficial and irrelevant; that all this capering about was more a matter of public preening than anything else, and that it left serious problems untouched. It is not going too far to say that the philosophers of that day made themselves hated in parts of their own university. Decades later bitter feelings against them, held in store by now for most of an adult lifetime, were still being confided to me by people who were themselves of great intellectual distinction. To the student of human nature it was a fascinating phenomenon. The most remarkable—and tragic—thing about it was how many people of first-class ability had been mis-taking an unimportant activity for an important one, and had wasted their lives on it.

The nearest parallel to this that I can think of in the history of ideas is the decadent strain of logic-chopping that developed within medieval philosophy and became known as scholasticism. Many intellectually brilliant people devoted their lives to that too. And, interestingly enough, they too drew down on the philosophy of their time a lasting opprobrium that extended to the not-guilty. It is a libel on medieval philosophy to regard only the schoolmen as

---

* "Saturday Mornings" by G. J. Warnock, in *Essays on J. L. Austin,* pp. 38–9.

representative of it. Much genuinely profound and original philosophy was done by other types of philosopher in the Middle Ages.

Between the Middle Ages and the twentieth century I do not think it entered the head of any philosopher whose name has survived to suppose that the subject matter of philosophy was linguistic. Even Bertrand Russell, who unwittingly fathered the approach and whose heirs some of the most prominent linguistic philosophers believed themselves to be, disowned it. Of himself he wrote that up to his mid-forties, by which time all his most significant work had been done, "I had thought of language as transparent—that is to say, as a medium which could be employed without paying attention to it" (*My Philosophical Development*, p. 14). That, I am sure, is what nearly all the great philosophers of the past had supposed. When Socrates asked *What is justice? What is courage?*, and so on, he did not think of himself as asking for definitions of the words, he thought he was probing into the true nature of phenomena that existed independently of language.

As an Oxford student at the high noon of Oxford philosophy I was scandalized by the disparity between, on the one hand, what my teachers were doing among themselves and in their published work, and were training me to do, and on the other hand what the dead philosophers whose names some of them were bandying about in the process, and whose works they were sometimes ostensibly expounding, had been doing. We would be told that Berkeley had been given to analysing certain kinds of proposition in a certain kind of way, as against Locke, who had analysed similar sorts of proposition in a different sort of way; and the pros and cons of the two modes of propositional analysis would be thrashed over, with perpetual reference to recent British philosophers, especially those living in Oxford. But when I opened the works of Locke and Berkeley themselves I found myself in a world unrecognizably different from that. Locke and Berkeley were simply not doing what my teachers said they were doing; still less were they doing what my teachers were doing. They were trying to understand the nature of reality, and the extent to which we human beings can gain knowledge of it, and the nature and limits of that knowledge. The degree to which the two activities were different was unaccountably hidden from some people by the fact that both were called "philosophy," and their practitioners "philosophers," though that was a matter partly of historical accident and partly of administrative convenience. On one side were people, mostly though not all dead, who were passionately involved in trying to deepen their understanding of the world, and on the other side were people involved, with admittedly great passion, in discussions about meaning, and the making of fine distinctions of linguistic usage. That the two were neither the same nor equivalent seemed to me patent, as did the fact that the former was as important as anything can be while the latter was little more than an intellectual exercise, like the invention of difficult crossword puzzles. It also seemed to me manifest that, as the crossword-puzzle analogy brings out, the fact that a person needs to be very clever in order to do something does not render it important. My contemporaries were having fun, in which indeed I often joined and found pleasure, but what they were doing was seldom if ever of the slightest consequence. Whenever I tried to turn the discussion to matters of substance they lost interest. They thought such things were "not philosophical."

My problem, when I was being serious about it myself, was that I felt a deep intellectual passion for traditional philosophy and for the questions it raised, whereas what was going on around me was a betrayal of it. Bertrand Russell—whom subsequently, in the late 1950s, I came to know—took the same view. In *My Philosophical Development,* published in 1959, he wrote (p. 230):

> The most serious of my objections is that the new philosophy seems to me to have abandoned, without necessity, that grave and important task which philosophy throughout the ages has hitherto pursued. Philosophers from Thales onwards have tried to understand the world. . . . I cannot feel that the new philosophy is carrying on this tradition.

Indeed it was not. Claims that it was, really, though in a different way, are uncomprehending, and I shall turn to those later. The truth is that the new philosophy had abandoned philosophy. And given that this was so, the manner in which it bewitched and captured the minds, and eventually in some cases the lives, of some of the people around me was an object lesson in the power of intellectual fashion. I first voiced openly what I had felt from the beginning when, about to read an extract from Kant, I was informed that the crux of his philosophy was the assertion that there were synthetic *a priori* propositions, and the central question about Kant was therefore whether or not this was the case. It was not possible, I declared with a confidence that I have ever since believed was justified, that the person most widely regarded as the greatest philosopher since the ancient Greeks could have gained that reputation chiefly by asserting that there were certain sorts of proposition.

The ur-question of philosophy throughout most of its history has been *What, ultimately, is there?* This was the dominant question for the pre-Socratics, and it has underlain, when it has not dominated, most of the best philosophy since. In pursuit of an answer, philosophers have asked a multitude of subsidiary questions, such as *What is the nature of physical objects? What is space? What is causal connection? What is time?* And by a natural progression from this they have become deeply exercised about the possibility of human knowledge: *How can we find out these things? Can we know any of them for certain? If so, which? And how can we be sure we know when we do know?* Before the twentieth century all these had been among the central questions of philosophy. Needless to say there was a host of more detailed and specialized questions too, not only in the theory of knowledge and the philosophy of science but also in philosophy of morals, politics, religion, history, sociology, law, education, mathematics; there were questions in logic, in aesthetics, and every other area of philosophical enquiry—which, as a whole, tended to be seen as coextensive with human experience. The nature of every experience we can possibly have, it was thought, can be questioned, and a deeper understanding of it sought. And for two and a half millennia most of the philosophers engaged in such quests would have found the view that all philosophical problems were ultimately questions about the use of language ridiculous, if not incomprehensible. One or two of them, for instance Locke, believed that considerations of language had a very important role in philosophical enquiry, but it never entered any of their minds to think that such considerations themselves constituted the chief subject matter of philosophy.

Oxford philosophy on the one hand, and philosophy as carried on by such figures as Plato and Aristotle, Descartes, Leibniz, Locke, Hume, and Kant on the other, are not only not the same activity but are not, at bottom, importantly related. The only contribution made to real philosophy by Oxford philosophy was at one remove: it gave to those who were trained in it a heightened critical self-awareness in the use of language which, if they then turned their attention to philosophical problems, paid off. Those who remained for ever within the confines of Oxford philosophy never set foot in the kingdom of real philosophy. I realized this as an undergraduate, but the full import of it came home to me in 1955–6 when I went to Yale for a year of post-graduate study. There I found philosophers immersed in such tasks as quarrying Einstein's Special and General Theories of Relativity, and quantum physics, for their full implications for our understanding of the nature of the world—for instance our understanding of the nature of time, and of space, and of the relationship between the two; our understanding of matter, of the nature of physical objects, and the question of the existence or otherwise of causality. They were asking what demands the supersession of Newton by Einstein made on us in the view we took not only of the nature of the world but also of the nature of knowledge itself. Separately from all that, the two most brilliant young logicians in the university used to spend their vacations in Washington working for the government on the development of computers, which were then in their infancy. And the general atmosphere among Yale philosophers contained something that was almost wholly lacking in the Oxford of that time, a living sense of philosophy's continuity with its own past. One of the most conspicuous features of Oxford philosophy was the low valuation it placed on past philosophy—the real reason for this, though not the one given, being that the two activities were largely unrelated. People whose job it was to teach philosophy would announce with obvious complacency, even pride, that they had never read some of the greatest philosophers. I knew some who claimed not to have read Kant's *Critique of Pure Reason*. At Yale this would have been considered like teaching Christian theology without having read the New Testament. There, even the scientists, to say nothing of the philosophers, would make germane references to Kant when discussing Einstein. I had never heard Oxford philosophers discuss Einstein at all.

One of the most valuable things for me about that year at Yale was that it enabled me to see Oxford from the outside, and to look at Oxford philosophers from the standpoint of other kinds of contemporary philosopher. Seen thus they appeared, it can only be said, provincial, superficial, self-admiring, and above all intellectually unserious. An illustration of all these characteristics is the fact that only one philosopher who had not practised in Britain was required reading for students taking the Oxford degree in philosophy, politics, and economics—even for those specializing, as did I, in philosophy—and that was Descartes (plus, if you like, Kant, though only for his little book on ethics). Others could be studied as options or as special subjects; but it was not only possible, it was usual, for a PPE student who got a first-class degree specializing in philosophy not to have read a word of Spinoza, Leibniz, Kant's *Critique of Pure Reason* (which was a special option), Hegel, Marx, Schopenhauer, Nietzsche, Husserl, Heidegger, or any other philosopher who had practised outside the British Isles. Most of the questions in the examination paper on the history of philosophy related to four philosophers only: Descartes, Locke, Berkeley and Hume. The only moral philosophy of the past that students needed to know apart from Kant's was British utilitarianism. For the rest, it was a question of studying the work of living British philosophers plus Moore and Wittgenstein (British citizens now dead). This had always seemed to me poky, but I now came to see it as risible. When I described it to a group of Yale philosophers one of them broke out jovially into the first verse of the song "There'll always be an England."

In the England to which I returned in 1956 only one well-known philosopher was carrying on philosophy in the way I had encountered it at Yale, and that was Karl Popper. As a direct consequence he suffered not only isolation but active discrimination. Both Oxford and Cambridge turned him down for professorships, despite the fact that he had a chair at London University and an international reputation. The linked articles that formed the successive chapters of his book *The Poverty of Historicism,* published in 1957,* had been

---

* When it appeared, Arthur Koestler wrote of it in the *Sunday Times* that it was "probably the only book published this year which will outlive this century."

rejected by the leading journal of philosophy in Britain, *Mind,* under the editorship of Gilbert Ryle—who also played the decisive role in keeping Popper out of Oxford.* The most scandalous aspect of a ripely scandalous situation was that several of the ablest philosophers in Oxford would admit in private, if the challenge were pressed, that Popper was the outstanding philosopher then practising in Britain. They knew he was better than they were, and did not want him on their territory. Even Ryle and Ayer regarded him as an equal, a view they extended to fewer than half a dozen of their contemporaries in total. But they did not want him as a colleague.

I got to know Karl Popper in late 1958 or early 1959, and we became lifelong friends, in spite of extreme disparities between us in personality, and deep divisions between our main interests, even within those loves we shared, which were notably music, philosophy and the history of ideas. Except for Bertrand Russell he was in an altogether different class intellectually from anyone else I knew. And to find myself at the end of the arid fifties sitting in his home not far from Oxford, discussing philosophy with him after years spent in Oxford itself, was like stumbling into an oasis after years of trekking across the Sahara. I still remember the tingling sense of excitement with which I would board the train at St. Marylebone on those journeys to Penn, where he lived in self-created seclusion so as to give himself wholly to work. His long years of rejection and isolation—first in his native Vienna, where he had lived until his middle thirties without getting a university post (he earned his living by schoolteaching—and decades later an Oxford professor who had come from the Vienna of those days said to me witheringly: "Popper? He's only a schoolmaster"); then in New Zealand, where he was cut off from Europe throughout the Second World War (and the person in the university with immediate authority over him objected to his spending so much of his time writing *The Open Society and Its Enemies* when what he was being paid for was to teach); and now again in Great Britain after the war—had bred in him the conviction that he should expect nothing from his environment and should just get on with his work regardless of others. Because of this isolation he seemed unaware that there were people in the United States working along similar lines—though he was better and more original than any of them—and in consequence he tended to suffer from the delusion that all his ideas were unique to himself. Our earliest conversations were bedevilled by his presumption that whenever I raised ideas I had absorbed at Yale, or perhaps in some cases might even have thought of for myself, I had got them from his work (most of which, at that time, I had not read). He was not, as he was so often accused of being, self-centred: he was unrealistically his-own-work-centred.

---

* This was hinted at to me by Ryle himself, and confirmed unequivocally by Ayer.

But his devotion to his work, although it cut him off, was selfless, and in this again he made a refreshing change from Oxford. There people performed: there there was a cult of brilliance, and individuals became famous by shining. For most of them philosophy was a means, with self-advancement as its end. Popper was the opposite of this: he was given up completely to his work, and sacrificed everything in his life to it. That he rode roughshod over anyone who got in its way, without concern for their sensibilities or convenience, was widely interpreted as arrogance or megalomania on his part, but in fact he was unthinkingly subjecting everyone else to precisely the same usage as he submitted himself to. It was a lesson in how someone can make his creative work the be-all and end-all of his life, and treat the social niceties as trivial by comparison. Among the pleasures of discussing philosophy with him, a pleasure unknown at Oxford, was that of watching the dissolution and disappearance of an outsize ego into the problem under discussion. He would lose all self-awareness, all sense of the impression he was making, and become at one with whatever it was we were discussing.

The high tide of Oxford philosophy began to recede in the sixties. I do not think it will ever occur to anyone again to go about philosophy in Austin's way. Only too obviously, it is a dead end. And the road it diverged from was one that led into fruitful paths, on which he had turned his back. It was a particular strand of development, encouraged by the work of G. E. Moore, of the kind of philosophical analysis of statements in ordinary language that had been put on the map by, above all else, Bertrand Russell's Theory of Descriptions, which had been published in 1905. There was far more to this theory than the meagre reflection of it in Austin's work, and it was to have an altogether wider influence, in fact a shaping influence throughout the English-speaking world, in which to this day one can say that the commonest single approach to philosophy remains "analytic" in a sense historically traceable to Russell's theory. But it is worth while being clear about what Russell himself thought the point of philosophical analysis was. He took it for granted that the central task of philosophy was the understanding of the world. This involved, as he saw it, having beliefs that we could justify, and this in turn imposed on us two philosophical necessities: first, the analysis of our most important beliefs, so as to make perspicuous to ourselves as well as to others precisely what it was they meant and entailed; and second, the provision of adequate grounds for believing them, which meant producing either good evidence or valid arguments for them, and being able to answer effectively the criticisms against them. It was within the framework of such a programme that analysis and argument had their respective places in Russell's philosophy. The linguistic philosophers were to develop his analysis of statements in ordinary language into a discussion of familiar words that came to be pursued for its own sake, and by the end this had degenerated into a nit-picking dissection of any and every commonplace utterance.

In universities other than Oxford, especially in the United States, there were philosophers who applied Russell's technique to the purposes for which he intended it, namely the investigation of our most important beliefs about the nature of reality. In such hands it was to prove a powerful instrument, precisely because it was only an instrument and never an end in itself. The upshot of the total situation as I have outlined it was that most philosophy in the English-speaking world became analytic in some sense of the term, though as a handmaid to serious activity in some cases but not in others. The three most important exceptions to this generalization were a persistent and sturdy devotion to German idealism in Scottish universities, the body of philosophy that grew out of the revival of interest in Marxism in the 1960s, and the philosophy that came to be pursued under the influence of developments in twentieth-century Germany and France. But what is best even in these has been influenced by analytic philosophy, and has greatly benefited from that influence.

"Analytic" philosophy in one sense or other, then, remains the commonest single approach. During the seventies and eighties it began to escape from its linguistic straitjacket even in Oxford, and came more and more to be applied to problems of substance. Under the influence of Chomsky first of all, then others, even its application to language took on a more scientific and interesting cast. And during the same period it began, for the first time since the thirties (when it had been anathema to Communists and fascists alike), to re-establish itself on the continent of Europe.

5

The Inadequacy of Linguistic Philosophy

During the 1950s and 1960s Oxford philosophers became used to accusations of trivializing the subject. The sort of reply they most often tended to give was exemplified in something said to me years later by A. J. Ayer (*Men of Ideas,* p. 127):

> . . . I think the answer is that the distinction between "about language" and "about the world" isn't all that sharp, because the world is the world as we describe it, the world as it figures in our system of concepts. In exploring our system of concepts you are, at the same time, exploring the world. Let's take an example. Suppose one is interested in the question of causality. We certainly believe that causality is something that happens in the world: I am bitten by the anopheles mosquito so I get malaria—and so on: one thing causes another. One could put this by saying: "What is causality?" And this is a perfectly respectable and important, indeed traditional, philosophical question. But you can also put it by saying: "How do we analyse causal statements? What do we *mean* by saying that one thing causes another?" And although you now look as if you are posing a purely linguistic question, you are in fact posing exactly the same question. Only you are putting it in a different form. And most philosophers would now consider this a clearer form.

When, after a few more sentences from Ayer, I went on to say, "What you've just said boils down to saying that an investigation of our use of language *is* an investigation of the structure of the world *as experienced by human beings,"* his reply was simply "Yes."

Now I would flatly deny that this is the case. If two people have an argument about causality they are disputing about what does or does not occur in the world, whereas if they have an argument about the analysis of a causal statement they are disputing about how a proposition in a humanly constructed language is to be understood. Furthermore, arguing about the world and arguing about what people say about the world are arguments at two different logical levels. In the technical language of logic, the latter is of a higher order than the former. And this is something that cannot be denied. It is not a matter of opinion. Logically, reality independent of human beings, people's experience of that reality, and what people say about either, constitute three or four different realms of discourse. In Popperian terminology they are World One (an objective world of material things), World Two (a subjective world of mental states), and World Three (an objectively existing but abstract world of man-made entities—language, mathematics, knowledge, science, art, the whole cultural heritage); so according to Popper an argument about causality is an argument about World One whereas an argument about a causal statement is an argument about World Three. As all these different formulations make clear, arguing about the structure of the world simply cannot be said to be the same as arguing about the structure of language. The classic statement of the view that it can—that the fact that we can talk about the world must mean that the structure of language corresponds to that of the world—is contained in Wittgenstein's *Tractatus Logico-Philosophicus,* the single text that probably had more influence than any other on the original logical positivists. But Wittgenstein himself came to regard the view as mistaken, and repudiated it.

Even so, the view of the matter expressed by Ayer remained typical of the generation whose outlook had been formed under the influence of logical positivism.* The generation that followed, the linguistic analysts whose outlook was formed under the presiding influences of the later Wittgenstein and J. L. Austin, met the challenge I put to Ayer with an altogether more radical and sophisticated view, the view that language was constitutive of experience. This was trenchantly expressed by John Searle (*Men of Ideas,* p. 184):

> I am not saying that language creates reality. Far from it. Rather, I am saying that *what counts* as reality—what counts as a glass of water or a book or a table, what counts as the same glass or a different book or two tables—is a matter of the categories that we impose on the world; and those categories

---

* See, for example, what Quine (who attended, as did Ayer, some of the meetings of the Vienna Circle in the early 1930s) has to say on pp. 178–9 of *Men of Ideas.*

are for the most part linguistic. And furthermore; when we experience the world we experience it *through* linguistic categories that help to shape the experiences themselves. The world doesn't come to us already sliced up into objects and experiences: what counts as an object is already a function of our system of representation, and how we perceive the world in our experiences is influenced by that system of representation. The mistake is to suppose that the application of language to the world consists of attaching labels to objects that are, so to speak, self-identifying. On my view, the world divides the way we divide it, and our main way of dividing things up is in language. Our concept of reality is a matter of our linguistic categories.

This is a view that continues to be put forward not only by philosophers but by specialists in other fields, in particular literature and linguistics, and even by some sociologists and anthropologists.

I would go along with Searle, as I think everyone must, that "what counts as an object is already a function of our system of representation, and how we perceive the world in our experiences is influenced by that system of representation," but I would interpret this in a Kantian sense (see pages 145–50). What I do not accept is that the categories of our system of representation are in any fundamental or primal sense linguistic. I understand the view: what I do not understand, and have never been able to understand, is how anyone can hold it. For I find (and I do not believe that I am differently constructed from others in this respect) that it is directly contradicted by my immediate experience.

If I look up from the writing of this sentence, my view immediately takes in half a room containing scores if not hundreds of multicoloured items and shapes in higgledy-piggledy relationships with one another. I see it all clearly and distinctly, instantly and effortlessly. There is no conceivable form of words into which this simple, unitary act of vision can be put. For most of my waking day my conscious awareness is a predominantly visual experience— as Fichte puts it, "I am a living seeing"—but there are no words to describe the irregular shapes of most of the objects I see, nor are there any words to describe the multiple, coexisting three-dimensional spatial relationships in which I directly see them as standing to one another. There are no words for the infinitely different shadings and differentials of colour that I see, nor for the multifarious densities of light and shadow. *Whenever* I see, all that language can do is to indicate with the utmost generality and in the broadest and crudest of terms what it is that I see. Even something as simple and everyday as the sight of a towel dropped on to the bathroom floor is inaccessible to language—and inaccessible to it from many points of view at the same time: no words to describe the shape it has fallen into, no words to describe the degrees of shading in its colours, no words to describe the differentials of shadow in its folds, no words to describe its spatial relationships to all the other objects in the bathroom. I see all these things at once with great precision and definiteness, with clarity and certainty, and in all their complexity. I possess them all wholly and securely in direct experience, and yet I would be totally unable, as would anyone else, to put that experience into words. It is emphatically not the case, then, that "the world is the world as we describe it," or that I "experience it through linguistic categories that help to shape the experiences themselves" or that my "main way of dividing things up is in language" or that my "concept of reality is a matter of our linguistic categories."

Corresponding things are true of our direct experience through all five of our senses. Imagine applying the phrases just quoted to the experiences I have when eating my dinner! Eating, like seeing, is part of our most elemental, everyday contact with the world of matter, even more necessary to our survival than seeing. I distinguish instantly, effortlessly and pleasurably between the taste of meat, the taste of potatoes, the taste of each vegetable, the taste of ice cream, the taste of wine. What is more, I distinguish instantly and effortlessly between different *kinds* of meat (beef, pork, lamb, veal, etc.), different kinds of potatoes (roast, boiled, French fried, mashed, etc.) and so on through each possible example. Can there be anyone who seriously maintains that the categories in which these experiences come to me are linguistic, or that my main way of distinguishing between them is linguistic? Is there even anyone who can put these experiences into words after he has had them—who can *describe* the taste of boiled potato, of lamb, of parsnip, in such a way that anyone who had not tasted those things would know from the descriptions what each of them tasted like?

We can, as I say, run through all the other senses in the same way. I know the individual voices of all my friends, and recognize most of them on the telephone after only a couple of words, but the categories in which I distinguish them are not linguistic, and it is beyond the possibilities of language to put the separate character of each and every one of them into words. This is illustrated by the fact that there is no way I could describe them to you that would enable you to identify them all immediately yourself. The plain fact is that *none* of our direct experience can be adequately put into words. And this is true not only of our sensory experiences of the external world. Going on inside me all the time is a complex and dynamic flow of ever-changing awareness, mood, response, reaction, feeling, emotional tone, perceptions of connections and differences, back references, side references, with flickering thoughts and glimpses and half-memories darting in and out of the various interweaving strands, all flowing endlessly on in some richly reverberating echo chamber of resonance and connotation and implication. I might be able to imagine this being translated into some kind of orchestral music but certainly not into words. Just as in the case of outer experience, even the most incisive and vivid of our private experiences are unverbalizable. Who can describe an orgasm? Or our response to a great work of art? Or the special quality of terror in a nightmare?

Try telling someone a piece of music. One of the most self-evidently false famous remarks in the recent history of philosophy, and one usually quoted with approval, is F. M. Ramsay's "What we can't say we can't say, and we can't whistle it either." This is typical, it seems to me, of the quite staggering blindness (or perhaps in this case deafness) of several familiar kinds of philosopher. *Everything* that can be whistled is something that can be whistled but cannot be said. Or was Ramsay able to say a tune? He might have been able to dictate the musical notation of one, but that would not have been voicing the melody. And when one considers the possibility of saying a Brahms symphony or a Mozart piano concerto . . . The same is true, of course, of other arts. How does one say the *Mona Lisa,* or Leonardo's *Last Supper?* The assumption that everything of significance that can be experienced, or known, or communicated, is capable of being uttered in words would be too preposterous to merit a moment's entertainment were it not for the fact that it has underlain so much philosophy in the twentieth century, and so much literary theory too.

What I am saying has radical implications for any philosophy that holds that empirical knowledge must derive from experience. For it means that this direct experience which is never adequately communicable in words is the only knowledge we ever fully have. *That* is our one and only true, unadulterated, direct and immediate form of knowledge of the world, wholly possessed, uniquely ours. People who are rich in that are rich in lived life. But the very putting of it into words translates it into something of the second order, something derived, watered down, abstracted, generalized, publicly sharable. People who live most of their outer or inner lives in terms that are expressible in language—for example, people who live at the level of concepts, or in a world of ideas—are living a life in which everything is simplified and reduced, emptied of what makes it *lived,* purged of what makes it unique and *theirs.* But although the unique character of lived experience cannot be communicated by concepts it can be communicated: by works of art. This explains why it is impossible to say what it is that a work of art "means" or "expresses" or "conveys," even when that work is itself made up of words.

I have talked so far only of the unverbalizability of direct experience, of what is immediately given. But it is also the case that the most important to us of our dispositions cannot be put into words either—being in love, for example, or our feeling for our friends, or what music means to us in our lives, or our relationship with our children, or our passion for philosophy (come to that a passion for anything, even golf). Then there are such things as our awareness

of ourselves as continuing beings, our apprehension of our own integral coherence and the unity of our apperceptions, our feelings about right and
wrong, our intimations of mortality. At every level, it seems to me, none, or almost none, of the things that matter most to us can be adequately expressed in
language, any more than our direct experience of the inner and outer worlds
can be adequately expressed in language.

I can only affirm, therefore, that life and the world as I experience them are
completely at odds with what language-oriented philosophers and literary
critics customarily say or seem to assume, in that both are largely inexpressible in language. Yet I am thinking all the time—I am observing situations and
perceiving movements and changes, noting contrasts and connections, forming expectations, making choices, taking decisions, feeling uncertainties, suffering regrets, and a thousand other things—but for the most part without the
use of language. And for me this is all a matter of directly apprehended experience, known with a certainty as immediate as I can know anything. Chomsky once said (*Men of Ideas,* p. 218): "I'm sure that everyone who introspects
will know at once that much of his thinking doesn't involve language," and I
should have supposed this to be self-evident were it not for the fact that so
many language-oriented academics of many kinds either deny it or proceed as
if it were untrue.

The everyday phrase "to put something into words," together with all its
common variations—"I don't know how to express this," "he has a very good
way of putting things," and so on—corresponds to my own directly apprehended experience. Normally I am absorbed moment by moment in the ever-
flowing Mississippi of my life, and this always includes as one of its currents
a perpetually ongoing flow of thinking without language. I rarely attempt to
put this into words unless I need to, and that is most commonly when I want
to communicate it to someone else. Then some part of me has to withdraw
from its immersion in immediate experience and extract itself from my direct
preoccupations in order to scan the public medium of language for ways of
saying what it is that I want to say. There is always that step involved. Sometimes the result comes effortlessly, sometimes I cannot find words that satisfy
me, but always there is an act of "putting it into words" of which I am directly
aware as being such—out of the concrete specificity of lived life, perceived
observations, felt feelings, thought thoughts, into the generalized, impersonal, public medium of language. And it is always, of necessity, an inadequate rendering, because the former is unique whereas the latter is general.
This means that *precisely* what it is that is lived and felt—what is uniquely
here, uniquely now, uniquely mine—has to be renounced if one is to say anything at all. What is *actually* lived, *actually* felt, *actually* thought, can never
find an equivalent in language, because the inescapably general nature of lan-

guage precludes that. One is forced into rough-and-ready approximations, the nearest one can get.

This separation appears to have a physical basis. As long ago as 1970 a Nobel Prize–winning geneticist, Jacques Monod, wrote in his book *Chance and Necessity* (p. 146 of the English edition): "I am sure every scientist must have noticed how his mental reflection, at the deeper level, is not verbal: it is an *imagined experience,* simulated with the aid of forms, of forces, of interactions which together barely compose an 'image' in the visual sense of the term. . . . However this may be, in everyday practice the process of simulation is entirely masked by the spoken word which follows it almost immediately and which seems inseparable from thought. *But, as we know, numerous observations prove that in man the cognitive functions, even the most complex ones, are not immediately linked with speech (nor with any other means of symbolic expression)."* I have placed that last sentence in italics because if what it states is true then the position put forward by Searle, and still widely advocated, was refuted scientifically more than a generation ago.

The fact that we do not necessarily think in words is demonstrated in public as well as private ways. We all have the experience sometimes of not being able to hit on the precise word we want in order to express something. We hesitate and stutter, and the people we are talking to suggest words to us, perhaps all those that in the thesaurus immediately surround the one we are looking for, but we say "No" . . . "No" . . . to all of them, until at last someone comes out with the right one, and then we exclaim, "That's it! That's the word I'm looking for!" If we had known less precisely than the focus of language what it was we wanted to say we would have accepted one of the words that were exceedingly close to the one we finally chose. But we did not. And that was because we *knew* what we wanted to say as exactly and precisely as language can say it, yet without the word; we knew that there was one and one word only that would do, and what is more we knew that it was a word we knew but could not think of at that moment. This shows that we can, and do, think with the utmost precision of which language is capable and yet without the use of the words themselves.

A lot of our connected behaviour is similar to that of animals, but no one supposes that animals think in language. Without having been trained by anyone to do it, a dog will by its spontaneous behaviour show that it knows that someone other than the people present is due to arrive soon to take it out for a walk, and as soon as it hears a particular noise from the garden gate outside it will know that the person in question is arriving for that purpose, and will go and fetch its own lead and take it to the door just before that door opens in order to place it into the hand of the newcomer. This demonstrates that a whole level of behaviour, which involves not only making valid connections

between one absent thing and another but being prompted to act on these connections at moments which are accurately co-ordinated with the behaviour of
different creatures in a shared time-frame, is effortlessly possible without the
use of language—and this, as I say, is a level at which an enormous amount of
human as well as animal behaviour goes on.

I hope I can be forgiven for a personal reminiscence that drives the point
more firmly home. I have stood for election to parliament several times, the
first two of them in a far-flung rural constituency some decades ago when political organization in such areas was well-meaning but catch-as-catch-can,
and for the most part things got reliably done only when the candidate specifically requested them. One night, towards the end of an exhausting campaign,
I was about to step out on to a public platform to make the final speech of a
long day when I was told that a whole family of my closest helpers had gone
down with food poisoning. This meant that all the campaign tasks for the following day had to be reallocated—who was to man the committee rooms at
each part of the day, who to preside over the various meetings, who to drive
me from one place to another at different hours, and so on. The changes required were small and many, and difficult to fit in with one another given the
limited number of helpers available; and all the people involved needed to be
told before they dispersed that evening—but, being unaware of the need,
many would slip away from the meeting as soon as I finished speaking. So I
went out in front of the audience and, while delivering my political speech, re-
arranged the next day's schedule in my head. As always in such matters, I
would start trying to put things together in one way, then find that this could
not be made to work out, so I would scrap it and start again, trying another
way, until after several attempts I found a way of fitting all the necessary requirements in with one another. Then, as I closed my speech, I asked those of
my campaign helpers who were affected to stay behind for a few minutes so
that I could re-allot their tasks for the next day.

Now I admit that from a purely practical point of view the fact that this happened towards the end of a campaign is not only relevant but crucial: I had
been through all the issues and all the arguments I was dealing with in this particular speech many times before, and it was only this fact that made it possible for me to voice them clearly and energetically while thinking in an
organized way about something unconnected with them. But the fact remains
that this is what I did. And I do not see how anyone can maintain that two unconnected streams of language were being produced by my brain simultaneously, both of them embodying tightly structured forms of organized thought.
And indeed I know from direct experience that this was not the case. I know
that I restructured the next day's schedule in my mind without the use of
words.

Furthermore, I know that there is nothing unique about my being able to do this. A lecturer at the University of Birmingham who went blind in mid-career, John Hull, has written a moving book about this experience called *Touching the Rock* in which he tells, among many other things, how he had to learn to deliver long and properly organized lectures without the use of notes. His account includes the following passage (p. 93):

> I now seem to have developed a way of scanning ahead in my mind, to work out what I am going to say. Everybody does this in ordinary speech, otherwise we couldn't complete a sentence. Somehow or other, and without effort, I have developed a longer perspective, and now when I am speaking I can see paragraphs coming up from the recesses of my mind. It is a bit like reading them off a scanner. While I am speaking, another part of my mind is sorting out into paragraphs what I am going to be saying in the next few minutes, and a yet more remote part is selecting alternative lines of argument from a sort of bank of material. This seems to give my lecturing style a greater sense of order than I had before, and people seem to be able to follow me more easily.

Hull's point that we would not be able to complete a sentence if we did not know what we had not yet said is another good demonstration of the fact that thought and knowledge precede the words into which they are put. Anyone who wants to deny it by saying that this sort of knowing-in-advance involves having the words in advance will find himself either involved in an infinite regress or committed to the view that when we embark on a long and closely interconnected argument we have all the words of which it is composed in our head simultaneously and instantaneously at the outset.

These processes are exemplified all the time in ordinary conversation. While talking to an aunt about the detailed state of her garden we are wondering whether to leave her house the next day or the day after, trying to work out which will be the more convenient in view of all the various other things we have to do, and examining each of the possibilities in the light of convenient train times—and all without pausing in our flow of meaningful, relevant and connected sentences about the garden. Or I might find myself suspecting that a stranger who has pushily forced me into conversation with him is trying to put something over. What is it, I wonder. Is he merely trying to impress me? Or is he going to try to sell me something? Or borrow money? Or could it be something else? And what shall I say to him in each of these eventualities? I consider the alternatives, form speculative expectations, make provisional decisions, without any hiatus in my conversation with him, which may be bowling along racily about holidays abroad or the price of houses. Surely all this sort of thing is familiar experience, as familiar as can be? And surely no one supposes that it involves two unconnected streams of rationally organized language going on in our heads simultaneously?

When Harold Wilson was at the height of his powers it was a fascinating experience to interview him on television, because he seemed to perceive simultaneously all the possible implications of the various answers it was open to him to give to each question. He cannot have run through them all in his head in language. (*"If I say {a long formulation} it'll lead to trouble with such-and-such a trade union, whereas if I say {another long formulation} it'll upset X in the Cabinet; on the other hand, if I try to get out of this by saying {a third long formulation} I'll be unable to reconcile it with what I said the other day in the House of Commons when I said {a fourth long formulation} . . ."* and so on and so forth.) Gilbert Ryle said something strikingly reminiscent of this once about Bernard Williams and philosophical discussion: "He understands what you're going to say better than you understand it yourself, and sees all the possible objections to it, and all the possible answers to all the possible objections, before you've got to the end of your own sentence." I do not believe that even the most famous linguistic philosopher then living can have supposed that Bernard Williams ran all those lengthy chains of reasoning and counter-reasoning through his mind in words during the course of a single Ryle sentence.

As a politician myself I have countless times faced tricky questioning in public, often cunningly designed to trip me up, and I have experienced the Wilson kind of reaction from inside. The conscious experience is of perceiving most of the traps simultaneously, analogously to the way one perceives many things simultaneously in a normal act of vision. One certainly does not do it in language, and indeed it is impossible to conceive how it *could* be done in language. And here again, does not everybody have a related experience as regards, shall we say, difficult arguments? If a person talking to us embarks on a convoluted chain of reasoning we sometimes do not see where it is leading, but then suddenly the penny drops and in an instant the whole of the argument lies before us with complete clarity. We do not run through it in our heads silently and super-speedily in words. It is just *there:* we have it before our mind's eye all at once. And it is not only in the form of such things as arguments that human beings are capable of apprehending long and complicated discursive structures in a single act. Mozart said that when he conceived a new composition the whole thing sometimes came to him simultaneously.

Talking of Mozart raises the point that there are many different modes of organized, complicated and highly sophisticated thinking which are everyday realities for some individuals—who do not need to be numerous to establish the point—and for which there are certainly no words: not only the composer composing music in his head, or a music teacher evaluating the nuances of a performance on the violin, but a motor-racing driver perceiving and seizing unexpected opportunities in the course of a race, and thereby changing his prepared strategy; a football coach working out a new and subtle manoeuvre; the choreographer of a Broadway show considering various possibilities for a new dance number involving several soloists and a large chorus; or someone selecting paintings for an exhibition from a larger body of competent work. In all these activities the decisive considerations are things for which there are no words—things which, even if time were not a factor (as it is in some of my examples), could not be articulated in language.

One reason why examples offer themselves in such profusion is that only a small proportion of our thinking or living is done in words. Yet if that is the case, how is it possible for so many undoubtedly clever people to assert, and believe in all sincerity, the opposite? This was my first reaction when, as an undergraduate, I first encountered language-oriented philosophers. *How can they possibly believe what they say? What must their inner lives be like? What must* they *be like?* Here, I think, is the key to the only possible explanation. Taking them to be sincere, which I do, they must be unlike most of the rest of us in the nature of their inner life and the way they experience it. Anyone who finds at all plausible such propositions as that we think in language, or that the world and our experience of it are amenable to adequate description in language, or that the very categories of our experience are linguistic, must either be someone whose direct experience is such as to render those propositions plausible, in which case he must be a quite abnormally language-limited person with no inner life that they contradict, or he must be someone who has never paid sufficiently close attention to his own direct experience to notice that these propositions contradict it. I think I have met examples of both types. And it goes without saying that they can have IQs as high as anyone wants to stipulate. It is not differences of intellectual ability that we are talking about here. Gilbert Ryle was a person of life-enhancing intellectual brilliance, but he had no inner life worth speaking of. (I say this from personal knowledge of him, but it was also a standing joke among his friends; and see *Modern British Philosophy,* p. 107.)

I do not think it is a coincidence that whereas most (not all, but a strikingly high proportion) of the great philosophers of the past came to philosophy from mathematics and the sciences, nearly all the Oxford philosophers came to philosophy from language studies. For many generations until recently most of the best schools in England took it for granted that their brightest boys would specialize in Latin and Greek. When those boys got to Oxford they found themselves following the course known as Mods and Greats. The first and shorter part of it, Mods, consisted of Greek and Latin literature, but Greats consisted of a combination of Greek and Roman history with Greek and modern philosophy. Thus most of the cleverest boys from the so-called "great" schools found themselves, if they went to Oxford, studying philosophy *not because they had chosen it* but because it came to them in the same package as the classical languages in which they were specialists. A. J. Ayer once remarked to me that it had never entered his head to choose to study philosophy, and that he would certainly not have done so had it not been presented to him as part of the Greats course. I strongly suspect that this is true of most Greats people who became professional philosophers—and most of the best-known ones were Greats men. It has had, I think, not one but several deleterious consequences of serious proportions.

First, it meant that most of the best philosophers at Oxford came to the subject after years of immersion in the detailed study of dead languages, a study which at the schoolmasterly level more often than not lacks imagination, and at worst can be pernickety and soulless. Secondly, and much more important, they took up philosophy not because they chose it or had any interest in it but because they were required to do so by a quirk of the English education system. It is my strong impression that most of them have never *had* philosophical problems in the sense that these have been traditionally understood, and in the sense in which I had them from early childhood onwards. This, I believe, goes most of the way towards explaining why they did not address themselves to such problems, and why what they did instead was to turn philosophy into another and more sophisticated extension of the study of language.

However, I would have retained a fundamental complaint against them even if I had conceded their approach. It was always a striking fact about them that although they declared themselves centrally if not exclusively concerned with language they left out of account the most successfully descriptive and communicative uses of language. About poetry, plays and novels they had nothing to say. The serious literary artist, whatever else he may or may not be, is a truth-seeker, exploring and trying to gain deeper insight into the world around us and our experience of it, its effect on us and on our relations with one another, and how we respond to these various phenomena; and conveying this, somehow, via language. The greatest of them have done it incomparably well. You might therefore have supposed that philosophers who declared their central preoccupations to be with the cognitive, descriptive and communicative functions of language would place great literature in the forefront of their concerns. But not a bit of it. Quite the reverse. They tended to be dismissive of literature as regards its relevance to philosophy. At one time it was even common to hear the word "poetry" used as a pejorative term for language put to emotionally expressive purposes, something that logical positivists in particular looked on as not worthy of philosophical analysis. This fits in with a fact that I have noted in personal relationships, the fact that most philosophers of the kind I am talking about have little interest in the arts. Not surprisingly, perhaps, the exceptions have tended to be among those who were the better philosophers.

There are two more damaging consequences that flowed from the fact that so many Oxford philosophers became philosophers only because they were floated into it on a current outside themselves that began in the schools. Most of them were not just the sort of boy who is top of the class, wins prizes, and so on: they were cleverer than their teachers, and tended to be admired and perhaps even looked up to by them. So it was programmed into them by experience at a highly impressionable age that they could bask perpetually in glory if they could bring their cleverness to their teachers' notice and thus win the respect and admiration of the authority figures of their world. These things carry over conspicuously into adult life. There is a marked tendency among professional philosophers to work at whatever will bring them the warmest approbation from the people they esteem most highly in the profession. This means they are slaves to fashion, albeit high fashion; and when the fashion changes, so does their work—indeed, so do their interests. They write not about problems which they have but about whatever it is that their most admired contemporaries are writing about. However, they also feel that to make their mark they have to show themselves to be cleverer than the run of their colleagues. The natural way for them to think of showing this is to do with a shared subject what others cannot do, or at least what others have not yet done. However, unless the abilities of the individual concerned are at the genius level they will not be able to address big questions in big terms without repeating what has been said before. So the logic of their situation drives them in the opposite direction, namely to work at a level of subtlety and refinement that others appreciate but cannot themselves manage, or have not themselves done. Many an Oxford philosopher won his personal reputation by drawing a distinction that no one had hitherto perceived. To decry such an achievement as necessarily valueless would be a form of intellectual philistinism, but the fact remains that most such philosophers have spent their professional lives buried in the small print of the subject, instead of, as I just put it, addressing themselves to big questions in big terms. Even when they have written about the great philosophers of the past they have usually felt under an absurd compulsion to eschew the obvious, so they have been greatly given to writing books saying that what was really important about Descartes or Locke, or whoever, was not what everyone had always thought it was but something else. If someone objected that these sophistications were all very well but what actually mattered to us fundamentally were the perennial questions, and that the various contributions to the discussion of these that had been made by the so-called great philosophers were important chiefly for the reasons people had always said they were, such a person would be written down as simple-minded, unprofessional in approach, impervious to the manifold subtleties of the questions themselves, and not up to appreciating the true intellectual sophistication of the work currently being done on them.

In my Oxford days, whenever I got into an argument with a philosopher about the validity of his approach or the worthwhileness of what he was doing, and asserted that what philosophers ought to be doing was trying to understand the world, I would most commonly bring forward the antinomies of time and space as examples of the sort of baffling problem they ought to be addressing. These antinomies, I then maintained, showed the commonsense view of the world to be unsustainable. Without any exception that I can recall, the philosophers would respond as did the adults to whom I had turned in childhood. They would say that such questions were unanswerable and therefore we ought not to waste our time pursuing them. They would evince a complete lack of interest in the questions and would change the subject. Trying to understand reality was not—specifically not—what they were interested in.

In the light of these *ad hominem* considerations I find it striking that all the philosophers active in Britain during the twentieth century whom I would without hesitation place in a higher class than the best of the Oxford philosophers made a conscious choice of philosophy and moved to it from an educational background that had not been centred on the study of dead languages. Russell and Whitehead came to philosophy from mathematics; Wittgenstein came to it from engineering; and Popper was a teacher of mathematics and physics before becoming a professional philosopher. In this, though unlike the Oxford philosophers, they were like most of the great philosophers of the past.

Since I have arrived at the point of using *ad hominem* arguments it is now open to a linguistic philosopher to turn the tables on me and say: "In what you have written about the character of human thought you have been generalizing from your own experience. This has misled you. It is we who are closer to the common experience. Your kind of experience is exceptional." There are two reasons in addition to everything I have written so far why I am confident that this is not so. First, I am to an unusual degree a verbal person myself, to the extent that I have all my life earned my living by the use of words, and in many different ways: I have taught in universities and schools, made hundreds of political speeches, been in hundreds of television and radio programmes, published scores of articles and sixteen books. And all my life I have been directly aware that I do not think in words. What I do is have the thought and *then* put the thought into words. To say that I think in pre-verbal images might be taken to imply that these are vaguer than words, whereas the opposite is the case. When I am concentrating—trying to work out a problem, or writing, or preparing a lecture or broadcast—my thinking is, just as music is, more tightly focused, more concrete and specific, than language is able to be; and I experience it in such an immediate way that there is no room for anything else to come between me and the experience. It is of its nature direct and instant. Experiencing it thus, I know it more surely and certainly than I can ever know anything in language. But, alas, it has to go without saying that I cannot express in language what thought is like before it is translated into language.

My second reason is that when one considers what proportion of the human race is illiterate or semi-literate, and how many of the rest, even in the best-educated societies, are only semi-articulate, it is not credible that all those hundreds of millions of people are continuously thinking in words. It is to them, too, that I would point if anyone were to say to me: "You may be a writer and a talker but you are not a very good writer or talker: your use of words is insensitive." Is it really more insensitive, I would be justified in asking, than literally *most* other people's, when you remember what "most" really covers?

Most philosophers since Bertrand Russell have credited language with an absurdly disproportionate importance in human life and experience. The same view has been shared over the same period by many language-oriented intellectuals in other fields. It was characteristic of the modernist movement in literature that what had hitherto been looked on as media and forms came to be seen as their own subject matter: books and poems and plays were interpreted as, at their *deepest* level, depicting things not about the world or people or relationships, but about language, sometimes indeed about books and poems and plays, not infrequently themselves. They were seen in this way not so much by their creators as by various schools of literary theorists, such as structuralists and deconstructionists. We have lived through an age that has preoccupied itself with language more than almost any before it, and has treated language as an object of interest, an end in itself, in a way few previous ages have done. But I believe that this era is ending, in literature as well as in philosophy, and for the same reason: the same error lies at the root of both. Both are treating a medium as if it were the subject matter of its own messages. And for only a small minority even among educated people can such an approach be given the illusion of credibility.

Two critical metaphors have been thrown at linguistic philosophers so often that their victims tend to get exasperated when they hear them. One is that they are like a carpenter who uses his tools all the time on one another—burnishing them ever more brightly, making the points gleam ever more brilliantly, sharpening the edges ever sharper—but never carries out any other tasks with them. The other is that they are like a man who sits all the time polishing his glasses but never puts them on his nose and looks through them at the world. I believe that the metaphors apply. Language is certainly problematic in a great many ways, and its uses impose limitations, but first and foremost—over and above everything else—it is a medium for expression, communication, description, explanation, depiction, narrative, argument, recording, the creation of works of art, the formulation of scientific theories, and other such practical or creative tasks; and it is for purposes such as these that it exists. In philosophy its chief functions are to embody insights and theories about the ultimate nature of reality, both the framework of it and its contents (including ourselves), and to formulate questions of all those kinds I instanced earlier as being characteristically philosophical, and to frame answers to those questions, and to voice criticisms of those answers, and answers to those criticisms. It is a medium for carrying on the public aspects of an activity whose proper focus is always reality, or some aspect of reality (including, if you like, language as one of its more detailed aspects).

This is a point over which Schopenhauer repeatedly took Kant to task, and in my view justifiably. Kant had characterized philosophy as the disciplined examination (*Wissenschaft,* which is usually translated "science") of concepts, to which Schopenhauer replied that although philosophical activity could be conducted only in concepts, and although it was only in concepts that any conclusions it might reach could be expressed, it was a science *in* concepts, not a (or the) science *of* concepts. Concepts were its medium, not its subject matter. Its subject matter was reality, and its aim was to deepen our understanding of the nature of reality.

There is a place for the philosophical investigation of language, as there is a place for the philosophical investigation of anything else—of mind, of logic, of science, of art, of morals, of politics, of sociology—but not more than that. To regard the philosophical investigation of language as more important even than, shall we say, the philosophical investigation of music seems to me a mistake. As for a linguistic approach to philosophy as such (as distinct from the philosophical investigation of language) there is, in my view, no place for that as anything other than a mental exercise in preparation for other tasks.

Anyone who truly believes that the real task of philosophy is to clarify utterance must believe that non-linguistic reality presents us with no philosophical problems. And this is precisely what Austin and the older Wittgenstein, and their followers, did believe. It has always seemed to me a manifestly erroneous belief, one which, for me at least, has always been contradicted by direct experience. In my heart I do not really understand how anyone can actually believe that there are no non-linguistic philosophical problems about the nature of time, or space, or physical objects, or causal relationships, or the existence of free will. Usually the view in question is either that our common-sense understanding of these things is basically right, and that all we need to do is clarify it—which was in practice the view held by most linguistic analysts—or that the discovery of new truths about the world is the province of the sciences, and therefore philosophy, properly understood, is for the most part the philosophy of science: this was the view held by most logical positivists. These attitudes are so impoverished intellectually that enough has been said against them now, and to go on attacking them would be to push against an open door. But although the schools that gave rise to them no longer exist as recognizable schools, the view of philosophy to which they gave rise, a view restricting it to clarification, remains with us all the time, held consciously and assertively by many distinguished professional philosophers. For instance Michael Dummett is on record as having said, in the 1990s: "Philosophy attempts, not to discover new truths about the world, but to gain a clear view of what we already know and believe about it." And it would be easy to cite an indefinite number of quotations from other contemporary philosophers to the same effect. The first definition of "philosophy" offered in *The Oxford Companion to Philosophy,* published in 1995, is "thinking about thinking."

I regard this attitude as a rejection of philosophy, and I reject it in return. For reasons which I hope I have by now made fully clear I believe that non-linguistic reality presents us with philosophical problems which are fundamental to the nature of the world and of our being in it, and are not to be explained in terms of our use of language. This being so, it cannot be the case that the problems can be solved by analysis. Analysis can do no more than clarify what we are already in possession of. Of course it is nearly always wise for us to formulate our problems as clearly as we can before we try to solve them, but clarification itself is not part of a solution, only a preliminary to it. The solution to a philosophical problem of genuine substance needs to be an explanatory theory, an idea that constitutes a new way of looking at things and casts fresh light on them, illuminates them, while remaining itself rationally criticizable and defensible. Such ideas are essentially creative personal achievements, and constitute the main content of worthwhile philosophy. It is only since the historically recent professionalization of the subject that the scene has been swamped with people who are categorized as philosophers but who are not capable of producing worthwhile philosophical ideas, and so have to make doing something else their chief activity—which then, because it is what most professional philosophers are doing, comes to be known as philosophy. Although this activity exists in superaddition to, and alongside, the traditional one, it has come, I think, to be mistaken even by most professionals for the real thing. In the course of my adult life I have encountered more serious interest in real philosophy outside the profession than in it.

6

The Problem of Perception

As an undergraduate student of philosophy at Oxford the only problem of substance I was officially required to tangle with apart from the philosophy of language was that of perception. This is a problem that has always obsessed empiricist philosophers and their legatees, the reason being that on the basis of empiricist assumptions it is insoluble.

The problem can be formulated as follows. If the world consisting of all other material objects apart from my own body exists independently of whether I exist or not, and in dimensions of space and time that are also independent of me; and if my knowledge of that world derives from the fact that those objects impinge on my body's senses in such ways as to cause effects in my brain which might be described as mental states in which the objects are represented; how can I ever know that the representations correspond to the objects, in other words that my perceptions correspond to reality? The only way one can check the accuracy of a copy is to compare it with the original, but in this case we have no independent access to the original, and therefore cannot make the comparison. We have access to the copy alone—indeed it is only from the copy that we infer the existence of the original at all. The question is made sharper by the fact that we know that there are times when our senses deceive us. If I have a visual image of a door six paces in front of me I infer that there is a door six paces in front of me, but at least once in a while I am wrong—I once found a brilliantly executed *trompe l'oeil* representation of a door painted on the wall. There are other reasons why I might have made the same mistake: I could have been deceived by the play of light in the shadows, or I could have been hallucinating, or I could have been walking in my sleep. The fact is that mistaken perceptions are commonplace in daily life—while driving, while playing games, and in all sorts of other contexts. Furthermore every object looks a different shade of colour in different lights and therefore at different times of the day; and every object looks a different shape from a different angle; so, we might ask, what is the object's real colour, and what is its real shape—and how do we know? Why should the colour in one particular light as against all the others be called the "real" colour, and why should the shape seen from one particular angle as against all the others be called the "real" shape? We know we are sometimes wrong. How can we be sure on each individual occasion that we are not wrong?

The question can be radicalized. If all I experience, and all I ever *can* experience, are mental states, what warrant do I have for believing that anything exists other than mental states? Indeed, what warrant do I have for believing that there are any mental states other than mine? I can never have direct access to anyone else's, so how can I be certain that there are minds other than my own?

These questions have been asked, pressed and pursued over hundreds of years, and there is now a substantial literature about them. Descartes, Locke, Berkeley and Hume are among those who have produced works of genius in their respective attempts to answer some of them; and although their proposed solutions have not withstood all subsequent criticisms their writings cast illumination on the problems. Hume in particular is deep and detailed in his understanding of how difficult the problems are, and in consequence has come to be generally regarded by students of philosophy as the greatest philosopher to have written in the English language, in spite of the fact that his works have not exerted the same breadth of influence as Locke's.

If the conclusions reached by these men are stated straightforwardly they have a way of seeming jejune and disappointing. The enlightenment to be got from studying them comes from the detailed working through of their arguments, which leaves one still searching but greatly helped forward in the search, not only by what they have to say but by the critical reactions and reflections to which one is oneself stimulated by the reading of them. Descartes believed that from the contents of his own consciousness alone he could prove that there must be an infinite, omnipotent and perfect being. He believed this because he thought that the greater could not be conceived by the less. Therefore I, a finite, weak, and imperfect being, would not be able by myself to form the clear concept of an infinite, omnipotent and perfect God. The fact that I have this concept means that something corresponding to it must exist and must have given me an apprehension of itself. A perfect being would not be a deceiver, and therefore would not order matters in such a way that I clearly and distinctly perceive things that are not there; and so the world must be as I take it to be when I am giving the matter my serious attention. This is to acknowledge that human experience itself cannot directly guarantee the existence of the external world, still less its correspondence to our perceptions. Our guarantee is indirect, and lies through the indubitable knowledge that we have of the existence of God. This conclusion follows in the train of another of still greater consequence: that, far from the objective being certain and the subjective uncertain, the only existences of which we can be indubitably sure are the immediate deliverances of our own consciousness.

This last conclusion is arrived at by Descartes through the application of a method which has become known as Cartesian doubt. This method consists of a suspension of belief *for purposes of the argument* in any proposition that could conceivably be wrong. I have put five words in italics here because there has been an extraordinary amount of misunderstanding of the point they make. Even many otherwise good writers have written as if Descartes actually doubted, or tried to deceive himself or others into thinking he doubted, his most basic commonsense beliefs, and have protested that this is an absurdity. Descartes did no such thing. If I may be allowed to put the point of what he was doing in my own words the account might go as follows.

We have before us in mathematics the very paradigm of indubitable and useful knowledge. The whole edifice is extraordinarily impressive at every level, from the farthest ranges of abstraction down to the most ordinary level of everyday practicality. If we could put our non-mathematical knowledge on a similar footing it would enable us to achieve the maximum mastery of reality, practical as well as intellectual, of which human beings are capable. Let us, then, examine mathematics for what gives it its compelling certainty, and see if this is something that can be brought over into non-mathematical knowledge. We find on examination that the whole of mathematics follows with the irresistible necessity of deductive logic from a startlingly small handful of premises that are so short, simple, elementary and obvious as to be indubitable. If we could find such indubitable premises for our empirical knowledge we could, so to speak, construct the whole world on their foundations. Let us, then, look at our empirical beliefs to see if there are any that *cannot possibly* be doubted.

We know, alas, that the direct evidence of our senses can be doubted, because we know that our senses do sometimes deceive us: the church spire at sunset looks golden when in fact it is grey; a straight stick looks bent in water; and so on and so forth. Sometimes we are deluded into thinking we are perceiving things when we are not perceiving anything at all: this happens when I dream—I take myself to be in my study doing this or that, only to wake up and discover that the entire thing is an illusion and that I am in bed. This is particularly disconcerting because it means that I cannot even be one hundred per cent certain that although I am confident that I am now sitting at my desk writing this sentence I will not wake up and find it to have been an illusion. On reflection, then, it appears that any experience can delude me as to its nature. However, there actually is something that it is impossible for me to doubt, and this is that I am having the conscious experience that I am currently having, even though I may be completely wrong as to its provenance. This was what was meant earlier by saying that the subjective is indubitable in a way that the objective can never be. So if I draw deductive conclusions not from the presumed provenance of the deliverances of my consciousness but solely from the bald fact that I have them then they cannot be wrong. Are there, however, any such possible inferences? Yes, there are. For instance, from the fact that I have the experience of conscious awareness at all it follows that I must exist, and, what is more, exist as being at the very least the sort of creature that has this sort of experience: I must be at the very least a thinking being.

So I can say with certitude: "I think, therefore I am; or, to be pedantically accurate, from the fact that I directly experience conscious awareness it follows indubitably that I am some sort of being (not necessarily the sort of being I think I am) that experiences conscious awareness (which may not necessarily mean what I think it means)." But I can go further than that and say that from the fact that I, conscious but limited, have the concept of a being that is conscious but unlimited, it follows that such a being must exist, and must have given me that concept, because the finite cannot give rise to infinity from within its own resources.

Then the rest of the argument follows as before. There are few philosophers more attractive to read than Descartes. He is the only great philosopher that France has ever produced, and his work exhibits the language of that country at its most compelling: the prose is pellucid, yet pervaded by his highly distinctive character; and although his most important work (the *Discourse on Method* and the *Meditations*) is written unrelentingly in the first person there is nothing alienatingly self-centred about it. On the contrary, the reader finds himself identifying automatically with Descartes's enquiry in all its urgency: "*Is there anything I can be one hundred per cent sure of?*" The clarity of it all, and the patience of the step-by-step search for a rock-hard, unshakable foundation from which a general view of the world can reliably be built up, make his work a first-class introduction to philosophy in general. The distinction of the writing, together with the pungency of the literary personality communicated by it, are so great that once read his work remains a permanent possession, like great art: for the rest of your life Descartes is someone you know. This is in marked contrast to, say, Kant, who is a greater philosopher: you can study Kant for years without acquiring any particular sense of a literary personality. Because of all this—and because Descartes is regarded, rightly, as the inaugurator of modern philosophy—he is one of the central figures of Western culture in general in a way that not even some of the greatest philosophers are. One has the feeling that all educated people ought to read Descartes. In France all educated people have.

His immediate successor in the central tradition of Western philosophy, Locke, was as unmistakably English as Descartes was unmistakably French. In his *Essay Concerning Human Understanding* Locke was inclined to give precedence to common sense over deductive logic; and his own ultimate conclusions seemed to him altogether more provisional, more fallible and less self-evident. He agreed with Descartes that a man cannot doubt that the deliverances of his consciousness are whatever it is they are, and therefore that this at least is something he directly and indubitably *knows;* and he agreed that the deliverances of our consciousness are such that we spontaneously take ourselves to be subjects in a world of objects that exist externally to us in the dimensions of space and time. But he saw it as demonstrable not only, as Descartes did, that our senses sometimes deceive us as to the true nature of physical objects, but that they always and systematically deceive us in some highly important respects, a situation which Descartes had denied was compatible with the benevolence of an omnipotent God. For instance, Locke argued that it was impossible that objects can be, independently of any perceiving subject, coloured, or sounding, or characterized by smells and tastes. There is a whole range of qualities such as these which appear to us to characterize the objects themselves but which in fact can exist only when there is an interaction between a perceived object and a perceiving subject. Therefore they cannot characterize an object as it is in itself independently of being experienced. These Locke called secondary qualities. The primary qualities are those characteristics that, in his view, an object can possess in itself regardless of whether it is perceived by a subject or not. It is under these latter aspects that the physical sciences deal with objects, and all of them are impersonally measurable or classifiable—the objects' location; their movements in time and space; their dimensions, weight, mass, material constitution; and so on.

A sceptic might say to Locke: "You tell us that objects have all these qualities, both primary and secondary; but you also say that it is only their qualities that we can ever apprehend. The object that those characteristics characterize, the substance in which they inhere, the underlying *thing,* is, you say, something to which we can never have access. It is, in your own phrase, a 'something I know not what.' But given this fact that it can never figure in experience, how can you know it exists at all? Surely it is a contravention of the fundamental principle of empiricism to assert that it does?" To this I think Locke would have replied somewhat as follows: "That qualities exist is something of which we have direct and indubitable experience. And it is not credible that these are just abstractions existing all by themselves, floating in mid-air so to speak. Still less is it credible that they free-float in the invariant combinations in which we experience them. To take a single example, whenever I do what I call 'eating an apple' I always have a very tight cluster of multiple and simultaneous experiences from within the same narrow range of sizes, shapes, colours, consistencies, tastes, smells, degrees of moisture, feelings in the hand and mouth, and all the rest of it. . . . Are you going to tell me that there are millions of these clusters just floating around in accidental yet permanent combination with one another, to which we deludedly give the name 'apples'? And are you going to go on to say that the same is true of all the innumerable other things in the world that we take to be physical objects? Surely no one can believe this. There must be some combinative something in which the qualities that we apprehend inhere, a substance that constitutes the substratum of each physical object."

But in logic this is not an answer. Even if it is accepted, it means that on Locke's own showing the ultimate nature of physical reality is an insoluble mystery to us, which indeed is what he believed. Furthermore, by parity of reasoning, the ultimate nature of experiencing subjects can be shown to be just as mysterious. We know how objects affect us—we have direct and indubitable experience of the visual, aural, tactile and other effects they have on us. But what it is that they thus affect—what the independent nature is of the subject that has the experiences—is something that can never itself figure in experience. It would appear to be a matter of logic that if we can have direct knowledge of experiences only, then we cannot, independently of those experiences, have direct knowledge of whatever it is that has the experiences. So we live in a world that consists solely of affects and effects. Those we experience directly. But what it is that has the effects lies permanently outside all possibility of experience, as does what it is that is affected. The view that we come out with is of a reality that consists ultimately of two different kinds of entity, minds and material objects, both of which are in their inner nature unknowable. Only interactions between them can we ever know.

One thing that will strike many readers about this view of total reality is that it corresponds to what a large number of people in practice believe. It is full of holes, but the holes are bunged with common sense—*of course* material objects exist, even if we cannot prove it; and *of course* we are continuous selves, even if our self is something we can never directly experience. It was the first view of the world to be publicly adumbrated that was not—or at least does not need to be—religious, and is still widely accepted. In that sense Locke can be looked on as the first modern man. When one adds to this the fact that as a political philosopher he is generally (and in my view rightly) credited with having laid the intellectual foundations of liberal democracy, his achievement appears gigantic. If he has come to be thought of as something of a plain, commonsensical thinker, perhaps even a bit pedestrian, it is because what he had to say has become so familiar that it may be in danger of seeming obvious to us now; but the truth is that when he put it forward it was profoundly original, and not obvious at all. The fact that it can seem obvious now is a measure of his influence. Indeed, it could be seriously argued that he is the most influential philosopher since Aristotle.

Locke's ideas constituted the first non-religious worldview since Aristotle's to sweep through the Christian West and find widespread acceptance. I do not need at this point to go into his impact on the Continent via Voltaire, Montesquieu and the French encyclopaedists, or his abiding influence on American society via the Founding Fathers and their drawing up of the American Constitution. The two philosophers from whom I have learnt most, Kant and Schopenhauer, repeatedly paid tribute to Locke for opening up the path of intellectual development that made their work possible. Indeed, more of the philosophy that is generally accredited to Kant had already been clearly stated by Locke than is generally ascribed to him even by professional philosophers. It is the severest of misfortunes that his writing is so lacking in literary qualities, because it means that in spite of its profundity and importance it is seldom read by anyone other than academics and their pupils. It has not directly become a part of the general culture, in spite of the fact that it has done so much to shape our heritage. This lack of literary attractiveness has also led, I think, to Locke's being underrated as a philosopher. He is closer in calibre to Hume than students of philosophy are generally inclined to place him.

According to Locke all abiding reality is hidden. But according to his most immediate successor in the great tradition, Berkeley, reality takes precisely the form that it appears to us to take, namely experience. Instead of, as Locke did, responding to the sceptic with an appeal to common sense that is really an abandonment of the argument, Berkeley takes the sceptic's objection seriously. What is more, he agrees with it. We have no warrant, he argues in effect, for postulating two separate but identical worlds, one the world of experience, the other the world of objects which are not experiences but which resemble our experiences to a hair and whose existence can only ever be indirectly inferred from those experiences. That whole inferred world of material substance is, he says, a superfluous hypothesis. We can never actually have adequate grounds for asserting its existence, so even if it did exist we could never know, because nothing in our experience would be different one way or the other. Since all we can ever apprehend is experience, all we can ever have sufficient grounds for asserting the existence of is experience. Why should we balk at that, or even regard it as presenting us with a problem?

It does not, he disconcertingly points out, present the man in the street with a problem. Ordinary human beings not engaged in philosophizing take it for granted that a so-called material object is the sum total of its observable characteristics. If you say to someone, "How do you know I'm holding a leather glove in my hand?," he might well reply with impatience, "Well, don't be silly, I can *see* it. And here"—reaching out—"I can touch it and feel it. And"—taking it and raising it to his nose—"I can tell from the smell that it's leather." And so on and so forth. And when he had gone through every attribute of the glove that was accessible to his senses he would think there was nothing left he could say about it. It would not normally occur to him to suppose that the real glove, the glove-in-itself, was an invisible, ineffable substratum that was for ever inaccessible to his observations even though it sustained the incidental characteristics he observed. He would, on the contrary, take the glove to *be* the sum of the characteristics he could observe. And in doing this, says Berkeley, he would be right. One of the most extraordinary features of this aspect of Berkeley's philosophy is that it appears at first sight to be wholly counter to common sense and then reappears, on re-examination, to be in line with it.

Yet for any kind of idealist philosopher a crucial question that has to be answered is this: how can he explain the fact that we human beings live in a shared world? Everyone who walks into this room where I sit writing these words will be able to perceive in any degree of detail you care to specify the same room: he will see me sitting here at this desk, and as he wanders around the room he will see all the same objects in the same places, and with all the same observable characteristics of size, shape, colour and so on. How is this to be explained if there is no independent world of material substance but only the experiences belonging to each individual? Berkeley answers that question by an appeal to the existence of God. All that is, he says, exists in the mind of God, and God is everywhere all the time. This explains why the same reality is experienced by all of us at any given point in space, and also why that reality is stable through time. Because all there is exists in the mind of God, and sometimes in our minds too, it is in that sense mental, with no other mode of existence attaching to it. There is an infinite spirit and there are finite spirits: the infinite spirit created the finite spirits and is in perpetual communication with them. We are the finite spirits, and our experience is God's mode of communication with us. No other reality exists.

I am sure there are religious people today who believe something of the same sort. But I take it that the great majority of people would be unable to accept an explanation of reality in any such form. Certainly I cannot, though I acknowledge it as a theory of audacity and beauty. Berkeley's consistent holding to the point that the data of experience are the only possible objects of our knowledge, and his demolition of what appear on a first encounter to be some of the obvious objections to it, have had a lasting effect on the whole of Western thought. Many years after his death it became, and for several generations remained, the central orthodoxy of science. One of Karl Popper's best-known papers is called "A Note on Berkeley as Precursor of Mach and Einstein," and in it he shows that at least twenty-one theses in Berkeley's philosophy are also embedded in what we think of as distinctively modern physics. Even for people who do not believe in God, Berkeley's philosophy has contemporary relevance and continuing interest: Bertrand Russell was an atheist, but many people have seen affinities with Berkeley in the position put forward in the famous book he wrote as an introduction to philosophy called *The Problems of Philosophy*. One way and another Berkeley has had considerable influence on twentieth-century thought.

The last in time of the quartet of "great" philosophers who were compulsory reading for PPE in the Oxford of my student days, Hume, is today the one most highly regarded by other philosophers. In some ways he conflated Berkeley and Locke. He agreed with Berkeley that all we can ever have direct access to is our own experience, that this remains permanently inside us, and that there is no way in which we can demonstrate the validity of inferences from it to the existence of a world separate from us and outside us in space—in other words we cannot prove the existence of the external world. But, like Locke, he took a different view of common sense from Berkeley: he maintained that unless we are making a strained and self-conscious attempt to be philosophers we cannot prevent ourselves from believing in the existence of an external material world, even though it cannot be proved. However, his appeal to common sense over the head of this unprovability is at one and the same time more practical and less confident than Locke's. He denies that there are grounds for any confident belief in the existence of a God—so, *pace* both Berkeley and Descartes, God cannot be accepted as the guarantor of the existence of anything independent of our experience. But at the same time the fact that it appears to us self-evident that we live in a world of material objects external to ourselves does not, *pace* Locke, constitute grounds for regarding the existence of such a world as *known* if it cannot—and Hume demonstrates that it cannot—be validated by either experience or logic. The arguments of the sceptic are, says Hume, valid. But only theoretically. Having conceded their validity *as arguments* he drives home the point that it is impossible for anyone actually to *live* as a sceptic, since to carry on our lives at all we have to be perpetually doing things, and this involves making choices and decisions, and these cannot but be based on beliefs about our situation. Furthermore, the stakes are often high, because our behaviour has practical consequences: every day we have innumerable opportunities of getting ourselves killed by stepping in front of vehicles, setting fire to ourselves, electrocuting ourselves, gassing ourselves, taking overdoses of drugs, or piercing our bodies with sharp implements. So we are all the time having to conduct our lives on the basis of important beliefs about reality, despite the fact that we can never be one hundred per cent sure that these beliefs are true. This leads Hume to advocate what he calls "mitigated scepticism." The wise course, he says, is to eschew all forms of dogmatism and be permanently prepared to revise our expectations in the light of experience, while at the same time acting as boldly and resolutely as getting the most out of life requires us to do. Inevitably there will be times when we fall flat on our faces, but when we do so the only thing to do is pick ourselves up and try again—and try also to learn from the experience. In practice the adoption of this approach has certain very large implications. One is a massive, humane tolerance. Another is a firm rejection of even the possibility of building a unitary system of explanatory thought—and therefore a rejection of total religions, ideologies and metaphysical systems *as such*—for if there is scarcely anything at all we can be sure of it is the height of absurdity to claim to have an explanation of everything.

Where Hume's thought is at its most disconcerting is in his detailed demolitions. He brings forward arguments of great sophistication and power in an attempt to show not only that we cannot demonstrate the existence of a world external to ourselves but also that we cannot validate the existence of causal connection in any realm; that there is no such thing as inductive logic; that we cannot even be sure of our own existence as continuous selves, and certainly not of the existence of God. His writing penetrates almost uncannily into the nooks and crannies of our certitudes, prising them apart. He genuinely succeeds, I think, in showing that almost everything we believe in, or take for granted, is not in fact *known,* and can never be known. He shows, I believe, that strict proof simply plays no part in human life outside mathematics, an activity he regards as secondary, albeit interesting. It is essential, though, to understand that he is not asserting that the commonsense world we take for granted does not exist, but only that its existence cannot be validated by rational demonstration or argument. In an important sense it thus emerges that what Hume is advancing is a critique of our human limitations, and in particular a critique of human knowledge—a critique of reason, in advance of Kant. What he shows is that most of reason's claims are invalid. We know almost nothing. Our thoughts are connected for the most part not by logic but by association of ideas, and our behaviour is guided not by genuine understanding of reality but by habitual expectation and custom. He was, it has to be said, entirely cheerful about this— he did not think of himself as holding a depressed view of the human condition.

On the contrary, he was an unusually well-disposed and happy person. His attitude to life was both down to earth and appreciative. In his relaxed, good-natured way he thought people would be happier if they could liberate themselves from the ignorance-mistaken-for-knowledge that filled most of the space in their heads, not to mention most of their books and most of their education systems. He had a number of contemporaries who thought he *ought* to be depressed, or frightened, and could not understand why he was not, but that is a fact about them, not a fact about him.

Hume is a writer whom far more people could read with pleasure and profit than do: modest yet witty, stylish and full of personality; serious but unpretentious; deeper than all except a handful of other philosophers, yet always clear. His work is a model of how a philosopher should write, and indeed some of the best philosophers since have made a conscious attempt to write like him. One thing I learnt from him was that my own problems went deeper than I realized. What Hume characteristically tells you when you go to him with a problem is: "It's worse than you think." I took mine to him for help, and came away with them in a more intractable state than before. This represents a considerable deepening of my own understanding, and for that I shall always feel a sense of gratitude to him.

One important respect in which I do not go along with Hume is in his doctrine of the self. He argued that when we introspect, all we can ever be aware of are the *contents* of inner experience: sensory perceptions, images, thoughts, memories, moods, feelings and all the rest of it. We do not also have cognition of some other sort of entity, a self, which *has* these things. As he puts it, "pain and pleasure, grief and joy, passions and sensations succeed each other, and never all exist at the same time. It cannot therefore be from any of these impressions, or from any other, that the idea of self is derived; and consequently there is no such idea" (*A Treatise of Human Nature,* Book I; by "idea" in this context he means any significant mental content). This presupposes that all direct experience consists of perception of an object, whether abstract or material. That may indeed be something that is arguable when what is under consideration is our knowledge of the external world, but I do not think it applies in inner experience. It mistakenly supposes, as philosophers are too often inclined to do when engaged in epistemology, that we are only knowing beings, only spectators of the world. One thing that seems to me to contradict it is agency. In addition to being knowing beings we are also willing beings and acting beings. We are not only spectators of the world but participants in the world, moving parts of the world (in both senses). Whenever I engage in willed activity I have a conscious experience of *doing* something, and that experience does not necessarily have an epistemological object. For instance, when I approach an important decision I may agonize over it for days or even weeks, lie awake at nights worrying about it, discuss it with friends, and so on. Throughout this period I am directly aware that I am doing something, and that I am involved, engaged; but I may have no idea what the decision is going to be (it may not even have come into being, not been formulated at all) until I arrive at the end of the process. In other words, there is direct and immediate awareness of the activity of a subject, and this awareness is prolonged and sustained. I believe it to be conscious and direct awareness of the activities of a self. This is not to say that the self is known through and through—on the contrary, it is so simple a matter to demonstrate that this is never the case that I need not bother with it here—but I do think it illustrates that being a continuing self is something of which we have immediate apprehension. This is not to say, of course, that the self is some sort of existential entity: it may be more in the nature of a process.

A philosopher who had a firm grasp of the argument I have just put forward—though it was to be many years before I discovered his work—was Fichte, who built much more on it than I have done. He concedes (indeed he rehearses the arguments for the conclusion in some detail) that no amount of epistemological analysis or argument can prove the existence of a world external to ourselves; but he goes on to claim that it is proved nevertheless by something categorially different from that, something that is not an argument at all, namely our agency. It would be impossible for us to act if nothing other than ourselves existed; and since we have direct, indubitable experience of our own agency this means that we have incontrovertible proof of the existence of a world external to ourselves. He hurls in his biggest attack on an even narrower front than this. Echoing Kant's *Critique of Practical Reason,* he asserts that we know ourselves directly and indubitably to be moral beings. But there could be no such thing as morality if we were never able to act otherwise than we do, that is to say if we were never able to exercise practical choices; and there could be no such thing as immorality if no obstacles ever existed to morally right action; therefore on both these grounds there must be a field of action containing entities that are not us—in other words there must be a real world external to ourselves. Fichte carries the argument even further forward than this, but we need not follow him beyond this point. He is a philosopher whose work yields many penetrating insights. Unfortunately he is also one of the most difficult to read and understand, as difficult in this regard as Hegel and Heidegger. In consequence, like those other two, he has sometimes been dismissed by genuinely gifted philosophers as a charlatan whose prose is little better than gobbledygook. A book of his which states a good part of his central position with untypical clarity is *Die Bestimmung des Menschen,* a title which has been translated as *The Vocation of Man* but which would have been better rendered *Man's Calling.*

I do not think there would have been any question of an undergraduate in the Oxford of my day being asked to read Fichte. Indeed, from Hume the compulsory syllabus in epistemology passed over Kant and the nineteenth century altogether and jumped straight to the twentieth century, to British-born philosophers (plus Wittgenstein) who were seen to be still grappling with the same problems as Locke, Berkeley and Hume. But whereas the great empiricists had couched those problems in epistemological terms, their modern counterparts translated them into problems about the logic of statements, and dealt with them in that form. As regards the substance of the problems they cannot be said to have made significant progress. As Bertrand Russell put it in his *History of Western Philosophy,* published in 1945: "[Hume] developed to its logical conclusion the empirical philosophy of Locke and Berkeley, and by making it self-consistent made it incredible. He represents, in a certain sense, a dead end: in his direction, it is impossible to go further. To refute him has been, ever since he wrote, a favourite pastime among metaphysicians. For my part, I find none of their refutations convincing; nevertheless, I cannot but hope that something less sceptical than Hume's system may be discoverable." In a sense the fact that so many important thinkers have found the philosophies of Berkeley and Hume impossible to accept and yet at the same time impossible to refute is a measure of the greatness of those two as philosophers. It shows that they have indeed confronted us with problems that are fundamental.

I regard the above Bertrand Russell quotation as illuminating in several ways at once. First, it brings out a striking and strange feature of the tradition of analytic philosophy inaugurated by Moore and Russell, namely that even its ablest practitioners did not regard themselves as having taken philosophy much beyond what it had been two hundred years before. Russell stated clearly what the difference was as things stood in the 1940s (*History of Western Philosophy,* p. 862): "Modern analytical empiricism, of which I have been giving an outline, differs from that of Locke, Berkeley, and Hume by its incorporation of mathematics and its development of a powerful logical technique." That he regarded himself and his colleagues as having refashioned the instrument but not having as yet carried out the task for which it had been intended is made clear by the sentence with which the same paragraph ends: "I have no doubt that, in so far as philosophical knowledge is possible, it is by such methods that it must be sought; I have also no doubt that, by these methods, many ancient problems are completely soluble." All I can say is that we are still, half a century after those words were written, waiting for signs of any such solution.

Most analytic philosophers after Russell seemed peculiarly unperturbed by the fact that they had made no substantial advance beyond Hume. With some this was because they believed that Hume had taken philosophy as far as it could go, and therefore that little was left to be done apart from a certain amount of clearing up. A. J. Ayer was the exemplar of this attitude. Once, when asked what the central doctrines of *Language, Truth and Logic* were, he replied: "They were very simple. They derived very much from Hume. In fact Logical Positivism, as its name would suggest, is a blending of the extreme empiricism of Hume with the modern logical techniques developed by people like Bertrand Russell."* In his writings generally, Ayer is constantly informing us that what he is about to say, or has just said, had already in its essentials been said by Hume. My favourite all-purpose quotation to this effect is: "Our reasoning on this point, as on so many others, is in conformity with Hume's" (*Language, Truth and Logic,* second edition, p. 126). There were some philosophers other than Ayer who were as cheerful as he was about this but for different reasons. They were untroubled about philosophy not having progressed much beyond Hume because they believed that the only problems philosophy could solve were unimportant. The most famous statement of this view occurs in the Preface to Wittgenstein's *Tractatus,* in which he claims for his book that it solves all the fundamental problems of philosophy, and then goes on to observe how little has been done when that has been done.

For different reasons again this was also, in general, the view of the linguistic analysts. They did not even accept that there were such things as philosophical problems, for they believed that what we mistook for serious problems were no more than puzzlements into which we had been landed by a mistaken use of language; and that once these linguistic misuses had been identified and cleared up, the apparent problems would be seen to have dissolved. So on the one hand they saw themselves excitedly as—as I put it earlier—disposing of the accumulated philosophical problems of two and a half thousand years, yet on the other hand they saw themselves as able to do this only because it was a comparatively small task. As one of the movement's Young Turks was later to express it: "In the face of this refined examination of actual linguistic practice, a lot of traditional philosophical theorizing began to look extraordinarily crude, like an assemblage of huge, crude mistakes. And it was, of course, extremely exhilarating to see huge and imposing edifices of thought just crumbling away, or tumbling down, to the tune of this fairly modest sort of piping" (Peter Strawson in *Modern British Philosophy,* p. 116).

This attitude in turn rests usually on an acceptance of the commonsense view of the world. The ordinary-language philosophers explicitly made everyday usage their criterion of what could or could not justifiably be said. To quote Strawson again: "I was greatly influenced and impressed by Austin,

---

* *Modern British Philosophy,* p. 49.

and, of course, and for partly similar reasons, by Ryle. There was something in common to their methods at that time, though the style was very different. They both gave careful attention to what could, or couldn't, be naturally or non-absurdly *said;* and also to the *circumstances* in which we could or couldn't naturally say such and such a thing. And this method, for reasons which seemed obvious enough once they were pointed out, was a very fruitful source of philosophical data" (*Modern British Philosophy,* p. 116). It was this method that led its practitioners to dismiss with instant derision such propositions as that there was no such thing as time. "But are you seriously going to deny," they would twinkle, "that I shaved yesterday after I got out of bed but before I had my breakfast? And that my lunch was later in the day than my breakfast but earlier than my tea? And that yesterday came before today, but after the day before yesterday?" If one said no, that one was not denying any of those propositions, they would, incredibly yet in all seriousness and sincerity, take themselves to have demolished the notion that time was unreal.

Not only this but all so-called philosophical problems were disposed of by them in such a manner. The piping was indeed modest. One wondered why they bothered with the necessary intake of breath. What they were doing, of course, was being anti-philosophical, for they were taking it for granted that already-familiar common sense was the arbiter of all things—the same common sense which Russell had observed to be the metaphysics of savages—when in fact the situations in which philosophical problems most characteristically arise occur when common sense is either questioned or pursued to its logical consequences.

Actually the assumption that common sense is basically *right* pervades the whole of empirical philosophy, and an appeal to it goes back through the whole empiricist tradition—even, as we have already seen, back through Hume and Berkeley to the founder of the tradition, Locke, though all those philosophers were more sophisticated and insightful in the way they framed the appeal than the moderns have been. It is this enslavement on the part of all of them to an unreflecting metaphysics that, for all the merits of the empiricist tradition, first led it into, and then left it in, the Humean cul-de-sac. For the plain truth is that common sense cannot be right. The antinomies of time and space alone are enough to demonstrate that, for although it is possible to argue that they have been dissolved and disposed of by Einstein it is not possible to argue that they can be dissolved and disposed of by common sense. Within the framework of a commonsense view of the world they are utterly insoluble. And they demonstrate that reality, whatever it is, cannot *but* be of an order radically different from the scheme of things presented to our minds by common sense. As a matter of fact, as we saw in the first chapter, the commonsense account of things seethes with self-contradictions and paradoxes. To anyone reflective, even if only a child, merely being in the world is an experience bristling with problems of a philosophically profound, baffling, and, it could be, insoluble character. Ever since the experiences I had while growing up, I have found it incomprehensible that anyone who thinks at all could regard the world as a place that is intelligible in terms of common sense. If you tell me that there are many indubitably clever people who do so, the only honest comment I can make is that their combination of high intelligence and unenquiring acceptance results in shallowness of a particularly distinctive and familiar kind: *clever* shallowness—self-congratulatory, complacent, a combination of intelligent self-assurance with blinkeredness. And I have to concede that this was a prevailing characteristic of the so-called Oxford philosophers. As much was admitted years later by Isaiah Berlin, who had been at the centre of it all, when he wrote:

> We were excessively self-centred. The only persons whom we wished to convince were our own admired colleagues. . . . We felt no need to publish our ideas, for the only audience which was worth satisfying was the handful of our contemporaries who lived near us, and whom we met with agreeable regularity. I don't think that, like Moore's disciples at the beginning of the century, of whom Keynes speaks in a memoir on his early ideas, any of us thought that no one before us had discovered the truth about the nature of knowledge or anything else; but like them, we did think that no one outside the magic circle—in our case Oxford, Cambridge, Vienna—had much to teach us. This was vain and foolish and, I have no doubt, irritating to others. But I suspect that those who have never been under the spell of this kind of illusion, even for a short while, have not known true intellectual happiness.*

---

* "Austin and the Early Beginnings of Oxford Philosophy" by Isaiah Berlin, in *Essays on J. L. Austin,* p. 16.

7

What Can Be Shown
but Not Said

Having taken my degree at Oxford in philosophy, politics, and economics I
was free at last to study whatever I chose. At once I set out to discover if there
were such a thing as a contemporary philosophy that was intellectually serious. (I had not yet discovered Popper's theory of knowledge.) What determined the direction in which I looked, I think, was that Oxford philosophers
had not only ignored the foundational metaphysical problems of time and
space and the nature of matter and its movements, they had ignored also what
were for me the most profound, illuminating, and engrossing human experiences to be found anywhere outside the immediacies of inner life, sensory response and personal relationships, namely those of art. Even accepting the
self-imposed limitations of their concern with language, they had disregarded
the very language that penetrated most deeply into human experience and our
understanding of it, the language found in the greatest of the world's drama,
poetry, and fiction. So my most immediate need was to find philosophers who
addressed themselves to questions raised by these things, and build, if I could,
some sort of bridge between what I had just been studying and what I felt to
be important—to build a bridge and then cross over it.

Without guidance, and therefore with what I see as remarkable good fortune when I look back on it, the first such philosopher I stumbled across was
the then still living American, Susanne K. Langer. I had never heard of her, but
I found myself one day thumbing through a paperback edition of her *Philosophy in a New Key* in a Malmö bookshop. Her tone of voice seemed to me at-

tractive, so I bought the book on impulse. Not long after I had finished it she (conveniently for me) published a successor volume, *Feeling and Form,* which evolved an aesthetic theory out of the chapter devoted to music in *Philosophy in a New Key.*

Those two books enriched my outlook in several ways that have lasted. The first involves Langer's distinction between discursive form and presentational form. To illustrate what this is one could take as an example a philosophical argument or a mathematical proof. Either is expressed in a symbolic language: in the former case words and punctuation marks, in the latter Arabic figures plus Roman and Greek letters, plus signs for logically constant relations. In either case, if the validity of what is being advanced is to be sustained it is essential that the symbols should be set down in some orders but not in others, and there are rules governing this ordering. In the case of a philosophical argument two sets of rules have to be observed simultaneously which are of an entirely different character, yet both are susceptible of almost unlimitedly complex and sophisticated application. The first of these are the rules of whatever language it is that is being employed, whether English, German, ancient Greek, or whatever: its vocabulary, spelling, grammar, syntax, idiom, usages both ordinary and technical, and so on and so forth. The second are the rules of logic. Both the sentences and their interrelationships have to embody both. Each is a separate example of what Langer calls "discursive form," a structure within which import is constituted and communicated by the placing of one symbol after another in significant order. The difference between one order as against another is of the essence, and therefore such forms can exist and be apprehended only sequentially, and therefore in the dimension of time. They can be, or they can fail to be, carriers of a great many interesting things simultaneously—most obviously meaning, truth, and relevance, but also emotional attitudes, impersonal elegance, economy, style, surprise, the distinctive personality of the human being putting them forward, even indications of his social class or the historical period in which he lived; and a great many other things besides. They can, for instance, have aesthetic value. Now, says Langer, once the philosophical argument (or the mathematical proof, or whatever it may be) which is thus constituted has been completed, it stands before us as a finished structure, and this then presents us with a form of an entirely different kind, a *Gestalt*—an organic whole, unitary, a single abstract object. This is what she calls "presentational form." Because it is—indeed it must be, and can only be—perceived as a unity and apprehended as a whole, the dimension of time is not constitutive of it. It too has many different properties—originality or conventionality, complexity or simplicity, balance, economy, poise, and so on—but because these are properties of the whole it has them in a different way from the way the discursive structure can be said to have the same properties. For example, a philosophical argument can be well balanced as an argument without the sentences of which it consists being well-balanced sentences—and vice versa. It can be highly original yet written in platitudinous prose. Or the sentences can be stylish yet the argument crude. And so on and so forth. One of the features of presentational form that is most fraught with consequence is that although it is displayed it cannot be communicated in any other way. The presentational form of a philosophical argument is something exhibited by the argument as a whole and not something stated in any, or for that matter all, of its sentences. There is little I can do to tell you what it is, except repeat it. You have to "see" it for yourself, and if you do not see it there is not much I can do to point it out to you.

One of Langer's most richly fruitful applications of this distinction is to the arts, not only to such works of art as are made up of words, like plays, poems and novels, but—most originally and profoundly of all—to music. One of her central theses is that in all the arts, the visual arts as much as the others, a work is first and foremost a presentational form symbolic of feeling, and this is why what it communicates can never be expressed discursively in words. I agree with her that a work of art is a presentational form in her sense, and I think her development of this distinction with respect to the arts is a major philosophical achievement. I also agree when she says that the *raison d'être* of presentational forms in art is to communicate not emotion but understanding, insight into the nature of something: she thinks that the something is emotion, I think it may be another something, but we agree that art is cognitive before it is expressive: it conveys to us first and foremost something about the way things are—and then, perhaps, and only secondarily to that, some of the emotions of the artist in response to it. If this is right, a philosophy of art needs to find its place in a wider philosophy about the nature of things. It was only many years later that I discovered one that had done this in a way which, for all its shortcomings, seems to me to be on the right lines, and that is the philosophy of Schopenhauer.

There is a link between Schopenhauer and Langer, and that link is the early philosophy of Wittgenstein. Schopenhauer was the greatest single intellectual influence on this philosophy, which in turn gave Langer the idea for her distinction between discursive and presentational forms. I am not sure she was aware of the connection in its full implications. She acknowledged in her writings that she had got her basic distinction between what can be said and what can be shown-but-not-said from Wittgenstein's *Tractatus Logico-Philosophicus,* where it is central to the book's most famous doctrine, the picture theory of meaning; but I do not think she realized that the *Tractatus* was thoroughgoingly Schopenhauerian. She does not say so, and I had no inkling of it myself until many years after reading her.

Another thing Langer did for me was to lead me to the writings of her mentor, Ernst Cassirer, in particular to his *Essay on Man* and his three-volume work *The Philosophy of Symbolic Forms*. The overriding vision here is of man as a symbol-creating animal—not only those symbols that constitute language but symbols of multifarious kinds—the whole range and use of them being what more than anything else defines man and differentiates him from the rest of the animal kingdom. Like many really big ideas, it seems unremarkable when stated. Not only each one of the natural languages but also mathematics and logic, and each one of the sciences, each one of the academic disciplines, each one of the arts, each one of the great religions, each one of the great ideologies, each one of the great mythologies, presents us with a world, a whole way of looking at things; and in each case it is a man-made world constructed and communicated in symbols; and in each case its chief purposes are to help us to represent, understand, interpret, come to terms with, and perhaps master our experience and our environment, and to orientate ourselves within them, and to communicate with our fellow creatures about them. Our understanding of ourselves and our environment can be increased only by extending these systems in significant ways, or constructing new ones, or establishing new connections between them; and the way to enrich our understanding of what we already know is to reflect upon and analyse both the systems themselves and what is articulated by and within them. This is an immensely rich way of looking at our understanding of the world, and at our attempts to articulate our experience and our knowledge, so rich that the whole of linguistic philosophy fits into a corner of it.

Because of Susanne K. Langer's special indebtedness to Wittgenstein's *Tractatus* I studied that book carefully. Although at Oxford it had been referred to constantly, undergraduates had not been encouraged to read it, because its understanding was taken to require a technical mastery of logic at an advanced level. However, logic had been one of my two special subjects in the degree examination (the other was political theory) so I felt ready to tackle it. I do not think I have ever been so astonished, either before or since, at the discovery of what *sort* of book a book was. At Oxford the *Tractatus* had always been held up to us as the founding constitutional document of logical positivism. When I read it properly for the first time I found that its central thesis was roughly speaking the opposite of logical positivism's.

The logical positivists had tended to assimilate all forms of truth-seeking about the world to science, and in consequence of this they judged all truth-seeking activities by the criteria governing those of science, and judged the validity of all utterance by the rules appropriate to scientific utterance. Only what could be verified by observation or experience could be known about the world, and only what we could produce valid grounds for stating could validly or justifiably be said. But everything important could, at least in principle, be said. And what could be said at all could be said clearly. The *Tractatus*, by direct contrast with nearly all this, maintained that almost everything that is most important cannot be stated at all but only, at the very best, indicated by our use of language. It may possibly be shown, but cannot be said. The *Tractatus* took a low view of science. All that propositional language is good for is to articulate empirical and analytic truths, that is to say matters of fact and logic. Outside those spheres it is more likely to mislead than to be useful, and therefore more likely to do harm than good. Therefore all the issues that matter to us most and have the greatest significance for us lie outside its scope. Questions about ethics and morals and values, about the meaning of life, about the nature of the self and of death, and about the existence of the world as a whole, are questions that can be settled neither by observation nor by logic, and are therefore such as propositional language cannot handle, with the result that if we insist on trying to deal with them in propositional language we get into a mess. Thus the view of total reality presented by the *Tractatus* is such that significant discourse in language is possible in two comparatively unimportant areas, but impossible throughout the rest. In accordance with this view, almost the whole of the book is devoted to those two areas—factual discourse and logic—and the main questions to which it addresses itself are what the nature of such utterance is (i.e., wherein its meaningfulness consists) and what the limits of its application are. However, so small is the area within which these questions even arise that it is essential for us not to lose our sense of proportion and forget how little has been achieved when these questions have been answered; so Wittgenstein stresses that point at the very outset of the book, in the Preface.

It is clear what the misunderstanding of the *Tractatus* by logical positivists and linguistic philosophers was, but it remains almost incredible how they could have perpetrated it. The nature of the misunderstanding has been well expressed by Paul Engelmann. "A whole generation of disciples was able to take Wittgenstein as a positivist, because he has something of enormous importance in common with the positivists: he draws the line between what we can speak about and what we must be silent about just as they do. The difference is only that they have nothing to be silent about. Positivism holds—and this is its essence—that what we can speak about is all that matters in life. *Whereas Wittgenstein passionately believes that all that really matters in human life is precisely what, in his view, we must be silent about.*"*

What nevertheless makes it almost incredible that Wittgenstein could have been so widely misunderstood on this point is that he states his position

* Paul Engelmann, *Letters from Ludwig Wittgenstein,* p. 97. His italics.

plainly and explicitly in the *Tractatus* itself. "It is clear that ethics cannot be put into words. Ethics is transcendental." What could be clearer than that? As for science: "The whole modern conception of the world is founded on the illusion that the so-called laws of nature are the explanations of natural phenomena"; and: "We feel that when *all possible* scientific questions have been answered, the problems of life remain completely untouched." Wittgenstein's attitude towards the ground-level problems that remain permanently untouched by science is at least in part a mystical one, and again he says so: "It is not how things are in the world that is mystical, but that it exists."

Reading this work only a few months after graduating from Oxford I was overcome by feelings of what I can only describe as retrospective disbelief. I did not see how all those people who had been talking and writing about the *Tractatus* could possibly have read it. To this day I find it hard to credit. Some indication, I suppose, of what the explanation is was provided by the most gifted of all the logical positivists, Rudolf Carnap, in his intellectual autobiography: "When we were reading Wittgenstein's book in the [Vienna] Circle, I had erroneously believed that his attitude toward metaphysics was similar to ours. I had not paid sufficient attention to the statements in his book about the mystical, because his feelings and thoughts in this area were too divergent from mine. Only personal contact with him helped me to see more clearly his attitude at this point."* If the explanation this suggests is the right one it means that a whole generation of intelligent people, serious students of philosophy and scholars, held a book in the highest esteem for saying the direct opposite of what it did say, and that they did this because they were locked so tightly into their preconceptions that they were unable to see what was staring them in the face. This added a powerful new lesson to those I had learnt already about the mesmerizing power of intellectual fashion, and it had an influence on me for the rest of my life. Never again did I suppose that the way a book or a thinker was generally, perhaps even universally, represented by professionals in the field could be assumed to bear a rough approximation to the truth. And when, on my return to Oxford after a year of teaching at Lund in Sweden, I got, or rather tried to get, into discussions with people about how the *Tractatus* was to be understood, I learnt another lesson still. They simply would not discuss it with me on my terms. When I started to say what I thought, they became acutely embarrassed, and it was me they were embarrassed for. It seemed self-evident to them that I must have got it all wrong. How could I be right and their friends wrong? The very idea was absurd. That I should keep buttonholing people about it was grotesque and—well, embarrassing. They were not willing to consider—not willing to let themselves even

---

* *The Philosophy of Rudolf Carnap,* ed. Paul Schilpp, p. 27.

countenance the possibility—that what they and their colleagues were agreed upon could be mistaken. In practice the notion itself was taken to be a form of self-contradiction, for their working hypothesis about the criterion of what was valid *was* that it was what they and the contemporaries they most admired were agreed upon. This circle could not be broken by an outsider: it was susceptible of change only from within the circle.

I read the *Tractatus* many times. It is a profound book, but at that period I mistakenly believed it to be also a highly original one. I could see that the unspecified presuppositions underlying it formed some sort of coherent framework of ideas, and I was all the time trying to break through to that unwritten level of the book and get a hold of it. This was the chief reason for the repeated re-readings. In fact, the presupposed framework is the philosophy of Schopenhauer, but nearly twenty years were to pass before I was to realize that. It is to this that Wittgenstein refers in the Preface when he writes: "I do not wish to judge how far my efforts coincide with those of other philosophers. Indeed, what I have written here makes no claim to novelty in detail, and the reason why I give no sources is that it is a matter of indifference to me whether the thoughts that I have had have been anticipated by someone else." The full extent of Wittgenstein's indebtedness to Schopenhauer is something I eventually laid bare in my book *The Philosophy of Schopenhauer,* published in 1983.

The nature of this indebtedness can be indicated briefly as follows. Schopenhauer agreed with Kant in dividing total reality for purposes of epistemology into such of it as is potentially accessible to us through the apparatus we contingently possess, and the rest. To the rest, by definition, we can never have any direct access. Therefore we can have no direct knowledge of it based on personal experience—though we may be able to make indirect inferences about it, in the way we can sometimes make informative inferences from what we can see to what we cannot see because it lies beyond the horizon. As for what we can directly know, it must remain permanently a fact that although this is limited first of all by what there is, it is limited second of all by the equipment we have for knowing it. Only what our equipment can cope with is knowable by us. From Descartes to Kant nearly all philosophers had seen the world thus apprehended as essentially an epistemological construction. Some of them had thought we could gain direct knowledge of reality by the exercise of reason, others that all the materials that the mind needed to work on must first be delivered to it by the senses; but in either case they believed that what resulted was a representation of reality that we put together in our minds, and that this was our empirical world. Kant and Schopenhauer had a radically new approach to this world, which I will not attempt to go into yet—all I need say at this point is that they regarded some of its negative features as among its most important, for instance that the subject for whom the world is object is nowhere to be found in that world; that no foundation for value judgments, whether moral or aesthetic, is to be found in it either; and therefore that those things, if they have any authentic existence at all, must have their foundations outside it, in that part of total reality beyond what is directly knowable by us.

All this was taken over from Schopenhauer by Wittgenstein. But Wittgenstein believed that the (for him) recent work of Frege enabled him to go a whole layer deeper than Schopenhauer had done in our understanding of the world of experience. The fact that we are able to represent reality to ourselves must mean that there is something in common between reality and our representation of it. Wittgenstein believed this to be their logical structure, manifested correspondingly in reality and in language. Logical possibility sets limits that reality cannot transgress, and in just the same way logical coherence sets limits that meaningful utterance cannot transgress. Not all combinations of fact are possible (for instance something cannot both be and not be at the same time) and what mirrors this in language is the fact that not all combinations of words are meaningful. Then again, not everything that is possible is the case, and this is mirrored by the fact that not all meaningful utterances are true. These facts yield a threefold classification of empirical propositions, or would-be empirical propositions: (i) statements to which nothing in reality could possibly correspond—these are meaningless; (ii) statements to which reality could correspond but happens not to—these are meaningful but untrue; (iii) statements to which reality corresponds—these are true. The picturing relationship that obtains between a meaningful proposition and a practical possibility is the same whether that possibility is actualized or not, but it does not correspond to any truth. It cannot itself be represented. This applies, by the way, not only to representation in words. A painter can paint pictures that correspond to actual scenes, but he cannot paint this picturing relationship. It is something that each of his works exhibits, and exemplifies, but could never itself be pictured. Similarly with meaningful empirical propositions: the relationship between them and the possibilities they represent manifests itself in them but cannot be put into words, i.e., cannot be expressed in other propositions. In this latter sense it is inexpressible in spite of the fact that it is displayed.

This picture theory of meaning, much scoffed at since, but in truth profound, was all that was original in the *Tractatus*. Everything else in the book came from other sources: most of it from Schopenhauer and Frege, a little from Russell. I never subscribed to the picture theory as adumbrated by Wittgenstein, because it was always clear to me that even descriptive propositional language, narrowly conceived, had uses other than to picture—though I must say that people nowadays seem much too inclined to forget the extent to which language *is* used to represent. In almost every speech-act there is a representational element: we see, hear, feel, hope, suspect, fear, and so on, *that* something or other is the case, and so a picture theory of meaning gets us a part of the way. As a theory it has genuine depth. Even so, and although Wittgenstein originated it, the most permanently enlightening use of it was made not by Wittgenstein but by Susanne K. Langer. However, I treasure the *Tractatus* for its superbly expressed insights; and also for its luminous prose, which has a supercharged intensity approaching that of Nietzsche. The fact that the Schopenhauerian insights were not original was something I did not know on my first several readings of the book, and such knowledge could have done nothing to diminish their value to me in any case, since to me they were new. Wittgenstein had repossessed them and made them his own, and he expressed them in sentences that have the capacity to smoulder in one's mind for the rest of one's life.

It was, most significantly, the picture theory of meaning that was repudiated by Wittgenstein in his next and most influential book, *Philosophical Investigations,* which was published in 1953. Just as *Feeling and Form* happened to be published conveniently for me soon after I had finished reading *Philosophy in a New Key,* so *Philosophical Investigations* came out when my immersion in the *Tractatus* was reaching saturation point. In the new work the metaphor of a picture was replaced by that of a tool: the meaning of a word was seen as consisting in what one could do with it, and was therefore the sum total of its possible uses. There was no longer any talk of an independent world of fact to which language could, or might fail to, correspond. The uses of language were rooted in diverse human purposes, and therefore grew ultimately out of differing forms of life. Each of the ways in which humans used language could be understood only from within such a context, and had a logic of its own which was perhaps appropriate only to it. Philosophical problems were conceptual confusions or muddles that arose when we used a word, or a form of words, inappropriately, that is to say in a context other than the one or ones in which it made proper sense; and the way to dissolve philosophical problems was to work patiently to untangle the conceptual knots thus created. It required the same sharp eyes and the same fine-fingered work, the same sustained application and patience, and perhaps the same ingenuity, as the untangling of tight little knots in a piece of cotton thread.

Philosophical Investigations introduced several terms and ideas into the common currency first of philosophy and then of a number of other disciplines. One such term that I used in the last paragraph was "form of life." Another such term was "family resemblance," as applied to the different meanings of a word. When we say of several members of a family that they have a family resemblance we do not usually mean (we can, but we do not normally) that there is a single facial characteristic that they all have in common, but rather that it is as if they had drawn varying combinations of features from a common pool. The point being made by Wittgenstein is that there is not (usually) one single feature that is common to all the legitimate uses of a word, but rather a family resemblance among its uses. The reason why this is so important is that human beings have always had a strong tendency to believe, perhaps because they have a psychological need to, that meanings are fixed, and that there is one thing for which the same word always stands if it is properly used. For example, the most famous philosopher of all, Socrates, went around asking questions like *What is courage? What is virtue? What is beauty?,* and there can be no doubt that he believed there were actual entities represented by these words—not material objects, of course, but nevertheless entities that had a genuine existence: what one might call real essences. Some belief of this sort has been deeply entrenched in many human minds down the ages, and it is this that Wittgenstein is attacking.

Another argument Wittgenstein put into circulation was to the effect that there can be no such thing as a private language. Before him two theories of meaning had been more widely held than any others—one that the meaning of a word is set by what the word designates, the other that it is set by the intention of the person using the word—and Wittgenstein is equally determined to demolish both. The meanings of words no more derive from the mental states of their users, e.g., their intentions, than from fixed entities outside language. Words have meaning only in so far as there are criteria governing their use, and for such criteria to be criteria they need to be inter-subjective, that is to say they have to have a social and therefore public dimension. No matter how apparently "inner" and "private" an experience may be to which we give linguistic expression—a dream, a drug-induced hallucination, a pain, a memory, whatever it may be—the fact remains that the language we use to describe it existed before we came on the scene, and it was from other people that we learnt both the words and how to use them. So even when I tell you my dream my use of language is a rule-governed social activity, and if it were not you would not be able to understand what I was saying. It is by extending the wider implications of this fact that Wittgenstein came to attribute the ultimate derivation of meanings to "forms of life." It also led him to compare the use of language in some detail with another rule-governed social activity, namely games. He coined the unfortunate term "language-game" not because he thought we were playing with words but because, just as the moves and terms and meanings in any game derive their significance from the rules governing the game, which are interpersonal, so the meanings of words derive their significance from the particular language-game in which they are used—philosophical, scientific, artistic, religious, academic, conversational, or whatever it may be. For example, what counts as "evidence" has an all-pervadingly different logic and structure in a court of law from what it has in a physics laboratory, and is quite different again for the historical researcher: to the historian hearsay counts as evidence, in fact it is very often the only evidence he has, whereas for the judge it is inadmissible as evidence, while for the physicist the question does not even arise. So the word "evidence" means something materially different in each context. Because of this, if we find ourselves in a muddle about what does and what does not constitute evidence it may be because we have tried to apply the concept in one set of circumstances in a way that is appropriate only to another. Because of the family-resemblance character of meaning this kind of mistake is easy to make, and Wittgenstein believes that it explains why philosophical puzzlements arise. The task of the philosopher is by patient investigation to trace the source of such puzzlements in the misuse of language; and when he has found it, and brought it to light, the problem will disappear for us—just as, when the psychoanalyst traces and brings to light the source of a neurosis in a conflict of which the patient had hitherto been unaware, it is supposed, according to Freud, to cure the patient. (This analogy, so often drawn, was made by Wittgenstein himself, who described himself as a "disciple" or "follower" of Freud—see Ray Monk: *Ludwig Wittgenstein,* p. 438.)

No comment on *Philosophical Investigations* can avoid saying something about the way the book is written. Like the *Tractatus* it is not in continuous prose but in separately spaced and numbered paragraphs. However, the later book is far the more loosely constructed of the two, so much so that almost every reader of it has difficulty sometimes in seeing what the connection is between a paragraph and the one before it; the sentences are clear, but the reader often cannot understand, at first, why they are there. The prose, though distinctive and compelling, has nothing like the blazing intensity of the *Tractacus.*

Wittgenstein is unique, I think, in that he produced two different and incompatible philosophies in the course of his life, each of which influenced a whole generation. Every possible way of evaluating them relative to one another has become familiar. For several years after the publication of *Philosophical Investigations* the generally held view in the English-speaking world was that both were philosophies of genius. However, as time passed and the later philosophy came more and more to be seen as having superseded the earlier the view became widespread that the later philosophy was indeed a product of genius but the earlier one not so. However, there had always been some, of whom Bertrand Russell was conspicuously one, who took the opposite view, namely that the early philosophy was the work of a genius, but not the later. And finally there had always been some, such as Karl Popper—and others, such as Anthony Quinton, came round to the opinion after a period of years—who took the view that neither of the philosophies was really of lasting substance or significance.

My own view has always inclined to the third of these four alternatives—what I think of as the Russell view—though with some qualifications. I do not judge the later philosophy to be quite as empty and worthless as Russell did. It seems to me to contain some thought-provoking ideas and suggestions. But in my view these have to be taken up and used for what they are worth more or less in isolation, since the context in which they are embedded constitutes a radically mistaken view of the role of language in human life and thought. Taken thus separately they are useful but scrappy. In the transition from the early philosophy to the later the most valuable things of all have been lost: the direct acknowledgement of a world of non-linguistic reality; the perception that there is something mystical about the very existence of such a world; the realization that any significance life has is transcendental, as must be also all values, morals, and the import of art; and that it is for that reason inherently impossible to give a satisfactory account in language of these things, the very things that are of greatest significance to us. Every one of these insights is valid and of profound importance. In the *Tractatus* they were masterfully seized and expressed. But, after that, Wittgenstein seems to have lost his sense of the authenticity of both sides of reality—the world of fact and the domain of the transcendental—and come adrift in a Sargasso Sea of free-floating language. His only frame of reference now is a means of communication, treated almost as if it were everything there is, without any of the things it communicates about or between. He has become like a fly buzzing around in a fly-bottle and unable to find its way out.

Since the later philosophy of Wittgenstein not only is not about philosophical problems in any traditional sense but denies their authentic existence, it is capable of appealing powerfully only to people who do not have philosophical problems. This explains two things about it that might otherwise be difficult to account for simultaneously: its great appeal to academic philosophers and its attractions for people outside philosophy. In this sense it is like those forms of music that appeal only to the unmusical, whether inside or outside the music profession.

In the same year as I read *Philosophical Investigations,* namely 1954–5, I read my first book by Karl Popper, *The Open Society and Its Enemies.* For the first time in my life I found myself reading a philosophical work by a living author that seemed to me to have something about it of the quality of greatness. Except for Bertrand Russell and Susanne K. Langer, virtually all the living philosophers I had read up to this point had taken conceptual analysis to be the central task of philosophy. But Popper declared roundly that what we ought to be questioning ourselves and one another about was not concepts but the way things are; that this means using our powers of insight and imagination to create theories that get us nearer to the truth than the theories we already possess; that in our pursuit of truth we ought, as scientists do in theirs, to carry on our discussions in such a manner that very little of importance depends on the way we use words; that significant knowledge about the world is not to be achieved by sharpening our use or understanding of terms; that there is no valid reason why definitions should be considered more important in philosophy than they are in physics; and that to get into long discussions about the meanings of words is not only boring but harmful, because it gets us into infinite regresses in which we find ourselves word-spinning and logic-chopping without end, enmired in an arid scholasticism that has taken us away from our real task. And all this was just by the way. What the book addressed itself to centrally were the problems of creating and sustaining what the author called an "open" society as against a "closed" one, that is to say a society that was an association of free individuals respecting one another's rights within a framework of law. It was written at the height of the Second World War, when the outcome of the war was uncertain and the two most gigantic armies that the world had ever seen to confront one another were those of the two most hideous totalitarian regimes it had ever known, the Soviet Union and Nazi Germany. Open societies were then, as they have been ever since, a small minority among the nations of the world, and their future at that time seemed in danger. For all these reasons the book was written with an enraged passion by an author who believed himself to be confronting the genuine possibility of a new Dark Age. It is, I believe, the best case for a free society that anyone has ever written.

At a first reading what struck me most about its qualities as a book was the spaciousness of it, not only in the largeness of its concerns but also in the breadth of mind and spirit pervading the whole thing. The problems confronted were the most important political and social problems there are; and the historical context in which these were viewed, pragmatically as well as intellectually, ranged from pre-Socratic Greece to the twentieth century, and also across disciplines in a way that embraced the natural as well as the social sciences. Yet none of it lacked logical rigour, and none of its energy was dissipated in rhetorical gestures. On the contrary, I had read few books so powerfully concentrated, so meaty in argument, or built on so solid a foundation of knowledge and reflection. The horizons were as wide as any I had encountered, but everything within them was held in proportion, and the grasp of detail was assured. The emotional force with which it was written gave it a sweep and bite reminiscent of Marx's *Das Kapital*. It is not easy to recapture at this distance of time the sense of exhilaration all this gave to someone accustomed for years to reading philosophers who brought high intelligence and impassioned intensity to spelling out in detail the differences in use between the expressions "namely," "to wit," "viz.," "i.e.," and "that is to say." It was like escaping from imprisonment in a fetid outdoor privy into the tingling fresh air, and finding huge, beautiful mountains all around.

One of the things that impressed me most, and has influenced me since, was Popper's way of dealing with opponents. I had always loved argument, and over the years I had become quite good at identifying the weak points in an opponent's defence and bringing concentrated fire to bear on them. This is what virtually all polemicists have sought to do since ancient times, even the most famous of them. But Popper did the opposite. He sought out his opponent's case at its strongest and attacked that. Indeed, he would improve it, if he possibly could, before attacking it—over several pages of prior discussion he would remove avoidable contradictions or weaknesses, close loopholes, pass over minor deficiencies, let his opponent's case have the benefit of every possible doubt, and reformulate the most appealing parts of it in the most rigorous, powerful and effective arguments he could find—and then direct his onslaught against it. The outcome, when successful, was devastating. At the end there would be nothing left to say in favour of the opposing case except for tributes and concessions that Popper had himself already made. It was incredibly exciting intellectually. The fact that he did this to Marxism, and on so generous a scale, was of great personal value to me. As an ardent young socialist—never a Marxist, but much influenced at one time by Marx—I had come to feel that the development of certain areas in my thinking was being held back by remnants of that Marxist influence, and I was engaged in trying to pin these down and think them through when I picked up Popper's book. It identified the most seductive elements in Marxism, made full acknowledgement of their appeal, gave a sympathetic account of the reasons for that appeal, formulated arguments as powerful as those to be found anywhere in support of them, and proceeded to demolish them. I and several years of my life were involved in this process. As in the case of Susanne K. Langer, though in a bigger league, here was a living philosopher writing about problems I *had—felt* problems, presented to me with agonizing sharpness by my life, my personality, my thinking. Here, at last, was the real thing, contemporary philosophy grappling with life itself, philosophy in the real world.

From then on, for several years, whenever Oxford philosophers asserted that the subject matter of philosophy was linguistic, my standard response was to say: "What about *The Open Society and Its Enemies?* That's unquestionably philosophy. And its subject matter is unquestionably not linguistic." To do them justice, none of them ever denied that *The Open Society* was philosophy, and none of them ever asserted that its subject matter was linguistic. But none of them ever gave me an answer to my question that could pretend to be even semi-satisfactory. Their commonest response was to give me no answer at all but to frown with calculated ambiguity and pretend to look thoughtful while remaining silent—and then either change the subject or drift away.

At the beginning of the academic year 1954–5 I returned to Oxford from a year in Sweden and began work on a doctorate under the supervision of Peter Strawson. The problem with which I was involved, and about which I proposed to write my thesis, had to do with metaphor. When human beings try to voice the deepest experiences of all, like being in love or facing death, they almost always resort to metaphor. Why? Is it because it is possible to *say more* in metaphor than in direct utterance? That this may be so is apparently supported by the fact that the most penetrating and expressive uses of language, those found in poetry, above all in poetic drama, make use of imagery throughout. Yet the whole point of an image is that it means something other than what it ostensibly says. A particularly puzzling thing about this is that although the meaning conveyed is not the one apparently stated, in practice this does not usually create confusion: we all, in normal circumstances, understand immediately what is meant, and understand it in the same sense. How does this come about? And why can what is conveyed indirectly not be stated directly? If what has been implied up to now is true, the following question is of fundamental importance: Is it ever defensible to use metaphors as premisses or links in arguments? If not, does this mean that the most informative uses of language have no place in rational argument?

Doctorate students then, as now, were asked who they wanted to supervise them. And because a supervisor could not be compelled to take on a student, the student was asked at the outset to name a second choice. This put me in a dilemma. Scarcely any professional philosophy had been published on the semantic and logical problems I wanted to study. All I found at first were two articles in academic journals from the pen of a young and little-known Oxford don called Iris Murdoch. So if I wanted any of the big guns in philosophy to teach me I would have to accept someone who had not written anything on my subject. I hesitated—but in the end nominated as my first choice the person I regarded as having the best analytic mind among the Oxford philosophers of that day, Peter Strawson, and put down Iris Murdoch as my second choice. I got Strawson, and to be taught by him was a privilege; but I sometimes wonder what it would have been like to be taught philosophy by Iris Murdoch.

Strawson employed the terror tactics of Oxford philosophy as a teaching method, which is what I gather his own mentor, J. L. Austin, had done. No sooner would I have completed any assertion to him, however small or slight, than I would find myself backed up against the wall and the bullets would be smacking round my head. And scarcely would I have got out of one tight corner before I found myself in another. The whole of each supervision would consist of Strawson gunning for me, and me fighting for my life. At the end of it I would emerge from his room vibrating with tension, convinced that he must regard me as a complete idiot. But the truth is that these supervisions did a great deal for me, because they brought home to me the fact that any ideas I might entertain on any philosophical subject would have to be such as to stand up to this sort of criticism; otherwise they would just not be good enough.

After two or three of these unforgettable supervisions I was offered—and accepted—a post-graduate fellowship in philosophy at Yale for the following academic year. The normal thing for me to have done would have been to continue work there on my doctorate thesis. Fortunately, I realized in advance that this would be to ignore most of what Yale was able to offer me. There was an alternative. My experiences with Strawson, which I found exhilarating in spite of the terror, like being engaged in a battle, had convinced me that I did not know enough, and therefore needed more sheer instruction. I felt a desire, quite simply, to study more across a broad front, not just in the philosophy that it came to me naturally to be interested in, like the work of Langer, Cassirer, Wittgenstein and Popper (I was marinading in this of my own accord), but from a position outside my limitations. I had no intention of becoming a professional philosopher, so a doctorate was not going to be of any use to me. And there would be nothing to stop me writing about the subject of my thesis, or anything else for that matter, after Yale. So I decided to put my plans for a doctorate aside and immerse myself for a year in general philosophical studies. It was the best academic decision I ever made.

8

A Yale Education

Post-graduate teaching of philosophy at Yale was based on seminars: eight or ten people would sit together round a table twice a week for two hours each time, with a professor in the chair. Most of them ran for two terms out of the academic year, but some for all three, though some for only one. The participants took it in turns to start the proceedings by reading a short paper about a topic of which everyone had been given notice. Discussion of this would then fill the remainder of the two hours, and spill over afterwards into cafés, clubs, bars, meals, walks, and private rooms. The students were some of the brightest graduates from other universities all over America, and almost without exception they were bent on making careers for themselves as professional philosophers.

There was an embarrassment of choice, and I shopped around, but the seminars I ended up attending regularly included a state-of-the-art appraisal of epistemology in the empiricist tradition, and studies in the philosophy of Kant, the philosophy of science, mathematical logic, symbolic logic, the philosophy of law, and (a sport, this) the conceptual analysis of foreign policy. There were a number of others that I sampled and dropped out of. Those on the empirical tradition and foreign policy required some but not much additional reading from me, because I was familiar already with most of the basic material; and nearly all the work involved for the two seminars in logic was done during the sessions themselves; so the reading load I was undertaking was manageable. In any case, it was of great value to me that, alongside the reading, I had to spend so much of my time immersed in discussion of material I had already absorbed.

Brand Blanshard, who led the seminar on empiricist epistemology, embodied a certain tradition. He was reminiscent of Bertrand Russell in his commitment to rational analysis and argument in forms that did not subordinate them to considerations of language. Like Russell's, his work was clear, elegant, stylish and witty—he had given a famous lecture, now published as a tiny book, on style in philosophy. In person he was old-fashioned, gentlemanly. The most important and interesting of the American empiricists in his eyes were the American pragmatists, whom I had rarely heard mentioned at Oxford; so now for the first time I started to learn something about C. S. Peirce, William James and John Dewey. However, most of what I had done at Oxford was included too, so what emerged for me overall from Blanshard's seminar was a clear-eyed assessment of a complete tradition with all its strengths and unanswered problems—including the phase of linguistic analysis, but seeing that as a distant and localized phenomenon. At first his teaching method struck me as a trifle chilly, but then I realized that it was the first philosophy teaching I had encountered that was not sectarian and excommunicative. The interpretations put on everything by Oxford philosophers had been analogous to the interpretations put on current affairs by active members of the Communist Party: partisan, belligerent, propagandist, intolerant, nakedly self-oriented and one-sided. Blanshard was quite different from this. Although he was himself in opposition to the tradition he was discussing he presented it with admirable fairness in its relationship to other traditions. We had long discussions of alternative sorts of philosophy, and the different ways in which they had approached the same problems. We talked about rationalists, and idealists, and existentialists, at each point comparing and contrasting what they had been doing with what the empiricists had been doing. At Oxford the assumption had always been that the empiricist tradition *was* philosophy. There had been one occasion when I had raised a question about the existentialist tradition as represented by philosophers like Kierkegaard, Nietzsche and Heidegger, only to have it explained to me that these were "not philosophers." Among other things Blanshard's seminar was for me an object-lesson in academic fairness, as well as being an illuminating and intellectually modest orientation course on a philosophy I had thought I was familiar with.

The insolubility of certain fundamental problems within the empiricist tradition constitutes Kant's point of departure in his later, critical philosophy. The seminar I attended on Kant, chaired by George Schrader, set itself the task of working through all three of Kant's critiques—*The Critique of Pure Reason, The Critique of Practical Reason,* and *The Critique of Judgment*—in one year, at the rate of a book a term. It was the most permanently enriching single thing I did at Yale, and possibly the most valuable single educational experience I have ever had. Throughout that year it was the main focus of my intellectual interest. A paper I wrote on Kant's Refutation of Idealism was the first thing of mine to be published in philosophy. From then until now I have believed not that Kant was right but that he had somehow managed to get hold of the right end of the stick, and that whatever the truth is about the world as we experience it, almost certainly it lies somewhere in the direction in which he pointed us. This is something I shall come back to at greater length.

The seminar on the philosophy of science was conducted by a brilliant if intellectually intolerant young man called Arthur Pap. He was a reconstructed logical positivist who—like, so it seemed, all the logical positivists in America—called himself a logical empiricist, perhaps to bring out both the fact and the emphasis of the reconstruction. The still-active older philosophers from whom he had learnt most included Quine and Carnap, who had, in different capacities, attended meetings of the original Vienna Circle, and were now teaching in the United States. Quine had been a young American graduate student on a trip to Vienna, Carnap had been the most intellectually gifted member of the Circle itself. Through them, Pap oriented himself within a still-living tradition that went back to Mach, a tradition that he was now actively engaged in propagating. His approach to the problems he dealt with was solidly science-based and mathematics-based, and in this he was at one with the original logical positivists, most of whom had been trained as scientists or mathematicians, not as philosophers. Half the people attending his seminar were practising scientists who were fascinated by the methodology of their subject. All this was in stark contrast to Oxford, where the teaching of logical positivism had been wholly language-based, and carried out by people with virtually no knowledge of science whatever. Pap's seminar brought home to me just how self-contradictory the situation at Oxford had been at the time when most philosophers had taught that scientific utterance was the paradigm of meaningful talk about the world, and that the only future left for philosophy was to become the handmaid of science, when those same philosophers were not only innocent of any taint of scientific knowledge but were not even sufficiently interested in it to acquire some. Indeed, in private conversation quite a few of them evinced what can only be described as an intellectual contempt for science, albeit a contempt based on ignorance. Their whole life-situation was what existentialists mean by "inauthentic." If they had *really* understood, and believed, and felt the truth of what they themselves taught, they would have lived differently. Their philosophizing was in bad faith.

For the first time I came to understand the problems faced by the original logical positivists in the terms in which they had formulated them for themselves. They mostly concerned the logical foundations of science, and such basic and interconnected activities fundamental to science as observation, measurement and calculation. It was in the context of this enquiry that apparently diverse matters such as the philosophical problems of perception and the logical foundations of mathematics were interrelated. However, I believe that the most enlightening thing I got from this seminar was not the taking on board of the logical positivist view of science in its authentic and not language-based form but the detailed working through of specific problems in scientific methodology—for example, what we are actually doing when we measure something.

Pap introduced me to many fruitful ideas in philosophy. To give only two examples, he was the first person I ever heard expound the argument that it is impossible to give an adequate definition of space-concepts without using time-concepts in the definition, and vice versa, and that this means that the concepts of time and space must be *logically* interdependent, whatever other relationships they may or may not have. He was also the first person I heard demonstrate that every discussion is bound to make use of undefined terms, since the attempt to define all our terms leads to an infinite regress. (The implications of this fact for a view of philosophy as linguistic analysis are of course quite devastating.) His manner of conducting his seminar was what was then, at a time still close to the Second World War, thought of as Teutonic, i.e., authoritarian in an aggressively assertive and clear-cut way, ruthlessly crushing any dissent. Yet so brimming over was he with energy, enthusiasm and ideas, always expressed with uncompromising clarity, that the rest of us were exhilarated by it and, whether we liked his manner or not, learnt an enormous amount from him. It was an intellectual as well as a personal tragedy that he died soon afterwards of a blood disease while still only in his thirties, leaving a wife and several children. (I think there were four of them—but saying that reminds me of a story he himself once told of his having asked an elderly Yale professor how many children he had, and getting the answer: "I think about five.")

The seminar I attended on mathematical logic was also conducted by an outstanding philosopher who was to die young, of cancer: Alan Anderson. He was a forceful but attractive personality who loved argument and invited dissent. He was one of the two logicians at the university who spent his vacations in Washington, D.C., working for the U.S. government on the early development of the computer. One particular argument of his (though for all I know he may not have invented it) that has stayed in my mind goes like this. Imagine lottery tickets, each with a different number on it, in a pile as big as you like—as big as the universe if you wish, if not bigger; infinitely large if you think such an idea coherent. There is nothing the slightest bit problematic about my plunging my hand into the pile and picking out a ticket. Nothing could be easier. Whatever ticket I pick out will have a number on it that is the only instance of that number in the whole pile. If at this point I clap my hand to my head and cry: "My God, this is completely and utterly incredible! The odds against my picking this number were infinity to one against, and I've picked it. It's im*poss*ible!"—I might *feel* goggle-eyed with wonder, but in fact this sense of wonder is totally misplaced, because whatever ticket I picked I could say exactly the same thing. And there is not the slightest difficulty about picking a ticket. So here is something that *feels* amazing but is not in the slightest bit odd. It is, as it were, a conceptual illusion. Now the important point is that this consideration applies to all questions about anything existing out of a wider range of possibility, however great—the sense of extraordinariness that this particular person should exist, or even that this particular universe should exist. Even if there were an infinite number of different possible universes there would not be *on that ground* the slightest room for surprise that this particular one exists. The only valid ground for surprise is that anything exists at all—e.g., that the lottery tickets are there in the first place (because *once* they are there, there is nothing left to explain). I made use of this fascinating argument in my novel *Facing Death,* in which I put it into the mouth of one of the characters.

Through Alan Anderson's seminar on mathematical logic, and Frederick Fitch's on symbolic logic, I pursued my studies in formal logic as far as I felt inclined to take them. The reason for this is that in each case I came to feel that I had followed the subject beyond the point at which it branched away from philosophy and became a discipline in its own right. The most recent developments in logic that are of indisputable importance to an understanding of philosophy in general are those associated chiefly with the names of Frege, Whitehead, Russell and the young Wittgenstein, and perhaps subsequently Carnap and Quine. After that it becomes a specialism.

It cannot be pretended that the conceptual analysis of foreign policy is a branch of philosophy, although at its heart lies situational logic, a concept adumbrated in a number of philosophical works. Arnold Wolfers, who conducted the seminar, had been one of the chief foreign policy advisers to the Truman administration, and I felt it would have been foolish not to take this opportunity of learning from him, especially as I expected one day to become a politician myself.

It is easy now to forget how overwhelmingly preponderant in the world the United States was in the mid-1950s. It produced more than half the world's entire economic output, so there were any number of things of which it could truthfully be said that there were more in the United States than in the rest of the world put together—and not only material goods, but goods in every sense: scholarship, scientific research, symphony orchestras . . . From the point of view of the rest of the world it was an unimaginable treasure-house of goods and services—in fact literally unimaginable, in that most people else-where did not know and refused to believe how wide the gap was between themselves and the United States. One consequence of America's vast power was that during that period it dominated world affairs to a greater extent than any single country had ever previously done, or has done since.

Wolfers's teaching method was undisguisedly manipulative, but highly effective. What he said was almost entirely abstract, yet paradoxically its concrete implications were all the more powerful for that. A typical seminar would get under way in something like the following manner. He would say: "Let's suppose there's a giant power on a continental land-mass." At this point he would draw a big, deliberately crude circle on one side of the blackboard. "And let's say that on the other side of an ocean there is another power of comparable size." Another big circle on the other side of the blackboard. "And let's say that the continental power has a lot of little countries on its borders, whereas the other one, because of its geographical situation, doesn't." Here he would draw a number of little circles on the edge of his first big circle. The design would now look like this:

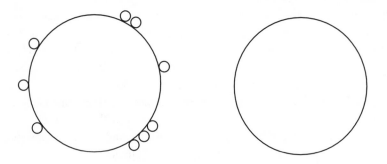

"Now," he would say, "regardless of what sort of societies they are, or what kinds of government they have, can you see any considerations that would be compelling as regards the foreign policies of any of the countries represented here?"

We would all sit and look at the diagram, thinking hard. Then perhaps someone would say: "No one of those little countries would stand any chance at all by itself in a war against its giant neighbour. It would either be swallowed whole or smashed. So its survival as an independent nation must depend on its not getting into that kind of conflict."

"Right," Wolfers would say, pleased. "Now can you see some of the alternative ways in which it might try to avoid that?"—and we were off. Discussion would begin, and each step would lead us to perceive some new consideration that we had not noted before. By the end of two hours we would have discussed all kinds of different possible ways in which each of the countries represented by a circle might be led by the logic of its situation to conduct itself with regard to each, or some, or all of the others. Then at the end of the seminar Wolfers would say: "Between now and our next meeting I'd like you to think which of the considerations we've raised apply in practice to China and the countries around her periphery in their relations to one another and to the United States"—and of course they all did, every one of them, while we all the time had been puzzling out the implications with regard to the Soviet Union. So now, freshly, we found ourselves starting to understand the underlying reasons for all sorts of things with regard to China—that this or that government was currently pursuing this or that policy *not* primarily because it was a Communist regime whose thinking was governed by Marxist categories, or because it was a right-wing dictatorship, or because of the personality of its leader, but because the logic of its situation led it to do so. As the mere contemplation of our crude diagram had led us to understand, any government of such a country, regardless of its makeup or ideology, would be bound at least to consider some such policy as this, if only in the end to reject it. And even if we believed there was a better alternative policy, we now understood what the pressures were towards this one, and what the chief considerations were in the minds of the people pursuing it (and what they would have to be reassured of before they would abandon it). The powerful underlying lesson that all this brought home to us was that foreign policy is largely (not entirely) to be understood in terms of the application of situational logic to self-interest in circumstances as they actually exist, regardless of what government is in power. There is a large number of things that a government cannot do without risking serious damage to itself, and a large number of other things that it is going to have to do whether it likes it or not; and in between not much room is left in which it can manoeuvre independently according to its own desires. There is, of course, some such room, and the various uses to which it might be put were among the things we discussed. One way and another I came to regard this seminar as a model of one particular sort of advanced education method: it was aimed first and foremost at making us think hard, logically and methodically, and then at getting us to apply our thinking to practical situations. It helped to remove the influence of prejudice and emotion from our judgments, and to get us to understand how very different the same situation can look from the point of view of different countries involved in it, and therefore why some such countries behave so inconveniently from our point of view. It seemed to me a lesson not just in foreign policy but in life.

The brilliance of Wolfers's teaching lay in its method, not in anything he actually said. As a personality he was self-effacing, and almost all his interventions took the form of Socratic questioning. Nearly all of the talking was done by the graduate students. In contrast, nearly all the talking in the seminar I went to on the philosophy of law was done by the man conducting it, F. S. C. Northrop, though in his case there could scarcely be said to be any method at all. In spite of that, he remains one of the only two people I have ever met with what tempts me to call it a genius for teaching (the other being my history master at school, David Roberts). Never have I known anyone so excited by ideas; and he was able to pass on not only the ideas but also the excitement. He would walk into the room already talking, and from then on perfectly formed sentences would come geysering out of his head as if he were a gusher blowing its top. It was the rest of us who did all the questioning. He welcomed questions, and accepted the fact that the only way for us to put them was by interrupting him; but it took determined and intrusive force from one of us actually to say much. Even so, because it was easy for each of us to get him to talk about whatever it was we wanted him to talk about, and then to listen to our critical questioning about it, and then to answer our questions at length, none of us felt dissatisfied. On the contrary, we were stimulated as I have never known any other teacher stimulate his students. Bright young graduates would emerge from his seminars thrilled by the prospects they had just glimpsed and impatient to pursue them—he was more than just a stimulator, he was a galvanizer, and they would rush straight to the library, lusting to get at the books. Over the years the heat of his intellectual passion had combined with his incredible energy to sweep him up to professional level in several fields—not only philosophy and law (in both of which he held chairs at Yale) but also international politics, sociology, physics, and the comparative history of ideas and culture. As a polymath he was in the same class as Bertrand Russell and Karl Popper. He lacked their creative originality, but what he did have was a compulsion to communicate—to communicate knowledge, ideas, and above all insights, especially as regards relationships between disciplines. To give an instance, he once launched into a spellbinding exposition of how the development of mathematical physics since the seventeenth century, the development of empirical philosophy over the same period, and the development of liberal democracy were organically interrelated, not only in ways to which others had drawn attention but in other ways too. He also talked at length, and with genuine knowledge and understanding, about how this development in the West was different from what had occurred in other cultures, notably those of India and China, which again were different from one another. And he ended by pointing out how all this related to the subject of his seminar. Over and again he would embark on what appeared at first to be digressions of almost unbelievable length, and on an astonishing multiplicity of subjects, but he always ended by demonstrating their connection with the matter in hand.

The subject of Northrop's seminar can be stated simply enough. With regard to every human community he distinguished between its positive law and what he called its "living law," and what he was concerned with was the complex relationship between the two. Positive law was enacted by the government and enforced by the administrative apparatus. Except where what obtained was arbitrary rule by an individual, the positive law was consciously considered, discussed with or among the highly placed, and made public in some form of words that would thereafter be referred to, and was capable of fairly swift change. But at the same time people in every community were brought up to do a whole host of things in particular ways that had nothing to do with the positive law: there was a rich mix of established procedure, custom, habit, mutual expectation, assumption, common language, family structure, folk memory, popular art and entertainment, public observances, rituals, possibly a religion, and so on and so forth, all woven into complex patterns that went on from generation to generation. These had not come into existence by any process of rational consideration or debate, they were not for the most part explicitly formulated in language, they could not be changed by any individual, and if they changed at all it was only slowly. This was what he meant by the "living law" of a community, and it was what more than anything else gave a community its unique identity. He argued that the attachment of human beings to their living law was always deeper, stronger and more emotionally felt than their allegiance to the positive law, with the consequence that if the two came into conflict people's spontaneous response was to break the positive law as much as they could get away with. If the positive law came too persistently into conflict with the living law the result would be serious social disruption and upheaval. Our analysis of the notion of living law led us into social psychology, comparative sociology, anthropology, and cultural history. Our analysis of positive law led us into politics, jurisprudence, comparative institutions, the development of science and technology, and the history of ideas. Over the course of a year our discussions in this seminar had the extraordinary side-effect of making me aware of organic below-the-surface interrelationships between all of my other seminars. It was like a mega-seminar tying the others together.

I think it was Northrop who first brought home to me the cultural centrality of science. I had always, obviously, realized that technology was of wide cultural significance because of its social consequences, but Northrop made me realize something quite different from that, namely that pure science was almost as fundamental as the arts to the spiritual adventure of Western man in his unending quest for insight and understanding about himself, and about the world in which he finds himself; that the treasure-house of already existing scientific knowledge and insight was so rich as to be surpassed in value and wonderfulness by that of the arts alone; and furthermore that science had an enormous amount in common with the arts—for instance both are self-disciplined truth-seeking activities attempting to probe the nature of reality, including the reality about ourselves, and to articulate the search and its findings in publicly accessible ways; and both depend for their success on the creative originality of rare individuals, above all on courageous and inspired leaps of imagination into the unknown. The sciences and their histories are thrilling in similar ways to the arts and their histories, and the two interconnect on multiple levels. It is impossible to have more than the most superficial understanding of ourselves and the world without a serious acquaintance with both.

Another thing I learnt from Northrop was how, and why, the two great revolutions in twentieth-century physics—relativity theory and quantum theory—impose on us the need to re-evaluate our view not just of the nature of science but of human knowledge as such; and what is more to look for answers in a Kantian direction, because so much that had always been taken for granted as lying out there in the external world independently of us was now understood to consist of explanatory structures that we ourselves bring into being, and then reify: not only explanatory models in science but the mathematics those embody, the logic of their arguments, and the categories of the natural languages in which they are articulated. This, of course, tied in with what I had learnt from Cassirer, but it was reached by a journey from an independent point of departure.

One general way in which I feel indebted to Northrop is that he helped to liberate my synthesizing proclivities, which had been brutally inhibited, indeed persecuted, at Oxford. I believe it was Plato who said that good judgment consists equally in seeing the differences between things that are similar and the similarities between things that are different. These are, of course, the two complementary forms of explanation that are now familiar under the names "analysis" and "synthesis," and Plato's remark was a profound one. A debilitating aspect of Oxford as I had encountered it was that not only did it concentrate exclusively on analysis, it was positively antagonistic to synthesis. The whole tradition was militantly analytic, critical, to the exclusion of all else. As a student of history as well as philosophy I was thundered down upon every time I tried to draw any kind of parallel, by a don who would itemize differences of which I was well aware—as if the existence of these negated all points of similarity. This reaction embodied the absurd assumption that anyone comparing two things in one respect was implying a similarity between them in all respects. The absurdity extended into private conversation. I was once asked what I wanted to do after leaving Oxford, and replied that I hoped to be able to combine writing philosophy and novels with an active involvement in politics—as, for example, Jean-Paul Sartre was doing at that time. My questioner snorted derisively and said, "Don't you think it's a bit ridiculous to compare yourself to Sartre?," whereupon I had to say, "I didn't compare myself to Sartre. I merely said I hoped to be able to combine the same three activities as he does."

It has always seemed to me that one of the most valuable things to be studied in history is the extent to which situational logic works itself out in unique, concrete terms in practical situations, and in the lives of individuals. Over and again one sees similar effects following similar causes in situations that are not unalike. Indeed, only because this is so is one able to acquire any general understanding of the world and of societies, and governments, and people. It goes without saying that one needs always to be on the lookout for significant differences too, and one ought never to leave them out of account. But at Oxford I was never allowed to "get away with" (as they always used to put it—"Oh, you can't get away with that!") drawing any comparisons *at all,* because differences also existed. Anyone who drew a comparison was assumed *not to know about* the differences, the assumption being that if he had known about them they are what he would have mentioned. In consequence the study of history was seen as only critical, only analytic, and attempts to relate one thing to another were regarded as doomed to failure because the two could never be the same. Historians elsewhere who wrote in comparative terms were seen as inherently inadequate, if not bogus, in that they were skating across a surface of similarities while being insufficiently aware of the differences underneath—the implication again always being that if you looked into the underlying differences more closely you would find them so extensive that you would no longer feel justified in drawing comparisons.

If I read out in one of my history essays a statement to the effect that in, say, mid-eighteenth-century London most X's had been *y,* I could almost rely on the tutor interrupting and saying, "What about So-and-so?"; whereupon something like the following exchange would take place:

B.M.: What about him?
T: Well he was an X, and he wasn't *y.*
B.M.: I know.
T: But what you just said implied the opposite.
B.M.: No it didn't.
T: Just read that last bit again.
B.M.: "Most X's were *y.*"
T: There you are. As I say, So-and-so was an X, but he wasn't *y.*
B.M.: I haven't said he was.
T: Well what you just read out seemed to imply it.

B.M.: On the contrary, the very fact that I wrote "*most*" X's were *y* clearly implies that not all were. And I'm aware that So-and-so wasn't.

T: Well I don't think the examiners would assume you knew it if you wrote like that in your examinations.

B.M.: What on earth's invalid about what I've said, exactly as I've said it? Surely it's *true* that most X's were *y?* Or would you reject that?

T: Well, no, if you insist on putting it like that—I expect it's true that most of them were, actually. But quite a few of them weren't.

B.M.: I know. That was the point of writing "*most*" and not "all."

T: I can see what you're getting at. Even so, it would be a good idea to shove in a reference to So-and-so at this stage, I think, so that people realize you're aware of him.

B.M.: But a reference to So-and-so would be totally out of place here—he's got nothing to do with the point I'm trying to make. In fact, as you say, he's an instance of something quite different.

T: Well all I can say is that if you don't make any reference to him your readers will assume that you don't know about him, and that you are making a false generalization.

When I made the move from Oxford history to Oxford philosophy I found the same muddled and crudely illogical response to generalizations of any kind, the same unselfcritical obsession with analysis to the exclusion of everything else. The philosophers carried on almost as if their profession consisted of nothing but the drawing of distinctions. Indeed, they actually *called* themselves "analytic philosophers," and proclaimed this conception of philosophy as the only proper approach to the subject—"the sole and whole function of philosophy," as Ryle had said. Not only did they declare that any form of system-building in philosophy was illegitimate and doomed to fail, they were hostile to the formulation of explanatory theories at any level. The self-contradiction at the root of this approach lies in the fact that distinctions of any kind can be made only with reference to criteria of some sort, and this involves having some sort of explanatory framework, in the background at least, if not in the foreground. In practice the explanatory framework to which Oxford philosophers were referring was either "ordinary usage" or "common sense," or a confusion of both; and the attitude to both was to an exceptional and unexplained degree uncritical. It was taken for granted that we all knew what both of them were, when in fact not much reflection is needed to realize that individuals are bound to have differing notions of both. It was also taken for granted that we all accepted and agreed with both. When I pointed these things out I was simply ignored—yet when I arrived at Yale I found precisely these as the standard objections to Oxford philosophy, obvious to everyone.

On my return to England, with my arguments to that effect enriched and enhanced, I received no more of a hearing than I had before. Years later, when linguistic analysts with doubts themselves started to say the same things, their pioneering spirit was much admired by their colleagues. Bernard Williams put the position well in the following recantation (*Men of Ideas,* p. 144):

> All [philosophical revolutions] tend to encounter the problems of their own methods before very long, and linguistic analysis was not alone in that. I think that its basic limitation was that it underestimated the importance of theory. It above all underestimated the importance of theory inside philosophy (though in the case of Wittgenstein this could scarcely be called an underestimation—rather, a total rejection). It had an ancillary tendency to underestimate the importance of theory in other subjects as well. I don't think it had a very clear idea about the importance of theory even in the sciences. . . . I think that what we tended to do was to pick up some distinction or opposition, and go very carefully into it and into the various nuances that might be attached to it, and order them, or state them, without enough reflection on what background made this set of distinctions, rather than some other, interesting or important. . . . "Piecemeal" was a term of praise. There was a revealing analogy which Austin used. When people complained about the multiplication of distinctions, he pointed out that there were thousands of species of some kind of insect, and asked: "Why can't we just discover that number of distinctions about language?" Well, the answer of course is that our grounds for distinguishing species of beetles from one another are rooted in a certain theoretical understanding of what makes species different, an understanding given by the theory of evolution. But unless you've got some background theoretical understanding, anything is as different from anything else as you like. . . . People did vary in the degree to which they said you could do philosophy bit by bit, but I think the acknowledgement that the problems were only set, the distinctions only given, by a background of some more theoretical or systematic understanding—that point, I think, was more generally overlooked.

This describes exactly the philosophical environment in which I had studied at Oxford, and against which I was in permanent revolt. To my misfortune I had the sort of mind that seeks illumination in parallels between things, sometimes at quite a distance from one another, and I was also seeking solutions to real problems, by which I was possessed. It was always clear to me that distinctions had no significance except in relation to a wider explanatory framework, so I was much more interested in the formulation, and the validation or criticism, of explanatory frameworks than I was in the making of the distinctions subsumed by them (though I was interested in those too). However, I was scarcely ever allowed to open my mouth on any such matter without somebody protesting not that the statement I was making was false but that I ought not to be making that *sort* of statement *at all*—vulgar comparisons were disreputable intellectually, low-grade, brash, tasteless ("like a chain of Odeon cinemas," as someone once described my contributions to a discussion) and revealed the fact that I did not understand what real philosophy was. Luckily for me, I never lost my ultimate confidence that the boot was on the other foot—that it was they who were intellectually unserious and I who understood what philosophy was, even if I was no nearer making a contribution to it than they were. But it was lonely being the only one in step. I had to take part in discussion on other people's terms, because they were the only terms available, and discussion is important to philosophy; but I never found anyone willing to talk in my terms about the problems that worried me. Any discussion of explanatory frameworks was taboo, and I could not find anyone willing to embark on it. Indeed, I could not get my philosopher friends to consider even thought-systems like Marxism and Freudianism, that were currently of immense importance in the world, and in our own culture, and in literature, indeed in academe itself. These were simply branded with a red-hot iron as "not philosophy," and that was the end of them. Most philosophers did not read Freud or Marx, since they were "not philosophy," and would have been incapable of sustaining a serious discussion about them.

In all these respects exchanging Oxford for Yale had been like stepping out of a dark cellar into the sunlight. For the first time I encountered people of my own generation who were of high ability, had first-rate philosophical training, and were in love with fundamental problems. Several of them have since become well known, one or two internationally. Some of the most intellectually satisfying hours I spent at Yale were passed not in seminar rooms but with friends like these, talking about whatever interested us. But the seminars themselves were richly nourishing; and it was wonderful to be in an environment in which philosophical problems were taken seriously by well-trained, well-informed people, and not just regarded as "an assemblage of huge, crude mistakes." It was wonderful, too, to be in an environment in which everyone saw that the pursuit of philosophy involved us all in science, especially mathematical physics, and that we also had to take seriously such contemporary thought-systems as existentialism, Marxism, and Freudianism. Where Filmer Northrop in particular was so liberating was in his clear realization that all these things, indeed all human attempts to understand mankind and its world, unavoidably have deep-lying relationships with one another by virtue of the fact that they are differing attempts to do the same thing. For instance, if Freudian explanations are even approximately right then the existentialist claim that individuals possess the freedom to create their own personalities must be false. However, if Marxist explanations of social behaviour are where the truth lies then Freudianism must be fundamentally in error. Yet again, Marxism as a system of thought that claims to be scientific, and is both materialist and determinist, is irretrievably at odds with the indeterminacy that lies at the heart of quantum physics. And so on and so forth. Almost any belief we adopt in almost any field has consequences for our relationship to other belief-systems. So if we are intellectually serious we cannot avoid considering them in relation to one another. This imposes on us a positive duty to think in an interdisciplinary way: nothing else is compatible with intellectual responsibility. We are, whether we like it or not, forced up against the fact that asserting anything in one place commits us to accepting, or ruling out, things in others. Not to face this is either ignorant or sloppy. And the idea that this form of thinking is itself sloppy is uncomprehending, indeed stupid, because it is blind to intellectual realities. Of course, this way of thinking can be *done* sloppily, but so can every other way of thinking, including (God knows) analytic thinking. However, at Oxford I had been encouraged not only to distrust it but to see it as inherently pretentious and phoney. I never swallowed this, but Northrop helped to free me from some of the inhibitions it gave me. In so far as my Oxford training has made me over-cautious about the making of connections, it remains a bar to understanding.

One last thing—and they are all big things—for which I have to thank Northrop is the perception that everything I have so far discussed in connection with him is related to a metaphysical problem of the relationship between what he used to refer to as the One and the Many. Not only religious people believe that everything there is is part of an ultimate unity, though I think I am right in saying that all the major religions of the world assert this. The self-same physical laws hold throughout the whole of the known universe, and every atom in that universe has the same basic internal structure as every other. The subjective experience of each one of us is characterized by what Kant called the transcendental unity of apperception: although it teems with a multitude of apparently unrelated elements of innumerable different sorts, there is a sense in which it is experienced by us as a unity. (Kant has characteristically profound things to say about what this unity consists in.) It is clear from the way people talk and write that many if not most assume the totality of what there is to be in some sense unitary. On consideration, though, any such unity is doubly mysterious, first in that it should exist at all, and second in that it is made up of an indefinitely large number of apparently disparate things. The first of these two mysteries has always held a particular fascination for me: the second of them held a particular fascination for Northrop. I do not think it was the case, as some people believed, that he had first of all been spontaneously interested in a large number of things and only then, secondarily, begun to seek for connections between them so that his outlook would not be a chaos. I think it is more likely that he had from the beginning had some sort of intuition that everything is ultimately connected, and so was led to pursue all the things that interested him to the point at which they began to reveal their interrelationships. He never lost his sense of excitement at the discovery of new ones, nor his sense of wonderment that they were there. In order to get the most out of him you needed already to know quite a lot yourself, but as a teacher in the upper reaches of higher education there was no one to touch him. If he had been creatively original on the same level as his knowledge he would have been in the Einstein class; but in that case the best of his energies would of necessity have been poured into research, not into teaching. It was only because he was not creatively original that he was an incomparable teacher.

9

The Discovery of Kant

As I have said, the most valuable single educational experience I had at Yale was being introduced to the critical philosophy of Immanuel Kant. The form in which this took place made an important difference: it was not only in solitary study, though I did a good deal of that, but as one of a small group of enthusiasts meeting twice a week for two or more hours of discussion throughout the year.

If you study philosophy for long enough you arrive at a stage where you can usually see for yourself the important things in someone's work that others are able to point out to you. After that you can go on picking up an unlimited amount of worthwhile detail from secondary sources, but far and away your most important perceptions about the work of a great philosopher are those you have for yourself. This is not so in the early stages, however, when you are groping your way: others can then point out highly important things to you that you might not otherwise have seen. This means that discussion is an indispensable part of philosophical training in those early stages. It is true that many great philosophers did their creative work in isolation, but that was not how most of them went through the learning process that was necessary beforehand.

It is a mistake, I believe, for beginners to think they can get very far by themselves in the study of philosophy. An essential part of the process for beginners is that their sincerely held beliefs—and, much more important than that, their assumptions, which are sometimes unconscious—should be challenged by people who are as intelligent and well informed as themselves; and they should have to meet those challenges head-on, and deal with them adequately, or else adjust their beliefs and assumptions accordingly, or abandon them altogether. This cannot happen if they are studying alone, no matter how intensely. Alone, they remain too much within the confines of their own limitations. It does not meet the case to say: "Ah, but the great philosophers that they read are massively breaching these limitations all the time, invading their heads from outside with new and exciting ideas." The student's understanding and interpretation of those philosophers is almost bound to be inadequate at first, and sometimes wrong; and without criticism he will have no way of knowing that he is in error. I know from my own experience, having taught philosophy to above-average students, not only that they all make serious mistakes but that they have a marked tendency to make the same mistakes, so they would reinforce one another in those errors if they had no guidance from someone more experienced (not necessarily more intelligent) than themselves. Later on, when—like trackers who have lived for years in the forest—they have acquired a whole armoury of intellectual skills that can be derived only from experience, they will be in a different situation. But not yet.

Discovering Kant was like discovering where I lived. Right at the outset he states that the nature of our reason is such that we cannot help asking questions about the world to which, *such is the nature of our reason,* we can never know the answers. He then goes on to set out the antinomies of time and space, arguing that it is possible to prove both that time must have had a beginning and that it cannot have had a beginning, and both that space must be unbounded and that it cannot be unbounded. I did not think that his particular formulations of these arguments were very good, as a matter of fact, but I saw how they might be improved, and in any case their faults paled into insignificance beside the fact that here was a philosopher who as his starting point was taking problems I had been struggling with all my life and not yet found solutions to. It was, as Goethe described the experience of reading Kant, like walking into a lighted room. I had discovered at last what I had come to philosophy looking for.

Kant makes the point early on that if reason leads us into self-contradiction and impasse, reality cannot correspond to it, and therefore it cannot be possible even in principle for us to understand reality by the use of reason alone. This knocks the bottom out of the programme of the rationalist philosophers who had preceded him, figures such as Descartes, Spinoza, and Leibniz. But Kant goes on to say that experience is no more able than reason to give us knowledge of independent reality, since the congruence of our sense-perceptions with external objects can never be validated; and what is more, the whole notion of our sense-perceptions being "like" objects as they are in themselves, independently of being experienced, turns out on analysis to be incoherent and unintelligible: we cannot form any conception of objects independently of the categories of experience and thought, all of which are subject-dependent. This last fact, however, gives Kant an entry into a wholly new way of approaching his problems.

Most philosophers before Kant seem to have assumed that objects exist more or less as we perceive them yet independently of us, and that they exist in a space and a time that are also independent of us. Furthermore, this is what one might call the commonsense view of things. But Kant realized that it could not possibly be right. All the ways we have of perceiving objects—sight, sound, touch, taste, smell—are such as cannot exist independently of sensory and nervous systems; and all the ways we have of thinking about objects are precisely that, namely ways of thinking, and can no more take place without brains than seeing can take place without eyes. If we abstract from our notion of an object all those aspects of it that are sense-dependent and mind-dependent we are left with, at the very most, the notion of a something, an x, to which we cannot assign any observable or conceptualizable characteristics. This notion of an object is metaphysical in the sense that, by definition, no such object could ever figure in experience. Kant believed that for us to have the experiences we do have, such metaphysical objects must exist as their causes. Locke also believed this, flagrantly though it breaches the fundamental principle of empiricism (which is that nothing about the world can justifiably be postulated that is not checkable by experience). In fact, it seems to me a matter of general observation that a great many people who hold what they take to be commonsensical views of the world also believe it. However, in Kant's case it involved a different sort of internal contradiction from Locke's.

As a young and middle-aged man Kant built a brilliant reputation as a teacher of mathematical physics. It was a field to which he also made an original contribution: at the age of thirty-one he published his *Theory of the Heavens,* the first book to give an account of the physical universe as having evolved and not just as having possessed more or less its present form throughout its existence (which had been both the Aristotelian and the Thomist view). He believed, as did almost everyone of his day who understood it, that the new science of the seventeenth century had set mankind on the highroad towards understanding the universe. He supposed, as again did others, that scientific knowledge was uniquely certain, and that what gave it its unique certainty was that it consisted of a combination of two processes neither of which admitted of error. The first was direct observation, not just on one occasion by one person, but observations repeated systematically by that person and then checked systematically by others. The second was logical deduction from observation-statements which had been arrived at in this way. So he took the whole of science to consist of things that were known infallibly to be true either because they had been directly observed—and, if appropriate, measured—under controlled conditions on many different occasions by trained and competent observers, or because they followed by logical necessity from what had been thus observed. Science, in other words, consisted entirely of immediate observation plus logic, and these were two processes which, if carefully and properly executed, yielded the highest level of certainty that there could be.

Kant was later to describe this state of mind as "dogmatic slumber." What woke him from it was reading Hume, and specifically, he says, reading what Hume had to say about causality. Hume taught him that causal connection is something whose existence is not only unobservable but impossible to derive logically from anything that is observable. When we talk of event A causing event B, we do not mean just that event A happened and then event B happened. We mean that event B happened *because* event A happened. However, all we can observe are the two events: we do not observe some third entity in the form of a necessary connection between them. And we cannot assert that there is known to be such a connection nevertheless, even though it cannot be observed, because every event of type A that has ever been observed has invariably been followed by an event of type B. For no matter how many events of type A have been observed and found to be followed by an event of type B, this does not mean that the next A will necessarily be followed by a B: it does not mean that there is any necessary connection. Necessary connection, then, cannot be observed, and nor can its existence be logically derived from what is observed. But necessary connection, as distinct from constant conjunction, is entailed by the notion of cause. Therefore our concept of causality has neither an adequate empirical nor an adequate logical foundation. Kant saw the validity of these arguments. But he saw also that if there were no such thing as causal connection there would be no possibility of an empirical world, whether the world of everyday experience and commonsense observation or the world as investigated and presented to us by science. Yet we do know there to be such a world, and therefore we know there to be such a thing as causal connection—and therefore we know that there are indispensable features of the empirical world that are neither observable nor logically deducible. This at once raises the questions: What are they? and How can it be possible for us to acquire knowledge of such things if not by either observation or logic?

In fact Kant, with a capaciousness of intellectual grasp unique among even the greatest philosophers, must have perceived on reading Hume that the concepts of time, space and scientific law are in the same boat as the concept of cause. Nothing that is infinite can, in its infinity, fall within the bounds of human experience, and therefore neither time nor space as presented to us by commonsense reflection and Newtonian physics—a uniform time, unbounded, stretching to infinity both forwards and backwards, and a uniform space, stretching outwards to infinity in three dimensions—could ever be established by observation, nor could they be logically derived from anything we could ever observe or experience. Similarly, Hume had demonstrated that no unrestrictedly general statement about the world, as all scientific laws are, is verifiable by any finite number of observations, however large, nor can its truth be derived by logical processes from any number of such observations. In short, Kant learnt from Hume that all of what had seemed to be the fundamentals of science—scientific laws, causal connection, absolute space, absolute time—were each of them unvalidatable both empirically and logically. He did not react to this astounding realization by concluding that science was invalid, though there have been others who have. That, in his opinion, would have been nonsense in view of the fact that science demonstrably gives us the most, and the most practically useful, knowledge that human beings have ever possessed. He reacted instead by saying, in effect (these are my words, not his): "We know that we live in a world of space and time, within which events are causally interrelated and can be accurately predicted if we apply scientific laws to the facts of observation. But Hume has shown that it is impossible for us to have derived this knowledge from any combination of observation and logic. Therefore we must have used something other than these in the acquisition of it. Therefore observation and logical derivation cannot be the only bases for reliable knowledge."

What else is there? In his Introduction to the *Prolegomena to Any Future Metaphysics* Kant tells us that the whole of his *Critique of Pure Reason* is an attempt to solve Hume's problem "in its widest implications." The attempt leads him into the most radical reconstruction of the theory of knowledge that anyone has ever carried out. At the end of it he pronounces that the whole nature of the world *as we experience it* is dependent on the nature of our apparatus for experiencing, with the inevitable consequence that things as they appear to us are not the same as things as they are in themselves.

Most characteristics that our experiences have are contingent: an object of perception can be of this material or that, of this colour or that, of these dimensions or those, and so on and so forth. We find out what they are by observing them and reading off their characteristics from our observations; and we do this both in our commonsense activities and in our science. But there are some characteristics of which we can say with certainty *in advance* that any object of experience has to possess them if it is to be an object of experience at all. We cannot, for instance, perceive any object without perceiving it to be *something,* and as being capable of being acted on causally by other things, and as having a location in three-dimensional space, and in one-dimensional time. These are not characteristics of the world that we learn about by reading them off from our experiences: they are things that we know with certainty in advance of all possible experience. They are preconditions that have to be met before anything can be an experience at all. And in this fact we find the solution to Hume's problem. Physical identity, location in space, location in time, propensity for causal interaction—none of these are concepts derived from experience, nor are they logical concepts: they apply to experience because they are constitutive of experience *as such,* and must characterize it if it is to be experience at all. Having this character, they constitute certain knowledge. So it is they that are the third component in human knowledge that we were looking for: they are what there has necessarily to be in addition to empirical observability and logical consistency for us to have knowledge of the world around us. They are the forms of all possible experience. If we think in terms of the metaphor of catching things in the network of experience, these are the meshes of our nets. Only what can be caught in them is available to us. Anything that passes through them untouched will not be picked up by us, and nor will whatever falls outside our nets altogether. Only what these nets catch will be ours, and only what they *can* catch *can* be ours. What they *do* catch is a contingent matter, depending on what there is to be caught, but what they *can* catch is determined by the nature of the nets themselves, and we live permanently with their capacities and their limitations.

This being so, if we carry out a painstakingly careful investigation of the forms of all possible experience we shall be discovering the limits of what can possibly be experience or knowledge for us; and anything that falls outside those limits cannot possibly be experience or knowledge for us. This is not to say that nothing outside those limits can exist, but only that if it does exist we have no way of apprehending it.

The way linguistic philosophers understood and expressed all this was to say that, before Kant, philosophical analysis had reached a stage of development at which two forms of meaningful utterance had been distinguished. First there were utterances about the empirical world. These were synthetic propositions, always contingent; which is to say that any such proposition was capable of being true or false, and therefore its truth could be known only *a posteriori,* that is to say after it had received validation from experience. Then there were analytic propositions, whose truth could be known *a priori,* which is to say in advance of experience, because if true they were necessarily true and not dependent on experience for their validation. According to Hume, all significant propositions must be either (i) synthetic and *a posteriori* or (ii) analytic and *a priori.* But now along comes Kant and tells us that there is a third category of significant propositions, namely the synthetic *a priori.* Such propositions are meaningful only as applied to the world of experience and possible experience, and for that reason are synthetic; but they are known to be true in advance of all possible experience, and for that reason are *a priori*. In the minds of linguistic philosophers, therefore, the decisive question raised by Kant's philosophy was: Can there be synthetic *a priori* propositions? Their consideration of this question seems to have led them to the conclusion that there cannot be, and this in turn led them to regard Kant's whole critical philosophy as a blind alley up which there was no necessity for a student (or anyone else) to go. They acknowledged that Hume had raised problems of a fundamental character with regard to human knowledge, and they agreed that Kant had offered a solution to them, but they denied that Kant's solution worked, so they regarded him as having left us back where we were, on square one, still looking for a solution to Hume's problem.

If we look on the Kantian analysis as telling us primarily something about the world and not something about propositions, its crucial points are that we human beings are embodied and that our bodies are equipped with certain mental and sensory apparatus, such that all experience must come to us through it. Therefore only what it can mediate is possible experience for us. Therefore untranscendable limits to the world of possible experience are set by the nature of the apparatus we have, and would have been so set whatever apparatus we might have possessed. Although the apparatus we have is contingent, the fact that it sets limits to our possible experience is not contingent but necessary. What it cannot mediate cannot be experience. This, to repeat, is not at all the same as saying that nothing can exist that it cannot mediate—to suppose this is the commonest error made by commonsense and scientific thinking, and also by empiricist and realist philosophers. There are no grounds whatever for supposing such a thing. The simple truth is that as far as we can ever know there is no limit to what can exist outside the possibility of our knowledge. Of course, because there is no limit on it, one of the infinitely many possibilities is that there is nothing outside the possibility of our knowledge. But that is infinitely unlikely. An additional assumption is needed to make it even in the smallest degree plausible, and that is that all reality is the product of our minds. Kant firmly disbelieved that. He believed as confidently as anyone can ever believe anything that there is an independent reality outside the world of all possible experience. He called this the world of the noumenal, the world of things as they are in themselves, and of reality as it is in itself. He called the world as it appears to us—the directly known world of actual experience with its penumbra, the postulated world of possible experience—the world of phenomena. And it is of paramount importance for those of us brought up in an Anglo-Saxon tradition never to forget that when Kant and his successors talk of the world of phenomena they are talking of the world as we ordinarily think of it, the actual world, the world of material objects in space and time, the world of common sense and of science: what we are used to calling the empirical world.

Kant left us with three as against two components of possible knowledge about this world: empirical observation, logical derivation, and the forms in which all instances of these are mediated by our mental and sensory apparatus. Among these last are time, space, the notion of an object, causal connection, and all empirical assumptions of an unrestrictedly general character. These characterize, and can characterize only, the world of experience, the empirical world, which we must also remember is a world of appearances, not of things as they are in themselves. What we are talking about are the structural features of experience, and they can no more exist independently of experience than a man's build can exist independently of his body.

All this has among its many consequences that Kant's notion of cause is such that causal connections can exist only between objects in the phenomenal world, the world of possible experience. And this in turn means that there can never be a causal connection between an object of possible experience and something that lies permanently outside the possibility of experience. If objects do exist in themselves independently of us they cannot, consistently with the rest of Kant's philosophy, be the cause of our experiences. But to say this is to abandon the only reason for postulating the existence of unobservable metaphysical objects. In that case philosophers, at least, are bound to ask: "What justification do we have for believing that they exist at all?"

If we give up the notion of independently existing objects this leaves Kant's philosophy looking very much like Berkeley's—a possibility that so disturbed Kant that when he issued a second edition of his masterpiece, *Critique of Pure Reason,* he mutilated it quite unnecessarily in order to emphasize his differences from Berkeley. He remained always insistent that total reality consists of two worlds, one (*pace* Berkeley) the world of things as they are in themselves, and the other the world of things as they appear to us. The latter is the world of objects of experience, manifesting themselves in three dimensions of space and one of time. Space and time are themselves conceived of as characteristics of a world of appearances only: an absolutely empty space in which nothing occurs or exists, and an absolutely empty time in which nothing occurs or exists, are both indistinguishable from nothing at all. Space "exists" only in so far as there are spatial relationships, and time in so far as there are temporal relationships. But since the entities which relate to one another are such as cannot exist independently of experience, nor, then, can space or time. They are what Kant calls forms of our sensibility, what we have been thinking of as nets; or one might call them frameworks within which we gather the as yet unprocessed raw material of experience together into the ordered, coherent world that is what we actually experience. Independently of that process they have no being.

By this route Kant arrived at an original solution to the problem that lies at the heart of empiricism and can never be solved on the basis of empiricist assumptions. If objects as we experience them exist independently, there is no way we can ever be justified in feeling sure that our experiences conform to them and give us accurate representations of them. Indeed—as Berkeley alone among the most famous empiricists seems fully to have grasped—there is no way in which our representations could intelligibly be thought to be "like" the objects at all, since the only notions we can form of *representation as such* are in terms of either concept-dependent or sense-dependent categories; and whereas objects as they appear to us are constituted entirely in these subject-dependent terms, any independent existence they might have would have to be entirely *not* in these terms, and that is something of which, in the nature of things, we are permanently unable to form any conception. Whenever a philosopher is heard to demand challengingly why objects as they are in themselves should not exist in forms that correspond to our apprehension of them he can be taken not to have understood this. Kant's demonstration of it is a contribution to philosophy of the utmost profundity. It underlies what he himself describes as his Copernican revolution in philosophy.

For thousands of years, it would seem, most human beings took it for granted that the earth was the centre of the cosmos and that the planets moved round it. It is, of course, perfectly possible to persist in seeing things this way, but it makes the actual motions of the planets so complicated as to be virtually impossible to imagine, and terribly difficult even to calculate mathematically. Even so, when Copernicus came along and pointed out that these problems disappeared if we dropped the initial assumption that the earth was at the centre, it was difficult for people even to take in the possibility of doing such a thing. The Church denounced it as sinful on the ground that it went against holy scripture, so that if it were valid the Bible would have to be inaccurate. Yet against all obstacles, including active persecution, the idea eventually established itself that the moon was revolving round the earth but the earth, and the rest of the planets, round the sun. And once our planetary system was looked at in this way, with the sun and not the earth as its centre, the difficulties melted away. Everything fell into place and made self-evident sense: the movements of the planets became easy to imagine and simple to calculate.

On the level of lived experience, though, all this remained deeply counter-intuitive. To us human beings it went on looking, as it always had, as if the sun were going round the earth, and to this day we find it impossible to *feel* ourselves (even though we know for a fact that we are) hurtling through space all the time at thousands of miles an hour on the surface of a revolving ball. This knowledge, even though it *is* knowledge, remains for us abstract, and is not at all contained, not even hinted at, in any of the experiences that we actually have—in fact the first people to say it publicly were dismissed as cranks or lunatics. Now Kant claims that all these things apply *mutatis mutandis* to the revolutionary approach to human knowledge proposed by him. For thousands of years human beings had generally taken it for granted that material objects possessed an independent existence in a space and a time that possessed also an independent existence. But from this seemingly self-evident starting point they had found it permanently impossible to explain how we could acquire knowledge of those objects, or, if we had knowledge, to know that we had it. And Kant pointed out that if, instead of assuming that knowledge must conform to objects, we looked at the situation from the opposite end, and thought in terms of objects conforming to knowledge, we would find that the impossibilities and self-contradictions vanished. Everything then falls into place and makes obvious sense. However, it will go on being counter-intuitive. We shall find it impossible to *feel* as if objects are conforming to our knowledge rather than the other way round. However, that ought not to get in the way of our knowing it to be true.

After all, Kant might have said, knowing in reality—knowing as actually experienced and lived—does *not* start from the object and then somehow make its way to becoming experience in a subject. It starts as experience in a subject. In other words, we have no choice but to start from where *we* are. We start with experience and then seek an explanation of it. That is what actually happens. Now, says Kant, if we keep sight of the fact that we can only ever experience objects through the mental, sensory, and other apparatus that we have for doing so, *and in terms of the forms and modes and categories mediated by that apparatus,* then inescapably it follows that *what* we experience can come to us wholly and solely in those terms. This is what Kant means when he says that objects conform to our knowledge of them. A writer can describe a scene in words, and then the representation you have of that scene is a verbal description. But the only representation of the same scene that a camera could make is a photograph, or a series of photographs; it could not possibly make any other sort, although there are in principle an indefinite number of radically different kinds of representation that could be made of the same scene. The only representation of it that could be made by sound-recording equipment would be a sound recording: it could not take a photograph. And so on and so forth—and so with our brains and our nervous systems and our senses: they represent reality in terms determined by their own nature; and that is all they can ever do; and this constitutes the only experience and the only knowledge we can ever have. If we start from this consideration we find ourselves able to explain what empiricism is terminally unable to explain, namely how it comes about that our knowledge conforms to its objects. What is actually happening is that what appear to us as the objects of our experience are being produced for us by our experiencing apparatus in the same sort of way as a photograph is produced in a camera and a sound recording in a piece of sound-recording equipment, and that is why they have the character they do. Things in themselves are not that way, any more than things in themselves are photographs or sound recordings, but all the ways we have of representing things are inevitably ways of representing, and are not the things themselves.

In responding to this sort of epistemology empiricists have tended to make—and persist in making—one huge mistake in particular. They represent Kant as saying that we ourselves synthesize reality, that we put it all together in our heads, that we make it up. He is specifically not saying that. On the contrary, he is always insistent that reality exists independently of us. What he is saying is something altogether different from that and incompatible with it, something about the nature of experience—namely that it has to be mediated by apparatus that is not itself the object of experience, and furthermore that it must inescapably take the forms determined by the nature of the apparatus, with the result that the representations it yields are categorially different from their objects. To be sure, *objects of experience* are "like" experience, but that is because they *are* experience, they are what we mean by the word "experience." But they are not the independently existing objects that constitute reality as it is in itself, just as the photograph is not the object photographed, and the sound recording is not the sound recorded. In the case of our experience its objects, as distinct from experience, are such as we can never perceive or form any conception of. We cannot apprehend objects without the intermediacy of our sensory and mental apparatus; and given its intermediacy its deliverances are what is immediate, and are all that can ever be immediate, to our consciousness. Although, says Kant, we know the objects in themselves to exist, they are outside the possibility of apprehension. Central to Kantian philosophy is the doctrine that precisely because reality exists independently of all possible experience it remains permanently hidden.

No one who understands the central doctrines of any of the world's leading religions ought to have any difficulty in understanding this idea, although of course such a person may disagree with it; that is another matter. The chief reason why so many empiricists misunderstand Kant is that the identification of independently existing objects (and therefore reality) with the objects of experience is so foundational a tenet of philosophy as they themselves conceive and practise it that they are not able to liberate themselves from the assumption, and so they import it into their understanding of Kant's philosophy, from which it is—equally foundationally—absent. As will eventually become clear, I am by no means in agreement with Kant about everything; but I do agree with him that whatever the nature of independent reality may be it must lie permanently outside all possibility of experience, and that all forms of experience are inevitably subject-dependent; so I agree with him that the empiricist approach as normally understood is radically mistaken. Empiricists may want to say something like: "But surely it is absurd to assert that the whole of our direct experience, and therefore all that we actually *know,* is not really real, while what is really real is something we can never know. Is that not standing everything on its head?" My answer to this is: "No, it is not, for the simple reason that all we can ever encounter in direct experience is *experience,* and experience as such is subject-dependent. Inherent in its logic is the fact that it is not objective. We know for the marvellously insightful reasons supplied to us by Kant that it is impossible that it should ever be independent reality. Indeed, precisely *because* it is experience it cannot be independent reality. *Experience can never be independent reality.* The error at the heart of the entire empiricist tradition is what you might call the reification of experience, the mis-taking of experience for reality, the mis-taking of epistemology for ontology."

Kant had some notable followers to whose work the mistaken empiricist view of his philosophy does in fact apply. Fichte, Schelling and Hegel each perceived that independently existing objects could not, compatibly with the rest of Kant's philosophy, be the causes of our experiences; and they took the view that since such things could never figure in our experience we had no grounds for postulating their existence, and what is more no need to do so. So they attempted, each in his different way, to produce a philosophy that derived from Kant without containing Kant's most conspicuous error. Of their work it can truthfully be said that they regard total reality as having the character of experience or thought, or consciousness, and as being synthesized either by our minds or by some sort of general Mind (in Hegel's case *Geist,* which lies somewhere between mind and spirit). They, therefore, are idealists in a sense in which Kant is not one. I have found it to be widely assumed that Schopenhauer too is this sort of philosopher, putting his particular concept of *Will* in the place of Hegel's *Geist.* This supposition is hopelessly wide of the mark. Schopenhauer was radically different from those others, not least because—like Kant—he believed in the existence of an independent reality. Because this belief was fundamental to his outlook he had a great deal to learn from the empiricists, without being one of them—and he learnt it: he revered Locke and Hume (like Kant again) and consciously tried to write German in the way Hume had written English. In some ways it is illuminating to think of Schopenhauer as if he were a philosopher of the British empiricist type who has taken Kant on board but perceived his mistakes, and then moved on accordingly, instead of retreating to Hume.

Up to this point in my outline of Kant's ideas I have dealt solely with his epistemology. Experience, he has been insisting, is precisely what it presents itself to us as being, namely experience. If it were anything else, a deep mystery would be involved, and perhaps an insoluble one, for how could experience, which of its nature can exist only in a subject, be at the same time also something else that exists independently of any subject? Fortunately, as matters stand, there is no need for us to trouble ourselves with such chimerical thoughts, and we can take experience to be what it seems to be, and not as being something with which it is incompatible.

This world of our experience, the empirical world, is not a chaos but is ordered. Every event in it is the causal outcome of antecedent events, and these interrelationships are so reliably consistent that vast numbers of them at every level of scale, from the formation of a snowflake to the motions of whole galaxies of our cosmos, are predictable, and are expressible in mathematical equations. No matter on what level we investigate our universe we find it saturated with structure, so much so that we pretty well know we shall find structure before we even begin to look. Kant believed that what happens within this world is governed entirely by scientific laws; indeed, he believed this to have been proved beyond any possibility of doubt by Newton. Much of his writing is devoted to systematic and detailed demonstrations of *how* it comes to be so. But this leaves him with one particular problem that has explosive implications. If the movements of all material objects in space and time are causally interconnected and governed by scientific laws, does this mean that we human beings, whose bodies are material objects moving in space and time, have no freedom of action? Is the new science incompatible with freedom of the will? There have always been some people who maintained that it was. Kant, by contrast, produced what he regarded as proof positive that it is not.

His argument, disconcertingly original both in starting point and in direction, proceeds from what he takes to be the undeniable fact that moral concepts and categories exist and are taken by us to have meaning. He undertakes to show that for this to be the case we must actually believe (whatever we may believe we believe) that we have free will. And he thinks that in demonstrating this he has proved that we are committed, again whether we like it or not, to the belief that there is more to total reality than the empirical world—that there must be a realm in which free decisions occur that impinge on the movements of matter but are themselves outside the governance of scientific laws. In other words we human beings are not physical bodies only but also something else; and the constituent of our being that freely directs some of the movements of our bodies is not in the empirical world, although our bodies are. The argument which we are about to examine, if valid, is of the profoundest significance for our understanding of ourselves. And one of the many important things about it is that it makes no use whatever of religious concepts, or presuppositions, and does not commit us to religious consequences of any kind: it consists of rational argumentation only, starting from the facts of the matter as we know them to be. It runs as follows.

Not only is it an undeniable fact, familiar to all of us, that we have moral concepts and categories: it is also an undeniable fact that there are times when most of us find ourselves unable to ignore these even though we want to. People who drive themselves to act against their own most deeply held moral convictions put themselves in real danger of some sort of personal breakdown, such as addiction to heavy drinking, or a nervous breakdown, or even suicide. All these are only too sadly familiar forms of response to intense inner conflict. And yet for our moral concepts and categories even to have any application there has to be some element of validity in notions such as *ought* and *ought not, right* and *wrong, duty, choice, obligation, integrity.* But this means that it must sometimes—not necessarily every time we think it, but sometimes—be possible for human beings to choose to do or not to do something; for if they are *never* at liberty to adopt, or refrain from, the courses of action they pursue, then none of the familiar moral concepts can ever justifiably be applied to any person or action. As Kant himself was the one to demonstrate— and the phrase has become famous in philosophy—"*ought* implies *can.*" If it is impossible for me to do something, then to say that I ought to do it is not meaningless, it is false. For this reason, if no human being ever had freedom of action, all moral propositions would be false.

Now at this point it is open to anyone to whom the argument is being presented to say: "That's right—I believe no human being ever does have freedom of action, and I believe all moral propositions are false." That puts him under a logical obligation to expunge every such falsehood from his own discourse and thinking, indeed from his whole conception of the world—all concepts of fairness, justice, praise or blame, good and bad, right or wrong, all morally evaluative terms whatsoever, in so far as they are ever applied to human beings and their actions, not only as individuals but through institutions. No determinist I have ever heard or read has faced up to what doing this would involve, or what the full consequences of it would be. Certainly none that I know of has tried to do it. If one did, and he succeeded, he would become a psychopath, because what we mean by a psychopath is somebody with no sense whatsoever of right or wrong. I am entirely confident that if you subjected any determinist who is not a psychopath, however amoral his life, to outrageous and cruel ill-treatment, he would become indignant with you and protest that you ought not to treat him in that way. *Ought* and *ought not* would spring to life for him then, and he would insist on attributing to you the ability to behave otherwise. In short, I simply do not believe that anyone does, or in practice ever could, consistently deny all elements of free will in other human beings, even if he denies them in himself. Even the wicked do not regard themselves as mere things, mere physical objects like a chair or a table, without rights or moral claims of any sort. Everyone wants to be treated with moral decency, even those who do not show it in their behaviour to others; and for this to be even possible it is necessary for others to have choice, at least sometimes.

Anyone who is not prepared to go consistently down the road of regarding both himself and others as completely without rights or moral claims, or even the possibility of praise or blame, has only one alternative, and that is to accept that moral concepts and categories do sometimes have content. And to accept this is to accept that human beings do sometimes have genuine choice, which is to say that they can sometimes act otherwise than they do; and this in turn means that the movements of their physical bodies in space and time at least sometimes take place freely in accordance with acts of will—"freely" here meaning not determined only by scientific laws. But if everything that occurs *within* the empirical world is subject to scientific law—and Kant regarded this as an inescapable truth—then those acts of will that we are talking about cannot occur in the empirical world. This means that that part of our being that chooses and decides, initiating physical movements (at least those movements that we designate as acts of will), has its existence in some way such that it is not part of the empirical world. Because this argument is of such central importance to Kant's philosophy, Schopenhauer was later to say that Kant had had under his very nose, for the grasping, the insight that the nature of the contents of the transcendental realm whose existence he demonstrated had the character of will, if indeed it was not will; and yet he had not perceived it, even though it was inherent in his own philosophy.

Once a physical movement has been initiated in the empirical world its consequences according to whatever the laws of science are will inevitably occur. If I throw a ball, its path through the air will be a parabola modified by air pressure, and what parabola it is will be determined by several factors combined: the mass of the ball, the angle at which I threw it, and the force I put into the throw. I cannot choose to throw that ball in that way without its describing that parabola. It is only *whether* I throw the ball *or not* that is up to me. I can choose to throw it, or I can choose not to throw it, and that is the extent of my choice. Once I have thrown it, the laws of physics take over, and they cannot be prevented from carrying the matter through to the end. The idea of free decisions or acts of choice *interfering* with the operation of what we now call scientific laws is the basic presupposition of belief in magic and miracles: it posits the operation of free will *within* the empirical world. Many of those of us who do not believe in magic or miracles believe that free decisions and acts of choice do not take place within the same realm as that in which scientific laws operate, but inhabit another domain that has a common frontier with it, and we believe that vital transactions take place across that frontier.

The complete chain of argument, therefore, runs as follows. We have, and know that we have, moral concepts and categories. In practice it is impossible for us to doubt that these have at least some significance. But for this to be so, human beings must possess some degree of freedom of choice in some of their actions. And in the empirical world it is not possible for the movements of physical bodies to be free, that is to say to be independent of scientific laws. Therefore the exercise of human freedom, which we know at least sometimes takes place, cannot take place in the empirical world, although it has consequences that ramify in that world. Therefore not every part of a human being is in the empirical world. That part which exercises freedom of choice is outside it. From these considerations we know that there is some part of total reality that is not the empirical world, and furthermore we know that there is a part of each person that belongs to it; and we even have a glimpse of some of the things that go on in it, namely decisions, choices, what might generically be termed acts of will. And all this is deducible by rational argument from the fact that moral concepts exist and have meaning. It is an astounding intellectual insight, fraught with consequence. For in this way, according to Kant, the fact of the existence of a transcendental realm, a part of total reality that is not the empirical world, is rationally demonstrable, and is therefore known by us with certainty.

However, no matter what the contents of that other realm may be, they are not themselves possible objects of knowledge for us. That they are outside the realm in which causal connection reigns means that there can never be any such thing as a causal explanation of them, and therefore we can never "understand" them. It is without any application to ask what causes them, why they occur, how it is that they come about, for they inhabit a realm in which *why?*, *how?*, and *cause* have no purchase. To ask those things is what philosophers call a category mistake: it is like asking whether green is triangular, and what triangles eat. We are already familiar with the truth of this with regard to the only instance of them that we have considered so far, namely acts of will. It is a matter of direct and immediate experience to us, as direct and immediate as anything can possibly be, that we decide, choose, and initiate bodily movements, and we do those things throughout virtually the whole time we are awake; yet we ourselves have not the remotest idea how we do them. These acts on our part seem perpetually to spring into existence out of nothing. However carefully we try to penetrate their provenance with the most sharply concentrated attention we find ourselves encountering nothing at all—no explanation, no causal connection with anything else, a void. The situation is as I described it on pages 3–4 of this book. It has exercised human beings throughout the history of thought. As Noam Chomsky put it:* "How can we decide to say things that are new but not random, that are appropriate to situations yet not under the control of stimuli? When we ask these questions, we enter into a realm of mystery where human science, at least so far (and maybe even in principle), does not reach. We can reach some understanding of the principles that make it possible for us to behave in a normal creative fashion, but as soon as questions of will, or decision, or reasons, or choice of action, arise, human science is pretty much at a loss. It has little to say about these matters, as far as I can see. These questions remain in the obscurity that has enveloped them since classical antiquity."

Although no one has ever been able to explain how these things occur, Kant has produced a rational explanation of why it is that they cannot be explained. If he is right, it will never be possible to explain them: there is no "how." (Hence Chomsky's parenthesis—he is self-awarely Kantian in his thought.) For us as inhabitants of the empirical world they are outside all possibility of explanation or understanding. If there are forms of apprehension other than those that are accessible to human beings, then for as long as we are human beings we shall not know what they are. If there is any sense, other than the indestructibility of the matter that constitutes our bodies, in which we shall continue to exist after we have ceased to be human, then perhaps it may be possible that we shall apprehend in some way other than the ways now available to us; but if there is no such sense then it will never be possible.

It is essential for the reader to be clear about the fact that whenever Kant draws a line of demarcation between what it is and is not possible for us to know he is never, never saying, or in any way at all implying, that nothing exists outside the realm of our possible knowledge. On the contrary, he thought that there had to be something, but that what that something was could never be an object of knowledge for us. Although we know *that* there is a part of total reality which is not contained within the empirical world, *the very fact that it is not so contained* means that we are permanently unable to have direct knowledge of its contents. This is a built-in part of the human condition, not something that just happens to be so and might one day change, a barrier we might one day break through. We shall never break through it as long as we are human. This has been the most historically influential of all the conclusions reached by Kant's philosophy. It rules out, permanently, any direct knowledge or understanding of a transcendental God, or any knowledge that we have souls—still less that they survive death. It provides an exceedingly powerful demonstration that there cannot *be* any such thing as specifically religious or theological knowledge, indeed any genuine knowledge of reality

* *Men of Ideas*, p. 214.

that is achieved by modes of thought that attempt to go beyond the possibility of experience. In doing this it demolishes many of the most important religious and theological claims—and much of the most "important" philosophy—of the last three thousand years. This awesome intellectual achievement caused Kant to be dubbed by one of his contemporaries *Der Alleszermalmer,* which means something like the all-destroyer, the all-pulverizer: "the demolisher of everything." In the history of human thought this is true to a unique extent—and yet at the same time Kant is the most positive and creative of all the great philosophers, the best of all the system-builders, the architect on the grandest scale. In my view he is the supreme understander of the philosophical problem of human experience. Even though he got important things wrong he set philosophy on the right path. He is the supreme clarifier—and as such the supreme liberator.

But so radical was Kant's thinking that we have still not caught up with it, nearly two hundred years after his death, just as most educated people still do not understand Einstein's Theory of Relativity, nearly a hundred years after its publication. I believe I am right in saying that it is still official doctrine in the Roman Catholic Church that the existence of God can be proved. I can see reasons why the Church does not wish publicly to renounce this doctrine, but it must know it to be false. The fact simply is that Kant has demolished the traditional "proofs" of the existence of God. Atheists, however, can take no comfort from this, for the same arguments demolish the intellectual foundations of atheism as well. For the same reasons that we can never know that there is a God we can never know that there is not a God, and people who regard themselves as knowing that there is not a God make exactly the same mistake as people who regard themselves as knowing that there is. One of the most important achievements of Kant's philosophy is that it demonstrates that permanently beyond the reach of human knowledge lies a realm of possibility such that, provided a statement is not self-contradictory, any assertion about what obtains in that realm is capable of being either true or untrue, and we humans have no way of knowing which. But he went on to point out that whereas it is unscientific, if not downright superstitious, to have faith in statements about the empirical world that have not been exposed to the normal tests of experience or observation, statements about the realm which is a realm of possibility only, being of their nature untestable, can be objects solely of faith, either positive or negative, if we are to entertain any degree of belief or disbelief in them at all. In other words, to take on trust something that is capable of being known is a provisional attitude: it is neither the most nor the best that we can do. But to take on trust something that may be true and yet is incapable of being known is indeed the most we can do; and therefore if we have better grounds for believing it to be true than for believing it not to be true, it is not irrational to invest a certain degree of faith in it. There is nothing unscientific about such an attitude, because the question at issue, concerning as it does the untestable, is not a scientific question. It is not a matter of possible knowledge. On a matter of such paramount importance as the existence or non-existence of God we may find it impossible not to incline towards a belief one way or the other, even though we ought to be well aware that we do not and cannot know. In a famous phrase, Kant said that he ruled out knowledge in order to make room for faith. And it has usually been claimed that Kant himself, who destroyed for ever our hope of knowing that God does exist or that we do have immortal souls, believed that God exists and that we have immortal souls.

Speaking for myself, I am more straightforwardly agnostic than Kant is said to have been, less inclined to put my faith in one possibility rather than another—perhaps partly because religion played no role in my childhood, as it so importantly did in his. In so far as I have an involuntary inclination towards one side, it is towards the opposite side from him, against belief in God. But what I feel more positively and powerfully than any such inclination to believe or disbelieve is the reality of unknowable possibility. I have a permanent and vivid sense of this. In a way it seems to me the most important thing about this human life of ours. All the things that are of the greatest importance to us are unknowable—above all whether after this life we shall be plunged into timeless oblivion or go on existing in some way that is unconceptualizable by us until it happens (and perhaps then too). It is *true* that we might have immortal souls, though I am inclined to doubt it. And it is *true* that there might be a God, though I am inclined to doubt that even more. The unknowability of such things is an ever-present reality for me. And of course, speaking selfishly, more for me depends on them than on anything else: above all, my survival or annihilation; and then, depending on that, the ultimate meaningfulness or meaninglessness of my existence. It has always baffled me that so many people are apparently unconcerned by these questions. But it baffles me almost equally that so many others think they know the answers.

I have little intellectual patience with people who think they know that there is no God, and no life other than this one, and no reality outside the empirical world. Some such atheistic humanism has been one of the characteristic outlooks of Western man since the Enlightenment, and is particularly common among able and intelligent individuals. It is the prevailing outlook, I suppose, in most of the circles in which I have moved for most of my life. It lacks all sense of the mystery that surrounds and presses so hard on our lives: more often than not it denies its existence, and in doing so is factually wrong. It lacks any real understanding that human limitations are drastic, in that our physical apparatus must inevitably mould and set very narrow bounds to all that can ever be experience for us—and therefore that our worldview is almost certainly paltry, in that most of what there is almost certainly lies outside it. It is complacent, in that it takes as known what it is impossible we should ever know. It is narrow and unimaginative, in that it disregards the most urgent questions of all. I think that I, like Kant, would go so far as to say that it is positively mistaken in believing that there is no reality outside the empirical realm when we know that there must be, even if we can have no proper understanding of it. Altogether, it is a hopelessly inadequate worldview from several different standpoints simultaneously; and yet it is one that tends to identify itself with rationality as such, and to congratulate itself on its own sophistication. Throughout my life I have found most of its adherents unable to understand that truly rational considerations lead to quite different conclusions. Such people tend on the contrary to take it for granted that anyone who adopts a different view from theirs does so from a standpoint of inadequate, or inadequately rational, reflection or intelligence—perhaps blinkered by convention, or religion, or superstition, or irrationalist beliefs of some more modern kind; or just plain muddle-headedness, if not thoughtlessness. Their attitude is what Schopenhauer called "shallow-pated rationalism." I have found that because its adherents identify it with rationality—and rationality with truth and enlightenment—everything said in rejection of it is misunderstood by them, supposed to come from a standpoint that is not arrived at, and cannot be defended, rationally.

As Voltaire once remarked, "It is the privilege of the real genius, especially one who opens up a new path, to make great mistakes with impunity." The Copernican revolution brought about by Kant was, I think, the most important single turning point in the history of philosophy. For that reason there has been, ever since, a watershed in understanding between those who have taken his work on board and those who have not. For a good many of the problems he uncovered, the solutions he put forward have not stood the test of time, but his uncovering of the problems remains the most illuminating thing a philosopher has ever done. Because of the fundamental character of these problems, and because Kant did not solve them, confronting them has been the most important challenge to philosophy ever since.

Tolstoy—who, if in a quite different way from Kant, was possessed of genius-level understanding of the complexities of human experience—referred once to "genuine philosophy, whose task is to answer Kant's questions."* I agree with that view. And I see Kant as having had one successor in particular who carried his philosophy forward with insights of the profoundest import, namely Schopenhauer. (Tolstoy took that view too.) From Schopenhauer there

---

* In a letter to N. N. Strakhov dated 30 November 1875—when he was in the middle of writing *Anna Karenina.*

is one direct line of succession to Nietzsche, and through him to modern existentialism; another direct line of succession to Wittgenstein, and through him to modern analytic philosophy; and a third to Popper, and through him to an essentially critical and science-based rationalism.* Other schools of thought that go back to Kant but not through Schopenhauer derive from Hegel, either directly or through Marx. Cassirer and Langer were self-aware Kantians, as is Chomsky. The only tradition of thought since Kant whose programme is not in any significant sense Kantian is neo-Humean empiricism; and although that has thrown up outstandingly gifted and interesting individuals such as Mill and Russell, it seems now to be running into the sand.

Until Kant's questions are satisfactorily dealt with (I do not say answered—it could be that a better way of looking at things can be put forward in which they are shown not to arise) they remain obstinately at the head of the agenda. Roughly speaking, it seems to me that we are faced with only two alternatives. Either we regard the fundamental Kantian insights as valid, in which case we must try to make progress on a basis that takes account of them, or we need to show why they are not valid, in which case we can then hope to make progress on the basis of whatever approach it is that successfully explains their erroneousness or inadequacy. What we cannot do is proceed as if we were not faced with this challenge. But precisely that, it seems to me, is what the tradition of neo-Humean empiricism has always done, and continues to this day to do—with the result that even the most intelligent work carried out along those lines is somehow beside the point, for in spite of being gifted it fails to meet the challenges that need to be met before we can make significant progress. There are many respects in which, at the very deepest level, our understanding of the human condition remains where Kant and Schopenhauer left it.

Readers of Chapter One will know that I grew up as a sort of natural Kantian before hearing of Kant, or attaching any accurate meaning to the word "philosophy." So I did not get my disposition to Kantianism from Kant. It was rather that when I discovered Kant I met for the first time a philosopher who was addressing himself to the deepest problems I had. Not only did he acknowledge them where others had omitted to do so, he analysed them incomparably better than I would have been able to analyse them myself, and proposed solutions some of which I found persuasive, others plausible, and nearly all thought-provoking even when I did not go along with them. In other

---

* Popper is a reconstructed Kantian, but with much more originality than that description implies. He once remarked to me: "It was through Schopenhauer that I understood Kant." Since it was also through Schopenhauer that Wittgenstein understood Kant, this means that Schopenhauer has been one of the most important influences on twentieth-century philosophy, while himself languishing unread by most professional philosophers.

words, here was someone who spoke my language, who saw things as I did, someone with whom I felt at home. He spoke not only to me but, surprisingly often, for me. It seemed to me self-evident that I needed to learn what he had to teach me before there was much point in my trying to go beyond him. With the help of subsequent philosophers I have moved quite a long way since, but the direction of my journey is the one he pointed me in, and many of the intellectual foundations of my worldview are in a recognizable sense Kantian. Let me at this point try to state what some of them are.

I believe that within the empirical world, the world of material objects in space and time, the principles of scientific explanation apply. They do not explain everything, but at the level of their applicability there are no limits other than those of the world itself to what they can help us to understand, and we should make active use of them to take us as far as they possibly can. However, the empirical world is the world of actual and possible experience, and as such is subject-dependent. Reality as it is in itself, unconnected with us, cannot possibly be of the character of experience, and therefore, since the only ways we can gain any apprehension of it are dependent on the forms of experience, we cannot apprehend or understand it. So independent reality is hidden. This in turn means that the empirical world cannot be all there is. We know this to be a fact for another reason, unconnected with this, namely that we have direct and unmistakable experience of initiating movements of our bodies at will, and this means that we know for certain that some of the movements of some of the material objects in the world do not have their complete explanations in terms of the laws of physics, although we remain at a loss to know how they are to be explained. Personally, I think that our immediate experience leaves no room for doubt that these things are so, but I am forced to take account of the fact that there are people who argue that the conviction we have of possessing free choice is a delusion; and because there are such people it becomes necessary to point out that we have confirmation of the existence of free will independently of our direct experience of it, since if we attribute any significance at all to moral terms, or to evaluative terms in so far as they refer to human behaviour (and I believe that in practice it is impossible for a human being not to), then that fact by itself commits us to asserting the existence of free will. So our knowledge that the empirical world is not the whole of reality is over-determined. For this reason, and especially because I have direct and perpetual experience of it as a fact throughout my waking life, I am unable seriously to regard it as being in doubt.

The Kantian account up to this point is a clearly recognizable description of reality as I find it to be in my direct experience of living. Included in this direct experience is the fact that we ourselves as human beings are partly in the empirical world and partly not. Our bodies as material objects inhabit the empirical world. However, there is a part of our selves which can initiate movements of our bodies at will, independently of the laws of physics (though not, of course, contrary to the laws of physics) and which must therefore be outside the empirical world. How it does it—what the relationship is between the willing me and the physical me—is a mystery that has baffled understanding since the beginning of human enquiry. But although I do not know what I am, I know that I cannot be only my body. I know myself to be a being that somehow combines the empirical and the non-empirical. In fact I am, so to speak, the embodied interface between the empirical and the non-empirical. Somewhere within the totality of whatever it is that I am, these two interact, and initiatives pass, or co-relationships exist, between one and the other. Questions about the nature of this connection—and, following on from those, questions about the nature of the non-empirical—are the most urgent and compelling of the questions we are left facing by the end of our study of Kant's philosophy. They are questions that Schopenhauer took up and tried to answer. That he did so, and the degree of originality and success with which he carried out the task, make him Kant's lawful heir.

There are some important things in Kant that I do not go along with. I have made no mention of his ethics, because it has never seemed to me even plausible that rationality could be the foundation of ethics, and this is the fundamental principle of Kant's moral philosophy. His aesthetics do not, in my view, get us far enough to be interesting. My conception of the nature of science is radically different from his. And whereas according to Kant the three overridingly important topics of transcendental metaphysics are God, immortality and freedom, I have never been able to feel very seriously engaged with the first two. I have never shared Kant's belief in God, and I do not see what such a belief would explain, since the existence of God would then itself require explanation. There is nothing I would love more dearly than to believe that I have an immortal soul, and it is possible that I have, but I have never been able to persuade myself as far even as a fifty-fifty conviction that it is so. What I do feel compelled to accept, however, is the existence of some measure of freedom, for the reasons I have given. And it seems to me that the trumpeting central insight of Kant's practical philosophy is his perception of the metaphysical implications to which any such acceptance commits us. What seems to me the inescapable fact that I and others sometimes have free choice—even that alone—forces me at the level of argument to the conclusion that an important part of total reality is independent of scientific law. I have to confess that in addition to this I have always been convinced of the same fact by my direct experiences of conscious awareness, of the exercise of choice and decision, of the initiation of willed action, of personal relationships (I have in mind particularly what seems to me the complete impossibility of regarding other people as nothing but physical objects), of sex, and of the arts, especially music. It seems to me self-evident that I live partially in the noumenal all the time I am awake, and perhaps even more so when I am asleep. What frustrates me almost beyond endurance is that it is possible for me to know so little about it.

10

Professional Versus Amateur Philosophy

September 1956 marks a watershed in my life. It was when my prolonged formal education came to an end and my non-academic life began. And it was when I arrived in London to live there for the first time as an independent adult. Since leaving school I had spent a year in Austria, a year in Sweden, a year in the United States, and five years in Oxford. I was now twenty-six. My feeling that I was entering real adult life for the first time was heightened by the fact that within weeks of my return from Yale to England the Suez Crisis erupted, followed immediately by the Russian invasion of Hungary: both these events have been regarded ever since as turning points in the history of the post-war world, and both plunged me immediately into political activity of a highly charged kind.

Within Britain the contemporaneity of the two invasions exposed the true political allegiances of individuals, or so it seemed to me: those who defended Britain's invasion of Egypt yet were outraged by Russia's invasion of Hungary were bigotedly right-wing, while those who defended Russia's invasion of Hungary yet were outraged by Britain's invasion of Egypt were bigotedly left-wing. Those of honest heart and mind were outraged by both. This flushed out those socialists, distressingly many, who had always put up a façade of liberalism and democracy but who now refused to criticize this flagrant act of aggression by the Soviet Union. Worse than that, many of them resorted to Machiavellian tactics aimed at obstructing or obfuscating the condemnation of Russia's behaviour by left-wing organizations and trade unions. It was in connection with these events that I as a member of the Labour Party found myself being swept along on tidal waves of political activity and passion almost immediately on my return to England from the United States. And no doubt it was partly in consequence of this that I was selected as a Labour parliamentary candidate about eighteen months later.

A question I had to face immediately was that of earning my living. And here I ran up against a problem. I did not want a career in the normal sense at all. Writing and politics were two kinds of work, both arduous, that I wanted to sink myself into for their own sakes, and all I could hope was that eventually a livelihood would come to me as a by-product of one of them. But in the meantime I would have to do some third form of work alongside the other two. Whatever this third job was, it would be bound to take me away for much of the time from what I thought of as my "real" work. And there was no point in my thinking about the long-term prospects of whatever the activity was, because as soon as I was able to leave it I would. So I drifted haphazardly—I say haphazardly because my best energies were concentrated all the time on politics and the writing of my early books—via part-time teaching into television, where I discovered that I could make as much money by working half-time as most of my friends earned in their full-time jobs; and that meant that I could share their standard of living and still devote half my working time to writing and politics. A pattern of commitment grew up on this basis which remained the foundation of my working life for most of the time between then and now. After I had achieved a measure of success in television, inducements of money and fame were dangled in front of me to work in it full-time, but I never felt any temptation to accept them. To me, television was a fortunately available way of earning a full-time living in half the time, leaving myself free to devote the other half to work of my own choice, work that I felt powerfully motivated to do. If I had not needed to earn money I would not have spent any time on it at all.

I had a certain envy of people with the self-sufficiency to live a bohemian life and be happy. I would have liked to be one of them. But what I found I actually wanted to do was to live comfortably in central London and go constantly to concerts and theatres; to have enough money to buy books and records; to travel abroad, and go every few years to the Bayreuth and Salzburg festivals. And it was essential for me to combine these activities with devoting most of my time to work of my own choosing. The attraction to me of working part-time for television was that it enabled me to live in this way—and I am not sure that any other form of work that was available to me would have done so. For as the years went by it was borne in on me with more and more strongly expressed feeling by my friends in the academic world that I was at greater liberty to pursue my intellectual interests than they were. Not only were they tied to the treadmills of teaching and administration: *what* they taught was not of their choosing. They had moral obligations to their students: they felt in duty bound to prepare them for the examinations they confronted, and this meant conscientiously teaching them the syllabus as laid down. And, of course, if my friends had to teach certain subjects then they had to keep abreast of those subjects, and this meant keeping up not only with a staunchless flow of academic journals but also every new book that created a stir in one of their fields of concern. So even most of their reading was not what they would have chosen if they had been free. I, by contrast, in what might be called my academic work, had the most precious freedom of all, the freedom not to devote any of my time or energies to matters not of my choosing. I spent no time at all on teaching or academic administration, and every book I read was a book I wanted to read. I could pour my working time and energies into my own enthusiasms for up to half of every year, enthusiasms which embraced not only philosophy and politics but music, theatre, travel, and a number of other interests, with the result that most of them developed rapidly.

It may be that an academic job in central London would have enabled me to live in much the same way, had I been determined enough; but there were two great advantages to my way of life that I could retain only outside academe. One was that it made philosophy not a compartmentalized "subject" but part of the warp and woof of my life, an inherent part of the texture along with, and in among, everything else. The other was that I was independent of intellectual fashions. Readers who have followed me up to this point will understand why both these things were important to me. With regard to the second I always remember Geoffrey Warnock, who spent his whole professional life as a philosopher at Oxford and became Vice-Chancellor of the university, saying: "Philosophers tend very much to take up the subject in the state in which they find it, and to swim contentedly along in the way the stream is going."* Doing what the others do is one of the most striking characteristics of academic life in general.

At any given time, in any major centre, certain topics or problems or (in the humanities) writers are in vogue, and others are out of fashion. Inevitably, the best of the jobs that fall vacant go to people with a reputation for doing good work in the fashionable areas. However indifferent to this an individual may be, he still cannot ignore it if he is in the profession, because he has to prepare his students for examinations, and they will be examined not by him but by others, and it will be the others who set the questions and judge the answers. In any case, his pupils will be, very naturally and properly, curious about contemporary discussions and controversies, and want to be able to take part in

* *Modern British Philosophy,* p. 88.

them. So even a teacher hostile to fashion is compelled to keep abreast of it—and this can be a disheartening burden to someone who feels it to be uninteresting and unimportant.

In general, discussion among colleagues in the same field is essential to what universities are for. In that atmosphere most people, including me, find it impossible to prevent themselves from ingesting some of the consensual priorities. This is illustrated by the fact that during the first flush of independence I still felt it important to keep abreast of what was going on in philosophy in my old undergraduate university, despite the fact that I had been militantly critical of it when I was there. Only after a period of reading what were obviously ephemera, and boring with it, did I realize the full valuelessness of this, and cut loose with a good conscience. That decision has been justified, if further justification were called for, by the fact that nearly all the Austinian and post-Wittgensteinian philosophy that was required reading for students at that time is now read by nobody at all. And in so far as I did read a great deal of it myself I gained almost nothing of lasting value by doing so.

Instead of reading what I came to think of as philosophical journalism I began to read, one after another, those great figures of the past that I had not yet read. In connection with this I developed a habit that grew with the years. If I found myself with a long weekend entirely free, and was in the right mood for it, I would shut myself up with some short philosophical masterpiece and soak myself in it for two or three whole days. Conveniently many of the classics of philosophy are very short: most of the dialogues of Plato, for instance, and some of the more important works of Descartes, Leibniz, Locke, Berkeley, Hume, Marx and Nietzsche. In subsequent years I would take longer works with me on my travels and soak in them for weeks at a time: Kant's *Critique of Pure Reason* during six weeks in the quiet heart of Majorca, the collected dialogues of Plato in Salzburg, Heidegger's *Sein und Zeit* in Bayreuth, the *Confessions* of St. Augustine in Sicily, Hume's *Enquiries* in Sweden, the works of Leibniz on Lake Garda, Pascal in the West of England. It became my favourite way of reading anything important: devoting myself to it full-time, reading all morning entirely without distractions, going for a walk in the early afternoon, reading again in the late afternoon, and then just unplugging and enjoying myself in the evening.

Against an ongoing background of this sort there were two special interests that I pursued during the late 1950s. One was political philosophy. This had been one of my two "special subjects" at Oxford, but I felt a need to revisit it now because I was immersed in political activity and wanted to clarify my thinking about the intellectual foundations of what I was doing. Apart from Popper's work—I re-read *The Open Society,* and read *The Poverty of Historicism* when it came out in 1957—new writing in political philosophy by academic philosophers was more or less worthless. In fact *"Political philosophy is dead!"* was a famous slogan among them at that time. The idea was that political theories as such had now been discredited, the age of ideology was over, practical politics had become a matter of problem-solving within changing institutional frameworks, and there was nothing left for the theoretician to work on beyond a certain amount of further elucidation by linguistic analysis of some of the more important political concepts. Even what you might call the official view was that the subject had become trivial. Given this, it is scarcely surprising that little work of significance was done in it, or that the gifted young were not attracted to it—except for those unfortunates who were seduced into following the Pied Piper of Marxism on what was to be his terminal outing. Some quite intelligent people went that way, but they were never heard of again. Nothing much came of their enthusiasm, and it was not really possible that anything much could.

However, all this left the classics of political philosophy untouched. They stood there like magnificent buildings from the past, still as available for use as they had always been, and made more imposing by the flimsy modern trash that had grown up around them. I read them now from the point of view of someone active in politics, and this led me to get more out of them than I had before. Those from which I gained most were Plato's *Republic,* Aristotle's *Politics,* Machiavelli's *The Prince,* Hobbes's *Leviathan,* Locke's *Second Treatise of Civil Government* and *Letter Concerning Toleration,* Rousseau's *The Social Contract,* Burke's *Reflections on the Revolution in France,* John Stuart Mill's *On Liberty,* Marx's *Das Kapital,* and Popper's *The Open Society and Its Enemies.*

The other special area in which I read was the work of Bertrand Russell. He was a contemporary figure then, high in profile for his activities on the political scene. His most recent contribution to philosophy, *Human Knowledge: Its Scope and Limits,* had been published only shortly before, in 1948. When I was an undergraduate his name was constantly bandied about in philosophical discussions, yet students were not required to read his books—except for those who were specialists in logic, and then it was not his work in general philosophy that they read. He was contemptuously dismissive of Oxford philosophy, openly declaring it to be trivial and boring, and Oxford philosophers in return were politely dismissive of him. They could not dispute his historic significance in the subject, but they talked of him as someone whose work had been important at one time but was now superseded by developments that he had failed to keep up with, namely their own work.

Russell's career as a philosopher is best understood step by step. He began as a mathematician. There is a charming and illuminating story in his *Autobiography* of how, when he was eleven, his elder brother Frank started to teach him geometry (Russell was educated at home until he was fifteen), beginning as usual with the axioms. Young Bertie at once demanded to be given a justification of these. Frank said he couldn't justify them, they just had to be accepted. At this Bertie jibbed. Frank, exasperated, announced that if Bertie refused to accept the axioms they couldn't begin. So eventually Bertie agreed to go along with the axioms *provisionally,* out of curiosity, just to see what followed from them. And what followed "was one of the great events of my life, as dazzling as first love. I had not imagined that there was anything so delicious in the world. . . . From that moment until Whitehead and I finished *Principia Mathematica,* when I was thirty-eight, mathematics was my chief interest, and my chief source of happiness."* His first degree examination at Cambridge was in mathematics, and the immediate reservations he had had about it as a child remained with him. Indeed, he tells us, they "determined the course of my subsequent work." He was profoundly—and, if one may so put it, creatively—puzzled about the foundations of mathematics as such. And it was in this field that he made his first really big contribution to philosophy.

Every argument of any kind whatever, including every mathematical demonstration, has to begin somewhere. It has to have not only a premiss (or premisses), but also a rule (or rules) of procedure. Now those premisses, and those rules of procedure, cannot themselves be validated by the argument, because if they were the argument would be circular—it would be taking for granted what it purported to prove. This means that every argument, every proof, every logical demonstration, no matter how rigorous, must inevitably assume at least one premiss and at least one rule of procedure for which it provides no justification. Someone may say: "Ah yes, but those premisses, and those rules of procedure, are not just arbitrary. They aren't just plucked at random out of the air. In every serious intellectual activity they have been chosen with self-critical care. It is perfectly true that they are assumed by *this* argument, but originally they were arrived at as the conclusions of other, earlier arguments, in which they were supported by a solid foundation of reasoning." But the reply to this is that those other, earlier arguments must themselves have started from unproven premisses, and must themselves have used unsubstantiated rules of procedure. So we find ourselves in an infinite regress. It is impossible ever to get back to arguments that justify themselves. There is no ground-floor of certainty—not on the level of argument, at least. Partly for this reason, philosophers in the empiricist tradition have asserted that all our valid reasoning about what is the case must go back in the end to direct observation or experience, that is to say to something that is known to be true not

* *The Autobiography of Bertrand Russell,* vol. i, p. 36.

because it is the conclusion of a chain of reasoning but because it has been directly experienced. On this view anything that purports to describe reality and yet cannot be traced back eventually to experience is, as it were, floating in mid-air. As Schopenhauer put it in a parallel case: "Concepts and abstractions that do not ultimately lead to perceptions are like paths in a wood that end without any way out."* For people who accept this description as applying to empirical statements there is still a separate question: Does it apply to mathematics? Is it contended that mathematics too is derived ultimately from experience? If it is, the question of what that experience is, or even could be, is a deeply puzzling one. On the other hand, if it is not so contended, then what are the foundations of mathematics—given that no self-sufficient premisses, and no self-justifying rules of procedure, can be established by chains of mathematical reasoning, or by arguments of any other kind?

This was the first great question to which Russell addressed himself. Unheard of by him when he began, a German mathematician who was a generation older than him, Frege, had been working in almost total obscurity on the same problem for many years at the University of Jena—so the young Russell applied himself to years of gruelling work making path-breaking discoveries which, unknown to him, had already been made. Independently, the two men converged on what was essentially the same conclusion, namely that the whole of mathematics was ultimately traceable back to the fundamental principles of logic. Both of them started by attempting to give an actual demonstration of this in the case of arithmetic, and they hoped ultimately to demonstrate it of all mathematics. Russell, indeed, declared openly that this was his aim. So if their idea was correct it would provide a validation of the whole of mathematics as a body of necessary truths deducible, impregnably, step by step, from purely logical premisses.

Russell laid out the groundwork of this theory in his great book *The Principles of Mathematics,* published in 1903. By this time he had, belatedly, discovered Frege, and tribute is paid to Frege in the book. Even so, announcing the reducibility of all mathematics to logic is one thing, demonstrating that reducibility by actually carrying out the reductions is another. Russell attempted to put this latter programme into effect in collaboration with his former tutor, Alfred North Whitehead, in a multi-volume work called *Principia Mathematica.* They worked on it together for something like ten years, and produced three enormous volumes. A fourth was projected but never appeared. Even so, and incomplete though it was, it was an epoch-making work which in the course of time was to make its effect felt across the whole range of philosophy, not only in the field of technical logic.

---

* *The World as Will and Representation,* vol. ii, p. 82.

It did this in more ways than one. Until the nineteenth century, at least, the foundations of logic had remained pretty well in the state that Aristotle had left them in more than two thousand years before. The Preface to the second edition of Kant's *Critique of Pure Reason* bears witness to this. "That logic has already, from the earliest times, proceeded upon this sure path is evidenced by the fact that since Aristotle it has not required to retrace a single step, unless, indeed, we care to count as improvements the removal of certain needless subtleties or the clearer exposition of its recognized teaching, features which concern the elegance rather than the certainty of the science. It is remarkable also that to the present day this logic has not been able to advance a single step, and is thus to all appearance a closed and completed body of doctrine." However, if the whole of mathematics can be shown to follow inevitably from the principles of logic then the whole of mathematics has to be regarded as incorporated in logic. But this is another way of saying that Aristotelian logic, which for all those centuries had been regarded as constituting the whole of the subject, now stood revealed as no more than a corner of it. Under the impetus of this realization an international renaissance of interest in logic took place that has continued to this day. Logic in the newly understood sense inaugurated by Frege and Russell is now actively pursued in every major university in the world.

It was, I think, a natural step for Russell to apply his new logical techniques to statements in ordinary language by asking himself questions of the form: "What exactly is it that we are saying when we say so-and-so?" For example, what exactly is it we are saying when we say "The King of France is bald" when there is no king of France? Are we saying *anything?* Although the example is trivial, there is a serious problem here concerning one of the commonest forms of empirical assertion; and all kinds of scientists, from medical researchers to nuclear physicists, want to be able to talk about possible entities of whose existence they are not yet sure. If my view of the solution is: "There is no such person as the King of France, and therefore the statement refers to nothing at all; therefore it is meaningless," you might plausibly protest: "But look, the statement *The King of Sweden is bald* is false, and must therefore be meaningful. Are you going to tell me that somebody has got to know (which lots of people don't, obviously) whether or not Sweden has a king before he can understand that statement at all, i.e., before it is even meaningful? Obviously that's nonsense. The fact is we all understand the statement perfectly well, regardless of whether or not we happen to know if Sweden has a king." But then if I allow that the statement *The King of France is bald* is meaningful, I am faced with a new dilemma: is it true or false? I do not see how it can be true to say that the King of France is bald if there is no king of France. But I do not immediately see how it could be said to be false either.

Does that mean I am driven to the view that there can be meaningful factual statements that are neither true nor false? I shrink from the thought of the can of worms that would be opened by any such admission. To cut a long disquisition short, Russell carried out a famous analysis of all statements of the form *The so-and-so is such-and-such* in an article "On Denoting," published in 1905, in which he concluded that the hidden logical structure of these statements can be expressed as: "There exists something which is unique in being the King of France and which is also bald." When expressed in this way the statement is exposed as false if there is no king of France. So Russell's analysis reveals the true logical structure of a common form of expression when this was far from being obvious in the first place, and thereby puts us in the position of being able to establish its truth or falsity, which we were not able to do before.

The implications of this new kind of analysis for our attempts to formulate true statements about the world were of historic significance. It opened up whole new vistas of possibility for us in our attempts to clarify and validate our beliefs. It launched a development that has dominated philosophy in the English-speaking world for most of the twentieth century, namely the analysis of statements with the purpose of bringing to the surface their unobvious logical structure, or unobvious distinctions of meaning contained within them. In this sense Bertrand Russell is the founding father of modern analytic philosophy. If every positive philosophical doctrine he ever proposed were to be rejected and forgotten he would still remain an important figure in the history of philosophy because of this. But as against many of his successors, about him there are two points that need to be driven home. First, he never regarded analysis as an end in itself. He put it forward as a method, a way of making crystal clear to ourselves what our statements really mean, or what accepting them would commit us to, so that we can accept or reject them with a fuller awareness of what it is we are doing. He took it for granted that this is worth while only with important statements, or with statements of a kind that baffle us, the aim always being to clarify our understanding of the world, of reality, of the way things are. Only if it matters to us whether a statement is true or false is there any point in our bringing such rigorous techniques to bear on it, and then the importance of the statement has to lie outside the process of analysis itself, unless the whole activity is to be viciously circular. It cannot be that the statement is important to us *because* we are analysing it: we can only be analysing it because it is important to us. Import cannot derive from analysis, though it can be brought out by analysis. An activity that consisted of analysis for no purpose outside itself would be without significance.

This leads to the second point that needs to be driven home about Russell: he could never make sense of a view of philosophy that saw it as consisting of analysis alone, and he could never see how any serious-minded person could take that view. To the end of his days he believed that the purpose of philosophy was what it had always been thought to be, namely the understanding of the true nature of reality, including ourselves. Work in widely differing intellectual fields could contribute to this understanding: the sciences, history, literature in many languages, psychology, and a great many other things. Because of this Russell took a spontaneous interest in these and many other subjects, and was a natural, unaffected polymath. As a matter of fact he was dogged for most of his life by the thought that he ought to have been a scientist. When he saw the sheer scale of the extension of our understanding of reality brought about by the work of Einstein he felt dissatisfied with his own achievement. But the fact remains that although he could easily have become a scientist—his understanding of modern physics was profound, and he had as great a mastery of mathematics as any physicist—he chose not to. And I think the reason why this is so is that what he was really in search of, in the end, was philosophical understanding. If he had become a scientist I think that sooner or later he would have embarked on the same programme with respect to science as he had done with respect to mathematics, namely an attempt to discover and establish its theoretical foundations. He might have become a great philosopher of science, but I doubt whether he would have done the sort of work that Einstein did.

Russell understood clearly—what many people to this day fail to understand—that science of itself does not, and never can, establish a particular view of the ultimate nature of reality. What it does—and this is one of the supreme cultural as well as intellectual achievements of mankind—is reduce everything it can deal with to a certain ground-floor level of explanation. Physics, for example, reduces the phenomena with which it deals to constant equations concerning energy, light, mass, velocity, temperature, gravity, and the rest. But that is where it leaves us. If we then raise fundamental questions about that ground-floor level of explanation itself, the scientist is at a loss to answer. This is not because of any inadequacy on his part, or on science's. He and it have done what they can. If one says to the physicist: "Now please tell me what exactly *is* energy? And what are the foundations of this mathematics you're using all the time?" it is no discredit to him that he cannot answer. These questions are not his province. At this point he hands over to the philosopher. Science makes an unsurpassed contribution to our understanding of what it is that we seek an ultimate explanation of, but it cannot itself be that ultimate explanation, because it explains phenomena in terms which it then leaves unexplained.

To many working scientists, science seems very obviously to suggest an ultimate explanation, namely a materialist one; but a materialist view of total reality is a metaphysics, not a scientific theory. There is no possibility whatsoever of scientifically proving, or disproving, it. The fact that it is held by many scientists no more makes it a scientific theory than it can be said to be an economic theory because it is held (no doubt) by many economists. Science is compatible with metaphysical outlooks of widely differing and mutually incompatible kinds. Some of the most path-breaking of twentieth-century scientists, including Einstein himself, have believed in God. The founder of quantum mechanics, Schrödinger, was attracted by Buddhism. For the individual there is not, and never has been, a conflict between fully accepting the claims of science and holding non-materialist beliefs. The realization that this is so seems to be spreading at last, though the number of people who assume the contrary is still large. For Russell the realities of this situation meant that no amount of personal scientific achievement would have taken him to the level of understanding that he hoped to penetrate. That, I am sure, is why he remained a philosopher. And as such he spent half a lifetime trying to provide satisfactory foundations for the view that the ultimate level of philosophical explanation of known reality is in terms of the philosophy of science and the philosophy of logic. He never succeeded. In fact, he failed separately with science and with logic.

In 1931 Gödel published his famous proof that in any consistent formal system it is possible to formulate propositions whose truth or falsity is undecidable without reference to criteria outside the system. This dealt a death-blow to our hopes of being able to establish a coherent and self-contained explanation of anything, let alone everything. Even if Russell and Whitehead had succeeded in reducing all mathematics to the principles of logic, that would still have left over, remaining outside the system, the validation of the principles of logic. And in fact Russell and Whitehead knew long before Gödel published his theorem that they had not succeeded in their aim. However, every great philosophy is a false theory which, despite being inadequate, has a lot to teach us. This is certainly true of the work contained in *Principia Mathematica*—and even more so of its application to the analysis of statements in natural languages.

Because mathematics and logic engrossed Russell until his late thirties it was not until the year in which he became forty that he published his first book of general philosophy. This was a short work called *The Problems of Philosophy,* published in the Home University Library in 1912 and intended as a popular introduction. To my mind it is a model of popularization in one specific respect: it is intelligible to the beginner while at the same time containing new ideas, and therefore is of interest and importance to the specialist as well. However, his next book—published in 1914 with the all-suggestive title *Our Knowledge of the External World as a Field for Scientific Method in Philoso-*

phy—remains for me his most fascinating single book of general philosophy. He continued to produce book after book—*The Analysis of Mind,* 1921, is of particular interest—until a long period came when his energies were diverted from philosophy into the popularization of left-wing social and political ideas. He continued to write books during this period, but they were crusading journalism. They had enormous influence, contributing to the personal development of some of the ablest members of rising generations; but in the nature of the case they are not of lasting interest. In the latter part of his intellectual career he returned to philosophy and produced three outstanding books: *An Enquiry into Meaning and Truth,* 1940; *Human Knowledge: Its Scope and Limits,* 1948; and *My Philosophical Development,* 1959.

It was not new for a philosopher to write a book about his own books. Perhaps the most familiar example remains that of Nietzsche, with his *Ecce Homo,* but the best I know is Russell's *My Philosophical Development.* Before I read it I expected it to be a lightweight work, an attempt at popularization, a very old man's reminiscent musings. (Russell was eighty-seven in the year it was published.) None of this is so. It is a solidly constructed, stylishly written, substantial work aimed at the serious student of philosophy and, while possessed of all Russell's legendary clarity, makes no concessions to a reader's possible ignorance. It is as if Russell had stepped three paces back and taken a clear, fresh look at his whole life's work, not just summarizing it accurately but tracing its developments clearly, and commenting on them with a rare perceptiveness. Containing as it does the fruit of more than sixty years of unusually hard thought it is packed with intellectual nourishment. It has, too, the advantage of privileged authoritativeness: if Russell says that the main thing he had been trying to get across in such-and-such a book was *p,* or that what he had really meant when he had said so-and-so was *q,* it is not the same as if someone else says it, and should in normal circumstances put paid to dispute about the matter. The book is an underrated one and will in the course of time, I suspect, come to be much more highly valued than it is now.

On the other hand Russell's *History of Western Philosophy,* published in 1946, is overrated. Its account of every important philosopher's work is inadequate even given its limitations of space. The treatment throughout is superficial, not to say flip—for example there are innumerable cracks that are amusing yet do the object of them an injustice, and although this sort of thing can be highly enjoyable in ordinary conversation it is not acceptable when introducing beginners to the subject. Nowhere in the book does Russell *grapple* with ideas, or even treat them with due intellectual and emotional seriousness. For all his genius he radically fails to understand Kant, and consequently the whole tradition of philosophy that has grown out of Kant's work. His entire chapter on Schopenhauer is consistent with his never having read that philosopher's main work. It is true that the book could have been written only by somebody with a vast store of historical and philosophical knowledge, but it is a farrago.

Russell himself was taken aback by its success. He had produced it casually. While he was doing so it never entered his head to think of it as an important book. He looked on it as a potboiler, a way of putting to further use a mass of notes he had accumulated for his adult-education classes. There was a period in his life when he was in the United States and unable to return to England because of the Second World War, but also unable to get a university job in America because a court there had judged that his published views on sexual behaviour made him unfit to teach the young. He needed to earn his living, so he was forced into adult education, in Philadelphia. And the enduring result was his *History of Western Philosophy.* In my view its having been conceived from the beginning as adult-education classes explains almost everything about it: its intellectual shallowness, indeed positive shying away from seriousness; its relentless determination to amuse; its declared programme (which is not carried out, and never could be) of relating philosophy to the political and social circumstances in which it is produced; the wildly disproportionate amount of space allotted to Christian philosophy (there, I suspect, may be something that relates to the social circumstances in which the notes for the book were compiled); and its worldwide best-sellerdom. Its unseriousness, combined with its amusingness and clarity, probably commends it to hundreds of thousands of readers who would not actually be prepared to take philosophical problems seriously. There may be others for whom it functions as an intermediate book: it may have the effect of bringing some people to philosophy. On the other hand it may persuade an equal number that philosophy is not worth bothering with, and give others the illusion that they know about it now that they have read the book. Considered on its merits, it is not really worth reading.

The last serious work of philosophy produced by Russell, before *My Philosophical Development* reviewed his output as a whole, was *Human Knowledge: Its Scope and Limits.* I think it was consciously intended as a summation of the position he had finally arrived at in his lifetime's quest for secure foundations for an empiricist view of reality. And it acknowledges that the quest has failed. Whether the reference of the title is conscious or not I do not know, but it has irresistibly Kantian evocations. After most of a long lifetime spent dismissing Kantianism and trying to move philosophical enquiry forward from the point at which it had been left by Hume, Russell feels himself compelled in the end, against his will, to admit that Kant was right, though significantly he does not name Kant in the confession but only Kant's most fundamental doctrine. He admits (his word) that attempts to acquire knowledge of the world are not possible at all unless we bring to them certain "causal principles" or "postulates" which are not *a priori* and yet cannot be derived from experience. It is only after we have done this that we can build up a system of the world exclusively and consistently on empirical principles. He starts the very last paragraph of the book with these words: "But although our postulates can, in this way, be fitted into a framework which has what we may call an empiricist 'flavour,' it remains undeniable that our knowledge of them, in so far as we do know them, cannot be based upon experience, though all their verifiable consequences are such as experience will confirm. In this sense, it must be admitted, empiricism as a theory of knowledge has proved inadequate."

When Kant had been dead nearly a hundred and fifty years this was the conclusion to which an empiricist philosopher of genius was driven after more than half a century of original thought on his own behalf, and in rejection of Kant. What makes it all such a tragedy is that the precise point that it took Russell most of his life to come to, and which he accepted only against his will, was the starting point of Kant's critical philosophy. If only Russell had taken Kant on board as a young man he could have begun his career as a philosopher from the point at which he ended it. Just as in mathematical logic he had devoted several years of hard, independent and deeply original thinking to work that had already been done by Frege, so in general philosophy it took him the whole of a magnificent career to reach the conclusion that empiricism is fundamentally inadequate for a reason given by Kant. The bitterest irony of all is that the philosopher to whom Kant himself directly owed this insight was Hume.

I think that this catastrophe is partly explicable in terms of intellectual history. There has never been a time when the philosophy of Kant gained general acceptance in Britain. The German idealism that dominated philosophy in Cambridge in the late nineteenth century was Hegelian, not Kantian, and the outstanding figures there, such as McTaggart, are rightly known as neo-Hegelians. Russell and Moore were brought up in that tradition. We easily forget that Russell's first published work was neo-Hegelian. It is a negative fact of extreme importance that when he and Moore rebelled against their intellectual background they were rejecting Hegel and neo-Hegelianism without ever having ingested Kant. They regarded themselves as having been through German idealism and come out the other side, but in fact at no time had they ever metabolised Kant into their living tissue. The criticisms with which they rejected German idealism applied to Hegelian philosophy but not, in essentials, to Kant. So in this whole process Kant was the baby that got thrown out with the bathwater. And because the young Russell had not learnt what Kant could have taught him it took him a lifetime of independent thinking to arrive at Kant's starting point. For this reason I doubt whether any of his books will be required reading for philosophy students in the future. Even his path-breaking work in mathematical logic has, inevitably, been superseded by subsequent developments.

In spite of all this, though, there is both pleasure and profit to be got from reading Russell, first of all because his work is sheerly enjoyable in a way that few philosophers have equalled (perhaps only Schopenhauer and Nietzsche since classical antiquity). Regardless of whatever difficulty may be inherent in the subject matter, his writing is always clear, sometimes amazingly so, without this clarity being bought at the cost of self-effacement: on the contrary, there is always a pungent personality in the prose. Whatever he is writing about, the broader background against which what he is currently saying is to be viewed is also conveyed, so that at every point there is a whole *Weltanschauung* present in the writing. It is always elegant and stylish, often funny—and funny philosophy is much to be welcomed. Altogether his writing is, most of it, a delight. Anyone who aspires to write about serious subjects can learn something from Russell, something about how this can be done with a light hand regardless of the technicality or depth of what is being said.

Secondly, Russell is the outstanding example in the twentieth century of a philosopher of the highest gifts trying to make an empiricist programme work. With all the great achievements of Locke, Berkeley, Hume, Mill, and the American pragmatists behind him he struggles heroically through book after book, first pursuing his aim in one way, then in another, each time being forced in the end to the conclusion that this particular attempt is leading him into unacceptable positions or contradictions—as a result of which he then changes tack in the next book, or the next sequence of books. His intellectual honesty in acknowledging and confronting the difficulties to which his own views give rise is exemplary. In fact to accompany him on these journeys is an educational experience for anyone interested in philosophy, the more so as it is pleasurable. In the nature of the case each book is a search that does not arrive at the hoped-for discovery, and is therefore not a statement of a tenable position, not even a position which the author himself would subsequently have wished, in most cases, to maintain. Yet in many respects the body of work as a whole is an object lesson in the ways in which philosophical enquiry should be carried on—and also in what the detailed and specific untenabilities of empiricism are. It is, after all, essential for anyone brought up in the empiricist tradition of the Anglo-Saxon world to know why it has to be abandoned.

Third, Russell is, so far, the most influential philosopher of the twentieth century. It was he who fathered analytic philosophy. He "discovered" the work of the hitherto little-known Frege, and propagated knowledge of it, and interest in it, internationally. It was Russell's work that brought Wittgenstein into philosophy—the young Wittgenstein threw up his studies in aeronautical engineering at the University of Manchester in order to go to Cambridge and study under Russell. Russell was, as I have said, the intellectual godfather of the Vienna Circle, whose members regarded him as having done more than any other individual to set them on the right path. The ablest of them, Rudolf Carnap, addressed himself to the task of constructing an artificial language in which rational thinking could be carried on and which had none of the logical impurities of a natural language; and in doing this he regarded himself as fulfilling a possibility and a need created by Russell. Quine began his professional career by imaginatively extending Carnap's work, and never ceased to revere both Carnap and Russell. When Karl Popper found himself confronting the challenge to stop writing books in his native German and start writing them in English he adopted Russell's prose style as his model. A. J. Ayer hero-worshipped Russell, and consciously imitated not only his prose style but his lifestyle. One way and another, then, Russell had a separate and direct influence on each of the most important philosophers who came after him in the English-speaking world.

Fourth, Russell was one of the outstanding personalities of his age. Like Voltaire in eighteenth-century France, he himself is one of the terms in which the society in which he lived needs to be understood. Grandson of a Prime Minister, whose earldom he inherited, he occupied from the beginning a privileged position in that society, one from which he was accustomed to meeting the famous and fashionable in all sorts of walks of life. He became the outstanding exponent of a certain set of radical-liberal social attitudes, perhaps best exemplified by his pacifist objection to the First World War, and his belief in sexual permissiveness, and in the abolition of censorship. This set of attitudes was not to come into its own until the 1960s, when as a very old man he became the hero of the radical young; but he had been making effective propaganda for it for decades before that, often so far ahead of his time as to be not just shocking but disgusting to contemporaries. He had, indeed, made propaganda for it in every way open to him: by perpetually bombarding people across the abnormally wide range of his personal acquaintanceship, many of them influential; by teaching and lecturing; by writing books and articles; by broadcasting, first on radio, then television; by standing for parliament; by founding a school; and by drawing attention to the work of whoever else held similar views. All this had been done with not only a seemingly unshakable self-confidence but also verve and style, together with that wonderful clarity, and that ever-present humour. He was the supreme prophet, and the supreme articulator, of a way of looking at life that became characteristic of liberal society in Britain in the last third of the twentieth century. It is difficult to see how any future historian of that age will be able to understand it without familiarizing himself with Bertrand Russell.

11

Getting to Know Popper

In the same year, 1959, I became personally acquainted with what I thought were the two best living philosophers in the English language, Bertrand Russell and Karl Popper. When I met Popper he was fifty-six and I was twenty-eight. When I met Russell he was eighty-seven and I was twenty-nine. These differences were to affect how the two relationships developed. Popper became a lifelong friend. Russell I saw quite a lot of for three or four years, but then I shared with many other people the experience of being cut off from him by Ralph Schoenman. Long before he died in 1970 at the age of ninety-seven we had lost contact.

The first time I set eyes on Popper was when he delivered the Presidential Address to a meeting of the Aristotelian Society in London on 13 October 1958. I had seen an announcement of this meeting in a philosophical journal, and was curious to see him in action. At that time there were only two books by him in the English language (compared with a dozen subsequently): *The Open Society* and *The Poverty of Historicism.* They caused me to think of him as a political philosopher, albeit a great one. I had read *The Open Society* twice, and already it had influenced my political thinking more than the work of any other writer. I was curious to see him in the flesh.

The audience, consisting almost entirely of professional philosophers, many of them well known, was seated and waiting when the speaker and chairman entered side by side, making their way along the back of the auditorium and down the centre aisle to the platform. At that moment I realized that

I did not know which of the two was Popper. It was an unsettling experience to be looking at them so closely, knowing that one of them was the person who had influenced me so much, but not knowing which. However, since one was a bulky, self-confident figure and the other small and unimpressive, it looked as if the former must be Popper. Needless to say, it was the latter, the little man with no presence. However, he lacked presence only for so long as he was not speaking—though even then what compelled attention was not his manner but the content of what he said. I listened to his paper utterly engrossed—and to the ensuing discussion with disbelief and dismay.

The address was called "Back to the Pre-Socratics" and appears under that title in Popper's subsequent book *Conjectures and Refutations,* published in 1963. Its main contention is that the only practicable way of expanding human knowledge is by an unending feedback process of criticism. Put like that it might seem self-evident, but the real clout of the thesis lies in what it denies. It denies that we get far if we attempt to base the extension of our knowledge on observation and experiment. Observations and experiments, it contends, play the same role as critical arguments; that is to say, they may be used to test theories, challenge theories, even refute theories, but are only ever relevant in so far as they constitute potential criticisms of theories. The way we add to our knowledge is by thinking up plausible explanations of hitherto unexplained phenomena, or possible solutions to problems, and then testing these to see if they fit or work. We subject them to critical examination, try them out on other people and see if anyone can point out flaws in them, devise observations or experiments that will expose any errors they may contain. The logic of the situation is this: we start with a problem—it can be practical, but it need not, it can be purely theoretical, something we wish to understand or explain; then we use our understanding of the problem plus our powers of insight and imagination to come up with a possible solution; at this stage our possible solution is a theory which might be true and might be false, but has hitherto not been tested; so we then submit this conjecture to tests, both the tests of critical discussion and the tests of observation and experiment—all of which, if they are to be tests at all, must constitute potential refutations of the theory. Hence the title *Conjectures and Refutations,* which encapsulates a whole epistemology.

How the pre-Socratics come into the picture is this. Popper claims it was they who inaugurated the tradition of critical discussion as a consciously used way of expanding human knowledge. Before them, he says, all societies regarded knowledge as something to be handed down inviolate and uncontaminated from each generation to the next. For this purpose institutions came into being—mysteries, churches, and at a more advanced stage schools. Great teachers and their writings were treated as authorities that it was impossible to dispute: indeed, merely to show that something had been said by them was to prove its truth. Dissent, in primitive societies, was normally punishable by death. The upshot of this was that a society's core body of knowledge and doctrine tended to remain almost static, especially if inscribed in writings that were regarded as holy. It was against this historical background that the pre-Socratic philosophers of ancient Greece introduced something wholly new and revolutionary: they institutionalized criticism. From Thales onwards each of them encouraged his pupils to discuss, debate, *criticize*—and to produce a better argument or theory if he could. Such, according to Popper, were the historical beginnings of rationality and scientific method, and they were directly responsible for that galloping growth of human knowledge that characterizes not only ancient Greece but the whole Western culture that has seen itself, since the Renaissance, as the legatee of the ancient world.

There are, of course, two theses here, one a commended method, the other a historical claim. And they are extremely unequal in importance. What matters most is whether the method commended has anything like the power Popper says it has. Compared with this the question who used it first is of very minor significance, and not even logically related to the main question. Whether the pre-Socratics did not use it after all—or whether they did but someone else used it before them—has no bearing on its validity or power. If the method is valid it overthrows an empirical tradition in philosophy of several hundred years' standing, a tradition whose most important single tenet is that all our knowledge of the world must begin with experience. It is therefore, despite appearances, a theory that is radical—revolutionary in a historic sense, and epic in its implications. It demolishes, almost incidentally, hundreds of years of philosophizing. And this was the first time that many of the people in that room, including me, had encountered it. It must be remembered that *The Logic of Scientific Discovery* had not yet been published in English; and although Popper had expounded some of these ideas in other lectures, those lectures were not to become generally available in print until several years after the event I am describing. I was intellectually thrilled by the argument—unable, of course, to know instantly, off the top of my head, whether I could go along with it or not, but finding it brilliantly argued and not at all implausible, perceiving many implications, longing to hear it discussed, and agog to see it pounced on by this particular audience, which contained some of the most distinguished philosophers in Britain (most of whom were identified, and identified themselves, with empiricism).

I simply could not believe it when, in the question and discussion period, not one single person raised this issue or referred to it. The entire discussion, which became impassioned, turned on whether or not this or that particular pre-Socratic philosopher had been correctly represented by Popper, which in turn meant arguing about whether an important fragment might be better understood in a different way, and whether the ambiguities of a key word in the original Greek had been properly accounted for. While this was going on I looked around the room, incredulous. These people were like passengers on the *Titanic* fussing over the deckchairs while the ship approached the iceberg. We had just been presented with a possible turning point in the ongoing history of philosophy, one which would have the effect of relegating to the past the foundations on which many of us had based some of our most important assumptions, and no one in the room was sufficiently interested even to discuss it. As the evening went by, and it became obvious that there was never going to be any discussion of it, I grew angry. This anger stayed with me, and caused me when I got home to write a letter to Popper. In it I said that although the intellectual frivolity of the audience was inexcusable, he himself was partly to blame for what had occurred. Instead of presenting his revolutionary idea head-on, he had presented it indirectly, in the form of a historical claim about the pre-Socratics, and this had misled the audience into thinking that his main thesis was something to do with the pre-Socratics. He had, I went on, made a similar mistake in the way he had written *The Open Society,* with similar consequences. Instead of presenting the most important arguments directly, he had put them forward in the course of discussing other people's ideas, chiefly Plato's and Marx's, with the result that most academics seemed to come away from the book thinking it was about Plato and Marx. He really must stop doing this, I said. His ideas were immensely important, but he was presenting them in a way that almost ensured that they would be misunderstood.

Popper replied, in a letter, that he was currently revising *The Open Society* for a new edition, and said that if I happened to have any criticisms of it that might be incorporated in it he would be pleased to see them. He obviously knew, as I did, that regardless of any inclination he might or might not have to agree with my basic criticism of the book, to accept it would have involved radically restructuring it, and this was not feasible. So I sent him several foolscap pages of detailed criticisms, which were incorporated in the fourth edition. It was after this that he wrote saying he would like to meet me, and invited me to visit him in his room at the London School of Economics, where he was Professor of Logic and Scientific Method.

My chief impression of him at our early meetings was of an intellectual aggressiveness such as I had never encountered before. Everything we argued about he pursued relentlessly, beyond the limits of acceptable aggression in conversation. As Ernst Gombrich—his closest friend, who loved him—once put it to me, he seemed unable to accept the continued existence of different points of view, but went on and on and *on* about them with a kind of unforgivingness until the dissenter, so to speak, put his signature to a confession that he was wrong and Popper was right. In practice this meant he was trying to subjugate people. And there was something angry about the energy and intensity with which he made the attempt. The unremittingly fierce, tight focus, like a flame, put me in mind of a blowtorch, and that image remained the dominant one I had of him for many years, until he mellowed with age.

All this was the grossest possible violation of the spirit of liberalism exemplified and advocated in his writings. Freedom is the heart of liberalism, as the word itself implies; and if you really do viscerally believe in freedom you accept that others have a right to do a great many things of which you disapprove, including the holding of a wide range of opinions with which you disagree. In a word, pluralism—a belief in the acceptance of the coexistence of the incompatible—is of the essence of liberalism. As a liberal in this sense I claim for myself the right to criticize others and argue with them: but if our argument reaches a stage at which we begin to repeat ourselves, then at that point we must usually agree to differ. All my life I have been that sort of liberal—by individual temperament, by education and personal development, and by the good fortune of national inheritance, having grown up in a country in which it is taken for granted that each individual has a right to his own opinion. Emotionally, Popper understood little if anything of this. He behaved as if the proper thing to do was to think one's way carefully to a solution by the light of rational criteria and then, having come as responsibly and critically as one can to a liberal-minded view of what is right, impose it by unremitting exercise of will, and never let up until one gets one's way. "The totalitarian liberal" was one of his nicknames at the London School of Economics, and it was a perceptive one.

I did not approve of this, and as a result all of Popper's early discussions with me were carried on by him in a kind of rage, regardless of the subject matter. Luckily I had a temperament that made me calmer and quicker-thinking the angrier he got. I believe it was this that made him change his behaviour towards me in the end, for he found that in spite of his greater knowledge and intelligence it was as often as not I who ended up in control of the situation. Only so as not to be at a disadvantage in that sense, which was intolerable to him, did he finally give in and accept the brute fact of my intellectual independence. After that moment I got on with him better than all but a small handful of people. In later years he said that in those early meetings I was frequently rude to him, but I do not believe this to be true: after I had grown out of the immaturity of my student days it was seldom my way to be personally rude in controversy. The truth, I think, is that I stood up to his intellectual bullying and hit back hard, and that he was taken aback by this, coming from someone half his age, and he resented it—and then, because he resented it, saw it as offensive.

What kept me coming back in spite of his outrageous attempts to domineer was the sheer bigness of the man, and of everything he had to say. As the biographer of Wittgenstein and Russell, Ray Monk, commented to me thirty-three years later, after his first meeting with Popper: "You knew you were talking to a great philosopher and not just a very clever man." Popper and I talked about problems we had, and addressed the biggest of them because we had them, without self-consciousness or affectation—no hint of Oxford self-consciousness here. Every question was met head-on, yet seen in the context of Western thought since the pre-Socratics, a living tradition that was in the room with us like a presence. There were invisible participants in every conversation: it was as if Plato, Hume, Kant and the rest were taking part in our discussion, so that everything we said had naturally to be referred to them, and then back again to us for our critical and often dissenting responses. In this situation Popper functioned as an independent thinker: he was, as it were, in his element. Everything he said was existentially *his,* something he had thought for himself because he cared about it; and then, driven by the same involvement, had thought through properly from the bottom up. The whole phenomenon had a quite different character from anything I had known. I felt as someone might who, having listened with passionate involvement to some of Brahms's piano music, visits Brahms and finds him composing a new work and impatient to try it out on the next visitor, to get a critical reaction. A visitor who finds himself in such a position may even exert influence by what he says. One quotation to which I drew Popper's attention, and which he put at the front of subsequent editions of *The Open Society,* was Burke's: "In my course I have known and, according to my measure, have co-operated with great men; and I have never yet seen any plan which has not been mended by the observations of those who were much inferior in understanding to the person who took the lead in the business."

A moment ago it came to me naturally to use a musical analogy because—not least on account of his defects of character—I came to see the relationship between Popper and his work as being more like an artist's than an intellectual's. It is quite common for an artist's work to be in some profound way compensatory, and thus to embody what the artist lacks in himself. For example, when Wagner decided to compose *Tristan and Isolde* he wrote to Liszt: "Since I have never in my life enjoyed the true happiness of love, I want to erect a monument to this most beautiful of dreams in which, from beginning to end, this love will for once be properly sated." He composed *Tristan* not because he was immersed in love but because he was not immersed in love. This is characteristic of how a lot of great art comes to be created (and helps to explain why the popular notion that artists are articulating their personal experience is so uncomprehending). The relationship between Popper and his writing has a good deal of this about it. His work is a monument to his deficiencies. Central to his philosophy is the claim that criticism does more than anything else to bring about growth and improvement, including the growth and improvement of our knowledge; yet Popper the man could not abide criticism. His political writings contain the best statement ever made of the case for freedom and tolerance in human affairs; yet Popper the man was intolerant, and did not really understand freedom. The input of the unconscious into anyone's intellectual work is great, but in Popper's case it was altogether exceptional; yet he believed we should put our faith in reason and make that our supreme regulative ideal. This high input of the unconscious into his work is, I am sure, related to its high emotional voltage, and also to the fact that it has the quality of genius. That he failed to live in accordance with his own ideas no more invalidates them than Christianity is invalidated by the fact that most Christians do not live in accordance with that. It is on their own demerits alone that ideas are to be criticized, not on the demerits of the people who profess them. As Schopenhauer put it, it is a very strange doctrine indeed to say that no one should commend any morality other than what he himself practises.

Popper's ideas go so deep, and are so unobviously revolutionary in their consequences, that it is rare to find someone who has a good grasp of them. In any case he is a thinker whom other thinkers tend to know about rather than to know—it is obvious that even most people in the world of professional philosophy have not read most of his books, though they think they know as much about him as they need to. Two or three big ideas are generally associated with his name—falsifiability, the denial that there is any such thing as inductive logic, assaults on Plato and Marx—but knowledge of his work rarely goes beyond that. He has never been in the eye of fashion; and, big though his reputation is, his time has yet to come. My guess is that it will come, though. Just as Wittgenstein's work is an object of special study in universities all over the world half a century after his death, so, I suspect, will Popper's be. And it is well fitted to stand up to this kind of scrutiny, for among its most striking characteristics are richness and wide-rangingness.

Popper considered it a waste of time for a thinker to address himself merely to a topic. If he does so, anything whatsoever that he then chooses to say about it is relevant. At the end there is often a feeling of so-whatness hanging in the air, since no particular problem has been solved, or question answered. The whole procedure is arbitrary. So Popper suggests as a general principle that a thinker should address himself not to a topic but to a problem, which he chooses for its practical importance or its intrinsic interest, and which he tries to formulate as clearly and as consequentially as he can. His task is then manifest, namely to solve this problem, or at least to contribute to its better understanding. This provides criteria of relevance that rule out most of what might be said on the topic in general, criteria by which we are also in a position to say at the end whether the discussion has achieved anything. The thinker's job is to identify a worthwhile problem, and then to propose a possible solution to it, and to perceive the wider implications of his own proposal, and to acknowledge the most powerful possible objections to it, and to provide convincing answers to those objections. Because this is the way Popper himself writes, every page of his work, at least of his best work, is rich in arguments, and always has a specific purpose and a sense of direction. It is always written in response to a challenge, and itself throws out challenges. This makes it not only exhilarating to read but thought-provoking. He achieves this across an extraordinary range of subject matter: the theory of knowledge, politics, sociology, history, the history of ideas, the philosophy of science, physics, quantum mechanics, probability theory, logic, evolutionary biology, the body-mind problem.

The best way to "locate" Popper is to see him as a reconstructed Kantian. To demonstrate this might have involved a lot of lengthy exposition were it not for the fact that there is one particular passage in his published writings in which he traces his own immediate descent from—and also what is in his own eyes his most important difference with—Kant. It so happens that this was not the purpose of the passage, and Popper was surprised when I pointed out to him that it does this, but he agreed that it did. Although the passage is two pages long in the original,* it is worth quoting in full. (Perhaps I should explain that the chapter in which it occurs started life as a radio talk, and it is this that accounts for what would otherwise be the puzzling fact that so many words and sentences are printed with emphasis: he wanted to remind himself to stress them in delivery.)

In order to *solve* the riddle of experience, and to explain how natural science and experience are at all possible, Kant constructed his *theory of experience and of natural science.* I admire this theory as a truly heroic attempt to solve the paradox of experience, yet I believe that it answers a false question, and hence that it is *in part* irrelevant. Kant, the great discoverer of the riddle of experience, was in error about one important point. But his error, I hasten to add, was quite unavoidable, and it detracts in no way from his magnificent achievement.

What was this error? As I have said, Kant, like almost all philosophers and epistemologists right into the twentieth century, was convinced that Newton's theory was *true.* This conviction was inescapable. Newton's theory had made the most astonishing and exact predictions, all of which had proved strikingly correct. Only ignorant men could doubt its truth. How little we

---

* Popper, *Conjectures and Refutations,* pp. 190–2.

may reproach Kant for his belief is best shown by the fact that even Henri Poincaré, the greatest mathematician, physicist, and philosopher of his generation, who died shortly before the First World War, believed like Kant that Newton's theory was true and irrefutable. Poincaré was one of the few scientists who felt about Kant's paradox almost as strongly as Kant himself; and though he proposed a solution which differed somewhat from Kant's, it was only a variant of it. The important point, however, is that he fully shared Kant's error, as I have called it. It was an unavoidable error—unavoidable, that is, before Einstein.

Even those who do not accept Einstein's theory of gravitation ought to admit that his was an achievement of truly epoch-making significance. For his theory established at least that Newton's theory, no matter whether true or false, was certainly *not the only possible* system of celestial mechanics that could explain the phenomena in a simple and convincing way. For the first time in more than 200 years Newton's theory became *problematical.* It had become, during these two centuries, a dangerous *dogma*—a dogma of almost stupefying power. I have no objection to those who oppose Einstein's theory on scientific grounds. But even Einstein's opponents, like his greatest admirers, ought to be grateful to him for having freed physics of the paralysing belief in the incontestable truth of Newton's theory. Thanks to Einstein we now look upon this theory as a hypothesis (or a system of hypotheses)—perhaps the most magnificent and the most important hypothesis in the history of science, and certainly an astonishing approximation to the truth.

Now if, unlike Kant, we consider Newton's theory as a hypothesis whose truth is problematic, then we must radically alter Kant's problem. No wonder then that his solution no longer suits the new post-Einsteinian formulation of the problem, and that it must be amended accordingly.

Kant's solution of the problem is well known. He assumed, correctly I think, that *the world as we know it is our interpretation of the observable facts in the light of theories that we ourselves invent.* As Kant puts it: "Our intellect does not draw its laws from nature . . . but imposes them upon nature." While I regard this formulation of Kant's as essentially correct, I feel that it is a little too radical, and I should therefore like to put it in the following modified form: "Our intellect does not draw its laws from nature, but tries—with varying degrees of success—to impose upon nature laws which it freely invents." The difference is this. Kant's formulation not only implies that our reason attempts to impose laws upon nature, but also that it is invariably successful in this. For Kant believed that Newton's laws were successfully imposed upon nature by us: that we were bound to interpret nature by means of these laws; from which he concluded that they must be true *a priori*. This is how Kant saw these matters; and Poincaré saw them in a similar way.

Yet we know since Einstein that very different theories and very different interpretations are also possible, and that they may even be superior to Newton's. Thus reason is capable of more than one interpretation. Nor can it impose its interpretation upon nature once and for all time. Reason works by trial and error. We invent our myths and our theories and we try them out: we try to see how far they take us. And we improve our theories if we can. The better theory is the one that has the greater explanatory power: that explains more; that explains with greater precision; and that allows us to make better predictions.

Since Kant believed that it was our task to explain the uniqueness and the truth of Newton's theory, he was led to the belief that this theory followed inescapably and with logical necessity from the laws of our understanding. The modification of Kant's solution which I propose, in accordance with the Einsteinian revolution, frees us from this compulsion. In this way, theories are seen to be the *free* creations of our own minds, the result of an almost poetic intuition, of an attempt to understand intuitively the laws of nature. But we no longer try to force our creations upon nature. On the contrary, we question nature, as Kant taught us to do; and we try to elicit from her *negative* answers concerning the truth of our theories: we do not try to prove or to *verify* them, but we test them by trying to *disprove* or to falsify them, to *refute* them.

In this way the freedom and boldness of our theoretical creations can be controlled and tempered by self-criticism, and by the severest tests we can design. It is here, through our critical methods of testing, that scientific rigour and logic enter into empirical science.

It was in relation to the philosophy of science that Popper worked out his most fundamental ideas: that we are never able to establish for certain the truth of any unrestrictedly general statement about the world, and therefore of any scientific law or any scientific theory (it is important to be clear that he is talking not about singular statements but about unrestrictedly general ones: it is possible sometimes to be sure of a direct observation, but not of the explanatory framework that explains it: direct observations and singular statements are always susceptible of more than one interpretation); that because it is logically impossible ever to establish the truth of a theory, any attempt to do so is *an attempt to do the logically impossible,* so not only must logical positivism be abandoned because of its verificationism but also all philosophy and all science involving the pursuit of certainty must be abandoned, a pursuit which had dominated Western thinking from Descartes to Russell; that because we do not, and never can in the traditional sense of the word "know," know the truth of any of our science, all our scientific knowledge is, and will always remain, fallible and corrigible; that it does not grow, as for hundreds of years people believed that it did, by the perpetual addition of new certainties to the body of existing ones, but by the repeated overthrow of existing theories by better theories, which is to say chiefly theories that explain more or yield more accurate predictions; that we must expect these better theories in their turn to be replaced one day by better theories still; and that the process will have no end; so what we call our knowledge can only ever be our theories; that our theories are the products of our minds; that we are free to invent any theories whatsoever, but before any such theory can be accepted as knowledge it has to be shown to be preferable to whatever theory or theories it would replace if we accepted it; that such a preference can be established only by stringent testing; that although tests cannot establish the truth of a theory they can establish its falsity—or show up flaws in it—and therefore, although we can never have grounds for believing in the truth of a theory, we can have decisive grounds for preferring one theory to another; that therefore the rational way to behave is to base our choices and decisions on "the best of our knowledge" while at the same time seeking its replacement by something better; so if we want to make progress we should not fight to the death for existing theories but welcome criticism of them and let our theories die in our stead.

It was only after Popper had developed these ideas to a high level of sophistication with regard to the natural sciences that he realized that their implications for the social sciences were also compelling. A political or social policy is a prescription based to an important degree on empirical hypotheses—"If we want to achieve x we must do A, but if we want to bring about y we must do B." We can never be certain that such a hypothesis is right, and it is a matter of universal experience that they are nearly always flawed and sometimes completely wrong. The rational thing to do is to subject them to critical examination as rigorously as circumstances allow before committing real resources to them, and to revise them in the light of effective criticism; and then, after they have been launched, to keep a watchful eye on their practical implementation to see if they are having undesired consequences; and to be prepared to change them in the light of such negative test-results. Again, the idea is to sacrifice hypotheses rather than human beings or valuable resources (including time). A society that goes about things in this way will be more successful in achieving the aims of its policy-makers than one in which they forbid critical discussion of their policies, or forbid critical comment on the practical consequences of those policies. Suppression of criticism means that more mistakes than otherwise will go unperceived in the formulation of policy, and also that after mistaken policies have been implemented they will be persisted in for longer before being altered or abandoned. On this basis Popper builds a massive structure of argument to the effect that even in purely practical terms, and regardless of moral considerations, a free (or what he calls an "open") society will make faster and better progress over the long term than any form of authoritarian rule. Fundamental to his political philosophy, as to his epistemology and philosophy of science, are the ideas that it is easy to be wrong but impossible ever to be certain that we are right, and that criticism is the agent of improvement.

In politics (as against economics) this is a profoundly original argument, and one whose practical importance is incalculable. Before Popper it was believed by almost everyone that democracy was bound to be inefficient and slow, even if to be preferred in spite of that because of the advantages of freedom and other moral benefits; and that the most efficient form of government in theory would be some form of enlightened dictatorship. Popper showed that this is not so; and he provides us with an altogether new and deeper understanding of how it comes about that most of the materially successful societies in the world are liberal democracies. It is not—as, again, had been believed by most people before—because their prosperity has enabled them to afford that costly luxury called democracy; it is because democracy has played a crucial role in raising them out of a situation in which most of their members were poor, which had been the case in almost all of them when democracy began.

Even this brief sketch will have given some idea what sort of relationship exists between Popper's political and scientific thought. But at the time when I met him this was not generally understood, and I did not understand it myself. This is because his seminal work in the philosophy of science was almost impossible to come by in its obscure pre-war German printing, and was not to appear in an English translation until later that same year, 1959, under the title *The Logic of Scientific Discovery.* It was then exactly a quarter of a century since its original publication in Vienna; but only after its appearance in English did it become generally familiar to philosophers in the post-war world.

The version current today in the German language is for more than half its bulk a translation back into German of the English edition. This unsatisfactory publishing situation is characteristic of Popper's work in general. His first book, *The Two Fundamental Problems of Epistemology,* was not published even in German until forty-six years after it was written, and as I write has not appeared in English yet, so it remains unknown in the English-speaking world. Three books that he wrote in English at the height of his powers— *Realism and the Aim of Science, The Open Universe: An Argument for Indeterminism,* and *Quantum Theory and the Schism in Physics*—languished for a quarter of a century in proof before being published. And some books have not yet been published at all. This excessive tardiness with which Popper's thought has crept out into the light is not unconnected with the tardiness of understanding and appreciation it has met with. Even I, who have a special familiarity with it, was unacquainted with his philosophy of science until after I got to know him personally—so it was only then that I was able fully to understand his political philosophy, despite the fact that I held it in high esteem.

In more ways than one, then, Popper has been his own worst enemy when it comes to the satisfactory propagation of his ideas.

Although I regard Popper as a great philosopher I have, and always have had, fundamental differences with him—as I do, if it comes to that, with every other great philosopher. He himself considered the most important of all philosophical issues to be that between idealism and realism, and he was a realist through and through, whereas I am some sort of transcendental idealist, even if I am not sure *what* sort. The most important experiences we human beings have in life—which I take to be first and foremost our awareness of our own existence, followed by our relationships with one another, especially those involving sex and its consequences, and then our experiences of the arts—are dealt with scarcely at all in Popper's writings; so he simply has not written about what interests me most. Like Kant, he believes that rationality is also the rationale of ethics, whereas I am sure that this is not so. In all sorts of ways, then, he and I are a long way apart in our thinking. The respect in which I am most Popperian is in my approach to political and social questions: there it would be difficult for me to exaggerate how much I have learnt from him. He is, I am sure, a political philosopher of genius. I think he has also made contributions of great profundity to the theory of empirical knowledge, and in particular to the philosophy of science—in fact I agree with Peter Medawar that he is the best philosopher of science there has ever been. These combined achievements make him, I should say, the outstanding philosopher of the twentieth century. But having said that, let me try to indicate where I think his limitations lie.

I hold the greatest single achievement in the history of philosophy to be Kant's distinction between the noumenal and the phenomenal. It embodied a fundamentally new, indeed revolutionary conception of how the limits of intelligibility were themselves to be understood; and although not in itself right, it was on the right lines. Since it constituted the longest forward stride in understanding of the human situation that there has ever been, it is scarcely surprising that in his pioneering formulations Kant made major mistakes. After him, philosophy's most pressing need was for correction of his chief errors, and for further illumination of what the relationship between the noumenal and the phenomenal is. There happens to be a philosopher who offers us these things, namely Schopenhauer, but I was not to discover his work until many years later, and meanwhile had an entirely mistaken idea of what sort of philosopher he was—I imagined him to be something like Hegel. Since in Britain virtually no professional philosophers read Schopenhauer he was scarcely ever referred to, so this mistaken assumption of mine was to continue uncorrected for many years. After studying Kant I knew what I was looking for, but did not realize how great a deal of it was already available. It was obvious that Popper did not provide it. He corrected one very important error of Kant's, the one dealt with in the long quotation on pages 186–8; and to a significant extent Popper's original contribution to epistemology consisted of his expansion of this insight, as he himself fully realized. But at no point does he write as if he believes in the existence of the noumenal in a sense relating to Kant's. He does, indeed, believe that reality is hidden, and permanently so, but he believes that this hidden reality is transcendentally real.

Kant was an empirical realist but a transcendental idealist: Popper is an empirical realist and a transcendental realist also. His epistemology centres on the relationship between what he takes to be a transcendentally real but not directly accessible material world (which exists independently of us) and the knowledge we human beings have of it (which is a human creation). He has thus given himself a new formulation of the classic and insoluble problem at the heart of empiricism. Because I believe that the empirical world is almost certainly transcendentally ideal I do not believe that Popper has effectively written about what he supposes himself to have written about. What I believe he has done is to provide a profoundly original and substantially correct analysis of the nature of empirical knowledge whose true place, unrealized by him, is within a larger *empirical realism/transcendental idealism* frame of reference, the necessity for which he does not acknowledge. In other words I think he has performed, better, one of the tasks the young Wittgenstein set out to accomplish in the *Tractatus,* even though Wittgenstein had greater self-awareness about the wider context in which what he was doing was embedded. Wittgenstein consciously took over from Schopenhauer the Kantian *empirical realism/transcendental idealism* view of total reality, and acknowledged that nearly all of what mattered most to us inhabited the transcendentally ideal part of it, within which nothing could be known and therefore no factual propositions asserted. Within this total frame of reference he tried to set the knowledge available to the human inhabitants of the empirical world on a philosophically defensible footing. He fully acknowledged how little would have been done when that had been done, but in spite of that he did not succeed in doing it, as he himself came eventually to acknowledge. Popper has had much greater success at the same task, though he does not see it as being the same task, because he does not accept the metaphysical framework. He does not so much reject as ignore the Kantian distinction which I regard as Kant's greatest achievement.

The reason why Popper's epistemology is able to be so successful in spite of what I consider an inadequate and mistaken metaphysics lies in the fact that he, like Kant and Schopenhauer, fully understands that ultimate reality is hidden and unknowable. The fact that he takes this view for reasons entirely different from theirs is beside the point. The crucial fact is that he does not see knowledge as attached to reality, or even as being in direct contact with it, and it is this that makes it possible for his account of knowledge to be painlessly removed from a framework in which ultimate reality is seen as transcendentally real and incorporated in a framework in which it is seen as transcendentally ideal. For these purposes it does not matter that the ultimate reality that Popper regards knowledge as condemned for ever to fall short of is a material world existing independently of our experience, whereas both Kant and Schopenhauer regard it as being an un-get-at-able level of non-material reality that stands *behind* the material world, something the material world hides from us, screens us off from, while being at the same time some sort of manifestation of. It is enough that Popper regards independent reality as something which human knowledge can approach only asymptotically, never to grasp or make direct and immediate contact with. This, as I say, renders his epistemology accommodatable within the *empirical realism/transcendental idealism* frame of reference, within which the ultimate reality with which it fails to make contact can be viewed as something different from what he takes it to be. In this crucial respect the underlying Kantianism of his epistemology saves it, and what is more is the chief source of its formidable explanatory power.

Taken on his own terms, what Popper has done is combine a fundamentally empiricist view of reality with a fundamentally rationalist view of knowledge—an empiricist ontology with a rationalist epistemology. Because he believes above all that knowledge is a product of our minds which has then to withstand and survive all the tests of confrontation with an independently existing empirical reality, the term he has coined for his own philosophy is "critical rationalism." It is worked out on such a scale, and yet in such detail, that it constitutes an intellectual achievement of the front rank. It is the most highly developed philosophy yet to have appeared that incorporates within itself a belief in an independently existing material world subsisting in independently existing space and time. It constitutes a huge advance beyond Russell, and embodies a depth of originality and imagination altogether outside Russell's scope. Anyone who is determined to cling to the empiricist tradition will find in Popper's philosophy the richest and most powerful instantiation of it that the ongoing development of Western philosophy has made available to us so far. At the point we have reached around the year 2000, to be a self-aware and sophisticated empiricist has to mean either being a Popperian or being a critical and reconstructed Popperian. And to be any sort of transcendental idealist ought to involve embracing something like a Popperian account of empirical reality. On either presupposition, he is the foremost philosopher of the age. On the first presupposition his work is itself the cutting edge of philosophical advance. Seen in the light of the second presupposition it appears somewhat incidental ("how little has been done when that has been done") but is still of significance, and a great improvement on the *Tractatus.*

The thing I tried hardest to get Popper to do, without success, was to bring his mind to bear on the interface between the phenomenal and the noumenal, perhaps even to indulge in what could only be temperament-based conjecture about the noumenal. But trying to get a creative person to do something different from what he does is hopeless, unless he feels within himself already the impulse to change direction. His creativity is not under the direction of his own will, let alone anyone else's. My motivation, mistaken though I may have been, was this. It seemed to me that what made Kant's philosophy uniquely great was that he for the first time delineated the limits of all possible experience and showed that although the content of our experience is determined by what there contingently is and what contingently happens, its forms, its structure, and its limits are determined by the nature of our apparatus; and so long as we are human beings at all this is a constant that cannot be transcended. The fact that he was mistaken in his specification of what some of the factors are, or how they work, creates a need for revision of his philosophy, but leaves his fundamental insight intact. And ever since Kant the most compelling issue in philosophy has been this question of the limits of intelligibility. One could give innumerable illustrations of this—it was the subject of Wittgenstein's *Tractatus,* the central preoccupation of the logical positivists, the title of Russell's last and culminating philosophical work, *Human Knowledge: Its Scope and Limits.* As the central question of Western philosophy, "What can I know?" goes back to Descartes, but Kant set it in a new light that has cast brilliant illumination on it ever since. It seems to me that if philosophy now can be said to have a most important single task it is to work on these limits and enrich our understanding of what they are and why they are limits—and perhaps even (greatest prize of all) by means of such increased understanding to occupy territory near the frontier which is at present unoccupied because we do not know where the frontier is, and thus extend our philosophical knowledge at the highest possible level. This is, after all, what Schopenhauer did; and the fact that it has been done once offers hope that it may be done again. It may be done more than once: there may be several great advances to come in philosophy, each of which will consist in just such an extension. And of course there may be other kinds of advance too.

In Popper I thought I saw the only contemporary who might possibly have the ability to accomplish this. So I tried to persuade him to address himself to the task. But my attempts were in vain. Since it was a fundamental tenet of his philosophy that reality is unknowable, he agreed that there must be some sort of no-man's-land within which what we know ends and reality begins; and that whether it was actually a fixed frontier (as Kant believed) or a perpetually moving one (as he believed) was a separate question. But it remains a striking fact that the things that are most important of all to us, which Kant (and for that matter also the Wittgenstein of the *Tractatus*) saw as rooted in the world of the unknowable—the meaning of life as a whole, the meaning of death; morality; values; the significance of art—are things that Popper has not written about, or at any rate not very much. Their supreme importance for us is something he not only conceded but asserted, and he was dismissive of so-called philosophers who denied their philosophical significance. Other philosophers, he said, might very well have something new and important to say about them: the only thing was, he did not. So he got on with work on the problems about which he did have something to say—and these were in any case the problems that fascinated him. It was this in the end that prevented him, I think, from being a philosopher in the Kant and Schopenhauer class. Unlike them, he did not offer us a view of total reality within which empirical reality was a part but not the whole. All his work was enclosed within the unattainable horizons of the empirical realm. Even the question of whether or not there is anything beyond those horizons was one to which he did not address himself, believing it to be inherently unanswerable. So he takes his place alongside those philosophers who have philosophized as if the empirical world were all there is. Having said that, I must add that I regard him as being as good as all but the very best of these (the best, I take it, being Hume and Locke).

This question of whether or not there is anything that lies permanently outside the range of all possible knowledge is one on which Popper remains unbudgingly agnostic to the end of the road. We simply cannot know, he says, and it is pointless to have an opinion in the matter one way or the other. It is possible that there is something, obviously, and anyone who denies that possibility is wrong; but it is possible that there is not, and anyone who denies that is wrong too. And there is no point in speculating, because we do not have even the concepts with which to do the speculating. The nature of concepts is such that if they are to have genuine content about what is or might be factually the case they need to be derived, if only indirectly, from somebody or other's experience, and no such concepts of the kind we are now talking about could be so derived.

From that point onwards the gap between Popper and me becomes one of personal temperament. I feel an ungovernable urge to grapple with these unanswerable questions: I am, whether I like it or not, infuriatingly baffled and perplexed by them, and cannot leave them alone; and because of this I am involuntarily involved with them, enmeshed in them; and there is a high energy-charge involved. With Popper none of this is so. Having satisfied himself that certain questions are unanswerable he is able with almost Buddhistic calm to turn his back on them and not think about them. His temperament has inclined him to proceed on the basis of what can be known (in his conjectured and testable sense of the term "known"); and so he has proceeded *as if* there were no more to total reality than what can be known. For instance, he has proceeded *as if* all morality and values are human creations—one of the respects in which he is most Kantian of all is in his insistence on viewing morality as an instantiation of rationality. Even so, he not just admits but argues at some length that in the last resort it is impossible to put rationality itself on rational foundations. When all analysis has come to an end, our belief in rationality is an act of faith, and an act of faith that can be justified, if at all, only by our success in meeting criticisms and surviving tests. He does not believe in ultimate foundations, neither for morality, nor for rationality, nor for knowledge, and his philosophy asserts that they do not need to be postulated in any of these fields. "Man has created new worlds—of language, of music, of poetry, of science; and the most important of these is the world of the moral demands . . ." (*The Open Society and Its Enemies,* vol. i, p. 65). This means he has to be ready to account for the existence of such things as human creations. He does in fact believe that they develop, like human knowledge, by processes of negative feedback in which perpetually revised attitudes and expectations are unendingly exposed to confrontation with experience, and changed again; that there is no more a beginning to this process than there is an answer to the question "Which came first, the chicken or the egg?"; and that there need be no end to it either. So although he regards values as instantiating human decisions, and not as being ultimately defensible in rational terms, he does not rest on a simple utilitarian analysis. Just as he had demolished the Verification Principle of the logical positivists and come up with falsifiability, not as an alternative but as a principle of something else, so he demolished the utilitarian principle that "the greatest good of the greatest number is the foundation of morals and legislation" and came up with "minimize avoidable suffering," not as the foundation of anything, since he does not believe in foundations, but as the first rule of thumb in the perpetually ongoing formulation of public policy.

There are some unknowable things about which Popper does have negative beliefs, by which I mean that there are things he does not see any grounds for believing, and therefore does not believe. In this sense he does not believe that there is a God, and he does not believe that our selves survive our deaths. Of himself, he said that he had no wish for an existence after his bodily death; and he thought that people who yearned for one were rather pathetic egotists— perhaps, as it were, collective egotists who failed to appreciate the near-nothingness of humanity in the cosmic scheme of things.

If there could be said to be one insight that pervaded Popper's metaphysical outlook as a whole it might be expressed in the words "We don't know anything." He regarded the special greatness of Socrates, and such figures as Xenophanes, as lying in their grasp of this. If one is in search of a reason why he did not, for all his gifts, address himself to some of the most important questions in philosophy, it lies here: he did not feel that he had anything to say—or at least not enough, and not enough that was new—about the problems involved. He once made a remark about Moore and mathematics that applied to himself on many important subjects. "First of all, Moore knew some mathematics. He didn't write about it because he didn't know enough, and he had no original ideas in the field. But he knew enough mathematics to understand quite a bit of what Russell was doing, and he even published some criticism of Russell's logic. . . ."* (Incidentally, in Popper's case it was not by him but by Imre Lakatos that his ideas were given their most fruitful application to mathematics. And when challenged to say why he had written so little about the arts, when in his intellectual autobiography he made it clear that considerations of music played a seminal role in the development of his fundamental idea about problem-solving, he replied that Ernst Gombrich had made a more imaginative and better-informed application of his ideas to art than anything he could have done himself.)

Our discussions and arguments about these questions were among the most interesting conversations I had with Popper over many years. After our first few meetings at his office in the London School of Economics he asked me to come instead to his home in Penn, Buckinghamshire, where we could talk at greater length and leisure. I would go there every three or four months, arriving either just before or just after lunch, and leaving in the late afternoon or early evening. Between these meetings we talked frequently on the telephone, sometimes several times a week.

When he first gave me directions about how to get to his home he told me I should take the train from St. Marylebone to Havacombe and then get a taxi. I had never heard of Havacombe, but saw no reason to anticipate difficulty. However, when I tried to buy the ticket at St. Marylebone they told me there was no such station as Havacombe. Only in the ensuing discussion did it emerge that what Popper had been saying was High Wycombe. From High Wycombe station the taxi was driven then, and for many years subsequently, by a driver of Greek extraction called Plato. He always asked with a great show of interest after "the Professor." A typical exchange between him and me was:

"What's the Professor working on these days?"

"He's writing an autobiography."

"Really? What about?"

* *Modern British Philosophy,* p. 137.

Usually, as soon as I entered the house, Popper would grab me by the arm and plunge with almost fearsome energy, but also bubbling enthusiasm, into whatever problem he was currently struggling with. Unless it was raining he would head straight out into the garden without the slightest pause in his flow of words, and there we would pace around slowly, he frequently pulling the two of us to a dead stop as he tightened his grip on my arm and stood there gazing fiercely into my eyes while he vehemently urged some point on me. His emotional input into these disquisitions was something of a phenomenon: "blazing intensity" would not be an excessive term for it. Not only was he existentially engaged with his problems: they had taken him over, he was living them from the inside. His expositions of them, and his urgings of their significance, were exhilarating. But his criticisms of his own first attempts at solving them could also be devastating. However, if I criticized him, or disagreed with him, he would become enraged. In that same conversation he would never yield, though weeks or months later he would sometimes revert to what I had said, and remark, as if we had not previously discussed it, that there was something to be said here that was interesting and strong. Occasionally he would then come round to my point of view. More often he would (as in his books) produce a substantially improved version of my case, on which it was obvious he had spent a good deal of trouble and thought, and then attack it savagely. When this happened I often got the impression he was saying what he wished he had thought of on our first encounter—he had not, so to speak, done my case enough damage the first time round and was now putting that right. These discussions stretched me to my limit, and I became uninhibited about hitting him with all the artillery I could muster. Needless to say, I won fewer battles than I lost. In competitive games the sort of opponent we most enjoy playing is one who forces us to give our utmost but whom we usually beat, and I believe Popper saw in me that sort of opponent. The degree of resistance I offered him was just about right for his needs: I forced him to give his all while only rarely inflicting on him what he felt to be significant setbacks. Although he turned every discussion into the verbal equivalent of a fight, and appeared to become almost uncontrollable with rage, and would tremble with anger, there is no doubt that he found a deep satisfaction in it all. He was always keen for us to meet again for more.

I discovered on these visits that there was almost nothing to be gained by my raising any matter in which Popper had not at some time in his life been involved. If I talked about what I had recently been doing myself, apart from philosophy—friends, music, theatre, travel, the current political situation—his lack of interest was unconcealed, and if I persisted he would find an excuse to bring our meeting to an early close. He needed to talk about what directly involved *him,* and could sustain interest only in what he himself had done at some time or other, or was currently doing. For a long time I thought that nothing of importance was lost by this, because the white heat of his involvement always gave the objects of his enthusiasm compelling interest for me, even if they were matters in which I had not been involved myself. For example, my interest in the philosophy of science had been ignited at Yale by Pap and Northrop, who had given me a grounding in it, but when I met Popper I was not actively pursuing it. However, the discussions of it I had with him over many years, combined with my study of his output on the subject, plus the sources his writings referred to, gradually gave me a first-class education in it. But in the long run I realized that although I learnt so much from him, a high price was paid for the exclusive intellectuality of our relationship, and the fact that it focused so much on his concerns and so little on mine. After thirty years of such meetings he knew almost nothing about my life, had met scarcely any of my friends, had never been to my home. And he was in this situation with regard to almost everyone he knew apart from the Gombriches, his lifelong friends. Yet he seemed unaware of this self-centred cut-offness. When he read my published memoir of Deryck Cooke, who died much too young after integrating Mahler's posthumous sketches with incredible skill into what is now the standard performing version of his tenth (and arguably greatest) symphony, Popper said wonderingly: "This man was obviously a master: why have you never talked to me about him?" The truth is that Popper was always snortingly dismissive of Mahler ("He never grew up beyond the age of sixteen") and if I had talked to him about Deryck's work he would have demonstrated his boredom and changed the subject. That was precisely the sort of thing that my experience of him had taught me not to do.

Popper said more than once that in all the years he had lived in England he had never been invited into anyone's home. I knew this to be false because I had invited him myself, and I knew others who had. Hennie, his wife, told me that they were invited frequently, but that Karl never wanted to go, because he preferred to spend his time working. He was the most intense workaholic I have ever known. On a normal day he would get up quite early in the morning and work solidly through the day until he went to bed again, with breaks for fairly spartan meals and possibly a walk. He refused to have a record player or a television set in the house, on the ground that they would waste his time, and he refused to have a newspaper delivered in case it distracted his thoughts. He knew that if anything important happened his friends would tell him about it, and they always did—I quite often telephoned him to tell him of some major public event. Well into his eighties there would usually be one night in a week when he got so excitedly involved in his work that he was unable to leave it to go to bed: many is the time I have been pulled out of a deep sleep at eight or so in the morning by the telephone, with Popper on the other end of it bubbling with excitement about what he had been working on all night, bursting to talk to somebody about it.

He did everything he could think of to isolate himself for the sake of his work. His house in Penn was in a private road with artificial bumps at short intervals to slow down traffic and make driving unpleasant. He told me that he deliberately chose to live several miles outside London, in as out-of-the-way a place as he could find, to discourage people from visiting him, and to eliminate casual dropping-in. When his colleagues at the London School of Economics presented him with a farewell gift on his retirement he returned it, saying he had not been there often enough, or played an active enough part in its affairs, to warrant it. When after Hennie's death he moved to Kenley, Surrey, he again bought an out-of-the-way house on a private road with bumps in it. There were other ways, too, in which he purposely made things difficult for people who wanted to see him. When, late in his life, he gave a regular seminar at Vienna University, he held it at a weekend, at a location on the outer edge of the city, so as to discourage (so he told me) all but those who were determined to come.

Several decades of self-isolation exacted a great toll on Popper's knowledge and understanding of the world around him, an isolation all the greater because he did not take up residence in his adopted country until he was in his midforties. There is the starkest of contrasts between his early and later lives as far as his sociability is concerned. As a young man in Vienna he was an active supporter of the Social Democratic Party, a dedicated voluntary worker with mentally disturbed children under the supervision of the psychoanalyst Alfred Adler, a chorister and junior helper with rehearsals in the Society for Private Concerts founded by Schoenberg (where he got to know Webern); and all this in addition to being one of the most enthusiastic and prominent young participants in the philosophical ferment taking place in Vienna at that time. He wooed and won a noted student beauty, and the two of them would often go mountaineering with their friends. One way and another he involved himself in a life of perpetual activity across an astonishingly wide range, along with others of his generation. It was a preparation for a life of exceptional richness. But psycho-emotionally he lived off it for the second half or more of his life. He abandoned it in 1937 to go to New Zealand, a decision which saved his life; but he felt himself cut off from the rest of the world throughout the Second World War. Then in 1946 he came to live in England, where his way of life was as I have described. That he became so unworldly is not in itself surprising, especially for so creative a person. What is surprising, at least to me, is that he did not realize it. *The Open Society* and *The Poverty of Historicism* were the products of prolonged and intensive thought applied to material which included a rich input of social experience throughout the 1920s and 1930s. After that he ceased to have much social experience; and because he directed his mind predominantly towards problems in the philosophy of science he also stopped thinking about social questions with his former degree of involvement. The result is that what he had to say on such matters became undernourished and thin. But that did not stop him from holding forth about them with the same burning self-confidence as he would have shown if he had known what he was talking about. He also had a tendency to give people firm-sounding advice about their careers or their private lives, though he had little understanding of either. All this, of course, was in direct contravention of his professed (and indeed genuine) beliefs, and practices, in philosophy.

Karl Popper died on Saturday 17 September, 1994, at the age of ninety-two. Next day three of the four leading Sunday newspapers in Britain described him, or quoted him as being described, as the outstanding philosopher of the twentieth century. By the end of the month articles in the same vein had appeared all over the world. Of course, who comes eventually to be seen as the greatest philosopher of the twentieth century will not be decided by the newspapers. But the short-list of genuine possibles is indeed short: Russell, Wittgenstein, Heidegger, Popper—it seems to me most unlikely not to be one of those. In any event Popper's work will be an object of growing interest for a very long time to come, I think, because so many of his ideas are radically original yet still comparatively little explored.

Up to now he has been seen primarily as a critic. This is not surprising, for he has been the most formidable and effective critic of not just one but several of the large-scale orthodoxies of the twentieth century. It was his magnificent demolition of Marxism, in his two-volume masterpiece *The Open Society and Its Enemies,* that made his international reputation. His destruction of claims to scientific status for Freud's ideas also achieved renown. Within the world of professional philosophy he was the first truly insightful critic of logical positivism, which in the end was destroyed by arguments which he had been putting forward all along. Most of his subsequent criticisms of linguistic philosophy, largely unpublished by him but given publicity in a somewhat brash form by his junior colleague Ernest Gellner, came in the end to be accepted by linguistic philosophers themselves. To this list of critical achievements are to be added many more. Popper and Einstein between them did more than anyone else to destroy a view of the nature of science that was almost universally held at the beginning of the twentieth century, the view that scientific knowledge is built up on the basis of direct observation and experience, and that what makes it special is its incorrigible certainty. This seems still to be the view of science most widely held by non-scientists, though in the upper reaches of science itself, as in philosophy, it has been superseded.

No other thinker of the twentieth century has come anywhere near matching this range of effectiveness as a destroyer of the dominant myths of the age, and this alone is likely to make Popper a figure of historical importance. But in each case he put forward an alternative to the thought-system he attacked— in politics, in logic, in philosophy of language, in psychology, in science, in every one of the fields in which he was active. To the end of his life he was astonishingly fertile in new ideas. However, his positive views have received only a fraction of the attention bestowed on his critiques. Yet they are of exceptional creative originality and richness. It is in the belated discovery, development and criticism of his positive doctrines that I expect the main future of Popper's ideas to lie.

To give only one example, he developed a theory of human knowledge that rejects the fundamental premiss of most epistemology in the English-speaking world, namely that all our empirical knowledge is built up ultimately on the basis of our sensory experience. In doing this he broke with a tradition going back to Aristotle, and one that has dominated most of the important Western philosophy of recent centuries. Such a denial is still unthinkable for many philosophers writing in English. If Popper is justified in it, and I think he is, the consequences for Western philosophy are seismic. He himself unpacked a great many of what these consequences are, and developed a radically new epistemology which sooner or later philosophers are going to have to come to terms with.

For a long time now a very large number of professional philosophers have believed that the true task of philosophy is analysis, the clarification of our ideas, the elucidation of our concepts and our methods. It is not to be expected that philosophers who take this view will put forward large-scale positive ideas. And it explains why, in the attention they paid to Popper, his contemporaries concentrated almost entirely on his critiques. But Popper himself rejected that whole conception of philosophy. He believed that the world presents us with innumerable problems of a genuinely philosophical nature, and that no problem of substance is to be solved by analysis. New explanatory ideas are what is called for, and they form the chief content of worthwhile philosophy, and have always done so. Because he believed this, and practised it, always from outside the main thought-systems of the age, he was never in the fashion. And because he spent so much of his time attacking and severely damaging the ideas of people he disagreed with he was never popular. But what matters is the quality of the work itself—and the sheer substance and weight, as well as originality and range, of Popper's work are altogether unmatched in that of any philosopher now living.

12

Getting to Know Russell

Most people must go through life without ever getting to know anyone of genius, so I count it a piece of great good fortune that I have known two. In 1959 I was earning my living as a programme maker for ATV, one of the independent television companies that had come into existence when commercial television began in Britain in 1955. I did not as yet appear on the screen: my designation was Editor, and my job was to think of subjects and contributors for features and documentaries, assemble the necessary components, and deliver them to a producer in such a form that he could turn the package I gave him into a programme without himself knowing much about the subject. Towards the end of the year I was allotted my first one-hour documentary, having previously made only half-hour programmes. I decided to devote it to the threat of global over-population. It seemed to me important in so long a programme to vary the content and pace, so in addition to assembling a good deal of dramatic and unusual film, and trying to think of ingenious ways of animating statistics by means of graphics, I also decided to include two studio interviews. My chosen contributors were Julian Huxley, who was at that time the best-known biologist in Britain, and Bertrand Russell.

Some time in December I telephoned Russell at his home in North Wales. He answered the telephone himself, which surprised me slightly. From the beginning of our conversation it was obvious that he was interested in the project, but before committing himself wanted to be sure that I and the enterprise were going to be serious. At that time so-called educated people were deeply suspicious of commercial television—indeed, in general, they did not watch it. It sounds absurd now, but the truth is that most of the middle and upper classes watched the BBC while most working-class people watched ITV. In the end Russell said, in effect (I do not recall the actual words): "I'd like to meet you and talk it over with you personally before saying yes." I agreed to this, whereupon he said that at eighty-seven he found the journey to London burdensome in winter, and would I be willing to come down and visit him in Wales? I said yes to that too; and the upshot was that at some point during the week between Christmas 1959 and New Year's Day 1960 I took a train to North Wales to visit him at his home in Penrhyndeudraeth.

By arrangement, I arrived not long after breakfast. My first physical impression of Russell was how tiny he was. Popper was no taller but gave an impression at that time of burliness and a certain strong slow forcefulness of movement, whereas Russell was bird-like and slight, light-boned, spry, quick-darting. The quickness of bodily and mental movement were extraordinary in a man of his age.

His wife, he explained to me, was in bed with flu and sent her apologies for not receiving me. He then proceeded to wait on me with a degree of attentiveness that I mistook for a desire to make up for his wife's absence: peeled the coat off my back, fussed about where and how to hang it, led me into a living room, took pains to see that I was comfortably ensconced on a sofa, plumped the cushions. In the course of time I discovered that he had the courtly manners of the Victorian age and invariably behaved as if whoever he were attending to were of nabob-like importance. We discussed the television programme at useful length, and he agreed to take part in it. When that was out of the way he questioned me about myself and sparked with new life when it emerged that I was a passionate student of philosophy.

For a long time he quizzed me about philosophers at Oxford and Yale whom I had come up against personally, people he had heard of but never seen. Then I began to ask him about philosophers he had worked with closely and also known well, above all Wittgenstein, Whitehead and Moore. Keen-edged comment, usually catty but affectionate, consistently funny, poured out of him— penetrating remarks, wonderful anecdotes. He was not at all like those people who make one's smiles creak by trying to be funny with everything they say: he just *was* funny with more or less everything he said. His normal mode of utterance was to use some sort of literal description for purposes of comic irony, with the result that his almost every remark was informative and funny at the same time. I do not think I have ever listened to anyone with greater delight. He had an ability unique in my experience to express himself in perfectly balanced and economically formed sentences that were strikingly satisfying, so much so that if they had been written down and published they would have constituted elegant, tightly constructed and almost unrevisable prose. It is true that I subsequently came across many of the same sentences in his writings, and of course a lot of the same points and anecdotes; but most of us are guilty of retelling our best stories in the same words, and in any case all this accounted for only part of his conversation: I said many things to which his response could not have existed in ready-cooked form, but his replies came out in the same spare, luminous, faultlessly constructed sentences as everything else he said. He was a little vain about this, and told me that for several decades he had dictated all his correspondence and everything he had published. "Not since the First World War have I used a pen for anything other than to sign my name." As a matter of fact I found him a little vain altogether, but in a vulnerable and lovable way, like an attractive and clever child seeking approval.

We were in agreement about a lot of basic things: that Wittgenstein's early philosophy was work of genius, whereas his later philosophy was a highly sophisticated form of intellectual frivolity; that the current orthodoxy in philosophy was deeply, deeply in error in treating analysis as the sole and whole function of philosophy, this being to treat a philosophical tool as if it were itself philosophy, and that to do this was an abuse not only of philosophy but of the tool, which could have been of immense power if put to better uses; that the central task of philosophy was still, as it had always been, the attempt to understand the world, or our experience of it; that in the history of this attempt one of the two or three supreme success stories so far was science, which must therefore have an especially important relationship to any properly conducted philosophy, and indeed that it was impossible to be a serious philosopher at all without a serious interest in science. He remarked that he often felt he had been mistaken in becoming a philosopher, and ought to have been a scientist.

His closest personal contact on the contemporary philosophical scene was A. J. Ayer. He spoke of Ayer with friendship and loyalty, but it became clear that although he regarded him as clever and quick he did not think he had anything original to contribute. He liked Ayer as a person, saw him as being on the right side of most controversial issues, and rated him a brilliant interlocutor, debater, critic and teacher, but did not see him as having important ideas of his own. Popper, whom he had met only briefly, he did see as an original, but knew only as the author of *The Open Society,* of which he approved highly. He had not read any of Popper's philosophy of science and did not think of him in the context of general as distinct from political philosophy. When I talked about *The Logic of Scientific Discovery,* which had just been published for the first time in English, it became clear that he had absorbed the common and mistaken view that Popper was advocating falsifiability as an alternative to verifiability as a criterion of meaning, this being the interpretation contained in, among many other books, Ayer's *Language, Truth and Logic.* When we brought this part of our conversation to an end Russell said I had stimulated him to read Popper's philosophy of science, but I do not know whether he ever did.

After some hours our conversation was still bubbling out of its natural spring when we were called away to lunch. This had been prepared by a couple who worked for the Russells but whom I did not see. It was waiting for us on the kitchen table, a hot boiled ham of Dickensian proportions, two steaming dishes of vegetables, and an open bottle of red wine. Russell put a hand on my shoulder and sat me down firmly on a wooden chair and proceeded to carve the ham with a certain flamboyance of gesture, continuing the conversation non-stop. He and the food were to my right, and since he insisted on serving me—first with ham, then with each vegetable in turn—from my left, it involved him in continually dancing round the back of my chair. As an able-bodied twenty-nine-year-old I felt embarrassed at sitting there being waited on in so elaborate a fashion by a man of eighty-seven. I confess that some notion of our relative status was also involved in this feeling: it seemed to me inappropriate that a person of historic importance in philosophy, world famous, winner of the Nobel Prize for Literature, and so on, should be dancing attendance like this on a total stranger young enough to be his grandson. At least I should be helping, I thought. So I tried to serve him with vegetables. For this I was sternly reproved. That was the host's job, he said.

"Well at least let me pour the wine," said I, reaching for the bottle.

"*No, no,*" he said emphatically, snatching the bottle before my hand could get to it. "If there's one thing the host absolutely *must* do it's pour the wine," and he poured the wine.

At this a resentment welled up in me. This man is being downright insensitive, I thought. Surely he must realize that his behaviour can only embarrass me. If he had real and not just token consideration for my feelings he wouldn't do it. I said something aloud to this effect, and he, unperturbed, replied: "I know, I know. A difference in age can have a quite irrational effect. When I was seventeen I had dinner alone with Gladstone . . ."*

The conversation changed direction over lunch, and it emerged that I was a prospective Labour parliamentary candidate. This galvanized Russell afresh, and launched us on a conversation about political and social affairs that swept us back into the living room and went on for the rest of the afternoon, so that by six o'clock we had been talking to each other with unflagging vitality for over eight hours. During this time a lot of things about Russell were revealed

---

* According to his writings this was artistic exaggeration. What happened was that at the end of a dinner the ladies withdrew and left the seventeen-year-old Russell alone with Gladstone over the port.

that are not evident from his writings, for example that he had an extensive knowledge of imaginative literature in English, French and German, and could quote large quantities of poetry in all three languages. Music was a blind spot (the one he regretted most, he said) but there seemed to be no main field of intellectual activity in which he did not possess as much knowledge as some people who pass for experts. He had known an extraordinary number of world-historic figures. Having grown up as a child in the household of his grandfather, a former British Prime Minister (his parents were both dead by the time he was four), he had always been accustomed to meeting international figures in informal surroundings; and his own eminence in adult life had caused this to continue. He referred to them spontaneously as people he knew, not in any spirit of name-dropping—he scarcely needed to drop names—but because our discussion brought them naturally to mind. For instance, when I mentioned what seemed to me an unsalvageable fault in Marxist theory he said: "I made exactly that point to Lenin, but I couldn't get him to see it." When I made some reference to Conrad it transpired that Conrad was the godfather of one of Russell's sons, and that both of them were named after him. And so on and so forth. He seemed to have met "everybody," and quite naturally so, in the course of his long life.

I found myself fascinated at talking to someone who had met so many of the people I had learnt about at school and university. It brought recent history alive for me in a new way and made me feel somehow in personal contact with it. I could ask Russell what he thought of Trotsky, Einstein, T. S. Eliot, and a whole host of very different other people, and he had actually *known* them, and I would get an answer based on personal acquaintance, sometimes surprisingly extensive. For instance, he had taught philosophy to T. S. Eliot at Harvard, and the poet had later come to live in his home in England. He did not tell me, what I subsequently discovered, that he had had an affair with Eliot's wife while the Eliots were living under his roof. One way and another most of the history of the last eighty-five years seemed to have passed through his private life. This had been brought about, I think, by a unique combination of factors. He had been born into one of the handful of most powerful political families in Britain when the country was at the apogee of its imperial might, governing a world-wide empire that embraced a quarter of the human race; and all the advantages that this conferred on an individual accrued to him. In particular, the fact that his grandfather had been Prime Minister meant that heads of government from all over the world visited their house, and he took this for granted. At the same time the young Russell had been possessed of world-class ability in his own right, and in a non-political field of activity. So he moved at the highest level in three different international worlds: political, social and intellectual.

Queen Victoria had died in the year in which Russell was twenty-nine, so he was in the literal sense a Victorian Englishman. More specifically, his first decade of adult life had been the 1890s, so he was a *fin de siècle* Englishman too. Since he was not the sort of individual to change his manners or accent to accommodate others his persona was quite simply that of a nineteenth-century aristocrat—he was, after all, an earl, though compared with his abilities this fact was so slight that people tended literally to forget it. In the age of democracy and modern political parties, trade union power, mass media and the rest, he was a creature from elsewhere, despite his success and fame, like an expatriate who keeps his original nationality yet rises to the top in his adopted country. It was, I felt, something for which he deserved to be greatly honoured.

One of the most dating and distinctive things about him was his way of speaking. His *o*'s were forward and open, not enclosed in the mouth but projected outwards. In the word "civilization" he pronounced the first three *i*'s the same, like *ee*. He referred to someone's family as "his people," someone's circle of close friends as "his set." The robust language of the Victorian novel came alive on his tongue. The actual sound it made in his case was high-pitched, nasal and reedy, yet always vigorous and emphatic. It was mimicked a good deal at the time, not only to imitate Russell but to stand for what was thought to be the archetypal philosopher, and even bad imitations of him were instantly recognizable.

I can still hear his voice in my mind's ear saying things he said to me at that first meeting, often summing up a whole argument or point of view in a single sentence. "Religious education is always an evil because it means teaching children to believe things for which there is no evidence." . . . "Aneurin Bevan considers it more important that he should become Foreign Secretary than that the human race should survive." And so on. When I asked him who he regarded as the most intelligent person he had ever met he replied unhesitatingly, "Keynes." When I asked, "Did you honestly regard him as more intelligent than yourself?," he said with equal lack of hesitation, "Yes. Every time I argued with Keynes I felt I was taking my life in my hands." When I said I was surprised by his answer because I had been more than half expecting him to say "Einstein," he replied that Einstein did not exhibit pure intelligence in the same way, but rather something akin to the gifts of a great creative artist: Einstein's work had come from depths of imagination rather than of intellect. When I asked him who he regarded as the greatest man he had ever met, he needed longer to consider his reply. In the end he came up with Lenin. When I asked why, he said it was because Lenin combined a brilliant mind with genius-level ability as a man of action, and this gave him extraordinary stature and effectiveness as a person. Also, he had changed the entire course of world history in a way few individuals ever do. However, he added, Lenin was not in the least morally admirable: he came near to boasting about the enormous scale of the death and suffering he was causing, and laughed about it in conversation with Russell.

My first day with Russell remains for me the most memorable day of talk I have ever experienced. For decades *Reader's Digest* used to run a feature in every issue called "The Most Unforgettable Character I've Met"; and Russell remains the most unforgettable character I've met.

After that first day, we met several times more, usually at his London house in Hasker Street, where he would invite me (again in the Victorian manner) to tea, on the ground that he became tired in the evening and needed to go to bed early. On the question of his vitality: I never ceased to be amazed not only by his mental energy but even more, if anything, by his physical energy. If in the middle of making a point he wanted to quote from a book he would leap out of his chair and prance over to the bookcase, go up on tiptoe, reach down a book from a high shelf and sweep back with it round the sofa to his chair, all in one single fluid line of movement, without the slightest appearance of effort or even hesitation in the flow of talk. He was so quick and light on his feet and so flowing in his movements that I always thought of the word "dancing" in connection with them. It was all, I believe, powered by his intellectual energy and his unflagging enthusiasm for what he was saying.

On one of my visits to Hasker Street I took him to task for having advocated the nuclear bombing of the Soviet Union to relieve mankind from any further threat of nuclear war. He denied that he had. He had been misrepresented, he said: what he had advocated was that before the Soviet Union developed nuclear weapons the West should use its monopoly of them to force the Russians to renounce any attempt to develop them. It is perfectly true that what would compel the Russians to accede to this demand would be the threat of nuclear attack if they did not, but since they would have no choice but to agree, there would in fact be no nuclear attack. But the proposal had led people simply to say of Russell that he advocated bombing the Soviet Union, and that, he said, was an utter slander. Next time we met I showed him a copy of an original source in which he had advocated bombing the Soviet Union. It was the only time I saw him flustered. He said he had genuinely and completely forgotten that he had said it, admitted that such forgetting was almost certainly Freudian, but insisted that he could have said it that once only, talking excessively loosely, and that on all other occasions he had said what he claimed he had said, this being his considered point of view. But I am afraid this is not true either. Russell had on a number of occasions advocated bombing the Soviet Union, over a period of two or three years.

This is an example of what was, in the end, my greatest reservation about him. He dealt in concepts, in words, in thoughts, with a wholly inadequate understanding of what they meant in terms of non-linguistic reality. Confronted with any human problem he looked for the right way of thinking about it rather than the right way of feeling about it, and consequently he tended to see both the problem and its solution in terms of ideas rather than in terms of flesh-and-blood people and effects on *them*. This led him not infrequently to believe and propose silly things—silly in the sense that they were out of contact with how life actually is, and how people actually are, and what it is actually possible to get people to do or go along with. This fact about him was at its most highly conspicuous in later life when he was publicly active in the cause of unilateral nuclear disarmament. (It always seemed to me fitting that the only person I ever met who had advocated the nuclear bombing of the Soviet Union was the most famous public proponent of unilateral nuclear disarmament.) It led many observers to say that he had become silly with age, but the truth is that age had little or nothing to do with it: he had been like this all along. During the First World War he had accused those of the bishops who were in the House of Lords of supporting the war because the Church of England owned shares in armaments factories. Of the ridiculous school, Beacon Hill, that he founded and ran between the wars he himself was subsequently to say that he had been "blinded by theory." He had always, from the beginning, had a tendency to say and do idiotic things when it came to practical matters, and always for the same basic reason: he treated practical problems as if they were theoretical problems. In fact I do not think he could tell the difference. I would even go so far as to say that he did not know that there was a difference. (It was a good thing for him and everyone else that he never went into parliamentary politics, as his family had expected him to, and as he himself felt until middle life that he ought—he stood for parliament two or three times.) Really, the explanation of how it came about that this man who was a genius in some ways could be so foolish in others was relatively simple. His whole genius was for solving theoretical problems, and—no doubt partly for that reason—he tended to see all problems as theoretical. When a problem really was theoretical he was masterly, but when it was not theoretical but a problem of private or public life he was a blunderer. And because he had so little practical intelligence he learnt almost nothing from the experience. He was as much (but no more) of a silly-billy when he was old as he had been as a young man.

An American called Ralph Schoenman became one of the voluntary helpers in his public campaigns, and rose to become his immediate assistant, and eventually took him over completely. I had personal experience of one of the ways in which this happened. After I had been in easy and pleasurable contact with Russell for a couple of years, exchanging letters, meeting him occasionally, chatting from time to time on the telephone, everything suddenly changed. If I wrote to Russell, the reply came from Schoenman, and it was obvious that Russell did not know of the existence of my letter. If I tried to talk to Russell on the telephone, my call would be answered by Schoenman, who had moved in with him. Schoenman would ask me what it was I wanted to talk to Russell about. Whatever I replied, he would say that Russell was too busy to attend to it, and I should call another time, or write. If I declined to discuss it but asked to speak to Russell, Schoenman would say he could not possibly pass me on to Russell unless I was prepared to say what it was about. If I wrote, I got another reply from Schoenman. If I telephoned again, I found myself talking to Schoenman again. The whole situation was Kafka-esque. I never met Schoenman—to me he was only a voice on a telephone. But all the means I used to make contact with Russell were effectively blocked by him, and it was clear that Russell had no idea what was going on. I naturally wondered whether this might be merely personal—perhaps Russell had come to the conclusion that he did not want to see me any more, and had instructed Schoenman accordingly—but I began hearing similar stories from other of his friends and acquaintances whom I knew. Indeed, such stories were beginning to appear in the press. Like everybody else, I suppose, I gave up in the end.

Meanwhile public declarations began to appear over Russell's signature that he could not possibly have written (if only because of their inadequate literacy) and which did not represent his views. This is itemized by Alan Ryan in his book *Bertrand Russell: A Political Life,* where the onset of this nightmarish development is described in the following words (pp. 196–7): "Many English readers doubted whether Russell had read, much less written, what he had put his name to; it read like the rantings of the student Left, not like Russell's own immaculate prose. . . . At times he began to sound like the Ayatollah Khomeini denouncing the 'great Satan'—in itself a reason for wondering how much he wrote of all the articles he put his name to." It was a terrible end for a philosopher of such magnificent gifts, a subject made worthy of Greek tragedy by the fact that it was the central figure who was responsible for his own downfall.

Schoenman was an appallingly sinister figure, like an evil dwarf out of Wagner's *Ring,* and his motivations were unquestionably calculated and manipulative. Whether they were of the far left or the far right I never knew, but it made little difference in practice because, as usual, it came to much the same thing. Many thought he was motivated by what later came to be called loony-left views plus an unbalanced hatred of his own country, the United States. Certainly these were what characterized the writings that appeared over Russell's signature once he was in Schoenman's clutches. But at least as many people suspected that Schoenman had been planted on Russell by the CIA with the mission of discrediting him internationally as the world's most prominent spokesman for unilateral nuclear disarmament—and certainly this was what occurred as a direct result of Schoenman's handling of him. If I had to bet on one of these alternatives I would opt for the latter, but it does not seem to me to be any longer a significant question.

13

First Attempts at
a Political Philosophy

I have told how, on my return to England from Yale in the late summer of 1956, I was plunged almost immediately into political activity by the crises of Suez and Hungary. This led me for the first time to attend one of the Labour Party's annual conferences, which was held in Brighton. The Labour Party Conference of 1957 turned out to be the historic one at which Aneurin Bevan made his famous "naked into the conference chamber" speech. The most charismatic figure ever to have emerged within the Labour Party, he had consolidated his reputation by creating the National Health Service as a Minister in the post-war Labour government. He had then resigned, in part out of protest against the introduction of charges in the Health Service, which seemed to him contrary to the principle on which it was based, but also partly because he knew that if he stayed in the Cabinet he would have to support the rearmament programme that had been put in hand after the outbreak of the Korean War, and this he was not prepared to do. From his new position outside the government he became the undisputed leader of the dissident left in the Labour Party and a brilliant spokesman for its most passionately held cause, unilateral nuclear disarmament. The 1957 conference was to be the occasion on which he publicly abandoned that cause and his left-wing followers, to throw in his lot as Deputy Leader of the party and Shadow Foreign Secretary with a new leader, Hugh Gaitskell.

Annual conference is the only occasion in the political year when the Labour Party meets as a whole. Representatives from the remoter areas use it as a unique opportunity of serving the interests of their otherwise neglected local parties, and they tend to do it opportunistically—for instance by inviting nationally known figures with whom they happen to find themselves hob-nobbing at the bars to come and speak in their out-of-the-way home towns. It was in this spirit that the representatives of the constituency of Mid-Bedfordshire came to Brighton that autumn on the look-out for a possible parliamentary candidate. Their constituency contained no town of significant size at all, but consisted of 250 square miles of villages, seventy-two of them all told. They had come to the conclusion that their local party did not contain anyone of sufficient calibre to be a parliamentary candidate and was going to have to find one from outside. However, Mid-Bedfordshire had always been safely held by the Conservatives, and this caused them to calculate that the only kind of person with the capacity to be an MP, serious about getting into the House of Commons and yet prepared to take on Mid-Bedfordshire, would have to be a young one keen enough on winning his spurs to be willing to lose an election. They thought, no doubt rightly, that there was bound to be a number of such people at the conference, and so they came looking for one. Their eye fell on me.

I had, naturally, to go through the selection procedure. At the Selection Conference, which took place in Bedford early in 1958, another person on the short-list of six was Betty Boothroyd. Thirty-four years later she became the first woman Speaker of the House of Commons. However, the key party activists had decided already that they were going to vote for me, and I was duly selected.

From then until the general election in the autumn of 1959 I spent every other weekend in the constituency, and quite often went there for an evening in mid-week. At the same time I continued to be an activist in my own local party in central London.* So during that period I got to know how local parties of very different sorts worked, as well as how to be a candidate, and how to fight an election campaign. In the general election of 1959 I lost in Mid-Bedfordshire. But less than a year later my successful opponent went to the House of Lords, so in the autumn of 1960 there was a by-election. Again I was the Labour candidate. Fighting a by-election was a different experience altogether from fighting a general election. Money and helpers came in from far and wide, there were daily visits from members of parliament, we were highlighted in the national media. I have ever since looked back on those years 1958–60 as my apprenticeship in party politics, the years in which I learnt the realities of it in among the grass roots.

---

* The leading lights of the St. Marylebone Labour Party were a couple called Pat and Kate Lucan. Many meetings were held in their house, and at these I often bumped into their teenage son, who later achieved fame as the Lord Lucan who committed murder and disappeared.

At one and the same time they were richly educative years and disillusioning. Learning about everyday politics, and how to function effectively as a part of it, was wholly to the good, but I was dismayed to discover how small a role ideas and ideals played in it all—and, to the extent that they did play a role, what shabby ideas and ideals they were, for the most part. Most political activity was actually a pursuit of self-interest in the light of situational logic. It was opportunistic in character, and in the Labour Party's case originated with the material interests of the trade unions in particular, and after them the less well-off fifth or sixth of society. Most of the ideas articulated were rationalizations of this activity, and they went out not in advance as a beacon and guide but after the event as a justification. Most of these rationales were based on rudimentary notions of common humanity, justice and fairness, and when expressed by ordinary party members came out as a form of wet liberalism. That, at least, was the case with the majority. Alongside them was a substantial minority who were tougher in practice and more astringent in theory, and they were the dissident left. Their guiding light was Marxism, expressly so with many intellectuals, though more often making itself felt as an unarticulated influence on people who were not primarily intellectuals—and on their many organized groups who acted as apologists for Communist regimes, and engaged in lying about them while savagely attacking anyone who told the truth.

I found all this appalling. It was not that I wanted the Labour Party to follow some different theory that seemed to me the right one. I could see it was neither possible nor desirable for politics in a free society to be theory-governed. Any such politics would always, naturally and unobjectionably, consist for the most part of the working out of conflicting views and self-interests in ever-changing circumstances, within a wider framework of morality and law; and the morality involved would always, again rightly, be the one commonly acknowledged in the society. However, what seemed to me desirable was, first, that this should be acknowledged, and an end put to the effluent-flow of claptrap that poured out unceasingly from socialist sources; and second, given that theoretical assumptions are presupposed by any activity, no matter what, we needed a better theory than Marxism to provide us with ours.

It seemed to me that much of the intellectual work required for this had been done by Karl Popper. The political philosophy published in *The Open Society* demolished Marxism beyond any serious possibility of its reconstruction, and offered in its stead a problem-solving philosophy designed to be a non-ideological guide to practical action for social democrats bent on rapid reform. So, exactly what the Labour Party needed lay ready to hand. From a position inside it I wrote a book that was critical of current Labour Party thinking and practice, and that recommended the—I hope it goes without saying, non-exclusive—adoption by the party of Popper's ideas. My book was called *The New Radicalism,* and was published in 1962 by Secker & Warburg. It was what many academics regarded as my first "serious" book, though it was my fourth to be published. As an undergraduate I had had a volume called *Crucifixion and Other Poems* published by Fortune Press. On my return to England from the United States I had written a travel book about America called *Go West Young Man,* published in 1958 by Eyre & Spottiswoode. Then came a spy novel called *To Live in Danger,* published in 1960 by Hutchinson. And now there was *The New Radicalism.*

With the writing of this book I adopted a practice I was to continue with most of my subsequent ones, namely to give a complete first draft to a number of carefully chosen friends with the request that they criticize it ruthlessly. I did not, I would tell them firmly, want to be told how good it was: I needed to discover what was wrong with it. When it came out it would be criticized in any case, so I would rather be told now of errors it contained, or ways in which I could improve it, while there was still time to make changes, than become aware of them when it was too late. This practice has been of great benefit to me. Not only has it saved me from many mistakes, it has shown me which passages in a book were, without necessarily being factually inaccurate, open to objections or reservations even from sympathetic readers, and given me the opportunity to acknowledge these objections in the book itself, and try to meet them. Often the usefulness of the criticism was different from what was intended. It quite frequently happened that a friend would express an objection that actually rested on a misunderstanding, but in these cases I never ignored what he said, nor did I assume that the misunderstanding was his fault rather than mine. Given that he was an intelligent and sympathetic reader, I took it for granted that if he misunderstood a particular passage then a number of other readers would do so too, and therefore I should change it. Sometimes I would alter the existing text, but sometimes I would leave it as it was and insert new passages, one beginning, let us say, "At this point a reader might object that . . ." and the next beginning, "But this would be to miss the point that . . ." All writing can be misunderstood. If one acknowledges the likeliest misunderstandings in the text itself, and meets them, it clarifies the writing to an exceptional degree.

Of the five friends to whom I gave *The New Radicalism* to criticize in this way, three were professional philosophers—R. F. (Ron) Atkinson, Ninian Smart and Bernard Williams. One of the other two, Anthony Crosland, was later to become Foreign Secretary in a Labour government; and the other, Tyrrell Burgess, was a pioneer in applying Popperian analysis to institutional studies. The sheer usefulness of the criticism of these five confirmed me in the practice ever after.

The core chapters of *The New Radicalism* were Chapters Three and Four, headed respectively "The Rational Basis of My Case" and "The Moral Basis of My Case." I sent a typescript of Chapter Three to Bertrand Russell while working on the rest of the book. He told me he agreed with it but had one important negative comment: it was, he thought, squarely in a tradition of radical liberalism that went back hundreds of years via John Stuart Mill to, at the very least, John Locke, and he therefore considered that the word "new" in the book-title was a false claim. The response I made to him was that I stressed within the book itself that I advocated the self-identification of the Labour Party with the central tradition of European rationality, a tradition that went back indeed to Socrates; that the Labour Party had never thought of itself in this way; that it would involve throwing out the legacy of Marxism, indeed of socialism itself in the traditional meaning of that word; that no one, so far as I knew, had ever advocated any such thing; and that much of my critique was new with Popper, to whom I paid full acknowledgement in the Introduction. What I was proposing was that the Labour Party should do something that was new *for it*. It seemed to me that liberalism as an actively radical, society-changing creed was what was needed in British politics; that the so-called Liberal Party offered no such thing, and had no prospect of getting into power anyway; and that, given this, the only alternatives were either to start a new party or convert one of the existing ones. At that time the chance of success for the first of these alternatives appeared considerably less than that of converting the Labour Party to a radical approach. So I gambled on the second course.

When I had said all this to Russell, and although it was all true, the fact remained that I felt his criticism to be justified. But I retained the title for seriously considered reasons of presentation: if there was going to be any hope at all of getting a party of reform to change its ideas, it could only be in exchange for ideas that were held out to it as new, not for ideas that were described even in the offer as old. Also, I was urging on the Labour Party some of the ideas of a still-living philosopher, and one that most of its members had never heard of. This seemed to me a not unreasonable excuse for describing what I was urging as new.

Popper, who read the book in proof, made several small suggestions and one big one. The big one was to my extended criticism of Hugh Gaitskell. I viewed Gaitskell as an inept leader who had created a brand of disruption within the party that was inimical to his own cause; and I also saw him as too conservative in temperament to lead the kind of radical party I was advocating. In this latter regard I objected to him on three counts: he would not have wanted to radicalize the Labour Party, would not have been capable of doing so if he had wanted to, and would not have made a good leader of any such party. Altogether I saw him as a major obstacle in the path I wanted the Labour

Party to follow. And I had said all this in the book, perhaps over-forcefully, and perhaps excessively personally. Popper felt strongly against my saying it at all—on uncharacteristically prudential grounds. What he saw Gaitskell as engaged in more importantly than anything else was a battle against the Marxist left for the soul of the Labour Party. It seemed to Popper essential that Gaitskell should be supported in that fight and should win it—and of course anything that weakened him would make him less likely to do so. If he were to cease to be leader he would be replaced by someone to his left who would not pursue the fight at all. Therefore, said Popper, if I sought the long-term good of the Labour Party I ought not to publish things which could serve only to undermine Gaitskell's position.

Popper and I had some hot-tempered arguments about this. My own position was disconcertingly weakened by the premature death of Aneurin Bevan, which took place while I was at work on the book—he was the person I had in mind as the best leader from the point of view I was advocating. The only politician in the party's history to possess a streak of genius, its biggest personality and best orator, and now its Deputy Leader, there was little room for doubt that if only he had been there when Gaitskell left the scene he would have become its leader. His left-wing past was a bonus, given that he was demonstrating a capacity to learn from experience and go on growing and developing in middle life. His ability to look at things freshly, and think for himself, was a rare one, and was the basis of his radical instincts. Now, with his unforeseen death, these hopes lay in ruins. In my arguments with Popper some of my strongest cards were now dashed from my hand. It was a racing certainty that, if Gaitskell ceased to be leader, his successor would be Harold Wilson—whom I despised, and from whom little that was good could be expected, least of all anything in the way of a sustained battle against the left, which would play an indispensable role in making him leader of the party. I was forced to concede that the best immediate hope for any of the internal party reforms I wanted was that they should take place under the continued leadership of Hugh Gaitskell, but I would have to expect them to be energized not by initiatives from him but by the party's ability to see what was needed for its own long-term survival.

My arguments with Popper divided my mind. My book as it stood in page-proof expressed the unvarnished truth as I believed it to be, without consideration for anyone's personal advantage or disadvantage, including mine. To tone down even one passage for tactical reasons would be to introduce intellectual corruption at that point; and this was something I wanted the book to be free of, since the Labour Party was so riddled with it, and this was one of my chief complaints against it, expressed in the book itself. On the other hand I could not offer an effective reply to Popper's argument: what he was saying was true. In the end, yet still somehow against my better judgment, I toned the anti-Gaitskell passage down. It was the only time in my relationship with Popper that I did something contrary to my own instincts under his influence, and I never felt right about it—in fact I experienced guilt, for I felt exactly as one does when one has done something one knows to be wrong. That particular pigeon came home to roost. When Gaitskell almost immediately turned his coat over Europe, and made a ridiculous little-England speech at Labour Party Conference, Popper said I had been right all along, and he regretted having persuaded me to change what I had written. Far from consoling me, this made me want to kick myself all over London, and I vowed never to make the same mistake again. That I would make mistakes was inevitable, and it was bad enough having to make my own, without making someone else's as well.

The publishers were confident that the appearance of *The New Radicalism* would create a furore. A hotly worded critique of the Labour Party from within was bound, they thought, to arouse interest and controversy not only in the Labour Party itself but in politics and the press generally. They looked forward with relish to the obloquy which they foresaw breaking over my head, and they pressed me to get myself ready for a period of high-profile public debate. It never happened. The book was prominently, lengthily and favourably reviewed by many leading journals—and then there was silence. The reviewers themselves made the same mistake as the publishers, in that they too took it for granted that the book was going to stir up a hornet's nest. The *Observer*'s began with the words: "This book is a dose of salts, to be taken at a gulp by the Labour Party and to blast its congested old innards clean." The *Economist* described it as "magnificently scornful and exact, in innumerable passages of cruel analysis that are a delight to read and will never be forgiven." *New Society* described it as "essential reading," and the *Financial Times* said it was "the best statement which has so far appeared of the beliefs and aspirations of the men and women who will shape the Labour Party of tomorrow. As such it is a document of considerable interest and importance."

Why were they all so wrong about the impact the book would have? By and large the events of subsequent years bore out the validity of its critique, so—especially since it was commended so highly by reviewers—one wonders why it did not attract more attention. Some of the fault must have been with the way I wrote it, despite what the reviewers said. But there was also, I fear, a prevailing lack of seriousness among people involved in Labour Party politics: most of them, with only a few exceptions, would not have been interested in any discussion of fundamentals, however it had been presented. The football-fan attitude to party affiliation—the assumption that what is required of one is to cheer one's own side, and to boo their opponents—was held by far more, and far more intelligent, people than I had dreamt. Many asked me why on earth, as an active member of the Labour Party, I had written a book criticizing it. Why had I not, they asked, written a book criticizing the Conservative Party? Others asked me why, if I thought the Labour Party had all the faults I mentioned, I stayed in it. The idea of critically evaluating an organization one cared deeply about with a view to improving it seemed wholly foreign to them. They saw my book quite simply as an attack on the Labour Party. Their view, often openly declared, was that if possible what I said should be totally ignored, and if it could not be ignored I should be counterattacked. The thought of actually considering what I said in case there were any truth in it occurred to very few people. One of them was the Chairman of one of the Paddington constituency Labour parties, who organized a special meeting for me to address. Nobody turned up to it at all, not a single person. So total a boycott of a well-publicized meeting in central London on a dry evening must have taken quite a lot of organizing, not least in view of the fact that at this time I was appearing regularly on the weekly current-affairs television programme with the biggest audience.

However, *The New Radicalism* did have an influence on individuals, and perhaps even on a generation of university students. Most of the current and future leaders of what may be called the social-democratic tendency within the Labour Party read it—one of them told me years later that his political outlook had been influenced by it more than by any other book. Also, it was translated into German and published in Vienna, under the title *Revolution des Umdenkens,* and seems to have had more influence in Austria than in England—there was a battle going on at the time between the liberals and the Marxists within the Austrian Social Democratic Party in which my book seems to have played a part, and which the liberals won.

One thing that came out of *The New Radicalism* was my next book, *The Democratic Revolution,* published in 1964. Not long after publication of *The New Radicalism* a total stranger came up to me one day in a literary club to which I belonged and put to me a publishing proposition. He told me that he edited a series of books that were read mostly in those Third World universities where English was the working language—his books were read typically, he said, by "the trousered African," a phrase I have relished ever since—and he invited me to write one. He pressed on me that in *The New Radicalism* I had written almost exclusively in terms of British domestic politics, and yet the central theme of my book—the advocacy of a democratic radicalism in opposition to both conservatism on one side and Marxism on the other—was a cause in urgent need of promotion in the Third World. Would I be willing to write a book in which I promoted this central idea in terms of issues facing Third World intellectuals? The proposal had a strong appeal for me, and so I wrote the book. It was published in 1964 by The Bodley Head, who published the whole series. Aside from whatever foreign sales the English-language edition may have had it was translated into Chinese, Hindi, Urdu, Korean, Spanish and German.

In it I argued that Communism was already a failed system, not only morally but economically and politically, and that this was clear to most of the people who lived in Communist countries, including most of the people who governed them. The same people also now understood that, for them, progress meant becoming more like the West. So continuing to think in Cold War terms of a global struggle between Communism and Capitalism was out of touch with an already changed reality. The outcome of the Cold War had been decided: the West had won. Both sides now faced the challenge of developing political democracy and social equality in non-Communist societies. The Communist societies themselves had already, without admitting it in their rhetoric, embarked on this task, and were seeking ways of finding the path of development on which the West was already much farther advanced. So, in ways that I instanced, the abandonment of Communism had already begun, and the reform of Communist societies in the direction of the West was quietly but firmly under way.

At the time when I was writing these things in 1963 I knew of nowhere else where they had been said in public. The conclusions were among those I had come to during my travels in Eastern Europe as a television reporter, and were based in the main not on study or reading but on personal observation. From these premisses I went on to argue that the appeal of Communism to Third World countries was delusive. For them to go Communist would mean fighting to get on board a sinking ship. Democracy, I argued, was an altogether more effective instrument for the transformation of their societies than any form of authoritarianism, whether Marxist or otherwise, though very few Third World intellectuals seemed to realize it. And I went on to make this thesis the main theme of the book. The political philosophy I advocated for those of the world's countries that had authoritarian governments was liberal democracy as a revolutionary creed, willing to overthrow dictatorships by force if necessary in order to establish free institutions, and dedicated to the radical transformation of society. I saw this not simply as the best way of doing so because Communism had shown itself incapable, but as better in any case. At that time I was travelling quite widely in black Africa as well as Eastern Europe, so I had first-hand knowledge of the applicability of my ideas to Third World countries as well as Communist ones. In spite of the fact (perhaps even because of it) that *The Democratic Revolution* was a short book, and presented its argument in bold strokes with a very broad brush, I have ever since gone on encountering people in remote parts of the world who refer to it when they meet me.

Today it needs to be remembered that in those days an almost entirely false picture of Communist societies was generally accepted throughout the West, even by most conservatives. When I returned from the first of my travels in Eastern Europe, in the early 1960s, and uttered such elementary truths as that the Communist regimes were cruel, repressive dictatorships; that they had no regard for human rights; that they showed undisguised contempt for the people they governed; that their normal methods had always included torture, the imprisonment of opponents, and judicial murder; that they were hated and feared by most of the people who lived under them; that they contained as an all-pervading feature inequalities of personal power wider than could be found in the West; that they did not even have the redeeming feature of being efficient, but were, on the contrary, inefficient to the point of near-shambles; and that they devoted colossal resources to trying to cover all this over by lies, including most of their official statistics—I found virtually no one willing to believe me. Most of my Labour Party friends thought I was passing through some sort of McCarthyite episode. Terms such as "reds under the bed," "hung-up about Communism," even "reactionary," were bandied about. Nor was it only left-of-centre people who reacted against the truth in this way. My conservative friends thought I was "exaggerating wildly," "going too far," "over the top," and so on; and they kept responding to my remarks with sentences that began "Come, come."

The fact is that in those days a widely held view among people in the West *regardless of their own political convictions* was that the generality of people in Communist countries were Communists, or at least that they willingly accepted Communism; that those societies had more or less achieved social equality; and that the regimes, though tough, were effective, well organized, and economically successful. They might be a bit brutal, and certainly they were insensitive about civil rights, but they operated with harsh efficiency, and might one day overtake the West materially. They offered a more promising model for Third World countries, which had never known democracy, than did the liberal democracies of the West. Some recognizable version of this picture was presented throughout the media and even, shamefully, in most academic work. Although the left was always claiming that people had an unfair view of Communism, and that the media presented a hostilely distorted picture of it, the truth of the matter was the diametrical opposite of that: the view of Communism accepted by most people, and reflected in the media, was so excessively favourable as to be divorced from reality. By and large people on the left tended to think that Communist regimes were pursuing laudable aims, but were using violent and repressive means, while people in the centre and on the right disliked the aims but thought they were being successfully pursued, and were even *afraid* of that success, seeing it as a threat to the acceptance of liberal and democratic values. Our own forms of society, they thought, were more civilized and liveable-in, but were pervaded by a sort of well-meaning incompetence (political and administrative as well as economic) of which the Communist countries were free, and we were therefore in danger of being supplanted by them. Anyone who insisted that this scenario was poppycock from start to finish found himself in the position of the child in the story of the Emperor's clothes. Given modern communications, the fact that it is so easy for people in general to sustain for decades so all-pervadingly mistaken a view about such a large-scale state of affairs in the world is baffling; but it is so, and it remains so to this day. Perhaps it becomes more intelligible when one considers what wildly differing views of our own society can be held by people who have lived in it all their lives.

Because left-of-centre people had a sympathetic view of what they took to be the goals of Communist regimes, and what they imagined to be the social equality those regimes had achieved, they were reluctant to criticize them in more than superficial ways. In fact they were perpetually apologizing for them. In response to important criticisms they would constantly utter sentences beginning, "Well, after all, you have to remember that . . ." This whole attitude was usually buttressed by a deep-seated anti-Americanism that caused them to see the two superpowers as equally delinquent; indeed, it was not at all uncommon for them to see the United States as a greater threat to world peace than the Soviet Union, and in terms of personal sympathies to dislike the United States more than they disliked the Soviet Union. Anyone who saw the United States, with all its faults, as being to the Soviet Union as cheese is to chalk was written off as naive. It is against some such background that many people in the West whose political attitudes within their own societies were unquestionably liberal connived at, or even actively supported, ugly and murderous totalitarian movements in the rest of the world, often against the liberal movements of their own countries. It was a *trahison des clercs* of gargantuan proportions, the supreme intellectual tragedy of the twentieth century.

Soon after *The Democratic Revolution* was finished I was again approached by a publisher with a proposition, this time that I should write a book in connection with a series of television programmes called *Towards 2000*. The theme of the series was the extent to which the world we live in had been, and was continuing to be, transformed by the development of science and technology. The making of the programmes had nothing to do with me, in fact they had been transmitted before I was asked to write the book; they had been so successful that they were to be repeated, and I was being asked to write a book whose publication would be synchronized with the repeat. I read through the transcripts and found that from my point of view the series contained a great deal of good material but had two conspicuous faults. First, the view of science that was propounded was pre-Popperian—the one Popper had, I believed, despatched into limbo. Second, there was nothing at all about the fact that the freedom of enquiry and criticism that are essential for the conduct of a successful science, and therefore for the achievement of a materially prosperous modern society, have inescapable libertarian implications in the political and social spheres. I saw here an opportunity to argue two cases that were close to my heart, so I agreed to write the book—but on condition that I was given a free hand, including freedom not to use half the material from the programmes. This was agreed, and the book, called *Towards 2000,* was published in 1965 by Macdonald. In it my chief concern was to show how the basic ideas advocated for domestic politics in *The New Radicalism,* and for international politics in *The Democratic Revolution,* were inextricably bound up with a tradition of rationality that went back to the critical thinking and Socratic questioning of ancient Greece, and whose most significant incarnation since then was its embodiment in science. This critical rationality I regarded as the most fundamental and distinguishing feature of Western thought, and I wanted a politics that positioned itself in the mainstream of it. Although I knew that the three books would be read by different people I regarded *The New Radicalism, The Democratic Revolution* and *Towards 2000* as the national, international and historical outline-treatments of the same approach. *Towards 2000* was the first book I wrote that could be categorized as "history of ideas." In it I made a conscious attempt not only to treat of ideas and their history but to integrate my treatment of both with a view of general history more broadly conceived. But even my historical narrative was concerned at bottom with ideas, and most specifically with a causal chain that went: "fundamental ideas about the world $\rightarrow$ science $\rightarrow$ technology $\rightarrow$ social change $\rightarrow$ social and political ideas."

It will be evident that by this stage of my life—I was thirty-four when *Towards 2000* was published—the experience I was having as a television reporter was a significant influence on my views. I was, after all, engaged in global travel with the express object of probing into important events, some of them historic, and bringing to light the truth below the surface. It was, I felt, like learning the world; and it was a quite different way of getting to know the world from reading about it, or from following the media. Although millions of people were getting their view of matters from reports like mine, I was not getting my view from TV reports but had to create it for myself on the basis of direct observation and experience. The difference is chasm-like, and it stretched all the way from my large-scale attitudes, such as the one I took towards Communism, down to my assessment of individual men and women in public life. My friends and acquaintances were given to forming confident opinions about politicians whom they saw only on television, whereas often I knew those individuals to be very different from the way they appeared on the screen.

I was getting this sort of direct, behind-the-façade education not only about international affairs but about the society in which I lived. Over the years I made programmes about such subjects as poverty in old age, the life of the unemployed, conditions in prisons, mental hospitals, comprehensive schools, the churches, the judges, small farmers, the boat-building industry, and all sorts of other subjects, some of them quirky; and always it involved me in strenuous attempts to find out what the truth really was—and led more often than not to the conclusion, supported by evidence, that this was different from what was generally supposed. I evolved a new, frank way of dealing on television with subjects hitherto taboo, like abortion, adultery, prostitutes and their clients, homosexuality, and so on. In this respect I was among the many midwives of the revolution in social attitudes that characterized the 1960s. Invariably I discovered not only that whatever social problem I was delving into was commoner than most people were ready to think but that the nature of it was different from what they supposed. It was in the logic of the situation that I should do a great deal more research for each of these documentaries than found its way into the programmes, so I was learning a lot more about each subject than I was passing on. In some ways this was frustrating, so I took to using the material for extended articles in journals such as *New Society.*

It says something about British attitudes at that time that the two programmes that created the most stir were both about homosexuality, one about men, the other about women. On the morning of the day of transmission of the one about lesbianism one of the country's most popular newspapers published an editorial clamouring for this filth to be kept off the nation's screens, thereby greatly increasing the viewing audience. The *New Statesman* asked me to write a special supplement on lesbianism, so I did, and for the first time that weekly journal sold out its entire printing before eleven o'clock on the morning of publication. Secker & Warburg, the book publishers, asked me to write a book about homosexuality. I refused, having by this time had enough of the subject and being unwilling to face the additional months of work on it that writing a book would require. David Farrer, the partner in the firm who had seen *The New Radicalism* through the press, begged me to reconsider. He confided to me that he was a homosexual, and spoke movingly—though not self-pityingly—about what it was like for people like himself to live their lives under permanent threat of imprisonment and blackmail. He thought a book at this juncture might make a contribution to getting homosexuality decriminalized. So I agreed to write it.

I tried to solve my problem by dictating the book, thereby avoiding spending too much time on it, but this turned out to be a mistake. By dint of dictating all day every day I was able (having the research at my fingertips) to complete the first draft in a week. At this point I was elated. "Amazing!" I thought: "I've written a whole book in a week!" It was too good to be true. And indeed it was. When the transcripts returned from the typist I found them unsatisfactory in almost every imaginable respect. The sentences were loosely constructed and full of stock phrases; the chapters had no structure but were just arbitrary lengths of prose; the vocabulary was impoverished; misplaced habits of speech, like repetition for emphasis, abounded. It might have been lively talk but it was not publishable prose. I settled down to sub-edit it into something acceptable, and there was not a single sentence that I did not either cut or rewrite. So I ended up rewriting the entire book by hand on the pages of a typescript, which took me three months. Unfortunately for me, this working method sacrificed what could have been the comparatively interesting task of minting new sentences for the dreary one of sub-editing a badly written text. And in circumstances like this, one never liberates oneself from what one starts out with, because that is what one is working on all the time, and the end product is the best thing one can turn it into—one cannot turn a sow's ear into a silk purse.

When the book appeared in 1966 under the title *One in Twenty: A Report on Homosexuality in Men and Women* it was extravagantly praised because of its content, but the truth is that neither the book as a whole nor its individual chapters were well constructed, nor were the sentences well written. Only one or two reviewers expressed any reservations on these counts, but they were the most perceptive ones. When a change in the law created the need for a comprehensively revised edition I took the opportunity to rewrite the book yet again. There is no doubt that the second edition is the better version, though I have never been other than dissatisfied with it. However, its practical consequences were good: it was generally credited with helping to get the law changed. And it may have contributed something in other societies too, for it was translated into German, French, Italian, Spanish, Dutch and Danish. When I visited Italy shortly after its publication there I saw it displayed on bookstalls and in bookshops everywhere I went. When eventually I asked the Italian publishers when they were going to pay me some royalties they told me there had been no sales.

I wrote two books by the same method, and at the same time. Since publishing *Towards 2000* Macdonald had been pressing me for another book, and eventually we agreed that I would write about the art of television interviewing, and how programmes of the kind I was involved in were made. There had been a remarkable public response to them, yet most of the viewers had little idea (and that little usually wrong, it seems) about how they were put together. So when I had finished dictating the first draft of *One in Twenty* and sent the tapes off to be typed I dictated the first draft of *The Television Interviewer*— then while that was being typed I got down to work on the transcript of *One in Twenty.* Working like this, moving back and forth between the two books, I produced them together over a period of six months. Everything I have said about the defects of *One in Twenty,* and my attempts to rectify them, applied to *The Television Interviewer.* Never since have I dictated anything intended for publication, no matter how short it might be. Letters, memoranda, notes, and all the rest, I am happy enough to dictate; but anything for publication I always write out carefully by hand—even if I am then going to dictate it.

The Television Interviewer was published only two months after *One in Twenty,* in May 1966. It was the first book of mine that was published simultaneously in hardback and paperback. Associated Rediffusion, the company for which I made most of my television programmes, sent a copy of it to every MP, and for many years gave it to each new person they hired, so there was a sense in which it became something of a handbook for practitioners.

During the five years 1962–6 I published five books while being involved with television in a way that included a great deal of foreign travel. To accomplish this I established a six-weeks-on, six-weeks-off arrangement with my television colleagues. This gave me complete control of half my time, and enabled me to know in advance when these independent periods were going to be. This had wider implications, for it enabled me to have a genuine private life. During my six-weeks-on periods of working for television I had no idea what continent I was going to be in from one week to the next, and sometimes from one day to the next. I went to my office one morning with my suitcase packed to fly to Germany that afternoon, and when afternoon came I was on a plane to Central Africa. For someone living all the time like this no normal private life is possible: when you arrange to see friends, or book tickets for a theatre, or make any other kind of social arrangement, you find yourself having to cancel at the last minute, not just sometimes but often. Even the most simple arrangement to meet another person can become insolubly difficult. This places a strain on ordinary friendships that most of them cannot survive indefinitely, and a dangerous strain even on intimacies. I saw the effects it had on the lives of people around me: they lost touch with all but their most steadfast friends, and many of their marriages came to grief. I lived like it full-time myself for one year, and found it intolerable. I found that a continuing private life, with true intimacy and friendships at its centre—and work outside that circle, not as the centre of it—was indispensable to me. I simply had to have time to digest experience, to think, to write books, to listen to music, to go to the theatre—and, if it comes to that, to study philosophy.

14

The Search for Meaning

Like a lot of other men, I went through a mid-life crisis in my middle and late thirties of cataclysmic force. No doubt on the surface I seemed to have everything I could reasonably want—good health, energy, an adventurous life, rewarding friendships, exhilarating love affairs, success in my work, exciting travel, the sustained nourishment of music, theatre, reading—but in the middle of it all I was overwhelmed, almost literally so, by a sense of mortality. The realization hit me like a demolition crane that I was inevitably going to die. This feeling, when it came, was not an ordinary fear or anxiety but was hyper-vivid and preternaturally powerful. As in a nightmare, I felt trapped and unable to escape from something that I was also unable to face. Death, my death, the literal destruction of *me,* was totally inevitable, and had been from the very instant of my conception. Nothing that I could ever do, now or at any other time, could make any difference to that, nor could it ever have done so at any moment in my life. Not only would being brave make no difference: gibbering cowardice would make no difference either.* I found this fact un-comeable-to-terms-with. I felt—as I imagine a lot of the people who have confronted firing squads must

* I was many years later to come across the following lines of poetry by Philip Larkin:

> Most things may never happen: this one will,
> And realisation of it rages out
> In furnace-fear when we are caught without
> People or drink. Courage is no good:
> It means not scaring others. Being brave

have felt—engulfed by mind-numbing terror in the face of oblivion. For several years this was my normal mode of existence, a nightmare from which it was impossible to awake because I was awake already.

The experience of being soaked in this realization for several years changed my life. And never afterwards was there any going back on that change. The first of many fundamental questions it raised was an urgent one about meaning. In the face of death I craved for my life to have some meaning. I found the thought that it might just mean nothing at all—might, in a long perspective, *be* nothing at all—terrifying. However, far from assuming for this reason that there must be some point to it, I was only too aware that there might be no point in it. The whole thing could just be contingent, arbitrary, accidental, meaningless. I hungered for it to have meaning, but from the fact that I hungered no consequence followed to the effect that it *did* have meaning. The meaninglessness of everything was a real possibility. Confronted with this fact, I felt what can only be described as existential terror, a horror of nothingness.

To anyone in this frame of mind nearly all human pursuits seem vain beyond all description. In the eye of eternity a human lifespan is barely a flicker. Death will be upon us before we know where we are; and once we are dead it will be for ever. What can anything I do mean or matter to me when I have gone down into complete nothingness for the rest of eternity? What can it matter to anyone else, either, when they too are eternally nothing? If the void is the permanent destination of all of us, all value and all significance are merely pretended for purposes of carrying on our little human game, like children dressing up. It is, of course, a willing pretence: we cannot bring ourselves to face eternal nothingness, so we busy ourselves with our little lives and all their vacuous pursuits, surrounded by institutions that we ourselves have created yet which we pretend are important, and which help us to shut out the black and endless night that surrounds us. It is all, in the end, nothing—nothing whatsoever. I am biologically programmed to want to go on living, so I do: I eat, drink, sleep, try to ward off danger, and all the rest of it. But the idea that it means anything is a pathetic little piece of self-delusion.

To anyone thinking like this the only human activity that seems to have any importance at all is the search for meaning in life. But unless such a search is

---

Lets no one off the grave.
Death is no different whined at than withstood.

The whole poem, "Aubade," expresses exactly the form of the fear of death that I experienced. No doubt for this reason it seems to me Larkin's best poem. The fact that it is also his last important one— poetry gave him up as soon as he had written it—leads me to suspect that the achievement of it was what he had been working towards throughout his life.

honest the result is likely to be illusory. And an intellectually honest search cannot start from the question *What is the meaning of life?,* for to do that is to take an answer for granted to not just one but three prior questions: *Can there be any such thing as a "meaning of life"?, If there can, have we human beings any possibility of finding out what it is?,* and *If finding out is a possibility for us, how should we go about it?* Only if there are good grounds for believing that we have positive and accurate answers to these questions are we likely to address ourselves to the fourth question, *What is the meaning of life?,* with success. If we accept a misleading answer to any of the first three questions the whole of the rest of our journey will be wasted.

In this frame of mind I read or re-read the central masterpieces of the great philosophers—of whom, after all, there are only somewhere between a dozen and twenty—and read them as if my life depended on it. I also read those figures on the margins of philosophy whose subject often comes close to being "the meaning of life"—such writers as St. Augustine, Pascal, Kierkegaard, Nietzsche, Tolstoy. From them it seemed a short and natural step to the mystics, of whom I found Angelus Silesius the most revelatory. And from those in turn it was only another short step to the basic texts of the religions to which the mystics so frequently referred: I re-read the Upanishads, the New Testament, and the more reflective parts of the Old Testament. This went on over a period of years, and in no sense was it a planned programme of reading. Rather was it a headlong, desperate search, as if my survival were at stake. I seized on and wolfed down whatever I hoped could help me. It was scarcely an intellectual activity at all but rather a practical, physical, almost animal one. It so happens—I thought then and think still—that what I was reading constituted the most important and valuable prose writings that there are: but in addition to that, the sheer emotional avidity with which I read them rendered them of unique importance to me. Quite a lot of what I then read was metabolized into my system and has been part of me ever since. Any attempt to summarize it, or to guide someone else through it, or even to say what I got out of it, would be jejune and hopeless, like a music-lover's attempt to particularize symphony by symphony what great music means to him.

There were certain assumptions which I knew from the beginning I was making but found it psychologically impossible not to make. One was that I am a part of whatever there is. No matter what the truth may be about the nature of reality, I must be a part of it, and therefore I must have a place in that account. I am not a detached observer looking at reality from outside, as something existing separately from myself: I am, whether in part of my nature or the whole of it, one of the material objects that inhabit the world, and it seems self-evident to me that if there is a spiritual dimension to reality I partake of that too. Because of this I had a deep conviction from the beginning that self-understanding and the understanding of the world and total reality are related parts of the same enterprise. This is not to say that I assumed that I as a human being must be especially important. Far from it. I was only too well aware that my whole existence might be the merest flicker of a speck of dust in the darkest corner of the remotest room of an empty house, as near to nothing as anything that is can be. This was indeed my fear, and I was more than half-way to viewing it as realized. But if that was so, it was still so because of the place of my existence in its overall context, its relationship to a wider scheme of things. So even my insignificance was something whose nature could be understood only in terms of how I stood in relation to the rest of reality, and therefore in terms of whatever else there was; and therefore I needed to have some understanding of that to have any hope of knowing what the truth was about myself and my situation.

Another assumption that I found it psychologically impossible not to make was that being now human was fundamental to the reality of my nature, such that metaphysically I was in the same boat as other human beings. The most foundational of all metaphysical questions presented themselves to me spontaneously not in the first person singular but in the first person plural: not "What am I?" and "What happens when I die?" but "What are we?" and "What happens when we die?" At first I tried to tell myself that in asking such questions I was making a colossal assumption and taking a giant step away from my own centre: in theory, at least, the only thing I could be certain of was my own existence, so I ought to put these questions in the form "What am I?" and "What happens when I die?" However, when I did this I found I no longer had the same interest in the questions. It was only in their first-person-plural form that they gripped me and held me. When I tried to analyse why this should be so it seemed to me that if the questions were *only* about me there was no way in which I could regard them as being of any interest or importance *in themselves*—important to me, yes, but not important other than to me. By contrast, I found it impossible to regard such questions about other people as of no importance even if (as was usually the case) the people themselves had little interest in them. So not only was it a simple and straightforward matter of fact that the first-person-plural questions were *felt* by me to be of intrinsic interest whereas the first-person-singular questions were not: it seemed to emerge on analysis that only in their plural form could they have any kind of impersonal importance.

I stress that these two suppositions—that the most urgent questions facing me are not questions about me individually but questions about the situation of human beings as such, and that any philosophical understanding of this would have to involve seeing it in the context of a wider reality of which it was part—were involuntary. I could not, in practice, think without them. This did not prevent me from subjecting them to analysis; but analysis seemed to confirm the validity of this view of them.

So, willy-nilly, I found myself involved with others in what was essentially a joint enterprise aimed at trying to understand whatever the reality is of which we human beings find ourselves to be part; and these others are a collection of widely differing people going back thousands of years. I did not ask to join, I just found myself in it. And I have had this feeling all my adult life, in particular during those recurrent periods when I immersed myself in reading the greatest philosophers of the past. Living daily with, shall we say, Hume, or Kant, I felt them to be closer to me than my friends, and I felt I knew them better, for I knew their insides, so to speak, their souls as revealed in their books. They have been among my lifelong companions, and I have personal feelings of gratitude to them for what they have meant to me, what they have done for me, the difference they have made to my life. My attitude towards them is very different from that of the scholar. What Kant scholars are trying to understand, I take it, is Kant; and what Plato scholars are trying to understand is Plato; and so on. In that sense such writers are not objects of ultimate interest to me. What I am trying to understand is the world in which I find myself, and myself. I read the great philosophers because they enlighten me about what I am trying to understand, often giving me insights of enormous depth that I could not have arrived at without them. But in the final analysis what matters to me is not what they believe but what I believe. I am interested in their work in so far as it is grist to my mill. So I treat them not as objects of study in their own right, as a scholar would, but as life-enhancing companions and guides, shipmates cannier than I in a voyage of discovery on which we are all embarked. As for scholars, I respect their labour and have drawn great benefit from it, but the fact is that at the banquet of philosophy they are neither the cooks nor the gourmets but the waiters that run between the two.

The basic drive behind real philosophy is curiosity about the world, not interest in the writings of philosophers. Each of us emerges from the pre-consciousness of babyhood and simply finds himself here, in it, in the world. That experience alone astonishes some people. What *is* all this—what is the world? And what are we? From the beginning of humanity some have been under a compulsion to ask these questions, and have felt a craving for the answers. This is what is really meant by any such phrase as "mankind's need for metaphysics."

The earliest answers that were arrived at seem to have been in terms of spirits—either that the world was a spirit, or that it had been made by a spirit, or that there were spirits in each individual thing and each activity of Nature, or that there was a more limited number of spirits who ran everything—perhaps together, perhaps in rivalry with one another. It might have been less surprising if primitive man had started out just simply seeing objects as objects, and only much later, at an advanced stage of sophistication, evolved the idea that they were inhabited or governed by invisible spirits. But it was the other way round; in fact the idea that there are no spirits at all is a highly advanced idea, only very recent in human history, achieved after thousands of years of intellectual development. We must not be misled by the explanatory primitiveness of materialism into thinking of it as historically, or developmentally, or intellectually primitive. Quite the reverse. My conjecture as to why this is so is that we know ourselves to be material objects endowed with conscious awareness, moved by acts of will, passions, thoughts; so perhaps, after all, it comes naturally to us to suppose that other material objects are like us in these respects, especially as this then provides us with a way of understanding their movements, a way that is intelligible to us precisely because of the analogy with ourselves. To this day children tend to be highly superstitious, to believe in all kinds of magic and fairy tales; and it is only slowly, as they grow older, that they learn not to be.

Inevitably, people's sense of orientation in the world depends on the view they take of it: so when everyone's view of the world was in terms of spirits, everyone's orientation to the world was what we might now call religious. With equal inevitability, such frameworks of orientation were basic to emerging forms of social organization—human beings must have organized themselves into groups in relation to what they took reality to be in order to cope with it effectively, perhaps even in part to master it. And since anyone who made the spirits angry was likely to bring their wrath down on the tribe—unless of course the tribe clearly dissociated itself from him and punished him—it must have seemed almost natural in such belief-systems to punish any dissenter dramatically.

As has been suggested earlier, what we now call philosophy begins at the point where dissent starts to be allowed. When people are permitted to criticize the prevailing worldview, and to put forward reasons for their criticisms, and thus inaugurate discussion and debate, the first stirrings of philosophy have occurred. Although the earliest developments of this kind that we know of seem to have been in pre-Socratic Greece, it seems to me that from a philosophical (as distinct from historical) point of view it matters little where it was. In whatever place, it was a turning point in human development when people began to think critically, and to voice their criticisms, and to argue with one another. Among so many other things, the practice of argument brings about the development of reason. People discover in practice that some forms of argument stand up to criticism better than others. They try to make their arguments as good as they can, and seek out weaknesses in arguments they oppose. They become ever more perceptive about what does, and does not, follow from what. One of the criteria of what it is possible to believe becomes what will stand up, i.e., what will withstand criticism. From such beginnings human understanding of the world and human reason develop side by side, interacting with each other at every stage.

To begin with, and for well over two thousand years, no distinction was made between what we now call philosophy and what we now call science. People were simply trying to understand the world—and learning in the process about their process of learning. Also from the beginning, philosophers occupied themselves with questions about the world as a whole. Thus Thales, who flourished around 580 B.C., and is traditionally regarded as the first philosopher, taught that the world was floating on water. It would appear from this that he equated the world with the earth, and earth with land: at all events his theory was an intelligent and imaginative one, but more important than that, it proposed an answer to an interesting and fundamental question, namely *What keeps the world in place?,* and then invited critical discussion of it. One of his pupils, Anaximander, a man of almost incredible insight, rejected the theory and proposed in its place a breathtakingly different one: "The earth . . . is held up by nothing, but remains stationary owing to the fact that it is equally distant from all other things. Its shape is . . . like that of a drum. . . . We walk on one of its flat surfaces, while the other is on the opposite side." One of *his* pupils, Anaximenes, rejected this theory in its turn, not in favour of a better one but in favour of one that was less good—in fact point-missing about Anaximander's, and poverty-stricken by comparison with it—namely that the earth is flat and that its "flatness is responsible for its stability; for it . . . covers like a lid the air beneath it." This is a regression half-way back to Thales—an improvement on Thales's theory but put forward just as if something better than either of them had not arrived in between. It was hundreds of years before Anaximander's theory was improved on, a period during which even the most gifted people worked to develop ideas from a position that he had got beyond. This "two steps forward, one step back" pattern of development over vast stretches of time has recurred ever since in the history of philosophy. Newcomers to it should never take for granted that the philosophical assumptions of their own day are an advance on what went before: what went before may be better, and better by a wide margin. I believe that this is the case today in our relationship to the Kantian–Schopenhauerian philosophy: we live in a one-step-back period.

Some insightful ideas were put forward by later pre-Socratic philosophers, ideas of lasting importance. Heraclitus taught that what we think of as things are more accurately understood as processes: they begin (come into existence) and are in a state of perpetual change, and therefore activity, while they last; their form may be constant but certainly not their matter; and then they pass away. What they are, then, is not stable material objects but something going on. Democritus produced an atomic theory of matter, and taught that the true basis of reality is hidden from us. Xenophanes taught that although we can never know the final truth about anything, it is open to us to get closer and closer to it over time. Pythagoras taught that of everything in Nature a deeper understanding than our senses can give us is expressible in numbers, or as we might nowadays say mathematical equations. Parmenides taught that the hidden reality behind the variegated world of phenomena is One. These are marvellous ideas whose importance in Western thought it would be difficult to exaggerate, and which more than two thousand years later stand in the forefront of what we like to think of as the most advanced conceptions, both in science and in religion.

Not only was the best thought of the pre-Socratics profound, it had also an aesthetic content. All writing was in verse before any was in prose, and they wrote in verse, some of it magnificent—for instance the following by Xenophanes:

> The Ethiops say that their gods are flat-nosed and black
> While the Thracians say that theirs have blue eyes and red hair.

> Yet if cattle or horses or lions had hands and could draw
> And could sculpture like men, then the horses would draw their gods
> Like horses, and cattle like cattle, and each would then shape
> Bodies of gods in the likeness, each kind, of its own.

Saying what is said here made Feuerbach's reputation when he said it more than two thousand years later.

One reason why the pre-Socratics are called the pre-Socratics is that Socrates consciously rebelled against them. It was not that he disagreed with their doctrines so much as that he disagreed with their choice of the questions to be raised. He maintained that what it is most important for us to know are not impersonal truths about the world but how we ought to live. So the vital questions are not "scientific" but "moral." He went around asking *What is justice?, What is courage?, What is friendship?, What is piety?,* and questions of that sort. As far as we know he never wrote anything: all his teaching was by word of mouth. It took a form that has become famous under his name as Socratic dialogue. He used to boast, disingenuously, that he had no wisdom to impart, but only questions to ask. He usually started by asking someone the meaning of an important concept, let us say "justice"; and then, whatever the person said, Socrates would go on questioning him in such a way that it became obvious that there were contradictions in the offered definition—and therefore justice could not be what the other person said it was—and therefore that the person did not *know* what justice was, even though he had supposed that he did. The victim would be left at the end profoundly troubled, the ruins of his previous assumptions littered around his feet, no longer knowing what is meant by some concept fundamental to his life. Needless to say this procedure disturbed many people, and was regarded as socially subversive by some. It all ended with Socrates being hauled up in court on a charge of corrupting the young; and in 399 B.C. he was condemned to death and executed. But by that time he had launched a mode of philosophical enquiry that has continued to this day, and is now inextricably associated with the very concept of Western civilization.

His ablest pupil, Plato, who was about thirty-one when Socrates died, was determined not only to clear his master's name but to continue his work, so Plato wrote and circulated dialogues in which Socrates was presented as a star performer who was always vindicated in the end. It is virtually certain that in the earliest of these, Socrates' actual questions and arguments were being reiterated. But Plato was a true pupil of his master in that he understood that being a philosopher meant not reproducing someone else's thoughts but thinking for yourself, criticizing your own ideas as well as theirs, questioning familiar assumptions, and so on. So once he had made sure that the best of Socrates' teaching was well in circulation, Plato went on to develop his own philosophy, and he did so in the form that he had so successfully established and created a demand for, namely published dialogues with Socrates as the protagonist.

This explains the fact that in Plato's early dialogues the "Socrates" figure expresses—largely, though not entirely, through the implications of his questions—one philosophical viewpoint whereas in the middle and later dialogues he puts forward another. They are in fact the two different philosophies of two different philosophers, in the first case the historical Socrates and in the second case Plato. The first is narrowly concerned with moral and personal questions. The second ranges over the whole of human experience: cosmology and science, mathematics, the arts, political and social life, personal morality and the rest. So close does Plato come to mapping out the terrain with which philosophers have concerned themselves ever since that the twentieth-century philosopher Whitehead was able to make a famous comment to the effect that the whole of Western philosophy is footnotes to Plato. Not only does Plato embrace the cosmological concerns that Socrates rejected, he puts mathematical physics at the centre of his account of the empirical world. However, he does not believe that the empirical world is all there is. On the contrary, it is, in his view, a world of appearances only, of fleeting phenomena that have no abiding reality. "Behind" it, so to speak, is a world of timeless non-material entities that constitute the only permanent reality there is. What the relationship is between that and the world of our experience is a question he has much to say about, as is also how human beings can hope to gain knowledge of the eternal. These aspects of his philosophy were later to have an incalculable influence on the early development of Christianity—so much so that some of the ideas widely thought of as most characteristically Christian come in fact from Plato.

Plato's are the first written works of any Western philosopher to survive in the form in which he wrote them. Socrates, as I have said, wrote nothing—most of our knowledge of him, and of what he said, is derived from Plato's dialogues. As for the pre-Socratics, not one of their complete works has survived: our knowledge of them consists entirely of quotations, summaries and references in the works of others, though some of these are quite long. Plato is the first philosopher whose works themselves we have, and we have reason to believe that we have them all. No philosophy before or since has had so great an influence, except arguably that of Aristotle; and since Aristotle was a pupil of Plato, Plato can even claim some of the credit for that. It is extraordinary that the first philosopher whose works we possess should remain to this day, in the minds of so many people, the best. The standard view among professional philosophers is that—of those whose writings we have—Plato, Aristotle and Kant are in a class above the rest; and it is hard to see how anyone steeped in the literature of philosophy could differ far from that judgment. Certainly I would not, though if I had to award a single prize I would give it to Kant. There is, however, something uniquely awe-inspiring about Plato's achievement in that he produced work of genius across the entire range of philosophical thought during the first half of the fourth century B.C., at a time when no one else had ever come remotely near to doing any such thing. And a great many of his ideas have remained at, or very near, the centre of Western thinking ever since.

He was a wonderful literary artist, as well as a great philosopher. It has long been the standard view among classical scholars that his is the most beautiful Greek prose ever to have been written. His dialogues display mastery of literary form, economic yet effective characterization, cunning use of dramatic irony, and other such qualities. There are some two dozen of them, varying in length between twenty and three hundred printed pages. The most moving are those concerning the trial and death of Socrates, which is to say the *Crito,* the *Phaedo* and the *Apology.* The most famous and influential are the *Republic* and the *Symposium.* Good English translations of nearly all are now easily available, and nearly all are well worth reading.

Most of the professional philosophers who do not regard Plato as the greatest philosopher of all time withhold that accolade from him because they give it to Aristotle. At the very beginning of philosophy's recorded history these two philosophers symbolize two approaches which, in various forms, were to confront each other down the ages. On the one hand there are philosophers who believe that the world of actual and possible human experience is not what is permanent, or permanently important, and therefore that we should try somehow or other to transcend it with our minds—or, if that is impossible, to think our way to the boundary between our world and what is of ultimate significance, so that even if we cannot cross that frontier we can at least pin it down and see where it runs—and perhaps even discover, from outside, the *shape* of the territory we cannot enter. (Cf. Wittgenstein's assertion in the *Tractatus,* 4.114 and 4.115, that philosophy "must set limits to what cannot be thought by working outwards through what can be thought. It will signify what cannot be said, by presenting clearly what can be said.") As against philosophers of this kind there are others who think that whether or not the empirical world is all there is, it is all we can experience or know, and if we try to soar beyond it on the wings of unsupported thought we shall talk nonsense during the flight and inevitably crash. Furthermore there is no need to pass beyond this world of experience in our search for something worth philosophizing about, for it is in itself an inexhaustible source of curiosity, wonder, richness and beauty. Trying to understand it will engross us, and reward us, for a lifetime. The difference between these two approaches has some relation to most of the great bifurcations in the history of philosophy—rationalism versus empiricism, idealism versus realism (or, in a different sense, idealism versus materialism), and so on. The temperament of individual philosophers has usually drawn them to one side or the other: most find themselves to be either Plato persons or Aristotle persons by some sort of natural inclination. The unique greatness of Kant was that he integrated the two, and in doing so showed philosophy its true path.

Aristotle was the first and the greatest philosopher of the second kind, the greatest of the natural empiricists. He was in love with experience, and he devoted his life to deepening and enriching his understanding of it, working always from *inside* experience, never trying to impose abstract explanations on it from the outside. In the course of a hard-working lifetime of doing this he became a sort of one-man encyclopaedia. He marked off the areas of the basic sciences for the first time, and did some of the earliest work in each of them (and, incidentally, gave some of them names by which they are known to this day). Not only did he seek scientific explanations, he had the insight to ask fundamental questions about what a scientific explanation *is,* and how we should go about formulating one. He codified all known logic into principles that remained in active use for two thousand years. He studied plants, animals, human beings and their many different forms of political organization, and made lasting contributions to ethics and aesthetics. He addressed himself at length to some of the most fundamental metaphysical questions concerning the respective nature of mind, identity, form, substance, continuity, change and causal connection, and said permanently important things about each. There was a period of hundreds of years, much later, when his work constituted the largest organized body of knowledge that Western man possessed. When universities came into existence in the Middle Ages they made Aristotle the foundation of the curriculum—which is why Dante described him as "the teacher of those who know." In the seventeenth century, when modern science began to emerge, the then-prevailing view of the world—two thousand years after Aristotle—was Aristotle's, and it was this that modern science had to combat in order to establish itself. A knowledge of it is altogether indispensable for an understanding of history. And to this day a lot of it remains either valid or interesting in its own right.

The works that Aristotle prepared for publication were praised throughout antiquity for their superlative beauty of style. Cicero described his writing as "a river of gold." Tragically, none of it survives. All we have of Aristotle is what was written up from his lecture notes, either by him or by his pupils who attended the lectures and passed their notes round. References in ancient literature to him and his published writings are so numerous that we have quite a lot of knowledge about what has been lost, and the calculation is that what we possess represents something like a fifth of his total output. It fills twelve volumes, and ranges over the whole of what was then human knowledge, a good deal of which it inaugurated. Alas, the fact that it consists of written-up lecture notes makes it stodgy reading, so it tends to be read only by students and scholars. Whereas one can imagine an intelligent person reading Plato for pleasure, it is difficult to imagine that sort of reading of Aristotle—or Kant. These last two are heavy going, and have to be worked at, indeed worked at *hard,* if they are to yield rewards. Students read Aristotle or Kant if they have to, or as part of a university course, but apart from them only the most dedicated lovers of philosophy are likely to read their works. This fact makes me feel forlorn, because it means that what are by any serious reckoning two of the four or five greatest philosophers of all time are never read by most intelligent or well-educated people, and never become part of their mental furniture. I am realistic enough not to expect this to change, but it makes me sad.

For reasons which I cannot explain fully enough to satisfy even myself, reading other people's accounts of the work of a great philosopher is inadequate as a substitute for reading the work itself. The number of indisputably great Western philosophers is less than two dozen, so anyone who wants to can read all their most important writings within a manageable period of time. In bulk, the literature *about* their work exceeds the work itself thousands of times over. Nearly all professional philosophers spend more of their lives concerned with this than they do with the originals. Almost by definition, it is not of anything remotely near the same calibre; but here and there are to be found penetrating commentaries or critiques or introductions that are genuinely deep in their understanding of the philosophy they deal with, lucid and accurate in their presentation of its arguments, perceptive in their criticisms, judicious in their evaluations. Why, then, can a high-quality secondary source not put us in possession of everything of importance about the original? If I turn this question round it becomes harder to answer: What is missing from a really good and full second-order exposition? Obviously the reader does not get from it the literary style and personality of the great philosopher himself—but then what has that to do with philosophy, strictly speaking? Aristotle and Kant are two of the greatest philosophers there have ever been—some people think the greatest—but in both cases the style of their work as we have it is terrible; and Kant, at least, has little literary personality or presence in his writing. Aristotle is merely written-up lecture notes anyway. So if in any area of their thought I make it clear to someone what the problems were to which they addressed themselves, what solutions they proposed to those problems, what arguments they used in support of their proposals, what potential objections they considered, and what their answers were to these objections, what am I failing to put him in possession of that he would have got from reading the originals?

I have discussed this question with many of my philosopher friends, and I have to say that none of us has a satisfactory answer to give. Yet we are all agreed that reading an original is an experience of a different order altogether from reading someone else's account of it, no matter how good. I can suggest only a few partial explanations. There seems to be something fundamentally interactive about the nature of philosophy—not only interactive between an individual and a problem but interactive between one individual and another. Questioning, dialogue, discussion, debate, argument—these seem to be, in some central way, essential to the nature of philosophy. So it is only when we are interacting with a philosopher and his work that we are really "getting" him. Also, no two people ever give the same account of the same work; so if we read Dr. A's account of Mr. X, what we are actually getting is not Mr. X but Dr. A—on the subject of Mr. X, admittedly, but it is still Dr. A that we are reading and not Mr. X. However accurate and persuasive his exposition, it always remains the case that what we are reading is what Dr. A considers important about the philosophy of Mr. X; and, what is more, in the terms in which Dr. A chooses to express it. If I read Plato I am in direct contact with Plato, but if I read Dr. A on Plato I am in direct contact with Dr. A. In the former case I am in direct contact with one of the greatest minds of all time: in the latter case with (no disrespect to Dr. A) a fairly run-of-the-mill one. And if instead of all this I decide to read Professor B on the same subject, that will be different yet again, and it will be different because Professor B is not Dr. A. For all these reasons it is only if I read Mr. X for myself that I am getting for myself what Mr. X says. Only then can I know that these are his actual words, this is his voice, and this his *tone* of voice. Anything else is not that. Only if we read a philosopher for ourselves can we really know how *we* react to him, what *we* think of him, and what, if anything, we consider important about what he is saying. It is a unique interaction that no other can clone.

Direct contact with originality is an inexpressible experience, like listening to great music or reading great poetry. Since it is the philosopher himself who is actually having the ideas, and bringing them to birth, traces of these processes are omnipresent in his writing. When we read original thinkers we are to some extent encountering processes, not being presented only with the finished products. For this reason what they say may be sometimes groping, and therefore less assured, more blundering or blurred, than an account of the same ideas given by someone who, coming along afterwards and finding them ready made, has only to think about how to put them lucidly, without himself having actually to *have* them.

There are other factors too. Each past philosopher was writing in a different historical and social context, and making use of a language at a particular stage in its development. More important, his *intellectual* orientation was different. It is impossible to see how Aristotle could have done his work if Plato had not first done his, and impossible to see how Plato could have done his had it not been for Socrates. Similarly, Schopenhauer's philosophy is unimaginable without Kant's, and Kant's without Hume's. Kant's philosophy is today only some two hundred years old: most "great" philosophy predates it, and had no possibility of incorporating its insights. An original philosophy carries its whole historical situation with it as a part of itself, including the situation of the language in which it is written. And all these things are lost in second-order expositions.

All these differences obtain between original thinkers and even the ablest expositors and commentators: what is not clear is why any of them should detract from the intellectual force of rational arguments clearly expressed. Having said this I must insert what might appear at first sight to be a qualification. I have had the experience of grappling with philosophers whom I have been unable to understand at a first attempt. The outstanding examples are Hegel and Heidegger. When I first read them they seemed to me little more than gobbledygook. I persisted, but got nowhere, and eventually became bogged down, and stopped. So I turned to commentators. Sure enough I was soon saying to myself, "*So this is what they're getting at!*" or even "*So this is what it's about!*" Eventually I returned to the philosophers and tackled them again— and found to my surprise that I could understand them, though sometimes I differed from the commentators about what it was they were saying. This means that there are cases when one needs to read commentators—and what is more to read them first. Even so, in those cases just as in all others, I found when I came to read the original philosophers that it was an experience of a different order—even more so in those cases than in others, because it felt like extracting gold from ore.

For all these reasons I have paid little attention to the secondary literature of philosophy, preferring to spend my time re-reading and re-re-reading the philosophers themselves. It has been my experience that if you want to deepen your understanding of a philosopher whose work you have read you will do it far more by reading it again than by reading a book about it by somebody else. Commentaries will draw your attention to innumerable details that you missed, or that you could not have known, but in the nature of the case it is not the details that really matter. Of course, if you are engrossed by something you will find the detail of it fascinating anyway, and if you are making a special study, or writing for publication, then it will be a necessary requirement for you to master detail. In circumstances such as these I have immersed myself in secondary literature. But philosophy is the extreme example of a field in which the big issues and big questions are of such preponderance that the rest is not really all that important by comparison. Time spent with secondary literature is life lived in the shallows; time spent with the great philosophers is life lived in the limitless depths of the ocean.

I fear that it is only people who are not really interested in the great issues who are happy habitually to devote their time to detail. Certainly, those are the people who most frequently get big things wrong. Of course, whoever you are, there will be times when you get things wrong: then it is essential for you to be put right from outside yourself, so you always need a certain amount of self-monitoring to be sure you are not making a significant blunder. But in most cases that is not a difficult thing to do, unless you are complacent about it: we do all err, and we do all need to be critically self-aware. There are several great philosophers whose works I have read and re-read but *about* whose work I have read only one book, often one widely referred to as "the best book on X," and that is usually enough to monitor my internal and external perspective on the philosopher and make sure I am not perpetrating some howler in the privacy of my mind. Of course, if the secondary literature itself gets the philosopher in question extensively wrong—as was for so many years the case with the early Wittgenstein—then the only standard to judge by is the thinker himself.

One of the worst things of all about subservience to secondary literature is that it means absorbing wholesale the mistakes of others, when it is bad enough having unavoidably to make one's own. I believe that most of the major misinterpretations of philosophers that find their way into print have something like this as their source, that the writer has absorbed from secondary sources a mistaken view of a philosopher that he has not yet read, and then when he comes to read him misinterprets him in terms of these already existing expectations, supported as they are by what he regards as "the recognized authorities." I have cited as an example Wittgenstein's *Tractatus,* and my discovery when I read it for myself that it was a different book from the one it was generally represented at that time as being. In those days the uncomprehending secondary literature about it was so extensive that I could have gone on reading it for years without realizing that the book itself was not like that. I do not believe that each and every one of those writers had read the *Tractatus* with true independence of mind and misunderstood it identically: I believe that nearly all of them had absorbed a mistaken view in advance from the same secondary sources and then interpreted the *Tractatus* in accordance with that, so that the misunderstanding was self-perpetuating. I was later to find that a similar situation existed with regard to Schopenhauer, only my discovery of it was the other way about. I came to Schopenhauer late and in a state of comparative ignorance. It seemed to me that he stated his views with exceptional clarity, leaving little room for doubt or disagreement about what it was he was saying. When then, out of sheer interest, I turned to the secondary literature, I found that nearly all the writers had got one of his fundamental doctrines (and the same one) wrong in a way that led them to misrepresent his philosophy as a whole. Again, I do not think that all those writers had coincidentally misunderstood Schopenhauer on the same point. With so lucid a writer—who goes to special lengths to make himself clear on the very point at issue—it is not credible. It can only be, I think, that the secondary writers thought before they read him that they knew what it was he had to say on that point, and then read him as saying it.

There are certain philosophers about whom opposing views are taken by large numbers of people, and in those cases you cannot know what you think unless you read them for yourself. Many who have read Hegel regard his work as consisting of trivialities and nothings decked out in oracular language to make them appear imposing—rather like a weak, ineffectual emperor who tries to impress his subjects by presenting himself to them in gorgeous apparel and grandiose ceremonies. Those who take this view include a number who are themselves gifted philosophically—for instance Schopenhauer, Bertrand Russell and Karl Popper—so you might suppose that as a view it cannot be lightly dismissed. But there are others, also greatly gifted, who regard Hegel as a profound and original thinker—Karl Marx, Kierkegaard (militantly hostile to Hegel yet regarding him as the most important thinker of the age), Heidegger and Jean-Paul Sartre. If you find yourself in agreement with the latter group, as I do, then it may be an interesting question how it comes about that philosophers of the calibre of Schopenhauer, Russell and Popper cannot see that there is significant content in Hegel. But of course that is not a philosophical question.

From the position we happen to occupy in the history of the Western world we find it convenient to divide that history into three broad eras: ancient, medieval and modern. How much longer these categories will last it is impossible to say, but at the time of this writing they are deeply entrenched, and have been for generations. Also, it has long been customary to see the history of philosophy in terms of the same three sub-divisions: ancient philosophy, medieval philosophy, and modern philosophy. Ancient philosophy is dominated by Plato and Aristotle to such an extent that if one studies the subject at a university these are quite likely to be the only two philosophers whose works one is required to read. For the newcomer to the subject it is quite reasonable that this should be so; but any avid student of philosophy is likely sooner or later to want to explore the work of other figures in the ancient world. He will find himself confronted with several hundred years' worth of insightful philosophy, from the pre-Socratics to the neo-Platonist philosopher Plotinus.

Medieval philosophy has one particular characteristic that differentiates it equally from ancient philosophy on the one hand and modern philosophy on the other, and that is its symbiotic relationship with established religion. Throughout the whole of the Middle Ages—the thousand years or more between the fall of the Roman Empire and the Renaissance—virtually all men of learning in the West were priests. The nearest equivalent of this was true even among Europe's small Jewish minority. And of course in those days no one could publicly admit to not being religious at all without running the danger of severe punishment, possibly death. So throughout the whole of that long historical period—as long as Greek and Roman history combined, and twice as long as the period between the Renaissance and now—all learning and all disciplined intellectual activities were pursued within a firmly established religious framework, in most cases within an actual religious institution. And since the ultimate truths revealed to us by God could not be questioned, this led almost inevitably to most philosophical enquiry's falling under two main heads: to what extent could the truths of religion be demonstrated by reason alone; and what was to be seen as the relationship of the great works of Plato and Aristotle to the Old and New Testaments?

It might be asked why any need was felt to raise these questions. With regard to the first: if God has revealed his truth to us, we are not dependent on our own unaided reason to arrive at it, and in that case what does it matter how far reason alone can take us? With regard to the second: surely the word of

God as given to us directly in the Old and the New Testaments supersedes all other sources of learning, and renders these superfluous? Serious thinkers in the Middle Ages had answers to both these challenges. In reply to the first they pointed out that Christendom was surrounded, perpetually threatened, often invaded, by peoples who rejected its religion. It was a pressing duty on Christians to persuade such people of the truths of the Christian religion; but obviously this could not be done by pointing to authorities which they did not acknowledge, or appealing to a revelation which they denied. The only hope lay in putting to them arguments which did not contain any Christian presuppositions, but which were nevertheless so good as to compel acceptance. With this aim thinkers in the Middle Ages made enormous strides in developing the purely rational arguments for religious positions. And the best of them showed great intellectual honesty in acknowledging the strength of the opposition, the power of some of the arguments *against* Christianity.

In reply to the second challenge, they pointed out that while a good deal of Plato and Aristotle was clearly in keeping with holy scripture, and some of it was in equally clear contradiction, the great bulk of it would appear, on the face of it, to fall into neither category. Therefore there would appear to be no reason why we should not take that over. However, before incorporating any of it into our thinking and our culture we needed to be sure that it was not going to turn out to have long-term consequences further down the line that were contrary to religion: if it did, then it should be rejected now. So before any of it could be accepted, a great deal of careful study was called for: consequences and implications needed to be thought through thoroughly, and pursued to the end. With this as a programme, an enormous amount of work was done in individual sciences and disciplines, across the board—far more than is now generally realized—with the general effect of establishing an Aristotelian worldview in what we now think of as the sciences. This rich and broadly based intellectual movement advanced with such vigour and purpose that in the late Middle Ages, around the thirteenth century, there was a glorious flowering of learning that in some ways anticipated the Renaissance— which was therefore not the clean break with the past that was at one time claimed. However, although the intellectual achievements of the Middle Ages have been undervalued, it has to be admitted that it was only when the pursuit of knowledge was freed from the Church that it recaptured the kind of growth-rate it had enjoyed with the ancient Greeks.

In our own day, people who study philosophy at university tend either to start with Plato and Aristotle and then (except in Roman Catholic institutions) pass over medieval philosophy entirely, picking up the threads with Descartes, who did his work in the first half of the seventeenth century; or else they actually begin with Descartes. In either case, medieval philosophy is omitted.

Although I find medieval philosophy attractive and interesting, and in many ways impressive, I cannot pretend that it is essential reading now. It contains, as does ancient philosophy, two figures who tower above the rest: St. Augustine (354–430) and St. Thomas Aquinas (1225–74). Aquinas's work—like Aristotle's, with whom it is massively preoccupied—is such as is likely to engage only the specialist or the serious student; in fact the best of it is contained in two compendia that were written as textbooks for students. Augustine is a different matter. His two most important books, *Confessions* and *The City of God,* are still accessible, and still to be found in every good bookshop. *Confessions* is, quite simply, one of the great books of world literature. In effect the first autobiography, it weaves together an exceedingly self-critical (hence the title) account of the author's life, in which is included a memorable portrait of his mother, and some profound philosophizing which retains its interest and importance to this day, especially that part of it which concerns the nature of time.

My own university study of the history of philosophy, as I recounted earlier, began with Descartes. In my middle and late thirties I re-read those of the great philosophers I had read as a student, and read others for the first time—not only moderns such as Spinoza but most of Plato and Aristotle. My second reading of Kant's *Critique of Pure Reason*—like the first, but separately from the first—remains one of the supreme intellectual experiences of my life. I had friends who lived in the middle of Majorca, far from any centres of tourist attraction, who were forever inciting me to come and stay with them for a long period; so I took the *Critique of Pure Reason* with me, and spent six weeks there just living my way through it. Sometimes I read no more than twenty pages in a day; sometimes I spent a whole day with the book in my hands without reading anything beyond the page I had got to the day before. I do not think there is a single one of the philosophical dilemmas I had confronted as a child that it does not acknowledge and illuminate, and these remain the most important ones. Its treatment of them is so rich and deep that no brief account could do it justice. For instance on pages 145–50 I offered a sketch of Kant's theory of perception: it was accurate as far as it went, but in order to keep it brief I left out altogether what Kant had to say about the role played in perception by imagination. As a warning example of how a clear and accurate account can be defective without this fact being betrayed by the account itself, let me return to that and indicate where imagination comes into the picture.

Our normal experience is of events happening, usually against a background of other things going on, and with both of these there is an indispensable time-dimension. As far as I can see, it would be impossible for us to have instantaneous experiences with no duration at all, for in that case we would have no way of knowing that they had occurred. This, I believe, is why Kant is insistent that time is the one indispensable form of inner sense, and that all experiences must occur in that dimension. Yet consider the following. If I watch somebody get out of a chair, or cross a room, or if I look at flowers waving in the breeze, or observe anything whatsoever *happening,* then at any given moment the objects of my observations can be in one and only one position. At that moment all the other positions that go together to constitute the movement or the event must either have occurred already, and already inhabit the past, or not have occurred yet, and still be in the future. So although when I have the experience of seeing something happen it is as if past and present positions of the same objects are presented to me in a single observation, this cannot be the case. Although the experience as I have it is a unitary one of seeing, say, someone lift a fork to his mouth, in order to have that I must be retaining in my mind's eye experiences I had one, two, three, and four instants ago and linking them all together with an experience I am having now; and what is more I must be retaining the past experiences as vividly as if I were having them now, because if I did not, my experience of seeing the fork go up to the mouth would not have the uniform and seamless character that it does. What actually must have been the input of a moment ago in what I experience as the perception of a single movement is so nearly as vivid as the current input that in practice I am scarcely conscious of any variation in sensory quality.

Corresponding things are true of experience by means of other senses. If I listen to a sentence or a tune, the actual sensory input at any given instant can consist of no more than part of a single note, or pause, or consonant, or vowel sound. For me to hear the sentence *as a sentence,* or the tune *as a tune,* I need at each point in it to retain in my mind's ear all the sounds that have gone before, and to link them with one another and with my current aural input into something that I then apprehend as a whole. Indeed, the truth is that I need to do all this to hear even so much as a single word. So the perpetually active exercise of imagination—by which Kant means the sustained maintenance before the mind of sensory imagery which is not the immediate product of current sensory input, though it has the same, or almost the same, degree of strength and vividness—is indispensable to the having of any experience whatever. On analysis it emerges that to have any experience at all of the world outside myself I need: (i) to have sensory input from that world; (ii) to sustain lifelike representations of these sensory inputs in imagination; (iii) to link the representations thus retained, one with another, and with new sensory inputs; (iv) to grasp the linked chains thus formed as wholes. When all this has been done I have experience. But it is only (iv) that constitutes the conscious experience—the hearing of a word, or a sentence, or a tune; the apprehension of an event, or of something going on. However, before (iv) can happen, (i), (ii), and (iii) need already to have happened; and this is true even if they do not and never can figure in experience in their separate and unsynthesized forms. From the fact that experience is of its nature a synthesis it follows that the elements necessary to create the synthesis cannot be independent objects of an experience in which the other elements play no part.

Kant pursues the analysis as far as he can take it. He excavates in his marvellously deep and detailed way the process of the bringing of experiences under concepts, which he sees as the function of understanding; and then our ability to use concepts, which he sees as the function of reason. One of his aims is to provide a fully analysed account of what reason is and can do, what all its available materials are, and how it acquires them, so that we shall understand in a fully supported way what its limitations are: what kind of thing it is impossible for us to know, what kind of thing it is impossible for us even to think or understand. As an intellectual achievement it is awe-inspiring, and it set the detailed agenda for most of the worthwhile philosophizing that there has been since, in the same sort of way as Plato set the broad agenda for more than two thousand years. In the nature of the subject Kant's work is exceedingly difficult to read and understand. No amount of clarity in the writing could have made its ideas easy to grasp, or its arguments easy to follow. But the rewards of studying it are incomparable. I honestly believe that, since the *Critique of Pure Reason* is unlikely to be read and understood by anyone who is not a serious student of philosophy, it is worth studying philosophy in order to read that one book. As Schopenhauer said: "Kant's teaching produces a fundamental change in every mind that has grasped it. This change is so great that it may be regarded as an intellectual rebirth. It alone is capable of really removing the inborn realism which arises from the original disposition of the intellect. . . . In consequence of this, the mind undergoes a fundamental undeceiving, and thereafter looks at all things in another light."*

There is a non-religious sense in which when I read the *Critique of Pure Reason* for the second time I was in search of salvation. Almost overwhelmed by terror at the prospect of inevitable death, I was looking for some shred of hope that I might not be totally and for ever annihilated, and that the world and my existence in it might not be meaningless and pointless. Kant's doctrine of the ideality of time and space, were I to believe it, offered me this. For it taught that the forms of time and space were inextricable from experience and its possibility and could have no purchase where they did not obtain. From this it follows that things as they are in themselves, independently of experience, are not in time or space. Without experience there can be no empirical world. If all human beings were to die, and also all other creatures with forms of ex-

---

* *The World as Will and Representation,* tr. E. F. J. Payne, vol. i, p. xxiii.

perience like ours, there would be no question of our world continuing without us in it, for it would cease to exist as well. Kant is explicit about this. "What we have meant to say is that all our intuition is nothing but the representation of appearance; that the things which we intuit are not in themselves what we intuit them as being, nor their relations so constituted in themselves as they appear to us, and that if the subject, or even only the subjective constitution of the senses in general, be removed, the whole constitution and all the relations of objects in space and time, nay space and time themselves, would vanish. As appearances, they cannot exist in themselves, but only in us. What objects may be in themselves, and apart from all this receptivity of our sensibility, remains completely unknown to us. We know nothing but our mode of perceiving them—a mode which is peculiar to us, and not necessarily shared in by every being, though, certainly, by every human being. With this alone have we any concern."*

One thing that has always struck me forcefully about this doctrine of Kant's is that it legitimates important components of a belief which he had held since long before he began to philosophize, namely Christian belief. It is a standard part of the traditional Christian faith that time and space and material objects are local characteristics of this human world of ours, but only of this world: they do not characterize reality as such. "Outside" the human world, so to speak (obviously "outside" is a spatial term, and therefore cannot apply literally where there is no space: it is being used here metaphorically), there is a timeless reality where God is, and the immortal souls of people in the human world. God and these immortal souls are not in time or space, nor are they constituted of matter, nor do they live in a world of material objects; but they are all that there eternally is; and since in the human world nothing is eternal—everything in it perishes—it is they that constitute what one might call "real" reality as against the evanescent world of time and space within which nothing lasts. If one ignores the religious references in the last three sentences they contain a plain statement of Kantian doctrines of space, time, and material objects. But the fact is that Kant had held such beliefs since he was a small child. For it so happens that he was born into, and grew up in, an unusually zealous Protestant sect, the Pietists, and was deeply and permanently influenced by this upbringing. Late in his adult life he produced a wonderfully rich system of rational arguments to support some of their beliefs, but he did not hold the beliefs because of the arguments, nor had he been led to them by the arguments; he had held them all along. This in no way invalidates his philosophy, of course, for that must stand or fall in the light of rational argument and criticism. But what he did, unmistakably (and unremarked on to an extent that

* *Critique of Pure Reason,* tr. Norman Kemp Smith, p. 82.

has never ceased to astonish me), is produce rational justification for many aspects of the religious beliefs in which he grew up.

Let me put it this way. We know for a fact that long before Kant started to philosophize he was dedicated, simply as a Christian, to the belief that the empirical world of time and space and material objects, within which everything is evanescent and everything perishes, is something that exists only for us mortals in our present life; that "outside" this world there is another, so to say infinitely more "important," realm of existence which is timeless and spaceless, and in which the beings are not material objects. Now it is *as if* he then said to himself: "How can these things be so? What can be the nature of time and space and material objects if they obtain only in the world of human beings? Could it be, given that they characterize only the world of experience and nothing else, that they are characteristics, or preconditions, of experience, and nothing else?" In other words, Kant's philosophy is a fully worked out analysis of what needs to be the case for what he believed already to be true. It is, I reiterate, none the worse for that. One of the most important of all philosophical activities is the investigation of presuppositions. *If I assert* p, *what does that mean I have already committed myself to?* is a question of which anyone who thinks philosophically needs to be perpetually aware. And the questioning in this way of the presuppositions of even a very simple statement often gets us immediately into deep water. For instance, nearly all of us have believed completely since early childhood that two and two make four, yet demonstrating the truth of that deductively is beyond the powers of most of us: to do it you need an advanced knowledge of mathematical logic. The fact is that most of what we take for granted is exceedingly difficult to validate, and much of it impossible.

Another thing that surprises me, in addition to the fact that the identity of some of Kant's fundamental doctrines with familiar religious beliefs is not more often remarked on and discussed, is the fact that most students of them find them difficult if not impossible to grasp. I am now talking not of the arguments or the analyses that support them—they are indeed difficult, sometimes almost impenetrably so—but of the conclusions which all this apparatus is there to validate, conclusions which in themselves can be stated quite simply. The reason I find this surprising is that the students already know these ideas perfectly well in a different context, that of religious belief. Even if not themselves religious they must be entirely familiar with the fact that millions of people who are religious believe that self-subsistent being is outside space and time, and does not take the form of material objects; that such things all belong to the empirical world only, and are not to be found in the timeless, spaceless realm where all permanence is. If these ideas are so utterly familiar in a religious context, why should so many students find it impossible to grasp that they are what Kant is saying, among other things? Perhaps they have come to associate these doctrines so exclusively with religious faith that it does not occur to them that a great philosopher might think it possible to establish them by rational argument.

Of course, it is one thing to spell out the necessary preconditions of a belief, and quite another to establish its (or their) truth. If I have pinned down preconditions in a particular case then I have demonstrated that *if* the belief in question is true then those conditions must obtain; but in this there is still an *if:* something remains still to be demonstrated. It is important for any serious thinker to realize this, because it applies to all arguments whatsoever. It comes as a shock to some people to be told this, but the fact is that no argument proves the truth of its conclusion. To say of an argument that it is valid is to say not that its conclusion is true but that its conclusion follows from its premises: *if* p *then* q, and therefore *if not* q *then not* p, and so on and so forth. No argument *can* establish the truth of its premises, since if it tried to do so it would be circular; and therefore no argument *can* establish the truth of its conclusions. Applying this to Kant, a lot of his arguments and analyses are as powerful as any that the human mind has ever developed—but are their conclusions, or their presuppositions, true? That is a very different matter. Of one thing I am certain. Kant has identified more clearly than anyone else what the most fundamental problems of experience are; therefore if we do not accept the solutions he proposes he puts us under challenge to come up with better ones. The unique position occupied by Schopenhauer in the history of philosophy since Kant is due to the fact that he appreciated this challenge more fully than anyone else, and also met it more fully. In consequence his attitude to Kant is what I believe to be the right one: on the one hand he venerates Kant as the greatest of his predecessors, and yet, on the other hand, most of his philosophy consists of working out with great freedom and independence of mind the consequences of seeing what is wrong with Kant. The rest of us should also, of course, adopt the same attitude to Schopenhauer.

15

Mid-Life Crisis

I must not give the impression that in my terror of oblivion my gaze was fixed chiefly on books. I did not expect to be able to read my way out of my death sentence. Far from it. For most of the time I was racked with unliterary and unintellectual thoughts about the direct realities of my situation: that my death was inevitable; that there had never been a time when this was not so; that death, for all I know, might be total oblivion, eternal or timeless nothingness; that although I could not be certain that this was so it seemed to me likelier than any alternative I could think of, and was therefore what I felt most inclined to believe; that compared with an eternity of nothingness the length of a human lifetime was not even so much as the twinkling of an eye; that if I was about to be swallowed up by an everlasting void, nothing I did was of the slightest significance, whether I went on to write great books or become Foreign Secretary, or get happily married or unhappily married, or prove a failure at everything—none of it would make the slightest difference to me or to anyone else when all of us were nothing, as everyone was going to be, including everyone not yet born; that it could therefore make no difference *when* I died, and would have made no difference if I had never been born; that I was in any event going to be for all eternity what I would have been if I had never been born; that there was no meaning in any of it, no point in any of it; and that in the end everything was nothing.

There are, evidently, contemplatives who would agree with all this and view it with calmness and serenity. I have never been one of them. I was terror-stricken by these thoughts. I felt like someone standing on the gallows with the noose round his neck, and the trapdoor under his feet about to open; or like someone facing a firing squad. I was on the point of being flung into eternal night. I raged against it with the whole of my being. And the impossibility of doing anything about it came close to sending me off my head with frustration and panic.

I used to look at people going about their normal lives with everyday cheerfulness and think: "How *can* they? And how can they suppose that any of what they're doing matters? They're like passengers on the *Titanic,* except that these people know *already* that they're headed for total and irremediable shipwreck. In a short time every one of them will be dead, either a heap of grey ash in an urn or a corpse rotting underground with worms wriggling in and out of its eye sockets. And that situation will be every bit as real then as their situation now is now; and it will last for very much longer. Why aren't they overwhelmed with horror at it? Why don't they seem even to mind?" In my London club—which unlike most of the others was something like a family—I would look at middle-aged and elderly members and think: "How can they sit there enjoying their lunch, telling jokes, laughing, their eyes sparkling with pleasure? In a short time now they'll be dead, all of them, and what's more they know it now. They're almost face to face with total oblivion. Don't they care?" I was baffled by the fact that almost all human beings knew what was in store for them yet lived as if it were not so—or as if it were something that they were perfectly happy about. Above all, I was baffled by the fact that the middle-aged, who were so close to death, tended to be even more cheerful than the young. In some of my moods they seemed to me like a lot of lunatics chuckling dementedly while the asylum burnt down and turned them to ash.

Under the influence of these thoughts my values went through sea changes. Everything that was limited to this life and this world came to appear insignificant. Only what might possibly point beyond them, or have its basis outside them—beauty, art, sex, morality, integrity, metaphysical understanding—could even possibly be worth anything. Of course this is related to what philosophy in the Kant–Schopenhauer–early-Wittgenstein tradition is saying, but when it hit me in this direct, overwhelming way it was not a theoretical conclusion but something felt, lived, acted on. Only in intimate relationships, and the privacy of one's own self, and experiences of art, and attempts to understand things, could there be any value. Success and fame were worse than nothing, because anyone pursuing them was actively throwing his life away. Quite apart from any considerations of self: politics, business and the professions were in themselves nothing, and the daily life and work of the world just a lot of meaningless vanity. People busied themselves in offices and factories, or hurried to and fro between these and their homes; markets and concourses teemed with crowds, traffic crammed the streets, buses and trains ran, airplanes flew, telephones rang; everywhere there was bustle and noise, strain and striving, people jostling and worrying and getting ill, pursuing leisure, pleasure and possessions as frantically as they worked. And to what end, ultimately? None at all. In fact, whether they realized it or not, they were just doing these things repetitively for their own sakes, and would go on doing so until they and everything else disappeared into total darkness. The whole thing was absurd in the most serious sense of that word.

Even on their own terms the politics and business of the world were absurdly evanescent. One week politicians, people who worked in the City, and people whose job it was to report their doings would all be kept out of their beds by a financial crisis which, six months later, would be little talked of. By that time perhaps there would be a rail strike that everyone was talking about, followed by a corruption scandal in local government, which would then be followed by a flurry of public concern over crimes of violence, which in its turn would be pushed out of people's minds by their fury over some proposed new tax; and so it would go on. Each of these things would seem important for a time, then each would pass away and scarcely matter again except to historians. In fact, the truth is that most of them made little or no difference even to the daily lives of most of the population living through them. People immersed in this stream of ever-changing events were filling their minds with what even on their own terms were ephemera and trivia, what people in electronics mean by "noise."

It is not as if there were no alternatives. Time spent listening to great music, or seeing great plays, or thinking about issues of lasting importance, was not in this category. In those cases the object of one's activities retained its interest and importance for the rest of one's life. If I spent an evening listening to Mahler's Third Symphony, that symphony was still going to matter to me in six months' time, or ten years, or thirty: it was part of my life, for always. In fact such things more often than not increased in interest and value with the passage of time. If I spent two or three months saturating myself in, let us say, recordings of Mozart's piano concertos, and then did not return to them like that for another four years or so, I would find when I came back to them that I engaged with them on a deeper level than before. And the same was true of most great art. I saw the same plays by Shakespeare, Chekhov, Ibsen and others over and over again, and the possession of them grew richer all the time. I marinaded in the standard works of the orchestral repertoire, saw the two or three dozen greatest operas repeatedly, and all these things were metabolized into my living tissue and became a permanent part of me, nourishing me more richly with every year that passed. And at the same time as I was deepening my relationship with the familiar I was also uncovering the new, hearing and seeing all sorts of great works for the first time. It was like being perpetually at large on an ocean of discovery, hearing such things as symphonies by Mahler and Shostakovich for the first time, watching Stravinsky conduct his own music, seeing plays I had not seen before by Ben Jonson, Molière, Strindberg and Pirandello, operas by Verdi and Richard Strauss, encountering unheard-of names like Feydeau and Janáček. There was something incessantly thrilling and marvellous about all that. There were times when I felt, after all, that I was living to the full in face of death. Many men of action who are also writers have described the bliss induced in them by the sound of bullets smacking past their ears, and said that it intensified their awareness of being alive to an intoxicating level. The things that came closest to doing this for me when I fully realized I was facing death were my love affairs and friendships, philosophy and the arts. Never have I reacted to these things more intensely than I did in my late thirties and early forties. It was as if Shakespeare and Mozart were addressing me personally. Sometimes I would go back to the same production over and over again. I found myself devoting every minute that I could to such things. Had it not been for my need to earn a living I would have immersed myself in them entirely. As it was I came as close to doing so as I could.

This change involved a big shift in my attitude to thought-systems. Those that treated political, social or historical levels of explanation as fundamental now seemed to me to be treating externals and surfaces as if they were foundations, and to be superficial and point-missing. In the world as it was at that time the most conspicuous example of this was Marxism, though there were others too. Marxism had a complete explanation of the arts in terms of political power, economic interests and social classes, and this seemed to me a grotesque attempt to explain the greater in terms of the less. Not only was there a lot of Marxist criticism around at that time, there were innumerable Marx-influenced stage productions which had the effect of superficializing the works they dealt with for precisely this reason, that they treated social and political externals as fundamental, while remaining oblivious to what actually *was* fundamental. Arguing with people who produced or supported this kind of thing was a dislocating experience, because it seemed self-evident to them that the metaphysical, personal and interpersonal dimensions of things were of secondary importance compared with the social and political. Indeed, they often denied that there was any metaphysical dimension at all, either to reality or to works of art.

I know from observation of friends and acquaintances that a large number of people, at least men, go through experiences in middle life not unlike mine. This is borne out by the existence of terms such as "metanoia," "mid-life crisis," "male menopause," and so on, all referring to some such phenomenon. It is also evident in the work of many creative artists—Dante's *Inferno* begins with lines that refer to it. Also, the lives of the artists themselves evince it. When they are young they are often ambitious for worldly success and fame, and perhaps they travel around a great deal performing, seeking exposure for their work, and putting themselves on show: and the work itself, at that stage, is socially aware, seeking acceptance, or aiming to impress, often referring directly to current social concerns. But later, at some sort of middle turning point of life, such an artist often changes his attitude and starts regarding success, fame, social ambition, worldly affairs altogether, as unimportant. He turns in on himself, perhaps turns towards religion, but in any case withdraws in some degree from the world, while at the same time becoming more otherworldly in his art. I am not saying that there is a single pattern of development through which every great artist goes, merely that a noticeably large number go through a recognizable version of this one. Observers who have not themselves been through it are sometimes inclined to see the change as a softening, or a falling away. People who are themselves locked into worldly values are inclined to see any such artist as having "opted out," even as having "sold out." Those committed to the view that the most important thing about art is its social significance are incapable of understanding that such artists have developed beyond precisely that—and, having done so, for them to return, if it were not impossible, would be to shrink and become shallower, and *that* would be really to sell out.

As applied to myself, I had these feelings not only as a producer of work but also as a consumer. I lost patience with the shallowness of most artistic productions, and even more so that of most socially aware comment on the arts, whether this came from prominent intellectuals or academics or journalists, or even, as increasingly it did in those days, from the artists themselves. In order to spend as much time as possible with what I now cared about most I shifted the focus of my paid work. First of all I changed the subject matter of my television programmes from the crises of news and current affairs to those of personal life—adultery, abortion, alcoholism, suicide, prostitution, crime, and so on. Then I extended it to the arts, and launched the first regular arts series on commercial television, and followed it up with a related series on BBC Radio. At the same time I became theatre critic of the *Listener* and reviewed recordings for the *Musical Times*. In so far as I could I tried to earn my living by doing what I wanted to do anyway: listen to music, go to the theatre, involve myself with my own and other people's personal problems. I felt I knew with some degree of certainty that if there were anything at all outside space and time we were at our closest to it in the private world of personal relationships, and of art and reflective thought, and were at our furthest away from it in the public world of social organization and politics. I abandoned, or so I thought, the idea of becoming a member of parliament, and declined approaches made to me to stand for parliament. In all these ways the centre of gravity of my life shifted from the public to the private, from the impersonal to the personal, away from whatever it might be that was currently going on in the world of affairs to things of a more individual and abstract nature, and of much longer-lasting interest. I knew that many of my friends and colleagues saw me as falling out of life's race in a way that was cataclysmic for myself. Indeed, some of them remonstrated with me about what they saw as my craziness in blowing a successful career.* But the truth is that I no longer regarded the considerations they cared about as mattering.

Perhaps I should stress that all this was not primarily an intellectual experience, and was in no sense whatever a reading experience. It was not a matter of studying certain writers and being influenced by their ideas. Books and study had nothing to do with the causes of it. It was an existential experience, one long permanent state of mental and emotional crisis, in which I came many times near to breakdown. It consisted of agonizingly direct experiences, felt feelings, thought thoughts. And it was from this state that I came to my reading. Given the overwrought state I was in, some of what I then read impinged on me as if I had been skinned. For instance, there seemed to be a certain body of doctrine that was common to nearly all the great religions and their famous sages, moralists, prophets, and so on, which I found self-evidently (and in that sense platitudinously) true and to the point, and which had an overwhelming impact on me, and yet which the world disregarded. Perhaps I might express it as follows.

The world is governed by false values. People in all societies seem anxious to do what they think is the done thing, and are terrified of social disapproval. They set their hearts on getting on in the world, being thought highly of by their fellows, being powerful, acquiring money and possessions, knowing "important" people. They admire the influential, the rich, the famous, the well-born, the holders of rank and position. But none of these things have any serious relationship to merit: as often as not they are ill gotten, and nearly always they are partly dependent on chance. None of them will protect a person from serious illness or personal tragedy, let alone from death. And none of them can be taken out of this world. They are not an inherent part of the person himself but are merely external decorations, hung on him. They are the tinsel of life, glittering but worthless. The things that really matter in human beings are things that can matter more than life itself: loving and being loved, devotion to truth, integrity, courage, compassion, and other qualities along en-

---

* It may be no more than a matter of the slang of the period, but several people on both sides of the Atlantic used the same words to me: "You've blown it" (or, years later, "I thought you'd blown it").

tirely different lines. But human beings are all the time sacrificing these true values to the false ones: they compromise themselves to get on, bend the truth to make money, demean themselves before power. In behaving like this they are pouring rubbish over their own heads. If they stopped abasing themselves in this way and started living in accordance with true values their lives would become incomparably more meaningful, more genuinely satisfying. They would even, to put it at its most superficial, be happier.

In the Hindu and Buddhist scriptures, in the Old and New Testaments, and almost everywhere I looked in the works of prophets and mystics, wise men and teachers—of any century and any society—some such message as this was to be found. Perceptive people seem to have been saying it since writing and teaching began. Even creative artists: the great ones seldom preach, and are diminished when they do, but, unspoken between the lines of what many of them write, these values are to be discerned. In the world's greatest opera and drama the conflict between private and public values is the most common theme of all, with the artist invariably enlisting the audience's sympathies on behalf of the private. And while the members of the audience are in the theatre, or reading the book, they respond almost universally in this way. But the moment they come out of the theatre, or close the book, they revert. It is true that in temples, mosques, synagogues and churches they offer lip-service to true values, and feel better for having done so; and those values may even sometimes be taught in schools; but, again, no sooner do people leave such places of instruction than they behave in their old ways. Worse than that: if any of them does not do so—if one of them sacrifices his interests to someone else's, tells the truth to his own disadvantage, declines to be sycophantic to people with a lot of power or money—the others remonstrate with him and tell him not to be a fool. If he persists, they lose respect for him: they come to look on him as stupid, someone who does not know how to manage his own affairs, someone making a botch of his life. The truth is, then, that the values people publicly acknowledge and pay lip-service to are in reality values that they not only repudiate but actively despise. It took me a long time to realize this, but when I did I came to understand in a new light the evident frustration and even despair of so many prophets and teachers, their isolation, and their characteristic tone of railing at people who they know are not going to take much notice of what they say.

Another body of writing to which I found myself unusually responsive was that of humanist existentialism. On the Continent this had been at the centre of attention in the years just after the Second World War. When I had gone to Versailles two years after the war as an exchange student, at the age of seventeen, it was what I had found the chattering classes there and in Paris talking about. The most famous philosophers then living in the French- and German-speaking worlds, Jean-Paul Sartre and Martin Heidegger, espoused it. But it was hopelessly at odds with Anglo-Saxon commitments to empiricism and linguistic analysis. In the philosophical circles in which I had been trained it had been dismissed by most people as pretentious nonsense unworthy of the attention of serious students of philosophy.

Three things in particular now attracted me to humanist existentialism. First and foremost, I had always believed that the most important questions in philosophy concern not knowledge but existence. Can it—and how can it—possibly be explained that anything exists at all? What *is* existence? If you like, what are we saying of something when we say that it exists? What is the nature of *our* existence? Are we wholly and solely material objects? If so, what is it to be a material object? Or is there perhaps something non-material about us that is more important than our bodies? If there is, what could it possibly be? Will it cease to exist when we die, or is there any imaginable sense in which it might continue? If the latter, what could such a sense, or such a continued existence, consist in? These are the most important questions *to us,* or so it seems to me. And it is in relation to them that the most important questions about knowledge begin to arise. Is there any way in which we can find out the answers to these questions? If there is, what is it? Or are the different questions to be answered in different ways? If so, what ways are appropriate to which questions? Or is it rather that some of the questions are answerable and others not? If so, how are we to tell which are which? These are the most important questions about knowledge as far as we human beings are concerned. And the crucial observation to make about them is that they do not relate to our sensory knowledge of material objects—unless we ourselves are material objects, and what we are asking about is our knowledge of ourselves through inner sense. Analytic philosophy never asked these questions. Not only that, it offered all sorts of complacent reasons why they were not permissible questions, and laughingly dismissed anyone who asked them as not being a serious philosopher. The fact that existentialism held these questions—and the implications for our lives of any answers we might seriously entertain—to be fundamental made it pertinent to me.

Second, to people addressing themselves to these questions, the following line of thought seemed naturally to suggest itself. "Although I don't know what I am, I do know that—whatever I am—I exist. All other existent entities seem to be in some way or other external to me, and the knowledge I have of them feels to me like knowledge from outside, and is, in that sense, indirect. But about myself I have a form of direct knowledge from inside. And I seem to myself to be the only existing thing of which I have such knowledge. Therefore, if I want to investigate the nature of existence *as such* it would seem that the most promising way to start, the way for which I am most fully equipped, is investigation into the nature of my own existence. So let me begin by analysing this immediate awareness that I have of my own existence, and see where it gets me." In this way many existentialist thinkers have been led to carry out a phenomenological analysis of their own conscious self-awareness. This is recognizably similar to something I had myself been given to doing since childhood, albeit in an unsystematic way, so I found it congenial.

It might have been supposed that because our conscious self-awareness is experienced as being direct and unmediated there is nothing further to say about it. But Heidegger shows in his masterpiece *Being and Time* that this is not so. He demonstrates by a long, slow, often pedestrian analysis that this apparently unitary experience must in fact contain a number of separable ingredients. First, for there to be any consciousness at all something needs to be apprehended as going on; there needs to be some area of activity, some field of happening, however vague, whether sensory, mental, emotional, imagistic, physical, or otherwise. There needs to be some sense, however limited and primitive, of some sort of sphere of events, some "world" of awareness, even though it may be nothing but a mental screen. "Worldishness" in this sense, then, is a necessary ingredient. Second, for anything to be *going on* in any sense whatever there has to be a dimension of time. Ongoingness of any sort would be impossible without time, though to say this is to leave open in all other respects what the nature of time is. Thirdly, for us to be aware of any of this at all it needs to constitute experience. So without in any way pre-empting the nature of whatever it is that is going on, or whatever the nature of time may be, I can safely say that I must have some awareness of being impinged on by what it is that is going on, of its somehow or other happening to me or for me or in me, and in that sense being my concern. For without *some* degree of involvedness on my part it would be nothing at all for me. So before going any further, even, than this, we already have three necessary ingredients for any kind of conscious awareness: worldishness, time, and involvedness. Heidegger's analysis as a whole is too painstaking and long and slow-moving for me recapitulate it here, but what I have said gives an indication of its nature. He unravels what seems at first to be a simple and unitary experience into separable strands, and in doing so digs down below what had hitherto been taken to be the basement level of experience—as Kant also does, in his different way.

Heidegger is appallingly difficult to read—in the same class as Hegel for obscurity—but I am in no doubt that *Being and Time* is of classic and lasting importance. Perhaps it would be more accurate to say that I think its contents are of lasting importance to philosophy, for it could be that they will one day be stated more clearly and interestingly by another writer, as a result of which *Being and Time* may cease to be read. This has not happened yet. Jean-Paul Sartre, though a would-be popularizer of Heidegger's work, was at the same time a misunderstander and distorter of it, mixing it with adulterations of Descartes and Marx, not to mention his own contributions. His work is unusually clever, well written, and attractive to read, but it is superficial and inadequate, which gives it the overall character of brilliant journalism. He did more than anyone else to propagate existentialism without being a satisfactory exponent of it. The best of his novels and plays are better than any of his philosophical writings: if he survives as a writer I am sure it will be for his creative and not his theoretical work.

The third thing that attracted me about the tradition of humanist existentialism is that my involvement with it led me back to its fountainhead in the work of Nietzsche. As an undergraduate at Oxford I had been instructed *ex cathedra* that Nietzsche was "not a philosopher." Only now, some fifteen years later, did I realize that outside the English-speaking world he was the most influential philosopher since Marx. Just as Kant had succeeded in identifying and posing the fundamental problem of experience in an unprecedentedly challenging way, so Nietzsche did something similar with regard to morality and values. And as in Kant's case, although the solutions Nietzsche proposed to his own problems were not proof against the criticisms of succeeding generations, his claim on our attention does not rest primarily on his positive doctrines but on his having posed the fundamental problem itself in such a radical and effective way that it can never again be ignored by serious thinkers, and is thus a challenge to all subsequent thought. This challenge might be expressed as follows.

Historically, human morality developed in relation to, among other things, belief in spirits, or a spirit, perhaps gods, or a God. In all human societies it was believed that certain things should be done, and certain other things should not be done, in order to propitiate spiritual forces by meeting their requirements and forestalling their anger. Historically, this is how morality began, and how it was taught. The West is not unique in this respect, though over the last two thousand years the thinking about the interrelationship between man and these forces has reached high levels of sophistication there. As a somewhat primitive basis for it the Old and New Testaments teem with divine instructions on how we should live: the Ten Commandments are precisely that—commandments, and from God. Even the meek and mild Jesus gave us a large number of direct orders about what to do and what not to do, accompanied by threats of hell fire if we disobeyed.

After a thousand years of the Middle Ages, during which the Christian Church ruled everywhere in alliance with the secular authorities, the entire culture of the West had become saturated through and through with Judaeo-Christian morality and values, supplemented by similar ideas from ancient Greeks such as Socrates, Plato and Aristotle, who had also believed in a God or in gods. However, as Nietzsche then disobligingly pointed out, by the late nineteenth century most educated Westerners had ceased to believe in the existence of gods or spirits. They had been won over to what they took to be a scientific view of the world, one in which gods and spirits had no place. Yet their traditional morality continued in full operation, dominating working moralities both public and private. Individuals were still as passionately attached to this morality as were institutions and whole societies.

Now, says Nietzsche, this situation is unauthentic and indefensible. You no longer believe in the foundations of your own value-system. You have specifically repudiated the religious beliefs on which it rests, yet you go on clinging to it. You cannot do this. You can justify retaining it only on the basis of a completely different set of reasons, reasons which you genuinely believe in. Consider. If there is no God, and no transcendental realm, no world at all other than this one, your morality and your values cannot come to you from a transcendental source. They are your creation. You—not you individually but human beings socially, and over time—decide what they shall be, bring them into existence, and change them. So the fact is that human beings are responsible for their own value-systems. Given this, and given that the beliefs which form the foundation of your present values have collapsed, you have no serious choice but to carry out a complete reappraisal and reconstruction of them. You need to re-evaluate your values, that is to say re-create your morality and your values from the bottom up, establishing new and solid foundations for them in which you have genuine belief, and accepting full responsibility for them as *your creation.*

Towards what proved to be the end of his working life Nietzsche planned and began work on a four-part book that was to be the summation of his thought, to be called *The Revaluation of All Values.* But in January 1889 he collapsed into total madness. The book was never written. Even so, from the hundreds of pages of material he had prepared for it, and from his already published works, it is clear how his answer to his own challenge had developed. It involved not providing traditional morality with an alternative basis but, on the contrary, repudiating it almost entirely. He believed that life itself was the touchstone of true values—the self-assertive reality of something or someone spontaneously being itself. He applied this to all living things. A fox devouring chickens is a fox being a normal fox. Hounds tearing that same fox to pieces are behaving perfectly naturally as hounds. This is the way things are: and if we want to say Yes to life it is to this, not to some non-existent liberal fantasy, that we have to say Yes, embracing it on its own terms, everything as it is, spontaneously, after its own nature. To say that it is morally unacceptable is like saying that bad weather is morally unacceptable.

All these things apply to human beings too. History is a beginningless catalogue of death-dealing conflict and struggle, and out of it culture and civilization have emerged. They have developed not in spite of it but because of it, via all those processes whereby the strong, the clever, the brave, the dedicated, the imaginative, the creative and so on persistently do down or eliminate the rest. It is and always has been conducive to the advance of civilization that the activities of such people should be untrammeled. Whatever opposes that is hostile to cultural development. But for something like the last two thousand years the great ungifted mass of the people have espoused value-systems that did precisely this, extolling the weak and meek (in other words, people like themselves) at the expense of the strong and self-confident (of whom they were afraid), and demanding of the powerful and bold that they live under law and not do what they like. The whole point of such value-systems is to put the strong in chains, to render superior types unthreatening by subjecting them to constraints, taking away their spontaneity and advantages, and bringing them down to the same level as everybody else. Nietzsche dubbed these views "slave moralities," and claimed, for example, that it was among the slave populations of the ancient world that Christianity had first become widespread. He often refers to Christianity as a, or the, "religion of slaves," by which he means also a religion of servility.

Darwin's theory of evolution, which Nietzsche seized on gratefully, described how higher and higher forms of life had emerged from the struggle of all against all in a natural world red in tooth and claw, through the operation of the principle of the survival of the fittest. To this Nietzsche added that after the emergence of humanity from this evolutionary process a similar story was gone through again, internally to mankind, that is to say the elimination of the weak by the strong, the incompetent by the competent, the cowardly by the brave, the stupid by the clever. And this was how human beings, by heroic exertions, raised themselves to the level of civilization. It was only, first of all, with Socrates among the ancient Greeks, then after him with Christianity, that so-called moralists appeared on the scene who denounced the very processes that had produced this upward march of evolution, and humanity, and civilization, as immoral, violent, cruel, selfish, and the rest of such nonsense. Such people tried to replace what were in fact true values by their opposite, by slave moralities which, if they had been followed from the beginning, would have prevented civilization from ever emerging at all. With arguments like these Nietzsche not only rejects the foundations of belief on which the established morality of the West is built but rejects the morality itself, wholesale. His writings are aimed at extirpating it, and establishing in its stead a morality based on uninhibited life-assertion, the triumph of the superior.

Although I think I am right in saying that Nietzsche is nowhere mentioned in Hitler's *Mein Kampf,* and that there is no evidence that Hitler ever read Nietzsche, it cannot be denied that Hitler put forward doctrines that are remarkably similar, though in his case argued in terms of race. And it is only too easy to see why Nietzsche's philosophy commended itself to the Nazis, who seized on it and proclaimed him the philosophical godfather of their movement. However, there are other reasons, and not only his fastidiousness and the quality of his mind, for believing that Nietzsche would not have approved of the Nazis. First, his doctrines had nothing to do with race, and equally nothing to do with nationalism. Although himself a German he took a contemptuous view of Germans in general, regarding them as uncultured, humourless and heavy-handed, not a patch on the French when it came to culture or civilization. He was constantly making witticisms at their expense; indeed German nationalism was something he regarded as itself a joke. Among the many things he objected to about it was its anti-Semitism, an attitude he especially despised, and frequently derided. The very last sentence he wrote that was published (and one typical of his sentiments on the subject) was: "I am just having all anti-Semites shot."* He is more likely to have thought that the Nazis ought to be eliminated themselves than do any eliminating.

Nietzsche was a superlative writer, one of the greatest among philosophers in any language—a literary artist, like Plato. His writings on any subject (like those of Wittgenstein, who writes in a way that is self-evidently influenced by him) consist not of arguments but of insights, semi-poetic in their use of metaphor and simile, and often laid out not in connected paragraphs but aphoristically, the observations separated by gaps on the page. It is not uncommon for native German-speakers to regard Nietzsche's written German as the best there is. No doubt this is one of the reasons why he has been read so widely by people who have not otherwise made a study of philosophy; and also one of the reasons why he has had such a great influence on creative artists.

Some of this influence has been, it can only be said, evil. Early in the twentieth century it was common for writers who were then or later of international reputation to advocate the mass killing of ordinary people in order to raise the standards of those remaining. The following is an example, from the novel which D. H. Lawrence regarded as his best, *Women in Love*. Speaking is the central character, Birkin, who was acknowledged by Lawrence himself to be an autobiographical creation. " 'Not many people are anything at all,' he answered, forced to go deeper than he wanted to. 'They jingle and giggle. It would be much better if they were simply wiped out. Essentially, they don't exist, they aren't there.' "† I once spent a morning in rancorous argument with

---

* Postscript to a letter dated 6 January 1889—though the date on the postmark is 5 January 1889. Nietzsche's collapse into madness had begun on 3 January. From later that month to the end of his life in 1900 he was hopelessly insane.

† D. H. Lawrence: *Women in Love*, p. 27 of the Penguin edition.

Robert Graves because of his attachment to the same sentiment. Bernard Shaw expressed it too, and so did H. G. Wells. In part it was the under-side of the influence of Darwin, and indeed such doctrines came to be known as Social Darwinism. But Nietzsche pioneered this line of thought independently, and was in many cases the most direct influence on those who voiced it, including Shaw and Lawrence. It is noteworthy that although what these people were advocating openly was mass murder they did not use the term "murder." Nor for that matter did the Nazis, who put the programme into operation and managed to wipe out not only most European Jews but most of the Polish professional class. Since these events, the advocacy of such views has come to seem inexpressibly shocking to most of us, and rightly so; but until they were put into practice, readers in general seem not to have been greatly perturbed by them. So although Nietzsche wrote of liquidating anti-Semites, not Jews, the fact that the Holocaust has occurred since his day has increased the horror with which all such aspects of his philosophy are viewed. It is an easy matter nowadays to bring arguments against them that most people will accept—again, in my view, rightly. But that does not dispose of Nietzsche. His challenge to us to re-evaluate our values, and to find a foundation for them in which we genuinely believe, stands. And, as Schopenhauer put it, to preach morality is easy, but to provide a foundation for it is hard.

Perhaps not surprisingly, it happens quite often with philosophers that they pose some important challenge to our way of thinking and then provide an answer to their own challenge that fails to meet with lasting acceptance. When such a thinker's positive doctrines are rebutted there are always some people who slide into the mistake of thinking that he has been disposed of, but of course this is not so. What great philosophers formulate for us unforgettably are the permanent questions, not their permanent answers. If, as in the case of Nietzsche, a philosopher confronts us with a fundamental challenge, and then attempts to answer it himself, but does so in a way that does not survive criticism, this increases, not diminishes, his challenge. The fact that he has failed to dispose of it himself means that it still confronts us. And Nietzsche's challenge will continue to confront us until someone is more successful than he was in meeting it.

There have been some quite different examples of the same mistake in our own day. For instance, Noam Chomsky has put forward a devastating criticism of the traditional view of how human beings acquire language. The alternative, positive account he has offered has not successfully withstood criticism; and this has caused a surprisingly large number of professionals to conclude that we no longer need take note of Chomsky. But the fact is that he has shown that the traditionally accepted account of something widely held to be fundamental to philosophy will not hold water, and this is a major intellectual achievement. The fact that his own positive account is not acceptable to us puts us the more under challenge to find an alternative explanation. The fact that Chomsky himself has not been successful in this search is a secondary aspect of the matter, and derogates not at all from his main achievement. It is worth mentioning, in passing, what this is.

The traditional view for a very long time was that children acquire language by imitation, by reproducing what the language-users around them are saying. Chomsky pointed out that acquiring a language involves mastering a large number of interrelated and complex rules governing grammar and syntax, and then applying these appropriately in circumstances that can differ from one moment to the next, thus generating an indefinitely large number of differing sentences, most of which the speaker is not conscious of having heard before and perhaps has indeed never heard before. Chomsky further pointed out that half the parents in the world are semi-literate and have no notion of what the rules are, still less any ability to teach them; that they are, too, semi-articulate, so that what their children hear from them is fragmentary, crude, simple, the merest bits, pieces and scraps of conversation; that quite often this linguistic input varies immensely from child to child, depending on the circumstances in which it grows up, some surrounded by people talking all the time, others hearing little talk; and that when one actually comes to examine these linguistic inputs in specific terms it becomes wholly obvious that most of them are inadequate to explain the practical mastery of the rules of grammar and syntax that almost all children acquire, and what is more acquire at an astonishingly early age, in an astonishingly short space of time—indeed at roughly the same age, and in roughly the same time—regardless of the wide range of arbitrarily varying inputs to which they are exposed, and regardless of the wide range of different ability-levels among the children themselves. Chomsky is justified in believing that he has shown that the traditional view of how we acquire language does not fit the realities of the situation and cannot be right. This means he has confronted us with a challenge which, if we reject his responses to it, we must meet in some other way, but cannot ignore.

The mid-life crisis was for me some sort of melt-down. Its existential challenge fused together parts of my inner life that hitherto had borne only loose connections with one another. If in the end the only individual activity that really mattered was the search for meaning in life, everything that contributed to that search was part of the same enterprise, and whatever made no contribution to it was something I could let fall by the wayside. Philosophy and the arts, my friendships and my sex life, all were felt by me as joint components of a unitary life. I do not want to exaggerate the extent to which this was new: there was some sort of taken-for-granted sense in which it had always been so—I had always had the feeling that my existence in this world was a single something composed of innumerable elements that were aspects of a whole—but now for the first time they fused together and focused on a single point. In a vividly present and immediate way, great music, great theatre, and great philosophy seemed to be articulating something to do with the same thing, something to do with the question of life's meaning; and something similar (an inner voice saying "This is really what it's all about") spoke to me from the heart of all deeply felt relationships, above all sexual ones, with their miraculous capacity to create new human beings. This realization, which came to me in a highly charged way during a frighteningly embattled period of my life, and not as a theoretical discovery but as something lived, turned out later to be merely one among many that I was to find stated with apparent ease by Schopenhauer as though it had cost him nothing. For instance, part of it is contained in the following passage: "Not merely philosophy but also the fine arts work at bottom towards the solution of the problem of existence. For in every contemplation of the world a desire has been awakened, however concealed and unconscious, to comprehend the true nature of things, of life, and of existence . . . For this reason the result of every purely objective, and so of every artistic, apprehension of things is an articulation of more of the true nature of life and of existence, of more of the answer to the question 'What is life?' Every genuine and successful work of art answers this question in its own way."* One reason why Schopenhauer's philosophy was to mean so much to me when I discovered it is that by the time I reached it I had already carved out most (not all, by a long chalk) of its special insights from the living rock of my own life, and possessed many of them only roughly and unordered, half comprehended. By the use of my unaided abilities I would never have been able to bring them all to the clear focus that he did. He showed me what was implicit, ungrasped, in much of my own experience.

This inner understanding that the arts, philosophy and my own life were all aspects of the same thing was experienced by me not just as a diffused general awareness but in specific terms. For example, I came to feel that the most characteristic distillation of the existentialist experience and sensibility was to be found not in the writings of any philosopher, nor in any plays or novels (as it might have been in those, say, of Jean-Paul Sartre) but in the symphonies of Mahler. These engaged with some of my own anxieties and insights with such force and precision that it was as if Mahler had buttonholed me personally. By the end of listening to one of them I would be wrung out, not *as if* I had been through an emotional experience that had drained me of my all, but because I had. Indeed, not only had I been through such an experience, I had shared to

---

* Schopenhauer, *The World as Will and Representation,* tr. E. F. J. Payne, vol. ii, p. 406.

the full in the existential depth of a personality, lived a life. Even the sometimes almost intolerable beautifulness of the music, demanding more of the listener than could be borne without distress, spoke directly of life and the world and experience as I knew them.

Mahler's music did not begin to find a wide audience until half a century after his death. In the German-speaking world this may have been partly due to the fact that he was Jewish, and music by Jews was banned under the Nazis, so that after their fall it was unknown to younger audiences; and perhaps then conductors who had complied with the ban were ashamed too suddenly to introduce the music. But even in Britain the first fully professional public performance of Mahler's Third Symphony did not take place until 1961. I was present at it, and found it a life-changing experience. The sixties were a decade in which I devoured, with unslakable appetite, the best in music and theatre that London had to offer, but even in the middle of such a welter of experience the discovery and absorption of Mahler were exceptional. Among other things they led me to the discovery of Shostakovich, a lesser but still great experience of a music replete with existential content. When many years later, in my fifties, I made a fifteen-part television history of Western philosophy I chose the opening theme music from Shostakovich's Eighth Symphony.

In the theatre, too, the metaphysics of the drama revealed itself to me in a new way. All of Shakespeare's greatest plays, comedies as well as tragedies, are, on one level, about the significance of life as a whole, and this now communicated itself with an almost painful directness—not so much through the words as through the inner life of the play, something within or behind the play that the play puts us in touch with. Drama is not literature but a performing art, and the words are only one element among several that have to be fused together to make a play; and the master dramatist conceives the whole of the final product, not the verbal input alone. I began to realize that this was where the greatest of Shakespeare's greatnesses lay: not in the multiple genius of the text itself but in a whole universe of unverbalized and unverbalizable insights which drama is able to present to us even though they cannot be stated. The words are spells that help to conjure up this magic, but they are not the magic itself. And the relaxed mastery with which Shakespeare uses them reveals that—to a considerable extent, at least—he knew what he was doing. In an effective production a hushed and magic stillness comes over the audience when the veil of phenomenal existence is lifted from what is happening on the stage. It is impossible to express in words what occurs in those moments, but everyone experiences it. Although no other writer compares with Shakespeare in this regard there are two or three more recent playwrights who are also able to distil this unverbalizable essence of drama in performance: Ibsen, Chekhov, and Pirandello. They give one the sense of seeing life as a whole from the outside, and from this perspective providing a deepened comprehension and compassion.

My strongest particular passion in the arts has always been my love of Wagner. It is stronger even (and only) than my love of Shakespeare. Both of them set my imagination and emotions alight when I was a child—pre-teenage, thanks to my father's huge enjoyment of them and his good judgment about when to expose me to them. During my second visit to Bayreuth, when I was thirty, the realization crystallized in me that Wagner's mature works are, in the profoundest sense, psycho-dramas, whatever else they may also be in addition to that. Before then I had reacted to them only emotionally, and with an almost exclusive concentration on the music; but from this time on I began to think about them, and also to pay serious attention to what was happening on the stage. During my thirties I saw them many times over, often taking in two *Ring* cycles in a year. Also I acquired many complete recordings of them, read about them, discussed them with friends. Eventually I came to feel that something close to the heart of them, one of the few such things that can at least be pointed to in words if not satisfactorily articulated, had not yet found expression in the literature that exists about them—in fact, two such things. First, the special emotional impact which everyone, including people who do not like them, acknowledges these works to have derives partly from the fact that they articulate forbidden feelings: greed for unbridled self-assertion, incestuous sexual passion, lust for power and domination, a hatred that wants to murder. They give us a hotline to what has been most powerfully repressed in ourselves, and bring us consciousness-changing messages from the unconscious. This point leads on to the next. The very fact that these works speak aloud of what is forbidden makes it possible for them to articulate emotional reality in all its fullness, in a way no art can that does not do this. Not only do they give full-blooded expression to love, delight in life, humour, compassion, tenderness, self-sacrifice, intimations of mortality and immortality, the beauty of the world, devotion to ideals: they express also cruelty and evil, brutality, sadistic enjoyment, triumphalism, lust, alienation, stark terror. What to my mind sets Wagner and Shakespeare apart from other artists is the fact that they deal with everything. Their works confront the totality of human experience, and present our emotional life as it is, in its wholeness. So much of even the greatest art is aspirational, concerned with, and aiming at, ideals. Bach said he was composing his music to the greater glory of God; Beethoven said he was trying to express the highest of human aspirations; and one could multiply these sentiments many times over by quoting from the mouths of some of the greatest of artists. Art that springs from such motives can be wonderful, but cannot articulate the realities of human feeling across more than part of its range. Wagner's work, by contrast, is not aspirational but cognitive, truth-telling; and he tells it like it is, down to emotions we disown. Shakespeare does the same, across an even bigger canvas. If Wagner is enabled to go deeper it is only because his chief expressive medium is music rather than words.

I wrote a short book saying some of these things, and touching on a number of other aspects of Wagner—in fact I called it *Aspects of Wagner*—which was published in 1968. On the whole it dealt with ideas rather than music: Wagner's theory of opera, his anti-Semitism, his influence on creative artists other than musicians, and ways in which his works ought and ought not to be staged. I also tried to explain why his music is both loved and hated more immoderately than that of any other composer. Because of the book's slimness, and what might be thought to be the particularized nature of its subject—not to mention the obscurity of its publisher, Alan Ross—I expected it to slip out into the world stealthily, attracting little attention. To my astonishment it was reviewed on every side, and selected by the chief music critic of *The Times* as his Book of the Year. In fact it became a sort of cult book, and ever since I have received enthusiastic letters about it. Of particular interest have been those from Jews commenting on the discussion of the place of Jews in modern culture.

The book was reprinted many times, and translated into Spanish, Italian (by a Jewish Wagnerolater), and Dutch. After nearly twenty years it was taken over by Oxford University Press, and came out in a revised edition in 1988. Since its first publication it has caused me to be thought of as an expert on Wagner, and in that capacity invited to lecture, attend conferences, and so on. I am sure one reason for its success is its extreme shortness—less than a hundred pages in the revised edition.

It is characteristic of what I have called the melt-down of my inner life that during this period I formed a close bond with someone who had no general interest in ideas at all and was in that sense not an intellectual, though he was one of the most gifted people I have ever known—and, among other things, the most knowledgeable Wagnerian I have ever known—Deryck Cooke. It was our shared love of Mahler that brought us together. When Mahler died in 1911 he was working on his Tenth Symphony, but had completed only two of the intended five movements. His sketches for the rest were scattered after his death among different owners in different countries, as various people who had access to them took them, kept them, sold them, or bequeathed them to others. This dispersal was compounded by two world wars and the Nazis' expulsion of Jews from Central Europe. Deryck succeeded in tracking down all the sketches, and when he had done so made one astonishing and one not so astonishing discovery. The latter was that they contained some of the most beautiful music Mahler had ever composed, especially in the last movement. The former was that when pieced together they constituted an unbrokenly complete outline for a symphony lasting well over an hour, with not a single bar missing. It seemed to Deryck unacceptable that this marvellous music, Mahler's conscious farewell to the world, should remain for ever unknown to anyone other than scholars. However, if it was to become known to music-lovers in general they would have to be able to hear it; and for the music to be heard it would have to be played; and to be played it would have to be rendered performable. In some places the sketch consisted of nothing more than a line of single notes without any indication of what the harmony was, or the orchestration, or the tempo; so decisions about a host of matters such as these would have to be made if the music was ever to be played.

After careful consideration Deryck set himself to the task of rendering Mahler's sketch performable. It never entered his head to think of himself as "composing" Mahler's Tenth Symphony; all he wanted to do was enable people to get an idea of this wonderful material, and of the unexpected direction Mahler was heading in after the Ninth Symphony. In any event, not a single bar of free composition was called for: all that was required at any point was the filling out of indications that already existed in Mahler's own hand. Naturally, Deryck tried in every way he could to do this in an authentic spirit of Mahler. To this task he brought profound love, and a profound knowledge not only of all Mahler's other works but of his working methods, in the sense of compositional techniques. But he was the first to say that if Mahler had turned the sketches into full score himself he would have done it differently, with all the unpredictability of genius and with a sense of complete freedom to change whatever he felt like changing. Deryck was also aware that those parts of the sketch where Mahler's indications are sparsest might have been not those about which he felt most tentative but, on the contrary, those for which he already had the most assured and detailed grasp of what it was he was going to do, and therefore needed the least reminding. In order that everyone could see precisely what it was that he himself had done, Deryck had Mahler's entire sketch printed in a smaller typeface along the bottoms of the pages with, above it in ordinary type, his own suggested version for full orchestra.

If I may be allowed to put words into Deryck's mouth, what he was saying to the rest of us was in effect: "I am not giving you Mahler's Tenth Symphony. There has only ever been one person who could do that, namely Mahler, and death prevented him from doing so. He left most of the work unfinished, and his Tenth Symphony is something we shall never have. However, the sketches for it contain some of the most beautiful musical material ever produced not just by him but by anyone. Isn't this an incredible find? And don't we want, somehow or other, to be able to *hear* it? Isn't it at least better than nothing to get an approximate idea of what the work as a whole might have been like—its length and proportions, the length and proportions of each movement, as well as the main thematic material for each of them, and the leading voice throughout the entire work? All this has been left to us in Mahler's own hand, and here it is. As you see, a lot of it is wonderful. Is anyone seriously going to say that it would be *wrong* for us to find a way of playing it? Surely such an attitude would be indefensibly puritanical and un-serious? How could anyone hold it who really loved Mahler? Let me suggest one possible way of doing it, of rendering this sketch performable. What about this, for example? I lay it out so that you can see in detail what I've done. And perhaps you can suggest a better way." He was entirely open to criticisms, and suggestions for improvements, and he incorporated large numbers of them from several different people in the published version. This was the spirit in which he presented the sketch. And indeed precisely the words he had printed on both the cover and the title-page of the full orches-tral score, which was published in 1976 by Faber & Faber, were: "Gustav Mahler: a performing version of the draft for the Tenth Symphony, prepared by Deryck Cooke." This is all he ever regarded himself as offering. The idea that he was putting himself forward as Mahler's collaborator on the Tenth Symphony, or acting as midwife to the completed work, is risible for anyone who knew him. He was, indeed, neurotically modest.

Several recordings of this performing version have now been made by major symphony orchestras from various countries, and it looks as if it may be on the way to establishing itself in the international repertoire as the nearest we are likely to get to a great but unrealizable work. This constitutes a truly wonderful achievement on Deryck's part. He has given to the world what is, even in this heavily edited form, a great symphony that it would not otherwise have had. It is not Mahler's Tenth Symphony as Mahler would have be-queathed it to the world—what Mahler would have given us would unques-tionably have been different and better—but it is a great symphony none the less. And are we never to hear it because the attribution of some of it is divided between Mahler and Deryck? To say this is to confuse scholarly considera-tions with artistic ones, because it is to say that we must never play certain very beautiful music on the ground that it cannot unambiguously be ascribed to its nominal composer. Music-lovers, as distinct from musicologists—people whose primary concern is music, not what can be said about it—must surely hold this to be absurd.

The defensive tone in which I write is explained by the fact that some, if not all, of the best Mahler conductors of recent decades have refused on purist grounds to perform this sketch: Bernard Haitink, Herbert von Karajan, Leonard Bernstein, Georg Solti. I once arranged a meeting with Haitink with the openly declared purpose of persuading him to try the experiment, but I failed. If I am to express my suspicions equally openly, they are not that these outstanding artists lacked appreciation of Deryck's achievement—on the contrary, when I met some of them I found them overflowing with obviously sincere admiration for it—but that they feared that their own reputations might suffer among the scholarly if they were to give the impression of treating Deryck's performing version of the sketch as if it were Mahler's Tenth Symphony. What makes this paradoxical is that there are thoroughly familiar works in the international repertory which are performed without the slightest objection by anyone and which contain long stretches of free composition by a person other than the nominal composer—of which, as I have said, there is none whatsoever in the performing sketch of the Tenth Symphony. When Mozart died leaving his *Requiem* unfinished it was completed by his pupil Süssmeyr, and it is in Süssmeyr's version that the work is performed, though we refer to it always as Mozart's *Requiem.* Puccini's opera *Turandot*—considered by some to be his greatest—was finished after his death by his pupil Alfano. The very names of Süssmeyr and Alfano are probably unknown to most music-lovers, including most of those who have enjoyed these works that were partly composed by them. I have never heard it suggested, not by a single soul, that we ought not to perform Mozart's *Requiem* or Puccini's *Turandot* on the ground that these are works that were brought to completion by others, nor have I heard it suggested that the *Requiem* is "not really" Mozart or *Turandot* "not really" Puccini.

But I protest too much. The future, I do believe, is on Deryck's side. His version has already been recorded several times, by conductors including James Levine, Eugene Ormandy and Simon Rattle (the first two with the Philadelphia Orchestra, and the last in an especially fine performance). I think the quality of the score is such that it is bound to acquire new adherents. What I would like is for it to be accepted into the international repertory as Mahler's Tenth Symphony alongside Mozart's *Requiem* and Puccini's *Turandot,* and for Deryck to join the company of Süssmeyr and Alfano.

Deryck Cooke's knowledge and understanding of Wagner were if anything more prodigious than his knowledge and understanding of Mahler. He knew the scores in the minutest detail, and he carried in the front of his mind a year-by-year—for some periods week-by-week and even day-by-day—biography of Wagner. "Yes, that was in the first week of April. Then towards the end of that month he . . ." And even: "He saw her on the Tuesday afternoon, and then again on the Wednesday morning . . ." I do not believe that Wagner knew his own scores so well, and I doubt whether he remembered his own life in such clarity of detail, or with such an assured grasp of chronology. Furthermore Deryck's knowledge was astonishingly alive: it did not just sit in his head like Fafner's hoard but was always at work, and he was always doing things with it. One thing he did constantly was relate detail to detail across wide expanses.

He would point out that at a certain moment in one of the *Ring* operas, when a certain character was saying a certain thing, one of the almost inaudible inner parts in the orchestra, let us say the second bassoon, played a certain configuration of notes, and that two operas later, when that character's son was saying a forlorn-sounding variation of the same thing, the second bassoon played a forlorn-sounding variation of the same notes. Incidentally, this persistent integration of almost unnoticeable detail into the close-woven fabric of vast and sometimes apparently sprawling structures is something Wagner has very much in common with Shakespeare. When Deryck drew attention to an example of it, it was seldom if ever an arguable, ho-hum sort of point. It was indisputably there. And Wagner's scores teem with this sort of thing. What, if anything, the significance of it might be in any given instance is perhaps open to interpretation, but the fact itself is usually not to be denied.

Another, connected gift Deryck had was for hearing that two pieces of musical material that no one before had heard as related were in fact related; and if the person he was talking to was sceptical he could always demonstrate what the relationship was, and show how one had been derived from the other. If the work in question was a Wagner opera he could show how this relationship was the musico-dramatic articulation of a change taking place in the relationship between two of the characters on the stage, or between states of mind within a single character, or between events—or that it related to words in the text. These gifts gave him a degree of insight into Wagner's art that was without parallel in my experience. Wagner had a limitlessly inventive capacity for musical metamorphosis, but his supreme achievement lay in putting it to work as a language of the theatre, infinitely expressive in its powers of psychological and dramatic revelation. And Deryck was the only person I have ever known who seemed to see precisely what it was that Wagner was doing at every moment, and how it was being done. This was what he regarded as his own most special gift, and he felt that what he had been sent on the earth to do was to pass his insights on in the case of *The Ring*.

His plan was to do this in a four-volume book. The first two volumes were to be about everything other than the music—the texts, the myths, the stories, the characters, the staging of it all, and so on and so forth. The last two, in which the true heart of the book was to lie, would relate all these things in close detail to the music, and furthermore analyse the music in and for itself. My conversations with him over a number of years revealed fathomless depths of understanding here, and suggested to me that by the time I met him most if not all the material had come together in his mind. The only thing that was holding him back at that point was his preoccupation with Mahler's Tenth Symphony, and he was waiting for his work on it to see itself through to its natural end before settling down to the monumental task of writing the *Ring* book. Alas, it was not to be. He had scarcely started work on it when at the age of fifty-seven he died of a stroke, leaving a pitiful beginning-fragment behind him that was published as a book under the title *I Saw the World End.* Next to the fact that Wagner himself did not live long enough to compose the symphonies he intended to write after finishing *Parsifal* it is the biggest single loss to serious lovers of Wagner that there has ever been.

In view of Deryck's towering abilities my readers may wonder why I have said he was not an intellectual. I say so because he did not function at all well at the level of conceptual thought. He was no fool, but conceptual thinking was not in his line. He found difficulty in following a philosophical argument, and also in grasping subtle logical distinctions. In any activity that consisted largely in the handling of verbalizable ideas he was like any other man on the Clapham omnibus. He was just simply not, more significantly than anyone else, a verbal person. There was something ordinary, and I mean that in a derogatory sense, about the way he used words. Above all else he was musical. The whole universe in which he functioned naturally, and felt at home, and moved at high speed with sure-footedness and assurance—seeming almost to take in everything and understand it all, grasping huge totalities not only as wholes but in their protean detail, exhibiting also a mastery of every level between the details and the whole, and able to relate those differing levels to one another; and all in realms beyond the reach of language, realms towards which words can at best point from a distance and then leave the traveller to find his own way—was musical. He was an object lesson in some of the realities of thinking without language.

16

A Philosophical Novel

Ever since I was taught as a child that our ration of life is threescore years and ten I have felt that if someone dies before the age of seventy he is being cheated, whereas if he lives beyond seventy he is being given a bonus. So once past the age of thirty-five I felt I was into the second half of my life. As I have recounted, for most of the time I had come to feel that this life was meaningless and pointless. But during the intervals when it seemed to mean something I was deeply dissatisfied with what I had done with mine up to that point. By conventional standards I had not been wasting my time. I had published eight books, stood for parliament twice, and for some years had been appearing on a regular peak-hour television programme. In a way I was a sort of minor celebrity: I was recognized by strangers in the street, addressed by name in shops and restaurants, asked for my autograph. But none of this had any value for me. I found being recognized shy-making, and did what I could to avoid it. I regarded my two latest books as journalism in stiff covers, not even properly written but dictated. Television I had always thought of as a superficial medium, inherently unimportant. I appreciated the international travel it brought me, and also the income, which enabled me to entertain my friends and enjoy as much music and theatre as I could happily consume. But I was not achieving anything that I myself valued. I even began to feel something of a fraud: my little bit of celebrity was based not on any solid accomplishment but on public exposure. I was well known for being well known. The conviction that I was wasting not just my talents but my life began to take root.

After trying in vain to remedy the situation by devoting my media activities to more worthwhile subjects I came to the conclusion that the only thing to do was give them up altogether, and occupy myself with something I believed in and wanted to do. The money I had in the bank would keep me for at least a year. So I turned my back—as I thought permanently—on the media world.

I wanted to write, and knew I wanted to write a novel, but did not know what novel. I felt I needed for a while to let my spirit breathe, and I trusted that, while I was doing this, what I wanted to write would come to me. So I spent a while doing other things. For six weeks I wandered around part of the Middle East—Beirut, Crusader castles, Jerusalem, Baalbeck, Damascus, Jerash, the Dead Sea, Cairo. While doing this I read the New Testament in a new English translation that enabled me to read it almost as if it were any book.

What came through to me most strongly was the radically "different" character of Jesus' moral teaching. So different is it, indeed, that it borders on the incomprehensible. Other moralists put forward rules of behaviour; other revolutionists in morals try to overthrow whatever are the existing rules and establish different ones in their stead; but Jesus is saying that rules, any rules, are not what morality is about. God, he says, is not in the business of awarding prizes to people who live in accordance with moral rules. You will not win any special favours from him by being virtuous, but are only too likely to find—to your great chagrin, no doubt, as well as your incomprehension—that he loves sinners just as much as he loves you. If this infringes your sense of justice you have not understood the situation. It is no use being good in the hope of getting a reward from God: this is pure self-seeking, and therefore a self-contradictory conception of morally admirable behaviour. Only if you are good when it is not rewarded is your behaviour morally admirable. But then there is indeed no reward: so the goodness has to be its own justification, regardless of consequences. God's loving you has nothing to do with your deserving it. He loves everybody, including the most undeserving, indeed he loves them as much as he loves you. Just as he loves the undeserving, so you also should love those who are undeserving of your love, including those who deserve it least, namely your enemies. Love is what matters, not deserving, and least of all rules. In fact, love matters above everything else. It is the ultimate reality, the true nature of existence, God. Perfect love is unconditional, and to unconditional love, deserving has ceased to matter or even have any significance. It is not that Jesus is against our living in accordance with rules. On the contrary, he recognizes that rules are necessary wherever human beings live together, and he believes that they should be obeyed; but he sees them as arbitrary, superficial things that should be made subservient to human needs, not human needs made subservient to them. If we had enough love and concern for one another there would be no need for rules. We need them only because we are selfish. They are not, in themselves, good.

These are only a few of the teachings of Jesus, but they are central to his message; and the fact that there was anyone at all going around preaching things like this two thousand years ago in a desert area of the Middle East is, to say the least of it, surprising. The extent to which they are original to Jesus is a matter that scholars dispute, and not one about which I know enough to have an independent opinion; but that the teachings themselves are unobvious, and full of deep moral insight, is clear to me. Jesus was also, although for some reason this is scarcely ever said, a profound psychologist. When, in addition to all this, one considers the audacity with which his views are expressed, and the poetically striking quality of many of his illustrations, he appears perhaps the most remarkable moralist there has ever been—a genius of a moralist, like Socrates: or perhaps even something in the way of a creative artist, like Plato. Like the historical Socrates, but unlike Plato, he confined his teaching to questions of morality. The nature of the world, and of our knowledge of it, do not appear to be concerns of his. In consequence he has nothing to offer that corresponds to the epistemological insights of Hinduism and Buddhism—and in that sense what he says might appear secondary, limited. But within the limitations of morality he goes as deep as anyone was to penetrate for the better part of two thousand years. When it comes to tellingness of moral insight, a question like "What will a man gain by winning the whole world at the cost of his true self?" is unsurpassed.

When I got back from the Middle East to England I decided to have a period, albeit short, doing something I had never done before, and that was to devote myself full-time to music, which had always been my ruling passion yet had always been a spare-time activity. I did so for only three months, but they were three unforgettable months. Since the age of thirty I had been paying visits to the home of the composer Anthony Milner for private lessons in harmony and counterpoint, and I now continued these lessons on a weekly basis in order to give some of my efforts a focus outside myself; but when I was not working for these, I gave myself up, which was for most of every day, to unguided composition. Most of my compositions were songs. They reconfirmed something I had known about myself since adolescence, namely that I had a flair for writing tunes—not great ones, alas, but whistleable ones. I had known this before, because when I was alone, especially on walks, I was given to whistling in a very free, improvisatory sort of way, and quite often I would hit on a good melodic idea, which I would then develop and put into shape. It is conceivable, at least to me, that if I had worked at it seriously I might have been able, when young, to develop the capacity to earn my living as a writer of popular songs. At best I might have been successful as what people dismissively describe as a tunesmith. Not even my finest efforts, I fear, would have had the distinction, still less the beauty, of the best of George Gershwin or Jerome Kern. Even so, I might, at my best, have managed to reach the level of some of their lesser known, more run-of-the-mill songs.

Those that I composed during this three-month period were not "popular" in this sense but "serious." Nevertheless they were faulty in a way that what I have been saying might lead one to suppose: they were sentimental—tuneful, yes, even memorable sometimes, but inclined to mushiness. They were rather like a modern equivalent of Victorian parlour ballads. At best they sounded like Richard Strauss on a bad day. I tried to remove this sentimentality by exercise of will, and by taking thought. But to no avail. I found it impossible to remove the sentimentality without removing the music, leaving nothing on the page but a dead exercise. My music was *inherently* sentimental. Either what I wrote was music and sentimental or it was not music, and that was the only choice I had.

Rarely have I found the process of work itself so absorbing or so satisfying as during those three months. I would get out of bed in the morning trembling with excitement at the prospect of going to work. I learnt a surprising amount about music. But I also learnt that I did not have it in me to be a self-respecting composer. One consequence of this was that my respect for certain other composers, particularly the good but lightweight ones, increased—people who produce easily enjoyable music with style and craftsmanship, people I might before have been inclined to feel patronizing towards but now knew I could not emulate, people I might once have felt superior to but now realized were superior to me. I discovered a new kind of pleasure in their music, a pleasure in its workmanship, its technical accomplishment and stylishly concealed ingenuities, sometimes its sheer professionalism, as well as its overt musical attractiveness. There was so much more to it than I had realized. And as for the truly great masters, my enhanced understanding of what it was they were doing gave me a kind of awe at what they achieved.

While I was drifting round the Middle East, and while I was composing music, a novel was forming in the darkness on the edge of my awareness. What is most curious about this process is that the book itself ended up as almost the opposite of what it started out as. I began by wanting to write a love story. My sex life was a never-ending pursuit of a reciprocal love that I had never experienced; and the reason I never experienced it was not that I was not loved, it was that I did not love. An inland sea of undirected and powerful emotion was dammed up inside me, blocked, unable to find expression, unable to flow freely, even when somebody loved me. The huge frustration this caused me built up a tremendous emotional drive for which I longed to find an outlet. I hit on the idea of writing a novel into which I would pour this drive, a novel in which the oceanic feelings could overflow and yet be slaked, giving me at last some sort of fulfilment of what I most lacked, not just in imagination but in something real, something that existed outside myself. I would call it *Love Story,* a title which up to that time, astonishingly, had never been used, at least not that anyone I knew could remember.

I was going to need at least two central characters, a woman and a man, that was obvious. But what was I going to do with them? Simply to say that they were in love, and try to express this love? Was I going to rhapsodize for two or three hundred pages, just that? It was not that I could not imagine such a thing being done successfully; I could, but by a kind of writer different from myself—a gigantic prose poem, a static and yet sustained celebration of love. But, to keep all that in flight without flagging, the impulse would have to be not just powerful but essentially poetic, and I knew that in this particular case my impulse had the power but not the poetry. The drive behind the book was, before anything else, psycho-emotional: what I was looking for was a way of channelling my libido. And I had a feeling that the outlet natural to me was going to have to be dramatic rather than lyrical—something eventful and (it was to be hoped) powerful. But this meant that something had to *happen* in the book. And if this something was to be central to the book's concerns it would have to impinge on the love relationship. And if it were not to be trivial it would have to be important. It would need to be this anyway to be dramatically effective. The more I thought about it the more I realized that it would need to be something that stood in the way of their love, some obstacle. I considered as many possibilities as I could of the eternal triangle; but if any of them were to have a real grip on the reader it would qualify the unconditioned nature of the central emotion, and this was something I did not want. So I tried to think of something that would constitute a huge, real, alarming threat to their love without involving another character. This led to the idea of a serious illness or accident. To be a mortal threat to their relationship it would have to be potentially life-destroying. Mulling this over, I realized that if the story ended with the danger being overcome after a period of touch-and-go this would be pure cliché, melodrama, silent film; and there would be a "and they all lived happily ever after" feel about it, at best fairy tale, at worst romantic novel. But what if the threat were not overcome? What if one of them died? The book could hold on to its reality and seriousness then. Something here clicked, and I knew I was on the right track. But still I had only a situation, not a story, still less a plot. I needed something to *happen:* I needed suspense, falls and recoveries, conflicts, misunderstandings, cross-purposes, deceptions, discoveries, revelations. Perhaps one of the two characters could be dying and know it, but not tell the other. I had known an American student at Oxford, a gifted poet, who had been in this situation. Told back home in the United

States that he had leukaemia and only a couple of years to live, he did what he had always longed to do and came to Oxford, but without telling anyone there his secret, and flung himself into life on all fronts simultaneously, trying to fit in everything he had ever wanted to do. He made a tremendous impact on other students, who were quite sure that he was going to become famous and successful later in life, perhaps even a great poet. Then he and another of the students fell in love. There came a time when he had to tell her the truth about his situation. She kept it to herself until after his death, and only then did the whole story come out. Meanwhile the only thing other people noticed was that the relationship between the two of them had a hyperintensity that others were much moved to comment on at the time, though nobody guessed at the truth.

For quite a while I thought of basing my plot on this situation, freely adapting it to my own needs, and I played with all kinds of variations along these lines. But then a powerful twist occurred to me. It would be possible for the one who was dying not to know while the other one did know. I knew this because it had happened to another friend of mine from Oxford, who had died in his late twenties from Hodgkin's disease. His doctors had told his mother the truth, but had not told him, and she had concealed it from him; and when he fell in love and declared his intention of getting married, his mother had told the girl. So both the mother and the girl had had to face the fact of his dying, and come to terms with it, each at a different time, each in her own way, while he himself knew nothing about it at all. There were all sorts of possible twists and turns available here that appealed to me as the basis for a plot, and this was the approach I settled on. Because the change in my intentions had happened only one step at a time it was a little while before I realized that my original plan to write a book about requited love had been hijacked by my obsession with the need to face death. I did realize it, however; and fortunately I wrote the book the novel had become, not the book I had started out intending to write. When it was published I called it not *Love Story* but *Facing Death*— a title which, I suppose, must have reduced the number of its readers.

I constructed my plot in such a way that each of the main characters in turn would have to come to terms with the young man's impending death, and would do so in different circumstances, ending with the young man himself; and I constructed the characters so that each would do it in a different way. The central couple did not bear any relation to the real-life couple I had known, nor had it ever entered my head that they ought to; also, I freely invented the incidents that constituted the plot, to meet my own needs. Since, therefore, both characters and story were made up, I was taken completely by surprise when large numbers of people who knew me, and therefore might have known better, assumed that the novel was fictionalized fact—that I had started out with the real-life story of those actual people and turned it into a novel. It is true that I made use of the real-life mother in creating my mother character; but apart from her the only character in the book for whom there was even a partial counterpart in real life was one who, in the book, had nothing to do with the plot, and in real life had never known the couple or their world—a doctor who, in the book, was privy to everything but at the same time a detached observer, and so acted as a kind of Greek chorus throughout the novel. I was thunderstruck when people started asking me in all seriousness what had "really" happened and what the "originals" were, not only of the characters but of everything else in the book. Was my Sunday paper based on the *Sunday Times* or the *Observer?* Or was it a combination of the two? Which actual pub had such-and-such a conversation "really" taken place in? To them it was all real; it had all happened to actual people in actual places, and they simply would not accept from me that this was not so. When I said that what they were asking about was made up, that only two of the characters in the book drew anything from real-life people, that none of the incidents or conversations had actually occurred, and that there were no "originals" to any of the fictional locations, I was simply not believed. People in general seem incapable of understanding that fiction need not have its origins in fact, indeed must not if it is to be true to itself, though it can be just as free in the use it makes of fact as it can be in the use it makes of anything else.

The way I, at least, had gone about it was as follows. I saw from the beginning that although each character in the book could be constructed in a variety of ways there were certain characteristics that each was going to have to have in order to make the plot work, and therefore make the book credible. And it was important that they should have not just these characteristics alone, otherwise they would seem undercharacterized, too much like working parts of a piece of machinery, manipulated puppets. Even so, they had to have at least these characteristics; and whatever others they had needed to be such as would be compatible with these. So I started from needful characteristics and worked outwards, turning the people this way and that in my mind, thinking of them from the point of view of the other characters, and the incidents of the plot, putting more and more flesh on them, trying to imagine their pasts, or guess their futures. I would ask myself all sorts of questions like: What does this person really want out of life? What does he fear more than anything else? Who does he love most? What makes him laugh? What does he do when he isn't working? Where does he go for his holidays? What sort of childhood did he have? And I would let my imagination play with complete freedom over the answers, filling out the characters further and further, until I knew a great deal more about them than ever got into the book.

For example, let us consider the central character, John, who is about to die. At the beginning of the book I wanted him to be immersed in the everyday, one might almost say in love with the everyday. And I wanted him then, very slowly and gradually, like the peeling away of the skins of an onion, to make the journey from being wholly involved in his outer world to the discovery of his inner self. On successive stages of this journey into the interior I wanted him to search for significance in life on deeper and deeper levels, for instance reflective thought followed by artistic experience followed by personal relationships. It was from considerations such as these that I started out on my construction of his character. To give him immersion in the everyday I made him a professional journalist who was in love with his job. And to give him a wide enough frame of reference for what was to come I made him the sort of journalist who is able to write about almost anything, who can review theatre and music interestingly as well as discuss politics informatively, and who has international experience. To provide plenty of scope for dramatic irony I made him someone for whom a great future was expected. Because it was my intention that late in the novel he should find himself pondering in a serious way, and to some purpose, whether life could possibly be said to have a meaning, and if so what sort of thing such a meaning could be, I made his education include a training in philosophy. But because I thought it would make the novel over-earnest and un-novel-like if he embarked on lengthy considerations of the doctrines of actual great philosophers I gave him the sort of philosophical training that would largely exclude any knowledge of them—I made him a Philosophy, Politics, and Economics graduate of Oxford. This in turn rendered it necessary that in the course of the book he was going to realize how inadequate such a training had been (another of my obsessions, you might say). And so on and so forth. In this way the character was created by the needs of the book itself. That is to say, every characteristic I gave him was one that I knew the requirements of the novel were going at some point or other to call for.

Something that turned out to have multiple consequences was his name. The most fundamental and universal truth about the human condition, in so far as we have knowledge of it, is that we are going to die; and I wanted in the book to bring out the fact that in facing death this young man, far from being in some specially traumatic or tragic situation, was in the same situation as everybody else, including the reader. The story was, at the most fundamental level, and shorn of all accidents of personality and contingencies of circumstance, everybody's story. So I wanted to give him an English name that was as near as I could get to Everyman. I decided to call him John Smith. But I was not happy about this. First, it was a blank, anonymous name to give to the central character of a novel—of course there are plenty of flesh-and-blood people called John Smith, and I have known several, but even so . . . More important: although each one of us is Everyman, each one of us is also a unique human being, unlike any other that has ever existed or will ever exist again—private, quirky, a mass of self-contradictions, unpredictable. The uniqueness of the personality is a great mystery; perhaps, for all I know, as great a mystery as death itself. So my John Smith, as well as being Everyman, was an inscrutably different and un-pin-downable individual. In keeping with this I wanted him to have his own distinctive name, a name that was not symbolic of anything, a name that was just him, *his* name. What a pity, I thought, that he cannot have two names—Everyman, and at the same time something individual. Then I realized: there is a way in which an Englishman can have two names, and that is if he is a peer. If Joe Bloggs is Lord Snookfish then he is equally Joe Snookfish. All three names, in fact, are properly his, and all three may be in frequent use. So if I made John Smith a peer I could give him another name, and he could then, if I liked, have not just two names but three. Because he was so young he would have to be a hereditary peer, not a life peer. Some readers might consider my making a young working journalist a peer a little high-handed, but in fact I could think straight away of several professional journalists who were hereditary peers: Wayland Young, John Grigg, Nicholas Bethell—there was no shortage of examples. So it was perfectly realistic, and I decided to go ahead with it. Thus John Smith became also John Winterborne. However, the side-effects were great. It meant that he would have to be from a socially privileged background, and have at least one foot in such a world, which would therefore have to figure in the novel. I could, of course, invent special reasons for this not to be so, but on reflection I realized that if I allowed it to go ahead I could give him every possible personal and social advantage for him then to discover the nullity of in the face of death, without this appearing arbitrary or strained. So it would enrich the possibilities of the book—not perhaps at the deepest level; but in a novel the social surface matters. So I went ahead and gave John an upper-class background that he was to some extent developing out of and reacting against. This in turn had many-sided implications—for his character and relationships, for locations, and for the plot in general.

Up to this point I have talked about the creation of John's character in isolation. But almost anyone writing a novel is going to find himself wanting to contrast one character with another, one episode with another; so I often found myself giving a certain attribute to one character because another lacked it, and my chief purpose might even be to point up something about the *other* character. Characters are constituted not only by the requirements of the theme and the plot but by the full range of all other elements in the book. In considerable detail you make each character everything that the book, at whatever point and for whatever reason, is going to call on him to be; and you want to do this without appearing to pull each characteristic out of a hat at the moment you need it. This involves planning, looking forward, all the time integrating the characters with one another and with their world. The great thing you have going for you is the fact that you have utter freedom of invention: you can simply make up whatever you need to to make the book work on its own terms—remembering that keeping it lifelike and credible is an essential part of making it work. For a long time during the gestation period of my novel I was afraid that the characters were being too arbitrarily created, too artificially synthesized; but there came a point when they took off on a life of their own. This was especially marked for me when I began to dream about them, which I did quite a lot. I took this as an indication that they had now escaped from the control of my conscious mind and were themselves acquiring unconscious characteristics. In fact I began to think of them as people, and I still do.

A plot, like characters, is constructed in accordance with a book's internal needs. *Facing Death* is dominated by the progress of John's illness and its treatment—which in my view (not all writers would share it) needed to remain faithful to the truth about medical conditions at the time in which the story was set. The length of the periods for which he felt well, what then went wrong with him, the length of the periods for which he was in hospital, the treatment he received, how he responded to it, all this created a detailed framework into which every element in the story had to fit naturally, including a pregnancy with whose time-scale I could also not arbitrarily interfere, once it had begun. Through doctor friends I got myself introduced to the chief consultant for Hodgkin's disease at one of London's teaching hospitals, and he agreed to become, in effect, the medical consultant to the plot. At every stage of John's illness I would confer with him about the possible next step, and he would say something like: "Well in those days I'd have had to do one of two things. Either I'd have done so-and-so, in which case he'd have had to come into the hospital for it, and he'd have been an in-patient for a week or ten days. Or I'd have done such-and-such, in which case he'd have been an out-patient, though he'd still have had to come in three times a week for injections . . . ," and so on and so forth, describing in detail, in response to my questions, exactly what was involved with each alternative, and the different ways in which a patient might respond to it. I would then choose whichever course of events best suited my story and the relationship between my characters, as these were developing under my hand. Sometimes I would put a request to the doctor: "I want to get John out of the way for a few days so that the other characters can unsuspiciously get together without him: is there anything for which I can realistically send him into the hospital, just briefly, at this point?" If there was, I would make use of it; if there was not, I would invent some other reason for John's enforced absence, perhaps something to do with his job. It was in ways like this that the sequence of fictional events came into existence and was made to fit together and interlock. That is why, when after publication a reader would say to me, "Who did this actually happen to?," I would find myself looking at him blankly. When I tried to explain that there was no "this," other than what I had invented; that my story was not an account of any actual events but was created by me, made up; the response was nearly always something like: "Oh, but one can tell from reading it that it must have happened— it's obviously real, a chunk of life. Come on, now, tell me who it was." To which one could only think, if not say: "Well, thank you for the compliment. I worked hard to give it life, and with you at least I seem to have succeeded."

The people most prone to the illusion that these are real human beings and events are those one would least expect it of, namely one's friends, who know quite a lot about one's life and might therefore be expected to know that it does not include the characters and events of the novel. An intriguing psychological process is at work here. Because those particular readers, unlike all the others, know the author personally, and yet share the widespread assumption that fiction is based on fact, they find themselves thinking as they read: "Now who is this character based on? Let me see, who are the women painters Bryan knows?," and so on. And they decide: "She must be based on Maria." So they then envisage the real-life Maria as the fictional painter, hear all her dialogue in the real Maria's tones of voice, and so on. In fact it is *they* who are rendering the painter as a portrait of Maria, in the privacy of their own minds. Such an attribution is self-fulfilling. At the end of the book they will say, "That was just like Maria, spot on all the way through—every word and every gesture," because they themselves have held Maria vividly before their minds all the time they were reading. However, different friends will attribute the same character to different models, and then they will argue with one another about which of them is right—and appeal to the author to settle the matter. Sometimes a friend will complain to the author that a portrait is inaccurate. "You've been a bit hard on Maria, you know—she's nothing like as self-centred as you've made her out." If the writer replies, "But if you yourself insist that this character is not like Maria why do you assume that she's meant to be?," the response, usually, is "Well in that case who *is* it meant to be?" The assumption that fiction has real people and real events as its starting point is not to be shaken in most readers. This constitutes, it seems to me, a radical failure to understand what fiction is, what it does, and why it is written. But I have long since given up trying to combat it with respect to my own novels.

By now a reader might want to start expressing accumulating doubts. He could say: "But in your own account you have already said that you once knew somebody who died young of Hodgkin's disease; that the doctors told the truth to his mother but not to him; that he then fell in love with a girl and declared his intention of marrying her; that at this point the mother told the girl, but not him; that the girl then had to decide whether to go ahead with the marriage, and whether to tell the young man herself. In the event, I hear, she decided not to tell him, just as in your book. And on top of all this you have admitted that you based the character of the fictional mother on the real-life mother of that young man. How, then, can you deny that what you have been doing is telling the story of those people? Surely it is inevitable that those who knew all of you should believe that this is what you have done?"

To this my answer is as follows. No one who knew the real-life young man, or the girl he married, could possibly imagine that the characters in the book are in any way at all portraits of them; they are not remotely like them. Nor do any other characters in the book have any connection, not even a distant one, with people I have known, except for the mother and one of the doctors—and he, as I said before, never met the real-life people at all. One qualification to this statement needs to be made, but it is not one that most of the misunderstanders would expect, although it is of the greatest psychological and artistic importance. Because I freely invent the characters, and use all the resources of imagination and understanding that I possess to get inside them, in order to feel what they feel and think what they think, and to look out on the world through their eyes, there are significant elements of me in all of them. And there is bound to be more of me in them than I realize, for two main reasons. First, it is not possible for me to bring to life in any of them, whether consciously or unconsciously, a thought or feeling or insight that I am incapable of having myself, and therefore all of them are in the last analysis limited by my limitations, which is of course not the case with any real-life person other than myself. The second reason is that, almost by definition, there must be a greater input from my unconscious in each of them than I am aware of. When people ask me, "Is John you?," or "Is Keir you?," my spontaneous reply is: "All the characters are me." The whole book is my creation: everything in it, including not only the characters but all the things I do not realize are there, is an expression of me. But it is only the book as a whole that is of this nature, only the book *as a whole* that I am, so to speak, uttering with my own mouth. *Within* it nothing is necessarily me at all: no opinion expressed by a character is necessarily mine, and no feeling or experience necessarily one I have had. All that these things need to be are things that, if only in imagination or unconsciously, I apprehend, and feel a need to do something with, whether by way of acceptance or rejection or transubstantiation.

What I am doing, and what I believe most writers of serious fiction are doing, is making full and free use of the entire range of material available for my purposes, regardless of its origin. And the very fact that I do not care where it comes from means that, of course, its sources can include people I have known and experiences I have had as well as the totality of what I can invent. But the real-life origin of material is purely incidental: it is never my concern, and certainly never the object of my writing. It is never my aim to transmit anything about real people or real events. *My starting point* is never somebody I have known, or something that has happened, which I then transmute into fiction. On the contrary, it is the other way about: my starting point is that I am writing a work of fiction; and to enable it to grow as it wants to grow I feed it with nourishment from any and every source, and in whatever form, however changed from the original, that is most gratefully welcomed by the novel itself.

Perhaps the point I am making will become clearer if I give a different sort of example of how real-life experience might come to be used in a novel of mine in a way that could then mislead even my friends. Suppose I start out by wanting to create a love-relationship between a boy and a much older woman, and from the point of view of his psychological development it is important that she should be the only woman he knows well. This will probably prompt the idea of setting my story in an all-male world. What all-male worlds are there for teenage boys, I would ask myself. Answer: training ships, any kind of reformatory, boarding schools, certain sorts of hospital, and so on and so forth. How does a mature woman come to be in such a world, usually? As the wife of a member of the staff—an officer, a warder, a master, a doctor. (I am now beginning to get my outline.) If I want to maximize both the stakes and the tension I could make the woman the wife of the supreme authority-figure—the captain, governor, headmaster, or whoever. This could lead naturally to making the husband a middle-aged man with a very much younger wife, so that the age-gap between her and the boy was no greater, perhaps even less, than that between her and her husband. I could make him an interesting person wrapped up in his work, or perhaps someone being especially challenged at the time of the story by a crisis in the institution—in which the boy could be implicated in some special way, and which could be used to heighten an all-pervading atmosphere of tension or danger throughout the book. Not just the situation but my story is now beginning to emerge out of nothingness. And so it goes on. At some point along this line, and quite soon, I would have to settle on the "world" in which all this was to happen. And there is one of the possible worlds that would have an enormous advantage for me over the others, in that I lived in a boarding school myself from the age of eleven until nearly eighteen, and know from experience what life in a boarding school is like. And it is more than just knowledge: I have the "feel" of it, my antennae for the subtleties of it are delicately tuned. However, I would be under no necessity to set my story in a boarding school: I am fairly confident of my ability to invent a setting on a training ship or in a reformatory, and to bring it to life. It is just that I would be able to give the background more authenticity and depth, and write about it from a deeper level of myself, with greater understanding, if I made it a boarding school. So I would probably decide on a boarding school.

When I continued with the working out of my story I might well discover that it involved complicated, clandestine comings and goings, meetings in the dark and so forth; and I would want to be consistent in my references to, or assumptions about, buildings, relative locations, distances, and so on. Also, such questions as what could be overlooked from which window might take on a special importance for the plot. At some such stage of a book's development many writers sit down and invent their school. They work out a sketch-map on paper, not usually to be included in the published volume but so that they can choreograph the movements of their characters and check them for consistency and plausibility. (Bernard Shaw used to do this on a chess board with pieces of paper on which the characters' names were written.) I might well do something similar, and would certainly do so if my story required it—for instance if the layout of the school needed to have certain special characteristics in order for the plot to work. But if that were not especially the case I might think to myself: "I can visualize the school I was at as vividly as any imaginary school of my own invention, and in more concreteness of detail; and it would cost me less energy to hold it in my mind's eye all the time I was writing. I know every nook and cranny of it, and would have no difficulty in finding my way around it in the dark. So that's what I'll do: I'll give the school in the book a different name, but what I'll have in mind when I'm writing is Christ's Hospital as it was when I was there. That'll guarantee unity and consistency to the setting, as well as feasibility to the characters' movements; and if some deep-seated feelings of mine about the school get into the writing, not necessarily consciously, that might help ensure that the 'world' in which the story is set has a life of its own and is not just a two-dimensional backdrop."

The point to stress is that this decision would be in no way a necessary one: I could very easily not make it. It would simply be a device of which I could, if I wished, make use in order to help me meet certain complicated inner requirements of the book that had no counterpart in reality. It might also be rather a lazy option, chosen to save me the concentration and energy required by invention, or to save time. But once I had made the choice I would feel completely free to use any material from my schooldays that would serve my purposes. If I wanted to give additional substance to the background I might draw on people and incidents that had made a lifelong impression on me; if I felt that the book needed humour I might make use of a zany schoolmaster about whom there were good stories to be told; if my plot needed, at some point, a dramatic stroke that hit the entire school simultaneously, like a fire or a bomb, I would be bound to remember that a flying bomb had fallen on the school while I was there, and might make use of my memories of that in my novel.

I am as sure as I can be of anything that when the book was published, many people who have known me all my adult life would take the main story as revealing a slice of somebody's personal history, probably mine. They would believe that I must have had a love affair, if not with the headmaster's wife, then at least with the wife of one of the other masters; or else, if it was not me, then it was a boy I knew, or one I had heard about. Readers who had themselves been at my school would say: "But it's Christ's Hospital to the life. There's even a description of that eccentric school doctor we had who was a Communist and used to hand out atheist pamphlets to people coming out of chapel." And when other readers heard these things they would see them as confirmation that the book was based on (*based on,* mind you) real-life people and events—and then the most interesting question would be: Who were the originals? Was the boy actually me? And was the woman really the headmaster's wife? (Come to think of it, the headmaster when I was there was a middle-aged man with a wife much younger than himself.) If someone were to say to me (as people, amazingly, do), "Well, if the main story isn't true, what made you want to write it?," I could reply only: "I had an urge to. I felt a need to create and explore that particular situation. If you insist on pressing the question why, perhaps it needs a psychoanalyst to answer it. And *he* might say it was because I was an unloved child who wanted to experience, more than anything else in the world, the love of an older woman, the only woman I knew when I was an infant, my mother. But of course it might not be that at all but something entirely different. I don't know."

Where the central characters and incidents of my fiction do make real-life contact with me and my experience it is at this sort of subterranean level. They are not autobiography; that would be a totally inaccurate word: they grow out of some deep-rooted need to experience something, or understand it, or come to terms with it, or exorcize it—or a mixture of these or other things. And at this level too the movement is directly the opposite way round from what most people suppose: I do not perceive or experience something and then write fiction about it; I write fiction in order to achieve insight and understanding. It is the writing that brings them about, not they that bring the writing about. The forces behind the urge to do it are of a psycho-emotional nature, and are for the most part unconscious. In the case of *Facing Death*—as it turned out in the end, and contrary to my intentions when I embarked on the project—I found myself writing out of the very depths of my own need to come to terms with death. I had to confront it fully and squarely, and at length, and to live through the process of dying as unevasively as it is possible to do in imagination; and in the very innards of that engulfment I had to ask myself: "Given the inevitability of all this, what point is there in life?"

My only other novel published so far, *To Live in Danger,* had a different aim, one that rested much more easily on the surface of my mind, yet the characters and incidents were invented to serve that aim in much the same way. In that case it was to show how intelligence work is morally corrupting for even the most decent of the people who engage in it, and at even the humblest of levels; and I suppose that the reality of that fact was disturbing to me in two separate ways: first, because I had been exposed to the corruption; and second, because the reality of it was so different from the books about it that I had devoured with such pleasure. The conclusion was one I had reached as a result of doing my military service in the Intelligence Corps. That was the autobiographical element there, and I made use of personal experience to fill in an authentic background to my story, give accurate descriptions of work procedures, that sort of thing. Again I drew freely on real life for some of the subsidiary characters. But the main character bore no relation to me or to any of my colleagues. Nevertheless, when the book came out most of my friends took the central story to be thinly veiled autobiography, and were unbudged by my denials. This reaction of theirs was so unconnected with the truth that it was a long time before I realized they were having it, and when I did I was incredulous.

Obviously the working methods of different fiction writers must vary very considerably, and it is a subject on which I can speak for no one other than myself. But over many years my concerns have brought me into contact with a great many writers of fiction, and from them I have heard observations similar to mine expressed again and again. Yet no matter how unambiguously these realities are stated it seems they are never believed. This refusal to believe is frontal and self-confident in a way that is, to me at least, perplexing. Even the greatest of all novelists, Tolstoy, is an object of it. The person most widely regarded as his best translator, and also best biographer, is Aylmer Maude, whose translation of *War and Peace* is published jointly by Macmillan and Oxford University Press. This volume contains, as an appendix, "Some Words about *War and Peace*" by Tolstoy, originally published in *Russian Archive* in 1868, in which he writes: "I should be very sorry if the similarity between the invented names and real ones should suggest to anyone that I wished to describe this or that actual person, more especially as the literary activity which consists of describing real people, who exist or have existed, has nothing in common with the activity I was engaged on. . . . All the other people are entirely invented, and have for me no definite prototypes in tradition or reality." To this Maude appends a footnote contradicting it. And at the front of the book he contributes a list of the principal characters written in such terms as: "Countess Véra Rostóva, their elder daughter (supposedly patterned after Liza Behrs, the older of Tolstoy's two sisters-in-law)," and so on. I would find such effrontery unbelievable if I had not experienced much the same from friends whose knowledge of me is closer than Maude's was of Tolstoy. A disturbing implication is that many readers who are as intelligent, gifted and knowledgeable as Maude fail radically to understand what creative writing even is, or what it does. One suspects that they do not know what art is. They are behaving as would lovers of painting if they self-confidently took it for granted that every painting of a Virgin and Child were really just a portrait of the artist's model, usually mistress, and their baby, and that denials of this from the artists themselves could safely be ignored; and if the labels in the galleries were then to inform us that this Madonna was in reality so-and-so, and that Madonna was really so-and-so (adding that in the latter case the child in real life was a girl, not a boy).

For four years the writing of *Facing Death* was my constant preoccupation. Psycho-emotionally it was the most demanding experience I have ever voluntarily undergone. It was the climax of my prolonged battle with the mid-life crisis, my struggle not to be overwhelmed by death and the fear of death, my war of liberation against these things. By the end I had been ravaged by the experience but felt I had come through. Just as the two or three people I know who have been in circumstances such that their imminent death (admittedly not at the hands of someone else) seemed inevitable and yet they survived have told me that it cured them for ever of the fear of death—they had been there already, so to speak, and found to their astonishment that they were not afraid—on the level of imagination something of the same sort happened to me. I do not claim to be cured of the fear of death, but I have confronted its terrors as honestly as I can, and, so far, I have survived. I am less frightened of it now than I was. The fear has ceased to be debilitating. And I suppose it was for this, more than for anything else, that I wrote my book.

Within the novel I pushed to its limits my ability, such as it was at the time, to pin down the level of ultimate significance in life, whether it be in the experienced realities of consciousness, or the unique self-awareness of the individual, or interpersonal relationships, or parenthood and family belonging, or involvement with a wider society, or in the satisfactions of work, or the creation and consumption of art, or contemplative thinking. In each of these directions I could get somewhere, but not far enough: each of them, as a path of exploration, however exciting in its early stages, petered out into frustration. None of them took me to the door of Aladdin's cave, with the key to the enigma of life sitting there quietly in its lock. They served in the end only to make the enigma appear more certainly inaccessible. None of them offered even in principle to endow life with a significance that would be self-sufficient in the face of death. So when I came to the end of writing the book I felt I had carried my search as far as I could and yet was still baffled, still frustrated. It was in this overall context that one of the concerns of *Facing Death* was with the limitations of philosophy. Both of the leading male characters had studied it at Oxford, which is how they met, but both find this not of any real use to them when they confront the fundamental questions in life. John takes longer to find this out than Keir, and there is a period during which they agree that philosophy as they have been taught it is inadequate, but disagree as to the nature of the inadequacy. Keir formulates his disagreement with John in these words: "You thought the techniques of Oxford philosophy constituted a marvellous tool kit, but that philosophers were using it for trivial tasks. I thought the tools themselves were the wrong tools, and that the right tasks couldn't be done with them."

That the tools of Oxford philosophy had characteristically been used for trivial tasks was certainly the case, but I was unsure whether there was nevertheless a worthwhile use to be made of them. When I finished the first draft of *Facing Death* my overwhelming desire was to re-read, from the perspectives I had now reached, the philosophy I had studied nearly twenty years earlier at Oxford, to see if there was any use I could put it to, anything I could get out of it. I made a rough calculation that it would take me between six months and a year to do the reading if I made it my prime task. But I had a financial problem: I had lived partly on savings to write *Facing Death,* and the savings were now gone. How could I keep myself for a year while reading philosophy, without constantly being taken away from the reading by the need to earn money? Answer: be paid to do the reading. It was this that led me to the idea of making a long broadcast series about British philosophy in mid-twentieth-century. The BBC would certainly agree that the preparation of such a series necessitated a lot of reading, and would include an allowance for that in the fee negotiated. At that time, the end of the 1960s, there was little or no chance of getting any such series on television, but radio was a different matter. I had done a lot of broadcasting for BBC Radio 3, had indeed had a series of my own devoted to the arts. So I made my proposal to the head of the Radio 3 network, Howard Newby (the novelist P. H. Newby, first winner of the Booker Prize), and he approved it. Thus began my association with the broadcasting of philosophy, an involvement which, unanticipated by me, was to stretch out across many years and eventually bring my face before millions of people in many countries. It also caused me, contrary to my intentions, to return to regular work in broadcasting as a means of earning my living.

When it was broadcast on the radio, that first series was called *Conversations with Philosophers,* but in book form it bore the title *Modern British Philosophy,* and that is what it is now known as. I would like to have called the book *British Philosophy in Mid-Century,* but there was already a book called *Philosophy in Mid-Century.* So I proposed *Contemporary British Philosophy,* and was talked out of it by the publisher, Fred Warburg of Secker & Warburg. "Contemporary," he argued, was a plonking word, lowering to the spirits, whereas "modern" was a bright, interest-arousing word which meant more or less the same thing. I allowed myself to go along with this. Like most young people I did not realize how evanescent the world as I knew it was, how quickly and badly both "contemporary" and "modern" would date my title. I fear that *Modern British Philosophy* has now been an inaccurate label for many years.

The broadcast series consisted of thirteen 45-minute programmes, each of which was not so much a conversation as an interview. The person interviewed, a philosopher well thought of in the profession, was different in each programme. The number thirteen was due to nothing other than the fact that the BBC planned its broadcasting schedules on a quarterly basis, and since a quarter contains thirteen weeks it had become familiar practice over many years for a long weekly series to consist of thirteen programmes almost regardless of its subject matter. My aim was to introduce listeners to recent British philosophy—to tell them something about what had been going on in each of the main branches, and introduce them to the leading figures. I realized that this would be intelligible only if they were given a certain amount of background, particularly as regards Russell, Moore, Austin and Wittgenstein, so doing this also became part of the project. Gradually, in the course of preparations, an overall pattern emerged. A few of the programmes would provide the background knowledge necessary for the rest. In some of these the current state of affairs in an important branch of the subject would be discussed by a philosopher involved in it—Bernard Williams on moral philosophy, Alasdair MacIntyre on political and social philosophy, Ninian Smart on philosophy of religion, Richard Wollheim on aesthetics. And finally the biggest figures of all, those whose work had become an object of study in its own right—A. J. Ayer, Gilbert Ryle, Peter Strawson, Karl Popper—would be invited to expound their own ideas, and reply to criticisms.

I asked the BBC for, and got, complete control of the making of the series, and every task that falls to a programme-maker I carried out myself—determining the length of the programmes, the subject matter, the participants; carrying out the interviews; editing the tapes; putting it all together down to the last detail. I even wrote the thirteen billings in the *Radio Times.* The nominal producer, George MacBeth, whom I had known since Oxford days and who had acquired by now a formidable reputation as a poet, was only too happy to let me make all the decisions and do all the work while he enjoyed a year of almost complete freedom to get on with his own writing. He was happier still when the series was a success with him credited as its producer. He had been through the Oxford philosophy mill himself, and had a first in Greats, so he was an appropriate "producer" for the series; but he and I held not a single conversation about programme content or contributors. What his office did was to lay on studio and other facilities as I asked for them, see contracts and expenses through the bureaucracy, and generally carry out the tasks of unit management; and nearly all of this was done by his secretary, Drusilla Montgomerie. As a way of working, it set the pattern for my subsequent television series about philosophy: I always made it an explicit condition of embarking on a series that I should have complete control of it, though I never took a producer credit.

When the tapes of the radio series had been completed there was the question of turning them into a book. One glance at the transcripts was enough to show that it would be a mistake to publish them as they stood. Everyone's sentences in spontaneous, unscripted speech, however carefully considered, are improvised, and therefore less precisely and concisely constructed than those of good writing: they also tend to go on too long, because additional clauses get tacked on, or spatchcocked in, as afterthoughts. There is also a natural use of stock epithets, familiar phrases, repetitions for emphasis, and other habits of ordinary speech, all of which look leaden on the printed page. Often an unsatisfactory formulation will be put forward but then improved on, so that the first can be removed; sometimes a point is made but then withdrawn or heavily qualified, so that again the first formulation can come out. People think afterwards of things they wish they had said, and want to put them in. For these, and all sorts of other reasons too, unscripted speech, no matter how intelligent, is not good enough for a serious book. So in any event I was going to have to ask my contributors to revise their contributions for publication. That being the case, I felt it worth going the whole hog and urging them to improve their transcripts to the fullest extent they could. I asked them to keep to approximately the same length, so as not to unbalance the book, and to preserve the conversational tone, this being conducive to clarity, as well as attractive in itself. I knew that most of the readers would be people who had not heard, and were never going to hear, the radio programmes, and this led me to want to make the book an independent production that was as good as I could get it in its own right, regardless of what had been said on the air—though of course it was the broadcasts that had provided it with its ground-plan and its tone of voice, not to say its existence.

While working on this I tried to broaden my understanding by making incursions into the professional world inhabited by my contributors. I joined two of their professional associations, the Aristotelian Society and the Royal Institute of Philosophy, and started attending meetings, and reading journals. I also started attending post-graduate discussions at the London School of Economics. Occasionally I would go to a philosophy conference—I began, for instance, attending the Joint Sessions. These are joint conferences of the Aristotelian Society and the *Mind* Association, and are the annual get-togethers of all those (who want to come) who are professionally involved in philosophy in Britain. They spread over three or four days in the second or third week of July, and take place every year at a different university. The attendance, usually, is somewhere around two hundred. I started going in 1970 or 1971, and have made a point of going most years since. I have now made some quite good friends at Joint Sessions whom I only ever see there, friends who teach in distant parts of the country, or abroad, and whom I look forward to seeing every summer. Another by-product of these conferences is that they have given me the experience of staying on campus, and in student accommodation, at most of the country's leading universities. The general effect of all this was to bring contemporary academic philosophy into my life on a broad front, and in ways additional to the reading of it. The result was to enrich the background to my understanding of contemporary philosophers and their works.

What did this most of all, however, was working with the philosophers themselves. Our prolonged co-operations were of inestimable value to me as regards the subject matter. Not only was I freshly reading or re-reading the works of the leading philosophers in Britain, I now had the chance of discussing their work with them personally; to probe their arguments and get them to enlarge on their views, to explain precisely what it was they had meant in this passage or by the use of that term, what their answers would be to the most commonly expressed criticisms of their work, what their own criticisms were of one another. If they endorsed as correct my interpretation of something they had written I knew I could henceforth assert it with authority—not as being true, of course, but as being what they meant—and this was an asset worth having in a field whose practitioners are perpetually in contention about what X means by saying so-and-so. If they told me I was mistaken, and explained why, I was thereby saved from an error that might have remained with me a long time if I had not had access to them personally, for I might well have insisted on maintaining the error against others arguing the correct view. One way and another I acquired an altogether deeper and more complex understanding of their thought than would have been available to me by the normal processes of study supplemented by discussion with others. And this strengthened me in the conclusion I finally reached, that except for Popper's their work constituted a bankrupt tradition.

It appeared to me that the nodal point at which the now dead branch had grown away from the main stem of philosophy was a point at which academics had taken off from Russell and Moore in the wrong direction. The logical analysis of statements in ordinary language that was pioneered by these two was transmogrified by others from a technique into a subject matter, and this—very strikingly—was something with which the two godfathers themselves would not go along. Russell disapproved ferociously: Moore was inclined by temperament to stop short at incomprehension. The disastrous change was made at first, obliquely, by Wittgenstein, who came to dominate philosophy at Cambridge, and then more directly by Austin, who came to dominate it at Oxford. In Strawson, who was a pupil of Austin's, but a formal logician in his early days, the influences of Russell and Austin were to some extent in conflict; but it seemed to me that Austin won out in the end, and as Strawson grew older he moved further and further away from the heartland of philosophy towards its frontier with linguistics (as, indeed, Austin had done: if he had not died at forty-nine I suspect he might have moved out of philosophy altogether). Ayer had remained faithful to Russell, if anything excessively so, but never had any original ideas. He was absent from Oxford through virtually the entire period of so-called Oxford philosophy, first in the armed forces during the Second World War, and then, from 1946 to 1959, as Professor of Philosophy at University College, London. Not until 1959 did he return to Oxford—but, as he said to me many years later, "I only went back to Oxford to do down Austin, and no sooner had I got there than he died." In succession to Russell, Ayer was the serious philosopher best known to the general British public,* but during the period following the Second World War his influence among professional philosophers at Oxford and Cam-

---

* During the 1940s there was a Reader in Philosophy at Birkbeck College, London, called C. E. M. Joad who became a household name in Britain for his weekly performances in a BBC radio programme called *Brains Trust*. He was an engaging but essentially fraudulent character. His popular books on philosophy thick-skinnedly recycled Russell's work without acknowledgement; asked once to write a recommendation of a book by Joad, Russell replied, "Modesty forbids." Joad, who was never a professor, came always to call himself Professor Joad. And his career ended in a public scandal when he was convicted of persistently cheating the railways over his train fares. Altogether he was something of a con man, and as a serious philosopher he never made a mark, yet there was certainly a period of years during which he was the most famous philosopher in Britain. To my mind he performed one immensely valuable service, and that was to familiarize the general public with the notion that when confronting a difficult question it is important to start by getting clear what the question itself means, and to make some necessary distinctions. Thus, if the Questionmaster asked, "Do you support the censorship of films?" he could almost be relied on to begin his answer with "It depends what you mean by censorship." Then he would make a few basic distinctions, and would probably end up saying something like (I am inventing these words, and putting them into his mouth) "If you mean the system we have for bowdlerizing every film we see in our High Street cinemas, no, I'm against that. But if you ask me, do I think people ought to be free to use children as models in pornographic photographs or films, no, I don't think they should be." Week after week he did this sort of thing with a wide range of questions, and I do believe it was the first time most of the population had heard such routine clarification carried out in a businesslike and unpedantic way. That it made a tremendous impact is evidenced by the fact that "It depends what you mean by . . ." became a nation-wide catch-phrase with Joad's name attached to it, and half a century later it is still quite commonly heard among the older generation. So the lesson stuck, with Joad still remembered as the teacher of it. This seems to me an almost invaluable service to have rendered to a population at large.

bridge was outshone by Wittgenstein, Austin, Ryle, and, from the late 1950s onwards, Strawson.

Ryle's career was a strange one. His first published articles were about Husserl and Heidegger, and broke new ground in the English-speaking world. He perceived that the work of these two men contained something new that was of substance and significance, and might undergo considerable future development. At that stage the young Ryle was enough of an admirer and enthusiast to write to Husserl and ask if he could visit him at his home in Germany, which he did. Then suddenly he turned his back on that whole approach to philosophy, and seems to have ignored it for the rest of his life, becoming instead the John the Baptist of linguistic analysis. It would have been wholly out of character for this to be an opportunistic decision: Ryle was as fearless as he was honest. But he was also impressionable, as witness his later domination by Wittgenstein, which continued even after Ryle came actively to dislike Wittgenstein. It may be difficult to credit that he can have had insights of fundamental significance and then lost them again, but I believe that this is what occurred. There is a known instance of it, and a much more important one, elsewhere in his life. As a student he read Schopenhauer, and a long time later, in his fiftieth year—having, as he thought, forgotten Schopenhauer almost entirely—published the book that made his name, *The Concept of Mind,* in which not only the central thesis but also what came to be the best known of the subsidiary theses come straight out of Schopenhauer, while all the time Ryle himself genuinely believed he was putting forward his own ideas. Only when someone pointed the fact out to him after publication did he realize that what he had done was recycle Schopenhauer. Of all long-dead philosophers the one who most influenced Wittgenstein was also Schopenhauer; but it is unlikely that Ryle knew that either.

Ryle's career was paradoxical in other ways. He was the first person to formulate and state publicly the programme of linguistic philosophy. He was an excellent teacher, and produced in A. J. Ayer a pupil more famous than himself, or for that matter than any of his colleagues. He held the most prestigious chair of philosophy at Oxford. For many years he was the Editor of *Mind,* which had been for generations the leading journal of philosophy in the English-speaking world. *The Concept of Mind* was received with acclaim, and for a few years was the most fashionable book in philosophy. He created the Oxford B.Phil. as a professional qualification for philosophers, and for a long period was the chief king-maker in academic appointments not only at Oxford but at universities all over Britain. It is difficult to see how, short of being a great philosopher, he could have had a more successful career. And yet in spite of all this he was overshadowed by Austin, who never published a book, and had nothing to set against most of Ryle's other achievements. That this was so was due chiefly to the assertiveness of Austin's personality, which not everyone found attractive. I think Ryle was angered and perplexed by the whole phenomenon: I know he resented it, and I know that he hated Austin. Most of Ryle's post-war career at Oxford was spent playing second fiddle to Austin, and it was a fact that he could never come to terms with.

During Ryle's later years I saw a good deal of him. One side-effect of the lengthy collaborative processes involved in making the programmes for *Conversations with Philosophers,* and then turning them into *Modern British Philosophy,* was the formation of lasting friendships between me and some of the participants—A. J. Ayer, Anthony Quinton and David Pears, for instance. Others had been friends already—Ninian Smart, Karl Popper, Bernard Williams. Peter Strawson had been my supervisor. The others remained what one might call friendly acquaintances—Alan Montefiore, Alasdair MacIntyre, Geoffrey Warnock, Richard Wollheim, Stuart Hampshire. The upshot was that the making of the series drew me more extensively than before into the personal and social worlds of Britain's leading philosophers: I became a familiar figure to them, someone they were used to seeing around, and I visited most of their homes. Unlike them, of course, I was not a professional philosopher; but I doubt whether in the Britain of that day there was any other non-professional who was as much involved with philosophy as I was. Ever since that time I have had one foot in that world, and have felt myself to be a link between it and the world outside it. To make use of a sporting analogy, I was a commentator rather than a player; but the commentator gets a better view of the game than any of the players.

It was because I was in this unusual position that Balliol College, Oxford, turned to me when it found itself in need of someone to teach philosophy for a couple of terms in order to fill a gap between two permanent appointments. I was delighted to accept their invitation, and spent the last term of 1970 and the first term of 1971 as a philosophy don at Oxford. This included the three months during which *Conversations with Philosophers* was broadcast for the first time on Radio 3. The fact that when the series went on the air I was a lecturer in philosophy at Balliol pleased the BBC, because they felt it gave me a recognized public status in the subject, but in fact there had been no thought of such an appointment in either their minds or mine when the series was made.

I taped all thirteen of the programmes quite a while before they were broadcast, so by the time they were heard by anyone other than myself the whole experience of making them was behind me and I had moved on to something else (teaching at Balliol) and was able to respond with a certain detachment when I heard them on the air. They seemed to me to come off well enough in the main, but I had an important reservation about them, and that had to do with their level of accessibility. Over and again while listening to them I found myself thinking things like "Not everyone will realize why we're discussing that at this point: I should have signposted it before we got here," or "I could have formulated this argument much more lucidly than he's doing: why doesn't he say so-and-so?" What nearly all my reactions came down to was the realization that I had left too much of the communicating to be done by contributors with little or no experience of communication to non-specialists. Most of them were used to discussing philosophy only with serious students of the subject; and in any case they were not experienced broadcasters. I, meanwhile, had many years of experience in the communication of serious subjects to non-specialists, not only through broadcasting but also in politics. Yet in these programmes I was saying very little—I was leaving the contributors to carry out tasks which, truth to tell, I was able to carry out better myself. And if I had carried them out myself, not only would the programmes have been clearer, and therefore accessible to more people, they would have been more in the nature of two-handed discussions, less like interviews, and to that extent livelier and (I would hope) more interesting, as well as more substantial. The programmes were, I realized, successful enough to justify themselves, but I saw many ways in which they could have been better, and this changed my subsequent practice.

I was astonished at how well the programmes were received. I had taken for granted that such a long series about analytic philosophy would be of interest to few people, and would trickle like a thin river through some remote and underpopulated outback of air time. Instead it was hailed by the press as a milestone in the history of radio, and listened to by an exceptionally large audience. The *Listener,* a widely read weekly journal published by the BBC, printed a long extract from each programme, thus filling several pages of each issue for three months. These extracts must have been read by more people than heard the programmes, though thousands of people made a point of first listening to the programmes and then reading the extracts. The *Listener*'s Editor, Karl Miller, allowed me to select and edit these extracts myself, giving me a different length to work to each week, depending on the interest of the material and what else was in the magazine. He was obsessional about detailed accuracy—it was said of him that he would make a transatlantic telephone call to change a comma—and this appealed to me very much, because so would I; in fact, like him, I had. So we worked happily together.

The general reaction of the academic philosophical community was an eye-opener. There had often been discussions among philosophers on Radio 3 before, but nothing to compare with this large-scale attempt over a period of three months to put the current state of the subject before a general audience. Academic philosophers were on the whole pleased that it was happening, and they were interested in (and enthusiastic about) the content of the programmes, but these reactions were secondary: far and away their most power-ful and intense concern was with who had been invited to take part, and to what degree this would enhance their personal standing. So unfamiliar were most of them with the techniques of broadcasting (this is less the case now) that they tended to assume that the programmes were being made week by week, as they were being broadcast; and a question fiercely discussed over quite a few dinner tables in North Oxford was: Who is going to be invited? Will X get the call, or will he find himself being passed over in favour of Y? Each time someone was seen as having been picked out there was a certain amount of sniping, but this was as nothing compared with the overflow of joy each time someone was seen as having been passed over—people actually rang up one another to relay the news from freshly delivered copies of *Radio Times.* Reports I received from eye-witnesses about incidents and conversa-tions of this kind were legion, and were reinforced by the distinctive tone of the questioning I was constantly subjected to about my intentions for the fu-ture. The whole Oxford-philosophy community was a-buzz about the series. Many took it for granted that I was luxuriating in being a power-figure be-stowing fame on those I chose to favour. When I tried to explain that this was not how it was at all, and that all I had tried to do was find out who would best help in making each programme, without it even entering my head that this would be seen as a feather in his cap, my words were often so much at odds with the values that motivated the speaker, and were assumed by him to moti-vate others, that he would receive them with undisguised disbelief. In fact I stopped giving this explanation and just let the false assumptions wash off me. One simple truth that all this brought home to me was that philosophy was in the state it was in at least partly because philosophers, by and large, were the sort of people they were.

The impact of the series was such that the BBC repeated it almost immedi-ately, in the summer of 1971. Secker & Warburg timed the publication of the book to coincide with this repeat, so a lot of listeners were now able to follow the programmes with the book in their hands. In order to bring home to them, and to subsequent readers of the book, my view that the decisive split in British philosophy as it had developed during the twentieth century was be-tween two incompatible ways of handling the legacy of Russell, I inserted into it a discussion that I had organized separately from the rest, also broadcast on Radio 3. The main subject of it was Russell's hostility to Oxford philosophy, and the broadcast dispute featured, on one side, Peter Strawson and Geoffrey Warnock (two of Austin's most gifted pupils), who defended Oxford philoso-phy against Karl Popper, who agreed with Russell. It seemed to me that Pop-per got easily the best of the argument in spite of being outnumbered by two to one. (As Chairman I was careful not to let my partiality show, as indeed I was throughout the series: if anything, I would lean over backwards not to be unfair, and often acted as devil's advocate.) It made me feel sad that because Wittgenstein was dead I could not stage a debate between him and Popper, who I am fairly sure are the only two antagonists who are likely to be of lasting interest in this schism.

The fact that the two most significant philosophers since Russell to have lived and practised in Britain were neither of them British by birth or upbringing but had both come from Vienna, where as young men they had haunted the fringes of the Vienna Circle, while themselves holding views that were incompatible with logical positivism, seemed to me to be not a coincidence. The education of both had been firmly rooted in mathematics (as had Russell's) and the natural sciences, and their earliest philosophical experience, in their teens, had been immersion in Schopenhauer, an experience which for both was to have lifelong consequences. Their existential involvement with philosophy was of a different character from that of people who came to it through an education system based on the study of the humanities, and an outmodedly conceived hostility to the sciences, as was England's. It would never have occurred to either of them that an active involvement with philosophy could be primarily a matter of reading books, or could be unconnected with scientific ways of understanding the world.

In one way, the success of the series put me in a false position. My own view of the matter was that I had given the best analytic philosophers of the day unlimited rope, and they had hanged themselves. Throughout the ages, until the twentieth century, philosophy had been pursued as an attempt to understand the world, experience, life, and ourselves; but analytic philosophers pooh-poohed all that, and turned their backs on it. What they were concerned with primarily was the analysis of propositions, and in particular of the basic concepts that we use when we speak—and they were inclined to represent *that* as being the investigation and deeper understanding of experience, if not of reality itself (as if either could be predominantly linguistic). I regarded my series as demonstrating what a hole-in-corner activity this was—not without interest, of course, and certainly not without difficulty, and therefore also not without opportunities for ingenuity and brilliance, but essentially unimportant. The series set this against the altogether more substantial approach of Russell, the early Wittgenstein, and Popper, and ended by informing listeners that what was going on in philosophy almost everywhere else was radically different from what was going on in Britain. To my mind, then, the series had exposed the triviality of the analytic tradition and its lack of a future, and had pointed up some of the other directions in which non-illusory advances could be made. But this was not how it was generally received. Listeners were entranced by the skill and apparent ease with which people like Freddie Ayer and

Bernard Williams navigated the difficulties of abstract thought: their stylishness in argument, and in criticizing the arguments of others, their ability to make subtle distinctions clearly, the economy with which they expressed themselves, their intellectual self-confidence. The more intelligent the listener was, the more likely he was to be impressed by these things, and to enjoy them. They were seen as justifying the broadcasts, indeed as being the point of the broadcasts. This intellectually entertaining demonstration of how brilliant the philosophers themselves were was sufficiently different from normal radio, and intellectually satisfying enough in itself, to content most listeners. What the content of it all was—what it was all about, or for—slipped by them unheeded: they were content to regard it as above their heads, too clever for them, while they sat back and relished the pyrotechnics. I received a good deal of praise myself for being ringmaster to such a galaxy of star turns. If I demurred at this and expressed my view of the matter I was usually thought guilty of false modesty. On those rare occasions when I was believed I was accused of fraud: "If that's what you really think, what on earth were you doing setting it all before the public like that, and on such a scale, and so seductively, without any hint that you yourself don't consider it worth while? What could possibly have been the point of doing that?" Really, I suppose, the prevailing attitude among listeners was the same as the prevailing attitude had always been among Oxford philosophers, and the more clever of their pupils: a concern with brilliance, performance, the making of reputations, without much real existential involvement with real philosophical problems. When the book came out only one reviewer, Kathleen Nott, saw it as I did, and wrote accordingly. The rest praised it in terms of the false values it exposed.

Secker & Warburg published *Modern British Philosophy* simultaneously in hardback and paperback. Subsequently it was published in a cheaper paperback by Paladin, and eventually, fifteen years after original publication, by Oxford University Press. There was separate American publication, and a translation into Italian. So the book had a reasonable life. Students made prodigious use of it—I have seen copies in university libraries that were literally disintegrating with use—because the conversational form rendered it accessible, and the accounts given by leading philosophers of their own work were so much easier to understand than their books. Inevitably, many students used it as a substitute for the books, and this was a cause of exasperation to some teachers; but there were others who used it as an introduction before getting to grips with the originals. It was my tenth book to be published, but the first that was categorized as "philosophy." Altogether it was with this series, the broadcasts and then the book, that my name became known in the world of philosophy and philosophers.

17

Groves of Academe

Between leaving Yale at the age of twenty-six and teaching philosophy at Balliol when I was forty I had no direct connection with academe, though of course I had close friends who were academics. When I returned to Oxford to teach I bumped into friendly acquaintances whom I had known as undergraduates and who had stayed on to make their careers at the university. When I remarked to Freddie Ayer that meeting them reassured me about having spent the intervening years in the way I had rather than in the way they had he said one would have to be out of one's mind to think anything else. This response astonished me, as he had been a full-time academic himself, except for war service. However, on getting to know some of my old friends better I discovered that their apparent complacency was more often than not a form of protective colouring, and that underneath it lay a good deal of self-doubt. Widespread in particular was the feeling that outside the university was a "real world" that they had never entered; and because they had not entered it they felt in some way inadequate. One or two confided a fear that they might not now be able to cope with it, having spent the whole of their adult lives within university walls.

I had shared these attitudes before leaving the academic world myself, but now no longer had them. It seemed to me that the world of university life was just as "real" as the world of politics, or business, or the media, or any other of the worlds I had moved in, and certainly as worthwhile. Where it fell short of the others was in the narrowness of its horizons. The supreme fault of academe lies not in its unreality, which I do not believe in, but in its littleness: there is always, somehow, something of Lilliput about it. For reasons I cannot quite put my finger on, academics seem generally to live in a reduced world, and it is their own apprehension of this that gives rise to the feelings I have described, the feeling that real life is going on somewhere else and that they are not participating in it. And yet their alienation is self-imposed. To this day I find that if I go to a party in Oxford or Cambridge nearly everyone in the room is usually "university," but if I go to a party in London there will be politicians, businessmen, lawyers, diplomats, bankers, authors, publishers, architects, actors, musicians, broadcasters—and of course academics too. There happen to be plenty of interesting people in each of these categories living in and around Oxford and Cambridge, but few of them are welcomed into the social world of the university; in fact dons often feel slightly ill at ease with them. It would be a good thing if a variety of such people were called in to nourish not only the university's social world but its cultural and intellectual world as well.

I soon noticed that a small minority of dons, including some of the most interesting and able ones, lived in a way that transcended these limitations. They had active social lives in London (sometimes they lived in London, though that was a breach of the rules), sat on the boards of national arts institutions or private companies, were members of government committees, did consultancy work, wrote for the newspapers, broadcast, gave help to a political party. But these were only a few—and their colleagues, instead of applauding their extended range of activities, resented it, and made ungenerous remarks about it. The two most common complaints were that such people were "spreading themselves too thin" and that they were "publicity seekers." In fact they usually produced as meritorious a body of academic work as their colleagues; and in only a trivial number of cases did publicity-seeking appear to be a significant motive for their actions. A more important one, usually, was the desire for a more interesting life.

I was struck by how often academics in middle and old age would confess, usually with embarrassment, that the part of their lives they had most enjoyed was the Second World War. They spoke of it as a liberation. Also, often, there was some other profession that they secretly wished they had followed. Freddie Ayer once said to me, completely out of the blue, "Do you think I ought to have been a judge?"; and when I questioned him about it he confessed that he frequently found himself wishing that this was what he had done. Peter Strawson wished he could have been a poet. Iris Murdoch, after fifteen years of being an Oxford philosophy don, gave it up to become a full-time novelist. Mary Warnock said publicly that if she had her life over again she would go into business or advertising, not academic life. Many philosophy dons remarked in my hearing that the cleverest pupils they had ever taught had gone into non-academic walks of life, and they were inclined to refer to such individuals with envy. According to academic folklore the most brilliant first-class degrees in living memory had gone to people now in politics—Harold Wilson in PPE, Quintin Hogg in Greats.

In anyone familiar with the history of philosophy, reflections of this kind were bound to prompt the recollection that both Spinoza and Leibniz had refused to become academics and had turned down professorships that were offered to them, and that Nietzsche had given up his professorship and left academe altogether in order to become a philosopher; that Descartes liked to think of himself as a man of the world, and always preferred the company of men of affairs to that of scholars; that Locke had been involved in political activity and medical research; that Berkeley had abandoned philosophy for the Church and education, and that Hume had left it for the writing of history, followed by active diplomacy and public service; that John Stuart Mill had been a member of parliament; that Russell had been dogged for the first half of his life by the feeling that he ought to have been in politics, and for the second by the feeling that he ought to have been a scientist; that Wittgenstein left philosophy intending to do so for good, and was brought back only reluctantly and incompletely. Academic life, it would appear, was not sufficiently attractive or satisfying to most of the best philosophers. And from what I knew about other intellectual fields the situation would seem to have been much the same in many of them too.

I found myself beginning to share this attitude. As I looked around me a life lived full-time in academe seemed uncomfortably confining. And this was true even for highly original and creative people, like Karl Popper. In fact, to take him as an example, it seemed to me that in spite of his enormous gifts, his personality had become unduly narrow since he had given up the range of activities he had pursued as a young man; and that this had had a deleterious influence on his thinking, particularly his thought about social problems. I do not mean by this *The Open Society and Its Enemies,* which arose directly out of active political concerns and involvements; I am referring to what his responses had become after writing that book.

When I expressed—tentatively, and taking genuine care not to offend—thoughts along these lines to some of my colleagues, they often surprised me by the vigour with which they agreed, sometimes going farther along the same lines than I did. Nearly all of them seemed to feel it, or if not that to see the phenomenon in others. So I realized that it was a reality and not just a subjective attitude of mine. This reinforced my feeling that I did not want to become a full-time academic. However, since ceasing to be a student I had developed serious academic interests which I was now bent on pursuing, and this meant being able, at least sometimes, to discuss them with others; so to find myself with one foot in the academic world was an enrichment of my life, and I welcomed it as such. This has been my attitude ever since. I have sustained long-term relationships with universities without being wholly part of them, going only to such meetings, discussions, seminars or lectures as I wanted to; teaching only occasionally, and then in subjects of my own choosing. Such periods as I have spent full-time in universities have been devoted to working on my own books, including this one. Always, even when actually living in an Oxford college, I have pursued a part of my life elsewhere, notably London.

However, during that early spell at Balliol I had to teach whatever was required, and this included philosophy of science, philosophy of mind, philosophical logic, two set books (John Stuart Mill's *Utilitarianism* and Bertrand Russell's *The Problems of Philosophy*) and "the history of philosophy" viewed as consisting of Descartes, Locke, Berkeley, and Hume. Far and away the most valuable thing in this as far as I was concerned was that it made me read or re-read the philosophy I was teaching. I also read a good deal of secondary literature, something that had never been my wont. This came about because my pupils were required by the examiners to show familiarity with quite a lot of unimportant books about important books, and I made a private rule with myself that I would never ask a pupil to read a book unless I could discuss it with him and answer questions about it. Sometimes this meant reading it after I had told him to, but before his next tutorial, which at first gave me an enjoyable feeling that the two of us were exploring it together. However, most secondary literature is on a level so far below that of the work it is about that I became irritated with it, and critical of a system of teaching—or perhaps I should say rather a system of examination—that required students to spend more time on the secondary than on the primary.

The fact was brought home to me in a new way that secondary writers are not carrying out the same activity as primary ones at a lower level but are engaged in a different activity. The great philosophers were not, except perhaps occasionally, writing about other people's work. They were grappling head-on with fundamental problems about the world and our understanding of it. "Do I directly perceive physical objects? What could that mean?," and so on. They actually had the problems, and were agonizing over them, wrestling with them. Secondary writers are not in this situation, and what is more are doing something which is usually not particularly interesting to people who have philosophical problems. The difference is concealed by the fact that both kinds of writing normally take the same literary form: books of philosophy and books about it are in both cases philosophical books, and can be of the same length, divided up into chapters with similar headings, written in the same terminology, and so on. In libraries and bookshops they will normally be shelved together under the rubric "Philosophy." The corresponding situation in another subject brings out the difference much more clearly. Academics in English literature often do strikingly similar things with regard to the works of great creative writers to those that academics in philosophy do with regard to the works of great philosophers. But academic writings about plays, novels and poems are not themselves plays, novels or poems. This fact makes the difference between the two activities obvious. No matter how distinguished, influential, and internationally famous a literary critic may be it is not possible for him to harbour the illusion that he is doing *the same thing* as Shakespeare, Milton or Dickens. He is plainly doing something radically different, and at a much lower level of importance. The same difference exists between the works of what one might call creative philosophers and the works of those academics who write about them. But in the case of philosophy it is easy for academics to live under the illusion that they are engaged in the same activity as the people they are writing about.

Academic life, at least in the humanities, is bedevilled by an obsession with secondary literature, most of it highly ephemeral. This secondary literature is provincial not only in time but in place. Students at Oxford are constantly having their attention drawn to work by local academics which would scarcely be on the periphery of people's consciousness in, say, a major American university, where the reverse situation is likely to apply. This has the effect of cheating the students. Instead of soaking themselves in the imperishable masterpieces of their subject and developing their powers of independent thought, judgment and criticism in relation to those, they spend half their time studying writings that will be considered scarcely worth reading by anyone thirty years later and are not studied even now in most other universities. A knowledge of such dispensable and ever-changing secondary literature is often seen as the hallmark of professionalism by people whose only distinctive intellectual possession it is. And their own concerns tend to relate primarily to it.

I realized for the first time from the teaching end, as distinct from the student end, how self-contradictory it is to treat philosophy as a curriculum subject. Only people who themselves have philosophical problems seem able to understand what they even are, and these people are going to want to, in fact have to, work on the problems they have. Nothing could prevent their doing so. The rest, inescapably, will see philosophy as something else. With these one finds oneself dealing with people who are mistaken as to the very nature of what they are doing, and will never be got to understand it, short of being infected with the problems. It was only my more intelligent pupils who found philosophy difficult. To the less intelligent it usually seemed comparatively easy, and my most difficult task with them was to get them to see that these problems were real and difficult problems. Their characteristic way of looking at them was to think that everything of real importance to be said for and against, let us say, utilitarianism could be said in three-quarters of an hour, and it was then really up to the individual to make his mind up as to which of the available attitudes towards it commended itself to him.

One principle of teaching that I came to espouse particularly strongly was that if you are serious about helping the pupil to develop within himself and not just to acquire a lot of extraneous baggage you must start from where he is, not from where you are, or from where the subject is. The great year of international student rebellion was 1968, and I began teaching in 1970, so I engaged with students who were in the fullest flush of Marxist intoxication. Often they had opted for PPE on the assumption that it would involve them in the serious study of Marxism—and perhaps also Freudianism, not to mention other Great Ideas of the Modern World. Too late they discovered that Marx had failed to make it into the required curriculum for philosophy, politics, and economics, and that not even if they had opted for philosophy, psychology, and physiology would they be studying Freud. Their unexpected immersion in formal logic and conceptual analysis at the age of eighteen was like having a barrel of cold water poured over them: in many cases their disappointment was immediate, their disillusionment with Oxford vast. A lot of them were in danger of being put off philosophy for good. So I seized on their enthusiasm for Marx and engaged them in discussion of him out of hours, which was a thing not difficult to do. Most of the fundamental objections to Marxism that I put to them were then encountered by them for the first time. I was able to persuade the more enthusiastic of them to subject Marx's central arguments to the analytic techniques that they were acquiring in their tutorials: to go through every argument carefully and ask themselves of each step whether it genuinely followed from the previous one or whether Marx just said that it did; to ask themselves what he meant by each of his terms, and to check that these were used consistently throughout the arguments in which they occurred; and so forth. In other words I got them to study Marx with the same rigour as I would have required them to study any other thinker. It cost me personally no sacrifice to do this, as I looked on Marx as a genius whose work was of great fascination, its influence without parallel in modern history. And I found I was able to teach a great deal more in the way of conceptual analysis and serious attention to logical argument by doing this, through ideas in which the pupils had an impassioned interest, than I was managing to do with the same people during tutorials about John Stuart Mill's *Utilitarianism* or Bertrand Russell's *Problems of Philosophy*.

The intellectually critical attitude to Marxism that inevitably ensued opened minds to alternative ways of thinking, and caused them to read with curiosity writers whom they would formerly have dismissed in advance. This was how I managed to get many of them interested in philosophy in general—and at that stage in their lives they could not have been so induced by anything that ignored their commitment to Marxism. Nor was this only a ploy on my part: I shared their view that Marx ought to be part of the required curriculum for PPE. It was merely an option, but no one had to do it. Yet in a world one-third of which was ruled by governments who called themselves Marxist, and proclaimed their determination to see Marxist government extended to the whole globe, a serious understanding of Marxism was indispensable to anyone interested in ideas or politics. Indeed, I took the view that it should be part of the mental equipment of every educated person.

My attitude to philosophy, for other people as well as for myself, has always been in this sense existential. Unless it is about issues that are real for you or could become so, about problems you actually have or could have, about ways of thinking that really are yours or are real options for you, then philosophy is existentially empty, for it is not about your understanding of yourself or your world. At this point it becomes a mental game, an abstract conceptual pursuit, or at the very best an attempt to understand how others think or have thought. As the last of these it can be an aspect of sociology, anthropology, history, biography, cultural enquiry or social psychology. These things are of interest and value, of course, and I have spent many years of my life studying them, so I cannot be accused of failing to appreciate their importance. But someone whose apprehension of philosophical matters is confined to them is like someone who becomes an expert on China without going there.

Although my informal relationships with students were good I tired fairly soon of formal teaching. This was for a variety of reasons. First, you owe it to your pupils to teach them what they are going to be examined on, however ill-chosen you consider that to be. You do not choose the syllabus yourself. You may teach all sorts of things outside the syllabus, of course, but you must teach at least that, and anything else is an optional extra, both for your pupils and for you. Second, you need to keep abreast of the secondary literature in the subjects you teach, and that means the permanent immersion of a part of yourself in ephemeral trivia. Third, you cannot, with the best will in the world, avoid repetition. The tutorial system, according to which you teach students individually, imposes it on you to an extreme degree. When I started giving tutorials I promised myself that I would never do what certain notorious tutors of my youth had done and say the same things to different pupils, but it was a promise I soon broke. If you are teaching, let us say, the philosophy of Descartes, then you have a duty to each pupil to make sure he has a firm grasp of certain fundamental aspects of Descartes's thought; so, given the one-to-one teaching relationship, you find yourself, at least sometimes, saying the same things to different people. This is reinforced by the fact that they tend to make the same mistakes, which you then have to correct, and to fall into the same misunderstandings, which you then have to help them find their way out of. One of my greatest disappointments was that I learnt so little from my own tutorials—I mean the tutorial itself, the hour with the pupil. I had some bright pupils, a couple of whom went on to become professional philosophers, and I was always hoping that they would raise some interesting question that had not occurred to me, or make some arresting observation that I had not considered; but they never did. Everything they said fell comfortably within the bounds of what was already familiar to me. I learnt a lot in the course of my reading in preparation for the tutorials, but little from the tutorials themselves—it may have been because of a certain basic lack of interest on the part of the students, especially the intelligent ones, in what the syllabus was requiring them to do.

The most valuable thing I taught my pupils, I believe, was that critical analysis, far from being an end in itself, is only a beginning. I had a pupil who turned in a couple of well-crafted essays on Descartes, subjecting *Cogito ergo sum* to effective and damaging criticism, putting his finger on the weaknesses of the so-called proofs of the existence of God, pointing out the circularity of the overall layout of the argument. His perceptions of what was wrong with Descartes were many and acute, and on the whole accurate, and his essays were stylishly written and solidly constructed. Having got to this point, he expected to go on to do the same with the next philosopher. This is the sort of thing the best students did, and it was thought to be Oxford intellectual training at its most sophisticated. But I said to him: "If all the criticisms you've made of Descartes are valid—and on the whole I think they are—why are we spending our time here now discussing him? Why have you just devoted a fortnight of your life to reading his main works and writing two essays about them? More to the point: if all these things are wrong with his ideas—and I think they are—why is his name known to every educated person in the Western world today, three and a half centuries after his death? Why are his writings studied in every major university in the world, as they are being studied by you and me here now? Why are clever people willing to devote years of their lives to writing books about him?"

The pupil saw the point straight away but was at a loss to answer. He realized the moment I spoke that there must be far more to Descartes than anything he had yet considered, otherwise we should not be discussing him; but he was unable to think what it could be, for he had subjected all of Descartes's best-known arguments to critical analysis, and there seemed nothing left to do. I put it to him that Descartes's programmatic division of total reality into observer and observed, subject and object, mind and matter, had got into Western man's way of looking at almost everything over hundreds of years, and in particular into the scientific way of looking at things; that at the dawn of modern science Descartes had developed thinking for oneself, independently of any authority, into a systematically constructed method of enquiry; that he was one of the world's great mathematicians, and saw mathematics as part of the built-in structure of material reality; that the putting to work of these methods in the world he postulated meant the investigation, by minds, of physically measurable phenomena such as matter and extension, and this led naturally to the idea of fundamental science as a mathematically based physics; that Descartes believed he had shown such a science to be possible, in the sense both of lying within human powers and of fitting reality; that along with such men as Francis Bacon and Galileo he played a crucial role in selling to educated Western man the desirability of developing such a science; that he believed it would have all the certainty of the mathematics that formed part of its foundations, indeed that it would be, would actually consist in, the quest for this very particular and certain kind of knowledge; and that in consequence, more than any other single person, he established the quest for certainty at the centre of Western science and philosophy, where it remained for three hundred years. Having suggested all this, I invited my pupil to consider that some of these things, even taken separately, represented major developments in Western thought. And scarcely any of this was to be learnt by analysing Descartes's arguments, or his use of concepts, though it was where his real importance lay. Ergo: an approach that confined itself to critical analysis had left him for the most part in the dark.

Along such lines as these I made it a conscious principle of my teaching, whatever the subject, to get the pupil first of all to do the necessary learning, and the necessary detailed work of analysis and criticism, and then to raise "Yes, but what is the point of all this—why are we doing it?" questions. And students almost invariably found that it was only when that stage was reached that the really exciting interest and importance of what it was they were doing opened up before their eyes. Many told me I was the only one of their tutors who did this; and the most important of all my criticisms of the Oxford tradition of education—not only in philosophy but in the humanities generally—is that it fails at this point: it treats analysis and criticism, and therefore the provision of a training in these activities, as ends in themselves, and so stops there, without considering what the point of them is. I have been told by innumerable people over the years, especially in response to my later television programmes, that they studied philosophy at Oxford without ever really understanding what it was about. They wondered silently why they were studying the writers they were writing essays on—why they were reading Locke, or Hume, when even their parents had never heard of them, and the tutor himself was carving up each philosopher's arguments with an air of great intellectual superiority, showing his views to be untenable. Where was the value in any of it? However, they kept their mouths shut, because they assumed that everyone else understood what was going on. Hoping that the light of understanding would break in them eventually, they just got on with doing what was expected of them; and some, having good minds, got first-class degrees, without ever understanding the point of what they were doing.

Perhaps in the light of all this it is not surprising that there seemed to be widespread agreement among tutors, in all subjects, that the best students sometimes did not do well in examinations. The chief reasons for this were not only the obvious ones: the element of chance in the questions, the current state of the student's private life, his temperamental responses to being examined (some are stimulated, others inhibited), the different markings of different examiners, and so on. A more interesting reason went deeper than any of these. It was that the highest marks tended to go to examinees who were good at doing what was expected of them—who read the approved books, and discussed them in the approved manner—and that these tended to be unoriginal people. More independent-minded students did not usually behave like this; and the more imaginative they were, and the more distinctive their intellectual personalities, the less likely they were to behave in that way. What these tended to do was to pursue with unusual intensity those subjects that interested them while neglecting those that did not, often with little regard for examination results. The consequence was that first-class degrees went to students with the mentality and temperament of high-grade civil servants, while many of those who thought for themselves, and had flair and imagination, got seconds. The two individuals who were probably the most academically distinguished ever to have passed through my own school, PPE, had been given seconds: John Hicks, who won the Nobel Prize for Economics, and Peter Strawson. One of the university Readers in politics used to say that all his best pupils got seconds. Someone in the English school pointed out that of the outstanding living authors who were educated at Oxford—W. H. Auden, Graham Greene, Evelyn Waugh, Robert Graves, Anthony Powell, William Golding (later to win the Nobel Prize for Literature)—none had firsts, and half got thirds. The head of one of the colleges once said to me: "I understand why we're teaching the students, but I don't understand why we're examining them."

The aspect of being a tutor from which I derived most satisfaction was the pastoral side. Some of the students had serious and unpleasant personal difficulties. Only rarely did they ask to discuss these. More often I would realize from their work or from their demeanour that something was wrong, and then a little gentle questioning would bring the trouble tumbling out. Sometimes their need was for professional advice, and then I saw to it that they got it.

Other times it was enough for them to have free access to a sympathetic older person who would keep their confidences and offer them commonsense advice that they felt at liberty to disregard. There were two or three for whom I did more in this way than any teaching could have given them. Not only was it of more use than teaching: it gave me, too, more satisfaction.

The pupils who interested me most were the most and the least able. This is because both categories called for special treatment, and constituted a challenge. Here—I felt in each case—was someone I could help in a way that might affect the rest of his life. The others, what I might call here the run-of-the-mill students (I never actually thought of them in that way, because I had a unique relationship with each), were neither going to profit all that much from extra efforts on my part nor be in danger of serious loss without them. With those I made the interesting discovery that their ability to do philosophy was not directly related to intelligence. In this respect it was like, say, being musical: some of the most intelligent ones were tone deaf to philosophy, and uncomfortably aware that they were not taking in what was going on, while others, less intelligent than they, were getting a tune out of it and enjoying themselves in the process. It taught me not to take for granted of any individual, however intelligent, that he would be able to see the point of a philosophical problem, and also not to get exasperated if, because of his inability to do so, he took philosophy to be rather pointless.

In addition to my relationship with my students I enjoyed the life of the Senior Common Room. This has to do with my temperament. I like London clubs for the same reason, and have belonged to several, just as I have to several colleges. In each case what I like is the fact that they provide an individual with personal freedom without this involving isolation. If you want to be left alone you can be, and yet have a wide range of useful services permanently available, to be used or disregarded at will. Everyone respects your privacy, no one bothers you, and if you wish, you can go for months on end without conversing with a soul, and nobody takes it amiss. But congenial company is always there: you can be sociable whenever you want, and for as long as you like, but you are equally free to be unsociable whenever you feel like it, and for as long as you want. Family life is not like this, nor is normal friendship, but it is something that a great many people feel a deep need for, as is shown by the fact that institutions providing it have existed throughout the history of civilization. It may be a need that is felt more widely among men than among women: I am not sure about that. But I know that I have it strongly myself.

Any Senior Common Room will contain specialists in the main subjects taught in the college, and although many of these individuals will be little more than schoolteachers for the grown-up there are almost bound to be some who have wider horizons, so there will always be good companionship to be had—interesting conversation at meals or at coffee time, drinking companions late into the night. You can find yourself discussing Russian novels with someone who teaches them, and of course knows them in Russian; or the economic recession with an economist, or the latest newspaper scare about AIDS with a medical researcher, or a play with someone who has written a book about the playwright. Equally, you may find yourself discussing your own subject with someone who has other kinds of knowledge that is relevant to it—in my case, say, metaphysics with a scientist, or political philosophy with a historian, or logic with a mathematician. If this goes on week in, week out, it enriches the soil of your mental life. I find it congenial in a profound way: it gives me a satisfaction that goes deep; it nourishes not just my mind but my spirit. So I have to say I greatly enjoyed the Senior Common Room life of Balliol, and made friends there that have remained with me ever since.

Students tend to take a student-centred view of what a university is for, and they get a distorted idea of what a university is. They think it consists of them, with a top-dressing of dons to teach them, and perhaps a few researchers. Because this is the view of it they form while they are there, they retain it when they are no longer there, and hold it, usually, for the rest of their lives. However, if you become a senior member of a great university you see it in a quite different perspective. All around you are colleagues, thousands of them, writing books and doing original work in the sciences, many with international reputations. At the same time they are having to run large-scale institutions in which you and they work, the colleges and institutes and laboratories, with their staffs and their budgets of many millions of pounds annually. And their work in these absorbs them decade in, decade out. Alongside it, of course, they have their private lives, their homes and their children. And then in addition to all this they have their teaching. At the bottom of a large pyramidical organizational structure are the students. Few of these stay for more than three or four years, so they constitute a perpetual flow through the bottom level of the system, always changing, arriving and departing with what seems like increasing speed. Their very evanescence as individuals renders their group-presence at the university insubstantial, and at Oxford this is reinforced by the fact that the three eight-week terms add up to less than half the year, so even when a student is there he is away for more than half the time. But your own work and that of your colleagues goes on just the same all the year round; and usually the more creative you are the more of your time you want to spend doing original work, and the less of it teaching. So, if you can, you delegate the teaching of all but your most rewarding pupils. Most good academics like to do a little teaching because, as they usually put it, it keeps them on their toes—it forces them to keep abreast of their subject on a broader front than they otherwise would. Also it keeps them in contact with the young, and what is more the intelligent young, and they like this for all sorts of reasons. More than a little teaching, though, gets in the way of what they tend to regard as their "real" work. So the most eminent do not teach undergraduates at all, only graduate students—a source of constant complaint from the brighter undergraduates and their parents.

Some of these generalizations apply to Oxford with special force. Although undergraduates past and present tend to assume that the university exists in order to teach them, this is untrue historically as well as actually. The university began as a community of scholars, each doing his own work; and only as a subsequent development did students go there to be taught by them. Today there are seven graduate colleges in which each individual is pursuing his own research, whether in the humanities or the sciences; and in the remaining colleges the proportion of post-graduate students is increasing all the time. Many observers believe that the university is in process, very slowly, of becoming a research institution which candidates will have to have a degree to enter. I think it not unlikely that this will happen in the twenty-first century.

18

In Praise
of Popularization

My period as a philosophy don at Oxford occurred at a time when there was a rare degree of intellectual ferment in society, and in the world at large. Advances in cosmology were overturning established conceptions of the universe. The incompatibility of relativity theory and quantum physics, while both of them obstinately went on yielding accurate results, remained an enigma that cut to the heart of empirical reality. The life sciences were undergoing a transformation. Historians were rebelling against the established professional practice of thousands of years of tracing the story of one small part of any social group they dealt with, and were reinventing the past. Sociology and anthropology were seething with new ideas—sociology must have been the fastest-growing academic discipline in Britain. A whole new approach to literary theory (in my view a mistaken one) was establishing itself in universities; while outside them the first broad wave of disillusionment with traditional left-wing ideas was seeping in, like the first shallow waters of an incoming tide, across the consciousnesses of people throughout the world who had hitherto thought of themselves as left. Keynesian economics, in accordance with which the economies of the West had been managed since the Second World War with unprecedented success, was in crisis. International concerns about the environment and the ecosphere were organizing themselves effectively for the first time. In Britain, age-old shackles of censorship had only recently been thrown off by literature and drama, and a new permissive attitude was taking hold not only about art but about life: the young were behaving like a liberated population. Society as a whole was becoming serious for the first time about equal rights for women and certain minority groups, while the old class distinctions were visibly disintegrating. The country was bringing its aboriginal isolation from the continent of Europe to an end. Altogether, the late 1960s and the early 1970s constituted an exceptional period in which big, fundamental ideas, many of them established for generations, were questioned, overthrown, replaced. But you would have tried in vain to engage most of the people teaching philosophy in the Oxford of 1970 in an interest in most of those things.

Paradoxically, there was more awareness of these great new waves of ideas among intelligent people outside the universities than among professional philosophers. This was reflected in a new kind of demand for intellectually serious but non-technical exposition and discussion. There had always been books of popularization by figures outstanding in their field, but for the most part popularization had been the province of journalists; this now changed, and books of high-level popularization by distinguished professionals became a recognized publishing category, one that has been growing ever since and includes many books of high merit. Cross-cultural journals like the *New York Review of Books* flourished and became part of a frame of reference common to many educated people. A series of paperbacks called Modern Masters was founded with the aim of providing introductions to recent thinkers who had influenced modern life. The overall movement was unmistakable, and intellectually exciting—and, it seemed to me, of social and political as well as intellectual and cultural significance.

In a way, my radio series *Conversations with Philosophers* and the book that came out of it could be seen as part of all this. Its unprecedented intellectual seriousness and scale was very much in the spirit of that time. It also, incidentally, made a reputation for me as being someone who could make successful broadcast programmes out of abstract ideas. This was to affect my immediate future. The first thing I did on ceasing to teach at Oxford was to present a long series of discussion programmes on television which, in some ways, I still regard as the best thing I have done in that medium.

Up to that time there had never really been any serious discussion of ideas on British television. In programmes like *Brains Trust* three or four people would talk about several unrelated topics in a single programme, so on average each of them spoke for only a couple of minutes about each. Even when a whole programme was devoted to a single topic the fact that several people were taking part always made it impossible for any of them to develop a single line of argument for long. Nothing intellectually serious was ever sustained. Interviews in the current affairs programmes were short, even when one of the most powerful people in the world was sitting in front of the cameras. People, like ideas, were never seriously probed. Because all discussion was so brief, it remained always on the surface. And because of that, most of it was carried on by broadcasters and journalists who knew only how to make it attractive at that level. One might have supposed that with the advent of television, figures like Karl Popper and Isaiah Berlin would have been asked to appear on it perpetually, since it was now possible, for the first time in history, for all the members of a complex society to see and hear its greatest minds and its most brilliant talkers. But this was not so at all; and because the medium dealt with ideas in such a frivolous way the people who could have contributed most to it were alienated from it: the leading intellectual figures in our society were seen on television either very little or not at all. This rested, of course, on judgments about the viewing audience made by the programme-makers: that the audience had a short attention span, that its levels of information and intelligence were not high, and that most of it would not follow a lengthy serious discussion but would switch across to another channel.

I challenged this by presenting a series called *Something to Say* in which, in each programme, a single issue was debated between two high-calibre opponents for an hour, with me acting as a self-effacing chairman. It was a high-risk approach. For the programmes to work, each topic needed to grip and hold the attention of viewers for that long period, and throughout the whole hour the participants needed to be pouring out an arresting flow of energy as well as ideas. The very simplicity of the format exposed it to failure. In ordinary discussion programmes, if one topic begins to run out of steam the chairman can shift to another; and if one of the participants is on disappointingly low form the discussion can be maintained, perhaps all the better, without him. But, in this series, if a subject failed to retain its interest the programme would collapse before its end like a cold soufflé; and it needed only one participant to be inadequate for the whole discussion to be shipwrecked. Everything had to go right all the time.

Luckily, the programmes came off. For the first time on television really big issues were debated at serious length by big intellectual figures. The outstanding international representatives of Marxist and liberal thought of that period, Herbert Marcuse and Raymond Aron, confronted one another on the question whether Communism was or was not compatible with democracy. Aron returned later in the series to argue with Roy Jenkins about whether a federal Europe was or was not desirable. F. A. von Hayek debated the merits of socialism with George Orwell's biographer, Bernard Crick. John Kenneth Galbraith confronted Anthony Crosland over whether the economies of the West should or should not pursue economic growth. Isaiah Berlin argued with Stuart Hampshire about whether, on balance, nationalism was to be considered a good thing. John Hume confronted Conor Cruise O'Brien over the future of Northern Ireland. The best-known behavioural psychologist, B. F. Skinner, discussed the possibility of free will. Two Nobel Prize–winning biologists, Jacques Monod and John Eccles, disputed the credibility of the existence of a human soul. A. J. Ayer and a Roman Catholic bishop disputed the credibility of the existence of God.

I made thirty-nine such programmes between February 1972 and August 1973. Because I presented them on the screen I received most of the credit, but behind the scenes the contribution of the producer, Udi Eichler, was equal to mine. Our other participants included the co-inventor of the transistor, William Shockley (there were several Nobel Prize winners in the series); the pioneer environmentalist Barry Commoner; Herman Kahn, Margaret Meade, James Baldwin, Barbara Wootton, C. V. Wedgwood, Denis Healey, Enoch Powell, Alan Walters, Keith Joseph, Lord Devlin, Raymond Williams, Anthony Quinton and Bernard Williams. The fact that Thames Television refused me permission to turn the best of all this into a book was a cause of sadness to me. Such a book might not have been a best-seller, but the financial risk would have been carried by the publisher, not by Thames; and given the calibre of the contributors, and the importance of the problems discussed, some of the material would, I think, have been of historical interest: here were some of the leading intellectual and public figures of our time arguing about issues that were exercising the minds of their contemporaries. Alas, most of the tapes have now been wiped: only a handful, and those not always the best, survive.

This is typical of the way television organizes, or fails to organize, itself. It seems to me self-evident that it should be shooting dozens of hours of material with each of the people whose ideas are most influential in our generation, not for immediate showing but for archival purposes—though it would be easy enough to edit programmes out of it for immediate showing that would pay the cost of the undertaking. It is breathtaking even to imagine what it would be like for us now if we had long and intellectually serious interviews on videotape with Voltaire, Adam Smith, Karl Marx, and so on. Yet for a long time we have been able to do the equivalent thing for our own historical period; and we shall have that ability permanently into the future. But we have not even begun to use it. On the contrary, we destroy most of the records of the historic figures of our own time that we acquire.

Good interviewing and chairmanship in programmes like *Something to Say* consists in raising the right questions in the right order. But before anyone can know what the most interesting, challenging or important questions are in any given area he needs to have a grasp of the issues. So my working method went something like this. I would study a subject or an issue, seek out the acknowledged experts, get their advice on what to read, do the reading, and then discuss the reading with the experts. (Up to this point it was an adaptation to my needs of the tutorial method of teaching.) This was designed to bring me to the point where I understood what were the most important things that needed to be said. I then tried to find out who would say these things most effectively on television. Having found him I would go and discuss the subject with him. Then, when we got into the studio, I would ask questions that enabled him to say what most needed to be said, and to say it in the most effective terms, the clearest order, and so on. This means that I gave a great deal of thought to the order in which I put my questions, because this would determine the whole shape and structure of the programme: my aim always was to place them so that the discussion of each appeared to give rise spontaneously to the next, with the result that the subject seemed to unfold naturally, of its own accord. Because this was the way I worked, it was rare for me to ask a question to which I did not already know the answer. If it was I who had chosen both the subject and the participants then I knew, at least in outline, when I walked into the studio, who was going to say what, and in what terms, and in what order.

On *Something to Say* I worked like this on equal terms with Udi Eichler. On my two subsequent TV series on philosophy I did it alone. Eichler remains to this day a gifted television producer who has never had the recognition he deserves, largely because the programme distributors do not want what he is best at producing. It is too good for them. In this they underestimate the viewing public. *Something to Say* acquired an unusually enthusiastic body of devoted adherents, and a quarter of a century later I find myself meeting total strangers who tell me they consider it the most intellectually stimulating TV series they have ever watched.

Udi and I gave endless thought and discussion to finding issues that would catch, straight away, and then hold for a full hour, the interested attention of an audience big enough to justify our place in the schedules. And we gave equal care to our choice of participants, concerned not only with their ability to articulate ideas but also with their quality as performers, their effectiveness as communicators to a non-specialist audience, their interestingness as personalities, their capacity to keep a long discussion energized right through to the end. Udi more than I (my subsequent practice came round to being like his) set special store on a contributor's being involved existentially in what it was he was saying, and not just giving a lucid but detached exposition of it in the way a skilful reporter or university teacher might. He talked a lot about what he called the "psychological warmth" of a discussion, as something different from its verbalizable content. He believed that this had a lot to do with getting viewers involved. He was certainly right in this, and we provided it; and all the quality indices, as well as the quantity indices, showed us to have met with an extraordinary response from our audience.

Because each of the programmes involved the kind of preparation I have described, and the making of the series was spread over a period of one and a half years, it gave me a wide-ranging education in many of the leading social and intellectual concerns of the day. I caught up, so to speak, on some of the issues that intelligent people outside the universities had been thinking about. It is the only time in my life that I have done this systematically and on anything like so large a scale. I read, in some cases re-read, the most influential current books, and discussed them with practitioners in their various fields of concern—and also, in many cases, with their authors: *The Affluent Society* with Galbraith, *The Constitution of Liberty* with Hayek, Marcuse's main works with Marcuse, nationalism with Isaiah Berlin, and so on. If contributors came from abroad, as many did, it was part of my job to arrange their visits to London, and entertain them while they were there. As a natural consequence of this some of them became friends, whom I met on subsequent occasions. At just the time in my life when I needed it the experience as a whole helped me on my journey away from academic philosophy towards other worlds in which fundamental ideas were lived, and lived passionately.

It goes without saying that on most of the social issues discussed on *Something to Say* there were many different positions that individuals could occupy. But I slowly realized that the majority of intelligent people's views could be seen as falling into one of four broadly recognizable categories. There were always plenty who more or less defended the status quo. Then there were people who wanted to see it reformed in a liberal direction, and by consent, even if an unreconciled minority should remain. Then there were people who wanted to sweep the existing state of affairs away altogether, by intolerant means "if necessary," and replace it with something radically different—and, they seemed always to be confident, better. In the Britain of the early 1970s most actual representatives of these three standpoints could be seen not unfairly as (using words in their traditional, not their party-political senses) conservative, liberal, and sympathetic to Marxism. On most specific issues my own views fell into the liberal category. Intellectually I was fairly self-confident in my attitude to the other two positions, which I saw as being on each side of my own, one to my right, the other to my left. They had been familiar to me all my life, and I thought I understood them. Acceptance of things as they are seemed to me a natural, indeed the normal, human attitude. And although my attachment to the cause of personal freedom had never been negotiable, in my early youth I had supposed it to be compatible with Marxism, and this meant that although I had never been a Marxist I had lived not far from a common frontier with Marxism, and did not feel afraid of it. So I was reasonably confident of my ability to come off best in argument with Marxists, of which I had a great deal of experience, and also in argument with conservatives—at least as far as my view of the merits of these arguments went, though no doubt not always in that of my opponents. This was not because I thought I was cleverer than they were, but because I was convinced I had the better cause. Those occasions when I realized I was getting the worst of it I tended to regard as being due to my own inadequacy as an arguer, or perhaps as I might have regarded a trick lost while winning a game at cards.

But now, for the first time in my life, I came seriously up against a fourth position, the position of the radical right, whose existence I had known of before but which I had never regarded with respect. In fact, the truth is that I had dismissed it as quasi-fascist, and had never given it serious examination. In various *Something to Say* programmes it was argued by, in their differing ways, Hayek, Alan Walters, Keith Joseph, Enoch Powell, Brian Cox (on education), John Sparrow (on censorship), Anthony Flew (on the causes of crime), Peter Bauer (on aid to developing countries), Peregrine Worsthorne (on racism). Roughly speaking, the view was that the status quo was unacceptable and ought to be changed, but not in a liberal or socialist direction because that would make matters worse. For generations, it was held, the countries of the West had been travelling down a road of ever-increasing government interference with the freedom of the individual: and whatever the case for this may have been in the past, it was now a cause of major social problems and evils. Liberals and socialists wanted to cure these ills by yet more government intervention, but this could only add to the trouble. What was needed was less regulation, not more; less government intervention, more freedom for the individual—and at every level: in the economic sphere through private ownership, free markets and freedom of enterprise; but not that alone: also in social life, through a corresponding openness of opportunity, so that individuals could seek their own path in life, and succeed or not in accordance with their merits; and in specific spheres like education, health services and pensions, through individual responsibility and private provision. One huge consequence of this was a firm commitment to equality of opportunity combined with a firm rejection of equality of outcomes. Put in these terms the whole attitude makes one think of the United States, and it might therefore be supposed to have been both familiar and sympathetic, but it did not begin to gain any significant number of adherents in twentieth-century Britain until the late 1960s. The chief reason for its powerful emergence at that time lay in the perceived failure of the alternatives.

In retrospect it is easy to see that post-war Labour governments made mistakes on a massive scale. They ought, as France and Germany did, to have given first priority to the rebuilding and modernizing of the economy after the depredations of war. Instead they diverted resources away from this to objectives that were either unattainable or irrelevant—the protection of sterling as a world currency, the preservation of Britain's pre-war position as a global military power with troops all round the world, the maintenance of an independent British nuclear deterrent, and so on. On the economic front they gave first priority to full employment, which they bought at the cost of inflation, overweening trade union power, and a degree of overmanning that resulted in artificially low productivity and the steady impoverishment of the nation. They nationalized most of the basic industries, which then ran with incredible inefficiency, many of them regularly incurring crippling losses that had to be paid with equal regularity by the taxpayer. And on top of all this they created an ever-expanding welfare state without anything like the wealth-creation sector necessary to sustain it. All this was done with the best of intentions, naturally, but it was disastrous. And the supreme fault of post-war Conservative governments, until Margaret Thatcher, was that they made no attempt to undo it. Each time they came back into power they devoted themselves to administering the status quo as they inherited it, except for a little tinkering here and there. So each Labour government pushed the country further down the wrong road, and each Conservative government accepted the new state of affairs thus created, operating what Keith Joseph called a ratchet effect in the process of national decline. Essentially, the resurgence of the radical right was a revolt against this whole situation, based on a desire to reverse it.

Neither then nor subsequently was I converted to the radical-right viewpoint. This was chiefly because I could not go along with its positive proposals, about which I shall say more in a moment. But I found its critique of the established alternatives dauntingly impressive. When spelled out in specific terms its critique of socialism and Communism was little short of devastating. And its critique of my own position was uncomfortably effective. Over and again the challenge it posed was the one I found most difficult to meet. I could answer the status-quo conservatives all right, and also the Marxists; but constantly I found myself emerging from argument with someone of the radical right with the feeling that I had not met his objections. I may not have lost the argument—I may have given as good as I got—but I had also got as good as I had given, and I could feel the bruises. I came to view the radical right as representing the strongest alternative to my own position. Here, I felt, was the case I had to answer, the one whose chief arguments I had to meet, and the one whose criticisms I was likely to find most difficult to deal with. Three things added especially to its power as far as I was concerned. One was the intellectual honesty of it, the down-to-earth common sense which contrasted so refreshingly with the ideology and bogus moralizing of the left. The second, following on from this, was its genuine populism, its closeness to the views, values, feelings, and aspirations of so-called ordinary people, which is something that socialists had always hungered for, and often deceived themselves into believing that they had, but never had had. (Many of them were utterly astounded when the dockers of London's East End marched in support of Enoch Powell, Britain's leading radical-right politician of the time—thereby exhibiting their total incomprehension of the actual views of such people.) The third was its ability to point to living examples of what it was proposing, namely in the United States—a country that I loved, admired, and felt at home in. Ever since my year at Yale I had believed that if a grown-up human being were to arrive on Planet Earth without ties, and had to decide where to live, the obvious choice would be the United States—which does indeed seem to be the first preference of more international émigrés than any other country.

The chief reason why I did not go along with the positive programme of the radical right is that the degree of economic libertarianism that they advocate would create, in effect, a free-for-all, and to that I have many objections. In an already advanced technological society most of the population would do quite well out of it, and some would do very well indeed, but many would come off badly. Those who have to cope with serious physical or mental health problems, either in themselves or within their close family; those who are simply no good at jungle warfare, the mild and the meek, or the ineffectual; also the unintelligent, the old and lonely, unmarried mothers with several children, ill-educated immigrants, the unlucky—these and all sorts of other disadvantaged individuals number several million in a country like Britain; and from them would breed an underclass in which crime, drug addiction, disease and slumdom were rife. The provision to them of adequate services in education, health, and old age, given their inadequate (often hopelessly inadequate) purchasing power, can only too plainly not be achieved by a free market. In fact, there are several areas of national life which are of fundamental importance yet whose requirements do not correlate with market forces. National defence is one. Intellectual and artistic life present others—if these were freely left to the operation of market forces our great national theatre, ballet and opera companies, our public art galleries and libraries, and our great universities (not to mention much of the research that goes on in them) would be shipwrecked. In these and multiple other ways a free-for-all would have the effect of destroying some of the most important bonds and activities that make for community, culture and continuity. I believe strongly in the principle of cost-effectiveness as applied to public expenditure, and I believe also that private providers of goods and services are usually more cost-effective than public ones, but I do not believe that it makes sense in any of the areas I have mentioned to allow the overall level of provision to be determined by market forces.

Even so, the cogency of the radical-right critique of centralized planning and much other governmental activity has to be acknowledged. When I first realized this it represented a seismic shift in the bedrock of my outlook, because I had hitherto been in favour not of public ownership but of transparent public management, that is to say the management by a democratically elected government of a largely privately owned economy—the kind of "democratic socialism" of which, at least in that one respect, Sweden was the exemplar. The experience of working on *Something to Say* helped to trigger off a reappraisal of my political attitude in a "social market" direction. It became clear to me that in the last analysis, macro-economic decisions had to be made either by the market or by an indicative planner, or body of planners; and that the former was in most ways more democratic than the latter. So I became convinced of the need for some sort of market basis to economic activity even when it was publicly funded; and I wanted to find ways of reconciling this with the prosperity of education, art and the sciences, and an acceptable level of well-being for the worst-off members of society. When eventually the radical right came to power in the person of Margaret Thatcher I developed the habit of saying that what I believed in was "Thatcherism plus Welfare." The difficulty of reconciling the two in a modern democracy has become the chief internal political problem facing many Western governments.

This rethinking of my political outlook was fed not only by the work I was doing on *Something to Say* but by the systematic re-reading of Popper's oeuvre that I was involved in at the same time. After *Conversations with Philosophers* the editor of the Modern Masters series, Frank Kermode, invited me to contribute a book on any thinker who was not already contracted for. My first response was to say that there was no appropriate person about whose work I knew enough to write a book, not even a short one. My second was to say that perhaps there might be one or two in whose work I could get interested enough to write a *very* short book. I suggested either Freud or Marx. Frank said he had commissioned books on both. I was unable to settle on anyone else, but he urged me to go on trying, and left the invitation open. It marinaded at the back of my mind, and after two or three months the idea surfaced of writing a short book about the philosophy of Karl Popper. At that time he was unknown, even by name, to most educated people, and I did not think there would be many who would want to read it; but once the project had established itself in my head it seemed worth carrying it out for its own sake, so I proposed it to Frank Kermode. He accepted it, and encouraged me to start work on it. In the light of the book's subsequent history it is ironic to remember that it came close to being aborted soon after its conception.

The Modern Masters were published by Collins, and it soon transpired that nobody in that firm had heard of Popper. Sales representatives were asked to test the water in the bookshops, and they reported back that no one in the non-specialist bookshops had heard of Popper either, and they seemed disinclined to order a book about him for non-specialists. Collins consulted Viking, the publishers of the series in the United States, who reacted in the same way. The two publishers then agreed that they did not want to have the book commissioned, and conveyed this to Frank Kermode. Since authors' contracts were made with them and not with him this placed him in a tricky situation. I do not think it mattered greatly to him whether his series contained a book on Popper or not, but he saw his control of the series as placed in jeopardy. He had verbally commissioned a book from me, and on the basis of his word I had started work on it: I think his fear was that if he now withdrew his invitation, effective control of the series would pass out of his hands into the publishers', and commissioning decisions would henceforward be based on commercial considerations, to the detriment of the series. So he protested, arguing that the series was already successful enough to carry two or three titles that were not good sellers—and that if it was to go on being successful he must be allowed to exercise his own judgment. I believe, though I do not know, that he let it be feared that if he were overridden he would resign and abandon the series altogether. At all events it was the two publishers who backed down, and I wrote the book. Viking made difficulties over the final manuscript, which at first, and without reference to me, they rewrote completely at the copy-editing stage in a quasi–*Time* magazine style, in the hope of making it saleable; but I insisted that they change it all back again, and there was a rerun of the earlier confrontation, with the same outcome. The book finally appeared as I wrote it.

All this means that I was writing it at the same time as I was making the *Something to Say* series: whenever television did not demand my working time I gave it to the Popper book. When at last it was published, in April 1973, it established itself immediately as one of the best-selling books in the series, second only to one on Chomsky by John Lyons. It overtook the Chomsky book within a couple of years, and remained the front-runner ever after. Viking truculently let it go out of print in the United States, but it was at once snapped up by another American publisher who kept it in print from then on. Translations appeared in German, Dutch, Danish, Swedish, Italian, Spanish, Portuguese, Farsi, Japanese and Chinese, and in Eastern Europe translations circulated underground in *samizdat,* sometimes two in one country. In some of these languages new words had to be invented for such key Popper terms as "falsifiability," "scientism," "historicism," and the rest. In some of them the appearance of my book led to the translation of his works, or of more of his works, and this was the most welcome development of all. But even as regards its own sales the book was the most commercially successful I had written so far. And I have to confess that this astonished me as much as it must have done the publishers.

It showed, first of all, that a wide and enthusiastic readership existed out-side the universities for some of the most substantial and fertile ideas to have come from a living philosopher. This cut across the assumptions of many aca-demic philosophers, including good ones, who believed that in the course of the twentieth century philosophy had become so professionalized and techni-cal that there was no longer any point in expecting non-specialists to read it—and therefore no longer any point in taking the trouble to write so that non-specialists *could* read it. In accordance with this, most philosophy now aimed at an academic readership or audience, and expected to have no other: philosophers wrote and talked for one another and for full-time students. From his earliest years Popper had condemned this approach. He believed that philosophers had a moral duty not only to deal with important problems but to do so as far as possible in a way that was open to understanding by any intel-ligent person willing to make the effort and give his mind to it. With him the achievement of maximal clarity was a matter of professional ethics, and he strongly disapproved of philosophers who made their work more difficult than it needed to be, or who wrote so allusively that only the initiated could under-stand. Especially did he scorn those among them who cultivated difficulty or allusiveness in the hope that it would enhance their status. He never himself implied this, but it was evident even to him that if someone of his stature, putting forward innovative and historically important ideas in epistemology and the philosophy of science, and also dealing with social and political phi-losophy on a very large scale, could write with the degree of clarity he man-aged to achieve in a language that was not his own, then it was not easily open to lesser figures to claim that what they were doing was so deep and so com-plex that they had no choice but to write about it tortuously. So it was not the case that first-class contemporary philosophy must inevitably be too difficult to be understood by intelligent general readers.

Because Popper demonstrated this there was a certain amount of resent-ment against him among professional philosophers for obstructing their aspi-rations towards priestcraft. They on the whole were not interested in writing about problems of general concern to intelligent people, and therefore did not want to write *for* them. But this was more a comment on them than on philos-ophy. When friends of mine who had studied philosophy with distinction at university, and then gone into other professions and lost touch with it, used to ask me whether they ought to read the book by X or Y which they heard was making a stir in academic circles, the only true answer I could give them in most cases was: "It doesn't matter. Read it if you think you'll enjoy it. But if you don't, it won't make any difference to you or to your life." It was not pos-sible for that sort of philosophy to be more than an intellectual pastime for anyone for whom it was not a profession. A contrast with this was deliberately highlighted by the opening paragraph of my book about Popper's work, a paragraph devoted to illustrating the fact that his philosophy changed the lives and work of some of the most gifted people who came under its influence in multifarious fields.

The unexpected success of the book taught me an important personal lesson: in a vivid way it brought home the fact that if you write something your heart is in, it is more likely to be well received than something you might have expected to be more popular but have written without the same commitment. Half a dozen years earlier, when I had dictated *One in Twenty* and *The Television Interviewer*, I had expected them to bring me in some money. That had not been my motive for writing them, but it was something I expected to happen, simply because the subjects were homosexuality and television. But in fact *The Television Interviewer* never earned more than its advance; so before I dictated the first word I had received all the money I was ever going to make from it. And although *One in Twenty* had better sales it was far outstripped by *Popper*. And yet I had written *Popper* expecting it to attract scarcely any attention at all: it had been a labour of love, something I considered worth providing for a handful of people because of the intrinsic merit of Popper's ideas. It made me realize that even if a writer covets high sales and financial success he is more likely to achieve these if he writes out of impulse and conviction than if he calculatedly produces what he thinks will succeed.

When I embarked on the writing of *Popper* only four of his books had been published: *The Logic of Scientific Discovery, The Open Society and Its Enemies, The Poverty of Historicism,* and *Conjectures and Refutations.* A fifth, *Objective Knowledge: An Evolutionary Approach,* came out while mine was in preparation. Because of his excessive reluctance to let any of his work go to the press—a reluctance due in part to perfectionism but at the same time bordering on neurosis—much of the material that went into the books that he published afterwards was already on paper in one form or another, and he gave me free access to it, so I was able to take it into account in what I wrote. This put me in the position of knowing, as it were, what his future development was going to be. However, the five books I have named were the only ones that anyone not close to him could have read at the time when my book appeared. And they constituted only about half of what his output had become even by 1983. Yet I discovered when I started going out of my way to discuss them with people, and also from some of the subsequent reactions to my own book, that they were a great deal more known about than known, especially among professional philosophers. Many who claimed to have read *The Logic of Scientific Discovery* voiced to me what were in fact elementary misunderstandings of its proposals about falsifiability, and did not seem to be aware that Popper had anticipated these misunderstandings and corrected them in the book itself. Others would bring forward objections without apparently knowing that these too had been considered and answered in the book, with the consequence that the kind of arguments they needed now were arguments against Popper's answers; or, of course, in the absence of those, new objections. People who said they had read *The Open Society and Its Enemies* often seemed unaware of the book's central arguments, and appeared to know only about its criticisms of Plato, Hegel, and Marx: often they gave the appearance of thinking that the book *was* a critique of those philosophers. And of course they had ready objections to Popper's treatment of them.

Popper had long been notorious for reacting to criticism of his work with impatient anger; but when I discovered from my own experience that most of the criticisms that were reiterated again and again were of such a low intellectual level as not to be worth serious discussion I developed a certain sympathy for him. How should he be expected to react when fellow professionals persistently attributed to him views he did not hold, or voiced criticisms to which he had already published a response that they did not take into account? He could only conclude that his work was not being taken seriously enough to be properly read, and decline to waste his time with such "criticism." I believe that the reality of the situation was something as follows. His work, like that of most of the so-called great philosophers, was to a high degree science-based. But most of his contemporary philosophers in the English-speaking world were ignorant of science, and therefore unable to engage with him on equal terms. However, they felt under little pressure to do so. Popper's head-on hostility to the successive fashions of logical positivism and linguistic analysis meant that he himself had persistently remained unfashionable, and therefore not someone whose new publications others felt it necessary to read. In any case, he was not writing about the sort of things they were writing about, and furthermore he appeared to take no notice of their work; and since no philosopher who understood what was really going on could possibly behave like that it confirmed that he was out of touch, no longer in the mainstream, no longer someone whose current work needed to be noticed. Finally, his open rejection of their whole approach to philosophy could only be branded as arrogance, and invite dismissal in return; indeed, it was an attitude that *had* to be dismissed, or they might be thought to be conceding that there could be something in it. So, altogether, a sort of corporate attitude towards him developed on the part of the rest of the profession. He was looked on as someone who had made an important contribution to philosophy a long time ago, but whom the history of the subject had now passed by. This enabled them to acknowledge him as a substantial figure without taking notice of his work. Because his contribution belonged to the history of the subject it was naturally part of everyone's background, something they all knew about by a kind of osmosis, without having read his actual works: everyone knew that Popper stood for certain things—falsifiability, anti-inductivism, the noisy dismissal of Plato and Marx—and everybody knew why his formulations of these positions were mistaken. And of course what everybody knew could be asserted with confidence, because everybody knew it. I was constantly struck by the assurance with which people who had clearly not read the work made assertions about it, an assurance based on a generally accurate assumption that none of their colleagues would challenge what they were saying. When an attitude of this sort towards an individual is firmly entrenched it becomes difficult to break it down, because the holders of it have a vested interest in sustaining it. Constant repetition makes it so familiar that it gains a kind of acceptance that makes it difficult for them to distinguish it from truth. Only over comparatively long stretches of time do such group evaluations change, usually when changes of intellectual fashion occur between generations.

I expect Popper's work to live when that of all but a small number of twentieth-century philosophers has faded. For unlike most thinkers, he never just chooses a topic for discussion and puts forward what he hopes are interesting observations about it. He addresses himself always to a problem, not a topic, a problem which exercises him and which he perceives as being of importance. He analyses it in a way that expands his reader's view of it, and then considers the possible solutions to it that have been proposed by other thinkers. In most cases he criticizes these in a way that is appreciative of their merits and derives suggestions from them. Then he puts forward his own solution. The use of this method means that his writing always has an aim in view, is rich in argument and the range of its references, and progresses (or tries to) beyond the most interesting work already done in the field by others. The view he takes of problems is normally a generous one, and the references he draws on are taken from a polymathic range of knowledge. He never published his work on a problem unless he believed it carried the state of the discussion forward, so all his published work contained new thinking about the problems with which it dealt; and these included many of the fundamental problems of philosophy. But in addition to these he believed that a serious philosopher had a social obligation to address himself to the major problems of his own time, problems under which his fellow human beings suffered, and to make whatever his contribution was to understanding those as accessible as he could by writing as clearly as possible. In consequence the problems he writes about range from probability theory to modern wars, and embrace democracy, socialism, language, music, sociology, history, the body-mind problem, the origins of life, Darwinian evolution, quantum theory, Einsteinian relativity, methodology of science, theory of knowledge, mathematics, logic, and a great many other things besides, including evaluations of the work of a large number of individuals. About all of them he has fresh, interesting, and sometimes profoundly original things to say. If I had to choose a single word to describe Popper's work it would be "rich." It is rich in subject matter, ideas, argument, suggestion, reference, and scholarly resource. And it is written in clear, vigorous English that is a pleasure to read.

But most of it, at the time these words are being written in the mid-1990s, remains unknown to most professional philosophers in the English-speaking world, who do not now even pretend to have read it. In their minds, Popper is still associated exclusively with some of the ideas of his early books, though not even with all of those. Bizarrely, such people tend to justify not having read the later works with the assertion that Popper merely goes on repeating the same things, and has nothing new to say—a fascinating example of people's tendency to believe that what they think they know is all there is.

The most serious aspect of this has to do not with giving an individual his due but with the intellectual loss involved. The work of the greatest recent philosopher is not being built on: progress is not being made that could be made. People publish uninhibitedly nowadays on specific subjects, such as the body-mind problem, or Wittgenstein, without knowing what Popper has said about them; so inevitably it often happens that they either repeat some of the essentials of what he has already published, or put forward positions he has effectively criticized without taking his criticisms into account, or discuss a subject without reference to what are in fact the most recent good ideas to have appeared in it. Little of his work has yet undergone the criticism and development which it merits. Admittedly the first important Popper publication to appear after my *Popper*—a massive two-volume compendium called *The Philosophy of Karl Popper,* which came out in the Library of Living Philosophers the following year—contained, among other things, thirty-three articles critical of his work, and his replies to them. But that was more than twenty years ago now. And it has to be said that not many of those criticisms were especially penetrating.

The Philosophy of Karl Popper contained also a book-length intellectual autobiography that was published as a separate volume two years later under the title *Unended Quest.* This contains engrossing material about the development of Popper's ideas. Central to it, surprisingly, are some comments on music, which turns out to have had an intellectual importance for him which few people would have guessed at. He argues that the arts generally, including music, are not primarily an expressive activity but a problem-solving one, and he relates how the conception of problem-solving which was to become the cornerstone of his philosophy came to him during his study of the historical development of music.

Popper's next important publication was *The Self and Its Brain,* an investigation of the body-mind problem written in collaboration with the Nobel

Prize–winning neurologist John Eccles. Here Popper reviewed the history of the conflict between materialist and dualist conceptions of the human individual, and argued for dualism. After that came three books that arose out of *The Logic of Scientific Discovery*. These were, in the order in which they were intended to be read, *Realism and the Aim of Science; The Open Universe: An Argument for Indeterminism;* and *Quantum Theory and the Schism in Physics*. The main text of *Realism and the Aim of Science* is the least fresh of Popper's writings, the only one of his books to merit the stricture of self-repetition to any really significant degree. Parts of it read like the work of someone who has not been properly understood and is repeating himself in the hope that if he does his message will get through. Other parts spell out what an intelligent reader of his earlier work might have expected him to go on to say next. The shock of surprise and discovery, the startling newness of original thinking that is such a prominent feature of his best work, is in evidence here only half the time. However, that is a good deal by most people's standards. And what the book says is of great importance, and is said well. It is certainly worth reading.

The title of the next book, *The Open Universe: An Argument for Indeterminism,* is, like many of Popper's titles, an indication not just of the book's contents but also of its programme. He had, many years before, put forward the argument that scientifically justifiable prediction of future discoveries is impossible, in a paper called "Indeterminism in Quantum Physics and in Classical Physics," published in the *British Journal for the Philosophy of Science.* He had then gone on to apply this argument to the social sciences, to show that a scientifically predictive sociology is impossible. So the argument actually became best known as part of his demolition of Marxism, whose claim to be scientifically predictive was central. In most of his readers' minds, therefore, it was now associated with *The Open Society.* But he still wanted to work it out at full length in the context in which he first formulated it, the natural sciences, and *The Open Universe* became this book. Thus its title not only indicates its programme but points up the fact that in one sense it is a balancing book to *The Open Society.*

The title *Quantum Theory and the Schism in Physics* refers to a battle of the giants among twentieth-century physicists over the "meaning" of quantum theory. On one side were ranged Einstein, de Broglie and Schrödinger, on the other Heisenberg, Niels Bohr and Max Born. The generally accepted verdict of subsequent generations has been to award victory to the second group, but Popper believes this to be a mistake. It is, he says, to accept an interpretation of quantum theory that makes nonsense of the world, when there is no necessity to do so.

One of the many problems about quantum theory is that it contains self-contradictions and yet yields results of unprecedented accuracy. Some scientists react to this by saying, in effect: "It works, yet it can't be right." Others, more seemingly radical, say: "The fact that it works shows that it must be right, and therefore that reality is self-contradictory by the standards of coherence that we have accepted hitherto. Reality is bizarre in ways we never dreamt of. So our past standards of coherence have been inapplicable, and have been misleading us." There are those who take some sort of bridging position, for instance Hilary Putnam: "I think we don't want to give up our standards of intelligibility altogether. We want to say: 'Quantum mechanics works, and the very fact that it works means there's something fundamentally right about it.' And, with respect to its intelligibility, we're willing to say, in part, that maybe we have the wrong standards of intelligibility, that we have to change our intuitions. Nevertheless, there are real paradoxes in the theory, and I think that it is important to find a satisfactory resolution of these paradoxes."* In *Quantum Theory and the Schism in Physics* Popper offers an interpretation which he believes enables us to take full account of the success of quantum theory without forfeiting a commonsense view of reality.

The subject is not one in which I feel very confident about defending an independent opinion, but I have to say I do not share Popper's respect for, and attachment to, common sense—in fact I am certain that a commonsense view of reality cannot possibly be right—so the incompatibility of quantum theory with our commonsense view of the world does not constitute for me the problem that it does for Popper. On the contrary, I am as sure as I can be of anything that will never be knowable that reality must be more bizarre than we shall ever be capable of conceiving. So if the verdict of the future is that his book does not succeed in carrying out its programme I will not be surprised. Until such time as the issue is settled, though, it remains a clear introduction to the problem, and a challenging exercise in attempting to reconcile what may be two irreconcilable thought-systems. What makes the book essential reading for anyone interested in Popper is its metaphysical epilogue. This is unique in his output, an attempt to put into words what his ultimate metaphysical beliefs were when he was at the height of his powers. I shall not attempt to summarize these beliefs, but offer merely a pointer to the direction in which they lie.

First of all, Popper is a realist. He believes that reality is not mental, that the cosmos exists independently of human beings, and that it includes among its contents us, our minds, and our knowledge. He believes that the growth of human knowledge is the open-ended process of extending our understanding of this independent reality in which we find ourselves, and takes the form earlier described: we frame hypotheses that we then test, and we go on using the

---

* *Men of Ideas*, pp. 230–1.

hypotheses that stand up best to tests until they are no longer that, in other words until we are able to replace them with better hypotheses. On this view our knowledge consists entirely of our theories, and our theories are products of our minds. (The world is not the product of our minds, but our knowledge is.) After the two great revolutions of twentieth-century physical science—relativity theory and quantum physics—we know that matter cannot be, as had been previously believed by so many people, the ultimate constituent of the universe, because elementary particles consist of energy. We also have exceedingly powerful grounds for believing that the universe is not deterministic. Popper incorporates these two extensions of our scientific understanding into the view that ultimate explanations need to be probabilistic in character, and that the basic elements that our probabilistic theories are most appropriately "about" are propensities. *A World of Propensities* is the title of one of his last publications. At one point in *Quantum Theory and the Schism in Physics* (p. 205) he says, for a moment adopting Aristotle's way of talking about these things: "To be is both to be the actualization of a prior propensity to become, and to be a propensity to become." In this part of the book Popper pushes his view of the way things are to the outer limits of intelligibility. But of course his view of the growth of knowledge is such that he would regard it as virtually certain that at some time in the future it will be possible for someone to reach a better understanding than is available to us now.

19

The Limits of Philosophy

When I had finished writing my Popper book, and the TV series *Something to Say* had come to an end, I felt at something of a dead end myself. The writing of *Facing Death* had assuaged at least the worst of my mid-life crisis, and carried me as far in my understanding of the human condition as I could see how to go. But I was still baffled by existence, and at a loss to understand how any further insight into it could be gained. I had no idea which direction to move in, or what to do. And I found this situation itself almost intolerably frustrating.

I had now entered my forties, and I think this fact contributed to the feeling. It so happens that my forties were to be the happiest and most fruitful decade of my life, but I did not know this when I embarked on them. What I chiefly saw was that I was no longer a young man, that directly confronting me now was middle age, to be followed by old age, and that I had reached this point without achieving anything like the understanding of life for which I hoped, longed and searched. On the surface of things I was still doing tolerably well: I had published several books that had received good reviews, and I was earning my living enjoyably as a broadcaster on radio and television. But beneath this surface I felt hollow and unsatisfied. I had no idea where I was going. I certainly did not want to *be* a broadcaster, though financial inducements were offered to me to do so. When I reviewed my general situation I seemed to have come to a dead end on all paths simultaneously.

Facing Death was still unpublished. It was turned down by something like fifteen publishers, and for each of them the process of reading and rejecting it took months. But I was untroubled by this: I knew it to be genuine, and I had an irrational faith that it would sooner or later find its own space. In any case I had written it not in order that it should be published but because I had felt a compulsion to write it; and in so far as it could it had met the needs responsible for its existence. I thought I would like to write another novel, but this time the true compulsion was not there: I made a start, but it turned out to be a false one.

In philosophy too I seemed to have come up against walls in more directions than one. Kant had provided me with an understanding of the nature of the limits of knowability that was now built in to my whole outlook. There were a lot of things wrong with Kant, and some of these were large-scale defects, but it seemed to me that some sort of corrected version of his analysis of basic problems of experience must be valid; and the very fact that many of his proposed solutions failed to convince me meant that the problems as he posed them still stared me in the face—or, if his formulations were, after all, mistaken, I needed to learn why they were mistaken. I have already mentioned that when I came across Tolstoy's phrase "genuine philosophy, whose task is to answer Kant's questions" it seemed to me precisely right. I had still not read any philosopher who dealt with Kant's questions to my satisfaction, and it did not occur to me to imagine that I had a level of ability myself that could produce viable answers. Several philosophers since Kant had made worthwhile contributions to philosophy, but their work found its place within his delineation of the bounds of sense; none that I knew of had pushed those boundaries back. The frontier between the knowable and the unknowable still seemed to me to be, with some qualifications, where he left it—and it would remain there until the next philosopher with a genius comparable to his came along. I could labour in the field of the knowable if I chose, and no doubt I would do interesting work, but at the end of the day I would have made no contribution to the most important question of all, and would not even have been addressing myself to it.

Nor could I see any living philosopher who seemed likely to carry out the job. I tried to persuade Popper to address himself to it, but he was not to be tempted. It was not that he needed any persuading of the centrality of the fundamental Kantian questions, but he was at a loss what to say in answer to them; and he always adhered closely to a rule of not writing unless he had something to say, and knew what it was. He could not help being aware that there were other problems to which he could contribute possible solutions, and it seemed to him more worth while to work on those in the hope of achieving something. As far as I was concerned there was no one else around whose calibre was comparable with his; and in any case none of the ablest philosophers elsewhere that I knew, or knew of, had his openness to the questions.

My re-evaluation of the tradition in which I had been trained, now published as *Modern British Philosophy,* had reconfirmed my conviction of its bankruptcy. American philosophy was more substantial than British, more rich and varied, but even the best American philosophers seemed limited to an analytic approach, and I knew that the problems to which they were addressing themselves could not be solved by that means alone. Such Continental philosophy as I knew seemed soft-centred and self-indulgent—in positive need, actually, of a bit of analytic self-discipline. It was notable for its rhapsodies about the Human Condition, understood in limitedly, not to say ridiculously, modish terms: contemporary politics, the current arts scene in Paris, and analytic psychology. Much of it was little more than rambles round Marx and Freud. The work of the best-known living Continental philosopher, Jean-Paul Sartre, did indeed seem to me clever and attractive, but it was essentially journalistic, and many of his underlying assumptions were repellent: for instance he was a persistent apologist for Communist totalitarianism, and its use of terror against its subject populations.

Perhaps what was needed, I was tempted to think, was a philosopher who addressed himself to Kant's questions in a manner that applied the disciplines of the empirical and analytic traditions without being limited to them. I would like to see such a philosopher give the arts a place near the centre of his considerations: I regarded art as the most important thing in life after people, and was puzzled at how little attention philosophers had paid to it. Sex, too: since it was the manifest means by which every individual human being came into existence I could not understand how it was possible for philosophers to give so little consideration to it—I mean, of course, to the metaphysics of it. Its metaphysical paramountcy stared them in the face, yet they had nothing to say about it. In their capacity as philosophers they did not even consider it, and would have been perplexed by anyone who suggested that they should. Any such thoughts were light-years away from what was being published by analytic philosophers in those days. Kant himself had said nothing about sex—and only one important thing about the arts that seemed to me genuinely helpful, namely that when we see an object as being beautiful this is a characteristic not of the object but of the way we are apprehending it.

All these were things for an extender of Kant's boundaries to do. If I had been able to formulate them more creatively I would have been such a person myself, and I knew I was not, but I could see big and (to philosophy) new problems that I wanted whoever it was to confront, in addition to repairing Kant's notorious self-contradiction in explaining the phenomenal as being caused by the noumenal. I felt rather as someone might who had come on the scene between Hume and Kant, and who felt the challenges presented by Hume's philosophy as compelling but was not himself able to come up with

Kant's solutions. I was, so to speak, waiting for the next Kant, the next philosopher big enough to change the shape of the questions and put the entire subject on a different footing. I did not for one instant believe that great philosophy had come to an end, as some people were saying it had, and as others were saying that great music had (I did not believe that either). With so many fundamental problems formulated but unsolved, serious philosophy could not possibly be at an end. But two thousand years had elapsed between Aristotle and Kant; so presumably it might be another two thousand years before the next figure of comparable calibre. Meanwhile, my life was running its course, and I had to live now. I began to think I might be compelled in practice to live *as if* philosophy had come to an end, simply because it had *for me.* I might just find that however hard I tried to think philosophically, and however much philosophy I read, my condition of frustrated bafflement was going to persist. It went without saying that I could continue indefinitely to learn from secondary masters—I was sufficiently interested in the subject to go on doing that in any case—but I had read, or so I thought, all the truly great ones, and I did not expect that my view of the world was likely to be transformed by any of the others.

Inevitably, in these circumstances, I began to look outside philosophy for a possible way forward in understanding how things are. Music and theatre had always played a more important role in my life than philosophy, so perhaps it was natural that I should look to them first, especially as among the many experiences I gained from them were intimations of something outside the empirical world, something timeless in which time was set. This was not an "as if" experience but an experience. It was an experience of there being something else, something timeless and universal to which this world related. Although music and drama have to—can only—exist in time, a good performance of a great work unfolds *sub specie aeternitatis.* And once I was absorbed in such a performance I was altogether outside myself, lost. Both the work and I were then independent of space and time: but its instantiation here, now, in this once-only performance, incarnated a relationship between, on the one hand, what went beyond space and time, and, on the other, a unique particular, concrete and specific, that existed in space and time. Along with this came a perception that somehow existence as such was like this; that this was the nature of everything. It was a direct, unmistakable piece of knowledge, like tasting. When I experienced it, it came to me nearly always from art, yet not quite always. Once as a child I looked at some horses in a field and saw them moving in another time. Every now and again I have had similar experiences in natural surroundings. But supremely great art, like that of Shakespeare, Wagner or Mozart, renders it a permanent dimension of my life.

I wondered, then, whether it might be through art that I could continue to explore and push back the limits of the knowable, extend my understanding of this world, and at the same time get glimpses of what might lie outside it. The trouble, though, was that I was doing that already. I had been marinading in music and theatre since boyhood. Most days I would work throughout the morning and afternoon and then go in the evening to a theatre, concert or opera. In a normal week I would go to something like five live performances, sometimes more; rarely less than four. It was like daily bread to me, nourishment that I came close to feeling that I could not live without. My favourite way of being with friends was to go with them to a theatre or concert and then have a meal with them afterwards, communing into the early hours, drinking, talking, making love. For me there was no imaginable way of life to compare with it, and I would not have dreamt of trading it away for any other—would not have dreamt, for instance, of accepting a job that involved living outside central London, or required me to get out of bed at a conventional hour and therefore consign myself to sleep at a time that would destroy the evening. Such an exchange, whatever its career implications, would have meant renouncing the greater for the less; and anyone who viewed my refusal to do this as frivolous I regarded as having frivolous attitudes. But because I was so passionately immersed in this as a way of life my consumption of music and drama was already, and had been for many years, as great as I could absorb. I do not believe anyone could have loved them more, and I was getting as much out of them as my capacities allowed. So I did not see how they could do significantly more for me than they were doing already.

Of course I could plunge into the *study* of drama and music, alongside going to live performances, and I could let such study take the same sort of place in my life as had hitherto been occupied by the study of philosophy. But of its nature this would be not an artistic or aesthetic activity but a conceptual and intellectual one. No doubt it would add interestingly to my knowledge about the works of art that I experienced, but I did not see how it could contribute to that experience itself, since it was essential to the whole nature of art that it was non-conceptual—unless a presentational symbol can be regarded as a concept. In the same way, there is a lot of great literature about the experience of being in love, but it is impossible to see how anyone who is in love can deepen his being so by reading books about it, wonderful though some of them are. To expect that kind of connection is to mistake the whole nature of the experience, indeed of both the experiences. Reading great literature is itself a highly worthwhile experience, and there is much to be gained from it, but the deepening of one's love for the person one is in love with is not one of them. There is something notoriously inauthentic about a love nourished by literature. It is easy to see how someone going through the experience of being in love might want to read about others doing the same, and might be especially responsive to what he read, but his true gains and experiences would be literary, and perhaps cognitive, scarcely amatory. The key analogies with the arts all hold: the creation of, and response to, authentic art are not activities of the conceptualizing intellect, and are not to be significantly furthered by an increase in intellectual understanding.

It may be that I am being too absolute here—perhaps what I should be arguing is not that there is no enhancement but that whatever enhancement there is is peripheral. But of that at least I am certain. In any case, because of my love of music I was already given to reading quite a lot about it. I had written a book about Wagner, which had required me to immerse myself in the relevant literature. So I was already getting much if not most of what was to be gained in this way, at least by me; and it was this already existing familiarity with such studies, and what I derived from them, that led me to the conclusion that they could not function as a continuation of, and still less as a replacement for, the study of philosophy, however valuable and interesting they might be in other ways.

The only remaining direction in which I could think to look was religion. In general my attitudes towards religious belief had tended previously to fall somewhere between the indifferent and the unsympathetic. My indifference was due chiefly to the fact that I had never seen any reason for taking religious assertions seriously: they had not of themselves commanded my attention, and I had never found myself confronting a problem to which any of them even looked as if it might be a solution. But perhaps I ought to look again. My lack of sympathy was due to the fact that religious belief had always seemed to me evasive. Instead of confronting the unknown, and struggling to master the fear this induced, and to come to terms with the frightening implications of our ignorance, and to live our lives with some degree of integrity in spite of our situation, it pretended that we were not in that situation at all—that we were not really as ignorant as all that, but in possession of some sort of quasi-knowledge of what the truth was, and knew furthermore that it was something we could take comfort in. All this flouted the most fundamental values by which I was trying to live: determination to do everything I could at the metaphysical level to find out what the truth is about what is; honesty with myself about the search and its findings; and absolute refusal to be lured away from it by any of the palliatives on offer to assuage the terror and frustration of not knowing. I regarded religion as a cop-out; and certainly without thinking of myself as courageous (on the contrary: I had been driven to the edges of mental illness, even suicide, by metaphysical terror), I thought of religion as cowardly. People who relapsed into it abandoned the search for truth. No doubt this made them easier in their minds, but as far as I was concerned it rendered anything they had to say on the subject of truth supererogatory.

Such, then, were my attitudes. But I knew that there had always been people of the highest intelligence who held religious beliefs, including some of the greatest artists, philosophers and scientists. And I knew that among these there were individuals who had come to religious belief from unbelief—for example St. Augustine, for whom I felt both respect and empathy. Tolstoy had, as it were, worked his way through philosophy, and then, when he discovered that it was not to be looked to for answers to ultimate questions, turned away from it disillusioned towards some sort of religion. And I had an idea that Wittgenstein had done something similar, though in his case the process was more veiled, ambiguous, uncommitted. In both of these last two instances it was only because philosophy was found wanting that religion was even considered: so perhaps I was now at the right point in my own life to find something in religion that I had not been able to see before. Anyway, I thought it worth exploring.

I realized, of course, that any intellectually serious study of religion would occupy me for a matter of years, and I was nowhere near wanting to make such a commitment. But I thought I could at least dip my toe in the water. Chiefly it was a matter of attitude: for the first time I felt willing to give serious consideration to religious doctrines in an open frame of mind. I decided to give an unhurried period over to the study of basic religious texts, and perhaps to some of the acknowledged classics among commentaries on them: and to discuss them with persons who believed in them. As before when I had wanted to do something of this kind, I looked to broadcasting to provide me with an income while I did it. In the ITV schedules there was a period early on Sunday evenings when the companies were required to broadcast religious programmes—in the trade it was known as "the God slot." They regarded this as a dangerous problem, for how were they to devise programmes whose seriousness would satisfy the Independent Television Authority without causing hundreds of thousands of viewers to switch across to the BBC and be lost to them for the rest of the evening? With the God slot in mind I devised a series for London Weekend Television called *Argument,* in which each programme consisted of an argument between me and one other person. With the head of the Roman Catholic Church in Britain, Cardinal Heenan, I argued about whether or not the existence of God can be proved—to this day the official Catholic view is that it can. With the Archbishop of Canterbury I argued about the relationship between Church and State. With Enoch Powell I argued that his Christian faith ought to commit him to a redistribution of wealth both at home and globally, and therefore to what might be called the politics of welfare, which was not at all what he believed. The unusual thing about the format was that there was no chairman, and therefore no one between the two protagonists: the viewer was presented with the argument raw, so to speak. This constituted an advance beyond *Something to Say.* I would introduce the subject by talking directly into the camera for about a minute, then introduce the other person, and then kick off the argument by posing a challenge—such as, to Cardinal Heenan: "I don't know whether God exists or not, and what's more I don't believe you do either." I made it my task to provide a certain amount of invisible chairmanship from one side of the argument—for example by keeping it moving unhurriedly along and never letting it get bogged down on one point; by making sure that all the most important issues were raised in the course of the programme; by seeing to it that anything that more than just a few viewers might not understand was explained; and by always allowing my opponent more time than I took myself, so that there could never be any question of my abusing my position in that regard. Learning to chair a discussion fairly and effectively from one side of it was to prove invaluable some years later when I came to make my television series on philosophy, for in those I consciously employed the techniques I had begun to develop in *Argument.*

One programme in the series was about Judaism and one about Buddhism, but the rest were devoted to Christianity. That imbalance, especially the absence of a programme on Islam, looks strange in retrospect, but it was in keeping with the assumptions of the time; indeed, to have had a balance very different from the one I had would have seemed strange, for to have programmes in the God slot about any religion at all other than Christianity was looked on as adventurously tolerant. The best of them was the one with Cardinal Heenan. With unusual forcefulness, precision and clarity he put forward the main classical arguments for the existence of God, while I put the main classical arguments against it (I had done my homework). The result was a paradigm debate that could have been used to set before university students both sides of an argument that has been going on for thousands of years. When I tried some years later to get a tape or transcript of it I was dismayed to be told that the tapes of the entire series had been wiped, and that there were no transcripts of any of the programmes. Suitably edited, it would have made a worthwhile little book. Enoch Powell had the good sense to make his own transcript, and included it in his book *Wrestling with the Angel,* published in 1977. Apart from that, the series has disappeared without trace.

However, as usual for me in my capacity as a broadcaster, the programmes were primarily not an end in themselves but a means, something I set up so that I could work at what I wanted to devote myself to, in this case religious studies. The period of preparation involved for me was always longer than the viewer would probably suppose. It is normal for the first office discussions of a broadcast series to take place months before the programmes go on the air. The broadcasting company needs to plan its schedules quite a long way in advance, and there are many practical matters to be discussed—staff to be seconded, money to be budgeted for, contracts to be negotiated; and before even these things can be settled the people responsible need already to have agreed among themselves what sort of programmes it is they will be making. Even for something as technically straightforward as a television discussion series there needs to be a studio set, and one whose design, colour scheme, lighting, and furnishings are appropriate to that particular series; so the set has to be discussed, agreed on, designed, built, tried out, and altered until it is felt to be satisfactory. The viewing public, most of them, never think about such things, nor do the programme-makers want them to, but they have to be done just the same, and professionals are right to regard them as important. In any case, such things cost money: with regard to every aspect of the programme money has to be carefully thought about, and is much discussed. So there are weeks or months of work to be done on a series, any series, before it goes on the air. Because of the nature of the programmes that I make, part of the invisible preparation for them includes a great deal of reading on my part: this too takes time, and that time too has to be paid for. Therefore someone like me cannot be contracted and paid for only the period during which the programmes are on the air; it has to be for a much longer period.

It is this fact that has enabled me to be, in effect, a self-employed scholar for so much of my life. On a series like *Argument* I would work full-time for several months, and most of this time would be devoted to study in libraries. On each of my subsequent fifteen-part series on philosophy I worked for two and a half years—and then spent another six months each time turning the series of programmes into a book. Of this total of six years an aggregate of four and a half must have been spent in solitary study. It would be quite impossible for a university teacher of philosophy to do that—unless he were a research fellow with no teaching duties; and there are not many of those. So, paradoxically, because I was not in the usual sense of the term a professional philosopher I was able to devote more time to the study of philosophy than all but a handful of professionals. This advantage was compounded by the fact that I was freer than they to choose what I studied. I have already made the point that if you teach philosophy you have to keep abreast of what you are teaching, and this is largely laid down for you by syllabuses and examinations. In practice you have to spend most of your time reading ephemeral secondary literature by contemporary authors, many of them people you know; so neither what you read nor when you read it is up to you. I have been able to ignore all this. I have read in response to genuine need—*what* I wanted, *when* I felt I needed it, or at least had a desire to explore it.

There is a world of difference between the two kinds of reading in the amount one gets out of them, including the extent to which one absorbs them.

With philosophy, as with other kinds of reading, one can come to things at the wrong time. Many of us have had the experience of trying to read a particular novelist and not being able to get on with his books—and then coming back to them some years later and revelling in them. In philosophy, so much depends on what the problems are that you yourself have, and what stage of development you are at in your relationship with them. A philosopher who illuminates those problems on the level you are at with them brings light into your life. If you have not yet got to that point you will not fully understand what you are reading; if you have passed it already it will be of little use to you. If a philosopher is writing about problems which you do not have, and with which he does not succeed in infecting you, you may understand him but are unlikely to find him interesting.

My self-interested tendency has always been to seek new light on problems with which I am struggling. Since only a few philosophers have ever produced thought of that kind it is not surprising that only one or two of them have usually been alive at any given time, and therefore that only one or two are alive now. It would be unreasonable to expect anything else. So, naturally, nearly all of the philosophers that I have devoted myself to studying have been figures of the past. I do of course read a certain amount of new philosophy, but "keeping up with what is going on" seems to me (and I have spent many years trying to do it) a pointless waste of time. The notion, for obvious reasons welcome to practitioners, that what is going on *now,* whenever now is, is superior to what was going on in the past, or is even necessarily "ahead" of what was happening twenty or thirty years ago, is just nonsense. Philosophy does not progress in the way technology progresses. No philosopher for two thousand years after Plato and Aristotle was as good as either of them; and in the two hundred years since Kant no philosopher has been better than Kant. The general truth of such remarks is so self-evident that one would have thought no one seriously concerned with philosophy could make the mistake of assuming that today's philosophy must be an advance on yesterday's; but many do, including large numbers of professionals. The truth is that whoever one is, and at whatever age, and whatever else one may have read, there is more insight to be gained from reading, let us say, Spinoza for the first time, or Schopenhauer for the first time, than anything that has been published in the last thirty years. Anyone who does not understand this does not understand the fundamental nature of philosophy.

For decades, then, I soaked myself in the greatest philosophy ever written while paying little regard to passing fashion. And my work on *Argument* made an unexpected contribution to this. My studies in the Christian faith quickly led me into medieval philosophy, of which I had read scarcely any after St. Augustine (I am referring to the texts themselves—I had read the usual accounts in histories of philosophy) and I found its richness, wide-rangingness, and "modernity" a revelation. So much of it anticipated developments that I had supposed began later. In fact, I now realized, I had scarcely thought of medieval philosophers as philosophers at all, but rather as apologists and propagandists for the Christian religion. However, a great deal of medieval philosophy was not about religion at all, but about logic, conceptual analysis, psychology, mechanics, and a whole range of other topics. The chief reason for its present neglect is that so much of the science-oriented part of it, and also the technical logic, has been overtaken by subsequent developments; but a lot of it was first-rate thinking out of which those developments naturally grew. And some of the metaphysics I found deep in a way that may have been associated in the minds of its authors with their religious beliefs but was not, on analysis, logically dependent on those beliefs. For instance John the Scot in the ninth century, a figure strangely isolated in time and place (Ireland), the only "great" philosopher anywhere in Europe between Augustine in the fifth century and Anselm in the eleventh, produced thought of extraordinary profundity that was capable of bringing illumination a thousand years later to an unbeliever like me.

Among much else John the Scot produced two permanently important arguments. One is to the effect that it is impossible for any sentient being to know, in the sense of understand, its own nature. I believe this to be true, and of immense significance for mankind, though still not widely appreciated. It was to take another eight hundred years before Kant worked out a fully satisfactory demonstration of it. The other, in direct consequence, is that even God does not know his own nature. John has been much mocked for saying this, and dismissed by many, but this means only that his argument has eluded his mockers. It is, I think, valid, and that means that if there is a God it applies to God. It may be that God has other attributes, un-understandable by us, such that this fact about him does not have the significance or the consequences that it would come naturally to us to infer. There may be reasons why it is beside the point, or is swallowed up and lost in other considerations, so that it has nothing like the meaning that we suppose; but, nevertheless, true it must be. John was a person of astounding gifts, not to mention the qualities of character he must also have had, and I was curious about him. But as regards his religion an unbeliever I remained. Here was exciting philosophy that was new to me, but the religious baggage that its author believed came along with it obstinately refused to arouse much interest on my part.

Some of my readers may find themselves thinking that the mere fact that millions of human beings, including many highly intelligent and deeply thoughtful ones, have had strongly held religious beliefs is itself a reason for giving them serious intellectual attention—not necessarily for believing them, of course, but for finding them interesting and for treating them with respect. I would agree with this if the reasons given for them commanded respect. But I have yet to encounter such reasons. What are claimed as proofs are not proofs, and all such "proofs" have long since been discredited, the most important of them by Christians themselves, such as Kant. Yet they go on being trotted out: assertions are made without evidence; mutually contradictory claims proliferate; historical knowledge is defied; mistranslations abound; language is used in a way that slithers unacknowledged between literal meaning and metaphor; the whole vocabulary rests on unsecured presuppositions. Superstitions and belief in magic are perennial in just the same way as religion, and something near to being universal among mankind; and *why* this is so may be interesting, but in most cases the beliefs themselves are devoid of interesting content, at least to me.

It is not the case that a belief is worthy of respect, or is even interesting, merely because it is widely held, though *that* it is widely held may give one food for thought. Of the religions I studied, the one I found least worthy of intellectual respect was Judaism. I have no desire to offend any of my readers, but the truth is that while reading foundational Jewish texts I often found myself thinking: "How can anyone possibly believe this?" When I put that question to Jewish friends they often said that no intelligent Jew did. To quote the precise words of one: "There's not a single intelligent Jew in the country who believes the religion." What they do believe, they tell me, is that it is desirable that traditional observances should be kept by at least some Jews because it is these observances more than anything else that give the Jewish people its identity, and therefore its cohesion; but that the doctrinal content or implications of the observances are not expected to be taken with full intellectual seriousness by intelligent people.

The religion I found the most attractive was Buddhism. There are many different varieties of it, and I know too little about any of them to say much, but it did seem to me that some of them were genuinely insightful and genuinely profound. These did not assert the existence of a God, or of a soul, or of immortality, and yet they confidently dismissed the claims of commonsense realism as trivial and wrong. If I may so put it, Buddhism came across to me as an agnostic religion, one that often did justice to the difficulty and complexity of fundamental questions facing human beings (which commonsense realism hopelessly fails to do) without attempting to impose dogmatic answers. It occurs often in philosophy that there is more insight in the formulation of a problem than in any of the proposed solutions to it; and it seemed to me that recognition of this was a distinctive characteristic of Buddhism. In this respect it is the opposite of the Christianity I have been acquainted with all my life. My most strongly rooted objection to Christianity is that its explanations fail so abysmally to take the measure of the mysteries they purport to illuminate: they offer simple-minded interpretations when what we are confronted with are almost impenetrable ignorance and bafflement. But I have this problem, if in lesser degree, with all religions, even the most attractive. They tell us things, but I find myself thinking: "How do they know? *Perhaps* what they say is true. I would like it to be. And it would be nice if it were. But what reason do they have for saying that it is?" And I have never heard a convincing answer to that question. People hold religious belief for umpteen different kinds of reason: because they have a deep conviction of its truth, or because it provides a welcome explanation of their experience, or makes them feel better, or comforts them, or makes them members of a sympathetic social group, or because they imbibed it at an uncritical age—or for goodness knows how many other reasons; but from none of these does it follow that the belief is true. And although I have pressed the question often enough I have never received an answer that really is an *answer*. In the end it usually comes down to one thing: people want to believe. But this has nothing to do with truth. Something I have had occasion to say many times is that ignorance is not a licence to believe what we like: it is ignorance, and renders believing what we like unjustified.

The two main positive things I got out of my period of religious study were that I learnt to find my way around medieval philosophy, and that I discovered enough about Buddhism to regard it as the most impressive of the major religions, more so than Christianity, which appeared crude by comparison. The big negative thing was that the (perhaps unconsciously hoped for) life-transforming step from recognizing the inherent inadequacy of philosophy to embracing religious thinking was one I could not make. I am told that in medieval universities students first of all studied philosophy and then graduated to theology if they were thought to be clever enough. I did not make the transition. For me neither the desire nor any sign of justification was there; and if the desire had been there, there would still have been no sign of any justification.

So on the central question I was no further forward. Worse, what might before have been perceived as options were closing. I knew of no unread philosophy that might conceivably carry me on its back into a new country of the mind. I did not have the genius to make such a journey unaided—to be the next great philosopher myself. The arts, though I valued them more highly than philosophy and always had, could not substitute for it. And I could not help still looking on religion as essentially a cop-out, for all its beguiling but incidental merits. So now I was unmoving, becalmed in the middle of the ocean of life without rudder or compass; I could see no prospect but to remain there, perhaps for several decades, in the middle of nowhere, until I died.

Words cannot express the appalled and appalling emotions that overcame me. The chief was a kind of claustrophobia of the spirit: I felt blocked, stifled, straitjacketed, bound, gagged, taped, unable to move even so much as an eye-brow. It was horrific. Indeed, it was intolerable, and I felt it to be so in a literal sense of the word: the conviction took control that I would not be able to go on living like this. I do not mean I became suicidal: I did not. The feeling was that my life had reached the limits of livability and was about to stop of its own accord, in the way a fire goes out when the fuel supply ends—that I would have a heart attack, or something of that sort, and die. And this seemed to me a fact, not merely a possibility. In the early summer of 1972, when I was forty-two, I knew in my bones that I was not going to live beyond the follow-ing winter.

I have since read that heart attacks can be psychosomatic, that they can hap-pen to people who are convinced in the kernel of their being that they cannot go on living any longer. The examples I read of concerned some of the pris-oners in arctic slave-labour camps in the ultimate depths of winter. My read-ers may smile at even so much as the whisper of such a comparison, but I believe it to be a fact that if I had not found an escape, and soon, I would not have survived for long. In some deep-lying way I had come to the end of the tolerability of a life whose horizons were bounded by this world. The claus-trophobia of it was more than I could bear, and I could feel my spirit dying of suffocation. What changed everything at the very last moment was reading the last of the so-called great philosophers that was left for me to read. Even more peculiar than the fact that he, of all philosophers, should be the only one left is the fact that this was not the first time I had attempted to read him: I had tried half a dozen years before, and persisted, but got nowhere, and given up.

20

The Discovery
of Schopenhauer

One day in May 1966 I was browsing in a bookshop when my eye happened to fall on a book called *Schopenhauer* by Patrick Gardiner. It was one of a series of introductions to philosophers under the general editorship of A. J. Ayer. I had read other books in the series, so I knew the sort of thing it was likely to be. The astonished thought hit me that I knew nothing at all about Schopenhauer: his name was known to every educated person, yet I had never read him. There was no other philosopher of whom that was true. So I thought it was time I learnt something. I picked up the book, browsed in it for a while, found the style clear and the tone agreeable, and bought it.

The very sight of the book made me feel guilty about my ignorance of Schopenhauer for a reason that had not occurred to me before. Since childhood I had had a special interest in Wagner, and nearly every general book about Wagner makes the point that the biggest non-musical influence in his life was the philosophy of Schopenhauer. But all such books as I had read had done this without attempting to tell the reader what the influence consisted in—so I had no serious conception of what it was. Even the doyen of Wagner scholars, Ernest Newman, at no point in his writings attempts a serious characterization of Schopenhauer's philosophy. Indeed, it was from his work that I had derived the false impression of Schopenhauer that I was now to find I possessed, namely that he was an impenetrably boring German metaphysician of a type similar to, let us say, Schelling. And just as I had known for years that Schelling had had an influence on a wide range of romantic artists whose work I enjoyed, from Weber to Coleridge, without this giving me the slightest desire to read him (and when I did read him it was not for this reason), so with Schopenhauer: I had accepted the fact of his influence on Wagner without this giving me any consciously felt curiosity to read his work. And I felt suddenly ashamed of that, and puzzled by it. Now that I had taken the decision to gain some acquaintance with him I was at a loss to understand how it was possible for this not to have happened before, and I felt not only ashamed but baffled by my own lack of curiosity—it seemed out of character. At bottom, I believe, it must have had something to do with my general attitude to art.

I do not regard art as an intellectual activity, and I do not believe that conceptual thinking has much to do with what matters most about a work of art: in other words, I do not think it has anything to do with whether it is good art or bad art. Of course artists think conceptually in the course of creating their work. But how good they are as conceptual thinkers has nothing to do with how good the art is. The familiar terms "academic painter" and "academic art" imply an artist who is well informed about the theory, the history, the aesthetics, and so on, of his art, and may be an excellent teacher of it, but is not himself a very gifted artist. And there are large numbers of such persons. Furthermore, art that is meant to convey a religious or political message may be produced by a highly intelligent person who is a genuine believer in, and intellectual master of, the thought-system involved, and still be poor art. Most such art is, I think; and there is a huge amount of it. Artists frequently espouse theories, aesthetic theories; but I do not believe that quality can derive from theory. In fact I believe that the relationship between artists' attachment to theory and their quality as artists is usually one of inverse proportion: the more attached they are to theory the less good they are as artists. I also believe that their theories are almost always rationalizations, and that their art, in so far as it is genuine art, is motivated artistically, not conceptually, and that their attempt to express what they are doing in terms of words and ideas is superfluous, and often erroneous. The ideas to which an artist is drawn are those that meet his needs *as an artist,* so even if he formulates or adopts the ideas before producing the works of art it is still art that decides his ideas and not the other way about. This is why you do not need to read Schelling to understand Coleridge, even though Coleridge appropriated, not to say plagiarized, large chunks of Schelling. The Schelling that Coleridge used is the Schelling that Coleridge needed for his own purposes, and these purposes are realized in his work.

All these things I felt with regard to Schopenhauer and Wagner. I did not believe I could be missing anything of artistic importance in Wagner through not knowing Schopenhauer. The same is true, for that matter, of other influences on Wagner, including even artistic ones. It so happened that I knew something about the influence of Aeschylus's *Oresteia* on his conceptualization of the *Ring,* but it did not occur to me to consider it essential for someone to know Aeschylus in order to understand and appreciate Wagner. The whole tradition of German romantic opera before Wagner, the tradition culminating in Weber, fed massively into Wagner's works, but it is not in the least necessary to have seen Weber's operas to enjoy Wagner's. This is partly a view of art and partly a view of the nature of influence. And it applies not only in art but in intellectual life. The philosophy of Karl Marx, for instance, is an explicit variation on Hegelianism, but many people have had a genuine understanding of Marxism without having read a word of Hegel.

Even so, and despite everything I have been able to say in my own defence, now that I was directly confronted by such a long-standing lack of curiosity I found it not easy to understand. After all, most writers on Wagner are specialists in music but not in philosophy, and it would not be reasonable to expect them to have studied Schopenhauer, whereas my love of philosophy was surpassed only by my love of music and theatre. And for years I had been actively looking for new philosophers to learn from. That this combination of factors had not brought me to Schopenhauer before caused me to wonder whether I might have had an unconscious unwillingness to deal in philosophical—in the true sense of philosophical—interpretations of Wagner's work. It was as if I had been in love with two women at the same time and—though not quite admitting it to myself—had not wanted them to meet.

Patrick Gardiner is a unique figure among Oxford philosophers of the middle and late twentieth century. The natural homeland of his intellectual life is what is often dubbed (not by me and not, I think, by him) German romantic philosophy—Fichte, Schelling, Hegel, Schopenhauer. His detailed knowledge is not confined to them: he knows a great deal about Kant, from whom they derived, and also about some of the philosophers who reacted against them, notably Kierkegaard. But except for Kant none of these writers has been read by most of his colleagues; and for the greater part of his career they were not accorded even elementary respect—indeed, Kierkegaard was not regarded as a philosopher at all. So Gardiner has followed his bent to an unusual degree in isolation. At the same time, he is trained and adept in the philosophical logic of his place and period, so his distinctive contribution has been to bring the armoury of analytic philosophy to bear on those particular philosophers. He analyses, expounds, and criticizes them in the sort of way he might if he were writing about Ryle or Wittgenstein. I suspect it is because they are written in this way that his books about Schopenhauer and Kierkegaard have been read as widely as they have by his professional colleagues: Gardiner has done a great deal to bring these philosophers to the attention of people who would otherwise have ignored them. But for all his gifts his work is subject to the limitations inherent in the analytic approach: it remains for the most part on the level of language and logic.

Isaiah Berlin once said something of the utmost significance in this connection. "The central visions of the great philosophers are essentially simple. The elaboration comes not in what I have, in perhaps too short-hand a fashion, called their models of the world, not in the patterns in terms of which they saw the nature and life of men and of the world, but in defending these conceptions against real or imaginary objections. There, of course, a great deal of ingenuity and a lot of technical language come in; but this is only the elaborate armament, the engines of war on the battlements, to fend off every possible adversary: the citadel itself is not complex: argument, logical power are, as a rule, a matter of attack and defence, not part of the central vision itself."* I do not for one moment agree that the central visions of, shall we say, Spinoza and Kant are essentially simple—on the contrary, I think they are exceedingly difficult to grasp—but nevertheless Berlin is saying something of great moment in the rest of his statement, namely that nearly all the conceptual and logical analysis, and detailed argument generally, with which less-than-great philosophers tend to preoccupy themselves are not central to the subject. Both the philosophers and the arguments are outside the citadel, on the battlements, making more or less skilful use of a lavish and intricate armoury. And I am afraid this applies to Gardiner's book on Schopenhauer. It clearly sets forth arguments and counter-arguments, considers objections and counter-objections, conjures up some of the point-missing criticisms an opponent might utter, and then answers them—but somehow the central vision is not there. I do not see how it would be possible, on the basis of Gardiner's book, to understand how it could come about that Schopenhauer had a life-transforming effect on so great a creative artist as Richard Wagner, or on so radically original a thinker as Nietzsche, and bowled Tolstoy off his feet, and hugely influenced the work of geniuses like Turgenev, Proust, Conrad, and Hardy. Iris Murdoch once complained that the world as envisaged by Gilbert Ryle was not one in which people fell in love or joined the Communist Party: Schopenhauer's is indeed such a world, full-bloodedly so, but Gardiner-on-Schopenhauer is not, it is Rylean.

Perhaps partly for this reason the quotations leapt at me out of the book in a way I have experienced neither before nor since: it was as if they flew up into my face off the page. When I read the words "the solution of the riddle of the world is only possible through the proper connection of outer with inner experience" it was as if someone had switched a light on inside my head. I became excited, and although continuing to read the book with care I began also

---

* *Men of Ideas,* p. 41.

to keep looking ahead to see when the next quotation was coming up. Some of Schopenhauer's comments on particular philosophers seemed to me marvellous; for instance on Spinoza: "To call the world 'God' is not to explain it, it is only to enrich our language with a superfluous synonym for the word 'world.' " His psychological penetration: "In order to deceive themselves, men pre-arrange seeming instances of precipitancy, which are really secretly considered actions." His profound images, as deep as those of Shakespeare: "We find our selves like a hollow glass globe, from whose vacancy a voice speaks." His analogies: "The man of talent is like the marksman who hits a mark the others cannot hit, the man of genius like the marksman who hits a mark they cannot even see." His invective, for example against imitative artists: "They suck their nourishment, like parasite plants, from the works of others, and like polyps they become the colour of their food." These things lit up the sky for me, and I rushed out to get Schopenhauer's works; and the moment I had finished Gardiner I plunged into them.

Alas, I made no headway. As soon as I started to read the man himself—his acknowledged masterpiece *The World as Will and Representation*—it all became different: heavy paragraphs, occluded arguments, sticky going. The quotations in Gardiner had seemed to blow out at me like an exhilarating wind from a world different from Kant's, but now that I was reading Schopenhauer direct I seemed to be back in Kant's world, yet not getting any further forward than Kant had taken me. Again, I cannot explain it. I now understand, in a way I did not then, that the philosophy of Schopenhauer starts from Kant, discards what it feels to be mistaken, keeps what it sees as important, and goes on from there to complete Kant's programme as thus reformulated; so in the early stages it is, inevitably, mostly Kant. What I still do not see is why that should have been an obstacle to me, since I was so familiar with Kant's work; or why I should have found Schopenhauer difficult to read. But I did. I tried to kick-start myself by absorbing treatments of Schopenhauer's ideas from other sources: histories of philosophy, dictionaries and encyclopaedias, essays; and in these second-hand versions I became familiar with them; but my engine refused to ignite. In the end I gave up. All I can conjecture is that because, six years later, when I did find myself responding to Schopenhauer, it was more in the way one normally does to a work of art than to a set of philosophical ideas, I was not yet ready for him. This kind of unreadiness is more familiar to us in our relationship to artistic than intellectual work. It is also more familiar to us with creative work than with study, and I may have been developing subliminally a need to write about these things myself. For whatever reasons, I put Schopenhauer aside for several years. During that period I regarded him as someone whose ideas I knew something about, and whose works were therefore not going to contain any surprises for me, despite the fact that I had not read his books.

By the spring of 1972 I was in the state described at the end of the last chapter—desperate. My feelings of frustration caused a physical reaction, a need to fly away and not be pinned down, to travel without constraint or plan or itinerary, just to be free. I packed a suitcase and took off for one of the Greek islands, where a family I knew had a house. After a stay with them I went to visit A. J. Ayer in his converted windmill in the south of France. From there I went to a former girlfriend who was spending the summer with her children in a deserted farmhouse not far away. (All of these friends, I hasten to say, had been pressing me with invitations to come and stay.) When I left the girlfriend I started knocking around in the south of France by myself.

I have mentioned that when I went on an extended journey I was in the habit of taking with me a single large, often difficult book that I might get the opportunity of reading in long, uninterrupted stretches. This time I had thought I might try again with *The World as Will and Representation:* it was six years since I had looked at it, so I put the two volumes in my suitcase. Now, I began to read it. And this time the experience was the direct opposite of the previous time. Not only did the book speak to me: it was as if it were speaking to me alone.

I have had only one other experience to compare with it in my life, but so similar was this that it may be worth recounting. When as a child I first heard of Mahler my father told me there was only one conductor for Mahler and that was Bruno Walter. I then discovered that this was the generally held view, just as it seemed to be agreed by everyone that the only conductor for Delius was Beecham. So I listened to broadcasts of Walter conducting Mahler. And the music meant nothing to me at all. It was just one meaningless phrase followed by another: the phrases themselves seemed to me without content, just arbitrary successions of notes; and I could hear no connections between them, either. The music sounded to me incoherent in the literal sense of that word. I would occasionally come back to it for another try, but it went on sounding like that to me until my late twenties. Then one day I went to an all-Mahler concert conducted by Otto Klemperer. And it was as if someone had fitted my brain with an unscrambler: the phrases had shape and point, and were piercingly expressive, each relating with absolute rightness to what came before and after. Everything fitted together, the music *cohered,* and was amazingly beautiful. Now, for the first time, it spoke to me, and in a voice unlike any other. I was transfixed. The whole experience was the aural equivalent of having a blindfold removed and finding oneself confronted by a wonderful sight. To this day, that evening remains one of the most memorable of my life. After it I went round looking for all the Mahler I could find. His music became one of the most treasured possessions I had. I then found it impossible to understand how it could have meant nothing at all to me for so many years. Even

Bruno Walter's performances meant something to me now, though I never cared for them much. And when I found myself listening to the great Mahler symphonies conducted by Jascha Horenstein they sounded to me as beautiful as any music there was.

Something corresponding to this happened to me with *The World as Will and Representation*. It was as if my hearing had been restored. Never have I had the feeling of being so directly and vividly in personal contact with an author: Arthur Schopenhauer was in the room there with me, sitting in front of me, talking to me, his hand on my arm or my knee, coining each new-minted phrase as he uttered it. This effect developed slowly, took hold of me only gradually: I read some of the book almost desultorily in Greece, then more in Avignon—and then came an unforgettable period of more than a week in Aix-en-Provence when I spent the whole of each day just sitting in my hotel room reading, emerging only briefly into the external world at lunch time for a stroll and something to eat, and again at night to spend hours loafing at open-air café tables in the summer darkness digesting what I had been reading. No other book has had so great an effect on my outlook, unless it be Kant's *Critique of Pure Reason*—and then it is a Kant that was given new life for me by Schopenhauer. Schopenhauer's intention was that the two books should merge together to form a single philosophy, and for me they have. Unless I make a conscious effort to draw the distinction for purposes of communication there are no longer two separate philosophies in my mind, Kant's and Schopenhauer's, but a single Kantian-Schopenhauerian philosophy which I regard as the most mind-stretching, capacious, illuminating and penetrating system of philosophical ideas that has yet been forged by human minds. I look at it, in other words, rather in the way Schopenhauer did, and as he hoped others would; and because of this I have sometimes slipped into discussing Kant's philosophy in Schopenhauer's terminology when this was at odds with Kant's—it is a thing I have to make a conscious effort to avoid.

Schopenhauer believed, along with a great many other people then and since, that Kant's most important insight was that what we human beings can think, perceive, know, experience, or be aware of in any way at all depends not only on what the reality is with which we have to deal but also on the apparatus we have for doing those things—our human bodies with their senses, nervous systems and brains. If this equipment can deal with something, it is by virtue of that fact an object of possible experience for us. As such it does not need to be a physical object: it can be all sorts of other things—the content of someone else's conversation, a piece of music or mathematics, the taste of fish, a thought, a memory, an intention, a belief, or any one of what is actually an indefinite number of other kinds of something. But whatever these are, the totality of them constitutes the outer limit of what we can have any thought or awareness of. However, it does not follow from this that it is also the outer limit of what exists. What is just *is,* I presume, independently of us and the apparatus with which we happen to find ourselves equipped; and we have no grounds whatsoever for believing that reality, the totality of what exists, coincides with what we are able to apprehend—and nor could we ever have any such grounds, for that would involve our being able to see on both sides of a line when that line is, as we have just said, an outer limit.

The fact is that anything that can possibly exist at all may exist and be outside the limits of all possible apprehension by us, and we can never know it. All we can know is limited to what our bodies can mediate. One may think, as I do, that it would be a simply incredible coincidence if what happens to be apprehensible by us happens also to coincide with the totality of what there is. To believe that it does goes against all common sense, all reason, and all the odds. It could not have a straightforward explanation in terms of evolutionary biology, because we are merely one of unnumberable thousands of different species which have developed widely differing sorts of physical equipment for surviving in the same tiny physical environment on, or not far under, the surface of this globe of ours. Many of the others have sensory equipment we do not have; and some of those that do have senses like ours have them in much more powerful and discriminating forms. Beyond all that, we have no way at all of knowing what lies outside the limits of our astronomy, nor has there yet been any possibility of our human equipment adapting itself to that, though it may have to one day. The only plausible possibility of a reality completely corresponding to our conceptions of it rests on the possibility that reality itself could be mind-like, or could be created by a mind, or by minds. Paradoxically, it is those philosophers who most confidently do *not* believe this, that is to say those in the empiricist tradition, who are most tightly wedded to an epistemological criterion of reality. That is one of the incoherences of their position.

The limit of human knowledge consists not only of a boundary beyond which we cannot apprehend anything. What we can and do apprehend within that boundary is also of a limited nature, though in a different way. If I look smack at the Empire State Building, head-on, I may feel that I am in the most immediate and direct possible contact with it—there it is, right there, straight in front of me, the Empire State Building, and I am looking at it right now—but the fact remains that it does not pop into my head. What is inside my head is not the Empire State Building but a set of visual data which I interpret as being the Empire State Building. The same is true of tactile data. The process of feeling a physical object—or, even more so, bumping into it—has something especially thingy about it, and can easily tempt us into believing that here is the brute reality of an independently existing world, the thing as it actually is; but of course such feelings of bumpings are as inside the head as visual data are, and as brain-dependent in the mode of their existence.

All our sensory perception of the external world is of this character. The direct and immediate awareness is in our brains, and must take a brain-dependent form to be awareness-material at all. This is what experience is: it is something in our brains and central nervous systems. But if there is a reality that exists independently of brains (and nearly all of us believe that there is) then it cannot exist in forms that are brain-dependent—despite the fact that these are the only ways in which we can apprehend it or form any notion of it. The world of our experience must in some fundamental, categorial way be radically different from independent reality. So as far as our knowledge of objects goes there must be at least two realms, one of things as mediated to us by our apparatus and the other of whatever actually is, independent of all such brain and body operations. And it is only of *things as they appear to us* that we can have any knowledge or awareness: whatever it is that they are in themselves must for ever remain inaccessible to us human beings.

These wonderful insights of Kant's constitute the core of what is known as transcendental idealism. They have, of course, been very much worked over since his day, constructively criticized, and developed. The most immediately famous of his successors—Fichte, Schelling, and Hegel—took the view that if so-called reality as it is in itself is beyond all possibility of apprehension then we can never have adequate grounds for asserting that there is any such thing. In keeping with this Fichte pushed Kant's Copernican revolution to its limits by evolving a philosophy in which the entire phenomenal world is explained not as the manifestation of an independent reality but as the creation of the ego, which both as perceiving subject and as moral agent creates a world for itself. This is idealism with a vengeance, perhaps the most thoroughgoingly idealist position that can be associated with a philosopher of note. Most of Fichte's writing is difficult to a point of near-unreadability, but he did make one attempt to express his central ideas in a book that was aimed at the general educated public, *The Vocation of Man*. Published in 1800, it is short—less than two hundred pages in most editions—and in my view a fine book, abounding in insights from which everyone can learn, including those who do not go along with the main thrust of Fichte's philosophy.

Schelling's writings are marked by an unnecessary obscurity not unlike most of Fichte's. In those days, as now, academic philosophers in Germany were frightened of losing the esteem of their professional colleagues if they wrote in a way that non-professionals would understand and want to read. Indeed, it was only because Fichte had been sacked from his academic job, and thought he was henceforth going to have to earn his living by writing, that he wrote *The Vocation of Man*. Schelling wrote no such book. Worse, he kept on changing his views, so there is not one Schelling philosophy but a succession of differing philosophies from the same pen. The most famous and influential was his *Naturphilosophie, The Philosophy of Nature*. Its central idea is that the empirical world is one single, ever-evolving entity within which, first, organic life emerged out of inorganic Nature, and then went on to develop successively as plant life, animal life, and human life. The main points here are that reality is not a state of affairs but an endlessly dynamic process of change, and that human beings have emerged wholly *within* that process and as an inherent part of it. They are matter become spiritual. But although one can thus think of human beings as spiritualized matter, equally one can think of Nature as materialized spirit, or latent spirit. The goal of this single upward-developing process is the achievement by Nature of self-awareness, and it attains this in the highest activities of mankind. The area of human life in which the highest levels of self-awareness are reached, including an understanding of the essential one-ness of human beings with the rest of what is, is creative art. Thus the ultimate aim of the existence of everything is realized in the creation of great works of art, and great artists are the incarnation of that part of total reality that reveals to itself the reasons for its own existence.

This philosophy had enormous appeal to the romantic movement, with which it was contemporary. The most characteristic thought of the seventeenth and eighteenth centuries had seen the natural world as an object submitted to man as knowing subject and would-be master, and had glorified the intellect as the means whereby both knowledge and mastery were achieved. But here was a revolt that overthrew that. Man was now seen as being at one with Nature, sharing with it the spirituality of his innermost being, which indeed was derived from it; intellect was dethroned; mathematics, science, and technology were devalued; art was asserted as "the highest" and made the object of what were in fact religious attitudes; the creative artist was seen as not just heroic but godlike. In the age of Beethoven and Byron, and the rebellion of the human spirit against the apocalyptic excesses of the First Industrial Revolution, here was the philosophy some of the rebels were waiting for. It was seized on not only by leading German romantics—Goethe, Weber, Hölderlin, Novalis—but in England by Coleridge, who plundered Schelling's works wholesale. Thus Schelling became the emblematic philosopher of the romantic movement. Many romantic artists regarded him as having organized into a philosophical system, that is to say a system of conceptual thought, fundamental truths that were expressed in other ways by works of art.

Schelling's philosophy of Nature saw matter and mind (or spirit) as interfused, alternative manifestations of the same thing, two aspects of a single world-process. Hegel's philosophy was in many ways similar to Schelling's, but was more unequivocally monistic. He too saw reality as essentially a process, but as one undergone by something that was a unity, and was mind-like or spirit-like rather than material. His word for the stuff of which reality consists was *Geist,* and unfortunately there is no satisfactory equivalent for this in English: it is, so to speak, midway between mind and spirit; more mental than spirit, more spiritual than mind. We use the German word *Zeitgeist* to mean the spirit of the time (*Zeit* meaning time) and in that form at least it is widely known among English-speakers. I suppose that most people who are religious and take their religious beliefs seriously think that all reality is ultimately spiritual; and those of us who are not religious are familiar with that thought in this context—and this in turn may help us to get a grip on it in Hegel's case. He believed that total reality consists of a single something, *Geist,* which is going through a process of change and development towards a goal of self-knowledge. But there are important differences from Schelling. First, Hegel had a specific doctrine about the pattern of development: it was, he said, dialectical. Every movement created an opposition to itself, every action evoked a reaction, and each such clash of opposing forces found resolution in a new, third state of affairs that carried the process forward—thereby, inevitably, evoking a new reaction. Thus, putting his technical terms for these successive stages into italics, he taught that every *thesis* inevitably conjures its own *antithesis* into being, and that the incompatibility between these two gives rise to a conflict which is resolved by a *synthesis*—which, because it then brings its own antithesis into being, becomes the thesis of a new triad. Two important points about the dialectic are, first, it shows that change, though perpetual, is not arbitrary but takes a rationally intelligible form; and second, it shows that change inherently involves conflict. The goal of self-knowledge towards which the world-process is developing is more philosophically cognitive with Hegel than with Schelling: it is the mind's (or spirit's) coming to recognize itself as the ultimate reality. Until that culmination of true self-knowledge is reached it will remain perpetually in some degree of alienation, mistaking what are in fact aspects of itself for elements standing in opposition to it.

These ideas have had incalculable effects on Western thought as a direct or indirect result of Hegel's influence: the notion of reality as a historical process, the idea of dialectical change, and the concept of alienation, are among the most influential ideas of the last two hundred years. The young Karl Marx was a Hegelian, and when he became a socialist in his mid-twenties he kept all the trappings of Hegelianism but harnessed them to a different horse. He too announced that reality was essentially a process of perpetual change, and therefore that everything needed to be understood historically if it was to be understood at all; that this unceasing change proceeded dialectically; that it had a goal; that the goal was maximal self-awareness, which would confer maximal freedom; and that until this was attained we would remain in a state of alienation. However, he saw all this as happening not to mind or spirit but to matter. I once tried to express it by saying that it was as if he had taken over a whole page of equations from Hegel, substituted a different value for x, but kept the equations themselves the same. A more dramatic way of putting it would be to say that he, the supreme materialist among thinkers of the modern era, took over the thought-system of the most famous of all the idealists and turned it upside down. He himself said, famously, that he had stood Hegel on his head. He never attempted to disguise the all-pervadingly Hegelian character of his thought, and for the rest of his life he continued, as when young, to express his ideas in Hegel's terminology. He called his philosophy "dialectical materialism," which to anyone familiar with Hegelianism is a well-distilled description.

When Schopenhauer discovered philosophy at university the outstanding philosophers then living were Fichte, Schelling and Hegel. Schopenhauer matriculated into the University of Göttingen in 1809 at the age of twenty-one—into the medical faculty, it so happens, but in his second year he changed to philosophy. And for his third year he changed universities and went to the University of Berlin, because that is where Fichte was. For two years he attended Fichte's lectures (and in the second of these years also those of Schleiermacher, whose reputation as a theologian continues to this day). He came to the conclusion that Fichte was not a genuine philosopher but a charlatan, someone using philosophy to make his name in the world. Fichte, he concluded, had perceived that the fact that Kant's philosophy was too difficult for most people to understand and yet was everywhere accepted as profound opened an opportunity for someone else to come along and put forward a philosophy which was too obscure to be understood and would be accepted as profound; and the very fact that it was too obscure to be understood would mask the fact that it was largely empty of content. People would think, in effect: "Here is another Kant"; or "Here is Kant's successor." Fichte was aiming precisely at having this effect, believed Schopenhauer: he was a sham, a rhetorician, a performer. Of course, to pull the trick off it was necessary for him to have an extensive knowledge of philosophy, so there was *something* there; but not very much; and it was all being exploited to corrupt ends.

In the course of time Schopenhauer came to feel the same about Schelling and Hegel. In the two-volume collection of his essays published in 1851 under the title *Parerga and Paralipomena* he wrote (vol. i, p. 21 of the English edition): "Fichte, Schelling and Hegel are in my opinion not philosophers, for they lack the first requirement of a philosopher, namely a seriousness and honesty of enquiry. They are merely sophists who wanted to appear to be, rather than to be, something. They sought not truth but their own interest and advancement in the world. Appointments from governments, fees and royalties from students and publishers—and, as a means to that end, the greatest possible show and sensation in their sham philosophy—such were the guiding stars and inspiring genii of those disciples of wisdom. And so they have not passed the entrance examination, and cannot be admitted into the venerable company of thinkers for the human race. Nevertheless they have excelled in one thing, in the art of beguiling the public and of passing themselves off for what they are not; and this undoubtedly requires talent, yet not philosophical."

As the brief remarks I have made about the ideas of Fichte, Schelling and Hegel will have been enough to indicate, I do not share Schopenhauer's view of them. There was, nevertheless, a lot of truth in that view. The three philosophers in question were career academics, and the universities in which they earned their bread were run by government officials. The Prussian state was not exactly liberal. If I were to look for a rough parallel to their position in my own lifetime it would be nearer to that of academics in totalitarian societies than in democracies. Unquestionably they were self-promoters, and they played ball with the people in power; but they were in a genuinely difficult situation, and their unscrupulousness in the methods they used to advance their ideas should not be too easily condemned. All of them, in my opinion, had genuinely valuable things to say and insights to convey—perhaps Fichte more than the others—and all had important historical influence as well as intrinsic merit. They are worth knowing something about. Having said that, I have to admit that the three main intellectual arguments that Schopenhauer brought against them were all valid.

First, he accused them of debauching language. Instead of writing as clearly as they could they deliberately chose to be obscure, because they wanted to impress. They put whatever they had to say into long, convoluted sentences full of abstract nouns and technical terms, sentences which it is difficult for even the most intelligent readers to think their way through clearly—though, when they have, it is surprising how often it turns out that not much has been said, and the little that has been is really quite ordinary. There is nothing, claimed Schopenhauer, about either the German language or the subject matter of philosophy to justify this opaqueness in the writing. Kant happened to be a bad writer who lacked a musical ear and was scribbling in a hurry to get his thoughts down on paper before he died, desperately trying to find ways of expressing profound ideas that were radically different from anything anyone had expressed before, and doing it in a language that had never yet been used for any such purpose. The only great German philosopher before him, Leibniz, had written always in either Latin or French. So Kant was compelled to pioneer terminology as well as philosophy. The result is an appallingly written prose that is not, however, obscure in the rhetorical, sacerdotal, incantatory way in which Fichte, Schelling and Hegel are obscure (if anything it is somewhat dry) but is just plain difficult to understand. In philosophy difficulty is not at all the same thing as obscurity. The prose style of Hume is so clear that more than one philosopher since has taken it as his model of clarity, and yet some of the ideas that Hume expressed in this model style are so difficult to understand that even now, more than two and a half centuries later, they are quite commonly not grasped. Kant's most fundamental ideas, which took off from Hume's as their starting point, are even more difficult to understand, and he had none of Hume's gifts of exposition. There is nothing inauthentic about Kant, nothing of the oracle, nothing of the performer, nothing of the poseur. He is honesty of purpose itself. But he is not much of a communicator, and his mind moves on a level of abstraction on which most readers find it difficult to secure a foothold. So he is not at all a model for anyone else, nor—and this is most important—is he an excuse. To anyone looking for a model, Schopenhauer was one of those who would point to Hume as the exemplar of how to write with optimal clarity and elegance about problems of the utmost profundity and difficulty, and he consciously set himself to write German in the same way as Hume wrote English. The result is prose of unexampled lucidity and wit, generally regarded in the German-speaking world as some of the best German that has ever been written.

The second intellectual indictment brought by Schopenhauer against Fichte, Schelling and Hegel was that they debauched logic as much as they debauched language. Knowingly and deliberately they exploit the obscurity of their style to try and slip pseudo-demonstrations past the reader, lulling him into accepting that one thing follows from another when, on a clear presentation, it does not. They *assert* that this follows from that, but as often as not the assertion is untrue, and very frequently it is ridiculous. At the level of logical argument their writing proceeds not, to speak metaphorically, a, therefore b, therefore c, therefore d, but a, therefore k, therefore d, therefore z; but it is all so clogged in impenetrable sentences that when the reader finds himself, perhaps to his surprise, at z, he would prefer to take it on trust that he got there by logically justifiable steps than attempt to go back through that rebarbative prose over the whole argument. This double exploitation of confusion, on levels of logic and language simultaneously, incensed Schopenhauer: he saw it as the most destructive of intellectual crimes. In particular he grieved over its effect on the young, on students who were having their brains addled by it for life. Hegel in particular he hated for this, and described him as "that clumsy and nauseating charlatan, that pernicious person, who completely disorganized and ruined the minds of a whole generation" (*Parerga and Paralipomena*, vol. i, p. 168). Those among the young who were sharp-witted enough to see through what was happening to them were at the greatest risk of being trained in the ways of intellectual dishonesty and turned into Artful Dodgers, the criminal masterminds of the ensuing generation. Schopenhauer was firmly of the opinion that bad thinking drives out good and, because it perpetrates harm, must not be ignored but has to be fought to the death. On almost any square foot of ground in the landscape of his writings a geyser of wrath may suddenly erupt, spewing out imprecations against the same three men. "What was senseless and without meaning at once took refuge in obscure exposition and language. Fichte was the first to grasp and make use of this privilege; Schelling at best equalled him in this, and a host of hungry scribblers without intellect or honesty soon surpassed them both. But the greatest effrontery in serving up sheer nonsense, in scrabbling together senseless and maddening webs of words, such as had previously been heard only in madhouses, finally appeared in Hegel . . ." (*The World as Will and Representation,* vol i, p. 429). Hegel, said Schopenhauer, was "a commonplace, inane, loathsome, repulsive and ignorant charlatan, who with unparalleled effrontery compiled a system of crazy nonsense that was trumpeted abroad as immortal wisdom by his mercenary followers . . ." (*Parerga and Paralipomena,* vol. i, p. 96).

I do not think anything in the whole history of philosophy compares with this invective by one now world-famous philosopher against another, especially when one considers that they were near-contemporaries and colleagues. (If we try to conjure up in imagination a credible example more nearly contemporary with ourselves, shall we say Karl Popper writing in this vein about Heidegger, it would certainly have damaged Popper's reputation, regardless of what anyone might think about Heidegger.) At the beginning of the 1820s, in order to save the young from Hegel's influence, Schopenhauer advertised a course of lectures at the University of Berlin to be given at the same time as Hegel's. Alas for him, the students went to Hegel's just the same. Nobody came to Schopenhauer's, and the course was unable to proceed. And that was the full extent of his career as a university teacher. He believed, nevertheless, that a time would come when the world would see through Hegel and would appreciate his own work. If he could have been told that the world would continue until at least the year 2000 to be more interested in Hegel's work than in his he would have been incredulous and baffled.

Yet the truth is, in my opinion at least, that the deliberate obscuration that Schopenhauer charged Fichte, Schelling and Hegel with is indeed there in their writings, and is a great evil. Moreover, it established a tradition that flourishes in our own day. There can be no doubt that, as Schopenhauer immediately perceived, it is connected with the professionalization of philosophy. Once the livelihood and careers of people studying philosophy came to depend on their acquiring paid jobs in universities it was no longer possible for most of them to forget themselves impersonally in their work. They had to convince others of its importance; and this meant making sure that the work itself *seemed* important, had an air of importance. It also meant establishing a name for the author of it, making his mark. Actually, there is not much academic work in any subject in which the desire to do these things is not discernible as a contributory motive, often the main one. But there is a special reason why philosophy is open to abuse in this regard, namely the comparative absence of generally accepted criteria by which the work in it is to be valued. A history scholar who may be little better than an academic hack can still do useful work: he may, for instance, edit and publish a medieval pipe-roll. If his editing meets accepted standards this is a genuine contribution to the subject, something that will be there for other scholars to use for all future time. But hack philosophy is of no use to anyone, except perhaps temporarily to teachers of the subject in the form of textbooks, or the latest idea on some particular topic. Here the comparison is more with the creative arts: unless a poet's or composer's work possesses the spark which unmistakably characterizes the real thing there is no point in his doing it at all. And if it has that spark it deserves our attention, no matter what its failings. In the English-speaking world the great majority of books that have been published in philosophy in the twentieth century are like academic paintings: they show unmistakable talent and are professionally competent, the result of long processes of learning, application and work; everything in them is accurate, in its right place, and as it should be; but it makes not the slightest difference whether they exist or not. In so-called Continental philosophy, however, the prevailing tradition remains the one established by Fichte, Schelling and Hegel. Obscurity prevails, even with those who have something to say; and for those who have nothing to say it provides a smoke-screen from behind which they make their advances in the world. Unfortunately, for people lacking in originality it is more pleasurably self-indulgent to write in this latter vein, and a great deal easier, than to write in the former; it also makes the triviality of what they are saying less evident, thus doing more to disguise their mediocrity; and the result is that the Continental tradition is now making inroads into the Anglo-Saxon world. There are whole university departments in which the uninspired and boring is being driven out by the pseudo-profound. This is not an advance.

Schopenhauer was the first now-famous philosopher to campaign against pseudo-profundity in philosophy. Like Hume, only more so, he is a model in this regard. His writing is even better than Hume's, because although no less clear it is strikingly rich in aesthetic qualities, with imagery which has the same shock-value and unforgettability as good poetic imagery; furthermore, it is brilliantly aphoristic, the two characteristics going together.

The third great intellectual accusation that Schopenhauer brought against Fichte, Schelling and Hegel is that—in addition to debauching, separately, language and logic—they debauched the legacy of Kant. As we have seen, in Schopenhauer's view Kant's supreme achievement had been to draw the distinction between the phenomenal and the noumenal. This distinction, Schopenhauer believed, opened up the way to discoveries of the highest value, which he himself was enabled to go on to make: the foundation of ethics; the nature of art and in particular of music; the true nature of religion; indeed, the true philosophy. But Fichte, Schelling and Hegel, each in a different way, repudiated the distinction itself. Instead of taking philosophy along one of the paths opened up by Kant they led it along false paths, thus throwing away Kant's achievement. Because Fichte believed that the natural world is the creation of a self that is outside space and time he did not believe that there was any hidden reality "behind" or "within" the natural world: he wrote of "nature, which exists only for me and for my sake, and does not exist if I don't." According to him I am an immaterial self which is "already" outside space and time, creating for itself a world in space and time. When I stop doing that, with my death, my spatio-temporal world will cease to exist, but *I* shall be what I always was. I shall die for others, but not for myself. I shall die for others because I shall cease to exist in their spatio-temporal world, but *my* spatio-temporal world will cease to exist in me. What exists timelessly is a community of selves. But they all exist "already," and each of us is one of them. There are no "things as they are in themselves"; the phenomenal world is the creation of such selves as myself; there is no room for the postulation of a noumenal reality for the phenomenal world to be a manifestation of.

Schelling in his *Philosophy of Nature* took the diametrically opposed view: not that Nature is entirely our creation but that we are entirely Nature's creation. But for him it is fundamental that the whole thing is a single process: there is no hidden reality. There is only the natural world, the natural process as a whole, which is everything. However, it would be a simple-minded mistake on our part to think of that as consisting of inert matter in space and time; it is much more like a huge organism abundant with life and potential, perpetually changing, evolving, developing, with us as a part of it, and with nothing outside it.

Hegel can be said at least partially to have conflated these two sets of ideas. What is crucial for him is the selfhood of what exists. For him, as for Schelling (but unlike Fichte), its existence is seen as essentially developmental, evolutionary in time, and there is nothing outside this process. Total reality, then, is the growth of a self-existent mental or spiritual entity towards self-recognition and self-knowledge. This is what natural history and the whole world of Nature are (which is what led Bertrand Russell to dub Hegel's view of matter "jellied thought"). However, for Hegel, like Fichte (but unlike Schelling), that which has always been is spirit, and it is not the case that spirit is something that has emerged within the natural order—an order which, if that were to have been the case, would have to consist at least partially of something else.

One argument offered by all three of the accused for rejecting belief in the existence of Kant's reality as it is in itself is that Kant felt we were bound to postulate it as the cause of our experiences while at the same time he put forward a view of causality such as could have meaning or purchase only within the phenomenal world. This was a flagrant self-contradiction. If Kant's general doctrine of causality were correct then nothing outside the phenomenal world could be the cause of anything. Schopenhauer endorsed that criticism of Kant, as I believe everyone must: the mistake is so glaring that I have never been able to understand how Kant could have made it, or, having made it, not have spotted it. But as Schopenhauer pointed out, if the Kantian doctrine of causality is accepted it does not follow that there is no noumenal realm, it follows only that if there is one the relationship, if any, between it and the phenomenal realm cannot be, and therefore is not, a causal relationship.

What Schopenhauer produced instead is what is now known as a double-aspect theory. He argued that the noumenal is not the *cause* of the phenomenal but that noumenal and phenomenal are the same thing understood in different ways. This notion of double-aspect can be clearly illustrated by the following example. An atomic physicist might view the table on which I am now writing as a concatenation of atoms within each of which subatomic particles are in perpetual motion at almost the highest possible velocities. This miniature cosmos of particles moving at speeds approaching that of light is not the *cause* of the table I am looking at, it *is* that table, exactly the same table, but conceived in a totally different way from the way I normally perceive it and think of it. The same object is being apprehended in two ways which are completely different, and yet both are valid—both, if you like, "true." As we learn more and more about the world, so we discover more and more phenomena which can be explained adequately only in terms of such alternative and yet equally valid descriptions. To ask: "Yes, but which is the table really? Is it really an aggregate of colourless particles moving practically at the speed of light, or is it really the solid brown object on which you are leaning your elbow?" is to miss the point entirely, perhaps by confusing descriptions with reality. "The table," whatever *that* is, is "really" neither—or else, equally, both; and no doubt a great many other things besides.

Schopenhauer was not the first great philosopher to bring a double-aspect theory to our understanding of reality as a whole. He had been preceded in this by Spinoza, who for that reason above all was held in high regard by Schopenhauer. Spinoza had argued that the totality of what there is, whatever that may be, is the only thing that cannot possibly be explained with reference to anything else. It is—it must be—self-subsistent, the one and only uncaused cause.

So if substance is to be defined (in the way Descartes had defined it) as that which requires nothing other than itself in order to exist, then the totality of what exists is the only true substance. The existence of everything depends on it, but it does not depend for its existence on anything other than itself. So it itself has not, and cannot have, been created, because there is nothing else that could have created it; but within itself it gives rise profusely and unendingly to all the known processes of creation. Looked at in this way it becomes obvious that this description of the totality of what there is corresponds with what people normally mean by "God." God is the one and only true substance, and is self-subsistent; and everything less than God is merely an attribute or aspect of God, and does not, could not, exist without God. In this rationally argued and not just mystical way Spinoza came to identify God with the totality of what exists, and it was this that has earned for him the reputation ever since of being the great pantheist among philosophers. It seemed evident to him that there was no reason why total reality should not have an infinite, or at any rate an indefinite, number of attributes, although only two of these are accessible to human apprehension. The two are (again in Cartesian terminology) thought and extension, by which is meant consciousness and occupancy of space—in other words, mind and matter. Spinoza was here offering a double-aspect theory of the relationship between mind and matter. For Descartes these had been the two irreducibly different components of reality—the famous "Cartesian dualism"—but for Spinoza they are not disjunctive in that way, not two fundamentally distinct and perhaps even opposed elements within total reality: they are the same thing apprehended in different ways, two aspects of the same single substance, the only true substance. The natural world—matter spread out in space, and moving in certain ways—*is* the world of interrelated perceptions and ideas that constitutes mental life, but under a different description.

Schopenhauer hailed this theory as constituting an epoch-making advance in philosophical understanding, and yet he regarded it nevertheless as falling short of what was required. Its key shortcoming, he thought, was that although it provides us with a basically true account of the nature of our perception of material objects (an account which he took up and enriched) it all remains confined to the natural world. The most important distinction drawn in Spinoza's philosophy falls not between the noumenal and the phenomenal but within the phenomenal, and that renders it, in the end, auxiliary. As a philosophy of the phenomenal world it was, thought Schopenhauer, marvellously informative and insightful, and he developed it a great deal further in the light of the advances made by Kant, whose work had fallen in time between Spinoza's and Schopenhauer's. But when all had been said and done, there still remained the immeasurably more important distinction drawn by Kant between the phenomenal as such and the noumenal as such. It was the mapping of this distinction, and the tracing of its consequences, that Schopenhauer regarded as the supreme task confronting philosophy, because to do it was to discover and make perspicuous the frontiers of intelligibility. And it was the successful completion of this task that Schopenhauer, with profuse acknowledgements to Kant for setting him on the right path, regarded himself as having achieved.

Schopenhauer agreed with Kant that the form taken by all and every experience we can ever have must depend on the apparatus we possess for having it, and therefore that the world of all actual and possible experience is a subject-dependent world that comes to us in the forms of experience, and cannot exist in those forms independently of being experienced. At the same time we are pretty well bound to associate reality with what we experience, even though it cannot, in itself, independently of being experienced, accord with the categories of experience, in other words with epistemological categories. Thus the intellect has a built-in disposition towards illusion, the illusion of realism. The real truth is that there must be an unconceptualizable difference between the world as it appears to us and the world as it is in itself. Having agreed on this fundamental point, however, Schopenhauer had many criticisms of the way Kant worked it out in detail.

Schopenhauer considered Kant too inclined to sacrifice concrete considerations to systematization. Over and again Kant elaborates detail to fill a space in his architectonic which is there only because his intellectual pattern-making creates it. If the symmetry of his vast and imposing system requires that there should be twelve *a priori* categories of experience, then twelve categories are what he postulates. Schopenhauer subjects this aspect of Kant's philosophy to detailed and damaging criticism. He ends, to continue the above example, by rejecting Kant's doctrine of the categories altogether—and therefore, *a fortiori,* his distinction between categories and forms of sensibility. He argues that in the last analysis the already existing frameworks in terms of which we render our experience intelligible to ourselves, and therefore render experience haveable, are no more than three in number: time, space, and causal connection. All others can be reduced to these. For instance, we do certainly have a predisposition to see space-occupancy in terms of material objects; but objects can be understood in terms of energy, energy in terms of force, and force in terms of causality. Incidentally, it speaks volumes for the penetration of both Kant and Schopenhauer that by purely epistemological analysis they arrived at the conclusion that a material object is a space filled with force, and that all matter is reducible to energy, a hundred years before the physicists reached it on the path of scientific investigation. When the physicists finally got there in the twentieth century they believed their own discovery to be almost uncomprehendably revolutionary, not knowing that two of the greatest philosophers had pre-empted them such a long time before. It reminds one of the British under Scott struggling to be the first to reach the South Pole when the Norwegians under Amundsen had already been there and left.

The first sentence of the Introduction to Kant's *Critique of Pure Reason* is: "There can be no doubt that all our knowledge begins with experience." And there can be no doubt that this belief was fundamental to Kant's philosophy. This being so, he had surprisingly little to say about direct experience. Instead, he persistently tended to write as if direct experience were some sort of under-labourer handing up raw materials to a superior intellect which used them in the manufacture of concepts and judgments, at which point the whole process starts to become meaningful and interesting. The central questions of his marvellous work are "What sort of thing is it possible for us to know?" and, following on from that, "What sort of thing is it not possible for us to know?"; and nearly all his discussion and analysis of these questions take place at the level of universal concepts and generalized knowledge, the sort of knowledge that can be taught in schools and universities, and would be taught in seminaries if what they were teaching were knowledge. But this means that the very subject matter of Kant's investigations is abstract—it is our knowledge, and the processes of understanding and reason by which we arrive at our knowledge. He believed that the main task of the philosopher was to subject conceptual thought to scientific investigation, and was even given to defining philosophy as a body of scientific knowledge derived from concepts.

For all of this Schopenhauer took him to task. What we want to find out, said Schopenhauer, is what actually exists, reality, the world. And this, all of it, is uniquely specific. It is concrete, not abstract. Even if in conducting our investigations we find it more advisable to talk in terms of our experiences, as being what we are directly conscious of, rather than in terms of the objects of our experiences—which, it may be argued, are at one remove from our experience, and their nature more problematic—it is still the case that each experience is specific and unique, and is differentiable from every other experience, if only in time (and usually much more than that). Surely, then, if what we seek to understand is the uniquely specific, the uniquely specific should be the chief focus of our attentions? Is it not, to put it mildly, peculiar that in our attempt to understand the concrete, specific and unique we should turn our attention away from the concrete, specific and unique in order to analyse the abstract, general and universal? For this is what Kant does. He proceeds as if reason, thought, judgments, concepts, are more informative than the direct experiences which he himself insists give them whatever reference they possess, so that more is to be learnt about the nature of reality from the analysis of those things than from attending to direct experience. But in that he is wrong, says Schopenhauer. Kant himself believes that meaningful empirical concepts can be derived only from experience. But in the very formation of those concepts what is unique about the experiences from which they derive has had to be sacrificed. So the very thing of which we are now in search has had to be left out, because only if concepts are detached from association with the uniquely particular can they perform the tasks for which they exist, namely storage and communication. There is, and there has to be, *less* information about reality contained in empirical concepts than in the experiences from which they derive. The analysis of concepts, therefore, can never possibly, even if carried out to perfection, give us an adequate knowledge of reality.

An all-pervading feature of Schopenhauer's philosophy is his insistence on the greater value, for our understanding of the world, of direct experience (and he includes in this our authentically own thoughts and emotions as well as our sensory perceptions) than of what is conveyed to us through the use of concepts from the experience of others via discourse, learning, reading, study, and the rest. "To perceive, to allow the things themselves to speak to us, to apprehend and grasp new relations between them, and then to precipitate all this into concepts, in order to possess it with certainty; this is what gives us new knowledge. But whereas almost everyone is capable of comparing concepts with concepts, to compare concepts with perceptions is a gift of the select few. According to its degree of perfection, this gift is the condition of wit, power of judgment, sagacity, and genius. With the former faculty, on the other hand, the result is never much more than possibly rational reflections. The innermost level of every genuine and actual piece of knowledge is a perception; every new truth is also the fruit of such a perception. . . . For this reason, the contemplation and observation of everything *actual,* as soon as it presents something new to the observer, is more instructive than all reading and hearing about it. For indeed, if we go to the bottom of the matter, all truth and wisdom, in fact the ultimate secret of things, is contained in everything actual, yet certainly only *in concreto* and like gold hidden in the ore. The question is how to extract it. From a book, on the other hand, we obtain the truth only second-hand at best, and often not at all."*

Contrasting his approach with that of Kant, Schopenhauer writes: "With me perception is throughout the source of all knowledge. . . . It is true that universal concepts should be the material *in* which philosophy deposits and stores up its knowledge, but not the source *from* which it draws such knowledge; the *terminus ad quem,* not *a quo.* It is not, as Kant defines it, a science *from* concepts, but a science *in* concepts."† Thus Schopenhauer strenuously criticizes Kant because, having made the most important distinction in the whole of philosophy,

---

* *The World as Will and Representation,* vol. ii, p. 72.
† *The World as Will and Representation,* vol. ii, p. 41.

the distinction between the phenomenal and the noumenal, he then proceeds as if the deepest understanding of the phenomenal world available to us is to be gained by analysis of concepts, when this cannot be the case.

However, if the greatest depth of understanding available to us is not communicable by concepts, does that mean that it is not communicable, period, and is to be gained, each person for himself, by nothing but our own unaided individual efforts? No, fortunately for us it does not. It does, of course, follow from Schopenhauer's views that fundamental insights that are gained from our own personal perceptions, feelings and thoughts are likely to be of more value to us than insights gained in any other way. But that, after all, is a commonly held, almost commonsense view. More to the point of the present discussion is the fact that he believes that although insight into the uniquely particular is not communicable in concepts it is, nevertheless, communicable. For there are, after all, non-conceptual forms of communication ranging across a far-flung gamut of sophistication from the dumb communion of animal companionship to the structural complexities of symphonic music. Schopenhauer believes that it is the specific function of the arts to convey profound and unique insights that are unamenable to conceptual communication. Even when a great work of art is constructed out of words, as is a poem, play, or novel, it is nevertheless impossible to say in words what it "means." To use a later terminology, though one derived ultimately from Schopenhauer's own thought, the meaning of a work of art is something that the work conveys but cannot state: it conveys it by virtue of being a presentational symbol, but what is thus conveyed is exhibited, it cannot be said. So the only thing that does or can articulate the work's meaning is the work itself, and that is just as true of the non-verbal as of the verbal arts, and for the same reasons. Art is a medium, a vehicle: there is something "behind" a work of art that the work conveys, and this is not anything *said* in the work, even when the work is in language.

Because these were Schopenhauer's views, a larger share of his philosophy is given over to detailed consideration of the arts than is the case with any other major philosopher. Another subject he writes about at great length which is scarcely more than touched on by any other great philosopher is sex. Because sex is the means whereby human beings come into existence he considers it astonishing that philosophers have not as a matter of course accorded it a place near the centre of their concerns. The parameters of the existence of every human individual are conception and death. Philosophers have written endlessly about death, yet they have given scarcely any attention at all to conception—which, to say the least of it, is just as important to us, and every bit as mysterious.

Schopenhauer's view of human life as one in which direct experience impinges far more powerfully on the individual than abstract thought, one to which sex is central, and one in which the arts have a uniquely valuable and important role to play, is light-years away from life as it is written about by most other great philosophers, but instantly recognizable as being what I myself live and know. We have not yet even come to the heart of Schopenhauer's philosophy, but I can say at this point that to a degree unmatched by any other philosopher he writes about the world as I encounter it, and about life as I encounter it. Added to this is the fact that what he says about them is always new-minted in his own perception, feeling and thought. He speaks to me, as no other philosopher does, direct and in his own human voice, a fellow spirit, a penetratingly perceptive friend, with a hand on my elbow and a twinkle in his eye. Although I frequently do not agree with what he says, I always listen to him.

21

The Philosophy
of Schopenhauer

Behind Schopenhauer's belief that his philosophy was to be understood as the correction and completion of Kant's lay the view that Kant had been right in dividing total reality into the phenomenal and the noumenal but wrong about what these were. As regards the phenomenal, although Kant had *said* that all our knowledge of it must derive from experience he actually directed most of his vast investigative enterprise not at the nature of experience but at the nature of conceptual thinking. As such it is of incomparable depth and value; and yet it very largely leaves out the uniquely actual, and our experience of it, when this is what life mostly consists of. In this part of his philosophy Schopenhauer tries to render whole the work of Kant by pushing the investigation into how we do in fact experience, know and communicate the uniquely specific; and, cognate with this, what the uniquely specific *is*.

With regard to the noumenal, Schopenhauer thought Kant's fundamental mistake was twofold: first, Kant had seen the noumenal as consisting in thing*s* (*in the plural*) as they are in themselves; second, he took these noumena to be the causes of our perceptions. The second of these mistakes has already been dealt with. As regards the first, Schopenhauer's reasoning went something like this.

For anything to be different from anything else, either space or time has to be presupposed, or both. In the case of material objects this is fairly obvious. For one object to be different from another it must either occupy the same space at a different time or a different space at the same time, or a different space at a different time: if it occupies the same space at the same time it is the same object (as turned out to be the case with the Evening Star and the Morning Star, or with the author of the *Waverley* novels and Sir Walter Scott). Less obviously, though, it is also true of abstract entities. Natural numbers, you may say, are different from one another and yet do not exist in space or time. But the very concept of number would be impossible without the concept of succession; and the concept of succession presupposes either spatial or temporal concepts, or both; and therefore only in a universe of discourse where either space or time is conceptualizable can there be natural numbers. You may say that poems or plays or symphonies do not exist in space and, properly understood, do not exist in time either; but, again, they are unconceptualizable without the notion of succession, for instance of words or of notes: this ordering is crucial to the identity of the work; indeed, without it the presentational symbol that is the work of art cannot be presented; but the very notion of any such succession presupposes either temporal or spatial concepts, or both. So on analysis, Schopenhauer insists, we find that the notion of differentiation *as such* can have meaning only if we accept the significance and relevance of the concepts of space or time. But, as Kant had shown, space and time are forms of sensibility. They have no purchase in a subject-less realm, the realm of whatever exists in itself independently of experience. Therefore differentiation can obtain only in the world of experience, and can have no being in the noumenal realm. Therefore there cannot be thing*s* (in the plural) as they are in themselves independently of being experienced.

This means, said Schopenhauer, that whatever it may be that exists outside all possibility of experience, we know that it must be undifferentiated. You can say, if you like, that it is "one" (or "One") but that could be misleading, because the concept "one" is significant only relative to some such concept as "many" or "more than one" (or of course "less than one"), and these can have no purchase either. The noumenal can be said to be "one" only in the sense that the very notion of differentiation *as such* can have no application with regard to it.

This argument provides Schopenhauer with another reason, in addition to those given by Kant, for believing that we can never have direct knowledge of the noumenal. Knowledge is, of its nature, dualistic: there has to be something that is grasped and something else that grasps it. If nothing existed but an undifferentiated something it would be unable to know itself. Since knowledge presupposes differentiation it follows that there can be such a thing as knowledge in the phenomenal realm alone, and that what exists in itself independently of being experienced is knowledgeless. Although we can know things *about* the noumenal, for instance that it is undifferentiated, we can never know *it*.

This difference between *knowledge* and *knowledge about,* or *knowledge* and *knowledge that,* is familiar in ordinary discourse, where it causes no confusion. I can know many things about a person, and therefore know that this, that and the other is true or untrue of him, without knowing *him* at all: he may have died before I was born. We have, all of us, huge amounts of knowledge about entities, abstract as well as concrete, of which we do not have direct knowledge. I would guess that most of our knowledge is of this kind: most of what we "know" we have been told, or have inferred, or read. There is no self-contradiction between saying "We know that the noumenon is so-and-so" and saying "We cannot have direct knowledge of the noumenon," unless the so-and-so were to be a particular something that could be attributed to the noumenon only by someone who had direct knowledge of it. I make a point of saying this because Schopenhauer has been widely, crudely and mistakenly accused of self-contradiction on this point. He does indeed tell us certain things about the noumenon while at the same time saying that we cannot have direct knowledge of it, but no self-contradiction is involved.

Schopenhauer's view of total reality, then, is that there is an immaterial, undifferentiated, timeless, spaceless something of which we can never have direct knowledge but which manifests itself to us as this differentiated phenomenal world of material objects (including us) in space and time. This conclusion is strikingly similar to the view taken within the mainstream traditions of Hinduism and Buddhism, but Schopenhauer did not know this when he arrived at it. He was not a religious person: he did not believe in personal survival of death, nor did he believe in the existence of God or the soul. He came to his views through rational argument in the central tradition of Western philosophy, carrying forward discussions inaugurated by the pre-Socratics and Plato, and contributed to very much later by Descartes, Spinoza, Leibniz, Locke, Berkeley, Hume and Kant. When he then discovered that Hindu and Buddhist thinkers had reached conclusions similar to those of Kant and himself he studied their works with enormous interest and began to refer to them in his writings, and this has caused it to be said that he was influenced by them, but that is not true in the sense in which it is usually meant: he did not derive any important ideas from them. He did, though, take the view that the fact that the same conclusions had been reached in such radically different ways in distant continents in unconnected cultures in widely separated historical epochs was a good reason for giving them serious consideration. When Christians took exception to his philosophy on the ground that it was incompatible with their religion he derived great pleasure from pointing out that the adherents of the religions that agreed with him outnumbered the Christians.

Like many Buddhists, but again independently of them, he came to the conclusion that the undifferentiatedness of the noumenal gives us the key to the explanation of the foundations of morality. We human beings are (perhaps among other things, but that does not matter to this argument) material objects in space and time, which means that like other phenomenal objects we are manifestations of an undifferentiated something that is spaceless and timeless, and therefore perforce non-material. In the phenomenal world we exist as individuals: we come into existence as material objects occupying space, and persisting for a time; but this differentiation can obtain in the phenomenal world only. Noumenally, in the ultimate ground of our being, outside space or time or embodiment, it is impossible that we should be differentiated. Therefore we must all be "one" in the sense stipulated earlier. So there is an ultimate sense in which if I hurt you I am injuring myself as well as you; if I do you an injustice I am sinning against myself as well as you. This, said Schopenhauer, is the explanation of morality, because it explains the compassion, fellow-feeling, disinterested concern for others, which as it were lie between us and morality, and on which morality is based, and which would be unintelligible if you and I were ultimately separate. Morality consists of the consequences for our behaviour of what the ultimate truth is about the human situation, and in this sense it is applied metaphysics. Its roots lie outside the phenomenal world, in the fact of our metaphysical one-ness. From this standpoint Schopenhauer dissociates himself from Kant's doctrine that rationality is the foundation of ethics; among his profoundest pages are those on which he criticizes Kant's categorical imperative and puts forward his own quite different view.

Kant elaborated his wonderful theory of our knowledge of material objects without showing anything like sufficient awareness of the implications of the fact that we ourselves are material objects. A human being is a material object that knows itself from inside. There is something awesome about this fact. Schopenhauer saw it as a fact that might possibly make available to us a degree of understanding of the inner nature of material objects as such, including therefore material objects that are not us.

Everything we apprehend that is not ourselves we apprehend from outside. We see and feel physical objects in space, see and hear their movements, and so on; and if we did not have knowledge of ourselves from inside we would build up a conception of the external world entirely on the basis of such input. Our only understanding of other people would derive from their appearances and behaviour, including what they say: we would observe them as material objects along with all other material objects, and understand them, or try to, in exactly the same way. And we do indeed make plentiful use of all such sources of information. But in addition to these we have another, quite different one. There is one unique material object that we know in all of these ways, and of which in addition we have direct, immediate, non-sensory knowledge from within. And it so happens that inside this material object all kinds of things are going on that cannot be seen or heard or touched—things like thoughts, feelings, moods and memories—but of which we nevertheless have immediate apprehension, although no one else does. This direct knowledge that we have of one physical object from within is so radically different in character from the indirect knowledge we have of all other objects from without that I am at a loss to express in language what the difference is. But every one of us is as familiar with it as he is with anything. And, as he knows from his own privileged and direct knowledge, inner experience can be as varied and many-sided, complex and difficult to understand, and profound in its implications and significance, as outer experience.

This being so, says Schopenhauer, then surely—if what we want to do is understand the inner nature and significance of the world—we need to pursue our investigations along the path of inner as well as outer experience, thus encompassing both of these lines of enquiry, rather than try to construct a conception of the world on the basis of outer experience alone. Already, in our understanding of other people, we find that we can make sense of their movements in space and time, and of the sounds made by some of these movements, only by assuming that they have—although it is not directly observed or observable by us—an inner life that is broadly similar to ours in the modes and forms that it takes, though different in content and detail. By analogy with ourselves we know (or, if "know" is too strong a word, we infer) that most of their observable behaviour is what we normally think of as willed behaviour. And we know, "from the inside" as it were (though again only by analogy), what this is like. If the human body seated opposite mine unfolds out of its chair into a standing position and walks across the carpet to a table, then opens with one of its hands a silver box that is standing on the table, takes out a cigarette, and inserts the cigarette into its mouth, I know that these things are happening because the embodied person wants a cigarette. I know what a cigarette is, and have some idea what it is like to want to smoke one, and would have some such idea even if I had never smoked myself. If I had no conception of these things, those movements of a physical object in time and space that I have been observing would be unintelligible to me. It is salutary to speculate what I might, in those circumstances, conjecture their significance to be.

In recent centuries there have been quite a lot of people in the West who believed, often as a matter of principle, that we should do everything we could to construct our total conception of the way things are out of what can be inter-subjectively observed. Such a programme constitutes a commitment to a scientific view of total reality. Schopenhauer sees this as an almost absurd error, not because he has anything against science, but because of its obvious and unnecessary limitations. Like almost every great philosopher since the pre-Socratics he had a passionate interest in science and was knowledgeable about it, as one of the most important sources of information and understanding available to us in our attempts to penetrate the significance of life. (Exceptions to this are few, the most notable being Socrates.) Like Kant, Schopenhauer believed that scientific methods and criteria must be given undisputed jurisdiction over the realm that is theirs, and that any denial of this is ignorant or obscurantist or irrational. The growth of scientific knowledge seemed to him among the few glories of mankind's history, one of not many things that human beings could be proud of. It perpetually astonishes us by revealing the world to be astoundingly different from what we had supposed, and does this over and over again in one respect after another. Its leading practitioners are geniuses of profound originality and insight. Nevertheless its explanations, though of prodigious richness, value and fascination, can never be exhaustive, because it is characteristic of science that it explains things in terms that are themselves left unexplained. In physics, for example, explanations tend to be in terms of scientific laws involving entities and concepts such as mass, energy, light, gravity, distance, time. If we press for an explanation of any one of these we are likely to be given it in terms of the others. So at this ground-floor level of explanation the explanations are circular. And physics goes no deeper than that: it ends there. If what you are after is an explanation or understanding of all of these things taken together, namely the world *as such,* it is in the nature of science that it cannot provide it. It is wonderfully enlightening and useful in what it tells us about what goes on in the phenomenal world, but what that world is, the mystery of its existence, is as great at the end of any such explanation as it was at the beginning—indeed greater, because the more we find out about the world in the course of scientific enquiry the more disconcertingly astonishing we discover it to be.

Ultimate explanations, then, are not to be looked for in science. The insistent belief that they are is not a scientific belief but a belief in science, a metaphysical belief, an act of faith whose inadequacy I should have thought it now fairly easy to demonstrate. At its crudest it takes the form of materialism, which Schopenhauer once described as "the philosophy of the subject who forgets to take account of himself." Unfortunately it seems to be characteristic of many people who have committed themselves to an act of faith in the ultimate ability of science to explain everything that they construe any denial of this as hostility to science. This is not so at all. Kant was a highly competent physicist who made a profoundly original contribution to cosmology; other great philosophers have been original and creative mathematicians, among them some of the most famous names in the history of the subject: it is not at all the case that such people fail to appreciate the nature and importance of science, or have any desire to belittle it (though that may be true of some academics in the humanities, and also of what one might call literary intellectuals). Most great philosophers have regarded an interest in, and knowledge of, science as being indispensable to an understanding of the world. Certainly Western philosophy has been intimately bound up with science throughout the whole of its history, and especially with mathematical physics, from Plato to Popper. Yet all great philosophers have had a clear understanding of the fact that not everything can be explained in scientific terms. Schopenhauer was explicit about this. It seemed very clear to him that in our attempts to understand the world we had to make full and enthusiastic use of all the resources of science but also of other sources as well.

To be publicly acknowledged source-material for a scientific understanding of anything, experiences need to be inter-subjectively available. It is no use anyone's appealing to observations that he alone can make as the basis for assertions claiming to be scientific. But it is in the nature of our subjective inner experience that each individual has access only to his own. And we have already seen how manifestly self-contradictory it would be for us in our search for a deeper understanding of the inner nature of the world to rule out as unusable the only direct knowledge of physical objects from the inside that we possess. It would constitute a deeper version of Kant's mistake in trying to understand the nature of things by analysing the process of formation of the abstract and universal concepts we have of them rather than addressing his attentions to the individual and concrete things themselves. Depending on the view you take of the nature of human beings, each one of us either *is* a unique material object or is embodied in one, and in either case he has sole access to immediate and direct knowledge of a large number of things that are going on inside that particular material object. This being so, it would seem that the royal road to a deeper understanding of the inner nature of things must pass through the investigation of inner as well as outer experience, and if anything more the former than the latter. But if this is so it will not be what is normally meant by a scientific investigation. As Schopenhauer expressed it in one of his notebooks: "Philosophy has so long been sought in vain because it was sought by way of the sciences instead of by way of the arts."

We have seen that although the most profound of our inner experiences cannot be articulated in the universal language of concepts they may be articulated in works of art, each of which is unique. Therefore what it is that is thus articulated is something of which philosophy needs an understanding. From this point of view Schopenhauer goes on to deal more fully than any other great philosopher, and also more insightfully, with what it is that art articulates, and how, and why, and what it means to both the artist and his audience; and why it matters to both of them so much. His treatment of these questions is in a quite different class of interestingness from that of any other philosopher's. But the treatment is in every way complementary with science, in no way antagonistic to it or wanting in appreciation of it. Although in Schopenhauer's day no one had yet talked of "the two cultures," he combines them more richly and harmoniously than any other philosopher. However, before I am in a position to go into this at any greater length I shall need to say rather more about his findings concerning the nature of inner experience.

He came to the view that if we dig down inside ourselves as deeply as we can, the ultimate thing we come to is some sort of will to live, to survive, just to *be*. This seemed to him confirmed by outer observation of the way other human beings behave, especially under stress or in extreme situations, when their ultimate motivation stands revealed. But, having said that, the more he examined emotions and feelings of every kind the more all of them seemed to him to be modifications of the will. Far from regarding this as a discovery he saw it as having been perceived by outstanding thinkers as far back as St. Augustine: "The will is in all of these affections; indeed they are nothing else but inclinations of the will. For what are desire and joy but the will in harmony with things we desire? And what are fear and sadness but the will in disagreement with things we abhor?" (*The City of God,* Book XIV, chapter 6). Schopenhauer saw the intellect as being the servant, not the master, of the will (as, for that matter, did Hume), and thus our whole inner lives as either consisting of or being dominated by will in one or other of its manifestations.

To put this in extreme shorthand, not only crude but metaphorical, it means that human persons, who present themselves to external observation as material objects in space and time, are in their inner being will, and a will that is not externally observable. In their observations of one another, all they can see and hear are material objects, and the movements in space and time of those material objects; it is only because they know from their own inner experience that their own physical movements in space and time are acts of will that they are able to interpret the movements of others as willed activity, and hence to understand it as behaviour. One important thing about this fact is that it is proof that what is inter-subjectively observable about material bodies in space and time is not all the relevant information that is available to us, and also does not give us all the information that is necessary to an understanding of them.

Someone following the investigation up to this point might easily jump to a conclusion and say: "Ah, Schopenhauer is about to say that the knowledge we have of ourselves from inside is knowledge of a material object, a thing, as it is in itself, and is therefore knowledge of the noumenon; and that what we thus discover the inner nature of things, the noumenon, to be is will—and that in the last analysis this will is will to exist, will to be." Generations of hasty readers of, or second-hand hearers about, Schopenhauer have leapt to this conclusion, and it has spawned unending muddle and misunderstanding. For Schopenhauer does not say, and does not believe, that the knowledge we have of ourselves from inside is knowledge of the noumenal. In fact he explicitly says that it is not, and he gives three reasons why it cannot be, reasons so powerful that any one of them alone would be decisive.

First, our inner sense exists in the dimension of time, and is unimaginable without time. Kant taught, and Schopenhauer agreed, that time is the very form of inner sense. Yet time can exist in the phenomenal domain alone. Therefore the knowledge that we have of ourselves in inner sense inhabits the phenomenal world, and does not constitute knowledge of the noumenal.

Second, knowledge of any kind at all can exist only in the realm of the phenomenal. This is because, as I have said, knowledge *as such* is inherently dualistic in structure: there has to be something that is known and something that knows it—something grasped and something grasping. Because this is so, and because the noumenal is undifferentiated and undifferentiable, there can never be knowledge in the realm of the noumenal. This is the most fundamental point of all in the present context, because it means that knowledge of the noumenal is inherently and for ever impossible. Schopenhauer is clear, explicit, and repetitive on this point; yet ever since he wrote he has been misunderstood about it. Any interpretation of his philosophy that ascribes to him the view that we have, or ever can have, cognizance of the noumenal, is mistaken about something that is foundational to his whole system of ideas.

His third reason is derived from empirical observation. His investigations of inner experience and of our knowledge of ourselves from within have led him to the conclusion that most of our perceptions and wishes and hopes and fears do not present themselves to conscious experience. Before Freud was even born, Schopenhauer expounded what is normally thought of as Freud's theory of repression, a theory which Freud himself pronounced to be the cornerstone of psychoanalysis. Furthermore, Schopenhauer provided all the necessary connecting links in the argument: at length and in detail, and with memorable examples, he spelled out that the greater part of our own inner lives is unknown to us; that it is unknown to us because it is repressed; that it is repressed because to face up to it would cause us a degree of disturbance that we could not handle; that this is so because it does not fit in with the view of ourselves that we wish to maintain; that this incompatibility is caused by high levels of such things as sexual motivation, self-seeking, aggression, envy, fear and cruelty whose presence within us we do not wish to acknowledge, not even in the secrecy of our own thoughts; and so we deceive ourselves about what our own characters and motivations are, allowing only such interpretations of them to appear in our conscious minds as we can deal with. This means that we are exactly as far from knowing our inner selves as our inner selves are unconscious, and we would be so even if such knowledge were theoretically possible on other grounds; and moreover that we would be unable to cope with it even if we had it—would indeed, many of us, break down under it. So we shall never know the true nature of our inner selves, not even of those parts of it that are so close to consciousness that they motivate our thoughts, our speech, our decisions, and our behaviour. So—far from constituting knowledge of the noumenal—the knowledge that we have of ourselves from inside does not amount even to an exhaustive knowledge of the phenomenal.

This means that within ourselves as well as without there is an underlying reality that remains hidden from us and can never be met with in experience. What it is in itself we shall never know. Knowledge of any kind at all, knowledge as such, can come to us only through the apparatus that we as phenomenal beings find ourselves embodied in, and in forms whose nature is determined by that apparatus. Unless we are in some way the creators of all the phenomena thus experienced—a proposition which most of us find incredible, though it was believed by Fichte—those phenomena cannot be all there is apart from us: there must be a sense in which they are manifestations of something other than themselves or ourselves, something whose existence accounts for them, but something with which we can never make direct contact.

This is what Kant believed, and Schopenhauer also. Kant seems to have allowed it to be supposed of him that he believed, in good faith (though he knew he could not know), that the unknowable and unexperienceable order of things included the Christian God as creator and law-giver, and also the immortal souls of men; but a reading of his works plus also, importantly, biographies of him has left me with the impression that he was more agnostic than he let it be thought. In particular he seems to have seen a question mark hanging over our survival of death. I am not insinuating intellectual dishonesty: I expect he was not sure himself what he believed or—which is crucially important in this context—what he did not believe with regard to the existence of God or of the soul. He was a passionately committed believer in the Christian ethic. He took the view that the true foundations of this lay in reason and not in either faith or revelation, which were therefore, in fact, superfluous in one important sense, though he never says so. He did take the view that human beings had arrived at what was more or less the right view of what morality contained, and had done it almost two thousand years earlier in the form of religious doctrine than they subsequently did in the form of rational demonstration—and indeed that the former step had facilitated and hastened the latter. In this and other ways he seems to have regarded the Christian religion as an importantly good thing even though insufficient; and of course the insufficiency is never explicitly asserted. When one considers that he lived in a time and place when any public questioning of the Christian faith could incur criminal proceedings and punishment; that even as things stood his writing fell foul of official censorship on religious grounds; that to get the censor off his back he felt constrained to promise his king that he would not publish any more on religious topics; and that his overriding concern was that his chief critical writings should be unimpededly circulated, and therefore that he should not facilitate their condemnation; he seems to have behaved with as much openness as one can reasonably expect of him.

Schopenhauer was explicitly atheistic, the first great philosopher of the West to be so. Others, such as Hobbes and Hume, may have been atheists in fact but could not have been explicit about it in their writings without incurring the wrath of the law. Schopenhauer published his view that there could be neither a personal God nor immortal souls, because both concepts were inherently self-contradictory. Our conception of personality, he argued, was derived from embodied human beings existing in space and time, with the consequence that no sense could be attached to the ascription of personality to a non-material entity outside space and time. In particular we could not conceive of personality without some such characteristics as feelings and thoughts and attitudes; and these, in any sense that we could attach to the words, were dependent on brains and central nervous systems. Also, the notion of a personal God involves individuation. Similarly with the concept of the soul: it was impossible to attach sense to the term without referring to characteristics like conscious awareness, which were dependent for their applicability on the existence of a material object, namely the brain; and it was also impossible to attach significance to the concept without the notion of individuation. So to talk of a personal God or an immortal soul was incoherent and therefore, literally, meaningless. He did say, though, that precisely because the noumenal was non-material, and outside all possibility of space or time or causal connection, and was unknowable and unconceptualizable, things were bound to be true about it of which we could form not the remotest conception, and that we should never lose sight of this even though in the nature of things there was little we could say about it.

What we do know about the noumenal is to an important degree negative. Because time and space are forms of sensibility, we know that reality as it is, independent of experience, cannot have temporal or spatial characteristics. Because differentiation presupposes time or space, or both, the noumenal cannot be differentiable. Because material objects can exist only in a time and a space the noumenal cannot be material. Because causal relationships presuppose succession, which in turn presupposes either time or space, or both, the noumenal cannot be involved in any causal relationship. Because knowledge involves differentiation the noumenal cannot be known. Because all categories of perception and understanding are subject-dependent, it cannot exist in itself in terms that correspond to our categories.

As for the positive things we know about the noumenal, the most fundamental and at the same time the most immediate is that the phenomenal world, the world of experience, is its manifestation. This term "manifestation" does not denote a causal relationship. It cannot be the case, as Kant had mistakenly supposed, that there are noumenal objects that cause us to experience phenomena. What we are concerned with here is a dual aspect: the many is a manifestation of the one. The connection is mysterious, not only in the sense that it is impossible to give an adequate account of it within the framework of a theoretical explanation such as the present one but, more to the point, in life. We find ourselves at a loss to give an account of those aspects of even our most immediate experience when they are direct manifestations of the noumenal: for instance the phenomenal world itself—it is notoriously impossible to prove that the external world exists; or the moral imperative; or beauty in music. There is nothing surprising in the fact of these things being mysterious, in the sense that we are all familiar with it: what Schopenhauer gives us is an explanation of why they cannot be explained.

Schopenhauer discusses the difficulty of adopting a linguistic term for the noumenal. On the face of it the fact that the noumenal can never be known, and is unconceptualizable, would appear to mean that whatever term is adopted will be merely a longer substitute for *x*. But he contends that the fact that we know certain things *about* the noumenal might have the consequence that we can do better than *x*. What we are looking for is a name for a fundamental drive that manifests itself in existence. The first term he considers is "force" (the word *Kraft* in German). But in discussing it he comes to the conclusion that this concept has a special association with the natural sciences; and since the applicability of science is confined to the phenomenal world alone, *Kraft* would be an inappropriate term: it would carry with it too many contradictory associations. So he considers a second term, will (*Wille*). After reflection, with a certain amount of hesitation and reluctance, he adopts it. He does so partly because, in our attempts to investigate ourselves from inside, the ultimate level of what we encounter is some sort of will to live, and it looks as if this may be the most elemental manifestation in experience of that metaphysical drive to existence that we take the noumenal to be. There is also the fact that in the case of those material objects to which we have uniquely privileged access from inside, what we discover their externally observable movements in space to be is willed activity—and, on analysis, we find that it is not the case that the act of will is the *cause* of bodily movement, but rather that the two are the same phenomenon under different aspects. "I say that between the act of will and the bodily action there is no causal connection whatever; on the contrary, the two are directly one and the same thing perceived in a double way, namely in self-consciousness or the inner sense as an act of will, and simultaneously in external brain-perception as bodily action" (*The Fourfold Root of the Principle of Sufficient Reason*, tr. E. F. J. Payne, pp. 114–15). Of course it has to be remembered that whatever knowledge we may have of ourselves from inside can never be knowledge of the noumenal. Even so, the suggestion is that the movements of all those material objects that are not self-aware, and constitute most of the physical universe, instantiate some sort of manifestation of a will that is not aware of itself.

The entire universe consists of matter in motion on a scale—the heavenly bodies of a number and size, the velocities involved of a speed, and cosmic space of an expanse—that beggars all human imagination; and it is difficult for us not to suppose that these unimaginable amounts of energy must be generated "somewhere." Yet there is nowhere "else" for that to happen. On closer examination it would appear that the energy of which everything material consists must just simply be. The physicists themselves now tell us that energy is the ultimate constituent of the universe, that all matter and motion are merely differing forms of it. So whatever the noumenal is, energy is its immediate manifestation in the world of phenomena, constituting the limitlessly differentiated manifold of material objects and their motions. If we want a word for the noumenal we are looking for a word for something whose phenomenal manifestation is a boundless, unconscious, impersonal, non-living, non-conative, utterly purposeless drive.

Schopenhauer ends up positing as the noumenal some sort of un-self-aware and not-in-itself-differentiated drive that is the same something manifesting itself in all the various phenomena that inhabit the world of experience. Some of those phenomena have developed in such a way that life has emerged within them. And some of these living formations of matter have changed further in such ways that they have developed personalities and minds. In this process mind, and everything to do with mind, and with conscious beings altogether, is tertiary. Foundationally, there is the noumenon, whatever that is; then there are the material phenomena as which this noumenal manifests itself; and then, some of those phenomena possess minds. In other words mind is something that characterizes a certain small sub-class of physical objects. It is much more immediately bound up with the material than it is with the noumenal, indeed it would appear to be either activity or epiphenomenon of matter: all the minds we know are instantiated in material objects. So if we end up calling the aboriginal metaphysical drive that manifests itself in existence "will," this is not to be understood as connoting anything to do with consciousness or mind or self-awareness of any sort; it is nothing to do with aims, wishes or intentions, nothing necessarily to do with life, which is highly contingent and might easily never have come into existence. It connotes something that is prior not only to life but to matter, a blind, non-material, non-personal, non-living force. There is as much will in a pool of water or a rock or a dead star as there is in a human being or human action. Human beings are of course embodiments of will also in this sense—embodiments of metaphysical will, the noumenal will—but it is exactly the same sense as that in which all physical objects are embodiments of will. The universe before there was any life was nothing but embodiment of will. The will to exist of which we may become aware within ourselves is not in itself this noumenal will but a manifestation of it in the world of phenomena, and so indeed must everything be that is a possible object of knowledge.

Having decided to use the word "will" in this way, Schopenhauer gives a serious warning to the reader. "Anyone who is incapable of carrying out the required extension of the concept will remain involved in a permanent misunderstanding" (*The World as Will and Representation,* vol i, chapter 22). Alas, this warning has been in vain, though Schopenhauer was only too right in realizing that it was called for. Explicit and repetitive on the point though he was, his philosophy has been misunderstood more widely than it has been understood, and all because of this: generations of non-readers and readers alike have taken him to be saying that the noumenal is will in something akin to our normal use of the word, and therefore that our direct knowledge of ourselves from inside, as agents, gives us knowledge of the noumenal. Although numerous quotations can be produced to show that these two fundamental misunderstandings *are* misunderstandings, whole books have been written that embody them, and such books continue to be written—not to mention entries on Schopenhauer in dictionaries and encyclopaedias, and chapters on Schopenhauer in general surveys. As in the more familiar cases of Hume and Kant, what the philosopher is saying runs so contrary to what we are accustomed to think that even intelligent readers can find, if they are not careful, that they have been understanding it in terms of ideas with which they are more familiar but which have been misleading them.

Schopenhauer was not the first great philosopher in the West to conclude that ultimate reality must be one and undifferentiable. Indeed, the idea stands at the very gateway to the recorded history of Western thought. Parmenides, who has been described as the most original and important of all philosophers before Socrates, held it. Schopenhauer mentions Parmenides a number of times, and interprets him persuasively in a sense that is congruent with his own thought—for instance, he cites Parmenides' contention that *Eros* is the ultimate principle out of which everything else emerges, in a way that relates it to his own doctrine of the metaphysical will. (On this point Parmenides anticipated the Freudian concept of Libido, but this derived more directly from Schopenhauer.) Plato gives us an account (which he may himself have invented) of a philosophical discussion in about the year 450 B.C. between Parmenides, who was then an old man, the middle-aged Zeno, and the "very young" Socrates. It is certain that Socrates learnt from Parmenides. And so, for that matter, did Plato—among much else, Plato took from Parmenides the view that ultimate reality must be something which is not cognizable by the human senses and yet is nevertheless apprehensible by human beings through their capacity for abstract thought.

In Plato's work this view developed into his famous doctrine of Ideas, a doctrine so unquestionably central to Plato's philosophy that the word "Platonism" soon came to denote it specifically, and has ever since done so. It was Plato's belief that ultimate reality consists of eternal, unchanging abstract forms that have their being outside any consideration of space or time, and which manifest themselves in all the individual things that come into existence and pass away in this world of our sensory knowledge and experience. In the empirical world nothing stays the same, indeed nothing lasts: all is perpetual change and eventual decay. But the fleeting things that constitute this world are degenerating copies of something permanent: it is only the copies that are ephemeral, and they perpetually replace one another; what they are copies of abides unchanging, eternal, immaterial. (This doctrine was to play a crucial role in the development of Christianity; and it is a historical fact that early Christian thinkers consciously took it from Plato.) In Plato's view the highest attainable state of human awareness was direct cognition of the Ideas, a state in which mind had soared above and beyond the material and was at one with the timelessly abstract. Mathematics, he believed, was the royal road to this mode of understanding of the spaceless, eternal entities that constitute ultimate reality. That is why, over the entrance to his Academy, he placed the words: "Let no one enter here who is ignorant of mathematics." And the key to the understanding of the world of experience, he believed, was mathematical physics. This belief has been fundamental to Western philosophy ever since, and is what chiefly differentiates it from other philosophical traditions. Among its consequences is the fact that every revolution in mathematical physics precipitates a corresponding revolution in philosophy.

The chief figures in two such revolutions are the two philosophers whom Schopenhauer revered above all others: Plato and Kant. His first book began with the somewhat startling words: "Plato the divine, and the astounding Kant . . ." He took this view of them for many reasons, but above all it was for the secure mastery of their understanding that the empirical world, including the objects of even our most direct perception and experience, is not ultimate or even independent reality. He was aware of the almost impossible counter-intuitiveness of this insight, which was one reason why he esteemed these possessors of it so highly, and he believed that the achieving of it was the most important single step in philosophy, the *sine qua non* of any philosophical understanding that could be considered worthy of the name. However, he thought that Plato, like Kant, had erred in allowing his conception of ultimate reality to be plural when this could not be the case: Kant had posited thing*s* in themselves, Plato posited Idea*s*. Schopenhauer did not respond to this by denying the existence of Platonic Ideas. He did not even deny that they were plural. What he denied was that they were ultimate. And it was impossible for them to be ultimate not only because they were plural—though that reason alone would have been enough—but also because they were undisentanglably associated with cognition. Nothing that is knowledge, or is knowable, is ultimate.

There is something disconcerting about the way Schopenhauer introduces Platonic Ideas into his metaphysics. He does so at an advanced stage in the exposition, and up to that point the reader has been led to expect a dualistic view of total reality as comprising the noumenal, which Schopenhauer has dubbed "will" in his specialized sense of that term, and the phenomenal world, consisting of the representations of sense and intellect—hence indeed the title of his masterpiece *The World as Will and Representation*. But now suddenly he introduces a third constituent of total reality in the form of Platonic Ideas. These, being plural and knowable, cannot be noumenal. But they are not phenomenal either. They are intermediate. It is only through their phenomenal manifestations that we can know of their existence at all, but, even so, their phenomenal manifestations are not *them*. Take, for example, a scientific law: let us say *at constant temperature the pressure of any body of gas is inversely proportional to its volume*. Only by observing the behaviour of actual bodies of gas in actual places and at actual times, and making inferences from such observations, do human beings arrive at knowledge of any such law. The law itself is not some sort of free-floating abstract entity that we can somehow directly "know." And yet each individual manifestation of the law is not the law. The law itself is abstract and universal. Even so, it would be obvious nonsense to talk of it as having any purchase outside the phenomenal world, outside the world in which there is space and gas and heat and pressure. Only in and through its concrete manifestations does it exist. Here, then, we have something which is abstract, independent of time and place, universal, and yet manifests itself in the phenomenal world of material in space and time—and in all these respects shares its nature with the noumenal—while being at the same time merely one among many scientific laws, and having no application or being whatsoever outside the world of phenomena, and being in those respects part of the stuff and substance of the phenomenal world.

Schopenhauer seems to think he needs a metaphysically intermediate category of this kind to explain how it is (not why—that would have no meaning) that the One becomes the Many. Scientific laws are the Platonic Ideas that stand behind the structure and motions of matter in space and time, and also behind the development of some of this matter as living organisms. Genera and species are the Platonic Ideas in terms of which each individual living thing is to be identified: this one is a cat, that one is a blade of grass, and so on. Schopenhauer also needs some such metaphysical category in order to explain how it is that a noumenal One which is a blind, impersonal, directionless force does not manifest itself in a jumble of objects without form or structure, a chaos in which everything is different from everything else. The phenomenal world exhibits deep, sophisticated structure at every level, both in the objects themselves and also in their behaviour, from a single cell to the unimaginably vast galaxies, and everything in between. Platonic Ideas are, as it were, the deep grammar via which the noumenal finds expression in the language of phenomena.

There is yet another context in which Schopenhauer seems to think he needs to call Platonic Ideas in aid, and that is his theory of art. It is characteristic of all the arts except music that they portray individual contents of the phenomenal world, including people, and yet do so in such a way that we are conscious of tapping in to something universal via the particular. The work of art in question may be a painting of nothing more decorative than a pair of old boots on the floor of a poverty-stricken bedroom, and yet it can seem to us to be expressing something of universal significance. What is happening here, says Schopenhauer, is that we are apprehending the Platonic Idea through a unique instantiation of it, and therefore we are in a literal sense perceiving the universal in the particular. Plato had believed that direct cognition of the Ideas was the highest form of awareness that human beings are capable of: Schopenhauer was agreeing with him, up to a point, and explaining that this is made possible for us by works of art. There is an irony in this, in that Plato had been anti-art, as Schopenhauer well knew. Plato had seen works of art as delusive semblances of objects which were themselves decaying and ephemeral semblances of Ideas, and therefore as delusive semblances of delusive semblances; and the more attractive they were, by so much the more did they divert our attention and aspirations away from the Ideas themselves, when cognition of these ought to be our highest aim. In this way Plato saw art as a lethally seductive threat to the immortality of our souls. In his view it would be banned from the ideal state.

Schopenhauer, however, did agree with Plato that Platonic Ideas are the dies with which what is noumenal stamps out the coinage of this world, creating innumerable objects that have their individual existence and yet are alike:

they are why every chaffinch is like every other chaffinch, every star like every other star, every blade of grass like every other blade of grass. He agreed also with Plato that it is possible for humans to attain direct knowledge of these Ideas, though he disagreed as to how: according to Plato it was by a kind of intellectual mysticism which, because it is intellectual, is a possibility for exceptional minds only; according to Schopenhauer it is through works of art. Beyond that there is only disagreement. Plato believes that Ideas are ultimate, and are divine, which is what makes direct knowledge of them a mystical experience; Schopenhauer believes that they are intermediate between this world and what is indeed ultimate, namely the noumenal, which is unknowable, uncomprehensible, non-intellectual (and is partly for that reason dubbed "will"), and one and undifferentiable.

It comes to us naturally, says Schopenhauer, to see the phenomenal world thus created as comprising four grades of object or entity—inorganic matter at the bottom and then, rising up, plants, animals and humans—and to relate ourselves in a different way to each of these. Human beings have always done this, he says, and on examining ourselves we find we cannot do otherwise. He agrees with Schelling that the second, third and fourth of these grades have emerged by a continuous process from the first. He sees the biggest single difference among them not as being between the fourth grade (humans) and the rest but as being between the first grade (inorganic matter) and the rest—in other words between life and non-life: this is the unique exception to Aristotle's maxim that Nature never proceeds by jumping across a gap. The second, third and fourth grades of the will's objectification consist of nothing but genera and species (each of which is a Platonic Idea). There is a developmental process running through them towards ever higher levels of complication and sophistication with regard to structure, and hence towards ever greater degrees of individuation, until with human beings the stage is reached at which each individual is itself (himself or herself) the instantiation of a unique Platonic Idea, and is therefore what one might call a universal individual.

By bringing together two of the formulations just offered—first, that the function of art is to provide us with cognition of Platonic Ideas via representations of individual phenomena that instantiate them; and second, that the phenomenal world instantiating the Platonic Ideas comprises four distinguishable grades—Schopenhauer provides us with a taxonomy of the arts. The differing arts, he says, relate characteristically (though not exclusively) to different grades of the will's objectification. What this gives us is a hierarchy of the arts. At the bottom we have the art whose subject matter is the first and lowest grade of the will's objectification, the inorganic elements of Nature: huge masses of stone, earth, water and the rest. This is architecture. No other medium can match it in the artistic use of natural elements—open air, real space, real light, real materials and not the symbolic representations of these to be found in paintings or in language. However, if what we want is to present objects in the second grade of the will's objectification—flowers, trees, plant life more generally—architecture is an inappropriate medium. The "natural" medium for those is painting. When we move up to the third grade, however, to the grade of animal life, the two-dimensionality of painting becomes a limitation. The body of an animal, its mass, weight, bulk, balance, poise, can all be rendered more effectively in sculpture: no painting of a horse can equal a good statue of a horse in its aesthetic impact. However, when we move up to the fourth and highest grade, even three dimensions are not enough. Portrait sculpture and portrait painting are fine arts, but their ability to represent human beings is limited by their lack of a time dimension. They represent fixed moments; but we also have need for a medium that can articulate the ebb and flow of human life and feeling, the development of emotions, character, relationships, the shifting balances within conflict, the building up and resolution of crises, the whole course and culmination of personal destinies; and for this the use of language is indispensable. A single leap of emotion may find expression in a lyric poem. But for the full-scale and ever-changing panorama of human life the most appropriate medium is drama, which can also draw on all the resources of poetry. It is in poetic drama, such as the great tragedies of ancient Greece, and above all the plays of Shakespeare, that the summit of literary possibility is scaled.

People who read Schopenhauer in the twentieth or twenty-first century are bound to think almost immediately of certain exceptions. Why does he not bring in novels at this point? The answer is that at the time when he was developing his ideas, very few of the novels that we think of as "great novels" had been written. And of those that had, not all were known to Schopenhauer. The medium was in its infancy, its time of greatness still to come. Schopenhauer loved Sterne's *Tristram Shandy* and Goethe's *Wilhelm Meister,* and saw them clearly as works of genius; but even if one adds to those the fictional works of Voltaire, Rousseau and Cervantes it adds up to very little compared with the vast corpus of poetic drama over a period of more than two thousand years between Aeschylus and Schiller, encompassing the greatest of the Latin, English, French, Italian and Spanish playwrights in addition to those of Greece and Germany. Between the two there is no comparison. So it came naturally to Schopenhauer to think of poetic drama as the apotheosis of literary art. But there would be no special obstacle to bringing the novel under his theories for anyone who wished to do so.

Another objection a modern reader might have is to the premiss that all the arts we have mentioned so far are essentially representational. What about abstract painting? Again, this had not come into existence at the time when

Schopenhauer wrote. Even now, it has not taken the visual arts over in the way it was expected to in the first half of the twentieth century: it now appears a much more limited phenomenon in time and place than it once did. But it nevertheless remains, I believe, an exception to Schopenhauer's rules. I think he would have to assimilate it to his theory of the purely decorative—though, again, it would be easier to do that than people seventy years ago would have wanted to admit.

The most obvious omission from the account of Schopenhauer's theory of art up to this point is music. This is because he did not regard the theory as applying to it. He saw music alone among the arts as being non-representational. Of course he knew that there is some music that imitates the sounds of Nature, as in Beethoven's *Pastoral Symphony,* or Haydn's oratorio *The Seasons,* but he regarded this as "sound effects" rather than music proper, and thought it a regrettable lapse of taste on the part of such great composers. True music is purely abstract, does not represent anything in the phenomenal world—and therefore does not give us cognition of Platonic Ideas through the depiction of concrete particulars. In fact it bypasses both Platonic Ideas and the representations of phenomena altogether. What it is, says Schopenhauer, is a direct manifestation of the noumenal. Just as the phenomenal world is the self-manifestation of the noumenal in experience, so is music. It is the voice of the metaphysical will. (This doctrine was to have enormous appeal to Wagner, not least because it put into words something that he intuitively believed already.) Music exhibits to us the insides of everything. "When music suitable to any scene, action, event, or environment is played, it seems to disclose to us its most secret meaning" (*The World as Will and Representation,* vol. i, p. 262). This puts it in a different category from the other arts, makes it what one might call a super-art. Far from being a depiction of anything in the world, it is itself an alternative world, and one that reveals to us the profoundest metaphysical truths that human beings are capable of articulating or apprehending, though of course we are not capable of apprehending them conceptually. "The composer reveals the innermost nature of the world, and expresses the profoundest wisdom, in a language that his reasoning faculty does not understand" (*The World as Will and Representation,* vol. i, p. 260).

Schopenhauer is aware that in talking in this way he is being driven to use language non-literally, and to say things that, on the face of it, are self-contradictory; but such figurative, almost at times poetic, use of language is the only way he can think of to convey what he wishes to convey. Conspicuously unlike Fichte, Schelling and Hegel, with their penchant for covert pseudo-demonstrations, he goes out of his way to draw his reader's attention both to his lack of any demonstrative argument and also to the self-contradictions in what he says. "I recognize that it is essentially impossible to demonstrate this explanation, for it assumes and establishes a relation of music as a representation to that which of its essence can never be representation, and claims to regard music as the copy of an original that can itself never be represented. . . . I must leave the acceptance or denial of my view to the effect that both music and the whole thought communicated in this work have on each reader" (*The World as Will and Representation,* vol. i, p. 257). Here he is making the same kind of appeal as art itself makes, and yet without attempting to deceive either the reader or himself into thinking that this will somehow do as a substitute for a logical process. His writings are almost uniquely rich in rational arguments—no philosophers' are richer—and yet he does sometimes call other forms of insight in aid, though when he does so he usually draws the reader's attention to the difference.

I mentioned earlier that I react to Schopenhauer's philosophy in some of the ways I am accustomed to reacting to art *in addition to* reacting to it as I am accustomed to reacting to philosophy. His philosophy is itself a work of art, as no other philosopher's is except Plato's. By saying this I mean that in addition to all the ideas and insights, arguments, doctrines, analyses and so on that go to make up any systematic philosophy, and which we can evaluate intellectually, the whole itself is a presentational symbol. And what it is a symbol of is total reality. I think Schopenhauer himself understood this, and I believe it to be the explanation of a statement that has baffled many people. Right at the beginning of the Preface to the first edition of *Die Welt als Wille und Vorstellung* he says of the book: "What is to be imparted by it is a single thought. Yet in spite of all my efforts, I have not been able to find a shorter way of imparting that thought than the whole of this book." Most readers seem to have reacted to this by assuming that the thought in question must be something to do with the assertion that the metaphysical will constitutes ultimate reality. Some have made efforts to put the thought into a single sentence. But I believe that the thought is the whole, and expresses a single idea in the same sort of way as a successful work of art embodies a single idea. In this case it is a presentational symbol of the way things are (not altogether unlike the way, for example, that Wagner's *Ring* is a presentational symbol of the way things are). Even at a purely intellectual level Schopenhauer's work needs to be read and understood as a whole more than that of any other philosopher—more even than Spinoza's—in that it is not possible properly to understand a single doctrine within it without having read the whole of it. This has damaging implications, I fear, for what I am trying to do at this moment.

It is common for imaginative writers to attempt to clinch their readers' understanding of something they have just said with the words "It was as if . . . ," followed by a metaphor that may then enable the reader to grasp for the first time what it really is the writer is getting at. Some of the most famous passages in literature are of this kind, extended metaphors designed to be understood not as factually true descriptions but as symbolic parallels casting light on something for which any literal descriptive words would have to be quite different. In ordinary conversation we do the same thing, and do it so often that some of the most familiar examples have become clichés, like "It was as if the floor opened under me." It has been said often that the more powerful an experience, or the deeper an emotion, the more likely we are to feel we need to resort to metaphor to give it adequate expression. Metaphor, it would appear, goes deeper than literal speech. That must be one reason why poetry can penetrate depths inaccessible to prose. And perhaps also it is why there is such an important element of "as if" in great philosophy.

The most famous passage in Plato, if not in the whole of philosophy, is the so-called myth of the cave in the *Republic*. It is an extended metaphor for the fundamental truth that we cannot help mistaking the objects of our direct perceptions for real and independently existing objects when in fact they are no such thing: they are, so to speak, passing shadows; but the circumstances of the human situation are such that it is not possible for us in our ordinary everyday situation to know what epistemological objects actually are, or how they come to be. In the *Timaeus,* which for hundreds of years was held to be the most important of Plato's dialogues, there is a creation myth about a divine craftsman imposing order on chaos. As Myles Burnyeat, one of our leading Plato scholars, has expressed it: "He wanted to see the entire universe as the product of order imposed on disorder, and by order he meant above all mathematical order. This, of course, is very different from the Book of Genesis. Plato's divine craftsman is mathematical intelligence at work in the world. . . . Of course such a very general proposition as the proposition that the whole universe is the product of imposing order on disorder is not something you can prove either in general or in all its detailed ramifications. Plato is well aware of this; it is a further reason for his clothing the proposition in a myth. All the same, the myth served as the guiding inspiration for something that Plato was very serious about indeed: a research programme for which he enlisted at the Academy the leading mathematicians of his day."* Yet another haunting myth of Plato's, this time in the *Symposium,* is that human beings were once unitary creatures but were then split into halves, female and male, and since that time every one of these incomplete creatures has been desperately seeking its other half in order to become whole.

Many other philosophers have coined myths or poetic metaphors that have endured: Heraclitus and the river in which you can never step twice into the

---

* Bryan Magee, *The Great Philosophers,* p. 27.

same water; Pythagoras and the music of the spheres; Descartes and the Malicious Demon; Hobbes and his State of Nature; Rousseau and his Noble Savage; Hegel and his parable of Master and Slave; Wittgenstein's fly trapped in the fly-bottle. There are quite a few. But there is a deeper sense in which any descriptive and systematic philosophy, being an attempt to capture reality in language, is metaphorical. The philosopher is saying "This is how things are," and this may be taken as meaning, or at least as including, "They are as if . . ."; and this mode of utterance, far from being evasive, enables the philosophy to go deeper than it otherwise could. There are well-known philosophical doctrines of which it is simply not clear whether the philosopher is putting them forward as literal truth or as enlightening metaphor. This is notoriously the case with Locke and his Social Contract: nobody quite knows whether he regarded it as a historical event or a legal fiction. But my point here is that this makes very little difference: what he is saying is that government is legitimate only if it has the consent of the governed, as if it rested on a contract freely entered into by both sides. This is how government is to be seen and felt about, he is saying; this is how best to understand it. And whether there ever actually was a literal contract made in some pre-historic time is (in my opinion) neither here nor there with regard to the central point. And this is how most people have viewed the matter.

But the same thing can apply in metaphysics. When Schopenhauer says that human beings interact and interrelate as they do because they are all, in their hidden inner nature, one, behind a delusory façade of separateness and differentiation, I have no way of knowing whether this is literally true or not. But I can see that human beings act *as if* it were true—and to perceive this is to deepen one's understanding of human behaviour. Schopenhauer's doctrine, metaphorical though it may be, even has predictive power: if you look at humans as if it were true you find you become better at knowing how they are going to behave. This seems to me to indicate that it contains important truth in some shape or form, even though that shape may not be literal, and the truth may be incomplete. It is not philosophy that we are trying to understand, after all, it is reality. And anything that increases our understanding carries us forward. So to turn one's back on a philosophical idea that illuminates reality because its formulation is logically or in some other way objectionable is to have forgotten what the purpose of philosophy is, and to have lost one's way. Unacceptable doctrines that illuminate are like crosses on maps that show where treasure lies hidden; they tell us where to start digging, in this case because they tell us where we have gone wrong about something important to us. But of course unacceptable doctrines that illuminate can be that only for people who look at reality in the light of them: for people who look only at *them,* and confine themselves to analysing them, there is only their unacceptability to be discovered, and no illumination to be gained.

Schopenhauer's philosophy possesses this characteristic for me more powerfully than any other. About the literal truth of many of his doctrines, including some of the most central, I am agnostic, but about their capacity to illuminate I have no doubt. Sometimes I find myself accepting his first and second steps as true in a literal sense and then withholding judgment about the third. For instance, he believes that Kant is wrong to argue that rationality is the foundation of ethics. The foundation of ethics, says Schopenhauer, is compassion; and the reason why we feel for and with one another, why we *identify* with one another, is that noumenally we are, as a matter of fact, one. Now I agree that Kant is wrong to see rationality as the foundation of ethics, and I agree that their foundation is compassion: I regard both of those propositions as true in a literal sense. But I do not know whether Schopenhauer's explanation of the apparently paradoxical fact that we experience compassion is true in the same sense. I find it, as I have said, surprisingly enlightening: human beings, including me, do tend to behave—and I myself to feel about other people—*as if* it were true. And if I look at interpersonal relationships in the light of it I find myself understanding them better. But of course it does not follow from this that it is true. And perhaps it is not true, not *literally* true. So I remain at the level of "as-if." This is more positive than rejection or disbelief, because it provides me with so much more understanding, but it is still not the same as belief.

I have this attitude also to Schopenhauer's doctrine of metaphysical will. I even have it to some aspects of the distinction between phenomenal and noumenal—not with regard to epistemology, but with regard to matters of value. To me it directly looks and feels as if our sense of morality, beauty, and the meaningfulness of life come to us from outside this world of observation and experience, and I cannot help regarding this-worldly explanations of them in biological, or historical, or social, or psychological terms as inherently inadequate, essentially mistaken. It just is as if the meaning and value of life have their roots in an order of being very different from this one, a realm to which we can never penetrate, which is destined permanently to remain mysterious to us. When Wittgenstein says in the *Tractatus* such things as "The sense of the world must lie outside the world . . . *in* it no value exists—and if it did exist, it would have no value . . . It is clear that ethics cannot be put into words. Ethics is transcendental . . . The solution of the riddle of life in space and time lies *outside* space and time" he puts into words the way things appear to me: but whether they actually *are* like that I have not so far discovered any way of finding out. So I live my life *as if* there were a noumenal realm of meaning and value outside this phenomenal world, without knowing—indeed, knowing that I do not know—whether there is one or not. It is an unsatisfactory situation to be in, but I am in it, and I do not see how to get out of it. I repudiate what I take to be the religious step of regarding my as-if perceptions as revelations, and putting faith in them as if they were truths. That seems to me unwarranted. The true explanation of them might be something I have never imagined, and may indeed be something I am incapable of imagining. To suppose that I know what the explanation is is to suppose I know precisely what I do not know.

There is, then, an available level of metaphorical understanding that runs throughout philosophy, not literal yet of great value, to be confused neither with religious faith on the one hand nor with knowledge on the other. In this respect philosophy is close to the arts. But this whole dimension seems generally not to be perceived by people who take an essentially logic-based, or language-based, approach to it.

There are many different ways in which philosophy can be approached seriously, but two in particular seem to be the commonest. Some people come to it seeking revelation, a new understanding of reality: what they are after is illumination, new insight, new truth. Others do not expect to get these things from philosophy: they derive their view of the way things are from other sources, such as common sense, or science, or religion, or a mixture of all three (but there are other sources too). What such people are seeking from philosophy is clarification, and perhaps justification, of what are already some of their most important beliefs. To such people analytic philosophy, whose central activity is the elucidation of concepts, is likely to have special appeal. But I am a person of the first sort: I come to philosophy in the hope of revelations about how things are. Analysis is interesting enough at a subordinate level, and I have devoted quite a lot of time to it, but as a conception of philosophy it is hopelessly inadequate, above all because no problems of substance are soluble by it. The solution of important and interesting problems always calls for new ideas, new explanatory theories, and it is for these, not for analysis, that we look to philosophers of genius. Many are the reliable professionals who can carry out a workmanlike analysis of any given set of arguments or concepts: all that this task requires, over and above a certain minimum level of professional competence, is time, concentration, thoroughness and assiduity. It is certainly hard work, and those who can bring to it an extra flair and a deeper than ordinary level of penetration make personal reputations. But the difference between doing this and producing new ideas is like the difference between being a musicologist and being a composer.

I would expect the sort of philosopher who pursues an analytic approach to note the self-contradictoriness of, let us say, what Schopenhauer says about the nature of music, and in consequence of that to reject it, and think no more about it. But Schopenhauer, as he makes clear, is as aware of the self-contradictoriness as anyone else. What he is trying to do at this point is give some sort of articulation in words to a perception that cannot be adequately expressed in language, and for this he needs not just the forbearance of his readers but their active co-operation in trying to understand what it is he is saying. Actually, what he is getting at is profound. At least two of the greatest composers since the time he wrote, Wagner and Mahler, have regarded his perception of music as the deepest and truest ever to have been formulated in words.

This provides an excellent example of two truths that apply to the work of the great philosophers in general. One is that anything that is difficult to understand requires effort, and therefore requires us to *try* to understand—but this calls for good will, without which understanding is not achieved. Therefore intelligence is not in itself enough for understanding: one must *want* to understand, and try, and be willing to sustain the effort. If one starts out being distrustful, guarded, critical, one often actively prevents oneself from understanding. I am not advocating an uncritical approach, I am drawing a necessary distinction between two stages: a person needs first to have a good grasp of something before he can criticize it intelligently and effectively; understanding has got to come before criticism. And from the fact that a person is trying to understand something it does not at all follow that he is going to have to agree with it when he does. So the good will required to achieve understanding involves only a temporary suspension, by no means the renunciation, of critical judgment.

The second important truth is that the most valuable things great philosophers have to give us are to be got at not by analysing the logic of their arguments or their use of concepts but by looking at reality in the light of what it is they are saying. It is noteworthy, for instance, that Schopenhauer says he must leave the acceptance or denial of what he is saying about music not just to the effect his writings have on the reader but also to the effect that *music* has on his reader: he expects the reader to consider music again in the light of this philosophical suggestion. So for me as a reader the question becomes: To what extent, if at all, is my understanding of the nature of music deepened if I look at it in the light of what Schopenhauer says about it? (The answer, it so happens, is "considerably.") The same is true of all, or at any rate most, philosophical doctrines, and also of philosophies as a whole: "Is reality illuminated for me if I look at it in the light of X's explanation of it?" There are few propositional truths in philosophy. Indeed, some philosophers have believed there are none. For the most part philosophy is about different possible ways of looking at things: its purpose is the achievement not so much of knowledge as of understanding. An original philosopher is saying to us, in effect, "You will find you understand things better if you look at them *this* way." When one gets to the later stage of squeezing the last drops of juice out of a particular philosophy it may be a good idea to resort to analysis, but seldom until then. First should come all the processes of intellectual empathy, shared vision, imaginative insight, and an "as-if" looking outwards from that particular standpoint.

Schopenhauer understood very well that in this respect philosophy can be like art. When we see a play or read a novel the work often takes us into a world of its own. Not only are we looking into the minds, hearts and lives of people different from ourselves, and in that sense beginning to understand what it is like to be them; we also find ourselves looking out at the rest of the world through their eyes. So we begin to understand how everything could look different from the way it normally does to us and still seem natural and real. Tolstoy's novels present us with a world that is distinctively their own, Dostoevsky's with a different world, and Turgenev's with a world that is different yet again. When I read any of these I am absorbed into that particular world, which I see through the author's eyes, and react to with his sensibility. This does not mean that I, Bryan Magee, see the world in the same way as Dostoevsky does, or that I agree with him about everything, or indeed that I agree with him about anything. I might, indeed, think that the world of his novels is quite unlike that of real life, and his people unlike real people, and that there are many important things that he fails to understand. But while I am reading his book I am inside his skin and his mind. And the result is an enhanced perception and understanding of my own world, my own experience, an enrichment of my vision. And precisely this is true with philosophers of genius. How does reality look to you if you see it through Descartes's eyes? Or Locke's? Or Spinoza's? Or Kant's? Each will present you with a different world, and you yourself may not agree that any of them is the real world, but you can learn from them all, just the same. You may even learn a great deal from a philosophy that you consider disastrously mistaken—as I, for instance, have from Marxism. What one gets from a philosophy consists largely not of true propositions but, more important than that, ways of looking at things, ways of *seeing* things. An approach that merely grubs along at the level of analysing the logic of arguments or the use of concepts lives a hidebound, blinkered existence on the lowest possible level of existence that the subject has to offer.

The metaphysical visions of philosophers are not empirically verifiable, and this is as true of those of the empiricists as of any of the others. When Locke, like Descartes, presents us with a vision of the universe as a vast cosmic machine made up of lesser machines, all of them subject to the same scientific laws, this is not a scientific theory that observers can investigate and test, it is a vision of how things are; yet it will have a thousand practical influences on whoever accepts it. And when, by contrast, Schelling comes along and says that reality is not so much like a machine as like a single great big living organism, and is therefore better understood as a quasi-organic developmental process rather than as something mechanical, and that in the highest products of the human mind this process achieves an understanding of itself, there are no crucial experiments by means of which scientific-minded observers can adjudicate between this view and Locke's to decide which of the two, if either, is "true." However, to conclude from this that such world-outlooks are nothing but words, and therefore fanciful, a lot of nonsense—a load, really, of meaningless metaphysics—is a profound mistake. It is those metaphysical visions that give rise to our research programmes, as they did in the case of both Plato and, two thousand years later, empirical scientists. The question with regard to each of them is: Do you find it illuminating, if only temporarily, to look at reality in this way? If you do, it has a value. If you find two models illuminating, they both have value. The fact that they are at odds with one another, so that if one of them is true the other must be false, does not alter that fact. It is true, incidentally, in the so-called "hard" sciences as well as in philosophy. The most famous example of this in our own day is the incompatibility between relativity theory and quantum physics, both of which yield accurate results, and both of which are used by the same scientists in spite of the fact that they cannot both be true. None of the philosophies I have discussed in this book is wholly acceptable by me as literal truth, or is taken by me at its own valuation, but all of them throw light, each from its own distinctive angle, on our view of the way things are.

It would be difficult for anyone to be more aware than I am of the inadequacy of the accounts I have given of individual philosophies. That is why I could not claim that this book is anything more than introductory. Schopenhauer's work in particular is so rich that I have written a separate book about it, and that too is no more than introductory. The most important aspect of Schopenhauer's philosophy that I have not attempted to go into is his pinning down of the ontological status of epistemological phenomena: if they are not objects that exist independently of our experience, and are also not creations of our minds, what can they possibly be? Schopenhauer's thinking here constitutes some of the profoundest philosophizing that has ever been carried out by anyone. But it would be impossible to give a coherent account of it here without extensive prior exposition, not least because it builds on some of the most prolonged and difficult analyses of Kant. I shall have to leave my readers to find it elsewhere, possibly in my other book but preferably in the works of Schopenhauer himself.

While writing my book about Schopenhauer I was in the unusual position of being able to discuss his philosophy with a philosopher of genius, Karl Popper; but this was not as useful as I might have wished. Popper had not read Schopenhauer for many years, and in each of the major disagreements that I had with him he came round in the end to my point of view. He did, however, make one or two remarks that are worth recording. As was the case with Wittgenstein, Schopenhauer was the first philosopher whom Popper read. Both of them did so as young teenagers, and for the same reason, namely that Schopenhauer was the most fashionable and discussed philosopher in the Vienna in which they were growing up. Popper's father, a distinguished lawyer, had a portrait of Schopenhauer on the wall of his study (as, incidentally, did both Wagner and Tolstoy) and gave a course of lectures on Schopenhauer's philosophy to the local Freemasons. It was because Schopenhauer instructed his readers to read Kant that Popper read Kant, who then became his lodestar until he found his own feet and his own way. He did once say to me, however, that it was from Schopenhauer that he had consciously adopted the method which he adhered to all his life of approaching every philosophical problem through its history: first you review everything of interest that worthwhile thinkers of the past have had to say about the problem, gaining from them everything that is to be learnt, but also criticizing them, above all clearly formulating the reasons why they have failed to dispose of the problem; and then you offer your own solution, and argue for it to the best of your ability. He also said that it was only through Schopenhauer that he came to understand Kant properly. (This last, for what it is worth, is true of me, too.) He once observed that there were more "good ideas" in Schopenhauer than in any other philosopher except Plato. And towards the end of his life he expressed the fear that his work was going to suffer the same sort of neglect as Schopenhauer's from professional philosophers. Knowing these feelings of his on the subject I was doubly moved when, at his death, he bequeathed to me a first edition of *Die Welt als Wille und Vorstellung* in which he had written "To Bryan, with love, to remember both Arthur and Karl."

22

Philosophy on Television

My book about the philosophy of Schopenhauer was a labour of great love, in which I was engaged continuously, though not exclusively, for ten years. It began in 1973, when I was a Visiting Fellow of All Souls College, Oxford, and came out in 1983, the month after I lost my seat in the House of Commons, where I had been an MP for nine years and four months. My chief aim in writing it was not to communicate Schopenhauer's ideas to other people but to get to the bottom of them myself. Throughout the time I was engaged on it, whatever else I might be doing I was marinading in Schopenhauer. In some ways it was the happiest period of my life intellectually, for I had at last discovered the heartland of my own wonderment. The involvement into which it plunged me was far from being confined to Schopenhauer: one of the things that fascinated me was his influence on others, and this made me look again, and through quite new eyes, at certain other thinkers—Nietzsche, Freud and Wittgenstein, for instance—and took me back to Wagner, and to a range of novelists that included Turgenev, Conrad and Hardy. I read the philosophers whom Schopenhauer attacked with such hate-filled venom—Fichte, Schelling and Hegel—and got a good deal out of Fichte in particular. I re-read the Up-anishads, which Schopenhauer turned to at the end of every day before going to sleep. I read Kant again, with an eye this time to his influence on Schopen-hauer. No other of my books has given me so rich an experience in the writing of it, except for *Facing Death*. As eventually published, it contained the most comprehensive treatments to have appeared so far in English of Schopenhauer's influence on Wittgenstein and Wagner. The latter was longer than the whole of my book *Aspects of Wagner.*

I managed to do this while being an MP by devoting every working morning to it, usually at home. I seldom went to the House of Commons until lunch time, but would then stay late, often into the early hours of the morning (as of course did all MPs). All my work with my parliamentary secretary was done in the afternoons: she would spend every morning typing what I had dictated the previous day, I would come into the office after lunch to sign it, and would then deal with that day's post. Every letter I received was replied to within forty-eight hours. At weekends I often devoted more than just mornings to my literary work, and during parliamentary recesses it became my main occupation—my first long summer recess was spent rewriting the first draft of *Facing Death,* which was published in 1977.

At that time there was nothing unusual about my devoting working mornings to an occupation unconnected with my parliamentary duties. Dozens of lawyers in the House of Commons did the same, and also dozens of MPs with jobs in the City of London, or with business interests. Quite a few were small businessmen with companies of their own which it was essential for them to keep in a healthy condition. The only unusual thing about my extra-parliamentary work was the nature of the work—though even then there were plenty of MPs who were writing books of one sort or another. It has always been common for British MPs to write books; and it has never been the case that all such books were about politics.

Another thing I did while I was an MP was make my first television series about philosophy, *Men of Ideas.* The then head of BBC2, Aubrey Singer, had read my book on Popper and found himself reflecting that this was the sort of thing his television network ought to be communicating to a wider public. His first thought, he told me later, was to invite me to make a one-hour documentary about Karl Popper and his work. But then, one morning in his bath, he found himself reflecting: Why only Popper? There were other well-known philosophers around: Jean-Paul Sartre and Heidegger were internationally famous, while within the English-speaking world there were such figures as A. J. Ayer, Isaiah Berlin, Chomsky . . . Why not devote a television series to contemporary philosophy, bringing some of these figures before the public at large and outlining their work, and explaining the most interesting and important current developments? By the time the project was put to me, this was its form.

Ironically, to begin with it was Aubrey Singer who was brimming over with enthusiasm for the project, and I who demurred. I did not see how it could be done. It seemed to me that if I were to keep faith with the subject matter, the programmes would remain unintelligible to a television audience—or, conversely, that if I rendered the programmes intelligible to a television audience they would have to over-simplify the subject matter to a point of near-travesty. So I declined Aubrey's invitation. But he persisted, and urged me to try out the idea in a pilot programme. I replied that a one-off success with a pilot would not mean that fifteen such programmes could be carried through successfully. All right then, he said: two pilots—though, for financial reasons, they would have to be made in such a way that if they came off they could be used as two of the programmes in the series.

This invitation was difficult to resist—though accepting it meant that I needed first to decide in outline what such a series as a whole would consist of. I asked for, and got, complete editorial control of the whole thing from that point forward, and in practice it was then in fact launched. As it turned out, my two pilots were not outstanding among the fifteen programmes that constituted the series; but perhaps for that reason they were reliable indicators. What was decisive about them as far as I was concerned was that they were intelligible and interesting to non-specialists without misrepresenting the subject. Contrary to my expectations—and indeed, not being always fully aware of how I had done it—I found I had drawn a very fine line between inaccessibility and over-simplification and marshalled the contributors along it.

The series as broadcast consisted of fifteen 45-minute programmes. Since I worked for several weeks on each one (most of this preparation consisted of reading) the whole series took two and a half years to make. The individual programmes were put on tape during the years 1975–7, and screened twice a week from January to April 1978—each being shown on a Thursday evening and then repeated three days later on the Sunday afternoon. Soon after it went on the air *The Times* wrote: "In seriousness and scope there has been nothing like it on any general network before." And by the time it finished the *Sunday Telegraph* said, "It has attracted worldwide interest."

The programmes fell into different categories. Some provided necessary historical background to contemporary developments, for instance in Marxism, logical positivism and the work of Wittgenstein—without some knowledge of which it would not be possible to understand what was currently happening. Some gave a state-of-the-art exposition of a well-known branch of philosophy—moral philosophy, political philosophy, philosophy of science, philosophy of language. Some gave an update on famous movements—the Frankfurt School, existentialism, linguistic analysis. And some consisted of pre-eminent individuals introducing their own ideas—Chomsky, Quine, A. J. Ayer, Isaiah Berlin, Marcuse. The whole added up to as full and lively a sketch of what was going on on the contemporary scene as could reasonably be expected from a television series. It was not ideal, of course. Some areas of the subject had to be left out altogether as being too technical for a television audience—logic, for example. Inability to speak English on the part of both Heidegger and Sartre led me, with the greatest reluctance, not to invite them, but to have their work discussed by someone else. My greatest regret of all was that Susanne K. Langer and Karl Popper were unable, for personal and health reasons, to take part. There was a certain irony about this in Popper's case, since it was a proposal to put some of his ideas on television that had led to the making of the series in the first place. And since I regarded him as the best living philosopher I felt a little as if I were putting on a production of *Hamlet* without the Prince of Denmark. But even without him it seemed to me that the project was worth while; and so I was undaunted, albeit disappointed.

In this series my years of immersion in philosophy and my years in television somehow flowed into one another. I had lived so long with each that I was able to move at ease in both at the same time. Every decision I made about content was taken from the beginning with an eye to the interests of a television audience, starting with the selection of subject matter and participants. Since it was needful for the programmes to be at an introductory level it was not at all necessary that a world figure in each particular field should be the protagonist: if someone less eminent could be relied on to give a much more interesting introduction which kept faith with the subject matter then he was my man. The television audience would not have heard of either of them, in any case. It is amazing how many professional philosophers were so status-minded (holding it essential to invite the foremost specialist, the "authority," taking it for granted also that he would compel the audience's attention by virtue of being the authority) and so indifferent to the realities of performance considerations as not to understand this. As one of them put it to me: "How could the person who has published the best book on Spinoza in the last twenty years possibly *not* be the right person for you to ask to do a programme on Spinoza?" Many possible participants, otherwise very gifted, were disqualified as far as I was concerned by having been devoted for so long to increasing their reputations by being publicly seen to master difficulty, subtlety and complexity that they had become almost incapable of expressing themselves in a manner that was simple, direct and clear—indeed were often afraid of trying to, in case it should cause them to lose status. The truly big figures—Chomsky, Quine, Berlin, Ayer, even Marcuse—were not like that, but the lesser, more insecure ones were more often than not. Chomsky was positively pleased after his programme because he thought he had expressed his central ideas with the greatest simplicity he had ever achieved; and Quine similarly said that nowhere else had he managed to articulate his underlying philosophical approach with such clarity and directness.

The desire to communicate and be understood as widely as possible often comes directly into conflict with the desire to impress. This gives many people an incentive not to be clear, because what they have to say does not amount to much, and so the more clearly it is expressed the more obvious that fact will be. Their only chance of giving an air of weighty importance to what they say is to avoid being fully clear while at the same time using impressive-sounding language. If their success in life depends on their making a mark, and if they have nothing in particular to say, it is genuinely difficult for them to resist the temptation to do this, even when they realize what they are doing (and in practice a certain amount of self-deception is usually involved too).

I had long meetings with my contributors, on days prior to our studio performance, in which we would decide how best to use our time—not only what issues to discuss, and what order to raise them in, but how to frame and word whatever was most difficult to express in such a way as to maximize clarity. Even in the discussions as finally taped I had no hesitation in intervening as often as necessary, and at whatever length, to ensure that what was being said would be transparently clear to as many people as possible. The lucidity I was aiming for was not only a property of the sentences; in fact it was not primarily a property of the sentences. It was a property of structure. It consisted in the viewers understanding at every moment precisely what the issue was that was under consideration, and why it was being considered at this particular point in the discussion, and how this point in the discussion had been reached. It was this, more than clarity internal to the sentences, that made clear to the viewers what was going on—though of course I wanted clear sentences too.

The public response was extraordinary. Several times a day during the period of nearly four months that the series was on the air I was buttonholed in the street, on tube platforms, in shops, restaurants, theatre foyers, and public places of every kind, with a frequency I had not experienced when I had been appearing on current affairs programmes with bigger viewing audiences. And from the way people spoke it was obvious that they had been enthused by the programmes in a way that was rare for them too, perhaps unprecedented—many said that these were the best television programmes they had ever seen. What so excited them was not the personalities or their performances but the ideas. Not only was such intense discussion of ideas new to them, the ideas themselves came as a revelation. Many asked me to suggest reading on subjects that had specially appealed to them. It demonstrated yet again what a large potential audience existed for serious philosophical ideas presented seriously.

For quite a few years afterwards my university friends told me that many of their candidates for admission, when asked why they wanted to study philosophy, said it was because they had seen my programmes. Within the academic community the series was well received too. There were criticisms, of course. One was that I had presented people talking *about* philosophy when I should have shown them *doing* philosophy, by which the critics meant carrying out on-the-spot analyses of concepts and arguments, this being their conception of what philosophy was. But that was a conception of philosophy that I had always rejected: as the title *Men of Ideas* was supposed to indicate, the main interest in philosophy is philosophical ideas, not their analyses, which are obviously important as well, but equally obviously must always be ancillary to the ideas. In any case it seemed obvious to me that it would not have been possible to retain the interest of a television audience in an extended piece of philosophical analysis, and certainly not in fifteen such analyses. And how little would have been achieved if only that had been done! The audience would have been left pretty well in the dark about the contemporary scene in philosophy, except for getting a Stoppard-like impression of what philosophical analysis sounded like.

There were some philosophers for whom professional jealousy was a problem. They found it hard to come to terms with the fact that while they, prestigious though their reputations might be within the profession, remained unknown to the public at large, I had become widely known in connection with philosophy. They felt it should have been them, not me; and this gave them a desire to take me down a peg. Three or four behaved in ways of which, I have reason to believe, they subsequently repented. But the rest acknowledged their jealousy with wry humour. There were one or two for whom there was no recourse but to make television programmes themselves, and these went to great lengths to do so; but when it came to the point they were let down by their lack of understanding of the requirements of programme-making and television communication. Their programmes made no impression on the public. One of them believed that because my programmes had consisted almost entirely of discussion I had not made proper use of the medium of television, and he set out to make programmes that were more like other television programmes. He succeeded, with the result that one started to forget them while watching them. Another was so intent on projecting himself as to be embarrassing. If the programmes made by these two had any effect at all it could only have been to weaken the demand for television programmes about philosophy.

However, the BBC were sufficiently satisfied with *Men of Ideas* to ask me to make another series. But the making of *Men of Ideas* had taken up so much of my time, and for so long, that I declined to plunge straight back into another such undertaking. We had exploratory discussions, though, and these resulted in an open invitation being left with me to make a fifteen-part history of Western philosophy. It was an invitation I was not to take up for several years. But when I lost my seat in the House of Commons in June 1983, and found myself having to earn money at something else, I chaired a long series of television discussion programmes called *Thinking Aloud,* and then, in the spring of 1985—exactly ten years after starting work on the making of *Men of Ideas*—started work on *The Great Philosophers.* Like its predecessor series it took two and a half years to make, and so went on the air during the winter 1987–8.

Three of the programmes in *Men of Ideas* had been devoted to expounding the work of dead philosophers—Marx, Wittgenstein, and, by the time the programme came to be made, Heidegger—and I now felt confident of my ability to make a whole series of such programmes. But more to the point, my experiences in making those earlier ones—in particular the specific forms taken by my dissatisfactions with them—had taught me a lot about how such programmes ought to be made, and this resulted in the individual programmes for *The Great Philosophers* being better than they would otherwise have been. In fact that series was better made altogether than *Men of Ideas,* and was, perhaps for that reason, more successful. It began with a programme about Plato and ended with one about Wittgenstein, dealing en route with Aristotle, medieval philosophy, Descartes, Spinoza and Leibniz, Locke and Berkeley, Hume, Kant, Hegel and Marx, Schopenhauer, Nietzsche, Husserl and Heidegger, the American pragmatists Frege and Russell.

I knew that viewers could not be expected to take in an ever-moving flow of new and often difficult ideas in each programme for forty-five minutes without respite. If I had been addressing the same people in a seminar room I could have allowed long pauses while they mulled over what was being said, and perhaps questioned me about it; but television does not allow long pauses, nor does it permit the viewer to question the screen and get an answer. My solution to this problem was to use repetition at specially chosen points. I tried to identify those moments in a discussion at which viewers were most likely to want to pause and reflect, or take stock, and at each of them I would bring it to a halt by saying something like: "This seems to me especially important. Let's just pause here and make sure I'm clear about what it is you're saying before we proceed any further." Then, instead of recapitulating what the other person had just said, I would give my own account of the philosophical doctrine in question; so what I was actually doing, though in my own way, was what the other person had just done; and this meant that what the viewer was getting was one account of a philosophical doctrine followed immediately by a differently presented account of the same doctrine. Because I had more experience of this kind of communication than my co-participant my account would usually be the easier one to follow; and in any case I had the advantage of coming immediately after an alternative explanation of the same thing. So it became a common experience on the part of viewers that they did not understand the other person but understood me—a fact which was to become a standard subject of jokes, in the press as well as in conversation, for many years to come. I received hundreds of letters from viewers asking laconically why I did not dispense with the other contributors and do all the explaining myself. Because I realized that this might be the response I was also aware that my obsessional pursuit of clarity could tempt me to talk too much, so I made a private rule that I would not take up more than a third of the time in any one programme (except for the one on Schopenhauer). Since I was in all fifteen of them, whereas my interlocutor was different in each one, if I had talked only the same amount as the others it would have come across as if I were talking all the time; but when the other person in each programme said more than twice as much as I did the balance came out about right.

Both *The Great Philosophers* and *Men of Ideas* were screened in all the major English-speaking countries except for the United States, where they were felt to be too highbrow. I am sure this was a mistaken judgment, for they elicited strong and favourable audience responses wherever else they were shown—even in some non-English-speaking countries, for instance Holland and Denmark. Both series were turned into books that had an independent life of their own, in hardbacks published by the BBC and in paperbacks by Oxford University Press. Between them they were translated into Japanese, Chinese, Korean, Spanish, Italian, Portuguese, Hebrew and Turkish. For several weeks the book of *The Great Philosophers* was in the best-seller list, the only book of mine ever to be so.

A few months after the book *Men of Ideas* came out I was invited by the then Prime Minister of Turkey, Bülent Ecevit, to be his guest in Ankara for a few days to discuss it. The book, he said, instantiated a kind of critical rationality that he wanted to propagate in Turkey, where all the most powerful traditions were against it. Islam had always punished critical dissent in a draconian way. Family structures were hierarchical—even parents deferred to their own much older parents in the making of family decisions. And at all levels of education, what the teachers said was repeated back to them uncritically by students, who did not dare to do anything else. As Prime Minister, he felt it would be equally disastrous for him to be seen as wanting to interfere in family life or get into a prolonged struggle with the authorities of organized religion; but among the things he really could influence, and in a systematic way, was the education system. So his question really came down to how the values of critical rationality could be introduced into the Turkish education system.

I was not under the illusion that I knew much about conditions in Turkey, so most of my reply had to do with questions and suggestions about teacher training, and I spent two days with members of the Cabinet and their advisers discussing the practicalities involved. Among other things, they asked me to recommend a list of key books for translation into Turkish, and I did that. However, our good intentions came to nothing, or at most to very little. Six months later a military coup ousted Ecevit from power for pursuing precisely such policies as these, and he never succeeded in getting back. (At the time of my visit, during which there were a couple of political murders every day, I was accompanied everywhere by a close personal bodyguard, who even stood outside the lavatory door.) For me, though, the whole experience was not only fascinating and instructive in itself but turned out to be invaluable some years later when I was asked to give similar advice for use in Eastern European countries as they found themselves emerging from decades of Communist dictatorship.

23

The Main Split in Contemporary Philosophy

The underrated philosopher R. G. Collingwood made much of the point that in any given historical period there are likely to be deep-lying assumptions that contemporaries share, not even conscious of them as assumptions, so taken for granted are they; and that these are sometimes not accepted by later generations. Because of this the great intellectual debates that go on between contemporaries are sometimes not what the participants take them to be. They believe themselves to be fighting for mutually contradictory positions; and if this were so, whatever the truth is would have to lie, at least broadly speaking, on one side or the other. Yet in the eyes of their own posterity they are sometimes both wrong, because of some fundamental assumption which they are both accepting.

It is salutary to reflect what such assumptions might be in our own age. I once put this question to an unusually intelligent friend, who answered immediately: "That we have minds." That he replied so quickly made me reflect that it was more likely to be something he had not thought of.

At a less deep level, and more numerous, are assumptions held within broad movements which are not universal even in their own day. Within most intellectual, or artistic, or religious movements there are certain assumptions that cannot seriously be questioned by anyone who is also serious about remaining a member of the movement. Until recently this was true of belief in God, and in the divinity of Jesus, for all the many different sorts of Christian. Even though the Christian Churches fought among themselves to the point of torturing and killing one another's members, every such member had to have a belief in God and in the divinity of Jesus if he was to count as a Christian at all; while at the same time there were people far removed from them and their wars who shared neither of those beliefs. In the twentieth century most Communists believed that you were a genuine socialist if and only if you believed in the basic correctness of Marxism; and there were different sorts of Marxist—Stalinists and Trotskyists, for instance—who tortured and killed one another over questions that were partly doctrinal; yet there were always large numbers of other sorts of socialist who were not Marxists at all.

There have, I believe, been not dissimilar, though of course much milder, such situations in the world of professional philosophy at various times in its history. There were several decades during the broad middle of the twentieth century when, in a great deal of the English-speaking world, a philosopher had to be thought to share the analytic approach if his colleagues were to regard him as a serious philosopher at all—although at the same time fierce and unforgiving battles went on among analytic philosophers. In these wars it was agreed on all sides that Continental philosophers (as they were usually dubbed in England) were not proper philosophers, in fact were mostly charlatans, not even so much as interestingly wrong, and therefore not to be engaged with. Within the analytic tradition fashions came and went as one overthrew another—early in this book I related what it was like when logical positivism held sway; and then how it came to be displaced by linguistic analysis. Both of those movements are now well in the past, a past sufficiently distant for other fashions not only to have reigned since but to have passed away in their turn. Having lived through these changes myself and observed them with particular interest, if always from outside, I feel a temptation to tell their story, but the truth is that such a narrative would be of interest only to a specializing few. I recall something said to me by the outstanding modern historian of English-language philosophy, the Australian John Passmore, at a time when he was re-reading works by the then leading figures so as to be able to give a public account of them. "If all these writers were to solve, to their own satisfaction and mine, the questions to which they are addressing themselves, I would have been enlightened about—what?" The implied answer to his rhetorical question was "Not very much," and I agreed with him heartily: I regarded the works of those writers as dangerously close to empty. This was not because they lacked ability, but because their assumptions were mistaken. At bottom it was the tradition within which they were working, the analytic tradition, that was empty. I do not believe that great philosophy can be done in it; and that is because I do not believe that any problem of substance is to be solved by analysis. (Nor, you may say, do analytic philosophers.)

I have already narrated how, after Moore and Russell broke away from the neo-Hegelian idealism in which they were brought up, the analytic approach which they then pioneered became entrenched in university philosophy to the point where it was widely held to *be* philosophy. Philosophy, it came to be thought, just *was* the analysis, clarification and justification of our interesting or important beliefs, and therefore of our reasons and arguments, our use of concepts, and our methods. That view of it has been foundational to all the competing schools and fashions that there have been within the analytic tradition ever since. It is the shared assumption that nullifies the efforts of them all. For to make that assumption is to be committed to the view that there are no first-order philosophical problems, or that, if there are such problems, they are of a technical nature, within philosophy and about philosophy. Apart from those, if philosophy consists only in the *analysis* of problems, and in the clarification of theories—and in the justification of our view of both problems and theories—then the problems themselves, and the theories themselves, are given to philosophy from outside itself.

In Moore's view most of the problems commonly called "philosophical" were caused by a failure to take common sense seriously, and could be dispelled by an appeal to, and vigorous application of, common sense—the assumption being made, if not always acknowledged, that a commonsense view of the world must be essentially right, and that what were felt by us as philosophical problems were artificially created by some sort of over-intellectualization. He once said that the world itself did not present him with problems that made him want to philosophize—that he had been turned into a philosopher only by the nonsense talked by philosophers.

Russell took a quite different view. He despised common sense, perceiving it to be superficial and extensively point-missing, and seeing, quite rightly, that most interesting truth is unobvious, much of it counter-intuitive. He thought that for hundreds of years now, far the richest sources of interesting and useful truths about us and our world have been the sciences, whose endless flow of discoveries come to us for the most part as revelations. But he also perceived that the sciences, and the mathematics of which most of them make extensive use, are not, and can never be, self-substantiating. Because of this, his most important philosophical work consisted of attempts to justify our belief in mathematics and science by excavating and laying bare their rational foundations. (He believed that mathematics was a body of knowledge about reality until the young Wittgenstein convinced him that mathematical truths were tautologies.) Where he overlapped with Moore and subsequent analytic philosophers was in his belief that a great many of our utterances are clothed in a grammatical form that misleads us as to their logical form, so that the latter—and therefore the meanings and truth values of our statements—stand clearly revealed only after analysis; hence the importance of analysis; but it never occurred to him to think that this was, as Ryle put it, "the sole and whole function of philosophy." To the last day of his life he believed that those who thought it was had abandoned philosophy's central task, our attempt to understand the world. It would follow from this that they had ceased, in essentials, to be philosophers.

The young Wittgenstein believed that all genuine knowledge of the world was derived from observation and experience, and that the richest corpus of it was embodied in the sciences. However, in what was very much a Kantian way, imbibed chiefly through Schopenhauer, he took the things that were of greatest importance to us to be unknowable—the nature of ethics and values, the meaning of life and death, the significance of the world as a whole. His attitude to such things was in some way mystical—the example that he himself offered of what constitutes the mystical is that the world exists at all. But he believed, partly under the influence of Frege's logic, that where no coherent answer can be formulated no coherent question can be asked, and therefore that what lies beyond any possibility of knowledge is also outside the range of philosophical enquiry. However, if the only meaningful questions that philosophy can ask are questions that can be answered, then philosophy is confined to the task of clarification within the sphere of the knowable; and this is indeed what the young Wittgenstein believed. He considered it, in principle, a completable task, and he believed himself to have carried it out "on all essential points"—but he conceded immediately "how little is achieved when these problems are solved." Thus his was, and consciously so, a minimalist conception of philosophy.

The logical positivists embraced the philosophy of the young Wittgenstein but were so oblivious of the mystical dimension of it that they did not realize it was there, and this made them unaware just how minimalist the philosophy was. They believed that the world of actual and possible experience is the only reality there is, and that everything in it is amenable to scientific enquiry. This led them to assimilate all meaningful utterance to scientific utterance, and therefore to take philosophy on board as the handmaiden of science, its task being the clarification of scientific utterance, in particular of science's use of concepts and argumentation, and also its methods and procedures. Philosophy could not itself give us any knowledge of reality: what it provided was clarification and justification. And because they regarded science as common sense writ large—and made more disciplined and more self-critical in the process— they were confidently of the view that their analytic approach was applicable to propositions in everyday discourse, indeed that such propositions stood especially in need of it owing to the lower level of self-critical discipline typical of their formulation. So they regarded the propositions to which philosophical analysis was to be applied as given to it by science and ordinary living, and both as being important; but for both it was science's standards of clarity and truth that were held to be the appropriate standards. Notoriously, the logical positivists tended to regard value statements and moral statements as would-be assertions of fact that lacked convincing evidence.

The linguistic analysts repudiated the notion that all forms of utterance were assimilable to the scientific, and asserted that we use language for a rich variety of purposes of which scientific utterance is only one. This led them to examine different uses of language, and to formulate different criteria of meaning and validity appropriate to each. This in turn led to their taking language as their subject matter, and they actually came to believe that philosophical problems were problems concerning our use of language. Bertrand Russell's comment on this was (*My Philosophical Development,* p. 216): "In common with all philosophers before [the later Wittgenstein], my fundamental aim has been to understand the world as well as may be, and to separate what may count as knowledge from what must be rejected as unfounded opinion. But for [him] I should not have thought it worth while to state this aim, which I should have supposed could be taken for granted. But we are now told that it is not the world that we are to try to understand but only sentences. . . ." The Oxford school of linguistic philosophers under Austin adopted what they called "ordinary usage" as their touchstone in this enterprise. "In what circumstances would so-and-so actually be *said?* And what would it ordinarily be taken to mean in such circumstances? If you ask what its meaning is, *that* is its meaning. And if there are no imaginable circumstances in which it would ever be actually said, then it has no possible use, and therefore no meaning." In the view of linguistic philosophers, philosophy was given its problems by the fact that we use language in ways that are at odds with its normally meaningful uses, thereby getting ourselves into a pickle: these conceptual tangles are philosophy's problems, and the function of philosophical analysis is to unravel them. When they have been unravelled, there is, characteristically, no problem left.

Eventually this was found to be unsustainable, for two main reasons. No truly reflective person felt able for long to justify this enthronement of ordinary language and ordinary usage. Again it was difficult not to agree with Russell when he wrote (*My Philosophical Development,* p. 241): "I, on the contrary, am persuaded that common speech is full of vagueness and inaccuracy, and that any attempt to be precise and accurate requires modification of common speech both as regards vocabulary and as regards syntax." But altogether apart from that, a human being needed to be brain-dead philosophically if, after muddles created by the misuse of language had been sorted out, he found himself confronting a world that presented him with no philosophical problems. A demand grew for a view of philosophy that saw it as being about something that matters more to men and women than fine discriminations of linguistic usage. The view of it taken by the logical positivists had at least paid it the compliment of giving it productive work to do in criticizing and reformulating the methods and procedures of science; but the linguistic analysts were mostly philistine about science, many of them being conspicuously ignorant of it and some of them downright hostile. Their activity tended to take the form of distinction-drawing for its own sake, and, what is more, in the minutiae of ordinary language.

It was this that brought about the greatest reaction of all against analytic philosophy. It was judged to be footling even by a number of professionals within the subject. At the same time it brought disapproval from outside, of unprecedented strength. During this period, more than any other, intelligent people were put off philosophy by its own practitioners. Young people went up to university intending to study it, but when they heard philosophers talking they came to the conclusion that it was a waste of time, and decided to do something else with their own. Intellectually distinguished academics in other disciplines found themselves forced to the conclusion that what their colleagues in philosophy were doing was unworthy of intellectual respect. The reputation of the subject (and, I would say, the subject as professionally practised) reached its nadir.

Unfortunately the reaction, when it came, did not go far enough. The desirable thing would have been for the analytic approach itself to be abandoned. If people then felt in need of some sort of model of what to do instead, one that lay ready to hand was the work of Karl Popper, who was then at the height of his powers and was acknowledged even by the linguistic analysts to be an outstanding figure. But instead they ignored his work while continuing to pay lip-service to him. Just as a generation earlier the logical positivists had taken his critique of them lightly, and then found that their position had to be abandoned for the reasons he gave, so now the linguistic philosophers did a similar thing. In both periods the unregenerate hung on to the intellectual leadership of Wittgenstein; the earlier generation to the Wittgenstein of the *Tractatus,* the later to the Wittgenstein of *Philosophical Investigations.* In a crude way philosophy's tragedy in the middle period of the twentieth century can be summed up by saying that the profession in general took its lead from Wittgenstein when it would have done better to take it from Popper. Even when finally it did move forward out of the trenches, it took its analytic impedimenta with it.

In the new, freer period, many individuals, including some of the ablest, pursued logico-linguistic investigations into the nature of meaning, reference and truth. Intentionality came in for a lot of attention, and so did problems of identity. All these areas taken together came to be thought of as constituting a field called the philosophy of mind, and came to be seen as the heartland of contemporary analytic philosophy. There were also increasing numbers of individuals who became interested in applying techniques of analytic philosophy to the central concepts of other non-scientific disciplines. A field in which this had occurred already, and recently, was jurisprudence: now came linguistics, psychology, welfare economics, and a number of others. There were some who brought analytic techniques to bear on specific social problems—abortion, experimentation on foetal tissue, genetic engineering, population policy, euthanasia, the use of nuclear weapons, even traffic control. The computerization of society brought into existence a whole new subject within philosophy, namely the study of artificial intelligence, which at bottom was an attempt to increase our understanding of the workings of the human mind by comparing them with the ways in which computers arrive at what are often the same results. On the face of it philosophy was now breaking out of its old confines and discovering a new freedom; and with this came a new diversity. Philosophers were writing about a range of subjects, from music to sexuality, that would not have occurred to the logical positivists, or even to the linguistic analysts, as promising subjects for philosophical investigation. They were more and more confidently mixing philosophy with other disciplines. And they were recovering great figures from the past whom earlier analytic philosophers had dismissed into the shadows—Hegel and Nietzsche most notably. It appeared to many that the scene could scarcely have been more diverse—by contrast with the bad old days, when philosophy kept itself to itself, largely ignoring its own past, and subordinating itself first to one passing fashion and then to another.

But what all such activities still had in common was an analytic approach. And this would have been enough to make them unsatisfactory, regardless of other defects. Analysis can clarify a problem, and this may facilitate its solution, but clarification cannot itself be the solution—not if the problem has any substance to it. Only if there is not a genuine problem at all, merely a muddle or confusion, can clarification remove what then only *appeared* to be a substantial problem. Otherwise clarification is at best ancillary to solution, never solution itself. But this has the drastic consequence that analytic philosophers are compelled to look outside philosophy not only for their problems but also for their solutions. Philosophy thus conceived becomes intermediate to the level of unimportance, being a possible source neither of serious problems nor of their solutions. Linguistic philosophers proclaimed openly that there were no philosophical problems, only pseudo-problems, and that their own so-called solutions merely consisted in tracking down misunderstandings. But analytic philosophers of all and every stripe are condemned to the view that philosophical problems as such can be problems of analysis only, and therefore problems in achieving clarification, not problems in achieving solutions. And this is what large numbers of them do in fact say: that the function of philosophy is to make our utterances perspicuous to ourselves, above all our statements of our beliefs and of our problems.

A solution to a problem needs to involve some sort of explanation, and an explanation that really does explain. To be in possession of any such thing we need to have an explanatory theory which is testable and which impressively survives tests. In other words what is called for are new ideas, ideas which have explanatory power and can stand up to critical evaluation, both theoretical and (where appropriate) practical. The heart of it all is explanation, understanding, insight. The core value of philosophical ideas lies in their explanatory power. Such explanatory theories are the chief content of intellectually serious philosophy, and are what we value most in the work of great philosophers. Their absence is what most conspicuously distinguishes the work of analytic philosophers from that of their predecessors.

Even clarification, if it is to be worthy of the name, needs to have an end in both senses: it should have an aim, such as to make a problem perspicuous, or an explanatory theory intelligible, and it should also terminate at that point for the time being. In principle there is always available space for more clarification: every distinction can be further refined, every explanation can be further elaborated (both in the sense of being made more detailed and in the sense of being further extended), and if these activities are pursued beyond the requirements of the matter in hand not only is this aimless but there is nothing to stop each of them from becoming an infinite regress. We are then word-spinning and logic-chopping for their own sakes. So we should make it a stipulation of method not to draw distinctions to no purpose, that is to say not to draw them beyond the point required for an understanding of either the problem under consideration or the explanatory theory being proposed for its solution; and the same goes for the elaboration of explanations. If further distinctions or further explanations are required they can always be sought when they are needed. To put them forward when they are not needed is obfuscatory, not only serving no purpose but actually getting in the way of understanding, since they reduce clarity. Because this is so, no genuine seeker after understanding behaves like that. The most common motives of those who do are to demonstrate ability, to take pleasure in the exercise of skill, and to gratify a fascination with the activity for its own sake. None of these are forms of the desire to understand the world.

What Bernard Williams, who had been perhaps the most notable of its younger practitioners, was to say in retrospect about analytic philosophy in its linguistic phase is so important that although I quoted it a while back, it is worth repeating in this different context: "When people complained about the multiplication of distinctions, [Austin] pointed out that there were thousands of species of some kind of insect, and asked, 'Why can't we just discover that number of distinctions about language?' Well, the answer of course is that our grounds for distinguishing species of beetles from one another are rooted in a certain theoretical understanding of what makes species different, an understanding given by the theory of evolution. But unless you've got some background theoretical understanding, anything is as different from anything else as you like" (*Men of Ideas*, p. 144). It is on the same page as this that Williams says something else important that I have quoted and is worth repeating: "I think that its basic limitation was that it underestimated the importance of theory. It above all underestimated the importance of theory inside philosophy (though in the case of Wittgenstein this could scarcely be called an underestimation—rather, a total rejection). It had an ancillary tendency to underestimate the importance of theory in other subjects as well. I don't think it had a very clear idea about the importance of theory even in the sciences."

To formulate a view of philosophy that rejects theory is to repudiate philosophy's most significant and valuable content, its very *raison d'être*. It is rather like basing a view of history on a denial that meaningful statements can be made about the past. Wittgenstein managed not only to hold such a view but to incorporate into it a rejection of the use of argument as well. Accordingly, his later work, which is what he is now best known by, contains neither explanatory theories nor arguments. It is scarcely surprising that Bertrand Russell should have written of it: "Its positive doctrines seem to me trivial and its negative doctrines unfounded. I have not found in Wittgenstein's *Philosophical Investigations* anything that seemed to me interesting and I do not understand why a whole school finds important wisdom in its pages. Psychologically this is surprising. The earlier Wittgenstein, whom I knew intimately, was a man addicted to passionately intense thinking, profoundly aware of difficult problems of which I, like him, felt the importance, and possessed (or at least so I thought) of true philosophical genius. The later Wittgenstein, on the contrary, seems to have grown tired of serious thinking and to have invented a doctrine which would make such an activity unnecessary. I do not for one moment believe that the doctrine which has these lazy consequences is true. I realize, however, that I have an overpoweringly strong bias against it, for, if it is true, philosophy is, at best, a slight help to lexicographers, and at worst, an idle tea-table amusement" (*My Philosophical Development*, pp. 216–7). It is also unsurprising that Karl Popper should have publicly associated himself with Russell's attitude (*Modern British Philosophy*, pp. 169–77).

Unlike Russell and Popper most analytic philosophers have not regarded themselves as primarily engaged in an attempt to understand the world, to understand non-linguistic reality—unless, of course, they believed that to understand our use of language *was* to understand non-linguistic reality. Their usual reaction when confronted by an explanatory theory of a philosophical nature has always been, and still is, not to look at it eagerly, sympathetically and with hope, re-examining their experience in the light of it in case it might deepen their understanding, but to examine its plumbing. That is to say, they do not attempt to evaluate the theory in terms of what it is for, namely to enlighten us about some aspect of the world, or of our experience of the world: that function goes by the board with them. Their concern is with whether it is conceptually well formulated and logically watertight—and investigating *that* is what interests them. And they think that doing that is philosophy. Their idea of a difficult philosophical problem is a difficult challenge in analysis. And their idea of a gifted philosopher is someone who is good at analysis. The production of new ideas is not, as they see it, their concern: that is a job for others. Often they reject insight even when it is offered to them, in a way that suggests either that they do not really believe that there can be such a thing or that they consider it dangerous, and therefore regard it with suspicion, to be kept at arm's length. One kind of personality structure not uncommonly found in professional philosophers is one that would be termed defensive by psychoanalysts: it does not embrace new ideas and new insights but fights them off, keeps them at bay.

In ways such as these, analytic philosophy in all its forms has contrived to exclude from its own activities philosophy's most significant and valuable content, the production of explanatory theories that could deepen our understanding of, and contribute to a solution to, the philosophical problems that confront us. At bottom the familiar charge that it is not really philosophy at all, and that its practitioners are not really philosophers at all, is valid. I know from decades of experience that it cannot even be taken for granted of individual analytic philosophers that they will be interested in the fundamental problems of philosophy (by which I mean, for example, Kant's problems), although of course some of them are. Nor can they be assumed to take an interest in the work of outstanding philosophers centrally concerned with those problems, be they figures of long ago, like Schopenhauer, or of our own time, like Popper. The fact that the current profession does not require them to take their own subject seriously saves them a great deal of trouble. One of the things that most commend analytic philosophy to its practitioners is that it can be done by anyone who is intelligent and interested in doing it—whereas what I am tempted to call real philosophy can be done only by people with ideas.

For that very reason, of course, it would not be possible to have a whole profession of real philosophers, because people with ideas are thin on the ground. In the whole of the Western world the number of philosophers in each century whose work is of widespread lasting interest cannot be expected to be more than half a dozen. This means that once philosophy had become professionalized it was inevitable that most members of the profession would need to be able to spend their working time at something other than producing good philosophy. It simply was not possible that they should actually be good philosophers, all of them. Their most obvious option was to teach the philosophy produced by those with a gift for it, and this is a worthwhile job that most of them have done. But confining themselves to that provided only derivative opportunities to make a personal reputation, which was what they needed to do if they were to have successful careers. They had to find a way in which they could be seen to be making a personal contribution. Analytic philosophy was ideal for this. There are two main ways of attracting attention through it: either you can do whatever is in the eye of fashion, so that people are predisposed to pay attention to your work, or you can find a corner of the field in which little or no work has been done and stake a claim on it. In both cases people will notice you; and then, if you perform well, you may advance in the world. In that case your work will have had the outcome at which it was aimed; and in those circumstances it is impossible not to see it as successful—not only you but others similarly seeking advancement will regard it, and you, as a success.

A familiar problem exists wherever something is taught in which creativity plays an indispensable role—be it art, music, imaginative writing, or whatever, and that includes philosophy. Is it to be treated as a subject or as an activity? One does not want to train students to be only passive admirers of the great. It is essential that they should be trained in the activity itself, trained to perform and to produce. Yet in the nature of the case ninety-something per cent of them are not going to be particularly good at that—one is not going to be able, with a straight face, to expect strangers to take an interest in their work. Nor are any but a tiny number of the people who teach them going to be all that good at the creative activity either. The danger then is that both teachers and taught will develop standards on the basis of what they live with in daily life; and to the extent that they do they will lose touch with the aim that their activity is supposed to serve, namely the production, consumption and appreciation of the best work there is. They can, in fact, quite easily develop a way of life in which such work plays little part. And from that point onward their perspectives will be awry, as in the familiar case of the schoolteacher who sincerely assures his friends that the Shakespeare performances put on by his pupils are as good as those at the National Theatre. The best way to avoid such a deep and yet common corruption of standards is to teach students *through* the best of what there is, so that this becomes what they live with daily, and shapes the standards they form.

The two approaches implied in what I have just said represent the parameters within which a creative activity can be taught; and an institution or university department may tend towards either extreme. Let us for a moment take a look at an example from outside philosophy. A music academy can conduct itself ultimately in one of two ways. It can base its teaching on the works of great composers, encouraging its students to learn by emulation: in their composition classes they can study such music, and as instrumentalists they can perform it. The advantages of this approach are that they become saturated with great music, getting to know some of it extremely well, deriving their own standards and models from it, and developing their own skills through it. But there will be critics of this approach who protest: "Your academy is a museum, if not an embalming parlour. You play only music by dead people. Your young people are slaves to the dead, and you are ignoring the fact that music is a living, breathing art. An academy of gifted people ought to be among the pioneers of progress, at the cutting edge of musical advance. You ought to be encouraging live composers; and your young instrumentalists ought to be playing the music of their own contemporaries. *Making* music is what this is all about. You and they ought to be breathing the air of practical innovation, the exciting and the new."

This sounds plausible and attractive, and goes hand in hand with the attitudes encouraged for most of the twentieth century by the modern movement in artistic and intellectual life, based as that was on the notion of sweeping away the past and starting afresh. Because of this, the more traditional approach has been seen for most of my lifetime as old-fashioned, confined, inimical to the creativity of the individual. Yet wherever the more "modern" approach is put into practice the students find themselves spending nearly all their time immersed in mediocre and uninteresting music—simply because all but a tiny amount of the music produced in any one generation is mediocre and uninteresting, including that which they produce themselves. They will be incited to compose it, and also to perform it, and in these most practical of ways to set great value on it. They will find, of course, that scarcely anyone outside the academy wants to listen to most of it, or even sustains for very long a continuing interest in what they are doing; but this is only too likely to develop in them a contempt for music-lovers in general as being unadventurous, stick-in-the-mud, past-bound, a lot of fuddy-duddies and stay-at-homes, uninterested in what real live composers are doing. Then a gap will appear, and will widen, between full-time music students on the one hand and music-lovers on the other. The full-time students will be blinkered and confined in their outlook by whatever happens to be the fashion prevailing at the moment, and will more and more be producing and playing such currently fashionable music for one another, and for a few trendies. Meanwhile ordinary music-lovers will continue to listen to the best music they can find, regardless of when it was composed or of what the more fashionable set may say about it.

A generation later, when such students are at the height of their powers and professional success, they will find that scarcely any of the music they favoured in their youth is remembered even by themselves, and that when they nostalgically revive it, it is not of much interest to anyone else; while the music of the masters is as often played and as much loved as it ever was, perhaps more so, and is still the music that they are most often asked to play for others. They will not find, if they remember to look, that what were thought to be the most modern academies have in the meantime produced more or better composers than the old-fashioned ones used to, or that leading instrumentalists are now noticeably better than they used to be. The worst thing of all will be that they will have lived their lives marinading in the formaldehyde of fourth-rate music, which is not something anyone who loves music could possibly want to do. Indeed, people in love with great music will by now tend to sidestep such academies as places where that love is not easy to develop, and will pursue it in another way, sometimes along a path that consists mostly of individual study and working at home.

Every point in this comparison has its counterpart in the world of academic philosophy. It sounds all very fine and large to say that philosophy is not a collection of great books, nor a conspectus of philosophical doctrines, but an activity, and therefore that teaching philosophy consists not in getting students to study the great philosophers of the past but to do philosophy themselves, and learn to think philosophically, and to engage with contemporaries who are also thinking philosophically. The trouble with it is that most of what they then do along these lines will be not very good, nor will most of the contemporary work they engage with. They would learn far more about how to think philosophically by studying the works of great philosophers; and furthermore these would then be valuable possessions for them for the rest of their lives, every bit as illuminating after thirty years as when first encountered—whereas if they immerse themselves in whatever happens to be the current literature they will find after thirty years that most of it is no longer of interest even to themselves. Worst of all, their continuing mental world all this time will have been a world of the third-rate and ephemeral, when it could just as easily have been a world of the lastingly valuable.

In both cases the more so-called modern approach flatters and elevates the current practitioner, who is therefore almost bound to have feelings in its favour. It encourages him to think that what is happening in his day, and what he personally is doing, are what really matters. It encourages him to produce, regardless of the quality of his work, and to set serious value on what he produces. He is led to believe that he and his contemporaries stand on the shoulders of all the past, and therefore stand higher than anyone has stood before—not in personal ability, of course, but in understanding. So their work, he will probably believe, is in advance of anything produced before. But all this time the harsh truth is that he will be a journalist with a longer timescale than most journalists, a producer of articles on topics of current concern which will be of no interest at all in a few years' time. And all this, together with its concomitant downgrading of the past, will be terminally distorting of his perspectives, and corrupting of his standards. He will, most probably, lose touch altogether with what are in fact real standards and achievements in philosophy as they have existed and endured over long stretches of time that include his own generation (whether he realizes that or not). He is likely to live out his life in an air bubble of the contemporary.

In philosophy I have seen this happen in several academic generations successively, and I expect it to go on happening. The fashions will continue to change, of course; and so, less often, will the underlying assumptions on which certain continuing traditions are based. This, incidentally, is what is now happening to the assumptions underlying analytic philosophy. They are visibly approaching the end of their period of acceptance. Because of this, analytic philosophy is on the way out. A reaction against it is gaining ground within the profession. But again, as in the past, reaction is not taking the form I would wish it to take. What I want to see is the re-espousal of philosophy by professional philosophers, their readoption of the task of trying to understand the world in its most basic and general features—the nature of time and space, and of physical objects and causal connection, and the relationship of all these to the subject of experience; the nature of this subject and of its consciousness, including its self-consciousness; the provenance of ethics and values. Such tasks ought certainly to be pursued with a critical self-awareness that extends to our use of language and of concepts, of logic and of argument; but those things must remain permanently among the auxiliaries of method. The activity as a whole cannot be analysis-led, or logic-led, or language-led, or concept-led, or topic-led. It can only be problem-led. And the problems are those presented to us by all the fundamental features of reality that baffle reason. It is difficult to see how the solutions we seek, unless we are going to appeal to authority or revelation, can at first take any form other than that of explanatory theories that go deeper or wider than any before them, and thus constitute new ideas of unprecedented reach and explanatory power. The best of these are not unlike works of art, in that both are truth-seeking attempts to understand and articulate the nature of fundamental experience in a way that requires creative imagination and exceptional originality—and therefore high talent, if not genius—in their originators. The best philosophy is like this, and it is primarily a creative—and in that sense synthetic, not analytic—activity. Of course, when we have it before us we can analyse it in a spirit that is both critical and appreciative, just as we do works of art; but the relationship of the analyst to philosophy is like that of the musicologist to music, or of the art critic to art. And just as the art critic is not an artist, so the analyst is not a philosopher.

The kind of philosophy now gaining ground in British and American universities at the expense of analytic philosophy is usually known, in Britain at least, as Continental philosophy. This is an umbrella term covering a number of differing traditions and strands within traditions. From the point of view of some of the people who use the term the chief thing these all have in common is that they are not analytic philosophy. What gives them such further unity as they possess is the fact that they have arisen out of, or been formatively influenced by, German philosophy after Kant, in a way that roughly parallels the relationship between analytic philosophy and the British empiricist tradition. Just as analytic philosophers continually hark back to Locke, Hume and Hobbes, so Continental philosophers continually hark back to Nietzsche, Hegel and Marx. And rather as today's analytic philosophers tend to look to Wittgenstein and Russell as their outstanding forebears in the twentieth century, so Continental philosophers tend to look to such figures as Heidegger and Husserl. Continental philosophy is nothing like so science-oriented as many strands of analytic philosophy, nothing like so interested in mathematics and logic, and (perhaps in consequence of that) nothing like so technical. It is more interested in Freudian (and post-Freudian) psychology, in literature, and in contemporary social and political movements.

Because of its interest in analytic psychology there is a great deal of personal reference to Freud and other leading figures in the psychoanalytic tradition from him to the present day. Because of its interest in literature there is extensive overlap between some forms of Continental philosophy and literary theory; some writers are of equal eminence in both, studied and referred to just as much in university departments of literature as in departments of philosophy. And then, because of the interest in contemporary social and political attitudes, there is a great deal of involvement with such contemporary movements as feminism, and gender concerns generally, including matters to do with homosexuality; and ethnic concerns, with a cognate concern with anti-racism (this previously took such forms as anti-colonialism). Before the shipwreck of world Communism brought with it a general disenchantment with Marxism a substantial amount of Continental philosophy was Marxist, or at least *Marxisant,* and this remains a significant influence—if only by reaction now, or through attempts to salvage whatever may be valuable from the wreckage.

These features taken together give Continental philosophy a profile that makes it repugnant to analytic philosophers for reasons quite apart from its non-adoption of the analytic approach. They see it as trendy, and as being riddled with partisan attitudes, usually with a left-wing bias, which breed politically correct agendas. Because of this, and a general absence of analytic self-discipline, they regard it as ridiculously self-indulgent, its most characteristic utterances being rhetorical—that is to say given to assertions of a position or point of view without anything remotely like adequate support in the way of rational argument, relying on obfuscation and the use of jargon, as well as intimidation and covert appeals to the unacknowledged wishes of their hearers, to win acceptance. All this runs counter to the analysts' own professional standards of impartiality and detachment, their determination to make everything they say perspicuous, and their commitment to rational argument. Continental philosophers have often been loud in their advocacy of "commitment," but by this they mean commitment to social causes, whereas the only commitment acknowledged by analytic philosophers, at least in their professional capacity, is to impartial rigour in the use of logic and language. Because of this they have a marked tendency to regard most Continental philosophy as rhetorical splurge, rubbish, bilge. A representative example of such attitudes was given to me by R. M. Hare in an exchange that was published in *Men of Ideas* (p. 156). Of Continental philosophers he said:

> They have more to say, in the sense that they say more words: their books are usually longer. Although there are some very good philosophers in these schools, the commonest sort do little but blow up balloons of different shapes and colours, full of nothing but their own breath, which float here from over the Channel or the Atlantic; and if you prick them with a sharp needle, it's very hard to say what was in them, except that it was probably inflammable and certainly intoxicating. I don't think these people do anything to solve practical questions. They may increase the head of steam a bit beyond what natural human group aggression produces anyway; but from faulty plumbing most of it gets on people's spectacles.
>
> MAGEE: In other words, you think these rival philosophical approaches tend to be colourfully rhetorical but lacking in transportable content. And this is partly because they also lack logical rigour.
>
> HARE: Rigour is the key word.

The absence of rigour gives the Continental approach to philosophy seductive appeal to many emotionally committed people who have a cause to promote. It allows them to give satisfying vent to highly charged and dramatic utterances without imposing on them the basic requirements of critical rationality. Anything goes, so long as it is clothed in language that impresses students, and a certain wider public, who will take what is being said to be profound. The result is sacerdotal philosophy in the worst traditions of Hegel,

Schelling and Fichte, but without their compensating content. Some of it tends to be oracular, as if in imitation of Nietzsche or Freud, or Marx, but has nothing like their quality or style, let alone their genius. Even so, uncertainty about what is being said allows everyone to share the illusion that this philosophy is difficult to understand because it is profound, and that they are weightily engaged with one another in great issues of the day. And if their habitation is an academic one they can enjoy these rewards without having to bother about any wider involvement or political responsibility. Intelligent people of intellectual integrity who have had some training in analytic philosophy are likely to be immunized against this, but those whose training is in the study of literature, and who are therefore accustomed to standards that may legitimately have little to do with logical rigour, are more vulnerable. If a writer conveys a great emotional intensity of concern, and with genuine rhetorical power, they may be swept away.

Speaking for myself, I object to Continental philosophy for most of the same reasons as analytic philosophers do. But in addition I object to it for the reason that forms my chief objection to analytic philosophy. Continental philosophy has abandoned what I see as philosophy's central task, the attempt to understand what is. The interests of Continental philosophers appear to be parochially confined to human affairs, and even then at a highly superficial level. In most cases this runs counter to their own larger beliefs; for most of them would agree, I take it, that human beings are a tiny and local phenomenon, a recent arrival on the surface of a planet that is unimaginably small compared with the universe at large; and that even this speck of a planet existed for aeons before humans emerged on it. But they are not interested in trying very hard to understand such matters. They take what happen to be our local, current and short-term human concerns and treat these as if they were everything. Even then they are more interested in comment than in understanding. All this gives an unmistakably journalistic character to much of their writings. For even if it should be the case, as I think it probably is, that the solutions to such cosmic enigmas as the nature of time and space, and the material objects these seem to contain, have something fundamentally to do with the nature of experiencing subjects, this involves the structural properties of human beings on a far deeper level than that on which these are engaged with by Continental philosophers, who write about humans at the level on which they visit their psychiatrist or go to the cinema, vote, read books and newspapers, or hold forth on cultural, social and political topics—in other words, at a level of ephemeral social concerns. As a conception of philosophy it is piffling, beneath any serious consideration, and could only possibly appeal to people for whom genuine philosophical problems have little or no interest. I have no objection to such people writing about the problems to which they claim to be addressing themselves—in fact (and I hope this goes without saying) I have no objection to anyone's writing about any problems at all. If it comes to that, I have written a good deal about such problems myself. But they have little to do with any serious conception of philosophy.

Despite, or perhaps even helped by, its superficiality, Continental philosophy is making inroads into many university philosophy departments in the English-speaking world, and has taken some over. It has also had an impact on literature departments, and made inroads into departments of psychology, anthropology, sociology and other subjects. In some places a war is going on between counter-balanced factions of Continental and analytic thinkers. Very noticeably, many of the individuals to whom Continental philosophy appeals are among those to whom Marxism once appealed. Its factions often possess the same sort of gang mentality, and behave in the same unlovely ways—being, among other things, intimidating and eliminative of dissent. In my view analytic philosophy is vastly to be preferred, partly because analysis is of some relevance and use in philosophy, and partly because a training in it can be genuinely educative. As a form of mental training Continental philosophy is counter-productive: it teaches students to express themselves inauthentically—in dead jargon rather than living language, portentously rather than simply, obscurely rather than clearly—and to abandon rational argument for rhetoric. It actively trains them not to think, and to be bogus; and in doing these things it debauches their minds.

However, the way to counter the influence of Continental philosophy is not to back analytic philosophy against it. The irretrievable emptiness of analytic philosophy—its inability to formulate fundamental problems of any kind, or to formulate possible solutions for fundamental problems of any kind—is the chief external factor that has allowed Continental philosophy to make its advances. The only effective counter is genuine philosophy—or, in such fields as literature studies, an uncowed insistence on authenticity in expression and response. In matters of this kind I am a short-term pessimist yet a long-term optimist. It could be that philosophy departments everywhere will be overrun by Continental philosophy. But it will never happen that real philosophy is driven out of the field of intelligent human concern, quite simply because the direct experience of reflective people will always confront them with philosophical problems that compel their active attention.

In any case, I do not think it will ever be possible to eliminate fashions in intellectual nonsense. As far as I can see they have existed for as long as human beings have existed; and I think they will exist for as long as human beings exist. They meet so many strong human desires, including the desire for extravagant emotional self-indulgence. They give us all the answers—and this in turn gives us a sense of mastery of the problems that we see as confronting us, as well as a sense of superiority to the uninitiated. Real thinking is hard—not only laborious but more often than not unsuccessful, leaving us with a frustrating sense of our own inadequacy and our ignorance, not to mention exposing these to the raised eyebrows of others. It will always be easier to flee in the direction of what is safe, and safe because approved already. Our lack of self-confidence will always incline us to believe that if what we think is at odds with what a lot of intelligent people are saying then they are more likely to be right than we are. This ignores, of course, the fact that original thinking can only ever be individual, never social, though criticism can be social. We shall never have any insight or understanding of our own if we renounce independent thought. But we shall be safe, and feel secure, perhaps even superior. In practice it is not usually the case that the chief recommendation of abstract beliefs is their truth.

24

Left Wondering

There have been great philosophers since Kant and Schopenhauer, and quite a few good ones. The distinguished company includes Kierkegaard, with his re-iterated insistence that only the uniquely specific exists, so that all real existence is individual, and therefore not to be captured in generalizing systems of abstract thinking; Marx, who, in spite of being so tragically wrong about so much, produced insights which have enriched the understanding of all intelligent people; Nietzsche, whose call to re-evaluate our values is the most challenging of all challenges for anyone who believes that the phenomenal world is all there is; Mill, the most effective of all propagandists for individual liberty; Frege, who sought to de-psychologize philosophy by replacing its epistemological foundations with logical ones; Russell, who did more than any other recent figure to make the implications of science, mathematics and logic a part of our everyday view of the world, and to absorb them into our ordinary use of language; the young Wittgenstein, who re-thought Schopenhauer in the light of Frege's work; Heidegger, who in order to help find out what it is we are actually saying of something when we say that it exists carried through a quasi-Kantian analysis of what it is we experience when we are aware of our own existence; Cassirer, who saw that we live most of our lives through symbols that we ourselves create, down to such ground-floor elements as concepts and sensory images, and that reason itself, logic, language, social and political thought, custom, ritual, religion, all the arts and all the sciences are man-made symbolic systems through which we try to come to terms with experience, to interpret it, store it and communicate it, so that man is most re-wardingly understood by philosophers not as a rational animal or a language-using animal but as an animal whose distinctive characteristic is the creation and use of symbols; Popper, who reconstructed Kant's thought on the basis of transcendentally realist assumptions, and by combining Kantian and empiri-cist approaches evolved the most fruitful and illuminating theory of empirical knowledge that has been developed so far, though he would have been the first to say that it is almost bound to be superseded by a better one, and perhaps quite soon.

All these philosophers are so good that if one reads their work with under-standing one's outlook is never the same again, because what they have to say feeds into one's own way of looking at things and becomes part of it, enlarges it, complicates it. In each case I have not only learnt from them but found doing so an intellectual turning point. Nevertheless, there is a sense in which all of them have been carrying out explorations and making discoveries in a continent whose coastline had already been charted by Kant and Schopen-hauer—with some preliminary help from Hume, needless to say. Passing the torch from one to the next, those three developed what seems to be a funda-mental insight into the nature of the limits of possible human understanding, and so the limits of intelligibility; and this insight still seems to be, broadly speaking, valid. In spite of arguments into which I do not need to enter here about whether a stretch of the sea has been reclaimed at this or that point on the coastline by this or that person, the great land-mass still seems to be roughly where Kant and Schopenhauer (viewing their work synoptically) said it was. Some of the best philosophy of the last hundred and fifty years has probed the limitations thus implied in the hope of characterizing them more accurately and acquiring a better understanding of their implications. And there always remains of course the hope of finding a way of pushing them back again as dramatically as Kant did, perhaps even of finding a point at which they might be broken out of altogether. In addition to that there is al-most endless scope for the criticism and correction of Kant and Schopenhauer, and plenty of room for development—space, indeed, for the creation of whole new subjects—within the continent whose coastline they drew, a continent which still contains unexplored areas of mesmerizing promise and fascina-tion. So there is no shortage of worthwhile challenges and tasks for philoso-phy, nor does it look as if there ever will be. But when that has all been said and done, the fact remains that in most of its essentials our metaphysical un-derstanding of the human condition is where Kant and Schopenhauer left it.

This does not mean that it has to remain there for ever. One of the greatest mistakes of those two philosophers was to suppose that it must. Yet just as they revolutionized philosophy, there is no reason in principle why some other person or persons should not come along and revolutionize it again, and no reason why this should not happen more than once. Kant and Schopenhauer thought they had good reasons for believing that this would not be possible, but their reasons were bound up with assumptions about the incorrigibility of the knowledge of the universe given to us by Newtonian physics, and these assumptions have turned out not to be valid. I cannot predict what the next philosopher of genius will do: if I could I would be him. But for several hundred years now, in Europe alone, each century has seen the emergence of at least one great, innovative figure in philosophy, and I take it that this will continue to occur—it seems more likely that it will than that the supply of such people should quite suddenly, unaccountably, dry up (though of course that is possible too). Between Aristotle and the next philosopher on the same level of ability, Kant, a period of over two thousand years elapsed. Perhaps there will be a comparable period before the next one. Or perhaps he has been born already. We shall not know until he makes his work public, and we may not recognize him even then—Schopenhauer was ignored for most of his lifetime, after all.

However and whenever it happens, if it happens at all, until the next philosopher comes along who changes everything in the sort of way Kant did, the rest of us will have to do the best we can in much the same situation as we find ourselves in now. There is something almost intolerably frustrating about this. And this frustration gives rise to a temptation. Since philosophy cannot, as yet at least, answer our ultimate questions—questions that are a matter of the greatest possible urgency to us, concerning as they do our annihilation or survival—we are tempted to look somewhere else for answers. And where better to look than somewhere that offers answers? This was the path followed by Tolstoy. He plunged into the philosophy of Kant and Schopenhauer with excited commitment, perceiving accurately that the task of genuine philosophy is to answer Kant's questions; but then he discovered that along this path no ultimate answers are to be reached. So he despaired of philosophy. What is the value of it, he complained, if it cannot tell us what the point of living is? So he turned his back on philosophy and embraced religion (I am tempted to add "instead"). But the substitution was illegitimate. Wonderful creative artist though Tolstoy was, not even he was entitled to conjure belief out of ignorance. There is a biting passage about this process in Freud's book *The Future of an Illusion* (p. 56): "If even the crabbed sceptics admit that the statements of religion cannot be confuted by reason, why should not I believe in them, since they have so much on their side—tradition, the concurrence of mankind, and all the consolation they yield? Yes, why not? Just as no one can be forced into belief, so no one can be forced into unbelief. But do not deceive yourself into thinking that with such arguments you are following the path of correct reasoning. If ever there was a case of facile argument, this is one. Ignorance is ignorance; no right to believe anything is derived from it." And that is the point: if we do not know, we do not know. Any talk about this opening up the way for faith is a dangerous playing with words. Ignorance is no justification for believing anything. Facing that fact, and living with it, and facing death with it, is the most frightening of all the existential challenges we have to grapple with in this life. In the grip of that fear and that challenge the most tempting of all temptations, for someone who cannot liberate his mind from thraldom to the problems, is to bolt in the direction of some religious or quasi-religious belief. For others, the supreme temptation is to avoid thinking about it, and I believe that this is what most people do.

Some of the best philosophers since Kant and Schopenhauer have consciously and deliberately put ultimate questions on standby while they got on with addressing themselves to intermediate problems that they were able to make progress with. Nietzsche did this, and so did Popper. The rewards are obvious and great, namely the philosophical works of those individuals. Yet in both cases it meant not addressing themselves to the biggest and most baffling questions of all. It meant—I do not know how to put this satisfactorily—settling for less (even in Nietzsche's case). It might have been better for them as human beings to have spent their lives wrestling with the most important questions, even if they were never to arrive at anything new to say about them. It is salutary to reflect how many people of high intelligence there must have been who have done this, leaving behind them no record of their thoughts or even of their existence. Actually, given the genius of the two under consideration, they might possibly in those circumstances have obtained some new insight; but even if they had not, their lives would have been more valuably spent, or so it seems to me, although the rest of us would have been the poorer.

So—what to do? The challenge is existential rather than intellectual. To spend a lifetime banging one's head against a brick wall is not an attractive prospect. Nor are years of inarticulate bafflement, with the level of frustration rising. Speaking for myself, I am not one of those people who are able to deal with the problem by ignoring the questions: it may be a matter of temperament, but for me the apparent unanswerability of the questions sharpens the persistence with which they nag at my mind. Scarcely a day has gone by since my childhood in which I have not thought about them. In fact, the truth is I have lived my life in thrall to them. They seem to me obviously the most important and interesting questions there are, and in my heart of hearts I do not really understand why not everybody sees them as such. And yet at the end of it all I have no solutions. I am as baffled now by the larger metaphysical questions of my existence as I was when I was a child—indeed more so, because my understanding of the depths and difficulties of the questions themselves is now so much greater.

No one reading this book can have imagined that I was going to end it by pulling out of a hat, in the last chapter, solutions to the fundamental problems of philosophy. The most I can hope to do is leave the reader with, like myself, a better understanding of some of them than he had when he started. The title I suggested to Karl Popper for his autobiography, *Unended Quest,* would have been even more appropriate for this book, and for me, applying as it does in a more all-embracing and metaphysical sense. I am on the way, journeying still, and no doubt will always be doing so, however long I may live. I do not even have much idea what it would be like to reach a destination, or what a destination would be like. If I try to grasp in imagination what it would be like to achieve an understanding of the world and its existence I find myself confronted by the idea of what amounts almost to a mystical experience, a sense of being wholly and completely at one with everything in a timeless state of fully achieved awareness—an experience which it would then be impossible to articulate in language, or any other medium, including artistic ones. I have never had such an experience, and perhaps it would not be like that after all. Far from thinking that I am going to have it one day, I do not believe that I shall, although I am prepared to believe that others may have had it, and therefore might be able to be sure, as I am not, that the possibility of it exists.

In the first chapter I told of the childhood experiences that hurled me forward into what has been a lifelong search for greater philosophical understanding. Since no fixed and final conclusions have been reached in this book I cannot round it off by reporting, after this lifetime of exploration, the triumphant end of the quest. So the end of this book has to be nothing more than that, just simply the end of this book, and not an end in any other sense, or of anything else. But it might at least give the sense of an ending if I tell where my beliefs now stand in relation to some of the questions with which I began. I shall not attempt to argue each one of them out at length—that would require a book as long again as this one—but will content myself with saying in what direction I believe the truth to lie.

Perhaps the best place to begin is by saying that I am surer now than I have ever been that no philosophy that equates reality with actual or possible experience can be right, or can even be on the right lines. The whole approach seems to me a sort of flat-earthism in which a large part of the human race is still enmeshed—a belief that may seem self-evidently true to insufficiently penetrating eyes, or insufficiently enquiring minds, but is hopelessly wrong. There are so many reasons why this is so. Because all the ways in which we can apprehend material objects, whether sensorily or mentally, are directly or indirectly experience-dependent, and therefore subject-dependent, such objects cannot exist independently of us and of our experience *in any of the ways in which we apprehend them.* If objects existing in time and space are, after all, independently real, then time and space must also be in some sense independently real; and this gives rise to insoluble self-contradictions in the concepts of time and space. The whole universe, including time and space, would then either have to have come into existence out of nothing or to have existed always in beginningless time; and it would have also to exist in infinite space, if not itself comprise an infinite number of objects. These extravagantly mystical notions are among the most immediate consequences of commonsense realism, and it is difficult to see how a reflective realist can remain unaware of them. Yet in practice realists tend to shrug them off with an unconcern that I find perplexing.

I suspect that the psychological mechanism at work is something like the following. For reasons discussed earlier, the tendency that we human beings have to embrace the illusion of realism is a compelling one. It might even be built in to us biologically: perhaps we react to our gauge-readings of reality as if they were reality itself because our survival so often depends on our taking instant action in response to them. If this is so then to cease to see them as real could be life-threatening, which in turn would explain why doing so is difficult for us, to the point of near-impossibility: as living organisms we have developed in the way we have for purposes of survival above all, and to go against this grain is rootedly counter-intuitive. So the idea that reality might actually be otherwise than it presents itself to us as being seems in itself unreal, dream-like, impossible to take seriously, no matter how compelling the rational arguments in support of it. Having that attitude ingrained in us, if anyone points out to us that our view spawns infinite regresses, antinomies and self-contradictions we find it easier to push all those considerations aside than to renounce our way of looking at things. If the worldview we have *must* be right then of course we can genuinely rest assured that any apparently insoluble problems to which it may seem to give rise can be left for solution at some future time, or indeed can be left permanently unsolved without distress. And this is how realists behave. Although they are unable to answer the sceptic, who has no difficulty in riddling their assumptions with objections, they nevertheless feel only a token concern about that. They accept with good nature and cheerfulness the validity of almost any serious objection to their position. Reality *must* be as they take it to be, so much is self-evident, and its self-evidence is undisturbed by their inability to produce arguments in support of any such contention. Since this whole situation arises out of our human nature there is obviously room for a conjecture that it is in our nature as human beings to be unable to solve these problems. If we adopt that view, which is widely held, we provide ourselves with a licence to stop troubling. And thus we can arrive in a position where we are taking a worldview riddled with ir-resoluble problems as self-evident, and remaining untouched by the com-pelling nature of some of the arguments against it.

The inability of a lot of otherwise intelligent people to think their way out of the apparent self-evidentness of realism has, as one of its consequences, an inability to understand what is being said when it is said that objects cannot possibly be as they appear to us. Large numbers of professional philosophers say that they do not understand it; and often they so misrepresent the view as to make it obvious that indeed they do not understand it. One of the common-est forms of misrepresentation is to describe it in some such terms as "poetic licence" or "mystical metaphor," apparently without realizing that it is the conclusion of an unexceptionably rational argument, and that commonsense realism has mystical consequences more difficult to believe.

It is revealing to consider Popper in this context, for Popper was a Kantian and yet a transcendental realist. He regarded as mistaken the propensity of empiricist philosophers to see the problem of perception as the cornerstone of the problem of knowledge. He put this mistake down to the fact that empiri-cists tend to be inductivists and to believe that we build our knowledge upon the foundations of immediate experience: we observe, and from what we ob-serve we generalize by the method of induction to formulate comprehensive views, whether they be those of common sense or of science. In this schema the authenticity of our knowledge depends on two things: the validity of our inductive procedures and the reliability of our observation statements, these latter being, so to speak, the foundations on which the weight of all our other statements ultimately rests. Popper denied the validity of induction, and ac-cordingly denied that our knowledge either was or could be inductively de-rived from observation statements. He put forward a wholly different schema of knowledge, one in which particular observations no longer provide the foundations of empirical knowledge but play a different role. According to him the expectations with which we approach reality derive from a wide vari-ety of sources, including a great deal of guesswork and hunch; and we are all the time testing these expectations against experience. Although a law-like ex-pectation cannot be reached from observations by any logical procedure it can be refuted by a single observation; and because of this we are all the time ad-justing and readjusting our expectations in the light of experience. In this schema knowledge is seen as "the best of our knowledge," a perpetually re-visable propensity to expect certain things to happen or to be the case; and ob-servation comes not prior to it, as something from which it is derived, but after it, as something against which it is tested, and in the light of which it is revised or abandoned. On this view we have no knowledge other than our hypotheses or theories, and these are products of our minds, not of our senses. It is very much a Kantian view. And anyone who holds it is able to carry on, as Schopenhauer attacked Kant for doing, as if sensory experience is not of the first importance in our scheme of things, indispensable though it may be. And precisely this is what Popper did. He never, so far as I know, addressed himself directly to the problem of the ontological status of epistemological phenomena, because his theory of knowledge did not require it of him.

From the fact that Popper saw all knowledge as being both theoretic and permanently revisable it followed that we never have grounds for certainty, but he was able to argue successfully that no alternative theory of knowledge gave us adequate grounds for certainty either. Certainty is simply not available to us. Descartes, by making the pursuit of certainty central to Western epistemology, sent it off on a fool's errand for three centuries, in the course of which even Kant and Schopenhauer were misled. However, once you accept that certainty is not available you are accepting that we are perpetually unsure what reality is, and therefore that the nature of reality is permanently hidden from us. So Popper is a realist who believes that reality is not something we can ever directly "know," but that our knowledge may get asymptotically closer and closer to it over the course of time. This is one of the features of his philosophy that give it a depth unavailable to most forms of empiricism: it is enriched by some of the most valuable insights of transcendental idealism without itself being idealist. This puts it at the opposite end of the realist spectrum from logical positivism, one of whose most famous proponents, Otto Neurath, proclaimed the philosophical slogan "Everything is surface." If I were a realist I would, I suppose, be some sort of Popperian: I certainly regard it as the form of realism closest to the truth. But it is only because Popper bypasses the problem of our knowledge of material objects in individual perception that he is able to cling to his view of himself as a realist at all. Not even in its Popperian form—which is, I think, its best-argued one—can realism actually be right.

Like Kant and Schopenhauer, I am an empirical realist while being at the same time a transcendental idealist. Within this framework, which he accepted, the young Wittgenstein tried to polish off the philosophy of empirical realism in his *Tractatus*. He protested how little would have been done when that had been done, but in any case he did not do it. Popper has come much closer to success—in fact his work seems to me altogether superior to that of Wittgenstein, although he did not feel at all inclined to acknowledge how little would have been done when that had been done. This is because he treats the empirical world as if it were total reality, even though he does not regard getting to know it as a completable task. He does this not because he believes that it is everything there is but because, in his view, we have no way of knowing whether it is or not, and can form no conception (no conception worthy of intellectual respect) of anything that might lie beyond it. Even *within* the empirical world, according to him, we know scarcely anything for certain: what kind of folly is it then to pursue knowledge outside it, where there is no ground for us to stand on? A phrase I heard from his lips as often as any other was "We don't know anything." He looked on this realization, which he attributed historically to Socrates, as the most important philosophical insight there is, one which ought to inform all our philosophical activity. One way in which it informed his own was to inhibit all speculation (even, I came to think, in the privacy of his own mind) about whether or not anything existed outside the empirical world. The result was that all his life he philosophized as if he were a transcendental realist, and he did indeed regard himself as such. My attempts to get him to address his mind to the possibility that empirical reality might not be everything were in vain. He would agree at once and without argument that this was a possibility, but he would always add that there was nothing anyone could say about it and no way in which we could make any use of it in our thinking, and therefore that we should proceed on our way without regard to it.

I see this as invalid both historically and actually. A number of philosophers, of whom Kant and Schopenhauer may be the greatest but are by no means the only ones, have said things of the utmost interest and perceptiveness about the nature of human limitations and their implications both for our thinking and for what might be outside the range of our understanding. They demonstrate by their example that a person can write about such things without departing from honest and open rational argument, without trying to express what is inexpressible or soaring into mysticism, and without resorting to poetic utterance or religious assertions, and without claiming privileged insight—and still say something worth saying. And if they can, others may. ("Well *I* can't," said Popper.)

The reasons we have for believing that reality extends indefinitely beyond our power to apprehend it fall into several distinguishable sets. One set has to do with the contingent and limited nature of the physical apparatus we have for apprehending. Another has to do with the large-scale ignorance and misunderstanding imposed on us by our location in time: when we consider the transformations that have taken place in mankind's knowledge of itself and the world in only the last four hundred years (the successive lifetimes of a mere four long-lived individuals) and when we remember that the pace of change, including intellectual change, is perpetually increasing, it is almost impossible not to believe that the next four hundred years are going to see changes at least as extensive and astonishing. A third set of reasons has to do with the boundedness of subjectivity: all perception, all experience, all understanding, all insight, can be only for a subject—and as Schrödinger once put it, "consciousness is a singular of which the plural is unknown" (*What Is Life?*, p. 95). A fourth has to do with the fragmented and narrowly limited nature of the cultural equipment through which we have to try to make our experience intelligible to ourselves. Taking them all in all, it is as certain as anything uncertain can be that reality as we apprehend it is not just different but massively and unconceptualizably different from total reality as it exists independently of us (as all those of us who are not solipsists believe that it does).

This at once reflects back in decisive ways on the conceptions and understandings that we do form. It means that none of our systematic sciences or philosophies can be adequate explanations of wholes in the way they so often take themselves to be: either they are wrong or they are pieces of an altogether larger picture of which we cannot yet get a conception, though it may come into focus at some future time. No doubt there are plenty in both categories. This has certainly been the pattern of the past until now, and common sense suggests it will continue. There is not a single science that has not been radically revised or extensively added to within living memory; and every well-known philosophy has familiar shortcomings. If we really do absorb into our thinking the fact that only fragmentary knowledge and partial understanding are available to us we shall stop making the mistake of supposing that everything can be explained in terms of the categories of understanding that happen currently to be available to us—and therefore that anything not thus explicable is in some sense supernatural. The idea that we have now come into possession of all the explanatory means required to make sense of everything is, on serious examination, so silly that I am at a loss to know how anyone can believe it, yet it is a widely held assumption, and held most confidently of all by people like philosophers and scientists.

The concept of the supernatural is a muddle, not because empirical reality is all there is but because total reality just is whatever it is: some of it apprehended by us, some of it not apprehended by us as yet but possibly becoming so in future, and some of it permanently inapprehensible by us. We can, if we like, call that part of it that is permanently inapprehensible by us "supernatural," but if that implies that there is something mystical about it, or religious, or magical, or occult, the implication has no evident foundation. Surely what would appear to be the obvious likelihood is that it is inapprehensible by us for the sort of reason that the visual world is inapprehensible by the congenitally blind, namely that we lack the apparatus required to apprehend it, but that it is as much "there" all the time as the visual world is "there" all the time despite being unperceived by the blind, and is as everyday a part of reality, neither more nor less mystical or religious than other parts. Our not apprehending it is a fact about us, not a fact about it. Indeed, it would appear fairly obvious that if we did apprehend it that would cause us to view what we apprehend already in an altered light—perhaps as a part of something of which at present we can form no conception.

The everydayness of unapprehended reality would seem to be the chief point of the most vivid dream I ever had, a dream whose high voltage and unforgettable impact cannot be conveyed in words. I was talking to a Mr. Average sort of fellow with a moustache, middle-aged, wearing a blue suit the colour of a children's book illustration, and carrying a walking stick; and I knew that he had died only a matter of days before. I was surprised to see him, and at once realized that here was a chance to find out what happens to us when we die. So I said to him: "What happens?" "We survive," he said: "[*Pause*] We survive as individuals. [*Pause*] We survive as souls. [*Pause*]" "Is it marvellous?" I asked. He shrugged his shoulders in a gesture that said: Okay, all right, nothing special. And that was the end of the dream. . . . There just is an obvious logical sense in which what is permanently the case cannot be exceptional. The implications of this for the so-called hereafter have been remarked on by others. Bernard Shaw once wrote: "In Heaven an angel is nobody in particular."

Not being religious myself, yet believing that most of reality is likely to be permanently unknowable to human beings, I see a compelling need for the demystification of the unknowable. It seems to me that most people tend either to believe that all reality is in principle knowable or to believe that there is a religious dimension to things. A third alternative—that we can know very little but have equally little ground for religious belief—receives scant consideration, and yet seems to me to be where the truth lies. Simple though it is, people have difficulty getting their minds round it. In practice I find that rationalistic humanists often think of me as someone with soft-centered cryptoreligious longings while religious people tend to see me as making token acknowledgement of the transcendental while being actually still far too rationalistic. What that means is that each sees me as a fellow-traveller of the other—when in fact I occupy a third position which neither of them seems to see the possibility of, and which repudiates both. What I want very much to see are two mass migrations, one out of the shallows of rationalistic humanism to an appreciation of the mystery of things, the other out of religious faith to a true appreciation of our ignorance.

Near the heart of the mystery of the world must be something to do with the nature of time. Whatever the truth about time may be, time cannot be what it seems. Neither the time of commonsense realism nor the time of Newtonian physics is given to us in experience, nor ever could be, since it stretches forward and backward to infinity, and nothing infinite can ever be encompassed in observation or experience. Any such time has to be an *idea*, something thought but never observed or experienced, a construction of our minds, whether it be a mathematical calculation or an imaginative assumption presupposed by the deliverances of our senses. The same considerations apply to space: the space of common sense, stretching as it does to infinity in all directions, is not a possible object of observation or experience—it too is a projection, a construct of some kind, as must also be the three-dimensional Euclidean space of Newtonian physics. Neither this space nor this time can be actual, because actual existence and identity require limits. Einsteinian space is without limits, even though it is finite, so it too could never be given in experience.

Limitless time and limitless space, then, are not the given, not experienced reality. What are they? It seems to me that the Kantian-Schopenhauerian answer to this question is somewhere along the right lines, even though their formulations cannot be accepted as they stand. The time and space of our experienced reality are, they believe, forms of our sensibility, and it is in that capacity that they appear as dimensions of experience. In the absence of experience they have no purchase, nothing to characterize. I know how deeply counter-intuitive this is—but so are many of the other most basic truths about our situation, such as the one I referred to earlier about our living on the surface of a giant ball that is hurtling through cosmic space while at the same time spinning on its axis at a thousand miles an hour. The first generations of people who encountered *that* idea found it crazy, completely impossible to believe—and then when people were forced to believe it they found it impossible to absorb into their everyday way of thinking about the world, and have still not done so. Of course it does not follow from this that there is anything subject-dependent about time and space, but it does show that the counter-intuitive impossible-to-believe may be everyday reality (another, and a different, respect in which everyday reality may be ungraspable).

My inclination to believe that there is something about time that is subject-dependent does not rest chiefly on considerations that have as yet appeared in this book. It is perfectly possible to form objective conceptions of time that are not dependent for any aspect of their structure on anyone's experience, and for much of our work in the sciences we do precisely this as a matter of course. But in any such time there is no place for a "now." No instant (whatever the units of measurement may be) is more privileged than any other. There is no problem at all about having an objective ordering of events, so that of any event or set of events it can be said impersonally and impartially which others it comes before and which it comes after; but there is no privileged event or set of events from whose position in the sequence all others are allotted their temporal location—unless, of course, we stipulate criteria for one, and then it is we who have done the stipulating. The point is that there can be no objective present in such a time, and thus no objective past or future. We can, if we like, say that all the instants in it are equally present, though I am not sure what that means—we could just as well say that they are equally not-present—but in any case to do so is to abnegate any such thing as a *passage* of time. If all time is present, or if all times are present, then something that we ordinarily regard as fundamental to our conception of the very nature of time—its movement along a single dimension, its "flow"—is absent. There have, of course, been a number of philosophers and religious people who taught exactly this, namely that the passage of time is unreal, an illusion, and that in reality all time is present. Whether this is the truth or not I do not know, but I am pretty sure that in a world without subjects there cannot be a "now," and that it is only from a privileged standpoint such as that of a subject of experience that there can be present, past or future; and therefore only relative to some such standpoint that there can be any such thing as the passage of time. I want to be unambiguously clear about what it is I am saying: as far as the present argument goes, because there can be temporal sequence without a subject there can be time without a subject, but there cannot be a "now" without a subject, nor can there be a passage of time without a subject.

What was to me the most fascinating of the issues between Popper and Einstein concerned the independent reality of the passage of time. Popper, in keeping with the extreme objectivism that characterizes his philosophy as a whole, maintained that the passage of time is objectively real, that there is a "now" independently of the existence of experiencing subjects. Einstein thought this impossible, and maintained that time, considered independently of the standpoint of any experiencing subject, must be tenseless. In private discussion Popper tried hard to change Einstein's opinion about this, but failed. I have to say that my view has always been on the same side of the question as Einstein's. In my arguments with Popper I never succeeded in extracting satisfactory answers from him to the objections that his view gives rise to. In this as in other respects he seemed to me too unperplexed about the elimination of considerations of subjectivity from his philosophical outlook. I am thinking not of personal subjectivity but of what one might call objective subjectivity, the fact that we human beings can never climb out of our minds and view anything from any standpoint more impersonal than that of the intersubjective. The notion of objectivity is, like so many others, a construct: no actually objective view of anything can ever appear in experience, could ever be given. This notion of objectivity is of incalculable value in science, and yet it is a metaphysical creation of our minds. Popper, it always seemed to me, used it too uncritically. If challenged he would always concede that it was a regulative ideal, not attainable in experience; but in practice he tended to proceed as if the self could and should be disregarded.

If neither a present nor a passage of time can obtain without a subject, and yet there is, or can be, time independently of subjects, this suggests that while only in experience is there present, past or future, and therefore passage of time, outside experience all time coexists. A striking thing about this conclusion is that we have been led towards it not by any considerations of the limitations inherent in the nature of subjective experience but by considering objective states of affairs and their ordering in time independently of experience. In my case I have been led to it by considerations of a purely philosophical, and I hope rational, character. In the case of Einstein the considerations were mainly if not wholly scientific. This deepens almost beyond measure the admiration I feel for Kant, who by armchair theorizing was able to penetrate so deeply into the nature of experience that some of the most revolutionary consequences of twentieth-century physics were unambiguously anticipated by him in a philosophy that went deeper than they. It is an object-lesson in what philosophy is capable of in the minds of its best practitioners.

What is most frustrating about the conclusion that being in unlimited space and passing time characterizes experience and the objects of experience only is that experience is all we have to test our empirical knowledge. As I have just been saying, we have no way of climbing out of this world of our experience and viewing it from the outside, still less of directing our gaze out of it altogether, like an astronomer with a powerful enough telescope trying to look not at but out of the universe. Yet only from outside the limits of this life could human experience ever be set against anything that was not human experience. This makes it imaginatively conceivable that death renders that possibility an actuality. But I see no grounds for believing that it does. In any case, we would still be left with the fact that within this life the relationship between the experienceable and the inexperienceable is inapprehensible. The truth about our situation is such that it can never give us any positive grounds for believing that there must be some other situation from which what is beyond us is apprehensible, still less for believing that if there is, there must be some way in which we human beings can get from where we are to it, if only by dying. This is wishful thinking, it seems to me.

If outside this world of our experience there is a time and it is tenseless then it must be assumed that relative to that tenseless time everything within the world of our experience coexists. In the minds of some people that thought seems to imply an impossibility of any freedom of the will. If it is a present fact that at a certain time in the future (relative to my present experience) I shall, let us say, impulsively invite a friend to lunch, then it is true now, in which case what makes it true will not come freshly into existence at that moment; so the feeling I shall then have of acting freely will be an illusion. There are many reasons why these fears are groundless.

First, foreknowledge is not the same as predetermination (in the sense of determinism). If it is possible for a being, let us say a God, to know what is going to happen in the future there is no more of a problem about his knowing that at some particular time in the future I am going to decide, entirely of my own free will, to do a particular thing than there is about his knowing any other kind of future event. Future free decisions, future free choices, are neither more nor less future than other future events: if there can be knowledge of future events at all then no special problem is raised about knowledge of future choices. Similarly, if we are able to view as tenseless the time-frame within which any given such series occurs then the objective temporal ordering of choices or decisions among other kinds of event presents no special problem. These two considerations are enough, I think, to still those particular doubts about free will. But I can see also a third possibility.

For reasons that have been discussed in unusually memorable ways by Hume, Schopenhauer and Wittgenstein, it would appear that the self is not a possible object of observation or experience, and therefore not a possible object of empirical knowledge. This fact, if it is a fact, has been found deeply baffling by large numbers of people, including me. Many have drawn from it the conclusion that there is no such entity as the self. But if we take into consideration three thoughts—first, that empirical observation and empirical knowledge are possible only within the bounds of possible experience; second, that time and space obtain only within the bounds of possible experience; third, that the realm of possible experience is almost certainly not the whole of reality—then that would appear to leave open a possibility that total reality includes a self or selves that are not in space or time, not within the realm of possible observation or experience, and therefore not possible objects of empirical knowledge. If this logical possibility is realized it brings with it an explanation of free will, and one that would meet the doubts we are considering.

The apparent possibility is that we are not wholly our bodies. These bodies of ours, like all other material bodies, are possible objects of observation and experience, and therefore of empirical knowledge, inhabit the realm of space and time, and are subjected to all the causal processes that are the concern of physics, chemistry, biology and the other sciences, from which there is no escape for them. But it is possible that in addition to bodies we are, or have, selves that are not material entities, are outside space and time, are not impinged on by the causality that governs the empirical world, and for all these reasons are not possible objects of empirical knowledge. The fact that our material bodies are subject to the regularities of Nature, in other words to scientific laws, would be incompatible with what we ordinarily think of as free will if it should turn out to be the case that our choices and decisions are enacted entirely by our bodies—are, for example, nothing but the redistribution of microphysical properties over space within our brains and central nervous systems. But if it should turn out that our choices and decisions are functions of an immaterial self then there would be no incompatibility between their being free ("free" meaning not subject to the regularities of Nature, not subject to scientific laws) and the movements of our bodies consequent on those decisions being subject to scientific laws. In those circumstances the supreme constraint on our freedom of decision would be the impossibility of any consequent movements of our bodies breaking scientific laws: we would not be able to effect any decision that carried with it that requirement. But we would, apparently, be free to choose or decide anything that did not have that consequence. Because physical movements consequent on my decisions would be subject to scientific law those movements would, in the ordinary way, be predictable, and responsibility for predictable consequences would normally lie at the point of their inauguration. Thus we have here a logically possible explanation both for freedom of action and for the ascription of moral responsibility: an immaterial self outside space and time inaugurates (some of the) movements of a material body in space and time, and is morally responsible for such of the consequences of those movements as are predictable.

Now the striking thing is that some such model as this appears, on the face of it, compatible with a very great deal of our experience, and can therefore be made to appear plausible if presented in a sympathetic way. But it gives rise to fundamental difficulties. How can an immaterial self move a material object? What is the ontological status of this immaterial self? Is its existence dependent on that of a material object, our body? If so, how does it come into being? If not, what is the nature of its apparently specific relationship to a particular body? Can it have only one such relationship, or can it have more than one? When the body dies, what happens to the immaterial self that is uniquely attached to it? Is this self in some way the, or at any rate a, connection between the empirical world and what lies outside the empirical world? Questions such as these would be the fundamental questions of philosophy if the logical possibility of a self's existence outside space and time were realized.

Many readers will find themselves reflecting that over the last few paragraphs I have been rehearsing, as logical possibilities, propositions a belief in which is central to some of the world's main religions. And they may begin to suspect me of advancing religious propositions behind the stalking horse of philosophy. But that is not what I am doing, nor would it reflect my attitudes: I am not religious, and I regard the adoption of religious faith as incompatible with openness to truth. What I have done is point out that certain possibilities exist, and that whether they are actualized or not is something we cannot know. This is something I take to be a fact. I certainly do not advocate belief in the truth of those propositions, given that we have inadequate grounds for any such belief. But nevertheless the possibility that they are true cannot be ruled out. And far from its being the case that they have been derived from religion, it is my belief that, historically, things have been the other way about, and that religious doctrines have been arrived at as a result of the possible truth of these propositions. It is because they could be true, and human beings have exceedingly powerful reasons for wanting to believe that they are, *yet the propositions themselves cannot be adequately supported by rational argument,* that they have become articles of religious faith. The drive behind the motivation comes, very obviously, from fear of death. That our bodies are destructible, and will quite certainly be destroyed sooner or later, is something we know. If we are only our bodies this means we confront certain annihilation. This prospect is terrifying. To the extent that the will to survive is the most powerful of all motivations, we therefore have the most powerful motivation possible for believing that we are not our bodies alone, that the real and essential "us" is something immaterial and indestructible that will survive the destruction of the body. I think this must be near to the heart of any explanation of how it comes about that most human beings throughout the ages have believed something of this kind, and have usually reacted in a seriously disturbed way, often savagely, to any suggestion that it might not be true. Belief that it *could* be true is not only justified but correct, though belief that it *is* true is unjustified.

I am fairly sure that whether the sort of possibilities I am talking about are actualized is something we human beings can never know. From this it would follow that they may not be actualized, and that we shall never know that they are not. Perhaps at death we shall go down into total oblivion, and never thereafter know anything about anything. It could be that the total scenario for human beings is insoluble mystery until we die, followed by nothing at all. On the basis of such knowledge as we have, that is certainly a possibility. *It might be true,* and I suspect that in practice, at least nowadays, as many human beings believe that it is as believe any of the alternatives.

Even so, although we must admit all possibilities, and genuinely so, not all possibilities commend themselves to us equally. To some we are led by rational considerations and processes of reasoned argument. Others are purely arbitrary postulates. For instance, I could proclaim that we have souls which are liberated from our bodies when we die and are at once transformed into invisible, intangible and inaudible hippopotamuses that then take up residence in the departure lounges of the world's airports, where crowds of living humans stream through them, perpetually, unawares. *This could be true,* and no one can prove that it is not. Indeed, I could claim, less than half jokingly, that it is no more unlikely than some actually held religious and superstitious beliefs. But there is not the slightest reason why anyone should waste a moment's consideration on it. (And that is indeed how I feel about many religious beliefs.)

But by contrast with this sort of thing there are possibilities that may lay claim to our attention, usually because serious rational arguments can be adduced in support of them. One is that there is no such object as a permanently existing human self or soul, or mind, and that for each of us the death of the body is the end of all conscious existence. This, I believe, could be true. Another is that there are selves whose existence is not wholly in space or time, and continue somehow after the death of the body. That, also, could be true. And there are others for which, as for these, intelligent arguments can be advanced. And I think it is self-deceiving to rule out any of those. A religious or quasi-religious faith to the effect that one is true and all the rest false seems to me out of place in any serious thinking, and out of place to the point of absurdity, given the state of our ignorance.

Someone might say to me: "That's all very well, but you can't, surely, be coldly neutral in matters of this kind? You can't view in a totally impersonal and detached way the question of what you yourself are. The very experience of being in the world must have given you an inclination to believe certain things as against other things when it comes to your own nature. Isn't that unavoidable?" Yes, at least for me it is unavoidable. I do have some such inclinations, though they are uncomfortably like those of a man who gambles his all on a horse when he knows that some other horse could perfectly well win, and is then on tenterhooks, and can scarcely bear to watch the race, fearing that only too soon he may find himself reeling away from the racecourse with his head in his hands having lost everything.

It does seem to me that I have a form of direct control of some of my bodily movements that involves free choice on my part. I still do not know how I do it, any more than I knew when I was a child, but *that* I do it is something I think I know. And I know this as directly and unmediatedly as I know anything—as directly and unmediatedly as I know that I see red when a red object is put in front of me. To express it the other way round, if I do not know this then I do not know anything, and do not know what knowing is. I am familiar with the arguments of determinists, which can be very sophisticated, to the effect that all my movements are determined and none of them the outcome of free decision-making, but these arguments seem to me to be contradicted by immediate experience. For I experience directly not only the making of decisions but also the apprehension of fields of possibility, of what it is open to me to do, and I often weigh up first of all whether certain options are open to me or not, and then, separately from that, the pros and cons of alternative courses of action, and then I consciously choose from among them—and then sometimes change my mind. Again, I am familiar with the arguments that each one of these processes is determined; but that is rather like saying to me that all my visual experiences are optical illusions, and I am not really seeing anything at all: there is an obvious sense in which it might be true, but it is a denial of the very possibility of the experience I am having, and in the present case that is the experience of agency. The fact of my own agency is something of which I have a knowledge so direct that it survives the most careful consideration of all the arguments to the effect that I do not have it, much as, if you gave a man with ten fingers an apparently cast-iron proof that he had eleven, he would doubt your proof rather than doubt that he had ten fingers.

There is another and totally different reason why I confidently reject determinism. If it is true, then none of us can ever *refrain* from anything we do. In that case any notions of good or bad, right or wrong, have no application with regard to human behaviour. It is false ever to attribute praise or blame to anyone, guilt or responsibility. "Ought" never applies, nor do such concepts as "duty," "justice," "fair." Conscience is an illusion. Every determinist, if he is sincere, must eliminate all such conceptions from his view of human beings, and also from his view of all human activities, arrangements and institutions. I have never known anyone who came anywhere near doing this. Certainly none of the people I have met who told me they were determinists did it. And the truth is, or so I believe, that it cannot be done. If it could it would leave us with a conception of ourselves that would not be recognizably human, not anything of which we could say that this was us. And if that is what the truth would have to be if determinism were true, it seems to me that determinism cannot be true.

I regard myself not just as believing but as knowing that I sometimes make free decisions and choices. It is from this fact—not from apprehending my self as an epistemological object, which I never do (and it seems I never can, however hard I try)—that I know that I either am or have a self. The fact that this self can apparently never be known as object but is unmediatedly known as agent has momentous implications, for it tells us that a self may indeed exist but evidently not as the sort of entity that exists as an object in the world. (The view that the self exists but is not an object is the basis of the positions argued in Heidegger's *Sein und Zeit.*) I have to say that I am pretty firmly convinced that the familiar arguments of Hume and others, from Locke to Ryle, to the effect that the self is not, and never can be, an epistemological object, are valid. If this is so, then if it were the case that the only way open to us of knowing the self to exist were the acquisition of knowledge of it as an epistemological object we could never know it to exist, and indeed would have no grounds for believing that it existed, and would therefore have to face the possibility that it did not. It is only because we exist as agents that we can be sure we have selves. I experience unmediatedly the fact that I (whatever "I" is) direct some of the movements of the physical object that is my body, and I know from experience that these movements, once inaugurated, have consequences in the empirical world for which I, having brought them about, feel myself to be responsible. Usually they are consequences that I wish to bring about, which is why I make the movements in the first place: I am perpetually bringing about, or changing, situations in the material world in accordance with my wishes, and that is a perfectly normal state of affairs during the hours when I am awake.

But this means that there is a dualism here. I have my physical body, a material object among other material objects, existing in space and time, subject to the same causal laws as other objects, coming into being and passing away in a material cosmos in which nothing ever stays the same; and I have or am a self that does not exist as an object in that empirical world but is an agent which directs some of the movements of one such object. This self, not being an empirical (and therefore not a possible epistemological) object stands in problematic relationship to both time and space, but especially to time. It is only from the standpoint of any such self that past, present and future, and therefore passage of time, can obtain. And it is to such a self that moral responsibility is ascribed.

I take all this to be true of other human beings besides myself. It is a striking, indeed compelling fact that I find it impossible to regard others as consisting of their bodies alone. Try as I might, even if only as a thought-experiment, I cannot encompass the idea that another person is a physical object in the same way as a sofa or a rock, one that happens to have powers of automation and conscious reflection. The notion is so contrary to what presents itself as being the case that I cannot get my mind round it: there is some sort of abyss between it and any possibility of its being true. In all my dealings with others I find myself compelled to treat them as if they are not only things, as if there is something essential to their nature that is not their bodies. And I observe that this is how they treat one another, and also how they treat me. A person who treats others as if they were things, physical objects, just so much matter, is a psychopath: and it is widely felt to be the most evil and horrific form of existence; and I sympathize with that view.

There are other and quite different illustrations, some eloquent, of the fact that it is abnormal, and for most of us impossible, to regard a human being as solely a physical object. If we enter a large, dimly lit room full of furniture, a room in which we take ourselves to be alone, we have a certain feeling about our relationship to our surroundings; but if suddenly we realize that a dark shape in one of the corners is a human being asleep in an armchair then that whole feeling is transmuted into something quite different. It is not as if there were one more piece of furniture in the room. It is as if the metaphysics of the space had been transformed. We ourselves now, as it were, have one foot in some other space as well: that room is no longer the only place we are, no longer the only context within which we are interrelating with something that is not ourselves. This has nothing to do with being observed or responded to: the person is fast asleep. We have suddenly realized that we are not alone, and with that realization we find ourselves, as I have just put it, in a different metaphysical space.

Some readers may think that what I am talking about without naming is the moral dimension to human existence, but this is not so. I am talking now about human beings purely as objects of cognition. There *is,* of course, a moral dimension, which we cannot ignore even when we wish to, and it does indeed constitute an insuperable reason why human beings cannot be treated as just so much matter; but that is not my present thesis. My point here is that we *know* human beings differently from the way we know anything else. We do not and cannot cognize them as physical objects on a par with other physical objects, material things only, wholly governed by scientific laws. Take, for example, the way we respond to other people's eyes. According to the laws of physics nothing comes out of anyone's eyes at all. Light rays go into the eye, and cause all sorts of things to happen inside a person, such as seeing and headaches, but there is nothing at all that comes out of the eye into the surrounding space. According to all the scientific knowledge we have, what I see when I look into someone's eyes is the light from the surrounding air reflected back to me from the surfaces of the person's eyeballs, and that light is outside the person, the light in the air around us coming back at me again. If it is dark I cannot see the person: it is only by the surrounding light that I see the surfaces of his eyeballs, with whatever degree of clarity that allows. And that, according to science, is the whole of the situation. But who actually believes it? Who *can* believe it? The truth of which most of us have indubitable experience every day is that when I look into another person's eyes I am in what is for the most part a reliable degree of contact with multitudinous things going on *inside* that person—and he with multitudinous things going on inside me: feelings, moods, thoughts, intentions, hesitations, doubts, fears, hopes, and a host of other highly variegated inner states, together with attempts to conceal or dissemble any or all of those, most of it fleeting and flashing past in flickering instants of time, the whole of it nuanced and inflected in subtle and sophisticated ways. Is there anyone who believes that this staunchless two-way flow of information is physically encoded on the surfaces of our eyeballs in a way that changes multitudinously instant by instant like a flow of orchestral sound (if so, how is it encoded?) and read off in the surrounding light by observers who instantly and accurately decode it in what is at both ends an essentially computing process? I have yet to hear of such a person. And this is only one example of the fact that in our daily lives, especially in our interpersonal relationships, cognition is all the time going on, and indubitably going on, that cannot be accounted for by any form of scientific explanation that is yet known. We are entirely familiar with this, we know few things better, and we do not normally regard it as mysterious. It illustrates not only the fact that we are all the time thinking, feeling, and behaving in ways which are incompatible with the assumption that other people can be accounted for, in the light of our present knowledge, as material objects governed by scientific laws; it illustrates also the fact that we are all the time having experiences that are incompatible with the assumption that the empirical world that science tells us about is the whole of the reality we know. It is deeply strange that so many of us ignore this dimension of our knowledge—so rich, so direct, so everyday, and not at all what we normally think of as magical or mysterious—in the formulation of our consciously held worldviews. People in general are guilty of the most extraordinary double-think in this regard: it is rare indeed for a thinker to take seriously into account, in his view of the way things are, forms of knowledge like those I have just been writing about, which in fact we make use of every day and would be unable to live without. There is something perverse about the way we try to build up worldviews on foundations which we already know to be inadequate.

I think I know that our situation is at least roughly as I have described it up to this point. Therefore I think I know that philosophies and thought-systems that are incompatible in more than detail with what I have said so far are mistaken. In the context under consideration the most important of the things that I think I know are that we human beings do not consist solely of our bodies; that in addition to having bodies we also have or are selves, and that these selves are not empirical objects in the natural world; also that morals and values do not have their existence solely within the natural world, and therefore (among other things) are not wholly products of human psychology, society and history, though they may be that to some degree.

However, at this point I falter and stand bewildered. Because my self is not a possible object of empirical knowledge I can never have direct knowledge of it. Actually, I do not believe I am ever likely to know what it is, in which case I shall die not knowing. It may be that a vital clue to its nature lies already before me, unperceived, perhaps even in what I have already written: I can only hope so, in which case there is a chance that the penny will drop before I die. Perhaps what is needed is to start from the premiss that the self exists but is not an object, and then proceed in a direction wholly different from Heidegger's.

At the heart of the mystery, it seems to me, must lie the relationship between the self and the empirical world in which it is not an object. In fact I am tempted to believe that the ultimate mystery *is* the relationship between the self and the empirical world. With his usual acumen Schopenhauer thought this. "The solution of the riddle of the world is only possible through the proper connexion of outer with inner experience, effected at the right point." The first time I read those words I got gooseflesh all over my body, my scalp prickled and tingled, and I knew I was going to read every word written by Schopenhauer. In his masterpiece he spells out what he thinks the solution is. It strikes me as being, on the whole—and with the usual plenitude of qualifications—as plausible a large-scale view of the way things are as I have come across; and yet I remain agnostic with regard to it. It could indeed be that something like that is true. But it could also be that the truth is nothing like that at all. The trouble is not just that I do not know but that I do not know how to go about finding out. Although I am sure there is an immaterial self I am far from being sure that it has any existence except in relation to a body. My own particular self may have come into existence when or after my body did, and may cease to exist when my body dies. It may be something that has evolved over millions of years in undisentanglable relationship with brains, and may have no way of existing separately from my brain. This was, for example, Popper's view. He was persuaded of its truth and untroubled by it. I am unpersuaded of its truth, and am deeply troubled by it.

If it is indeed the case that we can never know what the answers to these questions are then they demarcate some of the limits of philosophy. If that is so it may be rational to engage with philosophy up to the frontier that they constitute and then disengage from it and do something else. This was what the young Wittgenstein believed, and what he tried to do. He did not succeed in escaping, yet even so, when he returned to philosophy it was not to grapple with fundamental problems but to dissolve what he regarded as pseudo-problems, mere puzzles which he believed impeded our serious thinking. We had no choice, he had come to believe, but to confine our questioning, and therefore our understanding, and therefore to some extent our lives, to the realm in which there are intelligible answers, because where no intelligible answer can exist there can be no intelligible question.

I do not agree with this. First, the history of philosophy holds me back from any final feeling of certainty that there are questions permanently incapable of answer. They may not have been answered *yet,* and we may not be able to see *now* how they could be answered, but it does not follow from this that they will never be answerable at any time in the future. Although we may have what seem to us watertight reasons for believing that we have come up against permanent limits, we should remember that such unsurpassed philosophical geniuses as Kant and Schopenhauer believed the same thing with respect to their philosophy, but a century later it turned out that they had been in error about it for reasons that it had not been possible for them to understand. And so may we be. Second, even if there are certain questions that cannot be an-

swered it does not follow from this that the questions cannot be clearly formulated. I think I can demonstrate this by formulating metaphysical questions
which are fundamental and coherent and yet which human beings may never
be able to answer. Let me try.

Whatever total reality may consist of it has to include among its contents us
humans with our individual self-aware consciousnesses. We have what seem
to be good reasons for believing that these consciousnesses do not in themselves comprise the whole of reality: if they did, the forms of all existence
without exception would have to be consciousness and mental contents. But if
our conscious selves do not comprise the whole of reality, what is the relationship between these conscious selves and the rest of reality?

That is my first question.

If someone counters with the question "Why should you regard that as especially problematic? Why not just accept that our selves are a part of the natural world along with all of its other parts?," my reply is that I have many
reasons for not doing that, some of them quite unlike the others. One is that
nobody seems able to locate a self—not even his own, to knowledge of which
he might be thought to have special access—as an object in the world. Another
is that my self, though apparently not an object in the world, has the capacity
to control the movements of one particular such object, and this is deeply
strange. However, the most powerful reason of all is that only in relation to an
experiencing self such as I find myself to be can there be a present in time, and
therefore past and future, and therefore a flow of time. If one considers the
whole of known reality apart from these selves there appears to be no way in
which it can be characterized by the sort of passage of time that selves experience. So it looks as if selves inhabit a tensed time-framework yet nothing
else does. But is that in fact the case? If it is, how does the tensed time of the
experience of selves stand in relation to the untensed time that seems to characterize everything else?

Now surely these are understandable questions? We may not know how to
answer them, but their significance—and, what is more, their fundamental importance—can scarcely be open to doubt. Of course it goes without saying
that in my ignorance I may have formulated them on the basis of mistaken assumptions, and in the course of investigation this may be discovered; but that
is precisely the sort of development one hopes for: it is part of the normal way
in which intellectual progress takes place; and we can make progress only if
we start from where we are. If believable and persuasive answers *or objections* to the questions I have formulated become available to us, our understanding of the human situation will cut deeper than it does, even if those
particular answers or objections should turn out to be mistaken; because it will
almost certainly mean that our understanding of the questions has deepened.

The philosopher of the twentieth century who addresses these particular questions in the most interesting way is Heidegger. Among his conclusions are that tensed time is constitutive of human being—the reference of his title *Being and Time* is ultimately to the claim that self-aware being *is* time, and that this is central to the explanation of why it is that selves are not objects. There is no "ground of being"—being, as tensed temporality, is not grounded in anything at all. This disconcerting conclusion may be a gateway to important truth. But if it is, it is not a gateway that Heidegger himself passes through. He never addresses himself to the relationship between the tensed time which (he says) is constitutive of all conscious being and the untensed time that appears to characterize everything else. And this is not because, as the empiricists do, he mistakenly equates existence with the capacity to be an object of conscious experience, and therefore mistakenly attributes to all existence the tensed temporality that characterizes experience. It is that he takes being-in-the-world as the starting point of his enquiry, and proceeds from there to investigate the structure of being. He is insistent that to be at all we have to be in a world; and of course our actual being is in an actual world. He believes that there is something disastrously mistaken about the common Western view of man as a subject in a world of objects which impinge on him, as it were, from outside himself, so that he looks at them as if through an invisible plate-glass window, trying to understand them as an observer. This model helps to give rise to many of the classic problems of Western philosophy, including how we can ever know that the world corresponds to the conceptions we form of it; how we can know what its true nature is independently of the categories of our experience—indeed, if we cannot do the latter, how we can *know* that it exists. Heidegger rejects the model, and proposes an alternative way of looking at these matters within which (he claims) such problems do not arise, and can be seen as delusory.

I am sympathetic to Heidegger's approach until he reaches this point, but here it seems to me that he fails to confront the problem of the nature, including the temporal aspect, of that part of reality that is not selves, and therefore also the problem of the relationship, including the temporal relationship, between it and the selves constituted by tensed time. In other words he does not avoid the problem but evades it: his model gives rise to it in a form that he fails to deal with. His conclusion that the most distinctive characteristic of conscious selves is that they are constituted by tensed time suggests some sort of implication that the rest of reality is not so constituted (so far so good) but he has nothing to say about the problems of understanding created by this. He writes only about the being of conscious selves: although he both starts from, and concludes with, a commitment to the view that there is a world that is not conscious self, and that it is not, or may not necessarily be, characterized by tensed time, he writes in between as if the being of conscious selves is the whole of his problem. In my opinion it is precisely the relationship between what is self and what is not self that presents us with the fundamental problem of philosophy (and I would agree of course that it is almost certain that this problem is bound up with the relationship between tensed and untensed time). More than that: one cannot understand the nature of self if only self is considered. For reasons given earlier in this book, it is only if something is seen from outside as well as from its own point of view that it can be understood; and therefore only if my self is seen and grasped in its relation to what is not myself can it be understood. It may well be that Heidegger was of the view that we simply have no way of penetrating the nature of whatever it is that exists independently of conscious experience. Certainly that is a view that can be formidably argued; but to accept it is to remain with the fundamental position established by Kant, albeit to have made (as Heidegger has made) significant clarifications (or clearings in the forest, as he would have said).

It looks as if whether or not death is the end of the self depends on the nature of the self, although it may turn out to be more accurately understood as something to do with the nature of time. To take the first of these possibilities first: if the self were an object in the empirical world it would presumably be, like all other objects in the empirical world, ephemeral, and so we would know for sure that we confronted extinction. It is only because the self is not an empirical object that the possibility exists that we may perhaps not be extinguished after all. Naturally I hope that this possibility is realized, because the prospect of extinction terrifies me; but as yet I have not found good reasons for believing that it is. Indeed, if death is the end of the self there are not likely to be very good reasons for believing that it is not, and that would explain why they are so difficult to find. And it could be that that is the situation.

If death is the end of the self it is not something any of us will live through, and therefore not something we shall experience. As Wittgenstein so well put it, death will not be an event in our lives. For us there will only ever be this kind of life we have now. It is all we shall ever know, and it will go on until it stops, but there will not then be something else that happens: precisely because the end will not be experienced by us, it will not be experienced as an end. The limits of our life will be as un-clear-cut, as unlike a drawn line, as the limits of our visual field (again an analogy drawn by Wittgenstein). Also, if death is the end, there is something absurd about human life, in the sense in which the French existentialists used the term "absurd"—ultimately without point or significance, in the end meaningless. This thought is also terrifying, quite separately from the terrifyingness of death—perhaps, in a strange way, even more so—but that does nothing to render it invalid or untrue. Again, it might simply be that that is the case, regardless of whether we like it or not:

there is no Law of the Universe that says that the truth must be something which we like. To deny a possibility on the ground that it is too distressing to contemplate is wholly unserious intellectually.

If death is the end then most of what matters to us is already known to us, even though we cannot know that to be the case. But if death is not the end we are in a situation which is unknown to us in its most important features. The self might continue as in some comprehensible sense itself, or it might change in ways unimaginable to us. A self not embodied in a material object in space and time is something of which we can form some conception, but we have no way of knowing what its mode of being would be, or how it might relate to what was not itself, or indeed what *what was not itself* could be, apart from us and our world. All our notions of personality, indeed of any sort of individual being, are drawn from this empirical world of ours—it is notoriously the case that even people who believe in an omnipotent, omniscient and omnipresent God can think of no further characteristics to attribute to him other than human ones. Perhaps this is why so many people believe in reincarnation—because the only way they can imagine a person's self continuing to exist after that person's death is in another person. But perhaps that does indeed happen. Or perhaps, as Christians believe, each individual soul goes on existing immaterially, outside time and space. Or perhaps, as some Hindus and Buddhists believe, individuality is transcended altogether, and the self merges with the rest of what is, like a raindrop falling into the ocean. Or perhaps something unrecognizably unlike any of these things happens, of which we can form not the faintest conception.

Of course, whatever the truth may be, it informs the situation now, is part of the ultimate explanation of this life of ours that we are living at this moment. The relationship of that truth to us might be not unlike the relationship of the visual world to the congenitally blind, something that is there all around us all the time without our having any way of apprehending it—in which case death might be analogous to the acquisition of sight, though of course in such a case it would do no more than reveal to us what had been there all along. Our situation is such that until we die we have no way of knowing what happens. Even then, we may or may not discover the truth, depending on what does happen. This means we may not discover. The last thing I shall ever know may be my last moment of conscious awareness in this world, and that could very easily be occupied by something utterly trivial, such as a moment of concern at dropping my watch. In this case my momentary concern at dropping my watch will be the end. It will be followed by nothing at all.

If the truth of our situation is to be understood more accurately than in any of these ways in terms of something to do with the nature of time, I have less to suggest. Since childhood I have had an intuitive feeling that everything that is real—everything and everybody that actually happens or exists—is real for ever and always; that nothing real ever goes out of existence. This is not a hypothesis but a feeling: the feeling that everything coexists in an eternal present. I have the feeling involuntarily—it is not something I can shake off, or talk myself out of. But I am only too well aware that this does not make it knowledge, and that it could be delusory—could, for example, have origins that are more to do with wishful thinking than with reality. In any case, I do not know how to apply it in actual cases or questions. How, for instance, can it help me to answer the question "What happens to me when I die?" If all forms of my existence cease, the fact that I exist now is nevertheless a timeless and eternal truth, yet there is all the difference in the world between the fact or truth of my existence being timeless (or eternal) and *me* being timeless (or eternal). The fact that I am alive now will certainly still be a fact after I die, but what I want to know is what will *I* be? People may talk in sentimental ways about us living on in other people's memories, and all the rest of it, but this is just evasive metaphor: we are not living on, we are being remembered.

The present is the form of all existence. In a tensed time, what is not now is not. What is now is real, but the past is something that can only be conceptualized, as is the future. In any time with a now in it, it can never be any time other than now, because there can never be a now which is not now; and therefore in any tensed time it is always now, a continuing present, but a present that precludes past and future. Only in untensed time can what would otherwise be past, present, and future be equally real and in any serious sense coexisting. But this means that in untensed time I am already dead, and not yet born, and that these situations are all one.

We may get a glimpse of what this means if we consider our relationship to anyone's life that was completed during the period that is past to our own. Napoleon, shall we say, was unborn throughout the whole of time before the year 1769; between 1769 and 1821 he was living; after 1821 he was dead, and he will remain dead for the rest of time. But the periods before, during and after his life are laid out equally and simultaneously before the gaze of our present-day historians. Some, for instance medieval historians, are devoting their lives to the study of a world in which there was no Napoleon and had never been one, and was no thought of one. Others study Napoleon. Others study societies on which a dead Napoleon has left his mark. All these fields of study coexist, and all are equally meaningful and valid, and people are simultaneously active in all of them. The differences do not present us with any problem of understanding. We can, if we like, make comparative studies that bring them together for some purposes and not for others, just as we wish. The period between Napoleon's death and now was completely unknowable to Napoleon, a blank, a nothing, but the we that are living now know more about it than we know about any other period of history. It must go without saying that our own lives in time will stand in the same relation to people of future centuries as Napoleon's does to us. Those people will be able to look equally and simultaneously at the period after we die, the period during which we are living, and the times before we were born, and it will all be continuous to them. If anything, they will know more about the period after we die, a time that is still future to us, than we ourselves know about our own pasts. There are bound to be historians not yet born who will devote the whole of their careers to the study of periods that have not yet occurred.

All this is not in itself what I want to say but is a metaphor for what I want to say, a metaphor that makes use throughout of tensed time; but it may carry us in the direction of a better understanding of what an untensed time is like, a time in which there is temporal succession and yet all of whose contents co-exist. If there is a God, it may be that he apprehends our time in an untensed way, which is to say all of it simultaneously, and from no particular temporal standpoint. That is certainly how many physicists since Einstein have conceived of time, so human beings have the concept already in a scientific form and are making practical use of it. Fully establishing what the relationship is between tensed and untensed time could constitute the next great revelatory and revolutionary change in philosophical understanding, the next change on a par with the Kantian revolution, involving as it must elucidation of the relationship between subjective and objective, experience and what is not experience, inner and outer, consciously aware self and what is not consciously aware self.

On the other hand it may be possible for different time-frames to be, to the very end of the road, incommensurable, just as it is possible for different values to be ultimately incommensurable. Ultimate incommensurability may turn out to be a feature of many different and unconnected elements in our lives, by which I mean there may be different and unconnected areas of incommensurability, not only the area of values. I believe we already know this to be the case with the phenomenon of consciousness and the existence of different and differing conscious self-awarenesses. In spite of all the many indications that the conscious experience of one individual differs from that of another in what might have been thought to be identical circumstances we have no way of carrying out the comparisons. Plurality of consciousness is not a possible experience. And yet we know it to be a reality. If we combine the two examples of consciousness and time the point becomes even more obvious: it is quite easy to understand that there may simply be no way at all in which the time-frame in a dream dreamt by one individual is related to the time-frame in a dream dreamt by another; yet both have their being.

In view of the incommensurability of different consciousnesses there is one feature of my own metaphysical thinking that I remain surprised by and do not fully understand, and that is that I still do it nearly always in the first person plural. I seem automatically to find myself thinking "What happens when we die?," not "What happens when I die?": "Do we have selves that are not empirical objects but nevertheless exist in some way? If so, what could they possibly be?"—and so on and so forth. When I want to make a point sharper for purposes of communication I often do so by personalizing it, and in the process I may make it singular, but the thought itself is scarcely ever in the singular. And I am at a loss to understand why this should be so. Fear of annihilation is one of the motives behind my philosophizing, and I am nothing like as afraid of the deaths of most other people as I am of my own. On top of that, I am motivated by bafflement at my own experience, and this experience is uniquely particular to me: I concentrate on my conscious self-awareness and try to understand what it is; I look enthralled at a physical object and try to grasp what the precise nature is of the experience I am having; and so on and so forth, endlessly. With all this intensity of concentration on experience that is mine and mine alone, why—even within the privacy of my own mind—do I couch my questions about it in terms of "we" and not "I"? That seems to me strange, and unwarranted by the facts of the situation as they are directly available to me.

The experiences that drive me to philosophize are pointedly personal, sometimes upsettingly so, and it would seem both natural and logical for the questioning of these experiences to be personal in a way that corresponds to that. I have direct and unmediated knowledge of what I myself think, feel and see, but I do not and never can have unmediated knowledge of what anyone else thinks or feels or sees; therefore it would appear to be a requirement of proper method to confine my questioning, at least in the first instance, to what I directly know. With this thought in mind I have tried to make myself concentrate on my experience as being personally and uniquely mine, and to frame my questions about it in terms of "I"; but this feels strained and unnatural, something I am forcing myself to do; and as soon as I stop being self-conscious about it I relapse into "we" again. It appears to be another of those apprehensions that I cannot account for and yet cannot shake off—that there is something that we all are, and that its sharedness is essential to what it is, and that my metaphysical questions are about it. I have tried to find justification for this conviction, but in vain, and yet I have it. Schopenhauer offers an explanation of it to the effect that we, like everything else in the empirical world, are noumenon as well as phenomenon, and therefore since the noumenon is undifferentiable we must all be, ultimately, in the ground of our inner nature, one; but I do not see how the validity of this explanation is to be tested. It seems to fit the facts; if true it would explain why things are as they are; but those conditions are met by an indefinitely large number of alternative explanations; and how are we to choose between them? In intellectual matters I am almost never justified in accepting an explanation by the fact that I cannot think of a better one, for that is merely a contingent fact about me—there may be any number of better explanations waiting to be thought of by *somebody*. The only defensible way to deal with a conviction such as I have described is to treat it differently on different occasions: to let it have its head sometimes, in case it turns out to lead to valuable insight, but also at times to be highly sceptical of it as a possible illusion.

There are so many different reasons why we cannot know what the nature of total reality is that I have no difficulty in explaining it as a fact. The difficulty is in living with it. If you ask me why I am so exercised that there is something I cannot know, my reply is that my annihilation or survival hangs on the question. If you then ask me, as Karl Popper used to, why I should regard my survival as mattering, all I can say is that it matters to me. All my life I have been brimming over with an almost uncontainably powerful desire to live. I feel it as an ever-present drive, thirst, lust, of which I have been inescapably aware since childhood. This drive would have to be somehow broken before I could calmly accept my own demise, which until then will mean accepting the unacceptable, coming to terms with the uncomeable-to-terms-with. As yet I cannot do it, so I go on trying desperately to increase my understanding of this impossible situation—in the hope, I suppose, that a deeper understanding of it will make it easier to come to terms with. I should not, however, misrepresent myself—it is not only with my personal survival that I am concerned: I have also a greedy, sharp-edged curiosity about how things are, a clamant need to understand, that will not let me relax; and about this there is something impersonal and objective. I believe I would still have it if I were indestructible.

Perhaps this book ought to end in mid-sentence. There is no stopping point. Now that I have carried myself up to where I am I shall just continue to wonder and reflect, and I do not expect to reach a natural end, ever—which is to say before I myself reach a natural end. The philosophical problems about which I might one day have something to say are chiefly connected with the limits of human understanding, and in particular with the boundedness of subjectivity, but that will be at best a subject for another book. In this one my concern has been to show how philosophy can be an indispensable part of the many-layered tapestry of a human life that consists of a great many other things besides, and for the most part has not been devoted professionally to philosophy. The basic philosophical problems are presented to us by living, not by books or by the education system. The notion that only those who have studied philosophy at a university can philosophize is on a par with the notion that only those who have made an academic study of literature can read a classic novel—an equally silly view which seems to be held in practice (they would never say it) by a surprisingly high proportion of those who study literature at universities. In this book I have tried to show how life itself hurled fundamental problems of philosophy in my face, what I tried to do about it, how I discovered what the geniuses of philosophy had said about my problems, and what use they were to me. Although this has involved me, inevitably, in a lot of discussion of books and writers, this book is not about study or reading, or writing, or teaching, but about a lived and anguished absorption in the most important and difficult of all the non-moral problems that are encountered in a human life.

I have omitted moral problems for good reasons. Throughout my life I have believed that I knew when I was doing wrong. The problem in those cases has not been knowing what was right but doing it. Because knowing what was right has not presented me with fundamental theoretical problems I have never taken much interest in theoretical justifications of ethics. Needless to say, I could no more have *provided* a theoretical justification of ethics than I could have provided a theoretical justification for my view that Beethoven's music goes deeper than Mendelssohn's; but in neither case did I feel any need to. I am conscious, and rather shame-facedly conscious, of having been lucky in not having had to face more than two or three traumatic practical dilemmas up to this point in my life. We live in a century in which large numbers of people have had to make the most terrible choices. If a Gestapo officer brandishing a gun in my face had said: "You know where those Jews are hiding. If you don't tell me, I'll shoot your daughter first of all, then your wife, and then you," I think I would have told him—and then found it impossible to live at peace with myself ever after. It is sheer good fortune, no merit of mine, that I have never been in such a situation. Thousands have. And yet even there I think I know what the right thing to do would be. The right thing would be not to tell. Indeed, it is because this is so that my peace of mind would be permanently shattered: I would know I had done something hideously wrong. So, again, the problem is not a theoretical one, not a problem of knowing: it is the problem of doing what one knows to be right. Moral problems, terrible though they may be, are not, it seems to me, philosophical problems, they are practical ones. The supreme philosophical problem with regard to morals and ethics is that of providing a rational explanation for them; but that is not a moral problem, it is an intellectual one.

With our moral convictions, as with our belief in logic, or in the reality of the external world, few of us arrive at our actual conclusions by a rational process. It is not that we discover what the correct rules of inference are and then apply them, and come up with our conclusions. On the contrary, in logic and morals at least we derive our notion of what the correct rules of inference are from our convictions about what is the case. This means that we can no more prove that our moral convictions are valid than we can prove that the rules of logic are valid, just as we cannot prove that there is a reality external to ourselves. The most we can hope to do in all such cases is to see to the heart of how things are; and this is a very different matter from proving anything. I think I know, as I just implied, that Beethoven's music goes deeper than Mendelssohn's, but no one could prove it. Our aim is, or should be, not to prove anything, but to find out, and properly to understand, what the truth is about what is. All my life I have been absorbed in this with regard to the metaphysics of experience. This book tells that story; and if it has conveyed anything at all about the help that can be got from the greatest philosophers of the past it will have repaid some tiny part of the debt I owe them.

Index

ABOUT THE AUTHOR

BRYAN MAGEE has taught philosophy at Oxford and been a Member of Parliament, a critic of music and theater, and a professional broadcaster. His academic appointments include Visiting Professor at King's College, University of London; Fellow of Queen Mary College, London; and Fellow of Keble College, Oxford. He has lectured internationally, including at several colleges and universities in the United States. His books include *The Great Philosophers, The Philosophy of Schopenhauer,* recently reissued in a revised and enlarged edition, and *Aspects of Wagner.* Bryan Magee has written and presented many radio and TV programs on philosophy in the United Kingdom that have been sold internationally. He lives in London.